EU-CHINA: COMPARATIVE EXPERIENCES AND CONTRIBUTIONS TO GLOBAL GOVERNANCE IN THE FIELDS OF CLIMATE CHANGE, TAXATION, TRADE, AND COMPETITION

JOSÉ MARÍA BENEYTO PÉREZ
JERÓNIMO MAILLO GONZÁLEZ-ORÚS
Directors

EU-China: Comparative Experiences and Contributions to Global Governance in the Fields of Climate Change, Taxation, Trade, and Competition

Coordinators
JAVIER PORRAS BELARRA
IGNACIO FORNARIS VALLS

Preface
Jorge Toledo

Editorial Aranzadi, S.A.U.
C/ Collado Mediano, 9
28231 Las Rozas (Madrid)
Tel: 91 602 01 82
e-mail: clienteslaley@aranzadilaley.es
https://www.aranzadilaley.es

Primera edición: 2024
Depósito Legal: M-14252-2024
ISBN versión impresa: 978-84-1162-006-2
ISBN versión electrónica: 978-84-1162-007-9
Incluye soporte electrónico

Diseño, Preimpresión e Impresión: Editorial Aranzadi, S.A.U.
Printed in Spain

Índice General

Página

Página

Página

Página

Preface

JORGE TOLEDO ALBIÑANA

EU Ambassador to China

Ancient philosopher Heraclitus once famously said: "there is nothing permanent except change". From establishing diplomatic relations in 1975, to the 2003 commitment for a comprehensive strategic partnership to the European Council Conclusions on China of June 2023, the balance of challenges and opportunities in the EU-China relation has shifted over time. The EU's China policy has been experiencing a period of recalibration, of reassessment and redefinition, to reflect changes in China and on the global stage.

China's extraordinary economic, technological, political, and military rise over the last decades has led to new geopolitical adjustments and alignments. There is a growing perception that this rise is no longer as "peaceful" as it used to be, especially in the Indo-Pacific region and particularly in the South China Sea. Also, that China is trying to use its economic power and influence to reshape, reinterpret, or even rewrite the international order. Besides, China's position on Russia's war of aggression against Ukraine has damaged China's image, reputation and political standing in Europe. Finally, we confront "systemic" issues like the respect of human rights that are enshrined in international law and their universality and indivisibility which are being challenged and or reinterpreted by China. We continue to be seriously concerned about the human rights situation in China and particularly in regions like Xinjiang or Tibet, or about the recent developments in Hong Kong. However, we have resumed our bilateral Dialogue on Human Rights, which had not taken place for the last four years (initially due to COVID and lately due to China's unilateral suspension following EU listings under the EU Global Human Rights Sanctions Regime). The fact that people to people exchanges, or in-person high level exchanges were all but cancelled for over three years due to the pandemic has not helped to reduce mutual misunderstandings.

The pandemic, and the weaponisation of energy supplies by Russia has brought about a rethinking of excessive dependencies in Europe and a determined policy of the de-risking the supply chains of critical materials and products, many of which are currently being supplied by China.

However, let me be very clear: as the President of the European Commission assured before visiting China last April: the EU does not want or seek to decouple from China. We want to continue trading with China, and our companies are more than willing to continue to trade and invest in China. Our strategy is about protecting ourselves where necessary, which requires that we identify those products and areas of economic flows that pose a risk to our security, and about addressing these risks. The Commission has put forward a proposal for an economic security strategy on 20 June 2023, which summarises different measures and actions foreseen to identify and address risks linked to the weaponisation of trade and certain economic interdependences.

The EU and China both profit from a broad-based economic relation, with bilateral trade in goods in 2022 reaching EUR 2.3 billion every day. European companies have been contributing to China's rise by investing into the Chinese market and by sharing technology and know-how. Therefore, it is unfortunate that at present there is a growing feeling that the Chinese proclaimed policy of "opening -up" and reform is not being translated into the removal of market access barriers that prevent our companies to do business in the huge Chinese market. Besides, new barriers and important areas of legal uncertainty are being erected in the name of "national security" or "self-reliance", and the negative effects of these on trade and investment in China by European companies is already being felt.

Meanwhile, Chinese companies take good advantage of one of the three largest markets in the world, the European "Single Market" and reach record trade imbalances, which are increasingly unsustainable and difficult to justify in the face of the lack of both a level playing field and of progress in the removal of market access barriers. In 2022, China's trade with the EU reached a "Guinness" historic world book of record surplus, amidst extremely slow progress in solving the myriad of market access issues which European exporters are faced with when selling their products and services in the Chinese market.

This is why we urge China to take concrete measures to address the long-standing issues that are hampering European companies' possibilities to trade with and invest in China. The High Level EU-China Economic and Trade Dialogue, that will be held after the summer 2023, is a key opportunity to make progress and to ensure a successful EU-China Summit towards the last quarter of this year.

These negative developments notwithstanding, there has also been a growing recognition of China's crucial role in addressing global and regional challenges. The fight against climate change, the preservation of biodiversity or the protection of the environment are the clearest examples of policy areas where coordination and cooperation between the EU and China create global value. Besides, other global challenges (such as the fight against pandemics, global heath, food security) or regional conflicts and issues (Korean Peninsula denuclearisation, Iran-JCPOA, among others), need or merit further joint efforts and cooperation between China and the EU.

This is why the European Union's description of our relation with China as one of partnership, competition and systemic rivalry, as included in the EU-China — A Strategic Outlook Joint Communication from March 2019, has not only not been changed, but reaffirmed and reinforced, most recently last June 29th by the European Council. The EU will continue to deal with China simultaneously as a partner for cooperation, an economic competitor and a systemic rival. Moreover, we remain determined to use dialogue as the key instrument across the board.

Despite our different political and economic systems, the European Union continues to believe that it can pursue constructive and stable relations with China, anchored on the respect for the rules-based international order, balanced engagement, transparency and reciprocity.

Turning to EU-China engagement on climate, biodiversity and environment, China's contribution is key for achieving the Paris agreement goals. With big power comes a great responsibility for the related emissions too. China has seen tremendous economic growth in the past few decades. Its per capita emissions now exceed the EU's by a third. This is another reason why ambitious emission reductions in China are vital. China made remarkable progress in renewable energy already. China may even surpass its own objectives. There is value in under promising and over delivering, but setting ambitious targets is important too: it inspires others to follow suit.

Throughout the dialogue we have with China on environment and climate, we are exploring avenues for collaboration in areas such as methane reduction, climate adaptation strategies, the circular economy, pollution control, biodiversity conservation, as well as combatting deforestation and wildlife trafficking. These have been the key issues that have been addressed in the successful last edition, in person for the first time in four years, of the High Level Climate and Environmental Dialogue that was held in Beijing, at the beginning of July 2023 by Vice-Premier Ding and Executive European Commission Vice-President Timmermans.

A major topic of EU-China discussion on climate is the Carbon Border Adjustment Mechanism (CBAM). It is important to underline that the EU's CBAM initiative is not at all a protectionist trade measure. It is exclusively a climate measure, the only aim of which is to avoid that Europe's strong efforts to reduce its own emissions do not lead to emissions being just moved ("carbon leakage") to other parts of the world. China is actually in a favourable situation as it already has in place an emissions trading system that, if extended to other important emitting economic sectors, would result in a CBAM exemption of Chinese exports to the EU.

To sum up, the European Union and China will continue to engage and cooperate to tackle global challenges, will continue to trade and invest with and in each other. However, the EU will also seek to ensure a level playing field, a trade and economic relationship that is balanced, reciprocal and mutually beneficial. We do not intend to decouple or to turn inwards. However, we will continue to build up resilience through reducing critical dependencies and vulnerabilities, including in our supply chains, and we will de-risk and diversify where necessary and appropriate. We also remain firmly committed to the promotion of respect for human rights and fundamental freedoms, an area where we remain systemic rivals with China due to the fundamental differences in our understanding and definition of such values and principles.

Finally, as a partner in strategic and international affairs, we look for a partner in China that — as a permanent member of the UN Security Council — fulfils its special responsibility in upholding the rules-based international order, the United Nations Charter and international law, namely with regards the unprovoked and unjustified Russian Aggression on Ukraine.

As we look to the future of EU-China relations, the challenge before us is how best to make our relations work and how to manage our differences. This will serve the interests of both the EU and China.

I. SETTING THE SCENE OF EU-CHINA RELATIONS

EU-China Relations in the New Global Scenario

JOSÉ MARÍA BENEYTO PÉREZ

PhD of Laws and PhD of Philosophy and Letters from the University of Münster (Germany). Professor of International Public Law and International Relations at the CEU San Pablo University. Director of the Royal University Institute of European Studies (CEU San Pablo University).

I. APPROACHING CHINA FROM THE PERSPECTIVE OF ITS COMPLEXITY

If there is one feature that characterises China today, it is that of complexity. It is therefore necessary first to move away from unilateral and undifferentiated perspectives. The People's Republic has created a new political system, in which the role of the state is central, but in which the dynamics of a multitude of internal and external actors and factors must be considered.

Chinese society is also complex. Sharp differences have emerged between urban and rural, rich and poor, older and younger generations. Economic growth has given rise to a new middle class, consisting of hundreds of millions of people, which is constantly expanding and has new demands and expectations. The assumption of economic development by both government and society as the main legitimising element of the system has established a new social contract, hardly recognisable to Marx or Mao, in which continued economic growth is critical to popular support for the current political order and its leaders. The reform process has unleashed a wide range of new social forces, which the Chinese Communist Party (CCP) does not always control and to which it accommodates with more difficulty than official propaganda projects[1].

But this complexity is not only visible at the social or political level, it also extends to the individual. The process of profound transformation experienced by Chinese citizens in four decades has dramatically changed

1. In this sense, Roberts, D. T., "How much support does the Chinese Communist Party really have?", in *Atlantic Council*, April 14th, 2021.

what it means to be a person in contemporary China, affirming the emergence of a new, more individualised, more globally connected "self", which answers questions such as: what does a good life consist of? in an unusual way. The new generations are asking new questions that would not have been framed in the same way by their parents: about the environment, state intervention in private life and the internet, religion and traditional family norms, the transformation of health care and the later stages of life, or the feeling of the better-off classes about how to give back to society some of what they have achieved[2].

However, despite being turned towards the future, today's China has not emerged from nothing, nor has the past ceased to play a role. It would be premature to claim that China's extraordinary transformation over the past forty years and the changing role of the CCP are totally unrelated to Chinese history. It is difficult to understand Chinese citizens' strong feelings about Taiwan, or Japanese leaders' visits to the Yasakuni Shrine, to take two examples, without implicit references to the past.

The historical and cultural perspective is relevant because it draws attention to some surprising historical continuities that have endured despite radical changes. History continues to play a relevant role in contemporary political discourse and in the self-perception of many citizens in China today. Certain characteristics, such as the tension between intellectuals and politicians, are permanent features of Chinese culture and can help to understand the political debates taking place in the People's Republic[3]. For all the differences between them, Xi Jinping has sought to insert himself in a line of continuity with Mao and with the trajectory and sources of the CPC[4]. The difficulties that Chinese leaders experience in preserving their power in the face of challenges from the elites is also a constant in Chinese history[5].

But perhaps the most striking demonstration of the way in which the past counts is the fact that the CPC takes it so seriously. Central to the continued legitimisation of the CPC are historical claims, to the extent that, for example,

---

2. Kleinman, A. et al., *Deep China. The Moral Life of the Person, What Anthropology and Psychiatry Tell Us about China Today*, University of California Press, 2011.
3. See, for example, on Confucianism, Bol, P. K., *Neo-Confucianism in History*, Harvard University Press, 2008.
4. Macfarquhar, R. *et al.*, *Mao´s Last Revolution*, Belknap Press of Harvard University Press, 2006.
5. Wang, Y., *Tying the Autocrat´s Hands: The Rise of the Rule of Law in China*, Cambridge University Press, 2015.

a Party Central Office document in 2013 banned public discussion of what it called "historical nihilism", i. e. critical assessments of the CPC's history. In fact, the CCP no longer claims to be just the heir to the ideas of a 19th century German philosopher, it also justifies its existence on the basis of being the legatee, transmitter and actualiser of 5,000 their years of Chinese people's history[6]. In this sense, statements about the unique origin of Chinese civilisation or about the historic Silk Road must be analysed in the light of their specific intentionality.

If it is true that history in China carries even more weight than in other countries, the challenges of the future open up a whole series of unknown challenges. Perhaps the most important question is the continuity of economic growth at a time when internal difficulties have been visibly shown, for example with the current mortgage and banking crisis. But there are many other open questions; among the most relevant, whether the fight against corruption will be successful; the progressive consequences of massive urbanisation and parallel abandonment of rural areas; dependence on foreign trade and investment; measures against pollution and commitment to climate change; or the effects of unbalanced demographics.

On the other hand, the West does not sufficiently highlight the many points on which the Chinese experience is a unique test bed from which to learn, as is the case the other way around. The ability of Chinese governments to respond to the challenges outlined above, to maintain high levels of economic growth and development while preserving political and social stability, are important laboratory tests from which other countries can learn, without implying that there is a "Chinese model" that can be transposed in its entirety to other contexts. The undoubted progress achieved — as well as the mistakes made — are lessons for other countries in analysing how to reduce poverty, how to deal with the problems of ageing or mental illness, and even how to restructure areas as diverse as education or energy production. Undoubtedly, along with the realisation of China's complexity, it is necessary to consider that the current confrontation with the West does not only take place in the security, economic or technological domains, but also in the cultural domain, and, in particular, in the process of setting international standards and attracting allies through the projection of its own values and models[7].

6. Saich, T., *Governance and Politics of China*, 4.ª edition, Palgrave, 2015.
7. For an analysis of the multidimensionality of the relationship with China, see Rudolph, J. and Szonyi, M. (eds.), *The China Questions. Critical insights into a rising power*, Harvard University Press, 2018.

Bearing these introductory caveats in mind, in the following sections we look at three dimensions of EU-China relations from the perspective of the new global scenario: i) the increase in Chinese military capabilities and the growing political confrontation with the United States; ii) the structural reasons behind the economic slowdown of China, and iii) the European strategy of de-risking.

II. THE REALITY OF CHINESE MILITARY POWER AND ITS CHALLENGE TO AMERICAN HEGEMONY

China is now the world's second largest economy and second largest defence budget. It has the largest conventional missile capability, the largest coastal defence guard and the second largest maritime navy, the result of the fastest shipbuilding in modern history. Particularly dramatic has been the growth of its nuclear armament since 2020[8].

For a better understanding of China's national security policy, it is necessary to consider the three components of the armed forces: the People's Liberation Army (PLA), the para-military People's Armed Police and the Militia. The policies that have guided the development of China's armed forces have been shaped by the development of Beijing's national security interests. Thus, having strengthened and centralised its domestic security and border security, the CCP has been expanding its security needs beyond Chinese territory.

At present, and most likely in the coming years, these Chinese "ripples of expanding security capabilities" are located in the three nearby seas, the South China Sea, the East China Sea and the Yellow Sea, which are the sites of maritime and island sovereignty claims.

In Chinese strategic thinking these sovereignty disputes in the adjacent seas could instigate a possible response from the United States or its allies. For this reason, in order to raise the risk threshold for US or allied intervention in Chinese sovereignty disputes, Beijing has been increasing its military capabilities in order to respond to US vulnerabilities. Reinterpreting the traditional concept in PLA's strategy of "using the territory to control the sea", Beijing has reinforced its missile systems and other armaments aimed at a possible counter-intervention, with the objective of "winning without having to intervene" and securing its long-term security interests,

---

8. Fravel, T. *et al.*, "China's Misunderstood Nuclear Expansion. How US Strategy is Fueling Beijing´s Growing Arsenal" in *Foreign Affairs*, November 10th, 2023.

probably through the goal of progressively becoming the preponderant power in East Asia[9].

To achieve these ends, China's security strategy pursues deterrence of any foreign military intervention, first by demonstrating its capabilities (ideally without having to use them lethally) and combining this tactic with incremental progress below the threshold of war, in "grey zones" where it exercises coercion against rival claims, primarily using its coast guard and maritime militia. Thus, on the basis of available data, experts conclude that the increase in capabilities to conduct operations in relation to the near seas is mostly focused on Taiwan and the Spratly Islands dispute in the South China Sea, and is much smaller beyond these boundaries. In other words, it is generally understood that over the next decade the United States will maintain its prevalence in the event of a war against the Chinese military, although the latter will be in a position to achieve temporary superiority in certain sea or air spaces, and US victory will become progressively more costly than it would have been years ago if the current pace of Chinese military build-up continues[10].

A scenario involving Taiwan remains the most far-reaching plan. The PLA is seen as being in a position to conduct significant military operations, occupying a Taiwanese sovereign island or directly attacking the main island with missiles, both of which, it is estimated, would nevertheless backfire on Beijing because of Taiwanese resistance and the likely military response from Washington and its allies. The alternative of establishing a blockade of Taiwan is also widely believed by analysts to fail if Washington's reaction is robust, thus making US intervention a decisive factor. Finally, an amphibious invasion of Taiwan is considered unrealistic, given the structural limitations of the PLA and Taiwan's ability to exploit its formidable natural defences.

Second, the South China Sea appears to be a more permissive theatre for Chinese military action. Here the objective is not to invade and conquer a sophisticated and morally resilient population of 23.5 million, but reefs and islets with, if any, a very small indigenous population. Given the relative weakness of the neighbouring countries with which the PRC has disputes over jurisdiction over the area, both the coast guard and the maritime militia can conduct a variety of operations in the "grey zone" with significant

9. McReynolds, J. (ed.), *China´s Evolving Military Strategy*, The Jamestown Foundation, 2017.
10. There is currently an intense debate in the United States on these issues, with partly contradictory views, see Hass, R. and Blanchette, J., "The Right Way to Deter China From Attacking Taiwan. American Hard Power Is Not Enough", in *Foreign Affairs*, November 8th, 2023.

results. Without US intervention, the PLA could prevail over neighbouring defences. In the hypothetical case of US action, for example in support of its Philippine ally, in a crisis or conflict with the People's Republic, both sides would nevertheless face significant operational challenges. For the PLA, the biggest obstacle would be to be able to deploy sufficient forces to the highly vulnerable Spratly Islands and secure supply. If it could operate with some element of surprise, however, it would confront Washington with an unattractive situation.

The other arc of capabilities that China has been weaving concerns the extension of its growing external interests through initiatives such as the Silk Road (One Belt, One Road), which seeks to expand China's zone of economic and political influence along the old overland Silk Road through Eurasia, but also by sea and cyberspace[11]. Through these initiatives and others of varying scope in the region, China has been weaving a web of substantial and influential capabilities, albeit of lesser intensity in their strategic value. In immediate security terms, this network has enabled Beijing to protect its citizens and assets abroad, including evacuations from Libya and Yemen, or anti-piracy maritime escorts in the Gulf of Aden.

These latter examples, as well as China's participation in UN peacekeeping operations, show, moreover, Beijing's interest in contributing to global security and its aim to shape the course of international organisations, in the latter case by assuming a greater leadership role in UN bodies and agencies. The projection of more robust maritime power, including carrier-based operations and the strengthening of access to overseas facilities, most likely through bases such as the one initially established in Djibouti, are generally seen as progressing more gradually[12].

Ultimately, the military build-up, which has undoubtedly already achieved remarkable development, will in turn depend heavily on the level of economic growth, leading to a more complex negotiation within the CCP to achieve the goals of security and continued modernisation of armaments. In addition, the Chinese government is expected to encounter similar problems — of a structural and organisational nature, in terms of the costs of more sophisticated weaponry and the adjustment of currently high salary and pensions for military personnel — as those faced by more advanced militaries.

11. See Beneyto, J. M. and Fanjul, E., *El papel de España en la Nueva Ruta de la Seda. Oportunidades, retos, recomendaciones*, Thomson Reuters Aranzadi, Pamplona, 2018.
12. MacDevitt, M. A., *China as a Twenty First Century Naval Power. Theory, Practice, and Implications*, Naval Institute Press, 2020

In particular, more sophisticated weaponry also requires greater technological innovation, higher investment intensity and higher maintenance costs in order to advance or even retain the position it has achieved vis-à-vis competitors. The advantages China may have gained so far from lower costs will weaken as military equipment becomes more dependent on advanced materials and technology, and less on manpower. Likewise, more sophisticated weaponry implies proportionately smaller gains from the acquisition of foreign technologies. These more sophisticated technologies would primarily be needed to conduct operations of greater geographic scope, whereas operations in the Spratly Islands or similar are demonstrably achievable with current Chinese military-technological capabilities.

China's emergence has presented the United States with an unprecedented foreign policy challenge. For the first time since the Second World War, the US is facing a major competing power with both military and economic capabilities that can quickly become a rival to its own. China is also the first world power since pre-war Japan to confront US maritime supremacy, a fundamental pillar of US national security and global power. China's emergence calls into question US security in a vital region, considering that the Americans entered World War II and the post-Cold War period with the aim of preserving a regional balance in Asia that would guarantee their security. Undoubtedly, the growing US-China rivalry is the crux of today's global geopolitics and the successive crises we are witnessing. Russia's invasion of Ukraine, Hamas' aggression against Israel cannot be easily explained without making them part of this broader equation. The US response and the dynamics of the Sino-US confrontation decisively influence the positions of other actors: US allies in the region, EU and other European countries, Russia, emerging regional powers, and countries not aligned with either of the two emerging blocs.

The rise of China has forced the United States to adopt two strategies that are not easily balanced and, on whose management, depends whether the confrontation between the two will intensify or moderate.

The first is the need for the US to counter China's strategic strengthening through its increased military capabilities in the region. The primary US national security imperative has become to neutralise China's potential with its own weaponry in order to prevent its alliances in the region from being substantially weakened, and thus its presence.

But, secondly, Washington also needs to preserve cooperation with China, and not only as a means to promote difficult stability in the region. Many

US bilateral and global interests require Sino-US cooperation. Increasing strategic confrontation between the two countries is leading to a significant erosion of many of these interests and a significant increase in US economic and security costs.

Since 2010 there has been a negative spiral in the relationship between the two powers, such that it is worse today than at any time since 1972, and the US strategic position in East Asia is now at its lowest ebb. There are frequent altercations between the two militaries in the air or sea in Southeast Asia, tension over Taiwan has been growing, as have territorial disputes with China's neighbours, and both Washington and Beijing have developed and are developing weaponry with the explicit intention of defeating the other in a military confrontation. It is no wonder that books advising to reflect on alternatives to escape the constraints of the "Thucydides trap"[13] have been so successful.

The main US response to Chinese government activism — its expansion into South China Sea islands and facilities, pressure on US allies, and surveillance of naval and air operations in the area — has been to expand its maritime presence in the area, strengthen its alliances and preserve the balance of power in defence of its security interests. This has meant first and foremost strengthening agreements with Japan, Australia, the Philippines and New Zealand, and increasing its military presence and cooperation with the Philippines, Australia, South Korea, Malaysia, Singapore and Vietnam.

The US containment strategy has not always been successful and it remains to be demonstrated that it has necessarily improved its security or that of its allies. The deployment of missile defence systems in South Korea in 2016, for example, did not enhance South Korea's security vis-à-vis North Korea, as it was primarily aimed at weakening China's nuclear deterrent in the area and showing to Beijing the US's determination to contain. Nor did pushing the Philippine government to bring a case against China before the Permanent Court of Arbitration (PCA) with the intention of isolating Beijing in its maritime claims against its neighbours achieve the desired result. Although the Philippines won the dispute before the PCA, it was Beijing that was ultimately victorious, successfully isolating the Philippines and forcing the Dutarte government into a policy shift away from the US.

Not all analysts, including Americans, agree on the wisdom of the successive governments' strategy, which they believe may have failed both

13. Allison, G., *Destined for War. Can America and China Escape Thucydides's Trap?*, Houghton Mifflin Harcourt, Boston, 2017.

to strengthen strategic ties with South Korea, the Philippines and Vietnam and to limit China's maritime presence in the South China Sea. Moreover, Chinese perceptions of Washington's objectives have only accelerated Beijing's reaction to what is seen as a clear desire to prevent China's further growth.

The need for a more effective strategy that seeks to keep the Chinese government engaged with world order, rather than contributing to its dismantling, has therefore been frequently stressed. In a nutshell, this strategy means, to stop framing the confrontation in existential terms, or in terms of China's continued collapse, but rather to emphasise the dangers and self-harm that such a situation would entail[14].

This presupposes that Washington assumes, on the basis of cohesive and sustainable domestic support, that the primary interest of the United States — and China — lies in preserving a functioning international system. This overall aim has been dramatically made visible once again by the two geopolitical crises in Ukraine and the Gaza Strip. Urgently needed is a global order that, in short, contributes to the security and prosperity of the different actors on the international stage: the G-2, Russia and regional powers, Europe and Western countries, the Global South.

This strategy, which should overcome the increasingly unilateral approach of containment, thus moves away from the Cold War objectives of isolating the Soviet Union and forcing its collapse under the weight of its own contradictions. The aim should rather be to ensure China's engagement with a global system that serves as a framework and constraint for domestic behaviour and facilitates the identification of Chinese national interests with the continuity — and development — of existing rules and norms. But in order to be acceptable to Beijing, this strategy would have to involve recognition of the diversity of political systems and cultures and the legitimate desire of Beijing — and other countries, starting with emerging regional powers — to influence the development of international standards and norms[15].

On the other hand, Washington has recently shown its ambivalence towards maintaining the existing order, in the design and evolution of

14. See, among the abundant bibliography, that stresses the need of alternatives to increasing tensions, Ross, R. S., *China in the Era of Xi Jinping: Domestic and Foreign Policy Challenges*, Georgetown University Press, 2017

15. Without accepting the elements of exaltation of a Chinese cultural primacy, the argument of the well-known book by Weiwei, Z., *The China Wave. Rise of a Civilizational State*, World Century, 2011, rightly points to the need to recognise the diversity of systems.

which it has been a major player. It would be very difficult to make China stay within the order if the United States itself is not confident of doing so. Whether on trade, arms control, international trade or global health, Washington has in recent times demostrated growing inability to accept the constraints and requirements of the current international system.

For all its imperfections, the contemporary international framework has helped to prevent conflicts between great powers and has enabled hundreds of millions of people around the world to lift themselves out of poverty. The counterfactual scenario to cooperation and détente is what we have begun to experience again since the aggression in Ukraine.

China's rise since the late 1970s ran parallel to its decision to integrate into the world economy and the institutions that underpin the global order. China's economic and social development would not have been possible if it had remained in the isolation of the Mao era. China's growth in the coming decades also depends on maintaining international linkages and networks within an inclusive system that facilitates the country's access to the markets, foreign capital and technology it needs. A breakdown or fragmentation of the international system would be devastating to China's modernisation goals. As the International Monetary Fund has pointed out, a severe fragmentation of the world economy could represent a 7 per cent cut in global output. Given that China is the world's largest trading power — along with the European Union — the two would be most exposed to such a contraction.

So, while the Chinese government is demanding greater recognition and re-positioning in the international order, a fragmentation between a West allied with the United States and a China allied with Russia — with which, let us not forget, it shares thousands of kilometres of border and a common past of conflict — as well as eventually with a heterogeneous group of countries, could not satisfy the technology, trade and security needs of China. It would be counterproductive for the United States to continue to isolate and encircle China with a web of alliances to contain it, rather than to harness its potential for global order.

III. THE DIFFICULTIES OF THE CHINESE ECONOMY AND ITS FUTURE

China has achieved the largest reduction in poverty in human history, with between 400 and 600 million people being lifted out of poverty, a continuous growth of 10 per cent for thirty years, which has led to an almost twenty-fold increase in its economy. This has created extraordinary new opportunities for a whole generation[16].

However, a number of the causes that made this unprecedented development possible have disappeared or are disappearing, which means that the pace of economic growth has modulated, possibly leading to anaemic growth, or even — in the most negative scenarios — recession, due to the current housing and mortgage crisis.

Since 1978, one of the main factors has been capital accumulation, with the improvement in labour (including higher levels of education and experience) contributing only around 10 to 20 per cent of the total increase, and counting the other elements that are part of the productivity improvement. What was the rationale for this massive capital accumulation?

Several reasons have often been put forward to explain this phenomenon[17]. The first has to do with the very significant shift by successive governments in the allocation of resources from a centrally planned socialist economy to a more market-based approach. This meant that both households and enterprises could make investment decisions on the basis of prices, which were strongly influenced by supply and demand on a product-by-product basis. In addition, domestic prices became more closely linked to the world economy.

The second reason was the shift from a purely domestic economy to openness to the global economy. Exports were favoured, initially through special economic zones (SEZs) with specific tax and regulatory regimes, and later on a more generalised basis. Contrary to what happened in Japan or South Korea, foreign direct investment was favoured and directed partly towards the SEZs, but also towards the rest of the domestic economy. This was initially done through joint ventures and later through subsidiaries of foreign companies. The initial objective was to increase the volume of scarce foreign exchange and then to attract foreign technology (including marketing and business management skills) to China.

A third factor for growth was the clever exploitation of China's large overseas diaspora, which had extensive experience in dealing with foreigners

16. A current perspective, with detailed scenarios for the future, Liu, X. and Yao, S., *Sustaining China´s Economic Growth in the Twenty-first Century*, Routledge, 2023.
17. Cooper, R. N., "Can China´s High Growth Continue?" in Rudolph, J. and Szonyi, M., *The China Questions*, p. 119-125.

and could act as a bridge between the isolated mainland and the rest of the world. A very significant part of the initial investments in SEZs came from entrepreneurs from Hong Kong, Taiwan and other overseas Chinese communities who knew how to sell goods and products in the US and Europe and were familiar with the marketing and distribution channels.

A fourth factor was the demographic dividend, as China's working-age population (aged 15-64) grew sharply in this period relative to the increase in the total population, from 66 per cent to 74 per cent between 1990 and 2012 alone. Their productive employment contributed effectively to economic growth and rising per capita income. In these years, the one-child policy proved favourable, before the problems of accelerated ageing set in.

The fifth factor was a dramatic leap from rural to urban and more productive activities, as it has been the case in all poorer countries that improve their productivity by reducing agricultural population rates. Whereas in 1980, 70 per cent of China's labour force was agricultural, by 2016 this had fallen to 30 per cent. Some studies estimate that this factor alone accounted for an annual improvement of between 1.1 and 1.3 per cent of GDP growth.

The sixth factor was particularly high savings-to-investment ratios, in some years close to half of national output. Some of the investments were carried out by state-owned enterprises or local authorities, but most were made by new entities not owned by the central government, such as initiatives set up by cities and towns. These were followed by purely private investments, including some by foreign companies, thanks to new legislation that made them possible. Approximately 65 per cent of total investments in 2012 came from private sources, providing buildings and equipment to the expanding non-agricultural labour force. But another large segment of investment went to building new homes for an increasingly urbanised and higher-wage workforce. Another part of the investments shifted to infrastructure, partly for civic needs such as water supply, roads and streets, transport, sanitation, etc., and for ports, airports and inter-city transport, such as highways and railways.

A seventh factor was education. Already in the 1950s, a newly empowered CCP made a strategic decision to provide primary education for all Chinese children, thus enabling peasants to acquire a minimum level of literacy and their children to gain access to factory jobs. From the mid-1980s onwards, free schooling extended to nine years, and higher education schools and universities multiplied their numbers, to the point that in 2016 around 30 per cent of young adults were receiving some form of university education, up from just 2 per cent in the early 1980s.

These are the main factors behind China's strong growth during the three decades since the start of economic reform. Of course, technological advances — mostly acquired from abroad — also played an important role, but technology was largely a product of the above factors: foreign investment (and advice), the contribution of the overseas diaspora, high investment ratios, as well as rising educational levels, including training provided by foreign companies[18].

Once China completed its transition to a market-based economy — with some exceptions, such as banking, oil and telecommunications — the potential for growth based on economic reforms was substantially reduced. Foreign investment has also been drastically reduced in recent years. China continues to be the world's largest exporter, having increased its exports at a rate of 17 percent annually between 1980 and 2010, but this factor can only reach more modest percentages and has been subject in the last decade to exogenous factors such as the financial crisis, the pandemic and geopolitical tensions. Nor is the contribution of diaspora Chinese still relevant, once mainland Chinese have learned to manage directly with foreigners.

The demographic dividend ended in 2012, when the ratio of the working-age population to the total population peaked. This ratio has been declining, first slowly, then more rapidly, and China's ageing population is a major current constraint, which will not be significantly affected by the two-child policy. It is estimated that the median age will rise from 35 in 2010 to 47 in 2040, a ratio only similar to that of South Korea.

As far as the agricultural labour force is concerned, much of the mobilisation to the cities has already taken place and the average age in the countryside has also grown rapidly. In addition, families tend to try to preserve some of their agricultural property, to prevent it from

18. While there is also much debate about the causes of China's stagnation, the factors highlighted by Richard Cooper in the above-mentioned article form part of a certain consensus on this issue. On other factors, including in particular the growing influence of the CCP and the "long-covid" policy, see, for example, Posen, A., "The End of China's Economic Miracle. How Beijing's Struggles Could Be an Opportunity for Washington", in *Foreign Affairs*, September/October 2023, p. 118-130, and the critical comments to this article by, respectively, Zoe Liu, Z. and Pettis, M. "Who Killed the Chinese Economy. The Contested Causes of Stagnation?", in *Foreign Affairs*, November/December 2023, p. 176- 183. As for studies indicating other specific factors, Zongyuan Zoe Liu has written an important work highlighting the influence and different functions carried out by China's sovereign wealth funds in relation to the country's economic growth, *Sovereign Funds: How the Communist Party of China Finances Its Global Ambitions*, Belknap Press, 2023.

being completely reallocated to others, according to the so-called *hukou* system. As a result, rural-urban migration is lower than in the past, thus contributing less to growth.

For years, the Chinese government has been aiming to rebalance the Chinese economy to make it less dependent on exports and investment and to encourage private and public consumption. But this policy has had no tangible success and has generated another series of collateral effects, such as favouring a more speculative economy, which has been one of the reasons for the current mortgage crisis and the collapse of some major financial institutions. Nor have returns on new investments, particularly in public investments (infrastructure) or by public enterprises, contributed to growth in recent years.

These are structural, policy-independent obstacles, which can nevertheless be accelerated or retarded by policy decisions. In other words, education alone could be a factor that continues to contribute to growth, but only if increasingly well-educated university graduates can find suitable jobs. It remains to be seen whether the Chinese education system and Chinese society in general can respond to the need for greater innovation. At the root of the success of the reforms was a strongly pragmatic and down-to-earth methodology: moving step by step through experimentation, keeping channels open for criticism and analysis of results, and adjusting policies on the basis of local successes and failures[19].

There was thus very little ideology. Several authors have recently pointed out how the major governmental intrusiveness of the last decades, and in particular the errors of the "long covid" policy, must be considered as a substantial cause in the current difficulties of the Chinese economy[20].

Thus, the reported effects of weak consumption, low business investment, rising debt, and growing financial anxiety among Chinese households have their root in the imbalances that have been dragging on for at least two decades, characteristic of the growth model followed by the Chinese leadership. While the economic growth based on high savings and investment rates advocated by Deng Xiaoping in the 1980s and 1990s was successful as long as these rates could be absorbed by the productivity requirements of the Chinese economy, this deficit closed around 2006. The regulatory and institutional changes — business, financial and political — that would

19. Perkins, D. H., *The Economic Transformation of China*, World Scientific Publishers, 2015.
20. Small, A., *No limits.: The Inside Story of China´s War With the West*, Melville House, 2022.

have led to a consumption-oriented economy, higher household incomes, and the building of a stronger individual and collective safety net were not implemented. During the period 2006-2011, household consumption as a percentage of GDP fell to 34 per cent, compared to 50 per cent in the rest of the world.

Thus, China's growth over the past two decades has been driven by growth in speculative assets, especially real estate, as well as an unsustainable increase in debt. Business investment has been strongly constrained in this period by low consumption, which in turn has weakened the interest of private companies in expanding production.

At the same time, the focus of economic activity has shifted from sectors subject to severe budget constraints and the need to make profits, basically the private sector, to areas with fewer constraints, such as the public sector and those areas of the private sector with secured access to finance, such as real estate. The Chinese economy has thus had to rely on an expansionary public sector, given weak private investment, in order to achieve the high levels of growth demanded by Beijing[21].

On the other hand, it is stressed — perhaps more complementarily than contradictorily — that the government's increasing intervention into everyday life over the last decade, since Xi Jinping came to power in 2013, has been an essential factor in the change in Chinese citizens' behaviour. The abandonment of pragmatism and autocratic self-restraint by Xi and the CCP leadership — reinforced by the 'long covid' policy — would therefore be at the root of the change in households and small businesses and their increasing aversion to consumption. The CCP leadership would reportedly have taken concrete measures in recent years to prevent the private sector from positively influencing growth in ways undesired by the Communist party[22].

As a consequence of all these factors, and mainly due to the real estate crisis, China is far from its growth targets, which, in the context of a political system whose internal legitimacy has been mainly based on economic growth, constitutes a threat to its stability. In a more medium-term perspective, economist Derek Scissors estimates that the Chinese economy will feel the

21. Pettis, M., "How China Trapped Itself. The CCP´s Economic Model Has Left It With Only Bad Choices", in *Foreign Affairs*, October 5th, 2022.
22. Picking up on some of the views already mentioned and broadening the perspective to include new factors to be taken into account, see Huang, Y., *The Rise and Fall of the EAST: How Exams, Autocracy, Stability, and Technology Brought China Succes, and Why Thay Might Lead to Its Decline*, Yale University Press, 2023.

full effects of an ageing population, rising debt and constraints on private sector innovation from 2030 onwards, a consequence of the government's centralised role in the allocation of capital, talent and technology[23].

IV. THE EU AND CHINA: THE STRATEGY OF DERISKING

Since the first EU-China summit in 1998, relations between these two trading giants have rapidly become institutionalised through dozens of official meetings held each year. A strategic partnership between the two was established in 2003 and, despite profound differences in their political systems and values, the two developed a dense network of interactions at many different levels, from political to people-to-people contacts, economic and commercial, accounting today for 30% of world trade[24].

From a diplomatic perspective, Xi Jinping's visit to the European institutions in April 2014 — the first by a Chinese president — was undoubtedly an important boost. The interest shown by the Chinese counterpart and the determination of Chancellor Merkel, in particular, made it possible to sign an ambitious Comprehensive Investment Agreement in December 2020, now suspended in the European Parliament as a result of Chinese government sanctions against several European parliamentarians and diplomats[25].

Statements by EU and Chinese leaders in the past have often referred to common interests, their perspectives have been relatively similar on global issues such as trade or climate change, and there has been a joint desire for greater cooperation and coordinated action throughout most of the relationship. In the face of China's growing confrontation with the US, the EU continued to maintain the concept of "partnership" in its strategic documents, while also underlining the complexity of the relationship by clearly pointing out that the two are not only partners and competitors, but also strategic adversaries[26].

---

23. Scissors, D., "Failure of the China Economics Field", AEIdeas, *American Enterprise Institute*, August 22nd, 2023.
24. For a comprehensive overview of how the EU-China relationship has evolved and its different dimensions, see Christiansen, Th., Kirchner, E. and Wissenbach, U., *The European Union and China*, Red Globe Press, 2019.
25. On the EU-China Comprehensive Investment Agreement and its geostrategic implications, vid. Beneyto, J. M., *"El acuerdo de inversiones UE-China y sus efectos sobre la creación de una corte multilateral de inversiones"*, in *Arbitraje. Revista de arbitraje comercial y de inversiones*, vol. 23, n. 1, 2021, p. 25-54.
26. The EU's initial document on EU-China "comprehensive strategic partnership" has been largely superseded by the EU-China Strategic Outlook, with the Joint Communiqué

The history of the People's Republic of China has little in common with that of Europe, and both sides have gone through unique historical experiences, with very different processes of political and economic development, and different geopolitical positions and interests. These diverse geopolitical and security contexts do not preclude the existence of growing economic interdependence. They also share a common, if differentiated, sense of their global responsibilities.

China is seen as more relevant to the EU and most European countries than Europe is to China, leading to an imbalance in the number of initiatives on both sides. In large part, this is due to the EU's decision in favour of multilateralism and a political culture that seeks to engage and expand its democratic values, as opposed to a Chinese foreign policy that favours autonomy and multipolarity. On the other hand, Beijing often seeks to cultivate bilateral relations with European countries — especially with some of them, especially if there is competition for certain benefits, such as lucrative contracts, attracting investment to China, or gaining their diplomatic support in international organisations — and develops its own strategic objectives without taking the EU into account.

The period of greatest cooperation between China and the EU was during the process leading up to the PRC's entry into the WTO. This was also the time when the contradictions between the two became visible. While for the EU China's accession to the WTO was merely the beginning that should confirmed how the path of interdependence would lead to political reform and Beijing was soon asked to go beyond its commitments, for China it was an end point and a hard-won victory over deep-rooted domestic interests. It is not surprising, therefore, that a progressive shift in the relationship followed shortly thereafter and trade disputes began to emerge.

The focus of Chinese governments during Hu Jintao's ten years in office was clearly not on international affairs or on making concessions towards a greater role for the market, but on extending economic growth from coastal areas to inland and rural areas, strengthening the Chinese economy and making it more resilient. Thus, the EU and China's agreement on a global trade agenda was only temporary, and the arrival to power of Xi Jinping, who from the outset showed much more interest in international

of March 12nd, 2019, and the "EU-China 2020 Strategic Agenda for Cooperation", with the Joint Communiqué of April 2020, "EU-China Comprehensive Strategic Partnership for Mutual Benefit and Win-win Cooperation", which advocated a differentiation in the relation according to specific areas -security, trade, climate change, humanitarian operations, etc.-.

influence and the projection of Chinese power, has meant a new chapter in the evolution of the relationship, but now on the basis of assertiveness on the Chinese side.

A central factor in the relationship between the EU and China has been the role played by the United States. As a consequence of certain European countries' positions on international issues — the reaction to the invasion of Iraq, or the usually French rhetoric on multipolarity and a "more European Europe"[27] — Chinese strategists at some point in the mid-2000s mused about the possibility that the EU could line up with China as a kind of counterweight to the United States in a multipolar world. But Europe has not only remained a staunch ally of the US — an alliance that has been reinforced within NATO following Russia's invasion of Ukraine [28]- but it has more generally maintained its unrestricted commitment to multilateralism, without playing the multipolar game.

Since 2021 the EU-China relationship has deteriorated substantially as a result of a number of irritants: Chinese countermeasures to European sanctions over human rights violations committed particularly against the Uighur minority, economic coercion measures and unfair trade practices against the internal market, the deterioration of Hong Kong's autonomy, cyber-security attacks against the EU from Chinese territory, sanctions over the opening of a Lithuanian diplomatic representation in Taipei, and Chinese positioning in support of Russia in the Ukrainian war. The EU has, however, maintained the strategy of cooperation and engagement, given China's crucial role in addressing global and regional challenges. Differences among member states in their positions on China have increased and this has prevented a new common strategy, leading some analysts to speak of a 'no strategy'[29]. While others insist on the need to build new economic ties and strengthen existing ones to reduce strategic dependencies by updating the EU Action Plan on China and a three-pronged approach: de-risk, engage and coordinate[30].

---

27. See Shambaugh, D., "China and Europe: The Emerging Axis", in *Current History*, September 2004, p. 243-248.
28. Beneyto, J. M. "La neutralidad ficticia de China", in Ibid.(ed.*) ¿Hacia un nuevo orden mundial? La guerra de Ucrania y sus consecuencias,* Deusto, Madrid, 2022, p. 145-169.
29. Esteban, M., and Otero-Iglesias, M., *"From a China strategy to no strategy at all — Exploring the diversity of European approaches"*, Real Instituto Elcano, retrieved from *https://www.realinstitutoelcano.org/en/monographs/from-a-china-strategy-to-no-strategy-at-all-exploring.the-diversity-of-european-approaches*
30. Chimits, F., Ghiretti, F., and Stec, G., *"Updating the Eu Action Plan on China. De-risk, Engage, Coordinate"*, MERICS report, June 2023, retrieved from *https://merics.de/studie/updating-eu-action.plan-china-de-risk-engage-coordinate*

It would be a mistake, however, if Western countries wanted to use a possible situation of Chinese weakness to try to isolate China. Neither further US nor European interests would be well served. A more anxious and internally unstable China could lead to a further strengthening of the autocratic power of the CCP and its top leadership. Countries such as Iran, North Korea, Russia or Venezuela could then benefit from more unrestricted support from Beijing and pose a greater security risk. Beijing would most likely deepen its current strategy of building an alternative order, consolidating rival institutions and perhaps, in the medium term, substitute international bodies. It could also use its resources to make the BRICS group, progressively enlarged from its initial members Brazil, Russia, India, China and South Africa, the main player in setting the international agenda, displacing the G-7 and G-20. Beijing's contribution to development would also be channelled more decisively towards institutions such as the Asian Infrastructure Investment Bank, to the detriment of the World Bank. Although China guaranteed its support for the BRICS expansion that was decided in August 2023[31], it remains to be seen whether this will achieve more than symbolic value in the medium term.

A growing number of members of the Biden Administration — as well as G-7 countries — have, since its first formulation in January 2023 at the "State of the Union" address to the European Parliament, taken up European Commission President Ursula von der Leyen's notion of "de-risking" rather than "de-coupling", the latter first announced by the Trump administration, with respect to China. Taken to its logical extreme, de-coupling would mean severing the ties between the economies. However, both the economies of the United States and China and of China and the European Union — and in particular of its two core countries, Germany and France — are more inextricably intertwined than those who advocate decoupling and greater protectionism are willing to accept. There is no plausible way to undo this interdependence without irreparable damage.

According to von der Leyen's interventions in 2023[32], "de-risking" should be carried out through diplomatic instruments on the one hand, and

31. *BRICS and Africa: Partnership for Mutually Accelerated Growth, Sustainable Development and Inclusive Multilateralism*, Johannesburg II Declaration, XV BRICS Summit, Sandton, Gauteng, South Africa, August 23rd, 2023, retrieved from *https://brics2023.gov.za/wp-content/uploads/2023/08/Jhb-II-Declaration-24-August-2023-1.pdf*

32. Initially, "2023 State of the Union Adress by President von der Leyen", European Commission, retrieved from https://ec.europa.eu/commission/presscorner/detail/en/speech_23_4426, later her speech at the European Council meeting of June 2023,

economic means on the other. While "de-risking" through diplomacy leads to "relationship management and an open and frank exchange with our Chinese counterpart", the economic aspect would be based on four pillars:

(i) Increasing the competitiveness and resilience of Europe's economy and industry, including greater independence and diversity of supply in key inputs needed for European competitiveness, especially in the health, digital and environmental technology sectors, and with the aim of strengthening resilience in maritime, cyber security, space, defence and innovation;

(ii) Better use of existing trade mechanisms, particularly those that have been put in place in recent years in the EU to address security issues, such as the Anti-Coaction Instrument or the Foreign Subsidies Regulation, by taking a more cohesive and assertive stance on their implementation;

(iii) Developing new defence mechanisms for some critical sectors where dual use cannot be excluded or where there are human rights implications;

(iv) Alignment in favour of EU economic security with other partners, in particular with members of the G7 and G20. The focus should be on concluding free trade agreements (e. g. with Australia, India), modernising them (e. g. Mexico), and making better use of them for cooperation in sectors such as digital or green technology (through, for example, the EU-India Trade and Technology Council or the EU-Japan Green Alliance), as well as infrastructure investment (the EU Global Gateway strategy).

The first of these points shows that it is actually very difficult to separate risk reduction from decoupling, as more strategic autonomy implies the decoupling of supply chains of Chinese origin in certain essential areas. However, derisking cannot be simply understood as entering a new era in which the actors have become securitised states, with economies dependent on strategic objectives, but about how the vulnerabilities generated by China's rise are adequately managed. In other words, the goal is to preserve as much as possible the benefits of the global economy and the interdependencies generated, while addressing common problems and dismantling the most pressing security threats.

29-30, retrieved from *https://www.consilium.europa.eu/en/meetings/european-council/2023/06/29-30/*

In other words, the "risk reduction" formula involves, first and foremost, diversifying resources and sources of supply — particularly in critical sectors such as energy, chips and raw materials — and making the economy more resilient, as well as combating trade practices deemed unfair, establishing a more robust system of investment monitoring in strategic companies, and working towards the removal of Chinese restrictions on essential materials for semiconductors and solar panels.

There is in this regard undoubtedly a danger that technological advances could intensify rivalries between the world's major economic powers, which would intensify geostrategic competition. The emergence of two or more economic blocs (US/West versus China), with divergent standards and regulations, as well as the regionalisation of supply chains and company operations, are possible scenarios, to the extent that quite a few European companies could find themselves in one or the other bloc, unable to meet the requirements of both or having to pay a high price for doing so. In recent years, there has been an intensification of measures in this direction, through the imposition of export tariffs, sanctions, or the establishment of incompatible standards, for example for data and cloud applications. Some European companies might then choose to create completely separate structures to try to remain in the markets of the two spheres of influence, with negative commercial and economic consequences.

There is, however, a second dimension to derisking, instead of decoupling. In his 'State of the Union' speech, von der Leyen argued for more dialogue and less polarisation of positions, while at the June 2023 European Council, she stressed the need to keep channels open for trade and dialogue on global issues such as global warming. Finally, in a lecture delivered in November 2023 for the European Council on Foreign Relations and the Mercator Institute in Berlin (MERICS)[33], — a think tank specialising in relations with China, with strong connections to the German industry and which was subject to sanctions by the Chinese authorities — after having stressed that "China is changing" and is moving towards "a new era of security and control" with the aim of "transforming the international system by placing itself at the centre", von der Leyen clearly insisted on the 'vital importance' of preserving diplomatic stability and open lines of communication with Beijing. This is not preclude her from pointing out "issues of deep concern",

33. "Speech by President von der Leyen at the European China Conference 2023 organised by the European Council on Foreign Relations and the Mercator Institute for China Studies", Berlin, November 16th, 2023, retrieved from *https://ec.europa/commission/presscorner/detail/en/speech_23_5851*

while underlying the need to generate a framework for discussion for a more ambitious partnership and fairer and more disciplined competition, without implying the relationship to China had to be defensive.

Summarizing, the EU's quest for greater strategic autonomy and economic security has recently been coupled with repeated calls to reduce critical dependencies on 'systemic rivals' such as China. The ambitious target proposed by von der Leyen aims, for example, at producing at least 40 per cent of its green technology autonomously.

However, China's dominance in key strategic sectors is so significant that progress has not been very successful. Europe's dependence on China may well have increased by 2023, rather than decreased. For every five containers transported from China to the EU, only one makes the reverse journey. Compared to 2012 figures, Chinese imports have tripled and the trade balance has continued to deteriorate during the Covid-19 years and as a consequence of the Russian invasion of Ukraine. In some sectors, the reality is that it is difficult to find alternatives to Chinese products. Dependence on rare earths is 98%, on antibiotics 79%, and nearly 90% of the world's solar panel production is in Chinese hands[34].

The difficulties for companies to find alternative producers have even led a number of companies to reinforce their presence in China, in order to continue serving their vast domestic market with local production, independently from the rest of the world and therefore resilient in the face of possible new sanctions or an abrupt decoupling, resulting, for example, from a serious crisis over Taiwan.

On the other hand, decoupling has the effect of reducing the already limited domestic competition in China and giving up even more market share to Chinese companies. The side effect is to make Europe more dependent on state aid, quite possibly increasing frictions between European countries and delaying not only the decarbonisation timetable in Europe, but also in the rest of the world. 'Risk reduction' as a strategy in the face of trade weaponisation — visibly highlighted in 2023 by the Chinese authorities' swift ban on EU exports of gallium and germanium to the EU as a countermeasure to the Dutch government's limitations on the export of semiconductor technology — appears to be a clearly more positive one. The problem is how to implement it.

34. Schaus, M., and Lanoo, K., *The EU´s aim to de-risk itself from China is risky…yet necessary*, CEPS, Brussels, September 7th, 2023, retrieved from *https://www.ceps.eu/the-eus-aim-to-de-risk-itself-from-china-is-risky-yet-necessary/*

First, the two transitions, digital and environmental, require greater coordination and integration of member states' research and development policies, increased EU funding, and a global alliance for decarbonisation, which would enable the development of technologies that are not dependent on China for the benefit of the EU and the rest of the world, including China. Given the increase in global green demand, it is difficult for Chinese manufacturing capacity to meet all demand. However, for more than a few potential members of such a potential global alliance, the EU's green policies are excessively unilateral and protectionist.

Secondly, there seems to be a lack of clarity about the actual supply chain diversification needs of European companies, as well as the other elements of derisking beyond raw materials and green technology. This would require a comprehensive plan devised between EU authorities and business that would set out clear lines on derisking and provide predictability and certainty in relation to new supply chains. The specific, on-the-ground knowledge of business, taking into account the huge variety of possible strategies, should accompany the identification of specific areas and those where cooperation with China may be less problematic. Diversification requires new markets and trade opportunities that can only be achieved through a unified EU approach, using wisely through the new generation of trade agreements.

Third, the EU needs to establish homogenous procedures on visits and statements by member states or individual leaders on China. The cacophony displayed during the first half of 2023 in high-level visits to the Chinese authorities was evidence of a lack of cohesion and the absence of an integrated foreign policy. In this regard, it is incumbent on the High Representative for CFSP to develop the capacity to build consensus in the Foreign Affairs Council and to act jointly with the European Commission, something that member state governments do not always seem to be very willing to do[35].

Derisking may indeed be a better way to deal with China and an opportunity for the EU to consolidate its own role, without reducing alignment with the US and favouring alliances with other countries, but it requires a balanced reassessment and strengthening of the EU's trade, industrial policy and foreign policy instruments targeting the most vulnerable strategic sectors and with a planning that integrates member states and business support. This can only be achieved through more determined EU action, aiming at the continued competitiveness and resilience of European countries and a robust contribution to preventing further fragmentation of the global economy.

35. *Ibidem.*

Eu-China Relations and the Belt and Road Initiative

JERÓNIMO MAILLO GONZÁLEZ-ORÚS & LUIS RODRIGO DE CASTRO[1]
Lecturers at San Pablo CEU University of Madrid

I. INTRODUCTION

China and the European Union are the world's largest economies and, together with the United States, the most prominent actors in the international sphere[2]. Over the last few decades, we have assisted to a strengthening in the EU-China relations, and they and they have the potential to become even stronger in the next years, despite the differences that we are nowadays facing and the potential disputes that could appear in the future. We are now at a new crossroads requiring a re-adjustment, a rebalancing and hopefully a new impulse to the relation.

A greater cooperation and understanding between China and the EU could be highly productive not only for them but also for a better global governance as these two actors have experienced significant changes in the past and they are facing enormous challenges in the present. A good knowledge of this relationship and its evolution over the time is one of the goals of this chapter as a precondition for studying the impact of the Belt and Road Initiative (BRI) "in" Europe, "for" Europe, and for the EU-China relations.

The BRI appears as one of the most prominent proposals led by China in recent times. There is no doubt about the relevance of this initiative for China and the political endorsement from the Beijing elites because of its economical and geopolitical potential. In this sense, China and the European

1. Dr Maillo is Full Professor of EU & International Public Law, as well as Jean Monnet Chair at Universidad San Pablo-CEU (CEU Universities). Dr Rodrigo is an Assistant Professor and Academic Secretary of the Law School at the same University.
2. Beneyto, J. M., Xinning, S. and Chun, D. (Eds.), *China and the European Union: future directions*, CEU Ediciones, Madrid, 2013.

Union could obtain mutual benefits from this modern version of the ancient Silk Road but only if they enhance their bilateral cooperation through the promotion of the development of the BRI. It has the potential to become a benchmark in the evolution of EU-China relations.

This raises some questions such as: how has China presented this initiative to the EU? How has China sought the European support and engagement for the BRI? What has been the role of the European Institutions throughout this process? Or what other actors have been involved? It is also appropriate to look into perceptions, reactions, and motivations of the European Union to join the BRI, to reflect about the extent that this initiative turns ideas into specific projects, and what are the attitudes of China and the Union with regard to the BRI and Europe. Answering these questions is the second of our goals.

With the aim of achieving all these objectives, after an historical overview on the EU-China relations we introduce the general components of this relation, its evolution over the time, and future perspectives to conclude the first part of this paper with a detailed analysis of the economic and trade dimension of the BRI. In the second part, we discuss about its impact in Europe with a brief review of its basis and motivations. We conclude analysing how China has presented this initiative to its European partners and how they have responded/reacted.

II. EVOLUTION OF EU-CHINA RELATIONS

1. HISTORICAL PERSPECTIVE

The EU-China relations have a long history: more than four decades of meetings, negotiations, agreements, and cooperation. This relationship has become more intense and ambitious over time[3]. Nowadays, China and the European Union are strategic partners and both play a crucial role in the evolution of global governance.

The establishment of diplomatic relations and the initial contacts date back to the 1970s with the first official visit to China led by Roy Jenkins, then President of the European Commission, in February 1979 after the first trade agreement was concluded between China and the European Economic Community in 1978.

3. For a detailed analysis, see, *inter alia*, Snyder, F., *The European Union and China, 1949-2008*, Hart Publishing, Oxford, 2010.

Subsequently, in 1985 they concluded a new trade and cooperation agreement and three years later, in 1988, the European Commission opened its first representation office in Beijing. However, at the end of the decade EU-China relations suffered a serious setback after the events in Tiananmen Square and the subsequent imposition of sanctions, which included a weapons embargo.

In the 1990s, the bilateral relations were relaunched; the European Commission intensified and reviewed it position towards the country issuing two major communications: the first one in 1995 called *"A long-term policy for China-Europe relations"* and the second, *"Building a Comprehensive Partnership with China"* published in 1998. Furthermore, the first EU-China summits were held by the end of the decade, in London in 1998 and in Beijing in 1999. Since then, 23 editions of these summits have taken place, the last one on April 1st, 2022, just a few weeks after the Russian aggression to Ukraine[4].

The EU-China Strategic Global Partnership agreement originated a huge number of solid and far-reaching dialogues that crystallised in the institutionalisation of political, economic, and peer-to-peer meetings held every year or even twice a year during the last few decades. Additionally, over the last decades, they have also published several statements about the strategic dimension of the EU-China relations[5].

In addition to the political (human rights, security, defence, non-proliferation of weapons, cyber security, etc.) and economic aspects (trade, business, economic policies, etc.), bilateral dialogues, exchanges and cooperation cover

4. See, *inter alia*, European Commission press release "EU-China Summit: Restoring peace and stability in Ukraine in a shared responsability" (2022) and EUROPEAN COUNCIL press release "EU-China summit via video conference, 1 April 2022" (2022).
5. On the European side, see, *inter alia*, the European Commission statements: "EU Strategy towards China: Implementation of the 1998 Communication and Future Steps for a more Effective EU Policy" (2001); "A maturing partnership: shared interests and challenges in EU-China relations" (2003); "EU-China: Closer Partners, growing responsibilities" (2006); and the conclusion of the European Council of July 18th, 2016, adopting the EU strategy on China as well as the joint communication of the European Commission and the High Representative "Elements for an EU Strategy on China" (2016) and the joint communication to the European Parliament, the European Council and the Council "EU-China — A strategic outlook (2019). The European Council has recently reaffirmed its position in its conclusions on June 2023". On the Chinese side, the first "China's policy paper on EU" (2003) and the most recent "Deepening the China-EU Comprehensive Strategic Partnership for Mutual Benefit and Win-Win Cooperation" (2014). Also, the "EU-China 2020 Strategic Agenda for Cooperation" (2016).

a wide range of subjects such as: copyright; public procurement; transports; fair competition and regulation; social and regional cohesion; development cooperation; migration and mobility; land-use planning; environmental protection and climate change; science and technology; culture; education, and health. As a result, our bilateral relations have been reinforced in those areas and approaches connected to the 'hard diplomacy' have progressively been enlarged to other fields of 'soft policies'[6].

The dialogues include European and Asian affairs, and at the same time covers as well other topics regarding different areas as Africa and Latin America where they are called to play a leading role as stakeholders resulting in a network of connections, exchanges and policies producing a greater level of interdependence between them, their businesses, and their peoples.

In 2007, the negotiations on the EU-China Partnership and Cooperation Agreement (PCA) were launched. However, since the beginning it was clear that their respective approaches were radically opposite. On the one hand, the EU claimed for a binding agreement on trade, investment, public procurement, copyright, and other related aspects to ensure a level playing field for the European businesses in China. On the other, China pursued a minimum agreement on cooperation and dialogue but without any prior commitments. Even though they agreed on half of the total chapters of the PCA during the negotiations, it was finally not adopted[7].

In 2012, China and the European Union explored the possibilities of negotiating and concluding an agreement on investments (the '*Comprehensive Agreement on Investment*', CAI) with two main objectives: allowing a better market access and reinforcing the future investment protection.

Two years later, in 2014, President Xi Jinping appeared to welcome an eventual creation of an EU-China free trade area, but the European counterpart preferred to foster the CAI as a first long-term step for a further free trade agreement. The then Commissioner for Trade, Cecilia Malmström, stated at that point that any free trade area with China could be possible only if two conditions were met: first, the successful conclusion of CAI

6. MEN, J., "EU-China Relations and Diplomacy: Introductory Note", *European Foreign Affairs Review*, n. 19, Special Issue, 2014, pp. 1-4.
7. For the negotiations, an impact assessment was carried out with almost 40 analysts: see: VAN DER GEEST, W., *et al.*, *Trade Sustainability Impact Assessment of the Negotiations of a Partnership and Cooperation Agreement between the EU and China*, DG Trade, European Commission, Brussels, 2008.

and, secondly, a substantial progress in a level playing field for European companies operating in China.

On defence issues, October 16th, 2018, marked a milestone in the EU-China relations with the first combined military exercise ever between the EU NAVFOR and the Peoples Liberation Army Navy in the newly inaugurated Chinese military base in Djibouti, under the scope of the 'Atalanta Operation' against counter piracy and protection of vulnerable shipping off the coasts of Somalia. In this regard, the EU NAVFOR's Force Commander, Rear Admiral Alfonso Pérez de Nanclares, concluded: "[t]his excellent interaction leaves me and the Operation Commander in no doubt that with these results we will be able to prepare further exercises which will consolidate the excellent relationship that has been built up with our Chinese counterparts"[8].

At the beginning of 2020, the COVID-19 outbreak and the spread of the virus all over the world added a new element to the EU-China relations: the so-called 'China's Mask Diplomacy'[9]. The idea behind this assumption was that through a mass donation of masks, sanitizers, and medical supplies to European health care systems in difficulties, Beijing would try to rehabilitate its damaged image in some particular areas. Furthermore, upon establishing long-term dependence relations and patronage networks, China would gain access to sensitive core infrastructures in those member States opening their systems. In other words, China would promote a sense of gratitude deepening at the same time into the internal divisions within the European Union. At this point, the EU High Representative, Josep Borell, stated that: "[China] is now sending equipment and doctors to Europe, as do others as well. China is aggressively pushing the message that, unlike the US, it is a responsible and reliable partner [...]. But we must be aware there is a geo-political component including a struggle for influence through spinning and the 'politics of generosity'. Armed with facts, we need to defend Europe against its detractors"[10].

In the second half of 2020, Germany took over the presidency of the European Union and among its priorities was the EU-China dialogue with

8. Defence Web, "EU NAVFOR conducts first exercise with Chinese Navy in Djibouti", October 17th, 2018, retrieved from *https://www.defenceweb.co.za/sea/sea-sea/eu-navfor-conducts-first-exercise-with-chinese-navy-in-djibouti/*
9. Wong, B., "China's Mask Diplomacy", March 25th, 2020, retrieved from *https://thediplomat.com/2020/03/chinas-mask-diplomacy/*
10. European External Action Service, "EU HRVP Josep Borrell: The Coronavirus pandemic and the new world it is creating", Brussels, March 24th, 2020, retrieved from *https://eeas.europa.eu/delegations/china/76401/eu-hrvp-josep-borrell-coronavirus-pandemic-and-new-world-it-creating_en*

a bilateral summit in Leipzig, which was initially rescheduled due to the COVID-19 pandemic and finally postponed *sine die*. The burning question of Hong Kong would have been one of the central issues. Even if national interests were opposed, finding a strong common position within the Council was the ambition of that presidency according to the priorities set by Heiko Maas, then German Foreign Minister. The 23rd bilateral summit was finally held by telematic means on April 1st, 2022, just some weeks after the Russian aggression to Ukraine.

On February 24th, 2022, Russia invaded Ukraine, an aggression considered as unjust and illegal by the international community demanding the end of the war as soon as possible according to International Law provisions [11]. Since then, the European Union has strongly supported Kyiv in military, economic, and diplomatic terms and, on June 23rd, 2022, the Council agreed to grant Ukraine the candidate status [12]. China has maintained a more sceptical position avoiding breaking relations with Putin. As a result, Beijing's diplomatic activity has been more intense than in previous decades having proposed even a peace plan to both the parties in the conflict.

In October 2022, after the abolishment in 2018 of the constitutional term limits, the 20th National Congress of the Communist Party of China ratified Xi Jinping as general secretary for a new period of five years, ensuring his re-election for a third term as President of the country almost until 2028. Consequently, he has become the most powerful leader since several decades ago.

2. GENERAL FEATURES OF THE EU-CHINA RELATIONS

China and the European Union consider their relationship as 'strategic' but what does this adjective mean? Does it mean the same for both? Under what attitudes, approaches and principles are they facing that relationship?

Whether 'strategic' is understood as a long-term relationship, stable over time, and essential because of its potential, weight and dimension, there is no doubt that the relationship between China and the European Union is strategic for both parties' interests. However, if we consider that 'strategic' involves that a given partner is more important for one than for the other,

11. United Nations, "Ukraine: UN General Assembly demands Russia reverse course on 'attempted illegal annexation'", October 12th, 2022, retrieved from *https://news.un.org/en/story/2022/10/1129492*
12. See: European Council, "European Council conclusions, 23-24 June 2022", Brussels, June 24th, 2022, retrieved from *https://www.consilium.europa.eu/media/57442/2022-06-2324-euco-conclusions-en.pdf*

as it is crucial in terms of economic and political interest, it is clear that what we have between China and the EU is another case of strategic relation, even though not all scholars agree on this perspective[13].

By contrast, under no circumstances may the term 'strategic' be interpreted as synonymous of close ally, one which shares with us, at least in part, a social model, ideas on social development, a conception about how the international relations operate, and what global governance should prevail. From this point of view, the differences between China and the European Union are evident in multiple issues. Ignoring or considering that just a matter of time before an alignment of models is simply unreasonable and probably wrong.

Whilst the European Union is founded on democracy; rule of law; protection of fundamental rights and citizen's freedoms; a robust, trusted, and independent legal system guaranteeing equality before the law, as well as a market economy with a leading model of social protection, China, on the other hand, stands for a completely different political and social model. From a political perspective, the country is not a democracy, it lacks an effective system of fundamental rights protection according to international standards, and the national judiciary does not meet the criteria of transparency, liability, impartiality nor certainty. At the economic level, the evolution from a communist full planned economy into a more market-oriented one is undeniable, but many traces of protectionism and State direction remain in many areas and sectors.

For the European Union, a Chinese political evolution towards a democratic liberal regime protecting fundamental rights and citizens' freedoms would result the most desirable scenario. Nonetheless, an attempt to promote the European (or Western) values within the Chinese dimension appears in every position paper and in every statement of EU leaders as if time and the economic development would necessarily lead to the 'Europeanisation' of China, as if one (liberal regimes) cannot exist without the other (economic progress). On the contrary, China seems to have a different idea: government policies, political organisation, control on dissidents, and the extension of fundamental rights and citizens' freedoms are solely a matter of internal policy and are not concerned with the international relations. That is why

13. Zeng, J., "Does Europe Matter? The Role of Europe in Chinese Narratives of 'One Belt One Road' and 'New Type of Great Power Relations'", *Journal of Common Market Studies*, vol. 55, n. 5, 2017, pp. 1162-1176. The author holds that Europe is a second-tier concern for China and plays only a minor role in the Chinese political debate.

China has been calling for a full respect and non-interference in home affairs and does not accept that stronger market economy could lead *per se* to a liberal democratic system.

China defends its own political and social model as well as its own way to deal with economic openness. In practice, what we have seen over the last few decades is that economic transformation did not go hand in hand with a substantial reform in politics, although it has had a significant impact on the relations of China with the rest of the world as values and internal organisation vary from one country to another.

China and the European Union agree on defending an international community with no hegemonic power (i. e., United States) but beyond that, their positions are quite different. The European Union promotes multilateralism and the credibility of the institutions as cornerstones of international relations, whereas China is deeply interested in multipolarism too but with a more pragmatic and 'realistic' position which sees international relations as a balance of power between different poles, one of them is and must be China.

Multilateralism and multipolarism seem to be similar but the differences between them are immense. Moreover, we should not forget that the European countries are founding members of the main multilateral international institutions while China is a relative newcomer to most of them.

When joining international institutions, China disagrees with the specific role conferred as member or with their particular scope and functioning. This has led China to claim the need to upgrade its role and sometimes to promote the creation of new and alternative institutions (even more if the new status does not meet the Chinese expectations or if these institutions are reluctant to accept changes).

Therefore, although they are quite different, China and the European Union need each other, and they have increasingly become interdependent as both of them are sharing a plethora of common interests in several issues.

Finally, it is necessary to insist on the importance of the economic and trade components in EU-China relations, even if they have not been the only components of these relations and even if political dialogues at different levels have been developed in many institutional and people-to-people exchanges (through a combination of hard and soft diplomacy). One example is the EU-China 2020 Strategic Agenda for Cooperation based on four pillars: peace and security, prosperity, sustainable development, and people-to-people exchanges.

III. EU AND CHINA: TWO CONSTANTLY CHANGING ACTORS. CURRENT SITUATION AND FUTURE PERSPECTIVES

Since the establishment of direct relations between China and the European Union, both partners have radically transformed. Understanding these changes, but also the future trends and expectations, is something necessary to re-align their relation in a new context.

From an economic and trade perspective, China has experienced enormous changes over the last few decades. However, the political situation remains unchanged. It has supposed a radical collapse of the Western assumption that the transformation into a market economy would serve as a pre-condition for political reforms in order to finally achieve a liberal and democratic system.

Without considering the case of the European Union, in only 30 years of sustained growth China has become the world's second largest economy[14] and the world's leading trader[15]. Moreover, since 2014 China is the leading economy in terms of purchasing power parity and, as forecasts suggest, China could become the world's leading economy in absolute terms before 2030. Nowadays, China, even after the difficulties already surmounted from the pandemic, is the main trading partner of most of its neighbouring countries, most of them with sustained economic growth rates.

We must not forget that, for the years to come, Asia will emerge as a primary focus of economic growth at global level with China in the middle of a regional economy more and more integrated and interconnected than ever[16]. Furthermore, Chinese interests in Latin America and Africa are growing and strengthening. On the other hand, China is the second most important outward investor in the world and holds the largest foreign exchange reserves. Despite the international economic impact originated by the COVID-19 crisis, according to the World Bank, in 2020 the Chinese GDP grew by 2.2% and by 8.1% in 2021, even if some restrictions were still applying, while the United States GDP shrank in 2020 by 2.8% and the European Union by 5.7%, shifting for a respective GDP growth by 5.9% and 5.4 in 2021. This background

14. These rates do not take into consideration the European Union as a whole, only those of each member States. If that had been the case, the European Union would be ahead China as second world's largest economy.
15. China is expected to replace the European Union as the world's leading trading power before 2030.
16. China has become the most relevant economy and the main market for the majority of Asian countries at the expense of the United States. Even more, China is on its way to becoming also the most important investor in many of them nearing to Japan.

predicts positive expectations for the years to come albeit notable challenges should be faced by part of China such as: the transition towards an expanded domestic demand and the development of services; a more innovative and knowledge-based industry; a restructuring and adjusted excess capacity sectors (cement, steel, aluminium, flat glass and shipbuilding); greater regional and social cohesion within the country, and an urgent need to get health and environmental standards improved not only to protect its population but also to fight against climate change at a global level.

This transformation can shake the international arena and affect the Chinese external dimension. For many years, China has been focusing on their economic development and maintained an international low profile. However, during the last few years, this attitude has started to change, in particular under the leadership of Xi Jinping, whose ambition is to reach parity with the United States according to its growing global influence[17].

The 'One Belt, One Road' Initiative (OBOR), later renamed as 'Belt and Road Initiative' (BRI), the creation of the Asian Infrastructure Investment Bank (AIIB), the compromise with the 'New Development Bank' (NDB), located in Shanghai and formerly referred as the 'BRICS Development Bank', the endorsement of the Free Trade Area of the Asia-Pacific (FTAAP), the new Fund for the Development of the Belt and Road Initiative, some additional loans to its public banks as well as the demands for a higher participation in international agencies (IMF, World Bank, etc.) are evidences of the new role that China is gradually conquering.

China keeps on cooperating and favouring a multipolar world by strengthening its role in international forums on all fronts, but mainly in the economic sphere. The challenge is to turn economic power into geostrategic influence, to limit weaknesses and to strengthen national security, promoting in this way its own interests with the aim of maintaining economic growth, development, and transformation. Without denying potential military aspirations, China has not been focused exclusively on improving its current short-term capabilities but on increasing its own security as an extension of its economic influence.

17. Delage, F., "China: diplomacia económica, consecuencias geopolíticas", *Cuadernos de estrategia*, n. 187, Geopolíticas del siglo XXI, Spanish Institute for Strategic Studies, Spanish Ministry of Defence, 2017, pp. 55-92; Deng, Y., "China: The Post-Responsible Power", *The Washington Quarterly*, vol. 37, n. 4, 2015, pp. 117-132; Yan, X., "From Keeping a Low Profile to Striving for Achievement", *The Chinese Journal of International Politics*, vol. 7, n. 2, 2014.

Since the establishment of bilateral relations with China, the European Union not only has tripled the number of its member States from nine to twenty-seven, but it has also seen how its competences and powers were increased throughout each new treaty, in particular, with the Lisbon Treaty. As a result, Europe has left behind the former division between East and West and it is nowadays more united than ever offering a common perspective for its more than 450 million inhabitants.

Enlargement negotiations are open with Türkiye (since 1999), North Macedonia (since 2005), Montenegro (since 2010), Serbia (since 2012), Albania (since 2014), Moldova, Ukraine, and Bosnia and Herzegovina (since 2022), but no major immediate enlargement is planned, although new perspectives are open for a new round in 2030, always based on merits. Regarding the Turkish candidacy, it has remained frozen since 2016 when the European Parliament adopted a resolution claiming for the European Commission to suspend negotiations[18] and, one month later, the European Council endorsed this position[19] as the president Erdoğan's autocratic tendency violated the article 6 of the Treaty on European Union.

The Union has broadened the European neighbourhood policy in the North of Africa, the Mediterranean, and in the East of Europe, but the results have not been as expected. The failure of the 'Arab Spring', the crisis in Crimea and, finally, the Russian aggression to Ukraine are some evidences. Towards the world, the European Union has pursued further trade liberalisation standards with the conclusion of new trade agreements with Canada, Japan, Singapore, or New Zealand[20]. However, the Transatlantic Trade and Investment Partnership (TTIP) with the United States was finally cancelled by the Trump Administration.

In parallel with this international evolution of the events, from an internal and legal approach, the European Union has substantially extended its competences and powers with each new reform of the Treaties: from the Single European Act to Lisbon, going through Maastricht, Amsterdam and Nice.

On the economic side, the European Union completed the internal market in 1992 and introduced the Euro in 1999. Nowadays, twenty member States

18. See: "European Parliament resolution of 24 November 2016 on EU-Turkey relations (2016/2993(RSP))", retrieved from *https://www.europarl.europa.eu/doceo/document/TA-8-2016-0450_EN.pdf*

19. See: "Outcome of the 3511th Council meeting". General Affairs. Brussels, December 13th, 2016, retrieved from *https://www.consilium.europa.eu/media/21524/st15536en16.pdf*

20. See Beneyto, J. M. (Dir.), *Acuerdos Comerciales de Nueva Generación de la Unión Europea. Implicaciones para España*, Thompson Reuters Aranzadi, 2022.

constitute the Eurozone and share a common currency that has consolidated its global position since then (in fact, the Euro is the second most important currency in the world after the US dollar).

The lack of progress in completing the European banking union and the European fiscal union as well as the strong asymmetries within the Eurozone economies were serious handicaps one decade ago to manage the crisis and exacerbated its negative effects. Furthermore, it also caused several difficulties in the Union and in some countries, in particular Greece, Ireland, Portugal, and Spain. Fortunately, we could overcome this situation and crucial steps were taken in order to heal the wounds that jeopardised the European system, even if some of them required considerable efforts for the population and national economies. In any case, the goal was clear: get the problems fixed for the future and not to repeat the mistakes from past.

From a foreign policy perspective, we should remember that trade policy is an exclusive competence of the European Union according to article 3 TFEU. It means that the Union is responsible for adopting unilateral measures on trade policy, participating in international and multilateral trade agencies (as the World Trade Organization, WTO), and negotiating and concluding bilateral trade agreements with third countries or whatever other area of regional integration.

All the aspects mentioned above are extremely important for the EU-China relations and for each one isolated not only because they are the two foremost trading powers at a global scale but also because of their mutual trade exchanges and investments with third parties. As a leading power, the European Union has played an active role within the WTO, promoting multilateral advances, supporting the creation of new areas of regional integration, and setting a network of bilateral and regional trade agreements with third countries, particularly over the last decade. The European Union would be willing to strengthen its bilateral trade relation with China through new agreements on investments, a greater commercial openness or, even, a potential free trade area[21], provided first there is substantial progress on a level playing field.

In Asia, the European Union has advocated too in favour of setting up free trade areas with other third countries such as South Korea, Singapore, Vietnam, Thailand, Malaysia, Philippines, and Indonesia.

---

21. Pelkmans, J., François, J., *et al.*, *Tomorrow's Silk Road. Assessing an EU-China Free Trade Agreement*, Centre for European Policy Studies (CEPS), Brussels, 2016.

From a political dimension, it should be mentioned, first, the consolidation of an area of freedom, security, and justice, with free movement of people and police and judicial cooperation in civil and criminal issues. In this sense, it refers to the two major challenges that the European Union has faced in recent times: fighting against terrorism and immigration flows towards Europe. Both of them have been creating tensions within the member States and raised populist discourse in some sectors.

Secondly, the common foreign and security policy reinforced with the figure of the High Representative for Foreign Affairs and Security Policy as well as the European External Action Service (EEAS), whose diplomatic activity achieved a major success in the Iran nuclear deal. The European Union contributes to international peacekeeping and security around the world through different common missions; disarmament, rescue, and humanitarian operations; conflict prevention, and crisis management. In the same way, the Union is the world's biggest donor of development aid with a privileged status on cooperation vis-à-vis developing countries.

In terms of defence, the first steps towards a closer cooperation have been already taken. As a result, despite the Brexit shock, the Union advanced further down the road of the European integration and remains not only as a global actor but also as a world benchmark in economics, security, peace, minority protection, respect for the fundamental rights, climate change, development cooperation, humanitarian aid, social cohesion, or regional integration processes, among others.

However, the European Union is still facing enormous challenges. The effects of the economic and financial crisis broken out in 2009 produced deep social inequalities and job insecurity. In this respect, structural reforms were implemented to support the economic union. They served to ensure national budget equilibrium, keep budgetary expenditure under control, modernise national labour markets whilst preserving the European social model, take advantage of the digitalisation of the economy by providing more effective public services, and promote clean energies.

Until early 2020, Europe experienced a period of moderate growth with decreasing unemployment rates. This trend ended when the COVID-19 pandemic infected the world, leading the global economy into the worst recession since World War II because of the preventive but necessary measures adopted to limit the spread of the virus and protect public health.

Despite experts' warnings, when in 2016 the United Kingdom voted for 'Brexit' Europe was taken by surprise. The British decision was deeply troubling and confusing not only because one of the most relevant member State decided to leave the Union, but also because it opened an uncertain and unknown landscape. A ripple effect in other States wanting to leave the Union was the main risk as it could trigger a dangerous process of disintegration. However, it did not happen, and the 27 remaining States were more united than ever reaffirming their strong commitment and support to the Union. Of course, the best way to avoid new *'-exits'* is by not creating incentives for the separation and re-discovering the value of our European unity.

As expected, Brexit negotiations were not easy, progressed slowly, and faced serious difficulties to such an extent that the 'Exit day' had to be postponed three times until it finally entered in force on January 31st, 2020. From that date, once ratified the 'Withdrawal Agreement', after 47 years of membership, the United Kingdom left the European Union and began the transition period that concluded on December 31st, 2020. During those months, the United Kingdom remained being part of the European market and the customs union but could not take part in the institutional architecture of the Union. The post-Brexit relation between London and Brussels is now regulated through the Trade and Cooperation Agreement, provisionally applied as of January 1st, 2021, and fully in force since May 1st, 2021.

The United Kingdom was not the only country hit by Euroscepticism within the Union. A wave of populism has spread all over Europe. Thus, some member States have suffered the consolidation and institutionalisation of old and new ways of Euroscepticism to such an extent that, in some cases, have affected to the formation of national governments and it is to be seen how they could influence the next Parliament after the elections scheduled for June 2024. The main risk and the most prominent example has traditionally been the *'Front National'* (renamed as *'Rassemblement National'* in 2018) headed by Marine Le Pen in France. Fortunately, even if she got enough electoral support as to achieve the second round both in the French presidential elections in 2017 and 2022, she was finally beaten by pro-Europe and moderate positions in the figure of President Emmanuel Macron.

In Germany, after 16 years as chancellor, Angela Merkel (CDU) left the power in 2021 being succeeded by Olaf Scholz from the traditional centre-left party (SPD) in a coalition with the Liberal Party (FDP) and the Green Party known as "traffic light" coalition. Compared with the previous election in 2017, the far-right populist party 'Alternative for Germany' (AfD), which had emerged at that time as the third-largest party in the Bundestag (lower chamber) with the 12.6% of national votes, kept in 2021 the 10.3% (-2.3%).

Despite this loss of votes at national level, AfD remained as the first party in Saxony and became the most voted one in Thuringia.

Building this new coalition, the three parties agreed a common government programme for 2021-2025 where they included the idea of developing the Union towards a federal state based on the European Charter of Fundamental Rights and governed by the principles of subsidiarity and proportionality. Furthermore, they were in favour of replacing the unanimity rule by qualified majority voting in those issues connected to the Common Foreign and Security Policy as well as making the '*spitzenkandidaten*' process binding and adopting a single European electoral regulation with transnational lists[22].

In September 2022, Italy held a snap parliamentary election after the collapse of the government because of the withdrawal of the populist 'Five Stars Movement', led by the former Prime Minister Giuseppe Conte, in supporting the Draghi's national unity coalition. As a result, Giorgia Meloni, the leader of 'Brothers of Italy' (right wing), formed a new centre-right coalition becoming the first woman heading the Italian executive. For his part, the eurosceptic Matteo Salvini (*Lega*) sworn as Deputy Prime Minister for Infrastructure and Transport, the same who during the Conte's Cabinet served as Minister of Interior from 2018 to 2019 being known for his obsession against the European immigration policy.

In addition to the economic crisis, the populist wave, the anti-liberal path followed by some member States, the massive migratory flows from Syria, the consequences of 'Brexit', the threat of international terrorism, the instability in the Mediterranean, and the COVID-19 pandemic, the war in Ukraine has emerged as the last challenge to the European Union and its partners. In this struggle for a western perspective for Ukraine, President Zelensky has emerged as a symbol of the common values set by article 2 TEU.

From the outside, the Biden Administration is more convinced than the previous Trump Administration about the positive aspects of the European integration process and the need of cooperating with Europe through a closer transatlantic relation, in particular after the Putin's last challenge to the western hemisphere.

22. See: Germany's Coalition Agreement between the SPD, the FDP, and the Greens for a new federal Government "Dare more progress. Alliance for Freedom, Justice, and Sustainability", 2021, retrieved from *https://portal.ieu-monitoring.com/editorial/dare-more-progress-agreement-of-germanys-new-coalition-now-online?utm_source=ieu&utm_medium=web&utm_campaign=portal*

It is undeniable that the European Union has experienced times of uncertainty and faced multiple and severe crisis which has sometimes been seen as a crisis of identity. However, the difficulties have spurred major progresses in several fields and the European Union not only has survived to these difficulties but also has finally strengthened. As a result, most of the European current and past leaders, as well as the huge majority of the European people, have realised that the unity could never be taken for granted as it happened in previous times.

IV. THE CURRENT AND FUTURE DIMENSION OF THE EU-CHINA TRADE RELATIONS IN A GLOBAL CONTEXT: MAJOR LITIGATIONS AND AREAS OF MUTUAL INTEREST

The EU-China relations have been traditionally dominated by trade and economy but also by some political and cultural aspects, as mentioned above. In this section, we will focus on trade issues in order to better identify major litigations, areas of shared interest and future perspectives.

The trade balance between China and the European Union shifted from a deficit in the early 1980s to a surplus since 2000. In 2022, even if the trade in goods total volume reached €856 billion, the European Union experienced a deficit of €395.7 billion. That year, the European Union exported goods exceeding €230 billion to China (9% of the extra-EU total exports) and imported goods reached €626 billion from China (20.8% of the extra-EU total imports). The most exported goods from the EU to China were mechanical appliances, electrical equipment, vehicles, medicinal and pharma products, aircrafts, optical instruments, agri-food products, and raw materials. On the other hand, imports from China to the European Union were telecommunications equipment and automatic data processing machines followed by clothing accessories, furniture, toys, games, raw materials, optical instruments, plastic articles, and organic chemicals[23].

In their mutual relations, the European Union and China could apply trade defence instruments such as anti-dumping or anti-subsidy duties in addition to both technical and tariff and non-tariff barriers. They are particularly relevant in the case of the EU single market because when European companies consider that a Chinese one is trying to sell at inappropriately low prices within the Union, they may claim to adopt anti-dumping or anti-subsidy duties. This is a common, legal, and consolidated practice under the

23. Data source: Eurostat.

WTO standards and rules whenever they were properly imposed. In fact, over the last few years, the European Union has implemented such measures against Chinese imports, what has caused various complains about how we, the Europeans, are using these instruments. Statistics seem to confirm that, in particular after the accession of China to the WTO. Thus, the application of anti-dumping and/or anti-subsidy duties rates against Chinese imports is around 30% of the total, even if sometimes they have reached the 47% of the total[24].

The main problem is determining when the price is too low enough and what criteria should be applied. Under normal conditions, reference prices would be those of the State of origin, but when it is not a free-market economy and prices are not freely established or are distorted, some other index must be considered. Because of that, the scope to levy higher anti-dumping and anti-subsidy duties is wider.

Determining if China should be recognised or not as a market economy under the WTO terms and if so since when was one of the main trade-related controversies discussed over the last few years. It is because the answer to that question have a decisive impact on the scope of imposing anti-dumping duties on Chinese imports. When China joined the WTO, article 15 of the Protocol of China's Accession excluded such recognition due to a clear State interference in the economy and to the resulting distortion of competition.

According to this article 15 (d), China should be recognised as market economy not later than 2016 (15 years after the date of its accession to the WTO). However, the literal meaning of that provision remains (maybe deliberately) unclear, and they could lead to some alternative interpretations, in particular one in which the need to proof being a market economy is required. For its part, the European Union has been reluctant to agree that status to China because, from its point of view, the five conditions laid down by the Council Regulation 1225/2009 have not been yet met[25]. One

24. Yalcin, E., Felbermayr, G., and Sandkamp, A., *New trade rules for China? Opportunities and threats for the EU*, Study requested by European Parliament's Committee on International trade, 2016. Nonetheless, according to Pelkmans, François *et al*, *op. cit.*, p. 81, other countries like India or United States had imposed a larger number and more restrictive anti-dumping and anti-subsidy duties measures than the European Union.

25. Article 2.7 (c) of Council Regulation EC No. 1225/2009 of November 30th, 2009 on protection against dumped imports from countries not members of the European Community set out 5 requirements in order to be considered as a market economy: first, "decisions of firms regarding prices, costs and inputs, including for instance raw materials, cost of technology and labour, output, sales and investment, are made in response to market signals reflecting supply and demand, and without significant State interference in that

reason behind this attitude could be the negative impact on the European economy[26]. In any case, this is a very sensitive issue about the best way of promoting reforms within China to achieve a level playing field for European companies in the country.

Some years ago, in order to better deal with these problematics, the Union reformed its trade defence regulation by establishing new criteria and proceedings[27] requiring a proof of a state interference to impose antidumping duties. In addition, to make this process less complex the European Commission delivers reports about different countries with the aim to offer assistance to the European industry. The first report was focused on China[28] and included both sectoral and transversal distortions highlighting that, even if they would be taken into account, they do not lead to an automatically application of any antidumping or anti-subsidy duties, as each particular case should be evaluated separately[29].

When presenting the reform, the then President Jean-Claude Juncker stated that "[t]he EU is and will remain one of the most open markets in the world. We are and will remain in the first line defending open, fair, and rules-based trade. This, however, should not be mistaken as naivety". The former Trade Commissioner Cecilia Malmström noted that: "[t]his is an important time in our trade defence policy. It signals the EU's commitment to strong and

regard, and costs of major inputs substantially reflect market values"; second, "firms have one clear set of basic accounting records which are independently audited in line with international accounting standards and are applied for all purposes"; third, the production costs and financial situation of firms are not subject to significant distortions carried over from the former non-market-economy system, in particular in relation to depreciation of assets, other write-offs, barter trade and payment via compensation of debts; fourth, "the firms concerned are subject to bankruptcy and property laws which guarantee legal certainty and stability for the operation of firms", and fifth, "change rate conversions are carried out at the market rate".

26. In this respect, see: Scott, R. E., and Jiang, X., *Unilateral Grant of Market Economy Status to China would put Millions of EU jobs at risk*, European Policy Institute Report, 2015; TAUBE, M., and SCHMIDKONZ, C., *Assessment of the normative and policy framework governing the Chinese economy and its impact on international competition*, AEGIS Europe, 2015.
27. European Commission Press Release, "EU puts in place new trade defence rules", December 20th, 2017, retrieved from *http://europa.eu/rapid/press-release_IP-17-5346_en.htm*
28. European Commission, Commission Staff Working Document "Significant Distortions in the Economy of The People's Republic of China for the Purposes of Trade Defence Investigations", December 20th, 2017.
29. European Commission, Fact Sheet, Questions, and answers "The EU's new trade defence rules and first country report", December 20th, 2017, retrieved from *http://europa.eu/rapid/press-release_MEMO-17-5377_en.htm*

effective trade defence instruments. The EU is open for business. Nevertheless, we must also protect our industry from unfair competition from imports, particularly from countries whose economies are significantly distorted owing to state interference. The publication of country reports will help us to put the new methodology into practice. It will also give the EU industry a basis on which to make its case concerning countries where distortions exist".

Despite existing entry barriers in China, trade in services has grown exponentially, reaching in 2021 a total volume of €97.7 billion. The European Union exported services worth €59.1 billion to China (6% of the extra-EU total exports), with transports and business being the main exported services to China followed by travel, manufacturing, ICT, maintenance and repair, constructions, and insurance. On the other hand, the European Union imported services from China reached €38.6 billion (4% of the extra-EU total imports) with business, travel, transport, intellectual property, ICT, financial, and insurance as leading services. Therefore, in contrast to the trade in goods, trade in services balance offered in 2021 a surplus of €20.5 billion in EU's favour[30].

Restrictions in services access are related to a lag in the development of the Chinese service sector (even compared with other BRICS countries) and the predominant position of the State-Owned Enterprises (SOEs), characterised by a high market power due to regulatory issues, access to public funding and a strong political endorsement[31]. According to article 7 of the Anti-Monopoly Law, SOEs seem to be excluded from control measures which, combined with a lack in the State aids supervision, damages the opportunities for establishing an equal level playing field and perpetuates (and in some cases also boosts) significant and unfair distortions of competition. The political commitment acquired by the Chinese authorities to push ahead a reform of the Anti-Monopoly Law[32] was finally drafted in 2020[33] and again in 2022[34] but, despite the amendments introduced, article 7 has remained undisturbed.

30. Data source: Eurostat.
31. Pelkmans, François *et al.*, *op. cit.*, p. 16.
32. *Ibid.* pp. 24-25. In this regard, see "Annual Position Papers" issued by European Chamber of Commerce in China or the "American Business in China White Paper" published by the American Chamber of Commerce.
33. Deng, J., and Dai, K., "A Practical Review of the Draft Amendment to the Anti-Monopoly Law of China: Highlighting Six Areas with Eighteen Changes", Dentons, 2020, retrieved from *https://www.dentons.com/en/insights/guides-reports-and-whitepapers/2020/february/27/a-practical-review-of-the-draft-amendment-to-the-antimonopoly-law-of-china*
34. Huld, A., "What Has Changed in China's Amended Anti-Monopoly Law?", China Briefing, 2022, retrieved from *https://www.china-briefing.com/news/what-has-changed-in-chinas-amended-anti-monopoly-law/*

Except in a few cases where technological knowledge could not be provided at national level, access to Chinese public procurement is practically inaccessible for European companies even if Europe guarantees that possibility for Chinese enterprises[35]. Similar asymmetries are applying in the field of copyright protection, not because an absence of appropriate rules (in fact some significant progresses have been made) but to a practical problem connected to a legislative inappropriate implementation[36].

Since 2015, China has been net exporter of capitals. According to UNCTAD's World Investment Report 2022, the stock of Chinese foreign direct investment in 2021 amounted to $2.06 trillion, representing 11.8% of Chinese GDP. Through these investments, China pursues the objective of strengthening its financial sustainability and competitiveness throughout a double strategy: on the one hand, by integrating assets acquisition from advanced sectors in OECD countries in order to defend its internal market position and, on the other, by attracting key raw materials and energy resources in non-OECD countries for the Chinese industry[37].

In the specific case of the EU-China relations, Beijing's foreign direct investments in Europe reached €69.9 billion while the European Union's foreign direct investment in China exceeded €233.6 billion in 2021[38]. Asymmetries in this field are also quite substantial. As shown by the OECD foreign direct investment regulatory restrictiveness index, China is the seventy-three most restrictive economy among the eighty-three considered[39]. Many sectors of the Chinese economy are close off to foreign investors while some others are partially restricted and foreign investments are only accepted if they do not have more than a maximum fixed shareholding, forcing the establishment of joint ventures with Chinese partners. By contrast, the European Union is, according to that same index, one of the less restrictive economies.

A centralised control system with a prior authorisation for foreign direct investments has been established regarding the Chinese industrial policy

35. Pelkmans, François *et al. op. cit.*, p. 18 and 267-268.

36. *Ibid*, p. 19 and 268.

37. Spanish Institute for Foreign Trade (ICEX), "China", 2020, retrieved from *https://www.icex.es/icex/es/navegacion-principal/todos-nuestros-servicios/informacion-de-mercados/paises/navegacion-principal/el-pais/informacion-economica-y-comercial/sector-exterior/index.html?idPais=CN#19*

38. DG Trade, European Commission, Brussels, 2023, retrieved from *https://ec.europa.eu/trade/policy/countries-and-regions/countries/china/*

39. OECD, Dataset, 2023. All OECD and G20 member states are included.

but it has created uncertainty and a risk of arbitrariness. In addition to a lack of transparency, corruption, a weak legal system, and an unfair treatment benefiting only Chinese actors have caused many other disadvantages for European companies[40]. In the same way, notwithstanding the promises of the Chinese authorities, the country remains as one of the most restrictive economies for foreign investments[41].

In this framework, China and the European Union started the negotiations on the Comprehensive Agreement on Investment (CAI) in September 2012[42] with two main objectives: improving market access and enhancing the future investment protection[43].

Until few years ago, the European Union had no control *vis-à-vis* the foreign direct investments and only fourteen of the twenty-seven member States had a similar but inefficient system operating at national level, giving rise to political and academic debates on how to close this gap from a European perspective[44]. Extremely concerned about this issue, in May 2017 the European Commission headed by Jean-Claude Juncker proposed a common European framework for screening foreign direct investments within the Union that was warmly welcomed by the European Council one month after[45].

The EU Regulation 2019/452 of the European Parliament and of the Council of 19 March 2019 establishing a framework for the screening of foreign direct investments into the Union was adopted in a context of a stronger growth rate of foreign investment in Europe's strategic companies just after the end of European debt crisis, when attracting new capital

40. US Department of State, *China investment climate statement 2015*, Washington, D. C., May 2015.
41. OECD, Dataset, 2023.
42. Even if it was finally concluded on December 30th, 2020, it has not yet entered into force as it has to be still ratified.
43. An additional purpose was to avoid fragmentation from pre-existing national agreements on investments. Such agreements are inefficient and do not meet current investment requirements. For further information on this issue, see: Pelkmans, François *et al.*, *op. cit.*, pp. 209-210.
44. See: Jungbluth, C., "Buying Europe? Chinese investment in the EU still low despite recent hype", 2016, a Bertelsmann blog, retrieved from *http://ged-project.de/topics/competitiveness/challenges_in_international_competitiveness/buying-*
45. European Commission, Press Release: "State of the Union 2017 — Trade Package: European Commission proposes framework for screening of foreign direct investments", September 14th, 2017, retrieved from *http://europa.eu/rapid/press-release_IP-17-3183_en.htm*

was crucial to inject liquidity in the market and was boosted by a weaker legislation. Although it did not apply until October 11th, 2020, as set in its article 17, this Regulation has established a common framework for all the member States and, in some instances, allowing the Commission to control all foreign direct investments made within the European Union on the grounds of strategic security or public order but considering each particular situation of every member State as well as national particularities.

Among other points, member States are allowed to maintain, amend, or adopt different mechanisms focused to screen certain foreign direct investments as well as to prevent their screening mechanisms evasion. For its part, the European Commission has acquired the power to control all those foreign direct investments likely to affect projects and programmes of common interest for the Union.

In the same way, member States are required to ensure: (i) that rules and procedures related to screening mechanisms are transparent and non-discriminatory; (ii) that timeframes are applied under their screening mechanisms; (iii) the protection of confidential information acquired in application of this Regulation; and (iv) the possibility to seek recourse against screening decisions of the national authorities.

The Regulation has also established a mechanism for cooperation between member States when receiving investments if other member State(s) or the European Commission could be potentially affected. Thus, according to art. 6.2, if "a member State considers that a foreign direct investment undergoing screening in another member State is likely to affect its security or public order, or has information relevant for such screening, it may provide comments to the Member State undertaking the screening. The member State providing comments shall send those comments to the Commission simultaneously".

In the same way, article 6.3 empowers the European Commission to provide its opinion when it considers that a foreign direct investment undergoing screening could affect to the security or to the public order in more than one member State or when it has relevant information related to that investment. Furthermore, the European Commission or any member State may be requested to deliver its opinion or to provide some comments if, as set in art. 6.4, they consider that an investment could affect its security or its public order. However, it does not grant a right of veto for the European Commission on any decision taken by member States in the field of foreign direct investments. The European Union has acknowledged having been somewhat naive and needing greater supervision of some activities of foreign companies in our territory (especially those of countries in which there continues to be a certain dirigisme and a very strong link with the State, such as the case of China and Russia). The Union has progressively become aware that it had to provide itself with better mechanisms against risks to public security understood in a broad and modern way, such as risks to critical infrastructure, goods or services.

Furthermore, it has become more demanding when it comes to demanding reciprocity and guaranteeing fair competition and the same rules of the game (level playing field) to open its market to the outside world. Finally, it has understood that it must avoid excessive dependence on the outside (and especially on single suppliers) for certain essential goods and services (most sensitive industrial ecosystems) and that, therefore, it must commit to the diversification of suppliers and the development of certain European autonomy in them to be better prepared for future crises[46]. It is also trying to green and make its trade policy more climate fair. All of this has been materialized in different initiatives and new tools such as the new instrument relating of International Public Procurement[47], the Carbon Border Adjustment Mechanism (CBAM)[48], or the Regulation on Foreign Subsidies[49]. China and the United States are nowadays the EU's most important trading partners, even though it is expected that China finally becomes by far the first one over the next decade[50]. Chinese commercial strategy has included multilateral, plurilateral and bilateral actions. The most important was the accession of China to the WTO in 2001 followed by its accession to other international organisations such as the International Organisation for Standardisation (ISO). By contrast, China has not yet met the European

46. European Commission, Joint communication to the European Parliament, the European Council and the Council on "European economic security strategy", JOIN/2023/20 final.
47. Regulation (EU) 2022/1031 of the European Parliament and of the Council of 23 June 2022 on the access of third-country economic operators, goods and services to the Union's public procurement and concession markets and procedures supporting negotiations on access of Union economic operators, goods and services to the public procurement and concession markets of third countries (International Procurement Instrument — IPI), OJ L 173, 30.6.2022, p. 1.
48. Regulation (EU) 2023/956 of the European Parliament and of the Council of 10 May 2023 establishing a carbon border adjustment mechanism, OJ L 130, 16.5.2023, p. 52.
49. Regulation (EU) 2022/2560 of the European Parliament and of the Council of 14 December 2022 on foreign subsidies distorting the internal market, OJ L 330, 23.12.2022, p. 1.
50. Gros, D., and Alcidi, C., *The Global Economy in 2030: Trends and strategies for Europe*, CEPS Paperback, CEPS, Brussels, 2013.

expectations in certain multilateral negotiations, in particular because of a lack of support in encouraging other BRICS countries to establish new arrangements. Substantial efforts have been made in the field of public procurement and services through plurilateral agreements but without any important success. It should be noted not only that China is a relatively recent partner and that the internal reform process is quite complex and awkward to implement, but also that China must play a leading role among the BRICS as a result of its new global leadership.

China has become a full member of other regional initiatives as well, such as the APEC, whose objectives include the promotion of free trade. However, China has intensified bilateral actions over the last years. The reason is that this dimension is more flexible than the multilateral and plurilateral ones, as it means a lower level of commitment and brings more opportunities to go forward. Thus, China has pursued a particular bilateral activity with the ASEAN community as well as with its neighbouring countries such as Singapore, Pakistan, South Korea, Japan, Hong Kong, Macao, Sri Lanka, New Zealand, and Australia. Furthermore, Free Trade Areas have been achieved with Australia, Japan, and South Korea.

From its part, the European Union considers China and other Asian strong emerging economies as of strategic interest[51], being interested in consolidating an intense activity in this area. As a result, the Union has concluded different agreements and created free trade areas with South Korea, Singapore, Vietnam, Japan, Thailand, New Zealand, and Australia. On the other hand, the European position about the Chinese proposal of establishing an EU-China free trade area is extremely cautious: at the time, it stated that it could only be possible if the CAI entered into force and substantial progress was achieved on the need to ensure a level playing field for European enterprises operating in China[52]. As the CAI was blocked by the European Parliament and, since then, the scenario has drastically changed, it is not feasible in the next future to attain it.

51. See European Commission, "Global Europe, competing in the world: A contribution to the EU's Growth and Jobs Strategy", Brussels, 2006; European Economic and Social Committee, "Trade, Growth and World Affairs: Trade Policy as a core component of the EU's 2020 Strategy", COM(2010) 612, Brussels, 2010; or European Commission, "Trade for All: Towards a more responsible trade and Investment Policy", Luxembourg: Publications Office of the European Union, 2015.

52. Malmström, C., "China EU, A Partnership for Reform", speech by the European Commissioner for Trade at a Joint Business Europe, EUCC and EUCBA event, January 28th, 2016.

China and the European Union seem to have differing perceptions about the ambitioned free trade area, in particular concerning the details, the scope of binding provisions and the creation of dispute settlement mechanisms. While many points agreed by China focus mainly on tariff barriers, those agreed by the European Union cover a broad range of issues such as: tariff barriers, technical barriers to trade, sanitary and phytosanitary standards, regulatory barriers, public procurement, copyright protection, competition (including measures on SOEs and state aid), services, and investments. In the same vein, while many agreements concluded by China provide operational guidelines, the European Union includes binding provisions or arbitration and dispute settlement mechanisms[53]. Such comprehensive and deep free trade areas could have far more positive effects but because of its ambitious objectives they require much more preparation and openness creating doubts in less liberalised and complex economies[54].

V. EUROPEAN UNION'S VIEW ON THE BELT AND ROAD INITIATIVE

1. CHINESE MOTIVATIONS FOR THE BELT AND ROAD INITIATIVE

In 2013, President Xi Jinping proposed the creation of a modern version of the ancient Silk Road to get Europe and China better connected by both land and sea[55]. It was originally called 'One Belt, One Road' Initiative (OBOR) but was later renamed as 'Belt and Road Initiative' (BRI).

The first BRI Development Plan, launched in 2015[56], identified the objectives, principles, and cooperation areas and designed the main features of the initiative. Regarding the objectives, the initiative "[...] is aimed at promoting orderly and free flow of economic factors, highly efficient

53. For further information on this issue, see: Pelkmans, François *et al*, *op. cit.*, pp. 64-67.
54. Dür, A., Baccini, L., and Elsig, M., "The Design of International Trade Agreements: Introducing a New Database", *Review of International Organizations*, vol. 9, n. 3, 2014, pp. 353-375.
55. "Xi proposes a 'new Silk Road' with Central Asia", China Daily, September 9th, 2013, retrieved from *http://usa.chinadaily.com.cn/china/2013-09/08/content_16952304.htm*; "President Xi gives speech to Indonesia's parliament", China Daily, October 2nd, 2013, retrieved from *http://www.chinadaily.com.cn/china/2013xiapec/2013-10/02/content_17007915.htm*
56. Ministry of Foreign Affairs of the People's Republic of China, "Vision and Actions on Jointly Building Silk Road Economic Belt and Twenty-First Century Maritime Silk Road", Beijing, 2015.

allocation of resources and deep integration of markets; encouraging the countries along the Belt and Road to achieve economic policy coordination and carry out broader and more in-depth regional cooperation of higher standards; and jointly creating an open, inclusive, and balanced regional economic cooperation architecture that benefits all". "The Belt and Road Initiative aims to promote the connectivity of Asian, European and African continents and their adjacent seas, establish and strengthen partnerships among the countries along the Belt and Road, set up all-dimensional, multi-tiered and composite connectivity networks, and realize diversified, independent, balanced and sustainable development in these countries".

Under the principles of peaceful coexistence, mutual respect of national sovereignty, territorial integrity, equality, and mutual benefit, BRI covers the ancient Silk Road, but it is open to all those countries and international organisations willing to join it. Moreover, it complements and supports other similar initiatives through the establishment of infrastructure and connectivity networks to such an extent that it might be seen as the 'hardware' of a regional economic integration and the EU-Asia relations[57]. As the initiative is susceptible to alter the period scheduled for its implementation until 2049 (centenary of the founding of the People's Republic of China), it encourages the incorporation of other proposals and projects. The relevance in economic terms is huge significant as it includes 65 countries comprising over 70% of the world population and 55% of the world GDP. As Fernando Delage has noted: "once completed, it has the potential to alter the current global economic balances, transform the global financial system and reshape Eurasia and the Indo-Pacific region as geopolitical space"[58]. This is one of the main reasons why the Chinese government considers the BRI as a key element of its foreign policy, a cornerstone of the Chinese geopolitical aspirations and a tool for an in-house development[59].

At this point, we consider of special relevance to mention some of the Chinese main motivations to put in practice the Belt and Road Initiative[60].

57. Dollar, D., "China's Rise as a Regional and Global Power: The AIIB and the 'One Belt, One Road'", Horizons, n. 4 (Summer 2015), pp. 162-172 https://www.brookings.edu/wp-content/uploads/2016/06/China-rise-as-regional-and-global-power.pdf

58. Delage, *op. cit.*, p. 82.

59. "Foreign Minister Wang Yi Meets the Press", Beijing, March 8th, 2015, retrieved from *http://www.fmprc.gov.cn/mfa_eng/zxxx_662805/t1243662.shtml*

60. For further information on this issue, see: Djankov, S. *et al.*, "China's Belt and Road Initiative: Motives, Scope and Challenges", PIIE Briefing 16:2, March 2016; Johnson, C. K., "President Xi Jinping's Belt and Road Initiative — A Practical Assessment of the

From the internal policy perspective, China needs to ensure a sustainable growth rate in order to retain systemic and governmental legitimacy in front of its population[61], reduce regional inequalities, and enhance territorial cohesion. In a period of change, as noted above, economic growth depends on stimulating domestic consumption and creating additional benefit through technology and innovation, but also on benefiting from similar growth rates in its neighbouring countries by developing technical infrastructures and connections to Chinese industry exports. In practice, it means new business opportunities to boost Chinese investments and currency reserves as well as to procure a higher internalisation of the Yuan[62]. At the same time, if well planned, these new infrastructures and connections may contribute to the development of the peripheral and poor regions of China, reducing inequalities and tensions and overcoming internal resistance against economic reforms[63].

Concerning the foreign and geostrategic dimension, China seeks deeper connections with the Eurasian region, being at the heart of this dimension and rebalancing the dynamics of the international relations, in particular those of the Euro-Atlantic axis[64]. A pan-Asian emergence would result in a more Chinese-oriented new order at the expense of the United States leading role[65]. In the short-term, this could enhance stability and security in the region through economic development, discover alternative markets for Chinese exports and obtain energy resources.

Chinese Communist Party's Roadmap for China's Global Resurgence", CSIS Report, March 2016; Delage, *op. cit.*, pp. 84-89.

61. Delage, F., "China: cómo cambiar un modelo económico", Economía Exterior, n. 80, 2017, pp. 83-88.
62. Nicolas, F., "The economics of OBOR: Putting Chinese interests first", in Ekman, A., Nicolas, F., Seaman, J. *et al.*, *Three Years of China's New Silk Roads: From Words to (Re) action?*, Études de l'Ifri, Ifri, February 2017, pp. 17-28, retrieved from *https://www.ifri.org/sites/default/files/atoms/files/ekman_et_al_china_new_silk_roads_2017.pdf*
63. Esteban, M. and Otero Iglesias, M. "¿Qué podemos esperar de la nueva Ruta de la Seda y del Banco Asiático de Inversión en Infraestructuras liderados por China?", *Real Instituto Elcano*, ARI 19/2015, April 9th, 2015, p. 7.
64. Wang, J., "Marching Westwards': The Rebalancing of China's Geostrategy, International and Strategic Studies Report", *Centre for International and Strategic Studies*, Peking University, n. 73, October 7th, 2012.
65. Brzezinski, Z., "A Geostrategy for Eurasia", Foreign Affairs, vol. 76, n. 5, September-October 1997, pp. 50-64; Kissinger, H., "Does America need a Foreign Policy? Toward a Diplomacy for the 21st Century", *Simon and Schuster*, New York, 2001, p. 52. A reactive attitude from China with regard to the Trans-Pacific Partnership, dominated by the United States, could be a possible motivation for China in launching the Belt and Road Initiative.

2. EUROPE AND THE BELT AND ROAD INITIATIVE

In order to better illustrate the impact of the Belt and Road Initiative on the EU-China relations, we should clarify, on the one hand, how China has sought the European support and engagement and, on the other, how Europe has responded.

Regarding the first question, China made substantial efforts to promote the BRI among the European partners (European Union and member States) at political and diplomatic levels as well as in economic and academic fora, think tanks and media.

Following a strategy based on division among the member States, China opted first for not to propose any specific project nor programme at a wide-European dimension presenting them at national level in some member States, even if it could jeopardise the initiative itself. In this sense, Beijing did not use institutional common channels with the European Union adopting a bilateral and/or multilateral strategy to promote the BRI in Europe. However, China finally realised that the best and the inevitable option was to get the European Union involved in the initiative assuming the coordination among the twenty-seven.

Regarding the European countries benefiting from the Belt and Road Initiative, we need to distinguish between two different groups: the so-called '17+1 countries'[66] and the Southern European countries[67]. In any case, all of them have received the China's attention as potential recipients of funding for concrete projects and have been particularly interested in such option as they saw it as a great (and the only) opportunity to modernise infrastructures or to build up new ones in a period of budgetary constraints. Thus, the Port of Piraeus in Greece, the Belgrade-Budapest railway, some Spanish and Italian ports in the Mediterranean and the Yiwu-Madrid Railway line were projects developed under the scope of the BRI[68].

Preliminary studies on the impact of the BRI demonstrated that the trade flow from the European Union to China had increased by 6% because of a transport costs reduction and that the countries benefiting most from it were Belgium, Netherlands, Slovakia, Hungary, Germany, Poland, and

66. Albania, Bosnia and Herzegovina, Bulgaria, Croatia, Czech Republic, Estonia, Greece, Hungary, Latvia, Lithuania, North Macedonia, Montenegro, Poland, Romania, Serbia, Slovakia, and Slovenia.

67. Cyprus, Italy, Malta, Portugal, and Spain.

68. ETCN Report, "Europe and China's New Silk Roads", Edited by Van Der Putten, F-P, Seaman, J., Huotari, M., Ekman, A. and Otero Iglesias, M., December 2016.

Denmark[69]. The reason is that such cost reduction in the case of the land route was higher than in the pre-existing maritime one.

In the same way, both China and the Chinese companies focused not only on the European Union and its member States but also on other stakeholders such as companies or regional and local governments. In addition to what has been called 'BRI activities', there were some other projects potentially connected to the objectives of the BRI but not directly funded by it, as well as joint projects between some Chinese and European actors beyond Europe (Africa, Asia, and Latin America). Nonetheless, China has been more confident when cooperating and funding individual projects than when doing the same throughout institutional plans (i. e., Juncker Plan).

Chinese narrative on the BRI has focused also on the inclusiveness and openness of the initiative itself, its interdependency with other initiatives and projects, and its pertinence for improving and processing external capacities resulting in a 'win-win' situation for all the parties concerned (and not only for China).

China has been launching different ideas and projects but has remained open to other actor's proposals. In this respect, the country has organised several discussion groups and conferences, created Institutes, and collected critical comments and ideas with the aim of developing the BRI for the long term.

Concerning the second issue mentioned at the beginning of this section, a distinction between the European Union, its member States, the European companies, and other European stakeholders is relevant as each of them could adopt different points of view.

The European Union adopted a cautious attitude versus the BRI. First, it considered that the initiative was connected to the process of internal reforms in China and, therefore, to the country's subsequent needs in this new stage of its development. From this perspective, the European Union has always supported and encouraged such process of reforms showing its willingness to cooperate in this effort, as it is rightly sensitive in promoting processes of regional integration.

Secondly, the European Union has been aware about the implications of the BRI. Of course, it means more cooperation and new opportunities, but it also

69. García Herrero, A., and Xu, J., "China's Belt and Road initiative: can Europe expect trade gains?", Working Paper, n. 5, Bruegel, 2016.

implies a stronger competition that could be in some cases and under some circumstances unfair or fraudulent. That is why the Union has required that the investments and the economic development originated by the BRI should be transparent, based on international rules and standards, in full respect with the principles of public procurement and anti-subsidy, and without any distortion of the level playing field. All these aspects were particularly crucial for the EU before getting involved in and supporting the BRI.

Thirdly, the European Union has also been fully concerned about the importance that China put in practice the BRI, as well as about its political support within the country. This is why the option of be sitting on the fence was considered as an error. Even in that scenario, the initiative would have been developed in Europe or with European partners, but the European Union would have not had any real influence. Thus, the Union opted for a more collaborative position and proposed a mechanism to coordinate that collaboration (the EU-China Connectivity Platform) which was accepted by China.

Fourthly, the European Union emphasised the need for a better coordination of the proposals concerning the development of infrastructures in Europe within the framework of the BRI. As a result, the Union took care about unilateral actions undertaken by some member States, regional governments, and local entities.

Fifthly, the European Union knew that the economic development of Asia could therefore provide higher stability and security rates in the region. This was another reason in favour of getting involved into the BRI and cooperating with China to acquire a decisive influence.

The general overview was that some specific member States or local governments, as well as private companies, were more open to the Chinese proposals, in particular at the beginning of the BRI, than some others. Therefore, many governments at different levels were neutral or even strongly in favour, as it was the case of the '17+1 countries', because they saw the BRI more as a source of business opportunities than a geostrategic risk. However, business opportunities in China and in other non-European countries depend on the financing conditions and the rules for those new infrastructures.

On the specific projects already completed or in progress, it is still to be seen what the impact could be due to the relative short period of time since the creation of the BRI and the medium or long-term perspective applying for infrastructures investments. Nevertheless, new transport corridors are flourishing and increasingly used, and the European Union emphasises on the need to coordinate the European position and, consequently, clarify its role in that process.

VI. CONCLUSIONS

1. EU-CHINA RELATIONS

First. China and the European Union are strategic partners, and their bilateral relations are crucial for the development of common interests as well as for the global governance in the future. Despite their differences, in particular those related to the social model and the approach to apply in the international sphere, the EU-China relations have been strengthening over the last few decades, not only in terms of 'hard diplomacy' but also in terms of 'soft diplomacy'. However, we are now at a new crossroads requiring a re-adjustment, a rebalancing and hopefully a new impulse to the relation.

Second. Since the establishment of bilateral relations between China and the European Union, both partners have considerably changed. Understanding this changes, but also future trends and expectations, is necessary to re-align that relation.

China has experienced significant economic and commercial changes but has preserved its political model. The challenge is to gradually transform the economic power into geostrategic influence, reducing weaknesses and strengthening security in order to consolidate higher economic growth, development, and transformation rates. From its part, the European Union has increased the number of member States from nine to twenty-seven and has acquired more competences. Despite the economic and financial crisis, the outbreak of the pandemic, and the war in Ukraine, the European Union remains as one the world's largest economies in terms of GDP, the world's leading trading power, and a relevant actor on the global scene. Even if significant differences still exist between China and the European Union, they share some common interests and responsibilities, and a closer mutual cooperation could be mutually positive for them.

Third. Regarding the EU-China trade relations, trade in goods has increased tenfold over the last few years with a substantial surplus of €396 billion in 2022 for China. On the other hand, trade in services has also increased substantially but not as much as the trade in goods did. The positive surplus for the EU reached €20.5 billion in 2021. However, some restrictions imposed by China still apply.

Mutual investments are very significant, in particular the Foreign Direct Investments (FDI), but also here the existing asymmetries are a serious problem: the Chinese economy is the most restrictive among the eighty-three evaluated by the OECD.

The main disputes and areas of mutual interest on trade are: first, the status of China as market economy under the WTO standards (something that the European Union has been reluctant to recognise) and, therefore, the scope of imposing trade defence measures against imports originating in China; second, the Chinese restrictions on trade in services and a predominant position of the State-Owned Enterprises; third, asymmetrical access to public procurement and protection of intellectual rights; fourth, restrictions to foreign direct investments, and, finally, a way forward on investments after the blockage of the Comprehensive Agreement on Investment (CAI). Overall, there is a need of substantial progress on the level playing field on the Chinese side. Furthermore, the new context requires to take more in consideration (social and green) sustainability objectives and security concerns. A diversification and de-risking (but not decoupling) seems unavoidable and is already underway.

Hopefully, trade relations between China and the EU can continue growing in the years to come. The creation of a free trade agreement between both partners could even be considered in the long term but not before the assurance of a level playing field for European companies in China. Also, some of the existing disputes could be easily solved if China makes new progresses on internal reforms and ensures a sustainable growth rate. For its part, the European Union should continue supporting those processes and insisting on achieving that needed level playing field referred before.

2. EU AND THE BELT AND ROAD INITIATIVE

First. In an early stage, China deliberately chose not to consider institutional common mechanisms with the European Union and decided to adopt only a bilateral and/or multilateral approach to promote the BRI in Europe. However, China finally realised that the best and inevitable option was to get the European Union involved as a whole in the initiative granting it a role of coordinator of the European partners.

Second. Regarding those European countries benefiting from the Belt and Road Initiative, we should distinguish between the '17+1 countries' and the southern European members States of the EU. Nonetheless, according to some studies carried out about the potential impact of the BRI, central European countries such as Austria, Belgium, Denmark, Germany, Hungary, Netherlands, Poland, and Slovakia would benefit the most. In any case, it is still to be seen what impact the ongoing projects could have.

Third. The European Union has adopted cautious attitude versus the Belt and Road Initiative. In general, it has been considered more as a potential source of business opportunities than a geostrategic risk, even if the European Union has stressed the need for a full compliance with the public procurement and anti-subsidy rules as well as with a proper level playing field. Nevertheless, the option of be sitting on the fence towards the BRI was considered as an error and, consequently, the Union shifted for a more collaborative position and proposed a coordination mechanism accepted by China: the EU-China Connectivity Platform.

A common orientation at European level has been a priority for the EU as it is highly concerned about the possibility that the BRI could result in an enormous economic influence of China and risk the security and the stability in Asia.

Finally, the European Union must therefore encourage the BRI, having a closer implication on how it is going to be fully developed and continue demanding an equal treatment for those European companies operating in China. In the same way, the BRI needs to prove to be a useful instrument not only to boost a political reform process in China but also to provide positive synergies for all those countries and companies taking part in this initiative.

China-EU Economic Relations in the New Era

DING CHUN[1] & JI HAONAN[2]
Centre for European Studies, Fudan University

I. INTRODUCTION: A NEW ERA OF CHINA-EU ECONOMIC RELATIONS

China and the European Union (EU) have an extensive and growing economic relationship over the past 30 years. The rise of China in recent decades has been an economic success story, both for China and for the world[3], and the EU is one of the biggest beneficiaries. EU-China trade in goods has reached 856 billion Euros according to the statistics by the EU Directorate-General for Trade[4]. Besides the growing volume of bilateral trade, a range of dialogues have been established with the political efforts of China and the EU, where China and the EU can negotiate economic issues as well as policies. These reflect significant achievements in the EU-China economic relations.

On the other hand, the growth of the Chinese economy has provided the EU with new markets while also bringing competition[5]. With the development of the Chinese economy, the EU seems to become somewhat more sceptical towards the economic relations with China. The 2019 Strategic Outlook famously describes China as a "negotiating partner…, an economic

1. Ding Chun is a Professor of Economics, and Director of the Centre for European Studies, Dutch Study Centre of Fudan University. He is also a Jean Monnet Chair and Secretary-General of Chinese Society for EU Studies.
2. Ji Haonan is a research assistant at the Centre for European Studies, Fudan University.
3. Schmucker, C. and Wolf, G., "Managing Risks in the EU-China Economic Relationship", German Council on Foreign Relations, 2022, retrieved from https://dgap.org/en/research/publications/managing-risks-eu-china-economic-relationship
4. European Commission, European Union, Trade in goods with China, 2023, retrieved from https://webgate.ec.europa.eu/isdb_results/factsheets/country/details_china_en.pdf
5. Hill, C. and Vanhoonacker-Kormoss, S., *International relations and the European Union*, Oxford University Press, 2023, p.174.

competitor..., and a systemic rival"[6]. China, meanwhile, also have concerns about the EU's growing interventionist approaches to economic issues. 2019 marked a turn for the EU's diplomatic approach to China. Both parties have made efforts to address the concerns, yet challenges remain. The economic relations are further shadowed by the huge impact due to the global COVID-19 pandemic. The pandemic has, from many perspectives changed the EU's perceptions on economic affairs, in particular its economic relations with China. Different voices have emerged on ways to handle trade and investment with China with many asking for de-risking and diversification. The continuous conflicts between Russia and Ukraine also have a profound influence on the EU's security and economic interests, and hence impact the economic relations between China and the EU.

Hence, it is time to examine the China-EU relations, for it might have entered a new era. The era is not only marked by any significant changes in the volumes or trends in China-EU bilateral trade and investment. Instead, it is marked by different potential trends and challenges behind the landscape of the China-EU economic relations, and the changing views about these economic relations, particularly from the EU side. Therefore, this paper will present the status-quo of China-EU economic relations by looking at the economic situation within the EU and EU-China bilateral trade and investment. Then it will analyze the factors behind the status-quo, particularly noting the growing competition in international industrial competition, especially in the manufacturing industries while also pointing out the policy shift and public opinion changes during the past few years. After that the paper will indicate the trends for China-EU economic relations, arguing that China and the EU shall stay patient and enhance mutual understanding to foster economic cooperation.

II. STATUS QUO OF CHINA-EU ECONOMIC RELATIONS

1. STATUS QUO OF THE EU ECONOMY

The COVID-19 pandemic has forced most of the EU member states to implement lockdowns in 2020 and early 2021, leading to a worst-ever economic recession in the EU[7]. The EU economy continues to face tough

6. European Commission, "EU-China: A Strategic Outlook", EC and HR/VP Contribution to the European Council, 2019, retrieved from https://eur-lex.europa.eu/legal-content/EN/TXT/PDF/?uri=CELEX:52019JC0005
7. OECD, "Economic Survey of the European Union and the Euro Area (June 2023)", *EA and EU Economic Snapshot*, 2023, retrieved from *https://www.oecd.org/economy/euro-area-and-european-union-economic-snapshot/*

recovery, high inflation and a significant level of government debt. As the International Monetary Fund (IMF) has pointed out, the EU now faces a difficult task "simultaneously bringing down inflation, sustaining economic growth, and preserving financial stability"[8]. Moreover, the Russian-Ukrainian conflicts have deeply affected the EU's economy, leading to the sharp rise of energy prices. This section will introduce the EU economy from the following perspectives.

First, the EU economy is still recovering from the shock of the global pandemic and is constantly impacted by the conflicts between Russia and Ukraine. In the second quarter of 2023, the EU's GDP remains unchanged quarter-on-quarter in Q2 2023, following a moderate 0.1% rise in Q1 2023, while the Euro area is at 0.3% according to Eurostat[9]. Among the four major EU economies, the economy of France and Spain gains quarter-on-quarter and Germany's economy remains stable, while Italy has a modest contraction in Q2 2023. This is far from a sign of relief, although it shows a better signal from previous concerns over the fact that the GDP of the Euro Zone has dropped 0.1% in both the final quarter of 2022 and the first quarter of 2023 from the previous quarter, showing a technical recession. The projections of the European economy remain cautious, as the OCED projects GDP growth in the Euro Area to slow to 0.9% in 2023 and then gradually strengthen to 1.5% in 2024[10] while the IMF projects 0.8% for Euro Area in 2023 and 1.4% in 2024[11]. Despite the slow rate of recovery, compared to its pre-pandemic level in Q4 2019, EU GDP is 3.1% higher in Q2 2023, demonstrating the effort of the EU's economic responses to the pandemic.

Second, inflation remains significant, although it has been on the decline. The euro area's annual inflation rate dropped to 5.3% in July 2023 from 5.5% in June, according to Eurostat's flash estimate[12]. Core inflation which excludes food and energy prices, however, was unchanged at 5.5% in July

8. IMF, "Europe's balancing act: taming inflation without a recession", Regional Economic Outlook, 2023, retrieved from https://www.imf.org/en/Publications/REO/EU/Issues/2023/04/09/regional-economic-outlook-for-europe-april-2023
9. Eurostat, European Statistical Recovery Dashboard, retrieved from https://ec.europa.eu/eurostat/cache/recovery-dashboard/
10. OECD, "Economic Survey of the European Union and the Euro Area (June 2023)", *op. cit.*
11. IMF, Europe's Knife-Edge Path Toward Beating Inflation Without a Recession, April 2023, retrieved from https://www.imf.org/en/Blogs/Articles/2023/04/28/europes-knifeedge-path-toward-beating-inflation-without-a-recession#Projections
12. Eurostat, EU GDP holds steady, while economic sentiment continues to weaken, August 2023, retrieved from https://ec.europa.eu/eurostat/cache/recovery-dashboard/data/202308/text-docs/commentary-text-en.pdf

2023, indicating the persistence of underlying price pressures. Inflation situations differ in EU member states. While most countries saw a decline in inflation, Greece, Finland, Luxembourg, and Spain saw an increase. In general, the current inflation rate in the EU area is still much higher than the 2.0% goal set by the European Central Bank. Tackling inflation continues to be one of the major tasks of the ECA and member states.

Third, despite the shock of the pandemic, unemployment in the EU remains historically low at 5.9% in June 2023, with a 0.7% decrease from the pre-pandemic level in February 2020. Only Spain and Greece have high inflation rates over 10% at 11.7% and 11.1% respectively[13].

Different from the continuous recovery of EU GDP, inflation and employment, the EU's foreign trade has not been recovering constantly. The first estimate for extra-EU exports of goods in June 2023 was 225.9 billion Euros, which increased by 0.4% compared with June 2022, and imports was 201.2 billion Euros, which decreased by 22.6% compared with June 2022. Interestingly, the EU recorded a 24.6 billion surplus in trade in goods with the rest of the world in June 2023, compared with a deficit of 34.9 billion in June 2022[14]. As for the Euro Area, the first estimate for exports of goods to the rest of the world in June 2023 were 252.3 billion Euros, a slight increase of 0.3% compared with June. Imports ware at 229.3 billion Euros, a decrease of 17.7% compared with June 2022[15]. The fluctuation of EU foreign trade is affected by many internal and external factors, particularly by the global pandemic, and the Russian-Ukraine conflicts and the consequent rise of energy prices.

Besides these important figures, there are significant concerns with the EU's economy. On the one hand, government deficit and government debt have significantly expanded in comparison to their pre-pandemic ratios. In Q1 2023, the government deficit-to-GDP ratio stood at 4.0%, showing a notable increase from 1.4% compared to the same quarter of 2019 before the pandemic. The government debt-to-GDP ratio increased to 83.7% in Q1 2023 from 80.1% in Q1 of 2019, much higher than the 60% suggested by the EU. On the other hand, bankruptcy declarations in the EU continued to rise at a faster pace in Q2 2023 compared to pre-pandemic levels. The number of declarations of bankruptcies in the EU increased quarter-to-quarter by 8.4%

13. Ibid.
14. Eurostat, Euro area international trade in goods surplus €23.0 bn, June 2023, retrieved from https://ec.europa.eu/eurostat/documents/2995521/17336679/6-17082023-AP-EN.pdf/098f7aeb-9297-d074-d263-484d51c9ca87
15. Ibid.

in Q2 2023, after a 4.2% increase in Q1 2023, showing the serious challenges posted for the business in the EU.

In summary, the current EU's economy is recovering from the pandemic with most of the economic indicators recovering to the pre-pandemic level, but also shadowed by the uncertainty of its external economic environment and the high inflation. This brings both the dynamic for the recovery and development of China-EU trade and the uncertainty of China-EU economic relations.

2. CHINA-EU TRADE

China and the EU have a strong trade relationship and it continues to grow in the last decade. China-EU trade in goods, according to the European Commission, has grown from about 382 billion Euros to about 856 billion Euros[16]. 2022 also marked the biggest trade surplus for China in China-EU trade so far at nearly 396 billion Euros[17]. Now taking 15.4% of the EU trade, China is the biggest import partner with the EU and the third largest export market. Manufactures are the biggest product group for both sides in the China-EU trade. The three largest importers from China in the EU were the Netherlands, Germany and Italy while the three largest exporters to China in the EU were Germany, France and the Netherlands. Among the 27 EU member states, only Ireland had a trade surplus with China whereas the other 26 EU member states all had a trade deficit with China. The largest deficit was held by the Netherlands, followed by Italy and Poland[18]. In contrast to the trade of goods, on trade in services, the EU currently has an about 20.5 billion euros trade surplus with China. Interestingly, the pandemic did not result in any decline in EU-China trade[19]. China and the EU have been important trade partners, and the trade relations seem to remain the solid aspect of China-EU economic relations.

Some concerns have also been raised in the EU about trade with China. The European Commission has been expressing its concerns over issues

16. European Commission, Trade in goods with China, 2023, retrieved from https://webgate.ec.europa.eu/isdb_results/factsheets/country/details_china_en.pdf
17. Ibid.
18. Eurostat, China-EU — international trade in goods statistics, February 2023, retrieved from https://ec.europa.eu/eurostat/statistics-explained/index.php?title=China-EU_-_international_trade_in_goods_statistics#Trade_with_China_by_EU_Member_State
19. Choro-Mrozowska D., "The Impact of COVID-19 on EU-China Trade Flows", *Comparative Economic Research, Central and Eastern Europe*, vo. 25, n. 4, 2022, pp. 161-178.

including significant trade deficit, market access for European companies, transparency, intellectual property, and state-owned enterprises (SOEs). The EU has also used trade defence measures against imports from China. Since April 2020, the EU has initiated 39 trade defence investigations against China[20], reflecting some turbulent elements in the China-EU trade. There have also been growing concerns over China's economic influence inside and outside the EU, especially over China's economic relations with Central and Eastern European countries. China has been accused of using economic power as a leverage to inject a trojan horse to interfere with the EU's internal affairs. On the national level, similarly, some EU member states such as Italy have expressed concerns over China's Belt and Road Initiative (BRI) while the Baltic states, particularly led by Lithuania, have withdrawn from the China-proposed "17+1" initiative, a cooperation framework between China and the central and eastern European countries.

3. CHINA-EU INVESTMENT

China-EU investment has been on the increase in general before the pandemic. According to the Chinese Ministry of Commerce, the stock of two-way investment between China and the EU has exceeded 230 billion US dollars. In 2022, Europe has invested 12.1 billion US dollars in China, a substantial increase of 70%, and the automotive sector continues to be the biggest investment hotspot[21]. The EU foreign direct investment (FDI) in China has become more concentrated in terms of sectors, investors and countries of origin. Five sectors including autos, food processing, pharma/biotech, chemicals and consumer products manufacturing make up nearly 70% of all FDI in 2021 with a increase from 57% in 2008-2012 and from 65% in 2013-2017[22]. Top investors play a major role in European FDI in China. For example, in 2019, the top 10 investors took up 88% of all European FDI[23]. Germany, the Netherlands, the UK and France made up 87% of the total investment value, on average, in the ten years between 2011 and 2021[24]. During 2022, China has invested 11.1 billion US dollars in the EU, an increase of 21%. The new investment was concentrated in fields such as new energy,

20. European Commission, Trade defense investigations, 25 August 2023, retrieved from https://tron.trade.ec.europa.eu/investigations/ongoing
21. Xinhua, The average trade between China and Europe exceeds 1.6 million US dollars per minute, 5 May 2023, retrieved from https://www.gov.cn/lianbo/2023-05/05/content_5754261.htm
22. Rhodium Group, retrieved from https://rhg.com/research/the-chosen-few/
23. Ibid.
24. Ibid.

automobiles, and machinery[25]. There seems to be a bounce back for Chinese investment in Europe, as Chinese foreign direct investment (FDI) in the EU (including the UK) peaked in 2016 (47.4 billion euros) but has declined since then till 2021[26].

Given the increase in EU investment in China, Chinese investors' confidence in investing in the EU has been low. In the 2021 survey of more than 100 Chinese enterprises and organizations by the China Chamber of Commerce to the EU (CCCEU), 20% of the respondents noted that the EU's FDI screening mechanism had a negative impact on their business, and 42% of them were concerned that the mechanism may have more negative implications in the future[27]. Meanwhile, the EU seems to be more defensive against Chinese investment. The foreign investment screening regulation seems to mainly target China. Moreover, the Comprehensive Agreement on Investment (CAI) which the EU and China, which has been concluded in principle, is now away from ratification by the European Parliament.

4. INTERGOVERNMENTAL MECHANISMS IN CHINA-EU ECONOMIC RELATIONS

China and the EU have established multiple mechanisms for political dialogue to discuss economic issues, allowing both sides to manage disputes in economic relations. On the highest level is the Annual EU-China Summit, a presidential-level exchange on the comprehensive relations between China and the EU. In the field of economic relations, the EU-China High-Level Economic and Trade Dialogue is for the EU Vice-president and the Chinese Vice Premier to discuss economic and trade issues accompanied by EU commissioners and Chinese ministers. There are also the Joint Committee on Trade where annual ministerial-level meetings are held, and the Trade and Investment Policy Dialogue and the Economic and Trade Working Group for experts. Policy documents following these meetings help to establish a systematic framework for settling economic disputes and economic policy coordination. These mechanisms have facilitated the political exchanges between China and the EU on economic affairs.

25. Xinhua, The average trade between China and Europe exceeds 1.6 million US dollars per minute, op. cit.
26. German Council on Foreign Relations, Managing Risks in the EU-China Economic Relationship, November 2022, https://dgap.org/en/research/publications/managing-risks-eu-china-economic-relationship
27. Euractiv, The EU-China trade headache, June 2023, retrieved from https://en.euractiv.eu/wp-content/uploads/sites/2/special-report/The-EU-China-trade-headache-Event-Report-2023.pdf

5. THE CHANGING DYNAMICS IN CHINA-EU ECONOMIC RELATIONS

The economic relations between China and the EU have always been a mixture of development and concerns. However, there are significant changes behind the overall picture of China-EU economic relations. The concerns of the EU over its economic relations with China go beyond traditional trade policy concerns and merge with political or, in particular, security concerns[28]. The changes are mainly caused by the EU's perception of its economic relations with China and the overall changes in the EU's perception of its economic relations with the rest of the world.

The EU and some of the major member states have been adding a security dimension to their economic relations with China. As President of the European Commission Ursula von der Leyen expressed in her speech on EU-China relations to two of the major European think tanks — the Mercator Institute for China Studies and the European Policy Centre, the way the EU manage its relations with China "will be a determining factor for our future economic prosperity and national security"[29]. It is now a consensus within the EU as the European Commission and the High Representative published a Joint Communication on a European Economic Security Strategy saying "With geopolitical tensions rising and global economic integration deeper than ever before, certain economic flows and activities can present a risk to our security"[30]. Although the EU policy documents hardly mention China, the EU's attempt to protect its economic security through "the partnering with the broadest possible range of partners to strengthen economic security"[31] certainly means to some extent distancing its major economic partner — China. Since the outbreak of COVID-19 in Europe in 2020, the EU has been constantly reviewing its economic dependence on China and has taken a series of actions aiming to reduce its reliance on China. The European Commission has published two in-depth reviews of EU strategic dependencies and capacities in 2021

28. Huotari, M., and Jean, S., "Bolstering Europe's economic strategy vis-à-vis China", *Notes du conseil danalyse economique*, vol. 72, n. 3, 2022, pp. 1-2.
29. European Commission, Speech by President von der Leyen on EU-China relations to the Mercator Institute for China Studies and the European Policy Centre, March 2023, retrieved from https://ec.europa.eu/commission/presscorner/detail/en/speech_23_2063
30. Joint Communication to the European Parliament, the European Council and the Council on "European Economic Security Strategy", June 2023, retrieved from *https://eur-lex.europa.eu/legal-content/EN/TXT/?uri=CELEX%3A52023JC0020&qid=1687525961309*
31. Ibid.

and 2022 respectively[32], identifying 137 products for which the EU is highly dependent on imports, especially from China. A further analysis by European scholars shows that China emerges as the primary source for these dependent products occupying the origin for half of the 204 products where the EU experiences foreign dependencies[33]. And the EU's attempts to diversify its imports will certainly have a negative impact on EU-China trade. The rising security dimension in perceiving economic affairs in the EU is not unique to EU-China relations. Instead, it seems like a trend of emphasizing economic sovereignty. Before the pandemic, the EU has recently reformed its foreign investment screening mechanism with an eye on Chinese activities. During the pandemic, the EU strengthened its defence of key assets, attempting to prevent them to be acquire by countries such as China. The EU has revealed its ambition in enhancing its economic sovereignty through a series of legislations including Digital Markets Act, the Digital Services Act, the European Critical Raw Material Act, the European Chips Act and the Net-Zero Industry Act. Many of these legislations and policies came out only in the past three years, marking a significant change in the EU's perception of economic affairs after the global pandemic. Similar moves were made by the EU member states. Germany, for example, has published its national security strategy in June 2023, openly urging to "reduce unilateral dependence in raw materials and energy provision by diversifying supply relationships"[34].

So far it is difficult to draw any conclusion on the level of economic impact of these changes. For example, scholars have argued that geopolitical diversification efforts by the EU and member states may also foster a subsidy race between countries and diversification strategies may risk supporting ineffective and costly policies[35]. Yet it is safe to say the political dynamics

32. See European Commission, Commission Staff Working Document: Strategic dependencies and capacities, May 2021, retrieved from https://eur-lex.europa.eu/legal-content/EN/TXT/PDF/?uri=CELEX:52021SC0352&from=EN and Commission Staff Working Document: EU strategic dependencies and capacities: second stage of in-depth reviews, February 2022, retrieved from https://ec.europa.eu/docsroom/documents/48878

33. Arjona, R., Garcia W. and Herghelegiu C, "The EU's strategic dependencies unveiled", *CEPR*, May 2023, retrieved from *https://cepr.org/voxeu/columns/eus-strategic-dependencies-unveiled*

34. German Federal Government, Presentation of the National Security Strategy — This is about all aspects of our security, June 2023, retrieved from https://www.bundesregierung.de/breg-de/aktuelles/national-security-strategy-2196356

35. Ghiretti, F. and Maull, H., "Diversification isn't enough to cure Europe's economic dependence on China", *MERICS*, 2023, retrieved from *https://merics.org/en/comment/diversification-isnt-enough-cure-europes-economic-dependence-china*

behind China-EU economic relations have been very different compared to the pre-pandemic era and the economic relations between China and the EU, now have different meanings.

III. FACTORS

1. THE CHANGING GLOBAL CONTEXT FOR CHINA-EU ECONOMIC RELATIONS

Many scholars and think tanks have pointed out that the global context of China-EU relations has been shifting. The uni-polar system has gradually given way to a "new multi-polarity"[36] marked by China's re-emergence and mounting influence. The EU, in contrast, the international status of the EU has suffered setbacks within the past two decades due to multiple crises, chiefly the sovereign debt crisis, the refugee crisis and Brexit. These crises not only impacted the EU's international image but also cast doubts on the EU's economic model on which the EU relies as an order-shaper[37]. The sharp contrast of China's economic success and the EU's struggle, and the essential difference in economic system and culture have led to concerns over relative gains in the EU. The EU has not changed China's economic system as it wished. As the Chinese economy shifts from an export-led to a domestic demand-led growth model[38], the EU may also be concerned about losing leverage in its relations with China. With China's economic influence further spread, the EU's concern over China has grown.

The rivalry between the United States and China has become the major global context for international relations in recent years. On the one hand, the United States regards China as a revisionist power and seeks to contain the Chinese influence. Conflicts in trade, technology and financial policies have broken out, directly and indirectly affecting the EU and member states[39]. The EU's economic relations with China are now more affected by the United States' rivalry against

36. Geeraerts G., "The changing global context of China-EU relations", *China International Study*, 2013, pp. 42-53.
37. Geeraerts G., "The EU-China partnership: balancing between divergence and convergence", Asia Europe Journal, vol. 17, 2019, pp. 281-294.
38. Dadush, U., Domínguez-Jiménez, M. and Gao, T., "The state of China-European Union economic relations", *Bruegel-Working Papers*, 2019, retrieved from *https://www.bruegel.org/working-paper/state-china-european-union-economic-relations*
39. Perthes V., "Dimensions of strategic rivalry: China, the United States and Europe's place", in Lippert, B. and Perthes, V. (eds.), *Strategic rivalry between United States and China: causes, trajectories, and implications for Europe,* German Institute for International and Security Affairs, 2020.

China. On the other hand, the increasing unilateralism in the United States has hurt the confidence of the EU in dealing with global issues. China remains an important partner for the EU in global governance and multilateralism.

Besides these wider contexts, the global consequences of the COVID-19 pandemic and conflicts between Russia and Ukraine constitute the more recent contexts of China-EU economic relations. As mentioned above, the pandemic has triggered the EU to review its economic dependence and contemplate "de-risking" from China. Yet this is not the only direction which the EU is moving towards. The Inflation Reduction Act (IRA) by the U. S. Biden administration, has led to concerns within the EU since the IRA provides tax credits as subsidies for US-based production and hence violates international trade rules[40]. The IRA stimulates European manufacturers to relocate in North America. This clearly shows that the United States' protectionism is not unique to the Trump administration and undermines the trust between the EU and the U. S. During the post-pandemic recovery, growing protectionism is likely to be more common between major economies. Thus, the EU still needs China in cooperation related to trade liberalization. The conflicts between Russia and Ukraine have also impacted the EU's relations with China. While the conflicts have a negative impact on the EU's economy so that the EU needs improving its economic relations with China, many Europeans hope China to take up a bigger role in mitigating the situation or even blame China for staying indifferent. The conflict also causes the increasing prices of energy throughout Europe, with Eastern European countries which depend nearly totally on Russian gas supplies suffering more. This context has complex effects on China-EU economic relations. The increasing energy prices may not only harm the EU's economy and further impact the EU's foreign trade, it also accelerates the EU's review of its economic dependence on other economies. The pressure of economic recovery after the pandemic mounted during the energy crisis might push the EU for deepening economic cooperation with China. Due to the fact that different member states suffer differently in the energy crisis, the impact of the conflict may vary.

2. MUTUAL COMPETITIONS

As China move up in the global production chain, more Chinese manufacturing companies enter industries that are predominantly European,

40. Bruegel, The EU response to the United States Inflation Reduction Act, February 2023, retrieved from https://www.bruegel.org/comment/eu-response-united-states-inflation-reduction-act

leading to increasing competition between China and the EU, consisting a fundamental element in the economic relations between China and the EU. To identify and measure the changes in competition in the manufacturing industry, the article will present results from quantitative analysis based on data from China and EU-28 (before Brexit)[41].

Based on the calculation of the revealed symmetric comparative advantage (RSCA) index, China's manufacturing industry shows symmetrical comparative advantages mostly in labour-intensive (textile, shoes and hats) and resource-intensive (furniture, metal) industries, while the EU's advantages are mainly concentrated in technology-intensive (chemical, mechanical instrument) industries. In addition, there had been an expanding positive gap of symmetrical comparative advantages year by year (especially in 2013-2017) between the China's manufacturing industry and the United States and Europe as a whole, but the expansion of this advantage has slowed down after 2017.

According to the calculation of the export similarity index (ESI), the total similarity of the manufacturing ESI between China and the United States is significantly higher than that of China and the EU. The intensity of competition in the US manufacturing market is stronger than that of China and the EU. What's more, China and the US have obvious competition in the computer and electronic equipment, chemical and non-metallic minerals, clothing, textile and leather industries, while the competition between China and the EU is mainly concentrated in the chemical industry followed by machinery. In addition, the ESI of China-U. S. and China-EU manufacturing industries in resource-intensive industries is significantly lower than that of technology-intensive industries. Finally, the ESI of China-U. S. and China-EU manufacturing industries declined year by year from 2011 to 2015, but the speed of decline in China-U. S. is lower than that of China-EU. That is to say, the development of the manufacturing division of labour in China and the EU is stronger than that in China and the United States. Therefore, the United States has a relatively stronger demand for competition because of China's rapid catching up with the United States in international competitiveness and the high level of manufacturing ESI. On the contrary, China-EU ESI has steadily declined. Although the EU and China still have manufacturing competitiveness race, the EU's demand for

41. See Ding C. and Chen. T, "Competition in Manufacturing Industry among China, US and EU: Current Situations, Counter Measures of US and EU and Prospects", *Chinese Journal of European Studies*, vol.39, n.5, pp. 6-35. The paper is originally in Chinese. The title is translated by the authors.

radical comprehensive competition is not high. Many of the current measures considered "confrontational" against China may be triggered by the shock of the pandemic and economic and social pressures within the EU such as debt and refugees. The EU's manufacturing competition against China is still driven by rational economic calculation, while the United States' approach contains more irrational and political factors.

More information is revealed based on the calculation results for the Global Value Chain Position Index (GVC) between 2007 and 2015. First, in terms of the industry-wide GVC status index excluding subdivisions, the EU occupied the highest position in the global value chain followed by the United States and then China while after 2013, the U. S. manufacturing GVC status surpassed the EU. Secondly, in the subdivided manufacturing industry, China's GVC position advantage is in the sectors of food, beverage and tobacco preparation, and chemicals and non-metallic mineral products. The EU's advantages are in the clothing, textile and leather industry, wood and paper printing industry, and machinery manufacturing and other manufacturing industries. The advantages of the United States are in the three sectors of clothing, textile and leather industry, basic and processed metal preparation, and computer and electronic equipment. Third, China's GVC position index continues to rise, and its gap from the United States and the EU continues to narrow. At the same time, China has caught up with the United States and the EU in the fields of clothing, textile and leather industry, wood and paper printing industry, basic and processed metal preparation, machinery manufacturing industry, etc., but in the computer and electronic equipment manufacturing industry, there is still a big gap between China and the United States as well as the EU. Fourth, China has obvious advantages in low-end manufacturing, and its mid-end manufacturing industry is gradually catching up, but there is still a big gap between China and the EU in high-end manufacturing.

More conclusions can be drawn after combining the RSCA index and the GVC position index. Firstly, Chinese manufacturing has a comparative advantage over the United States and the EU, but this advantage is not reflected in GVC participation. Secondly, China's manufacturing advantages compared with the United States and the EU, both in terms of GVC position and in terms of comparative advantage, are all concentrated in labour-intensive and resource-intensive industries while disadvantages existed in technology-intensive industries, although this gap has gradually narrowed in recent years. Thirdly, the overall advantage of China compared with Europe has expanded, and the EU's manufacturing industry has experienced a relative "decline". Fourth, given that China's GVC position is less advantageous, China's manufacturing industry can still have a comparative advantage over the United States and the EU, showing that most of China's manufacturing industry realizes the international competitive advantage through the economies of scale in low value-added middle and downstream labour-intensive industries.

In conclusion, the international competitiveness of China's manufacturing industry is constantly catching up with that of the United States and the EU, and the source of competitiveness is gradually shifting from downstream with lower added value to upper stream with high added value. China is gradually getting rid of its over-reliance on labour-intensive and resource-intensive industries and increasing investment in technology-intensive industries. The advantages of the EU in technology-intensive industries (especially high-end manufacturing) are still an insurmountable gap for China at the moment, and their traditional manufacturing advantages have changed little. The competition in manufacturing industries between China and the EU has driven the EU to implement policies to improve industrial competitiveness and protect its manufacturing industries, adding to the competing dimension of the China-EU economic relations.

3. EU STRATEGIC AUTONOMY AND NATIONAL PRIORITIES

The concept of European strategic autonomy has gradually occupied a central position in the political discourses in the EU. In response to the changes in the economic and geopolitical changes near the EU, the concept is about "the capacity of the EU to act autonomously — without being dependent on other countries — in strategically important policy areas"[42]. Originating in the realm of security and defence, the term has now expanded to the discussion around the EU's economy and its economic relations with other economies. For example, in June 2020, HR/VP Josep Borrell and European Commissioner for the Internal Market Thierry Breton published an opinion piece, arguing for the EU to become more resilient and independent facing the pandemic supply shortages, urging for a "united, resilient and sovereign Europe"[43]. The Trade Policy Review published by the European Commission

42. European Parliament, EU Strategic Autonomy Monitor, July 2022, retrieved from https://www.europarl.europa.eu/RegData/etudes/BRIE/2022/733589/EPRS_BRI(2022)733589_EN.pdf
43. Borrell, J. and Breton, T., For a united, resilient and sovereign Europe (with Thierry Breton), retrieved from https://www.eeas.europa.eu/eeas/united-resilient-and-sovereign-europe-thierry-breton_en

in 2021 introduces the term "open strategic autonomy" as a goal in the field of trade. The term has also been associated with the EU's internal economic resilience demonstrated by its appearance in initiatives such as the Next Generation EU[44]. There seems to be a trend that the concept of open strategic autonomy is going to be the directive term for the EU's economic policies.

Economic relations China has now been a notable part of the strategic autonomy discussion in the EU. Both the EU collectively, and many member states individually, "act as if Chinese ownership of critical infrastructure assets is inherently more threatening" than other states[45]. Compared to the dependencies on energy from Russia, the EU's dependencies on China are more complicated and therefore receive profound discussions. In May 2021, the European Commission published an update to its 2020 industrial strategy outlining the dependencies of the EU on products and technologies from third countries[46]. The European Commission has investigated in detail dependencies in key technologies and research & innovation and in strategic areas with proposals for reducing these strategic dependencies.

However, just like much of the discussion of European strategic autonomy has been shattered by the priorities of different member states, the strategic autonomy debates around China have not yet come out with a consensus. While the European Commission has urged the EU to reduce its dependence on China and protect key assets, there have been few tools for the EU to realize its ambition. Instead, the "de-risking" process has to rely on member states who take diverse stances on economic cooperation with China. For instance, while the Netherlands joined the United States and Japan in imposing new export controls on microchips technology, restricting the sales of advanced chips machinery to China,[47] France has been openly against de-coupling with China and called for enhancing its economic cooperation with China. The different level of member states' dependencies on China also contributes to the difficulty of EU coordination. The Dutch Foreign Trade Minister Liesje

44. European Parliament, Next Generation EU A European instrument to counter the impact of the coronavirus pandemic, July 2020, retrieved from https://www.europarl.europa.eu/RegData/etudes/BRIE/2020/652000/EPRS_BRI(2020)652000_EN.pdf
45. Poutala, T., Sinkkonen, E. and Mattlin, M., "EU Strategic Autonomy and the Perceived Challenge of China: Can Critical Hubs Be De-weaponized?", *European Foreign Affairs Review*, vol. 27 (special), 2022.
46. European Commission, Commission Staff Working Document: Strategic dependencies and capacities, May 2021, retrieved from https://eur-lex.europa.eu/legal-content/EN/TXT/PDF/?uri=CELEX:52021SC0352&from=EN
47. Dutch Government, Staatscourant 2023 18212, retrieved from https://zoek.officielebekendmakingen.nl/stcrt-2023-18212.html

Schreinemacher said Greece makes an effective China policy more difficult in the European context due to its reliance on Chinese investment in ports[48]. This reflects the dilemma in promoting European strategic autonomy in economic fields. On procedure, the progress of strategic autonomy is often by trade-offs between leading states and member states unwilling to change. In essence, moreover, strategic autonomy in itself is complicated as it could translate into independence from other entities or independence in capacities. The former may require the EU or the member state to reduce economic dependencies on China yet this may harm the capacities for hedging.

To conclude, the EU's pursuit of strategic autonomy is a double-edged sword in China-EU economic relations. On the positive side, it emphasizes the EU's capability in developing its economy and defend against external economic shocks. As the President of the European Council Charles Michel stated, "Autonomy is not protectionism"[49]. It opens up space for economic cooperation between the EU and China — one of the EU's major economic partners. In addition, European strategic autonomy requires the EU to preserve its autonomy and not to comprehensively follow the U. S. economic policies against China. On the negative side, strategic autonomy, as some European politicians translated, includes reducing imports from China and tightening control over Chinese investment in Europe. The concept may evolve to include more policy implications and further influence the economic relations between China and the EU.

4. CHANGING PUBLIC OPINIONS TOWARDS CHINA IN THE EU

Public opinions on China in European countries have been on the decline according to Pew surveys. Unfavourable views about China have been at or near their historic highs in many of the advanced economies since 2020[50]. Most of the respondents in European countries except Italy held a negative view on China's responses to the coronavirus. They also tend to hold a

48. Eurativ, Dutch FM: Greece makes EU China policy 'difficult', Sept 2023, retrieved from https://www.euractiv.com/section/politics/news/dutch-fm-greece-makes-eu-china-policy-difficult/
49. European Council, "Strategic autonomy for Europe — the aim of our generation", speech by President Charles Michel to the Bruegel think tank, September 2020, retrieved from https://www.consilium.europa.eu/en/press/press-releases/2020/09/28/l-autonomie-strategique-europeenne-est-l-objectif-de-notre-generation-discours-du-president-charles-michel-au-groupe-de-reflexion-bruegel/
50. Pew Research Centre, How Global Public Opinion of China Has Shifted in the Xi Era, September 2022, retrieved from https://www.pewresearch.org/global/2022/09/28/how-global-public-opinion-of-china-has-shifted-in-the-xi-era/

negative attitude towards China's international actions[51]. Regarding the economy specifically, in 2020, European countries surveyed by the Pew Research Center, including the United Kingdom, France, Italy, Germany, Spain, Denmark and Sweden, saw China as the dominant economic power instead of the United States[52]. Surprisingly, the Europeans' perception of China has changed little in 2023 compared with 2021 according to the European Council on Foreign Relations (ECFR), showing very little impact of the Russian-Ukraine conflicts on European perceptions of China[53]. Most Europeans still see China as an ally or a partner to Europe and to their own country rather than a rival or an adversary[54]. From a broader perspective, it seems that most Europeans want to remain neutral in a potential US-China conflict and are reluctant to de-risk from China even if they recognize the dangers of China's economic presence in Europe[55].

These results reflect the complex attitude of European citizens towards China and its economic influences. Although this may not directly impact the trade and investment between China and the EU, it generates political forces to push political parties and institutions to employ tougher policies against China while remaining cooperative with China in some policy areas.

IV. TRENDS

1. RESTRICTED BILATERAL INVESTMENT

There is little sign of decoupling in the trade between China and the EU. The pandemic only resulted in a decline in China-EU trade in goods in the first half of 2020. Trade has increased again substantially after a slowdown during the Covid-19 pandemic. Investment between China and the EU, however, is worrying. The EU FDI in China remains relatively modest

51. Pew Research Centre, China's Approach to Foreign Policy Gets Largely Negative Reviews in 24-Country Survey, July 2023, retrieved from https://www.pewresearch.org/global/2023/07/27/chinas-approach-to-foreign-policy-gets-largely-negative-reviews-in-24-country-survey/
52. Pew Research Centre, How Global Public Opinion of China Has Shifted in the Xi Era, September 2022, retrieved from https://www.pewresearch.org/global/2022/09/28/how-global-public-opinion-of-china-has-shifted-in-the-xi-era/
53. European Council on Foreign Relations, Keeping America close, Russia down, and China far away: How Europeans navigate a competitive world, June 2023, retrieved from https://ecfr.eu/publication/keeping-america-close-russia-down-and-china-far-away-how-europeans-navigate-a-competitive-world/
54. Ibid.
55. Ibid.

with respect to the size and the potential of the Chinese economy[56]. With the CAI "frozen" by the European Parliament, European investors may stay cautious in investing in China. Chinese investment in Europe now faces severe challenges. According to the report of the Rhodium Group, Chinese investment in Europe (EU-27+UK) continues its multi-year decline. Chinese foreign direct investment in Europe reached a decade low of just 7.9 billion Euros in 2022 with a 22 percent decrease compared to 2021, taking the amount of Chinese investment in Europe back to its 2013 level. A lack of Chinese mergers and acquisitions (M&A) activity may be the prime reason for the fall[57]. Investment remains heavily concentrated on the three major powers (Germany, France and the United Kingdom) and Hungary as 88 percent of investment flowed to just four countries[58]. While the end of China's strict lockdown policy against COVID-19 could boost Chinese outbound investment in 2023, Chinese investment in Europe is unlikely to bounce back as Europe continues to tighten investment screening measures.

2. COOPERATION POTENTIALS

There is still potential to be unleashed in China-EU economic relations. This paper will name a few of the major fields where China and the EU may further cooperate. With the exploration of these fields, the interdependence between the economies would improve and add to the stability of China-EU economic relations.

Strengthening its economic ties with China can help the EU in its Green Transition. Both China and the EU are committed to dealing with climate change. The EU-China Partnership on Climate Change was established in 2005 and supported by renewed commitment to climate cooperation in 2010, 2015 and 2021 with the participation of officials and experts in technical dialogues and joint research projects. In 2021 the High-Level Environment and Climate Dialogue was established to foster high-level coordination in climate issues. Given the fact that China has been dominant in most renewable technologies[59], expanding technological cooperation with China

56. European Commission, Key elements of the EU-China Comprehensive Agreement on Investment, December 2020, retrieved from https://ec.europa.eu/commission/presscorner/detail/en/IP_20_2542
57. Rhodium Group, Chinese FDI in Europe: 2022 Update, May 2023, retrieved from https://rhg.com/research/chinese-fdi-in-europe-2022-update/
58. Ibid.
59. E3G, Islands and oases: EU-China climate diplomacy in times of geopolitical challenges, Sept 2023, retrieved from https://www.e3g.org/news/islands-and-oases-eu-china-climate-diplomacy-in-times-of-geopolitical-challenges/

in the research and exchange application of renewable technologies would be helpful for the EU in pursuing its Green Transition. In fact, Chinese and European companies have already carried out investment cooperation in offshore wind power, fuel cells and other technologies. And there is huge potential for cooperation in renewable energy.

The digital field is also full of potential for advancing China-EU economic relations. China and the EU have formed good examples of digital cooperation in innovative technology industries such as autonomous driving and new energy vehicles. Information and communication technology, e-commerce and other fields can be expanded to become new growth points.

China and the EU may enhance cooperation based on existing mechanisms. For example, it has only been two years since China and the EU signed the China-EU Geographical Indication Agreement (GIA) and 244 products have been mutually recognized. More products will benefit from the GIA as long as efforts continue to be made by both sides. Connectivity between China and the EU has been intensified with efforts such as the development of China Railway Express. By the end of 2022, the CR Express trains had completed over 65,000 trips since its start in 2011 and shipped 6 million TEUs of freight worth $300 billion[60]. On the global level, both sides might foster the WTO reform which will benefit the bilateral trade.

3. LACK OF DYNAMICS FOR CHANGES

Most of the factors mentioned above are unlikely to change in the short term. On the global level, the United States has defined China as a long-term competitor and is very unlikely to reverse its approach even if a new U. S. Government emerges after the 2024 US Presidential Election. The contrast between the EU economy and the Chinese economy is also unlikely to change in the near future. Instead, the competition is going to be more fierce between China and the EU. The concept of European strategic autonomy has established its position in EU politics. Even though its meanings remain flexible, the recent pandemic has led to the EU's reduction in dependencies on China. The past decade has also witnessed the deteriorating European public opinions on China, and the trend seems to persist.

60. CGTN, *Graphics: China Railway Express, the modern Silk Road*, June 2023, retrieved from https://news.cgtn.com/news/2023-06-28/Graphics-China-Railway-Express-the-modern-Silk-Road-1kZZUNviOPu/index.html

Moreover, unlike the previous obstacles in the economic relations between China and the EU in which individual policies, administrative orders or court decisions lead to temporal obstacles, the current policy shift on the EU level and in the major member states is forming a policy system where Chinese businesses, investment and imports would find it difficult to secure a safe place. It is now EU laws, policies and plans instead of individual political leaders and policies that get in the way of the EU's economic cooperation with China. Therefore, election results or other internal political changes would have less impact on lifting the economic policies targeting China despite politicians like French President Emanuel Macron holding a more conciliatory position. The EU's "de-risking" policies targeting China are in building process. There leaves little dynamic for the EU to improve its economic relations with China. Nevertheless, a strong de-coupling strategy is not in the EU's interest. The EU relies much more on foreign trade than the US and China is becoming an increasingly relevant trading partner for the EU[61]. The EU has no fundamental geopolitical conflicts of interests with China and would be unwise to subordinate its interest by following the US. As Ursula von der Leyen pointed out, the EU focuses on "de-risk" but not "de-couple" because the latter is neither in the EU's interest nor viable[62].

V. CONCLUSIONS

The economic relations between China and the EU have been a mixture of intensive development and political concerns. On the one hand, as reflected by the statistics of bilateral trade and investment, the economic relations between China and the EU have been closer despite the negative impact of the pandemic and the geopolitical conflicts. On the other hand, the concerns over future economic relations have been growing, as the EU has been increasingly leaning towards geopoliticization of external economic relations and moving towards a tough and defensive position against China. The status quo is due to a complex mechanism where competition increases between the economies of China and the EU, as well as the EU's changing perception of its economic relations with China against the background of rising China-US rivalry, the lesson of the global pandemic and the changing European public opinion on China. The changing perception of economic

61. Leonard, M. et al., *Redefining Europe's economic sovereignty*. Brussels: Bruegel, 2019.
62. European Commission, Speech by President von der Leyen on EU-China relations to the Mercator Institute for China Studies and the European Policy Centre, March 2023, retrieved from https://ec.europa.eu/commission/presscorner/detail/en/speech_23_2063

relations with China in the EU has been gradually realized by a series of policy documents. Nevertheless, such competition shall not be exaggerated and the potential for cooperation still exists.

Looking into the future, there are still areas for China and the EU to enhance economic relations, such as climate change. China and the EU have technologies to share and common goals to pursue. But in general, the relations between China and the EU is unlikely to change significantly in the near future because: a) reducing the economic dependence from China has been an EU-wide consensus and measures are in the process of implementation; b) the global context, especially the stagnation of Russian-Ukrainian conflicts increases the EU's dependence on the US while the U.S. may further assert its influence on the EU to confront China; c) the elections for European Parliament, and changes in leaders of major EU institutions and in major EU member states leave little space for EU leaders to change its position. Yet there are no fundamental conflicts in the economic relations between China and the EU. Therefore, economic relations could stay solid if both sides manage their concerns properly and preserve momentum for the improvement of China-EU relations.

Careful What You Wish for: China Encourages European Sovereignty

RICHARD MCMAHON[1] & GAO YUXUAN

I. INTRODUCTION

The very last day of 2020 saw a crucial development in the international governance of investment. Two of the world's three biggest economic powers signed a Comprehensive Agreement on Investment (CAI) after seven painstaking years of negotiation. The EU and People's Republic of China (PRC) chose the moment of maximum American distraction, the transition between the Trump and Biden presidencies. This allowed the EU to evade criticism in Washington, where a rare bipartisan consensus represented Beijing as an existential threat to American global leadership or even the liberal democratic world order. Within three months however, the CAI ratification collapsed, in an EU-China row over human rights and sanctions.

This chapter examines Chinese socially constructed narratives about EU-China cooperation on global governance. Prospects for cooperation depend heavily on the same complex interactions among European and Chinese narratives that were at the heart of the CAI drama. Chinese commentators see America's China threat narrative as the core of its broader New Cold War (NCW) narrative. This disguises American defence of its declining global hegemony as an ideological crusade of democracy against dictatorship. The CAI by contrast was nested in an older set of narratives, of "win-win" EU-China bilateral or multilateral collaboration to manage common challenges and profitable interactions. The chapter identifies complex interaction among the NCW and collaboration narratives and between them and other narratives of Chinese and European identity and China-Europe relations (see table 1).

We identify what we call China's multipolar partnership narrative (MPN) as its core narrative justifying collaboration with the EU. The MPN

1. PhD in History and Civilisation at the European University Institute. Associate Lecturer in EU Politics at University College London.

welcomes a sovereign Europe as another pole in a multipolar world and a partner against American unipolar hegemony. It has long been under strain, but we argue that it is now particularly challenged by the recent intensification of European sovereignty narratives (ESN), which demand that the EU act internationally as a sovereign actor. We argue that their mobilisation against China may fatally undermine one of the MPN's key prerequisites, that an autonomous Europe would support China against the US.

Key narratives	**New Cold War (NCW)**	**"Win-win" collaboration**	**Multipolar Partnership Narrative (MPN)**	**European Sovereignty Narratives (ESN)**
Content	China-West ideological struggle	China-West "constructive engagement"	China & EU partners vs US unipolar hegemony	EU should be sovereign international actor
China attitude	**Proposes: this is how US thinks**	**Wants to preserve**	**Proposes: main traditional narrative on EU**	Welcomes to support MPN
EU attitude	A rising option	A declining option	Narrative unknown in West	**Proposes**
US attitude	Increasingly the consensus	Increasingly rejected		Ambivalent
sub-narratives (details in body of chapter)	China Threat (West)	Multilateral Global Governance (MGG)	China "stands up" (China)	Strategic autonomy (EU)
	Divide & rule (EU)			
		"Wandel durch Handel" & "End of History" (West)	ESN (China)	European sovereignty (EU)
	Wolf Warrior (China)			

Table 1. Key Narratives in China-EU relations. Main proponents of narratives highlighted.

The chapter focuses empirically on the narratives of Chinese academics about EU-China relations regarding trade, investment, and climate change, three crucial spheres of globalisation and global governance.

For three reasons, Chinese scholarship provides insight into broader Chinese discourse and especially the very opaque official Chinese policy debate[2]. First, Chinese academics influence policy by training elites and because they are expected and often commissioned to provide confidential expertise, especially through "internal reports" and "think tanks with Chinese characteristics"[3]. Second, Chinese academics and officials may share representations due to common socialisation, politicised universities, public engagement by academics and the revolving door between diplomatic and academic work[4]. Third, to avoid "immediate trouble" with the strict constraints on academic expression in China, but also due to their strong national service ethic, Chinese ES scholars "try to follow… government guidelines and policies', declaring themselves 'committed' to the 'fundamental', 'urgent' mission to 'serve the country's interests"[5].

As a result, some highly cited Chinese academic articles contain regime propaganda language, for example praising the "assiduous whole-of-government execution of" China's Belt and Road (BRI) initiative "with enormous political resolution… diplomatic ingenuity and intellectual elucidation" making "steady strides forward… thanks to Beijing's all-out efforts"[6]. Statements such as "China under the leadership of the new president Xi Jinping has demonstrated confidence" hint at a cult of personality[7]. Other

2. McMahon, R. and Zhang, Y., "A geopolitical triangle: How China's European Studies scholars represent the EU", *Comparative European Politics*, vol. 21 (2023).
3. McMahon, R. and Zhang, Y., "A geopolitical triangle: […]", *op. cit.*; Weber, R. and Tarlea, S. "Politics of Immobility: Global Knowledge Production and the Study of Europe in Asia", *JCMS: Journal of Common Market Studies*, vol. 59, n. 2 (2021), p. 383; Jones, L. and Zeng, J., "Understanding China's "Belt and Road Initiative": beyond "grand strategy" to a state transformation analysis", *Third World Quarterly*, vol. 40, n. 8 (2019), p. 1418.
4. Weber, R. and Tarlea, S. "Politics of Immobility: […]", *op. cit.*, p. 383; Shambaugh, D. L., "China Eyes Europe in the World: Real Convergence or Cognitive Dissonance?", in *China-Europe Relations: Perceptions, Policies and Prospects*, Routledge, London (2008), p. 128.
5. Dai, B., "European studies in China", in *China — Europe relations: perceptions, policies and prospects*, Routledge, London (2008), pp. 113-115; Men, J. "Chinese perceptions of the European Union: a review of leading Chinese journals", *European Law Journal*, vol. 12, n. 6 (2006), pp. 789 and 791; Song, W. "European studies in China and its Chinese characteristics", *European Political Science*, vol. 11, n. 3 (2012), pp. 359-361; Xu, G., "Studies on Central and Eastern Europe in China since Reform and Opening-up: Preliminary Thinking Based on Disciplinary Construction", *Russian, East European & Central Asian Studies*, vol. 1 (2020), p. 29; Weber, R. and Tarlea, S. "Politics of Immobility: […]", *op. cit.*, pp. 374 and 383; McMahon, R. and Zhang, Y., "A geopolitical triangle: […]", *op. cit.*
6. Ji, X., "Conditional endorsement and selective engagement: a perception survey of European think tanks on China's belt and road initiative", *Journal of Contemporary Central and Eastern Europe*, vol. 28, n. 2-3 (2020), p. 175.
7. Lai, S. and Shi, Z., "How China views the EU in global energy governance: A norm exporter, a partner or an outsider?", *Comparative European Politics*, vol. 15 (2017),

articles openly declare they are offering "a Chinese perspective"[8] or writing to suggest policy reforms that improve the prospects of Chinese policy[9]. Nevertheless, scholars express a less constrained diversity of views than official and probably also press discourse, indicating more comprehensively the content of China's Overton window for policy debate.

We systematically identify narratives in the introductions and conclusions of the most highly cited academic articles since 1999, whose lead authors were mainland PRC-based scholars (e. g. excluding Hong Kong). To capture their communication directed at both international and Chinese audiences, we compiled "canons" of 25 articles in English from Google Scholar (GS), the most comprehensive Western database of academic texts, and 26 in Chinese from the Chinese National Knowledge Infrastructure (CNKI), its Chinese equivalent. We searched these databases in Feb 2023 for texts containing the search-words "European Union" (欧盟) and, for the GS texts, "China" plus one additional search term. These additional search terms referred either to the three issue areas, "trade" (贸易), "investment" (投资) and "climate" (气候), or to the narratives that interest us. These included "governance" (治理), if the referent was global/international or EU governance and "sovereignty" (主权) and "strategic autonomy" (战略自治), if the referent was the EU. We also searched for "belt" or 路 because the BRI, constructing connectivity infrastructure across Eurasia since 2013, has been the most prominent and contested element in the China-EU trade and investment relationship.

We only included texts in which the EU played a major role and there was a strong focus on regulation or other political issues, rather than just private actors or political theory. We halved the thresholds for harvesting texts published since 2020 to two citations (GS) and 20 citations (CNKI), because recent texts have less time to build up citations.

The chapter structure reflects our argument. We first set out China's hopeful representations of the EU in the MPN, including ESN and multilateral global governance (MGG). The second part considers how these hopes are increasingly challenged.

---

p. 81; Liu, Z., "The role of Central and Eastern Europe in the building of silk road economic belt", *Međunarodni problemi*, vol. 67, n. 2-3 (2015), p. 184; Ji, X., "Conditional endorsement and selective [...]", *op. cit.*, p. 175.

8. Pan, Z., "Managing the conceptual gap on sovereignty in China — EU relations", *Asia Europe Journal*, vol. 8 (2010), p. 228.

9. Ji, X., "Conditional endorsement and selective [...]", *op. cit.*, p. 176.

II. CHINA SUPPORTS THE EU

A very widespread Western narrative, including among academics, represents China's divide-and-rule tactics among EU member states as sabotaging European integration "with something close to contempt"[10]. In particular, the BRI is accused of undermining EU influence and democracy promotion in central and eastern European (CEE)[11].

However, although Chinese scholars in our canon occasionally acknowledge European fears that BRI could "divide" EU "cohesion"[12], they generally praise and support European unification. Only one article explicitly declares that "China should continue to support European integration"[13], but of all 49, 34 are positive about the EU as either a partner for China (18 articles) or in other ways (20 articles), such as a policy model, as a global actor, as important for China or in terms of supporting integration. They sustained this enthusiasm well over time, especially for China-EU cooperation. Since 2017, despite mounting European disenchantment with China and worries about an NCW, fewer GS scholars criticised the EU and they increasingly appreciated it as a model. Since 2019, GS articles largely stopped mentioning EU weakness and European criticisms of China.

Far from welcoming a divided EU, articles complained that the insufficient integration and "self-interest"[14] or "state-centric" response of member states to the Covid pandemic, brought "greater economic loss and a crisis of unity, exacerbating doubts about the EU's existence"[15]. The EU should be less passive in guiding member state engagement with the BRI[16]. JIANG Qingyun praises the CAI for replacing "the current fragmentation"

10. Jakóbowski, J., "Chinese-led regional multilateralism in Central and Eastern Europe, Africa and Latin America: 16+ 1, FOCAC, and CCF", *Journal of Contemporary China*, vol. 27, n. 113 (2018), pp. 668-669; Maher, R., "The elusive EU-China strategic partnership", *International Affairs*, vol. 92, n. 4 (2016), pp. 975-976.
11. Gabusi, G., "No Losers? The BRI Factor in the China — EU Relationship", *China: An International Journal*, vol. 17, n. 4 (2019), pp. 100-101.
12. Yin, W., "Challenges, issues in China-EU investment agreement and the implication on China's domestic reform", *Asia Pacific Law Review*, vol. 26, n. 2 (2018), p. 172; Ji, X., "Conditional endorsement and selective [...]", *op. cit.*, p. 192.
13. Pan, Z., "Managing the conceptual [...]", *op. cit.*, p. 241.
14. Xin, H., A, "Structured Analysis on the Strategic Implications of the European Economic Sovereignty and Technological Sovereignty" ["欧洲经济主权与技术主权" 的战略内涵分析], *Chinese Journal of European Studies [欧洲研究]*, vol. 38, n. 4 (2020), p. 29.
15. Xie, N. and Zhang, X., "'Europa Geopolitica': Is the EU Transforming into a Geopolitical Power?" ["地缘政治欧洲":欧盟力量的地缘政治转向?], *Chinese Journal of European Studies [欧洲研究]*, vol. 38, n. 2 (2020), p. 32.
16. Ji, X., "Conditional endorsement and selective [...]", *op. cit.*, p. 193.

of EU member state policies with an EU "common investment policy"[17]. BO Yan appreciates how member states "pool their diplomatic resources" and make "systematic use of EU diplomatic power" to save costs, "be more flexible" and expand EU influence in global environmental governance[18].

Chinese scholars sometimes advocate exemplary cooperation with specific pro-Chinese member states, but only to improve overall China-EU cooperation rather than to outmanoeuvre and undermine the EU[19]. LIU Zuokui urges "wide-ranging communication and multi-tiered cooperation" with "local leaders" of BRI partner countries in Central and Eastern European (CEE) to promote EU-China cooperation and economic links[20]. Another canonical paper identifies BRI partners countries as "the indispensable anchor of the BRI in the European context"[21]. There is also little emphasis on intra-EU intergovernmental manoeuvring, aside from one mention of Germany ensuring that the CAI benefitted its companies[22].

1. MULTIPOLAR PARTNERSHIP NARRATIVE (MPN)

We argue that Chinese scholarship has generally remained pro-EU because China's dominant geopolitical narrative of Europe is the MPN rather than divide-and-rule. Research suggests it has been the dominant prism through which China's media, elites and general public interpret Sino-European cooperation in global governance and broader relations since the 1990s[23]. The MPN mobilises an IR realist geopolitical logic that is as implacable as physics. China and Europe, as two rising global powers, should quasi-

17. Jiang, S., "Chinese investment in the EU: a win-win game. A view from China", *European Policy Centre*, vol. 25 (2013), p. 82.
18. Bo, Y., "The leader of the Kyoto process: why the EU instead of the US" ["京都进程"的领导者：为什么是欧盟不是美国?], *International Forum [国际论坛]*, vol. 59, n. 05 (2008), p. 6.
19. Zhang, J. and Chen, Z., "China-Eu Cooperation Under the "One Belt One Road" Initiative: From a Two-Level EU perspective" ["一带一路"倡议的中欧对接:双层欧盟的视角], *World Politics and Economics [世界经济与政治]*, vol. 423, n. 11 (2015), p. 52.
20. Liu, Z., "The role of Central and Eastern Europe [...]", *op. cit.*, pp. 85 and 93.
21. Ji, X., "Conditional endorsement and selective [...]", *op. cit.*, p. 176.
22. Xu, Q., "Scoping the impact of the Comprehensive Agreement on investment: liberalization, protection, and dispute resolution in the next era of EU — China relations", *Asia Pacific Law Review*, vol. 30, n. 1 (2022), p. 122.
23. McMahon, R. and Zhang, Y., "A geopolitical triangle: [...]", *op. cit.*; Zeng, J., "Does Europe matter? The role of Europe in Chinese narratives of 'one belt one road' and 'new type of great power relations'", *JCMS: Journal of Common Market Studies*, vol. 55, n. 5 (2017), p. 1167.

automatically balance against the unjust US "unipolar hegemony"[24]. As a Chinese newspaper argued, the "Warmongering US will have to accept a new world order with China, Russia and the EU alongside"[25]. In our canon, JIN Ling welcomed the EU seeking "relative independence" from the US as "conducive to balancing" American unilateralism and fostering "world stability" in "increasingly uncertain" times[26]. For LI Huiming, "strategic intention... to become an important pole" was a "fundamental" driver for EU "proactive" emission reductions and international climate policy leadership[27]. Two earlier texts expressed the MPN even more explicitly, welcoming a more united Europe that could support China on the world stage[28]. CHEN Zhimin hoped the EU and China, as demographic, military, and economic superpowers could collaborate as "key order-shapers"[29].

A few canonical scholars consider Europe's "important role", affecting "the balance of power" within the "US — China — Europe" "strategic triangle"[30]. While the CAI should "weaken the US-EU transatlantic cooperation"[31], the planned "transatlantic trade and investment partnership" would "inhibit China's development momentum" in the global economy[32].

This required a powerful China. Twenty-three canonical articles stressed the importance of China to the world (18 articles) or the EU (eight),

24. Sears, N. A., "China, Russia, and the Long 'Unipolar Moment'", *The Diplomat* (2016), retrieved from *https://thediplomat.com/2016/04/china-russia-and-the-unipolar-moment/*; Men, J. "Chinese perceptions of the European Union: [...]", *op. cit.*, pp. 798-801.
25. Su, T., "Warmongering US will have to accept a new world order with China, Russia and the EU alongside", *South China Morning Post* (2021), retrieved from *https://www.scmp.com/comment/opinion/article/3129207/warmongering-us-will-have-accept-new-world-order-china-russia-and*
26. Jin, L., "'Sovereign Europe': European Union Turning to 'Hard Power'?" ["主权欧洲":欧盟向"硬实力"转型?], *International Studies [国际问题研究]*, vol. 195, n. 1 (2020), p. 87; Jin, L., "'Sovereign Europe', Covid-19 and China-EU Relations" ["主权欧洲", 新冠疫情与中欧关系], *Foreign Affairs Review [外交评论]*, vol. 37, n. 4 (2020), p. 94.
27. Li, H., "Eu's Position in the International Negotiations on Climate Change" [欧盟在国际气候谈判中的政策立场分析], *World Economics and Politics [世界经济与政治]*, vol. 354, n. 2 (2010), pp. 48 and 66.
28. Pan, Z., "Managing the conceptual [...]", *op. cit.*, p. 241.
29. Chen, Z., "China, the European Union and the fragile world order", *JCMS: Journal of Common Market Studies*, vol. 54, n. 4 (2016), pp. 775 and 788-789.
30. Wang, L., and Li, Y., "The negotiation of EU — China comprehensive agreement on investment and its potential impact in the post-pandemic era", *Journal of Chinese Economic and Business Studies*, vol. 18, n. 4 (2020), p. 372.
31. Xu, Q., "Scoping the impact of the Comprehensive [...]", *op. cit.*, p. 95.
32. Cui, H., "European and American TTIP: origin, goal and impact" [欧美TTIP:由来、目标与影响], *Contemporary International Studies [国际问题研究]*, vol. 157, n. 5 (2013), p. 60.

focusing on economic strength. Seven vaunt China as the world's second largest economy and still growing rapidly[33] or as a trade and investment partner[34]. One notes that in 2020 China became "the EU's largest trading partner"[35]. Two emphasised Europe's "urgent need" for China's economic "helping hand" during the Eurozone crisis[36]. The first line of one canonical article introduces China as "the largest developing country", one of "the world's two biggest markets" and an important representative of "Eastern civilization"[37].

Broad enthusiasm for cooperation with Europe is also very common among canonical texts. ZHANG Ji and CHEN welcomed the "'solid foundation', 'rapid warming' 'new high level' and even 'signs of a new 'honeymoon' in China-EU relations, with cooperation in 'many contents, wide fields, large scale and high feasibility'[38]. SUN Yihao and DONG Yifan welcomed 'a new historical starting point' in relations, 'where consensus outweighs differences and cooperation outweighs competition'[39]. Other articles identified 'tremendous potential'[40], promising developments[41] or 'mutually beneficial results' from the 'many times' these 'important...

33. Ying, F., "An analysis of China's outward foreign direct investment to the EU: Features and problems", *International Journal of Management and Economics*, vol. 41, n. 1 (2014), p. 45; Xu, Q., "Scoping the impact of the Comprehensive [...]", *op. cit.*, p. 94; Wang, L., and Li, Y., "The negotiation of EU — China comprehensive agreement on investment and its potential impact in the post-pandemic era", *Journal of Chinese Economic and Business Studies*, vol. 18, n. 4 (2020), p. 371; Su, W. *et al.*, "Sustainability assessment of energy sector development in China and European Union", *Sustainable Development*, vol. 28, n. 5 (2020), p. 1063; Wang, W. and Picciau, S., "How to strengthen EU-China cooperation based on Belt and Road", *Revista de Relaciones Internacionales, Estrategia y Seguridad*, vol. 13, n. 1 (2018), p. 23.
34. Wang, L., and Li, Y., "The negotiation of EU — China [...]", *op. cit.*, p. 365; Ying, F., "An analysis of China's outward [...]", *op. cit.*, p. 45; Yin, W., "Challenges, issues in China-EU [...]", *op. cit.*, p. 171; Wang, W. and Picciau, S., "How to strengthen EU-China [...]", *op. cit.*, p. 23; Xu, Q., "Scoping the impact of the Comprehensive [...]", *op. cit.*, p. 94.
35. Wang, L., and Li, Y., "The negotiation of EU — China [...]", *op. cit.*, p. 365.
36. Ying, F., "An analysis of China's outward [...]", *op. cit.*, p. 58; Jiang, S., "Chinese investment in the EU: [...]", *op. cit.*, p. 365.
37. Wang, W. and Picciau, S., "How to strengthen EU-China [...]", *op. cit.*, p. 23.
38. Zhang, J. and Chen, Z., "China-Eu Cooperation [...]", *op. cit.*, p. 52.
39. Sun, Y. and Dong, Y., "New Developmnts of US — Europe Relations: Strategic Competitions and Prospects within the Framework of Alliance" [美欧竞争新动向:同盟框架下的博弈与前景], *Contemporary American Review [当代美国评论]*, vol. 4, n. 2 (2020), p. 121.
40. Wang, W. and Picciau, S., "How to strengthen EU-China [...]", *op. cit.*, p. 23.
41. Wang, L., and Li, Y., "The negotiation of EU — China [...]", *op. cit.*, pp. 365-366.

partners' 'managed to cooperate'[42] in high-level economic diplomacy or other 'political, economic, cultural' spheres. LAI Suetyi and SHI Zhiqin described China — EU relations as 'a priority'" for Chinese foreign policy[43].

Scholars downplay challenges to the relationship, such as the 2008 finance crisis. They say this was not clearly the EU's fault[44] and in its aftermath, the Chinese retained higher expectations than other Asians of the EU[45].

Thirteen articles encouraged further "mutually beneficial projects"[46]. China and the EU could build on long-established ties to "improve their relationship"[47] in the "long run" and achieve "concrete implementation" of economic cooperation[48]. LIU urged China to revive the ASEM diplomatic "cooperation and communication platform" with the EU[49]. Articles sought "common grounds"[50] or stronger "dialogue, exchanges and cooperation"[51] on climate or technology issues. BO and CHEN believed both Brussels and Beijing "emphasize the importance of jointly addressing climate change"[52]. At least three canonical articles emphasised the "high complementarity"[53] of at least partially "mutually compatible" Chinese and EU policies[54] and the Commission's desire to link them[55]. Both sides shared "the mutual goal of

42. Wang, L., and Li, Y., "The negotiation of EU — China [...]", *op. cit.*, pp. 365 and 372; Yin, W., "Challenges, issues in China-EU [...]", *op. cit.*, p. 172.
43. Lai, S. and Shi, Z., "How China views the EU [...]", *op. cit.*, p. 81.
44. Zhang, M. *et al.*., "Comparison of carbon emission trading schemes in the European Union and China", *Climate*, vol. 5, n. 3 (2017).
45. Chen, Z., "China, the European Union and the fragile world order", *JCMS: Journal of Common Market Studies*, vol. 54, n. 4 (2016), p. 788.
46. Chen, Z., "China, the European Union [...]", *op. cit.*, p. 789.
47. Wang, W. and Picciau, S., "How to strengthen EU-China [...]", *op. cit.*, p. 24.
48. Jiang, S., "Chinese investment in the EU: [...]", *op. cit.*, p. 3; Ying, F., "An analysis of China's outward [...]", *op. cit.*, p. 58.
49. Liu, Z., "The role of Central and Eastern Europe [...]", *op. cit.*, p. 193.
50. Li, S. and Kit, C., "Legislative discourse of digital governance: a corpus-driven comparative study of laws in the European Union and China", *International Journal of Legal Discourse*, vol. 6, n. 2 (2021), p. 350.
51. Wang, W. *et al.*, "The Geopolitical Pattern of Global Climate Change" [全球气候变化与能源安全的地缘政治], *Acta Geographica Sinica [地理学报]*, vol. 69, n. 9 (2014), p. 1264.
52. Bo, Y. and Chen, Z., "China and the European Union in Global Climate Change Governance" [全球气候变化治理中的中国与欧盟], *Contemporary International Relations [现代国际关系]*, vol. 232, n. 2 (2009), p. 50.
53. Wang, W. and Picciau, S., "How to strengthen EU-China [...]", *op. cit.*, p. 23.
54. Yin, W., "Challenges, issues in China-EU [...]", *op. cit.*, p. 200.
55. Ge, J., "EU strategic autonomy and European version of Indo-Pacific strategy" [欧盟战略自主与欧版"印太战略"], *Asia-Pacific Security and Maritime Affairs [亚太安全与海洋研究]*, vol. 30, n. 2 (2020), p. 50; Yin, W., "Challenges, issues in China-EU [...]", *op. cit.* p. 172.

further… strengthening economic ties" and "flows"[56]. ZHOU Hong urged them to seek "complementarity" and a "win-win" developing "partnership"[57].

Chinese scholars generally agree that China and the EU "can cooperate" on climate, trade and investment, our case study policy areas, including through the BRI and equivalent European Commission programmes[58]. Their "leaders have long" promoted economic cooperation as a "strategic" priority, for example through dialogue on industrial product rules[59]. Canonical authors recognised "significant" EU-China trade links[60], advocated stronger "economic and trade cooperation" to promote a "win-win" partnership[61] and mutual economic benefit. Some pressed for a free trade agreement[62] or more trade coordination[63].

Two articles advocated more cooperation on investment rules[64]. For one, growing Chinese investment in the EU "primarily through mergers" was "a win-win"[65]. Chinese comments on the CAI, the focus of four[66] of the twelve canonical texts on investment, were glowing. This "most ambitious and advanced" treaty was "a brilliant opportunity" and "landmark step" for "both trade partners", "to ease… tensions"[67] and bring "economic cooperation and bilateral investment" to "historic heights"[68]. Others identified "a lot

56. Wang, L., and Li, Y., "The negotiation of EU — China […]", *op. cit.*, pp. 365-366.
57. Zhou, H., "Sino-European Partnership: Symmetries above Asymmetries" [论中欧伙伴关系中的不对称性与对称性], *Chinese Journal of European Studies [欧洲研究]*, vol. 2 (2004), p. 1.
58. Yin, W., "Challenges, issues in China-EU […]", *op. cit.*, p. 200.
59. Zhou, H., "Sino-European Partnership: Symmetries above Asymmetries" [论中欧伙伴关系中的不对称性与对称性], *Chinese Journal of European Studies [欧洲研究]*, vol. 2 (2004), p. 10.
60. Yin, W., "Challenges, issues in China-EU […]", *op. cit.*, p. 200; Qian, J. *et al.*, "Food traceability system from governmental, corporate, and consumer perspectives in the European Union and China: A comparative review", *Trends in Food Science & Technology*, vol. 99 (2020), p. 410.
61. Zhou, H., "Sino-European Partnership […]", *op. cit.*, p. 10.
62. Zhang, J. and Chen, Z., "China-Eu Cooperation […]", *op. cit.*, p. 52.
63. Qian, J. *et al.*, "Food traceability system from […]", *op. cit.*, p. 410.
64. Jiang, S., "Chinese investment in the EU: […]", *op. cit.*, p. 3; Ying, F., "An analysis of China's outward […]", *op. cit.*, p. 58.
65. Ying, F., "An analysis of China's outward […]", *op. cit.*, pp. 46 and 58.
66. Three of these are from the GS canon, despite slightly more CNKI (seven) than GS articles (five) focusing on investment. However, too many actors are involved in publication and citation decisions to draw any definite conclusions from this and some other GS-CNKI differences.
67. Xu, Q., "Scoping the impact of the Comprehensive […]", *op. cit.*, p. 122.
68. Wang, L., and Li, Y., "The negotiation of EU — China […]", *op. cit.*, p. 372.

of potential for mutual benefit"[69], including by unlocking "many… under-explored" two-way investment opportunities and improving the "protection and treatment" of Chinese investors abroad[70]. "Earlier authors reported both sides" "intention to start negotiating such a treaty as soon as possible"[71] or encouraged China to advance the negotiations[72].

Four canonical articles[73] focussed on the BRI. CNKI articles exaggerated the EU's "docking" relationship with the BRI which the EU "as a whole" "established" or the European Commission "proposes to prioritize"[74]. ZHANG and CHEN claimed the EU was the BRI's "most dazzling cooperation partner", and that "all" EU "member states could theoretically be classified as countries along the 'Belt and Road'" [75]. "[C]ontinuous clarification and deepening" had taken this cooperation from "limited docking of interconnection and transportation infrastructure construction" to "full docking" in "trade and investment policies, RMB internationalization… new multilateral financial institutions, and educational and cultural exchanges"[76]. Other articles saw "benefits" for China-EU relations or "win-win" cooperation in the BRI[77], which offered "great opportunities" to "influence the future EU-China relationship profoundly"[78]. Three articles noted Europe's key role as the "geographical end" and "an indispensable part" of the BRI, targeted as "the next phase of BRI implementation"[79]. "European countries were China's 'crucial… economic and political partners'"[80].

Probably recognising that the BRI is very controversial in Europe, Chinese scholars most often emphasise China-EU policy compatibility and the Commission's desire to collaborate when they discuss it[81]. JI Xianbai

69. Jiang, S., "Chinese investment in the EU: […]", *op. cit.*, p. 3.
70. Yin, W., "Challenges, issues in China-EU […]", *op. cit.*, p. 2018; Xu, Q., "Scoping the impact of the Comprehensive […]", *op. cit.*, p. 122.
71. Jiang, S., "Chinese investment in the EU: […]", *op. cit.*, p. 3.
72. Zhang, J. and Chen, Z., "China-Eu Cooperation […]", *op. cit.*, p. 52.
73. Three from GS.
74. Zhang, J. and Chen, Z., "China-Eu Cooperation […]", *op. cit.*, p. 37; Ge, J., "EU strategic autonomy and European […]", *op. cit.*, p. 50.
75. Zhang, J. and Chen, Z., "China-Eu Cooperation […]", *op. cit.*, pp. 37 and 52.
76. Zhang, J. and Chen, Z., "China-Eu Cooperation […]", *op. cit.*, p. 52.
77. Yin, W., "Challenges, issues in China-EU […]", *op. cit.*, p. 202.
78. Wang, W. and Picciau, S., "How to strengthen EU-China […]", *op. cit.*, pp. 23-24.
79. Ji, X., "Conditional endorsement and selective […]", *op. cit.*, pp. 175-176; Wang, W. and Picciau, S., "How to strengthen EU-China […]", *op. cit.*, p. 23; Zhang, J. and Chen, Z., "China-Eu Cooperation […]", *op. cit.*, p. 52.
80. Ji, X., "Conditional endorsement and selective […]", *op. cit.*, p. 192.
81. Ge, J., "EU strategic autonomy and European […]", *op. cit.*, p. 50; Yin, W., "Challenges, issues in China-EU […]", *op. cit.*, p. 172.

believed European BRI partners strove to "harness" it "to their advantage" and their think tanks "generally" favoured it[82]. Scholars often narrated the BRI as a public-spirited project benefiting the wider world. If China and the EU could "join forces"[83], it would expand "connectivity of all forms", including between the Asia Pacific and Europe[84]. The Chinese and European "two zones of peace and stability"[85] could expand "regional cooperation", "stability and development" across Eurasia or even "the vast Afro-Eurasian supercontinent"[86].

Because canonical authors generally discussed climate change in terms of global governance, only two explicitly encouraged EU-China cooperation on climate policy[87]. However, two articles underline their similar strategies, "concerns and interests" on energy security[88] and climate change, where occasional differences "do not seem to lead to confrontation"[89].

Chinese scholars most freely represent one key element of the MPN, the US as an adversary, to Chinese audiences. Eight CNKI but just three GS canonical texts contain hints of anti-Americanism, such as complaints that "the USA has garnered" EU and Japanese support against Chinese forced technology transfers[90]. However only one article made the explicit geopolitical analysis that the US, to maintain hegemony, was increasingly sliding towards "containment", increasing "competition" and characterising China as a strategic "competitor and challenger"[91]. It insisted that Europe had "quite different" "strategic doubts about China", emphasising "economics and rules"[92].

82. Ji, X., "Conditional endorsement and selective [...]", *op. cit.*, pp. 179 and 192.
83. Chen, Z., "China, the European Union [...]", *op. cit.*, p. 789.
84. Wang, W. and Picciau, S., "How to strengthen EU-China [...]", *op. cit.*, p. 23.
85. Chen, Z., "China, the European Union [...]", *op. cit.*, p. 789.
86. Ji, X., "Conditional endorsement and selective [...]", *op. cit.*, p. 192; Yin, W., "Challenges, issues in China-EU [...]", *op. cit.*, p. 172; Liu, Z., "The role of Central and Eastern Europe [...]", *op. cit.*, p. 185.
87. Bo, Y. and Chen, Z., "China and the European Union [...]", *op. cit.*, p. 50; Zhou, H., "Sino-European Partnership: Symmetries [...]", *op. cit.*, p. 11.
88. Yang, G., "EU Energy Security Strategy and its Inspiration" [欧盟能源安全战略及其启示], *Chinese Journal of European Studies [欧洲研究]*, vol.147, n. 5 (2007), p. 56.
89. Bo, Y. and Chen, Z., "China and the European Union [...]", *op. cit.*, p. 50.
90. Qin, J. Y., "Forced technology transfer and the US — China trade war: Implications for international economic law", *Journal of International Economic Law*, vol. 22, n. 4 (2019), p. 744.
91. Sun, Y. and Dong, Y., "New Developmnts of US — Europe Relations [...]", *op. cit.*, p. 121.
92. Sun, Y. and Dong, Y., "New Developmnts of US — Europe Relations [...]", *op. cit.*, p. 121.

2. WHY CHINA HOPEFUL: EUROPEAN SOVEREIGNTY AGAINST AMERICA

The MPN requires European capacity, unity and will to be an assertive and independent global actor. The Chinese nationalist *Global Times* tabloid (2022) therefore welcomed EU "strategic autonomy" "independent from the US" and Nato to create "an important pole in a multipolar world". European impotence during the 1990s Balkan Wars, opposition to the 2003 US invasion of Iraq, fear of abandonment since Barack Obama's "pivot to Asia", and the US Trump presidency's hostility and alien values all stimulated Europe's demands for strategic autonomy as a global military geopolitical actor that acts independently of the US and Nato[93]. Trump expanded American unreliability to commerce, institutionally crippling the WTO. One canonical author noted his "unilateral" "America First" trade wars against both the EU and China[94].

The CAI prominently expressed European sovereignty from the US, directly confronting the growing Washington consensus on the China threat. German Chancellor Olaf Scholz was then criticised for breaking the West's "united front" against China by visiting XI in Beijing in November 2022[95]. Multiple European leaders met XI over the subsequent six months, some accepting Chinese mediation in the Ukraine war[96].

Of the six conical articles that discussed European strategic autonomy or sovereignty, all in the CNKI canon, three were positive about it. Under the banner of "sovereign Europe", a "breakthrough in integration", which responds to popular "demands", the EU aimed "to protect Europe, to seek autonomy and independence externally", and avoid relegation to a "spectator in the game of great powers" "completely losing its international influence"[97]. GE Jianhua made the EU "a stakeholder" even in China's

93. Fiott, D., "Strategic autonomy: towards 'European sovereignty' in defence", *European Union Institute for Security Studies (EUISS) Briefs*, n. 12 (2018), pp. 1-2.
94. Ge, J., "EU strategic autonomy and European […]", *op. cit.*, p. 49.
95. Hunter, F. and Impiombato, D., "Olaf Scholz Is Undermining Western Unity on China", *Foreign Policy*, n. 23 (2022), retrieved from *https://foreignpolicy.com/2022/11/23/germany-china-eu-scholz-xi-meeting-economy-trade-g-20/*
96. Wintour, P., "'China can play mediating role': Macron to visit Xi Jinping over war in Ukraine", *Guardian* (2022), retrieved from *https://www.theguardian.com/world/2022/nov/16/emmanuel-macron-visit-xi-jinping-ukraine-china-mediating-role;* Caulcutt, C. and Lynch, S., "EU's von der Leyen to join Macron in visiting China", *Politico*, (2023), retrieved from *https://www.politico.eu/article/ursula-von-der-leyen-emmanuel-macron-china-trip/*
97. Jin, L., "'Sovereign Europe': European […]", *op. cit.*, p. 67; Jin, L., "'Sovereign Europe', Covid-19 […]", *op. cit.*, p. 72.

"Indo-Pacific" neighbourhood, where its strategic autonomy "starts with maintaining a free, open, prosperous and stable" order and "solving... security issues"[98]. Another article worried that if "Sino-US relations deteriorate", the Transatlantic military alliance may give the EU "no choice but to fall firmly to the US camp without realizing its strategic autonomy"[99].

Rather than anticipating a China-EU alliance, the MPN merely welcomes an autonomous EU, not "forced to take sides between China and the US"[100]. Four canonical articles reference Brussels seeking "strategic balance" between them[101], which would be "positive" for "stability" in "an increasingly uncertain world"[102]. As "a geopolitical actor" or "distinct force", the EU could transcend "ideological barriers" to "find a third way" in the China-US "game" and "relative independence" from the US in "a balanced transatlantic relationship"[103]. Under the MPN, China also retained the strategic autonomy to exploit US-EU disagreements, allying with one party or the other[104].

III. MULTILATERAL PARTNERS?

If realist IR thinkers such as John Mearsheimer are correct that international relations are fundamentally driven by unending geopolitical power struggle[105], then MPN is probably the best Chinese narrative that the EU can hope for. However, the EU's own official identity narrative represents Europe as having transcended the violent realist logic of waring nation states by gradually building up a dense network of multilateral international and transnational institutions, including international and European law[106]. The

98. Ge, J., "EU strategic autonomy and European [...]", *op. cit.*, p. 38.
99. Sun, Y. and Dong, Y., "New Developmnts of US — Europe Relations [...]", *op. cit.*, p. 121.
100. Global Times, "A strategically autonomous France is important for Europe: Global Times editorial", *Global Times* (2022), retrieved from *https://www.globaltimes.cn/page/202204/1260329.shtml?id=12*
101. Ge, J., "EU strategic autonomy and European [...]", *op. cit.*, p. 38.
102. Jin, L., "'Sovereign Europe', Covid-19 [...]", *op. cit.*, p. 94.
103. Jin, L., "'Sovereign Europe': European [...]", *op. cit.*, pp. 67 and 87; Jin, L., "'Sovereign Europe', Covid-19 [...]", *op. cit.*, p. 94.
104. Li, X., "The Shift of Leadership Pattern in Global Climate Governance and China's Strategic Choice" [全球气候治理领导权格局的变迁与中国的战略选择], *Journal of Shandong University (Philosophy and Social Sciences) [山东大学学报社会科学版]*, vol. 220, n. 1 (2017), p. 77.
105. Mearsheimer, J. J., "The inevitable rivalry: America, China, and the tragedy of great-power politics", *Foreign Affairs*, vol. 100 (2021), pp. 48.
106. Manners, I. and Murray, P., "The end of a noble narrative? European integration narratives after the Nobel Peace Prize", *JCMS: Journal of Common Market Studies*, vol. 54, n. 1 (2016), p. 188.

EU projects this powerful internal identity narrative beyond its borders to promote MGG of profitable globalisation and transnational problems such as climate change through institutions such as the UN and WTO[107].

Three prominent discursive elements in the canonical articles suggest that many Chinese scholars now couch win-win cooperation with the EU more in terms of these narratives of liberal multilateralism than of the realist MPN. First, many authors are more preoccupied with the interests of referents such as business or the climate rather than of the Chinese state in its geopolitical struggle with the US. Second, articles advocate multilateral global governance. Third, they propose the EU as a model for China.

1. REFERENTS OTHER THAN THE CHINESE STATE

Of the eight GS canonical articles largely focused on the environment all but one clearly emphasised environmental over nationalist preoccupations. They portrayed emissions reductions as the "right direction" to protect the "deteriorating environment" from climate change[108], a "severe" or even "existential" challenge for "human society"[109]. China therefore prioritised "reducing reliance on fossil fuels and environmental damage"[110]. Articles blame "human activity and consumer requirements" for unchecked climate change[111] and threats to "global food security and health"[112]. One article explicitly claimed to address "alarming" environmental effects of China-EU trade rather than to "fuel a blame-game"[113]. Others emphasised different

107. Yang, L. *et al.*, "The Impact of China-EU trade on climate change", 2011 International Conference on Management and Service Science, IEEE (2011), pp. 1 and 3; Niţoiu, C., "The narrative construction of the European Union in external relations", *Perspectives on European Politics and Society*, vol. 14, n. 2 (2013), p. 243.
108. Bo, Y. and Chen, Z., "China and the European Union [...]", *op. cit.*, p. 50.
109. Wang, D., "A comparative study of firm-level climate change mitigation targets in the European Union and the United States", *Sustainability*, vol. 9, n. 489 (2017), p. 1; Zhao, X. *et al.*, "Challenges toward carbon neutrality in China: Strategies and countermeasures", *Resources, Conservation and Recycling*, vol. 176 (2022), p. 1; Wei, Y. *et al.*, "Exploring public opinions on climate change policy in "Big Data Era" — A case study of the European Union Emission Trading System (EU-ETS) based on Twitter", *Energy Policy*, vol. 158 (2021), p. 1.
110. Lai, S. and Shi, Z., "How China views the EU [...]", *op. cit.*, p. 95.
111. Tang, D. K. H., "Climate change policies of the four largest global emitters of greenhouse gases: their similarities, differences and way forward", *Journal of Energy Research and Reviews*, vol. 10, n. 2 (2022), p. 20.
112. Qian, J. *et al.*, "Food traceability system from [...]", *op. cit.*, p. 402.
113. Yang, L. *et al.*, "The Impact of China-EU [...]", *op. cit.*, p. 3.

common global or Sino-European concerns such as Covid[114] or building "a stable, economical and clean energy system"[115].

Twelve articles acknowledge China's responsibility to reduce its emissions[116]. TANG Kuok Ho not only recognised China as the largest emitter but unfavourably compared its "sharp increase" in emissions with the US and missed an opportunity to justify China's position by discussing per capita emissions[117]. His conclusions focussed on the changes "developing countries" must make[118]. LI praised EU targets which "require large developing countries", presumably including China, to reduce emissions[119]. Another article described "dangerous and ever increasing" Chinese exports of high-emission products to the EU as "alarming" and advocated a "better trade balance" with more EU exports to China[120].

These non-nationalist preoccupations also appear among the trade, investment, and BRI-focused articles, though less prominently. Four primarily emphasised the interests of business, consumers, global governance or the environment. By supporting engagement with global governance to advance liberalising pro-business reforms within China, three articles implicitly welcomed constraints on arbitrary actions by an autocratic government, which has placed itself at the centre of nationalist narratives. They welcomed the CAI as an "important" possible "driving force" to accelerate and deepen China's "domestic reforms" and "opening up", including by liberalising investment and "market access"[121]. As a tool for "non-discrimination", the CAI could safeguard investors rights, bring "new hope to businessmen" on both sides[122] and help introduce "a unified, open and orderly competitive market system", including by making state-owned enterprises (SOEs) more transparent[123].

114. Wang, L., and Li, Y., "The negotiation of EU — China […]", *op. cit.*, p. 372.
115. Yang, G., "EU Energy Security Strategy and its Inspiration", *op. cit.*, p. 56.
116. Tang, D. K. H., "Climate change policies of the four largest […]", *op. cit.*, p. 31; E. g. Zhang, M. *et al.*, "Comparison of carbon […]", *op. cit.*, p. 13; Xu, L. and Chen Y., "Global Climate Governance and China"s Strategic Choice" [全球气候治理与中国的战略选择], *World Economics and Politics [世界经济与政治]*, vol. 389, n. 1 (2013), p. 132; Su, W. *et al.*, "Sustainability assessment […]", *op. cit.*, p. 1073.
117. Tang, D. K. H., "Climate change policies of the four largest […]", *op. cit.*, p. 20.
118. Tang, D. K. H., "Climate change policies of the four largest […]", *op. cit.*, p. 31.
119. Li, H., "Eu's Position in the International Negotiations […]", *op. cit.*, pp. 65-66.
120. Yang, L. *et al.*, "The Impact of China-EU […]", *op. cit.*, p. 3.
121. Xu, Q., "Scoping the impact of the Comprehensive […]", *op. cit.*, pp. 95 and 122; Yin, W., "Challenges, issues in China-EU […]", *op. cit.*, pp. 200-201; Jiang, S., "Chinese investment in the EU: […]", *op. cit.*, p. 81.
122. Xu, Q., "Scoping the impact of the Comprehensive […]", *op. cit.*, pp. 95 and 122.
123. Yin, W., "Challenges, issues in China-EU […]", *op. cit.*, pp. 200-201; Jiang, S., "Chinese investment in the EU: […]", *op. cit.*, pp. 81 and 93.

At the most extreme, liberalisers verged on explicitly advocating pluralism and accountability. CHEN claimed China is "building a rule-of-law society"[124]. Other canonical articles praised "strong public participation" or "stakeholder engagement"[125] or warned that "government control should be cautiously used" in particular policy areas[126].

2. ADVOCATE MULTILATERAL GLOBAL GOVERNANCE

No fewer than 34 canonical articles[127] enthusiastically endorsed multilateral global governance, especially to protect the environment (19 articles) and business (11). This implies a decisive rejection of untrammelled nationalism and at least a redefinition of the MPN. YIN Wei entreated Chinese and EU decision-makers to "support regional and international cooperation" and "the good operation of the multilateral system", respecting "internationally widely recognised standards and principles of customary international law"[128]. A China-EU investment deal would be "important" for this, countering "rising protectionism, populism and anti-globalisation"[129]. Scholars believed China and the EU "have advocated multilateralism" and "peaceful settlement of international disputes through" diplomacy[130] and hoped their cooperation could contribute to "a more peaceful, prosperous... just" and "progressive world order"[131]. Three articles emphasised the central role of the UN[132] for example insisting that "China must always adhere to" its climate change mechanism[133].

Scholars anticipated or proposed "new multilateral" mechanisms to manage technology transfer[134], make foreign investment more secure while

124. Chen, Z., "China, the European Union [...]", *op. cit.*, p. 789.
125. Wei, Y. *et al.*, "Exploring public opinions on climate change [...]", *op. cit.*, p. 2; Qian, J. *et al.*, "Food traceability system from [...]", *op. cit.*, p. 409.
126. Fang, G. *et al.*, "How to optimize the development of carbon trading in China — Enlightenment from evolution rules of the EU carbon price", *Applied energy*, n. 211 (2018), p. 1048.
127. Twenty from CNKI.
128. Yin, W., "Challenges, issues in China-EU [...]", *op. cit.*, p. 200.
129. Yin, W., "Challenges, issues in China-EU [...]", *op. cit.*, p. 172.
130. Wang, W. and Picciau, S., "How to strengthen EU-China [...]", *op. cit.*, p. 23.
131. Chen, Z., "China, the European Union [...]", *op. cit.*, pp. 775 and 789.
132. Pan, Z., "Managing the conceptual [...]", *op. cit.*, p. 241; Li, H., "International leadership and China"s strategic options in an era of fragmented global climate governance" [全球气候治理制度碎片化时代的国际领导及中国的战略选择], *Journal of Contemporary Asian-Pacific Studies [当代亚太]*, vol. 202, n. 4 (2015), p. 128.
133. Wang, W. *et al.*, "The Geopolitical Pattern of [...]", *op. cit.*, p. 1264.
134. Qin, J. Y., "Forced technology transfer [...]", *op. cit.*, p. 744.

supporting sustainable development[135] or protect "global food security and health"[136]. YIN considered it "high time for China" to create "sound domestic" investment rules "to match" "widely recognised international" principles" and facilitate the CAI talks[137].

A few texts even feared the "crisis of multilateralism", the "stability of the international system"[138] or the "American-led liberal hegemonic order" as a "threatening scenario", and advocated Sino-European collaboration to reform and reinforce "the existing main global institutions" such as the IMF[139]. For GE, the Trump presidency and rising "global trade protectionism" exacerbated fears for "the free trade order that underpins the world economy"[140]. JIANG advocated investment agreements with Europe and the US rather than confrontation in response to prospective US trade deals with Pacific (TTIP) and European (TPP) allies[141].

Climate change stimulated multilateralism most strongly. Of the canonical texts, we judge 23 to directly advocate, defend or welcome multilateralism or global governance in this area. Several CNKI articles insist that "China should adhere to multilateral climate governance"[142] "and not take any unilateral "side"[143]. Chinese scholars consistently advocated[144] or at least welcomed[145] stronger governance or "cooperation" by "every country" to reduce carbon emissions. Articles praised Chinese readiness "to make sacrifices for"[146] or "actively participating in and promoting" global climate governance[147]. Two articles argued that trade interdependence required internationally "coordinated action" or "a united framework" in emissions trading[148].

135. Xu, Q., "Scoping the impact of the Comprehensive [...]", *op. cit.*, p. 122.
136. Qian, J. *et al.*, "Food traceability system from [...]", *op. cit.*, pp. 402-403 and 410.
137. Yin, W., "Challenges, issues in China-EU [...]", *op. cit.*, pp. 200-201.
138. Jin, L., ""Sovereign Europe", Covid-19 [...]", *op. cit.*, p. 71.
139. Chen, Z., "China, the European Union [...]", *op. cit.*, pp. 775 and 789.
140. Ge, J., "EU strategic autonomy and European [...]", *op. cit.*, p. 49.
141. Jiang, S., "Chinese investment in the EU: [...]", *op. cit.*, p. 82.
142. Xu, L. and Chen Y., "Global Climate Governance [...]", *op. cit.*, p. 132.
143. Wang, W. *et al.*, "The Geopolitical Pattern of [...]", *op. cit.*, p. 1264.
144. Fang, G. *et al.*, "How to optimize the development of carbon trading [...]", *op. cit.*, p. 1040; Zhao, X. *et al.*, "Challenges toward carbon neutrality [...]", *op. cit.*, p. 1.
145. Wei, Y. *et al.*, "Exploring public opinions on climate change [...]", *op. cit.*, p. 1; Zhao, X. *et al.*, "Challenges toward carbon neutrality [...]", *op. cit.*, p. 1; Su, W. *et al.*, "Sustainability assessment [...]", *op. cit.*, p. 1063.
146. Zhuang, G., "Copenhagen climate game and re-understanding of China"s role" [哥本哈根气候博弈与中国角色的再认识], *Foreign Affairs Review [外交评论]*, vol. 26, n. 6 (2009), p. 18.
147. Xu, L. and Chen Y., "Global Climate Governance [...]", *op. cit.*, p. 134.
148. Liu, Y. and Wei, T., "Linking the emissions trading schemes of Europe and China-Combining climate and energy policy instruments", *Mitigation and Adaptation Strategies*

Several authors encouraged EU-China cooperation to address climate change[149] or protect and strengthen a global order[150] based on mutually beneficial "multilateralism, international rules, balanced development" and peace[151]. Articles described this partnership of demographic, military and economic superpowers as "an important platform" to build "a workable world order"[152], having already helped reform and improve "the global governance system"[153].

Seven articles[154] expressed an absence of nationalism by recognising EU climate change leadership, including in global governance[155]. One contrasted the EU's "leading role" in the Kyoto climate negotiations with China's "active and prudent" participation[156]. Two texts expected the EU to continue carrying this "banner of "leadership"", occupying "a dominant position in international morality" by proposing "more radical and clear emission reductions for developed countries"[157] BO attributed Europe's willingness to prioritise this "leading role" to its "greater awareness" of these issues and multilateral philosophy, "often" using compromise, "guidance, persuasion, encouragement and demonstration" to promote "international environmental cooperation"[158].

Several canonical scholars framed Chinese global leadership as a "responsibility"[159] to promote "the public interest", for example by "actively" participating in global environmental governance and reducing emissions[160].

for Global Change, vol. 21 (2016), p. 136; Zhang, M. *et al..*, "Comparison of carbon […]", *op. cit.*, p. 13.

149. Bo, Y. and Chen, Z., "China and the European Union […]", *op. cit.*, p. 50.
150. Chen, Z., "China, the European Union […]", *op. cit.*, p. 789; Jin, L., ""Sovereign Europe", Covid-19 […]", *op. cit.*, p. 71.
151. Zhou, H., "Sino-European Partnership […]", *op. cit.*, p. 15.
152. Chen, Z., "China, the European Union […]", *op. cit.*, pp. 788-789.
153. Zhang, J. and Chen, Z., "China-Eu Cooperation […]", *op. cit.*, p. 52.
154. All but one from CNKI.
155. Bo, Y., "The leader of the Kyoto […]", *op. cit.*, p. 1; Zhuang, G., "Post-Kyoto International Climate Governance and China"s Strategic Options" [后京都时代国际气候治理与中国的战略选择], *World Economics and Politics [世界经济与政治]*, vol. 336, n. 8 (2008), p. 7; Wang, D., "A comparative study of firm-level […]", *op. cit.*, p. 2; Zhou, J. and He, J., "EU climate change policy and its economic impact" [欧盟气候变化政策及其经济影响], *Contemporary International Relations [现代国际关系]*, vol. 232, n. 2 (2009), p. 38.
156. Bo, Y. and Chen, Z., "China and the European Union […]", *op. cit.*, p. 44.
157. Li, H., "Eu's Position in the International Negotiations […]", *op. cit.*, pp. 65-66; Bo, Y., "The leader of the Kyoto […]", *op. cit.*, p. 6.
158. Bo, Y., "The leader of the Kyoto […]", *op. cit.*, p. 6.
159. Zhao, X. *et al.*, "Challenges toward carbon neutrality […]", *op. cit.*, p. 3; Pan, Z., "Managing the conceptual […]", *op. cit.*, p. 241.
160. Zhuang, G., "Copenhagen climate game […]", *op. cit.*, p. 24.

China should therefore be a "torchbearer" rather than a Western style "leader" in constructing "a global ecological civilization"[161]. YIN added that China and the EU should "bear in mind" their "enormous weight and impact on… the global economy" when "designing rules or taking actions"[162].

3. THE EU AS MODEL

Rather than nationalistically rejecting the potentially humiliating discursive role of student to the Western teacher, ten canonical articles[163], including seven published since 2017, welcomed Europe as a policy or developmental model. As well as revealing Chinese thinking, this facilitates collaboration in global governance with the EU and wider West. It confirms hopeful Western "Wandel durch Handel" (change through trade) narratives of economic engagement and development encouraging liberalisation and ultimately democratisation in China[164]. These excuse profitable commerce and cooperation in global governance with an abusive autocracy, if it can be persuaded to comply responsibly with rule-based MGG[165].

One article praised EU "data governance" as "a global legislative benchmark"[166]. Four believed "China should learn" from the EU's "advanced experience" in environmental and climate policy[167], including sustainable energy development[168], policy implementation[169] and its Emissions Trading System (ETS)[170]. As the world"s largest and earliest, the EU"s ETS played a "significant role"[171] and offered "a flagship reference" for other countries[172].

161. Zhuang, G., Bo, F. and Zhang, J., "China"s Role and Strategic Choice in Global Climate Governance" [中国在全球气候治理中的角色定位与战略选择], *World Economics and Politics [世界经济与政治]*, vol. 452, n. 4 (2018), p. 7.
162. Yin, W., "Challenges, issues in China-EU […]", *op. cit.*, p. 200.
163. Seven were from GS.
164. Umbach, F., "Strategische Partnerschaft oder multilateraler Kotau? Die EU-China-Beziehungen und die Aufhebung des Embargos", *Internationale Politik*, vol. 60, n. 3 (2005), p. 77.
165. Umbach, F., "Strategische Partnerschaft oder […]", *op. cit.*, p. 77.
166. Li, S. and Kit, C., "Legislative discourse of digital […]", *op. cit.*, p. 372.
167. Fang, G. *et al.*, "How to optimize the development of carbon trading […]", *op. cit.*, p. 1040.
168. Lai, S. and Shi, Z., "How China views the EU […]", *op. cit.*, p. 95.
169. Cheng, C., "The New EU Energy Policy and Energy Security" [欧盟新能源政策与能源安全], *Journal of Graduate School of Chinese Academy of Social Sciences [中国社会科学院研究生院学报]*, vol. 269, n. 1 (2009), pp. 117-118.
170. Xu, L. and Chen Y., "Global Climate Governance […]", *op. cit.*, p. 132.
171. Zhang, M. *et al..*, "Comparison of carbon […]", *op. cit.*, p. 12.
172. Wei, Y. *et al.*, "Exploring public opinions on climate change […]", *op. cit.*, p. 2.

Three of these four environmental articles were published in 2017-18, following the 2015 Paris Climate Agreement, a European diplomatic triumph.

Some GS texts admired the EU's "normative" commitment to "vigorously" promoting transformative multilateralism through "flexible and pragmatic" coalition-building[173]. As a pioneer in "fast-developing" global governance, its CAI "spearheaded" "avantgarde" "innovations", introducing a "new era" for the global investment regime[174]. Two articles advocated Chinese learning from the EU"s "multilateral diplomatic cooperation"[175].

China's self-understanding as a developing country legitimised this learning. Scholars argued that economic "asymmetry" made "developed Europe", which had "perfected and tested" policies "over a long period"[176], "an advanced model" for China since the 1980s with "strong" Chinese press support[177].

IV. CHINA-EU TENSIONS

Despite intensifying connectivity between China and Europe, including in international governance, many Westerners argue that relations have increasingly deteriorated from optimistic constructive engagement to suspicion and tense confrontation[178]. In radical contrast to the GS canon, CNKI authors since 2014 criticise the EU more and cease mentioning the EU as a model.

1. EUROPE DECLINING, CHINA RISING

The shifting global balance of power is a key challenge to relations, weakening the EU"s credibility as a multipolar partner and a model for China's transition to capitalist modernity. Canonical scholars claimed China "weathered well" the "prolonged" global "financial crisis since 2008", becoming stronger

173. Jin, L., ""Sovereign Europe": European [...]", *op. cit.*, p. 67; Jin, L., ""Sovereign Europe", Covid-19 [...]", *op. cit.*, p. 71.
174. Xu, Q., "Scoping the impact of the Comprehensive [...]", *op. cit.*, pp. 94-95.
175. Fang, G. *et al.*, "How to optimize the development of carbon trading [...]", *op. cit.*, p. 1040; Cheng, C., "The New EU Energy Policy and Energy Security", *op. cit.*, pp. 117-118.
176. Yang, G., "EU Energy Security Strategy and its Inspiration", *op. cit.*, p. 71.
177. Lai, S. and Shi, Z., "How China views the EU [...]", *op. cit.*, pp. 81-82 and 95.
178. Huotari, M. *et al.*, *Towards A "Principles First Approach" in Europe"s China Policy. Drawing lessons from the Covid-19 crisis*, MERICS — Mercator Institute for China Studies, Berlin (2020), p. 8.

and "more and more proactive" in "world affairs"[179] and "more cautious and realistic" about the role of an EU faced with immense internal challenges[180].

Out of twelve articles mentioning EU weaknesses, nine referenced the financial crisis. It "deeply harmed" the European economy, leading Europeans to ask China for economic help and become "more materialistic and short-sighted", which then sapped their external "normative power"[181]. JI described the EU's response to "growing Chinese influence" in BRI countries as "passive and reactive instead of pro-active and enterprising" and lacking "any coherent policy"[182]. Another article claimed "China has not yet perceived the EU as a key partner" in global energy governance[183].

Several canonical works highlighted eroding EU leadership in climate policy[184], reducing the EU to "a bystander" at the 2009 Copenhagen Conference[185] and undermining its ETS[186]. Two articles criticised the EU's "insufficiency" and "slow" response to the Covid pandemic[187].

LAI and SHI argued that post-crisis, China "interacted more confidently" in its "norm sender–receiver relationship" with the EU, ending mentions of EU development aid to China[188]. This accelerated a broader shift in the China-EU "balance" since 2003, and a "decline" in EU "global influence" that meant it may now be "normative no more" to China and broader Asia[189].

2. REALPOLITIK IN MULTILATERAL GLOBAL GOVERNANCE

Mark Leonard argues that the intensifying interdependencies of globalisation, including global governance, are increasingly becoming both a cause and arena of Chinese-Western tensions (2021). PAN Zhongqi in China

179. Li, X., "The Shift of Leadership Pattern in Global Climate […]", *op. cit.*, p. 78; Lai, S. and Shi, Z., "How China views the EU […]", *op. cit.*, pp. 81 and 95-96.
180. Chen, Z., "China, the European Union […]", *op. cit.*, pp. 788-789.
181. Lai, S. and Shi, Z., "How China views the EU […]", *op. cit.*, p. 81.
182. Ji, X., "Conditional endorsement and selective […]", *op. cit.*, p. 193.
183. Lai, S. and Shi, Z., "How China views the EU […]", *op. cit.*, p. 95.
184. Lai, S. and Shi, Z., "How China views the EU […]", *op. cit.*, p. 81; Zhuang, G., Bo, F. and Zhang, J., "China"s Role and Strategic Choice […]", *op. cit.*, p. 26; Bo, Y. and Chen, Z., "China and the European Union […]", *op. cit.*, p. 44.
185. Zhuang, G., "Copenhagen climate game […]", *op. cit.*, p. 19.
186. Zhang, M. *et al..*, "Comparison of carbon […]", *op. cit.*, pp. 2 and 13.
187. Xin, H., A, "Structured Analysis on the Strategic […]", *op. cit.*, p. 29; Xie, N. and Zhang, X., ""Europa Geopolitica": Is the EU […]", *op. cit.*, p. 32.
188. Lai, S. and Shi, Z., "How China views the EU […]", *op. cit.*, pp. 80 and 96.
189. Lai, S. and Shi, Z., "How China views the EU […]", *op. cit.*, p. 81.

similarly attributes "frictions", including on global governance issues, such as climate change, to the China-EU relationship now transcending the "tyranny of distance" and "primacy of trade"[190]. JIN in our canon identifies intensified China-EU frictions just as China-EU "economic and trade cooperation... multi-level exchanges" and "demand for strategic cooperation" are all increasing[191]. Another article criticised the EU's "excessive demands" when cooperating with China on "technology and low-carbon development"[192]. Whereas almost all GS canon works on China-EU environmental relations, speaking to an international audience, adopted a purely environmentalist position, only one of the 15 CNKI articles with a focus on the environment did so. Nine of these were instead realist international relations analyses, primarily concerned with China's national interest. LI for example feared an EU-US "low-carbon economic alliance [圈]" could impose "intense pressure" for Chinese emissions reductions and "severe challenges"[193].

One way that Chinese scholars made multilateralism an arena of great power realpolitik was by demanding more Chinese influence in global governance. They urged China, "as a major power"[194], to "raise its voice", "provide its own approach" and "ensure its interests" as "a trend-setter rather than a trend-taker"[195] on issues such as "the economic crisis, climate change, nuclear proliferation, protectionism, piracy" and "regional instability"[196].

Positive-sum MGG particularly shaded off into the MPN when Chinese scholars supported China-sponsored minilateral or bilateral governance initiatives. CHEN for example foregrounded EU-China cooperation on global order-shaping through China's Asian Infrastructure Investment Bank and the BRI, which extends "China's bilateral networks" to Europe[197].

Of the 17 canonical articles focused on international trade and investment governance, 13 were primarily concerned with China's interest, including all three BRI articles. Chinese scholars argued for less constraining climate rules, making them more "polycentric" and "voluntary"[198] or giving "equal

190. Pan, Z., *Conceptual gaps in China-EU relations : global governance, human rights and strategic partnerships*, Palgrave, Houndmills (2012), pp. 2018-2019.
191. Jin, L., ""Sovereign Europe", Covid-19 [...]", *op. cit.*, p. 71.
192. Wang, W. *et al.*, "The Geopolitical Pattern of [...]", *op. cit.*, p. 1264.
193. Li, H., "Eu's Position in the International Negotiations [...]", *op. cit.*, pp. 48 and 66.
194. Zhao, X. *et al.*, "Challenges toward carbon neutrality [...]", *op. cit.*, p. 3.
195. Yin, W., "Challenges, issues in China-EU [...]", *op. cit.*, pp. 171 and 200.
196. Pan, Z., "Managing the conceptual [...]", *op. cit.*, p. 241.
197. Chen, Z., "China, the European Union [...]", *op. cit.*, p. 789.
198. Wang, D., "A comparative study of firm-level [...]", *op. cit.*, p. 1.

importance to economic development"[199]. An economics article rejected EU imposition of climate costs on Chinese airlines and welcomed the need for "long-term sustainability" in air travel for giving "the industry a license to grow"[200]. Julia QIN's multilateral solution to "forced technology transfer" (in inverted commas) advocated an "equitable" "proper balance" between Western insistence on "fair competition" and China's desire for technology dissemination and negotiated "country-specific" rules for different development levels[201].

Seven[202] articles emphasised China's emerging, "significant" or even "decisive" role as a "leader" of global climate governance[203], making it "more just, reasonable and orderly" as Beijing's "hard power and soft power have been continuously enhanced"[204]. China had "been pushed to the center of the stage"[205] by its large ETS or greenhouse gas emissions[206]. Its importance in climate policy had been "on an equal footing with the US", since 2009 and "cannot be overemphasized"[207]. As "a responsible major country", ready to make sacrifices for global agreement[208] and take "the lead in providing" climate assistance, it used "intelligent and inclusive leadership", "green diplomacy and smart power" to coordinate relationships among "major countries"[209]. As "the largest developing country"[210] it was also the "leading force in safeguarding" developing country interests[211].

---

199. Zhao, X. *et al.*, "Challenges toward carbon neutrality [...]", *op. cit.*, p. 9; Fang, G. *et al.*, "How to optimize the development of carbon trading [...]", *op. cit.*, p. 1039.
200. Li, Y. *et al.*, "Has airline efficiency affected by the inclusion of aviation into European Union Emission Trading Scheme? Evidences from 22 airlines during 2008-2012", *Energy*, vol. 96 (2016), pp. 8-9.
201. Qin, J. Y., "Forced technology transfer [...]", *op. cit.*, pp. 744 and 762.
202. Six on CNKI.
203. Zhuang, G., "Post-Kyoto International Climate [...]", *op. cit.*, p. 6; Zhang, M. *et al..*, "Comparison of carbon [...]", *op. cit.*, p. 12; Zhuang, G., Bo, F. and Zhang, J., "China"s Role and Strategic Choice [...]", *op. cit.*, p. 4.
204. Xu, L. and Chen Y., "Global Climate Governance [...]", *op. cit.*, p. 134.
205. Li, H., "International leadership and China"s strategic options in an era of fragmented global climate governance" [全球气候治理制度碎片化时代的国际领导及中国的战略选择], *Journal of Contemporary Asian-Pacific Studies [当代亚太]*, vol. 202, n. 4 (2015), p. 156.
206. Wang, D., "A comparative study of firm-level [...]", *op. cit.*, p. 16; Lai, S. and Shi, Z., "How China views the EU [...]", *op. cit.*, p. 82, Zhang, M. *et al..*, "Comparison of carbon [...]", *op. cit.*, p. 12.
207. Zhuang, G., "Copenhagen climate game [...]", *op. cit.*, pp. 15 and 19.
208. Zhuang, G., "Post-Kyoto International Climate [...]", *op. cit.*, p. 18.
209. Li, X., "The Shift of Leadership Pattern in Global Climate [...]", *op. cit.*, p. 78.
210. Bo, Y. and Chen, Z., "China and the European Union [...]", *op. cit.*, p. 50.
211. Xu, L. and Chen Y., "Global Climate Governance [...]", *op. cit.*, p. 134.

Chinese scholars also inserted great power rivalries and alliances into MGG. Four[212] "articles from 2011-16 acknowledged that the world economy", international institutions[213], "global climate politics"[214] or whole "hegemonic order" remained Western or "American-led"[215]. One article thought Western "influence" in climate governance had increased since 2008[216]. Of the 23 canonical articles that highlight China's rise, therefore, just eleven vaunted its importance in global governance, accelerating "global progress"[217] and shaping international relations[218].

Three articles criticised Donald Trump's "America First" unilateralism, "wide-ranging trade war" or "apparent WTO-illegality" against Europe, China and "many countries"[219]. This "seriously eroded… multilateral mechanisms and traditional Atlantic relations"[220]. Seven articles complained about the poor US record on global climate change governance since the 1990s[221]. Washington was "passive"[222] or "less willing" to lead and had been replaced by the EU "as an active leader"[223]. ZHUANG Guiyang excoriated Americans as "unwilling to change their extravagant and wasteful lifestyle", demanding "concessions from others" while "drastically" reducing climate funding, withdrawing from agreements and causing "turmoil" in international climate negotiations[224].

212. Three from CNKI.
213. Cui, H., "European and American […]", *op. cit.*, p. 69.
214. Li, Y. *et al.*, "Has airline efficiency affected by the inclusion of aviation into European Union Emission Trading Scheme? Evidences from 22 airlines during 2008-2012", *Energy*, vol. 96 (2016), p. 66.
215. Chen, Z., "China, the European Union […]", *op. cit.*, p. 775.
216. Bo, Y. and Chen, Z., "China and the European Union […]", *op. cit.*, p. 44.
217. Zhao, X. *et al.*, "Challenges toward carbon neutrality […]", *op. cit.*, p. 3.
218. Chen, Z., "China, the European Union […]", *op. cit.*, p. 775; Lai, S. and Shi, Z., "How China views the EU […]", *op. cit.*, pp. 81-82.
219. Ge, J., "EU strategic autonomy and European […]", *op. cit.*, p. 49; Qin, J. Y., "Forced technology transfer […]", *op. cit.*, p. 744.
220. Jin, L., ""Sovereign Europe", Covid-19 […]", *op. cit.*, p. 72.
221. Tang, D. K. H., "Climate change policies of the four largest […]", *op. cit.*, p. 21; Wang, D., "A comparative study of firm-level […]", *op. cit.*, p. 2; Li, Y. *et al.*, "Has airline efficiency affected by the inclusion […]", *op. cit.*, p. 66.
222. Bo, Y., "The leader of the Kyoto […]", *op. cit.*, p. 1.
223. Xie, L., "Why the EU Led the World against Climate Change?" [为什么欧盟积极领导应对气候变化?], *World Economics and Politics [世界经济与政治]*, vol. 383, n. 8 (2012), p. 73; Bo, Y. and Chen, Z., "China and the European Union […]", *op. cit.*, p. 44.
224. Zhuang, G., "Post-Kyoto International Climate […]", *op. cit.*, p. 7; Zhuang, G., "Copenhagen climate game and re-understanding of China"s role" [哥本哈根气候博弈与中国角色的再认识], *Foreign Affairs Review [外交评论]*, vol. 26, n. 6 (2009), p. 19; Zhuang, G., Bo, F. and Zhang, J., "China"s Role and Strategic Choice […]", *op. cit.*, p. 5.

Several articles discussed China's potential allies in global governance geopolitics. JIN explicitly applied an MPN framing, claiming the EU, by "vigorously" promoting multilateralism, helped balance American unilateralism[225]. However transatlantic tensions could not be guaranteed. CUI Hongjian believed Europe and the US "hope to use" and preserve their "dominant position" in "global economic governance" by shaping multilateral trade and investment rules together[226]. His critique of the TPP offered the canon's sole and ambiguous argument that the EU damaged multilateralism, by weakening the WTO[227].

Anti-Western and developing country partnerships were more promising. Ten articles underlined the competing developing and developed country agendas. One noted that since 2003, China had been "gaining a larger role" in international politics "through active participation in the G20, the BRICS" (Brazil, Russia, India, China, South Africa) and bilaterally[228]. Scholars particularly identified this dynamic in climate politics, pitting BRICS and the Group of 77 developing countries against the developed countries[229]. ZHUANG advocated a G77 "unified stance" to "safeguard the development rights of developing countries" to continue emitting greenhouse gases[230]. Whereas some scholars recognised a continuing "large gap in power between China and developed countries in global climate governance"[231], others expected BRIC, "headed by China" to "inevitably play a more important role" due to the "rise" of "emerging countries and the relative weakness of Western countries" since 2008[232].

China's developing status meanwhile helped explain "conflicting" approaches between "China and its developing countries camp" and "the EU and its developed countries camp"[233]. China's increased assertiveness on

---

225. Jin, L., ""Sovereign Europe": European [...]", *op. cit.*, p. 87.
226. Cui, H., "European and American [...]", *op. cit.*, p. 69.
227. Cui, H., "European and American [...]", *op. cit.*, p. 62.
228. Lai, S. and Shi, Z., "How China views the EU [...]", *op. cit.*, p. 81.
229. Zhuang, G., "Copenhagen climate game [...]", *op. cit.*, p. 15.
230. Zhuang, G., "Post-Kyoto International Climate [...]", *op. cit.*, p. 10.
231. Xu, L. and Chen Y., "Global Climate Governance [...]", *op. cit.*, p. 132.
232. Li, X., "The Shift of Leadership Pattern in Global Climate Governance and China"s Strategic Choice" [全球气候治理领导权格局的变迁与中国的战略选择], *Journal of Shandong University (Philosophy and Social Sciences) [山东大学学报社会科学版]*, vol. 220, n. 1 (2017), p. 78; Bo, Y. and Chen, Z., "China and the European Union [...]", *op. cit.*, p. 44.
233. Liu, Y. and Wei, T., "Linking the emissions trading schemes of Europe and China-Combining climate and energy policy instruments", *Mitigation and Adaptation Strategies*

"international rule-making" would be "in line with the view of other emerging economies"[234]. In climate negotiations, "unity" with "developing countries will always be China's priority"[235]. However, scholars have decisively abandoned revolutionary anti-capitalist leadership. YIN praised the developing "South" for "actively... promoting trade and investment cooperation and embracing economic globalisation, while the North is getting stuck and facing frictions" due to increasing immigration, foreign investment and protectionist trade restrictions[236]. She stressed that the "South sees China becoming an important capital exporter" and "shifting from a conservative... to a more liberal and open" position on investment and investor protection[237].

Chinese scholars demanded special treatment for developing countries, including "support" from developed countries "to address climate change"[238]. A number of articles insisted that as a developing country, China was simultaneously "active and cautious" towards global climate governance[239], requiring "justice", "inclusive development"[240] and a "trade-off"[241] between "green transformation" and economic growth[242]. Producers "in developing countries such as China" should not be forced to price-in their emissions[243]. China's late conversion to environmentalism was justified because from the 1950s it prioritised "state-building and feeding its huge population" and, since the 1980s, "economic reforms and development"[244].

3. INCOMPATIBLE IDEAS

A crucial obstacle to China-EU cooperation is their vast "conceptual gaps" regarding sovereignty, human rights, democracy, and stability[245]. In our canon, LAI and SHI explicitly claimed that China rejected EU "definitions

for Global Change, vol. 21 (2016), p. 147; Lai, S. and Shi, Z., "How China views the EU [...]", *op. cit.*, p. 83.

234. Yin, W., "Challenges, issues in China-EU [...]", *op. cit.*, p. 171.
235. Zhuang, G., "Copenhagen climate game [...]", *op. cit.*, p. 21.
236. Yin, W., "Challenges, issues in China-EU [...]", *op. cit.*, p. 171.
237. Yin, W., "Challenges, issues in China-EU [...]", *op. cit.*, p. 171.
238. Fang, G. *et al.*, "How to optimize the development of carbon trading [...]", *op. cit.*, p. 1040.
239. Bo, Y. and Chen, Z., "China and the European Union [...]", *op. cit.*, p. 50.
240. Li, X., "The Shift of Leadership Pattern in Global Climate [...]", *op. cit.*, p. 78.
241. Su, W. *et al.*, "Sustainability assessment [...]", *op. cit.*, pp. 1063-1064.
242. Zhao, X. *et al.*, "Challenges toward carbon neutrality [...]", *op. cit.*, pp. 1 and 3.
243. Yang, L. *et al.*, "The Impact of China-EU [...]", *op. cit.*, p. 4.
244. Lai, S. and Shi, Z., "How China views the EU [...]", *op. cit.*, p. 82.
245. Pan, Z., "Managing the conceptual [...]", *op. cit.*, pp. 227 and 241.

of... norms like liberty, democracy and human rights"[246]. Chinese writers argued that EU attempts "to impose" these, and especially the intensified "promotion" of norms from 2005, "inevitably" create "policy conflicts" with China, "turbulence and turmoil"[247]. Four canonical articles advised mutual tolerance, "compromise", "consensus" seeking or "foresight and insight" to "understand each other's "conception" and "transcend the asymmetry"[248].

To justify compromise, PAN dismissed the EU's disruptive norm-based foreign policy as "primarily" for its own "identity-building"[249]. However, the EU has difficulty compromising on its norms, precisely because its own identity is built on them. Established to suppress bellicose nationalist dictatorship, the EU represents universal liberal values of democracy and human rights as prerequisites for peace[250]. They are inscribed in the EU's foundational treaties, accession criteria and agreements with partners and are considered vital for the EU's democratic legitimacy and rule-of-law and therefore its single market.

European identity narratives prime publics and elites to frame belligerent, repressive, nationalist dictators, such as XI, within the EU's foundational historical narrative of an existential struggle against Hitler, Stalin and now, Putin. Since taking power in 2012, XI has repulsed Europe by suppressing civil and press freedoms in Hong Kong and mainland China, establishing concentration camps in Xinjiang, encouraging caustic "Wolf Warrior" diplomacy, and clashing militarily with neighbours in the South China Sea and elsewhere.

The hopes of one canonical article that China, under XI, could export its norms through the BRI, are therefore anathema to the EU[251]. Europeans worry that high-profile BRI investments undermine the EU's use of aid conditionality to promote liberal democratic norms among EU candidate countries such as Serbia and Montenegro and democratic backsliding member states such as Poland and Hungary[252]. Democracy promotion is

---

246. Lai, S. and Shi, Z., "How China views the EU [...]", *op. cit.*, p. 95.
247. Pan, Z., *Conceptual gaps in China-EU relations* [...]", *op. cit.*, pp. 218-2019.
248. Pan, Z., "Managing the conceptual [...]", *op. cit.*, p. 241; Zhou, H., "Sino-European Partnership: Symmetries [...]", *op. cit.*, p. 1; Yin, W., "Challenges, issues in China-EU [...]", *op. cit.*, p. 200; Jin, L., ""Sovereign Europe", Covid-19 [...]", *op. cit.*, p. 71.
249. Pan, Z., *Conceptual gaps in China-EU relations* [...]", *op. cit.*, p. 218.
250. Niţoiu, C., "The narrative construction of the European Union in external relations", *op. cit.*, p. 244.
251. Lai, S. and Shi, Z., "How China views the EU [...]", *op. cit.*, pp. 82 and 96.
252. Gabusi, G., "No Losers? The BRI Factor [...]", *op. cit.*, p. 102.

embedded in Western liberal narratives of development from poor, corrupt, unstable autocracy towards wealthy, peaceful liberal democracy, but also in the EU's history[253]. The bloc helped most of its present member states escape right or left-wing dictatorship in southern and eastern Europe, respectively.

Chinese framing of norm competition and its no-strings approach to investment is equally embedded in core national identity narratives of a post-colonial rising great power, determined to assert the equal validity of its distinct norms. Seventeen canonical articles emphasised the legitimacy of China's specific political conditions. Norm compromises with Europe must be on an "[e]qual footing", involving "mutual respect"[254], including for "China's traditional concerns over" sovereignty and "insistence on non-interference"[255]. Though PAN encouraged China to "adapt to European concerns on the human rights", he insisted that the EU must avoid "instigating potential separatist movements" and "challenging China by receiving the Dalai Lama"[256]. CNKI climate governance articles, in particular, emphasised norms of justice and inclusivity to underpin China's post-colonial solidarity with other developing countries[257].

China scholars emphasised the policy studies truism that policy details "vary across geographies, cultures, and products"[258]. Borrowed policies such as an ETS must therefore be adapted to "local conditions", "specific characteristics and national situations"[259] rather than "simply imitating" foreign examples[260]. China therefore "selectively" adopts EU norms, "ideas and practice"[261]. Rejecting "bias or prejudice" against China's "state-owned system", YIN rooted diversity in the sovereign right of states to choose their own development model and insisted that Europeans "respect" China's "economic model" and policy-making traditions[262]. Gradual opening, "national security

253. Niţoiu, C., "The narrative construction of the European Union in external relations", *op. cit.*, pp. 240-255.
254. Lai, S. and Shi, Z., "How China views the EU [...]", *op. cit.*, p. 96.
255. Pan, Z., "Managing the conceptual [...]", *op. cit.*, p. 241.
256. Pan, Z., "Managing the conceptual [...]", *op. cit.*, p. 241.
257. Xu, L. and Chen Y., "Global Climate Governance [...]", *op. cit.*, p. 132; Li, X., "The Shift of Leadership Pattern in Global Climate [...]", *op. cit.*, p. 78; Zhuang, G., "Copenhagen climate game and re-understanding of China"s role" [哥本哈根气候博弈与中国角色的再认识], *Foreign Affairs Review [外交评论]*, vol. 26, n. 6 (2009), p. 21.
258. Qian, J. *et al.*, "Food traceability system from [...]", *op. cit.*, p. 409.
259. Yin, W., "Challenges, issues in China-EU [...]", *op. cit.*, p. 200.
260. Lai, S. and Shi, Z., "How China views the EU [...]", *op. cit.*, p. 95; Zhang, M. *et al..*, "Comparison of carbon [...]", *op. cit.*, pp. 12-13.
261. Lai, S. and Shi, Z., "How China views the EU [...]", *op. cit.*, p. 95.
262. Yin, W., "Challenges, issues in China-EU [...]", *op. cit.*, pp. 200-201.

exceptions" and partial reciprocity were therefore "legitimate" In China-EU investment relations[263]. LAI and SHI said EU "norms-export has been always difficult" to large, "non-democratic... countries such as China and Russia"[264]. By pushing unwelcome ideas, the EU "has induced negative feeling in China" but could make "its norms attractive" by highlighting how they "are suitable and essential" for Chinese needs[265].

Technical works focusing on policy outcomes were far more likely to advocate European policy models. Fewer than 19% of canonical articles advocating European models focussed on China's national success, compared to over 37% of the remaining texts.

Chinese assertiveness almost exclusively focused on the right to vet European norm exports to China. Only LAI and SHI went on the normative offensive. They argued that effective dialogue and "concrete cooperation" also depended on China's "own set of norms to send to the EU"[266]. Rather than "passive recipients of information" from outside, "[t]he Chinese" since the 2008 financial crisis "want to shape the information for consumption at home and abroad"[267]. Under XI, therefore, China "has attempted to be a norm-setter and sender" for example through the BRI and "insistence on the principle of non-interference"[268].

Some canonical scholars downplayed problems of normative difference. They acknowledged sovereignty[269] and peaceful foreign relations as shared Chinese-European values[270] and compatibility between the principles of Chinese "harmony but not Sameness" and EU "diversity and unity"[271], which ZHOU contrasts with the rejection of diversity in "American culture"[272].

PAN mixed pessimism and optimism on whether EU-China conceptual gaps were "likely to be managed"[273]. Though political "wisdom", shared values and respect for multilateral institutions and sovereignty had so far made "most" sovereignty issues "manageable", "well entrenched" conceptual

263. Yin, W., "Challenges, issues in China-EU [...]", *op. cit.*, p. 201.
264. Lai, S. and Shi, Z., "How China views the EU [...]", *op. cit.*, p. 81.
265. Lai, S. and Shi, Z., "How China views the EU [...]", *op. cit.*, p. 95.
266. Lai, S. and Shi, Z., "How China views the EU [...]", *op. cit.*, p. 82.
267. Lai, S. and Shi, Z., "How China views the EU [...]", *op. cit.*, p. 95.
268. Lai, S. and Shi, Z., "How China views the EU [...]", *op. cit.*, p. 96.
269. Pan, Z., "Managing the conceptual [...]", *op. cit.*, p. 241.
270. Lai, S. and Shi, Z., "How China views the EU [...]", *op. cit.*, p. 95.
271. Wang, W. and Picciau, S., "How to strengthen EU-China [...]", *op. cit.*, p. 23.
272. Zhou, H., "Sino-European Partnership: Symmetries [...]", *op. cit.*, p. 11.
273. Pan, Z., "Managing the conceptual [...]", *op. cit.*, p. 241.

gaps made "consensus implausible" and tricky, casting "a shadow over" future China — EU relations[274]. Other articles linked the stalled CAI talks[275] and doubts about EU-China ETS collaboration[276] to their "great difference" in business methods and "economic systems". LI Siyue and KIT Chunyu attributed China-EU divergence on data laws to fundamentally "dissimilar principles" on "basic human rights" and balancing privacy, free transmission of data, "national security and sovereignty"[277].

Some Chinese optimism about relations with the EU, especially expressed to a Chinese CNKI audience, was unrealistically hopeful about European opinion. WANG and LI for example emphasised "timely and mutually cooperative" aid during the Covid pandemic by China and EU countries[278]. ZHOU believed China's strengthening "market capabilities" would help improve the "China-EU economic partnership"[279]. In practice, China's reputation plummeted among Europeans during the pandemic[280] and fears of a rising China have stimulated European demands for "de-risking"[281].

Canonical articles held similarly mixed views on the impact of normative diversity on global order. CHEN believed "a common order" should be shaped by "divergent historic experiences and values"[282]. Optimistic articles believed shared China-EU faith in UN dispute resolution "facilitates mutual accommodation in practice"[283] or hoped, in line with the MPN, that the EU "can transcend ideological barriers" to choose neutrality in America's ideological new Cold War against China[284]. Pessimists noted that China preferred "multi-polarity" to EU-style multilateralism[285].

274. Pan, Z., "Managing the conceptual [...]", *op. cit.*, pp. 241-242.
275. Yin, W., "Challenges, issues in China-EU [...]", *op. cit.*, p. 200.
276. Fang, G. *et al.*, "How to optimize the development of carbon trading [...]", *op. cit.*, p. 1040.
277. Li, S. and Kit, C., "Legislative discourse of digital [...]", *op. cit.*, p. 373.
278. Wang, L., and Li, Y., "The negotiation of EU — China [...]", *op. cit.*, p. 372.
279. Zhou, H., "Sino-European Partnership: Symmetries [...]", *op. cit.*, p. 10.
280. Krastev, I. and Leonard, M., "Europe"s Pandemic Politics: How the virus has changed the public"s worldview", *ECFR Policy Brief*, n. 326 (2020), p. 16.
281. Von der Leyen, U., "Speech by President von der Leyen on EU-China relations to the Mercator Institute for China Studies and the European Policy Centre", *European Commission press release* (2023), retrieved from *https://ec.europa.eu/commission/presscorner/detail/en/speech_23_2063*
282. Chen, Z., "China, the European Union [...]", *op. cit.*, p. 775.
283. Pan, Z., "Managing the conceptual [...]", *op. cit.*, p. 241.
284. Jin, L., ""Sovereign Europe", Covid-19 [...]", *op. cit.*, p. 94.
285. Lai, S. and Shi, Z., "How China views the EU [...]", *op. cit.*, p. 95.

4. EUROPEAN SOVEREIGNTY AGAINST CHINA

Two of the six canonical authors discussing European strategic autonomy or sovereignty worried that it will make China-EU relations "more complicated and dual-faced", with less "strategic mutual trust", intensified economic frictions and "politicization and security risk" in cooperation[286]. XIN Hua predicted that European economic and technological sovereignty "will strengthen" "bilateral competition" and EU negativity and "reduce its economic 'dependence' on China"[287]. YU Nanping meanwhile warned that European "strategic security" and industrial chains that "selectively" exclude "the outside world" could damage the European and global economies[288]. Other scholars recognised that von der Leyen's declared "geopolitical Europe" framed China as its "main rival and competitor" and a key challenge[289].

The recent reformulation of European strategic autonomy as European sovereignty has helped redirect it against China. The recruitment of Germany's Scholz government to the European sovereignty agenda helped entrench ESN in the language of EU statements[290] but also deemphasised the French focus on projecting military power abroad autonomously from the US[291]. Atlanticist Germany has shifted ESN towards a more economic and foreign policy oriented "strategic sovereignty" that defends Europe's internal affairs from foreign coercion. Beijing's deployment of diplomatic and economic tools in geopolitical competition encourages this shift[292].

In our canon, JIN frames the paradox of simultaneously intensifying China-EU frictions and economic and diplomatic interchanges within Europe's sovereignty drive[293]. By broadening ESN to the commercial, environmental and global governance spheres where Chinese and European societies interact

---

286. Jin, L., ""Sovereign Europe", Covid-19 [...]", *op. cit.*, p. 71.
287. Xin, H., A, "Structured Analysis on the Strategic [...]", *op. cit.*, p. 1.
288. Yu, N., "An Analysis on Europe"s Strengthening of Economic Sovereignty and the Reconstruction of Global Value Chain" [欧洲强化经济主权与全球价值链的重构], *Chinese Journal of European Studies [欧洲研究]*, vol. 39, n. 1 (2021), p. 101.
289. Xie, N. and Zhang, X., ""Europa Geopolitica": Is the EU [...]", *op. cit.*, p. 33.
290. Hoff, H., "The Quest for European Sovereignty", *Internationale Politik Quarterly* (2022).
291. Lefebvre, M., "Europe as a power, European sovereignty and strategic autonomy: a debate that is moving towards an assertive Europe", *European Issue*, n. 582 (2021), pp. 5-9.
292. Fiott, D., "Strategic autonomy: towards "European sovereignty" [...]", *op. cit.*, p. 2; Leonard, M. *et al.*, *Redefining Europe"s economic sovereignty*, Bruegel, Brussels (2019), pp. 2-3.
293. Jin, L., ""Sovereign Europe", Covid-19 [...]", *op. cit.*, p. 71.

in multiple ways, EU *sovereignty* narratives encourage targeting of China. Campaigns for European digital, technological, economic or data sovereignty problematise European dependence on Chinese markets and supply lines, especially for medical equipment during the Covid pandemic, and vulnerability to Chinese exports, investments, disinformation and cyberattacks[294].

Technology is particularly sensitive. The controversies surrounding the construction of 5G mobile networks by Chinese company Huawei and perceptions of China's selective and propagandistic provision of PPE during the Covid pandemic were key stimuli for demands for European technological sovereignty[295]. In 2019-20, the EU coordinated member state assessments of security risks in 5G networks and influenced several to freeze Huawei out of contracts[296].

Europeans remain far more ambivalent about China than Americans do. However, XI's nationalism and authoritarianism have powerfully stimulated ESN[297] and China threat narratives in Europe[298]. Beijing has fostered European solidarity by weaponizing transnational links, using economic and judicial coercion to discipline Western or EU countries such as Norway, Japan, the Czech Republic and Australia. In 2018-21 China seized two Canadian hostages to force the release of an arrested Huawei executive. In 2022-23, the EU used ESN language to respond collectively to unofficial Chinese trade sanctions against Lithuania for opening a "Taiwan Representative Office"[299]. Brussels coordinated within the G7, referred China to the WTO and, in 2023, agreed an EU Anti-Coercion Instrument.

294. Crespi, F., *et al.*, "European Technological Sovereignty: An emerging framework for policy strategy", *Intereconomics*, vol. 56, n. 6 (2021), p. 352.
295. Crespi, F., *et al.*, "European Technological Sovereignty [...]", *op. cit.*, p. 348.
296. Euractiv. with AFP, "EU auditors worry about divergent policies on 5G suppliers", *Euractiv*, (2022), retrieved from *https://www.euractiv.com/section/digital/news/eu-auditors-worry-about-divergent-policies-on-5g-suppliers/*; European Commission & Finnish Presidency, "Member States publish a report on EU coordinated risk assessment of 5G networks security", *European Commission press release* (2019), retrieved from *https://ec.europa.eu/commission/presscorner/detail/en/IP_19_6049*
297. Fiott, D., "Strategic autonomy: towards "European sovereignty" [...]", *op. cit.*, p. 6.
298. Huotari, M. *et al.*, *Towards A "Principles First Approach" in* [...]", *op. cit.*, p. 9.
299. European Commission, "EU strengthens protection against economic coercion", *European Commission press release* (2021), retrieved from *https://ec.europa.eu/commission/presscorner/detail/en/ip_21_6642;* European Commission, "EU refers China to the WTO following its trade restrictions on Lithuania", *European Commission press release* (2022), retrieved from *https://ec.europa.eu/commission/presscorner/detail/en/ip_22_627;* Ozer, D., "China"s Sanctions against Lithuania Go Almost Unnoticed", *Politics Today* (2022), retrieved from *https://politicstoday.org/china-sanctions-against-lithuania-go-unnoticed/*

Russia's 2022 invasion of Ukraine, by reinforcing transatlantic reconciliation and ideological NCW narratives, has encouraged this redirection of ESN against China. Not only do Europeans see parallels with China's threat to Taiwan but Beijing has reinforced this impression by maintaining its close partnership with Putin and refusing to condemn the invasion.

The BRI particularly drives Europeans to protect their sovereignty against China by undermining a crucial Chinese advantage in relations with Europe. Unlike the US in the Western Pacific, no direct strategic or territorial conflicts impeded China-EU friendship[300]. However, some Europeans experienced the BRI, which XI welcomed for making China and EU like "neighbours"[301], as a geopolitical power projection into their neighbourhood. Canonical authors acknowledged that Beijing "initiated... and coordinated" the BRI to broaden China's "influence in the world", whereas European "partner countries" were on the "receiving end" and should "balance between Beijing and Brussels"[302]. LIU recommended that China, through the BRI, should be "actively involved" in European infrastructure planning[303]. Publishing shortly after Russia first invaded Ukraine, he added that China should continue "cooperation with Russia" in BRI, despite this being economically inefficient[304].

Two GS articles acknowledged "drastically different"[305] Chinese and EU views of the BRI, leading to clashes[306]. Europeans increasingly worried about its openness, transparency, adherence "to market rules and international standards", and especially the "potential negative impact" on EU "cohesion" of its "16+1" cooperation framework with central and eastern European (CEE) countries[307]. A recent canonical article therefore feared EU deployment of "market and financial instruments", such as its investment banks, "to counter" China and the BRI's "growing economic presence and political influence" in "geopolitical 'shatterbelts' such as CEE"[308].

300. Pan, Z., *Conceptual gaps in China-EU relations* [...]", *op. cit.*, p. 223; Sun, Y. and Dong, Y., "New Developmnts of US — Europe Relations [...]", *op. cit.*, p. 121.
301. Fallon, T., "China"s Pivot to Europe", *American Foreign Policy Interests*, vol. 36, n. 3 (2014), p. 179.
302. Wang, W. and Picciau, S., "How to strengthen EU-China [...]", *op. cit.*, p. 24; Ji, X., "Conditional endorsement and selective [...]", *op. cit.*, pp. 176 and 193.
303. Liu, Z., "The role of Central and Eastern Europe [...]", *op. cit.*, p. 194.
304. Liu, Z., "The role of Central and Eastern Europe [...]", *op. cit.*, p. 194.
305. Ji, X., "Conditional endorsement and selective [...]", *op. cit.*, p. 176.
306. Yin, W., "Challenges, issues in China-EU [...]", *op. cit.*, pp. 172 and 202.
307. Ji, X., "Conditional endorsement and selective [...]", *op. cit.*, p. 192; Yin, W., "Challenges, issues in China-EU [...]", *op. cit.*, p. 172.
308. Xie, N. and Zhang, X., ""Europa Geopolitica": Is the EU [...]", *op. cit.*, pp. 32-33.

Canonical scholars identify sovereignty tensions with the EU in climate, trade, and investment policies. On climate, one canonical article criticised EU efforts to include foreign airlines flying to the EU in its ETS, which caused "great controversy" and was blocked in 2012 by "great diplomatic pressure"[309] from the US, China, and others[310].

In trade relations, canonical scholars complained that the EU's "unfair", "discriminatory" antidumping policy, which was even "more stringent" than America's, targeted China[311]. European firms meanwhile increasingly criticised China's high tariffs, non-tariff barriers, low environmental and labour standards, forced technology transfers, weak legal protections, and strategic state support for China's huge SOE sector[312]. Canonical authors occasionally recognise this China-EU "divergence" on China's "level of openness (restrictive regulatory regime)"[313].

Canonical articles acknowledged EU complaints about European investors in China facing "limited" market access, "unequal regulatory treatment", insufficient regulatory reform[314] and forced technology transfers[315]. Three articles, all from GS, acknowledged doubts, "rising concerns" or "growing fear" "in recent years" about the "political hot potato" of "rapidly growing" Chinese investment in Europe[316], possibly because "some local media" "misled" Europeans, causing "unnecessary" "apprehension"[317]. Others recognised that BRI investment "may present... challenges" for EU-China relations or expected tough negotiations on investment. Scholars complained about "EU officials" or member states recently deploying "defensive measures", discrimination and "national security as a protectionist "tool" against Chinese investors[318].

309. Li, Y. *et al.*, "Has airline efficiency affected by [...]", *op. cit.*, p. 8.
310. Buckley, C., "China bans airlines from joining EU emissions scheme", *Reuters* (2012), retrieved from *https://www.reuters.com/article/us-china-eu-emissions-idUSTRE81500V20120206;* Meacci, L., "China and the United States Could Sabotage EU Emission Efforts Again", *Foreign Policy* (2021), retrieved from *https://foreignpolicy.com/2021/09/17/china-united-states-european-union-greenhouse-gas-emissions/*
311. Wang, J., "A critique of the application to China of the non-market economy rules of antidumping legislation and practice of the European Union", *Journal of World Trade*, vol. 33, n. 3 (1999), pp. 117 and 144.
312. Dadush, U. *et al.*, "The State of China-European Union Economic Relations", *Bruegel Working Paper*, n. 9 (2019), p. 21.
313. Yin, W., "Challenges, issues in China-EU [...]", *op. cit.*, p. 172.
314. Yin, W., "Challenges, issues in China-EU [...]", *op. cit.*, pp. 171 and 201.
315. Qin, J. Y., "Forced technology transfer [...]", *op. cit.*, p. 744.
316. Yin, W., "Challenges, issues in China-EU [...]", *op. cit.*, p. 172; Jiang, S., "Chinese investment in the EU: [...]", *op. cit.*, p. 1.
317. Ying, F., "An analysis of China"s outward [...]", *op. cit.*, p. 46.
318. Yin, W., "Challenges, issues in China-EU [...]", *op. cit.*, pp. 171 and 201-202; Xu, Q., "Scoping the impact of the Comprehensive [...]", *op. cit.*, p. 95.

Some canonical articles therefore counselled Chinese investors and exporters to "change"[319] or make "substantial efforts"[320] to "reduce the increasing political backlash in Europe"[321]. "Extra care" in BRI investment was "essential" to "avoid conflicting with the EU", as the CEE rail network "is mainly within" a "pan-European" "framework"[322].

V. CONCLUSION

Amid intensifying suspicion and nationalist belligerence on all sides, is the world sliding towards a NCW between China and the West? We identify competing and interacting narratives by Chinese scholars about cooperation with Europe in MGG. This intricate and ambiguous pluralism may provide insights into China's opaque official policy debate.

Despite rising China threat rhetoric in the West, the signing of the CAI suggests that in Beijing and Brussels, MGG remains an important narrative alternative to NCW. In 2019, the EU, reluctant to decisively chose confrontation, labelled China an "economic competitor" and "systemic rival" but also "a negotiating" and "cooperation partner" with some "closely aligned objectives"[323]. Beijing demonstrates similar ambivalence by claiming to continue "normal economic and trade cooperation" with Russia and condemning sanctions punishing Putin's invasion of Ukraine while apparently complying with sanctions in practice[324].

The Chinese scholars we studied are hugely enthusiastic for globalisation, MGG, the EU and China-EU cooperation, especially when publishing abroad. Several welcome international engagements to advance liberalising reform within China and protect business or the environment. Strikingly,

319. Jiang, S., "Chinese investment in the EU: […]", *op. cit.*, p. 1.
320. Wang, J., "A critique of the application to China […]", *op. cit.*, p. 145.
321. Yin, W., "Challenges, issues in China-EU […]", *op. cit.*, p. 172.
322. Liu, Z., "The role of Central and Eastern Europe […]", *op. cit.*, p. 194.
323. European Commission & High Representative, "Commission reviews relations with China, proposes 10 actions", *European Commission press release* (2019), retrieved from *https://ec.europa.eu/commission/presscorner/detail/en/IP_19_1605*
324. Zhao, L., "Foreign Ministry Spokesperson Zhao Lijian"s Regular Press Conference on June 29, 2022", *Ministry of Foreign Affairs of the People"s Republic of China* (2022), retrieved from *https://www.fmprc.gov.cn/mfa_eng/xwfw_665399/s2510_665401/202206/t20220629_10712209.html#:~:text=China%20and%20Russia%20conduct%20normal,restriction%20by%20a%20third%20party;* He, L., "4 ways China is quietly making life harder for Russia", *CNN Business* (2022), retrieved from *https://edition.cnn.com/2022/03/17/business/china-russia-sanctions-friction-intl-hnk/index.html*

those who publish abroad increasingly propose borrowing policy from Europe, including its approach to multilateralism. The scholars strongly emphasise China's emergence as a world power, but overwhelmingly stress its economic power, perhaps reflecting our economic cases studies. Fewer claim a powerful Chinese voice in MGG and fewer still demand that this be strengthened. Some even worried about disruption to the existing world order.

However, the MGG narratives of Chinese scholars are riven with ambiguities. Western and Chinese academics warn about competing interpretations of MGG[325]. Chinese hopes for a multipolar world ruled collectively by a few competing great powers clash with Europe's preference for institutions and laws constraining great powers and safeguarding the rights of smaller countries. Beijing is often ascribed a "Hobbesian view on power... all about absolute sovereignty, stability and control"[326]. The BRI ties smaller countries to a Chinese hub[327]. The main referent of trade and investment governance articles and those published in China on the environment was China's national interest. Only environment scholars publishing abroad prioritised environmental preoccupations. Some of the articles we studied geopoliticised MGG as an arena where China, often leading the developing countries, confronted the US or West. One canonical scholar recognised that even liberalisation in China serves the purpose of boosting Beijing's international economic power[328]. Chinese nationalists may support MGG for the same reason.

Rather than scheming to "divide and rule" the EU, Chinese scholars generally advocate EU's unity, sovereignty, and international role. They mostly hope that conflicting values on human rights, democracy, rule of law and non-interference can be overcome on Chinese terms, through Europe tolerating China's autocracy, while accepting that China must also make compromises.

However, some anti-Americanism and references to the China-EU-US "strategic triangle" suggest that pro-Europeanism may express China's traditional geopolitical MPN, which hopes for EU neutrality in the China-US struggle. Though the MPN is rarely expressed in explicit terms, its

325. Pan, Z., *Conceptual gaps in China-EU relations* [...]", *op. cit.*, p. 219; Gabusi, G., "No Losers? The BRI Factor [...]", *op. cit.*, p. 100.
326. Yu, J., "The belt and road initiative: domestic interests, bureaucratic politics and the EU-China relations", *Asia Europe Journal*, vol. 16 (2018), p. 232.
327. Gabusi, G., "No Losers? The BRI Factor [...]", *op. cit.*, p. 100.
328. Yin, W., "Challenges, issues in China-EU [...]", *op. cit.*, p. 171.

habits appear robust. European strategic autonomy from the US is therefore welcomed by the few scholars who discuss it. However, there are also early inklings of worry about ESN morphing towards protecting Europe's economic and technological sovereignty from China and some recognition that Europeans find the BRI threatening.

China's MPN anchored China-EU relations in a certain stability for decades. Which new core narrative rises to replace it will have profound implications for global governance. Though the behaviour of the XI regime and increasing criticism of the EU in works published in China suggests the NCW is in the ascendant, our research reveals more pluralism and support for MGG in Chinese policy debate than is often appreciated. This pluralism supports calls in the West for engagement rather than an ideological NCW[329].

The MPN-driven "wishful thinking"[330] of some scholars that the EU will welcome the BRI and China's Covid "mask diplomacy" demonstrates that China is susceptible to the same delusional groupthink as Chinese scholars bemoan in Western narratives of China. Chinese scholars who hope the EU will be their multipolar partner against America are as likely to be disappointed as those Westerners who resent Beijing for rejecting Western narratives of China's liberalisation and democratisation.

---

329. E. g. Chen-Weiss, J., "The China trap: US foreign policy and the perilous logic of zero-sum competition", *Foreign Affairs*, vol. 101 (2022), p. 40.
330. Chen, Z., "Europe as a global player: a view from China", *Perspectives: Review of International Affairs*, vol. 2 (2012), p. 7.

Challenges and Prospects of China-EU Partnership for Global Development

ZHANG MIN

Senior Research Fellow at Institute of European Studies, Chinese Academy of Social Sciences

I. INTRODUCTION

Profound changes unseen in a century are met with the COVID-19 pandemic. The Russia-Ukraine conflict has created a rapidly changing and complex international situation. Severe shortages in supply chains and industrial chains caused by a period of shutdown and a lack of transport capacity have led to widespread economic slowdown and recession, as well as compounded social problems such as high unemployment and new poverty. Therefore, how to promote the global socio-economic development will remain a major practical issue facing all countries around the world from now on.

President Xi proposed the Global Development Initiative on the 76th session of the UN General Assembly, which is now becoming a major guiding principle for solving global development issues and building a global partnership. The GDI focuses on six fronts: first, putting development as a priority; second, people-centered development; third, inclusive development; fourth, innovation-driven development; fifth, harmonious co-existence between man and nature; sixth, taking concrete actions[1]. This is another major contribution to promoting global development made by China following the Belt and Road Initiative (BRI) in 2013. Some Chinese scholars believe that "The Global Development Initiative echoes with the call of the times for peace and development, confronts urgent issues on development facing the world today,

1. Xinhua News Agency, *Bolstering Confidence and Jointly Overcoming Difficulties to Build a Better World — Statement at the General Debate of the 76th Session of the United Nations General Assembly*, 2021, retrieved from *https://www.gov.cn/xinwen/2021-09/22/content_5638597.htm* on 28/09/2023.

and reflects the aspiration of people around the world for development and happiness. This is not only an important innovation in global development theories, but also a guideline and encouragement for all countries to cooperate, to focus on development and to pursue common development together"[2]. And thus a deep interpretation and a systematic analysis of the Initiative are necessary for reshaping the post-pandemic global development paradigm and constructing the China-EU partnership for global development.

II. CHINA-EU COOPERATION IS AN IMPORTANT FORCE FOR GLOBAL DEVELOPMENT

In the current complex and volatile international situation, stable growth in China-EU relations will not only benefit the China-EU practical cooperation across all boards, but also contribute to the long-term stability of the world economy and the sustainable development of the international community. However, COVID-19 is still ravaging the world, and the journey to global economic recovery remains a difficult and tortuous one, followed by the Ukraine crisis. These factors will produce negative impacts on the stability and development of the China-EU relations. To implement the GDI, grasp the direction of the China-EU relations in time and create new opportunities for deeper China-EU practical cooperation, leaders of China and the EU reopened the China-EU Summit on April 1st, 2022. During the video meeting with President Charles Michel of the European Council and President Ursula von der Leyen of the European Commission, President Xi reiterated the global meaning and value of the China-EU cooperation: "China and Europe should foster a China-EU partnership for peace, growth, reform and civilization and build a China-EU comprehensive strategic partnership with more global presence. China's vision remains unchanged. If anything, it has become more relevant under the current circumstances. China and the EU share extensive common interests and a solid foundation for cooperation. China and Europe are two major forces, two big markets and two great civilizations, and thus should enhance communication on major issues such as China-EU relations and global peace and development. China and Europe should play constructive roles and add stabilizing factors to a turbulent world. Stable China-EU relations are of vital importance for maintaining world peace and stability"[3].

---

2. Xu, X, *Important Innovation in the Global Development Initiative*, 2022, retrieved from *http://opinion.people.com.cn/n1/2022/0530/c1003-32433280.html* on 28/09/2023.
3. Xinhua News Agency, *Xi Jinping: China and Europe should add stabilizing factors to the turbulent* world, 2022, retrieved from *https://www.gov.cn/xinwen/2022-04/01/content_5683023.htm* on 28/09/2023.

1. THE RESILIENCE AND VITALITY OF CHINA-EU COOPERATION WILL BRING STABLE GROWTH TO THE WORLD ECONOMY

The primary goal and core of the GDI is staying committed to development as a priority. Since the start of the COVID-19 pandemic, China-EU relations have achieved new development from challenges, and China-EU cooperation has made new progress in overcoming difficulties. It is proven that China and the EU share extensive common interests and a solid foundation for cooperation. The fundamentals of China-EU cooperation remain sound, vibrant and resilient, leading the world economy towards stable growth.

1.1. First, the Bilateral Trade Between China and Europe Maintains a Good Upward Momentum, Serving as a Stabilizer and Anchor of the World Economy

In 2021, resurgent global COVID-19 cases slowed down the recovery of the world economy, while China-EU bilateral trade saw a rapid growth. According to the General Administration of Customs of China, China's national trade with the EU reached USD 828.11 billion, up by 27.5 percent year on year. China remained the EU's largest trading partner and the EU was China's second largest trading partner[4]. China and the EU saw positive trends of cooperation in many areas. Growth in bilateral trade spoke for the complementarity and interconnectivity of the economic structures and industrial structures between China and the EU. The positive trend where the mutual linkage and supplement between Chinese and European industrial chains and supply chains will leverage the collective advantages of the China-EU cooperation, pulling other countries around the world out of economic downturns. In the first two months of 2022, China-EU bilateral trade reached USD 137.16 billion, up by 14.8 percent year on year, USD 570 million higher than that between China and the Association of Southeast Asian Nations (ASEAN). The European Union surpassed ASEAN to become China's largest trading partner again in the first two months of the year[5]. It is still a convincing judgement that China-

4. Xinhua News Agency. 2022a. *New heights in China-EU bilateral trade, showing great vitality, resilience and potential*, retrieved from *http://www.gov.cn/xinwen/2022-01/29/content_5671188*.htm on 28/09/2023.
5. Ministry of Commerce of China, *China-EU trade: full of resilience and vitality*, 2020, retrieved from *http://chinawto.mofcom.gov.cn/article/e/r/202203/20220303295730.shtml* on 28/09/2023.

EU economic and trade cooperation enjoys solid foundation, large scale and strong resilience and they remain each other's important partners and provide huge opportunities for each other.

1.2. Second, Though the China-EU Comprehensive Agreement on Investment (CAI) is Still on Hold, China-EU Mutual Investment Shows Growth Momentum

Negotiations on the Comprehensive Agreement on Investment was completed on December 30th, 2020 as scheduled. But the EU deliberately put its approval on hold under the pretext of protecting the huge market of Europe, resulting in a delay in materialization of the CAI. However, in terms of the reality of China-EU investment, the bilateral investment remains a positive trend. According to statistics from the Ministry of Commerce (MOC), by the end of 2020, China had an investment stock of USD 83.02 billion in the EU. In 2021, China-EU bilateral investment crossed the USD 200 billion threshold[6]. By April, 2022, China-EU bilateral investment has exceeded the USD 270 billion, focusing on vaccine R&D, renewable energy, new energy vehicles, logistics, finance, etc.

Multiple reports in recent years show that European companies still have confidence in the Chinese market. According to the *European Business in China: Business Confidence Survey 2020*[7]from the European Union Chamber of Commerce in China, European companies maintained great enthusiasm about investing in China, attracted by its huge market and an economic environment increasingly conducive to research and innovation. According to its *Business Confidence Survey 2021*, 60 percent of the surveyed enterprises planned to expand their presence in China, up by 10 percentage points from 2020. A quarter of the surveyed companies said that they were strengthening their supply chains in China or would soon do so, and nearly half said that their profit ratios in China were higher than the global average, much higher than those in 2020[8]. As COVID-19 is still wreaking havoc on the world and the world economy is pushed into a deep recession, these data shows us

6. Wan, Z., "Stable China-EU relations in response to the turbulent world", *Guangming Daily*, 2022.
7. European Union Chamber of Commerce in China, *Business Confidence Survey 2020*, 2020, retrieved from *https://europeanchamber.oss-cn-beijing.aliyuncs.com/upload/documents/documents/BCS_EN_final[917].pdf* on 28/09/2023.
8. European Union Chamber of Commerce in China, *Business Confidence Survey 2021*, 2021, retrieved from *https://www.europeanchamber.com.cn/cms/page/en/publications-business-confidence-survey/368* on 28/09/2023.

the resilience and vitality of the China-EU economic and trade cooperation and its bright future.

1.3. Third, China-EU Connectivity Made New Headway Under the Belt and Road Initiative with Transportation Protection for China-EU Economic and Trade Cooperation and Bilateral Investment Provided by the China-Europe Railway Express

The China-Europe Railway Express became an important symbol for China-EU cooperation, played a pivotal role as an artery for international transportation, and facilitated the flow of goods and services between China and Europe, providing necessary supplies for the resumption of work and production and smooth operation of industrial and supply chains for some European countries. As the pandemic broke out and continued to spread, port logistics like shipping, air transport and roads were hindered or overstretched, which led to a huge transfer of logistics to railway transportation. The China-Europe Railway Express witnessed rapid growth in its orders despite the disruption of the COVID-19 pandemic and dispatched 15,183 trains throughout the year, with a year-on-year increase of 22%. At the same time, a new foreign transportation network of the China-Europe Railway Express was formed, connecting land and sea and extending to multiple directions in an effective way. It successfully explored new ways and new channels, crossing the Caspian Sea and the Baltic Sea and passing Ukraine, Finland and other countries. By 2021, the China-Europe Railway Express has laid out 78 operating lines, reaching 180 cities in 23 European countries, adding two more countries and 88 cities than 2020, a 96 percent[9] increase in operating cities. It is like the "lifeline" in the pandemic, which ties the world together for common development and a shared future.

2. THE CHINA-EU GREEN DIGITAL PARTNERSHIP IS BECOMING A NEW DRIVER AND HIGHLIGHT FOR CHINA-EU COOPERATION

As China-EU cooperation keeps expanding, cooperation on green development and digitization has become new highlights. On September 14, 2020, leaders of China and the EU decided to establish a China-EU High Level Environment and Climate Dialogue and a China-EU High

9. National Development Reform Commission. 2022. *Information about the China-Europe Railway Express Release*, 2022, retrieved from *https://baijiahao.baidu.com/s?id=1725107209702846572&wfr=spider&for=pc* on 28/09/2023.

Level Digital Cooperation Dialogue, and forge China-EU green and digital partnerships. The transformations led by green development and digitization have created a broader space for China-EU economic and trade cooperation. China's green development philosophy dovetails with that of the EU: In 2019, the EU proposed their development strategy for the next decade — the *European Green Deal*, in which it was proposed for the first time that efforts would be made to ensure Europe becomes a net-zero emitter of greenhouse gases by 2050; China is taking an active part in global governance for green development, practicing the green and low-carbon development philosophy, and promoting the development of the China-EU green market. In September of 2020, China announced its aspiration to achieve carbon neutrality before 2060. By deepening the China-EU green partnership, companies in China and Europe will have the opportunity to engage in each other's development of green economy. This will also benefit the practical cooperation between China and Europe in renewable energy, carbon market, carbon pricing, green finance and efforts under the Global Biodiversity Framework (GBF). Digital economy is accelerating in China and Europe, triggering rapid digitization in traditional industries. The scale of China's digital economy was second only to America in 2020, nearing a total of USD 5.4 trillion, up by 9.6 percent year on year, topping the world in terms of growth speed[10]. The EU released a series of action plans on digitization, covering areas such as industrial digitization for manufacturing, infrastructure construction in tele-communication, semiconductor, cloud-computing, Artificial Intelligence (AI), Internet of Things (IoT) and cyber security, among others.

3. CHINA AND THE EU COOPERATE IN SCIENCE AND TECHNOLOGY TO INCREASE INTERNATIONAL COMPETITIVENESS

Technological cooperation is an important channel to enhance international competitiveness in science and technology between China and Europe. Cooperation on science and technology sits at the core of the China-EU comprehensive strategic partnership and the EU is a major source of China's technology import. As China-EU relations get closer, cooperation on technological innovation is becoming increasingly diversified, innovative and far-sighted. New highlights and trends keep emerging in China-EU cooperation on technological innovation: new milestones achieved in

10. Wang, Y., *How will China-EU digital economy develop in a state of competition and cooperation in this post-pandemic era?*, 2021, retrieved from *https://www.163.com/dy/article/GLNLFOE00514BQ68.html.*

China-EU cooperation on technological innovation; a new mechanism for coordination and cooperation on China-EU *Horizon 2020*; development and innovation in technological ties between China and the UK and the release of *The UK-China Joint Strategy for Science, Technology and Innovation Cooperation*; a new model of innovation cooperation between large and small countries in the East and West as China and Switzerland built an innovative strategic partnership. These characteristics reflect new directions for new cooperation on science and technology between China and Europe, laying a solid foundation for upgrading the "China-EU comprehensive strategic partnership" to "China-EU comprehensive innovative strategic partnership"[11].

III. NEW DILEMMAS OF CHINA-EU RELATIONS UNDER MAJOR CHANGES AND THE PANDEMIC UNSEEN IN A CENTURY

1. CHINA-EU RELATIONS: FROM COOPERATIVE COMPETITORS TO SYSTEMIC RIVALS

In an increasingly interdependent world, the relations between countries, especially major countries are far from fixed and smooth. Since diplomatic relations were formally established between China and the EU in 1975, China-EU relations have withstood profound changes in the international community, and we managed to explore new mechanisms and models for cooperation amid ups and downs. To date, China-EU relations have the following characters in the current stage: First, our relations have experienced three leaps based on the mutual understanding of seeking common ground while shelving differences and respecting each other's systems, from "constructive partnership" in 1998[12] to "comprehensive partnership" in 2001 and then to "comprehensive strategic partnership" in 2003. And other major European countries such as the UK, France and Germany also followed suit and established comprehensive strategic partnerships with China in 2004[13]. Under the comprehensive strategic partnership, China-EU relations have witnessed multi-dimensional, multi-level and all-round cooperation and development, as well as the building of multi-pillar relations covering

11. Zhang, M., "New highlights and trends in China-EU cooperation on technological innovation" in *Blue Book of Europe: Annual Development Report of Europe (2017-2018)*, Beijing: Social Science Academic Press, 2018, p. 282.
12. In 1998, China and the EU built the Long-term Stable Constructive Partnership Between China and the European Union.
13. Zhou, H. and Jin, L., "Seventy Years of China-Europe Relations: The Formation of Multi-facet Partnership", *China Journal of European Studies*, 2019, pp. 1-15 and 165.

economy and trade, science and technology, politics and people-to-people exchange. "China-EU relations demonstrate a three-layer framework between China and the EU, China and EU members, and China and EU Sub-regions"[14]. Second, as China-EU relations grew closer, the EU became wary of China and started to regard China as a competitive partner. In its sixth resolution on China-EU relations, the EU announced to enhance competition with China, breaking the virtuous interactive cycle where China and the EU are interdependent on each other and both have a stake. As the EU's suspicion escalated, China-EU relations became more complex. Third, by repositioning China in its strategy, the EU unilaterally reshaped China-EU relations from competitive partners to rivals. On March 12, 2019, the EU released *EU-China — A Strategic Outlook,* in which they reviewed China's role: a partner for cooperation and negotiation, an economic competitor, and a systemic rival. This marks the first time that the EU viewed China as a systemic rival. Before and during the Russia-Ukraine conflict, China-EU relations saw some turbulence. EU's growing doubts about China clearly indicated that China-EU relations were deteriorating[15].

2. FACTORS CONTRIBUTING TO THE CHANGING TREND OF CHINA-EU RELATIONS

Despite that China-EU relations are developing fast, but the amicable days when the two sides cooperate more and more closely with each other have been shattered. The change owes to: First, Europe's wrong perception and false strategic judgments towards China; second, a new competition paradigm brought by China's increasing overall national strength; third, external factors including the United States that stayed in the way of China-EU relations.

2.1. Europe's Wrong Perception and False Strategic Judgments Towards China

Since the establishment of China-EU relations, the sustained growth and growing closeness is an inevitable result of the principle of mutually beneficial cooperation based on mutual needs. Both sides needed the support and cooperation of the international community, no matter it is the EU's building of the European single market or China's attempt to integrate into

14. Ding, C. and Ji, H., "70 years into China-EU Relations: Achievements, Challenges and Prospects", *Forum of World Economics & Politics*, 2019, pp. 134-153.
15. European Commission, *EU-China Relations Factsheet*, 2022, retrieved from *https://www.eeas.europa.eu/sites/default/files/documents/EU-China_Factsheet_01Apr2022.pdf* on 04/09/2023.

the international community with its reform and opening up policy. The EU saw China as a new destination for foreign investment as it carried out its single market, and a pilot zone for its new regulations. It met the internal needs of the EU to promote the cooperation with China across all areas and deepen their relations with China; as China continued its reform and opening up, trying to be part of the global economic system, it also generated new opportunities for the EU's foreign development. At the same time, China also needed external funds, new technologies and concepts, etc. So those technologies, funds and new concepts from the EU can provide new stimulus to China's development.

However, this cooperation model that benefits both sides changed with the EU's new orientation towards China. Especially after China became the world's second biggest economy, the power dynamics shifted drastically between China and the EU and the EU saw China's rapid development as its threat and challenge. The EU has changed its answer to the question whether there are more challenges or more opportunities in China-EU cooperation, and even believed that China brought more challenges than opportunities, though they recognized China's important role in solving regional and global issues. From its perspective, China has become a challenger for its international position and regional presence. "Some people in media and politics in Europe keep spreading the 'China Threat Theory', claiming that China is becoming a competitor for some Western countries in terms of economy, science and technology, and even political system"[16]. "Fundamentally, Europe is still understanding China with its traditional western mindset, which leads to a misconception that China would seek hegemony once it becomes stronger"[17].

The EU is less enthusiastic about China-EU cooperation and warier of China, and sees China as a competitive opponent. As a consequence, agreements reached in negotiations in China-EU cooperation find it hard to land and materialize, and barriers are set against China in terms of major strategic investment. "This new positioning of China has already hit China-EU relations, with important bilateral agreements put on halt before implementation, rounds of sanctions and countermeasures on Xinjiang-related issues, and the delay of the 23rd China-EU Summit, among others"[18].

16. Mei, Z., "Stay clear-headed and Promote steady growth of China-EU relations", *World Affairs*, 2020, pp. 15-17.
17. *Ibid*.
18. Long, J., *Prospects and Review of EU's Policy on* China, 2022, retrieved from *http://www.siis.org.cn/sp/13764.jhtml* on 28/09/2023.

2.2. The Western Value-Oriented Diplomacy Led to Closer US-EU Relations While Deteriorating China-EU Relations

External factors have been dominated by value-oriented diplomacy, especially since Biden took office, championing western version of democracy, freedom, human rights and other values, as an attempt to bring European countries closer ideologically and repair the damage during Trump's administration on US-EU relations. As a result, transatlantic relations heated up across the board. The trade war between the US and China started by Trump's administration dealt a severe blow to China-US relations, which didn't seem to recover in Biden's administration. It is very clear that the US was bent on treating China as a target to be contained strategically. On March 3, 2021, the US released *The Interim National Security Strategic Guidance,* first of its kind for Biden's administration. Although this guidance made responding to the COVID-19 pandemic a priority, it still managed to mention "China" for more than twenty times. By repeating their old tricks of the "China Threat Theory", they were determined to build partnerships in Africa and Asia with their allies from NATO, New Zealand and Australia, Japan and Korea and others, so as to build a so-called "more effective international norm". China was defined as "the only competitor with a comprehensive power to challenge the international order" and "the biggest geo-political challenge in the 21st century". According to the report, China has emerged as the only competitor potentially capable of combining its economic, diplomatic, military, and technological strengths to mount a sustained challenge to a stable and open international system[19].

Bewitched by the US, the EU stayed high alert against China, and allowed the US to exert a bigger influence on China-EU relations, which may be a major constraint on the development of China-EU relations.

2.3. The Simmering Conflict Between Russia and Ukraine has Accelerated the Pace of Joint Security and Defense Cooperation Between the United States and Europe and Enhanced the EU's Sense of Strategic Autonomy

After the Cold War, NATO defense union led by America kept expanding eastwards. This not only enhanced US dominance in EU security affairs, but also put Europe at the center of major country competitions again after the Cold War. The outbreak of the Russian-Ukrainian conflict is a direct consequence of the US domination of European security affairs.

19. The White House, *Interim National Security Strategic Guidance,* 2021.

European Union member states showed exceptional unity in opposing Russia, supporting Ukraine and imposing sanctions on Russia. China has been encouraging peace talks and political negotiations, and stood firmly against war, maintaining a rational and neutral position in issues related to Russia-Ukraine relations which has triggered a cold shoulder from the EU. Recently, the European Council publicly stated that "Over the past year, EU-China bilateral relations have deteriorated, notably related to a growing number of irritants: China's counter-measures to EU sanctions on human rights, economic coercion and trade measures against the single market, and China's positioning on the war in Ukraine. So the EU will constantly re-position the China-EU relations"[20].

IV. PROSPECTS FOR CHINA-EU GLOBAL PARTNERSHIP FOR DEVELOPMENT

It is undeniable that the development of China-EU relations is facing multiple challenges. A lot of efforts need to be done to increase trust and dispel misgivings to bring China-EU relations back to the normal track. To strengthen political trust, China and Europe should reach more consensus in strategies and explore new ways for development. From a new strategic perspective of global development with development at its core, the Global Development Initiative proposed by President Xi Jinping pointed out the direction for promoting socio-economic development from all respects for all countries. This will help to weather negative impacts induced by the pandemic, in the context of profound changes unseen in a century. Based on this initiative, we can work on the following sectors to build China-EU partnership for development and enhance practical cooperation.

1. CHINA-EU PARTNERSHIP OF CIVILIZATION SHOULD BE BUILT TO LEARN FROM EACH OTHER AND ACCOMMODATE DIFFERENCES FOR MUTUAL BENEFITS

China and Europe, which represent the world's two great civilizations, have made tremendous contributions to the progress and development of human society. The China-EU partnership for civilization will bring huge moral strength for promoting the GDI. Both humanism from ancient Greek and the people-based thought from ancient China advocated a "people-centered" approach. Traditional Chinese culture values "paramount importance of peace" and "seeking harmony without uniformity". China

20. European Commission, *EU-China Relations Factsheet, op. cit.*

is not a threat but an opportunity, not a rival but a partner for other countries in the world. "As the birthplace for Western civilization, Europe boasts profound traditions in philosophical critical thinking and rational reflection, making it the most capable and possible trailblazer to understand and accept China in the West and conduct sincere dialogues and equal engagements with China in terms of economy, system and civilization for mutual learning. 'China Model' and 'Europe Model' enjoy different characters, but can coexist and accommodate with each other"[21].

Despite the different systems between the East and the West, China and Europe have created ethical advancement and material wealth in many fields such as science, philosophy and humanities, and have promoted the development of the world and the progress of mankind. Therefore, China and Europe should build a partnership for civilization, learn from each other through dialogues and exchanges, continuously improve mutual understanding, and promote the construction of a new paradigm featuring mutual learning and harmonious development of civilizations in China and Europe. With peace and development as a general trend, China and Europe should enhance the research and dialogue between the two sides on the history of Chinese and Western civilizations with people-to-people exchanges as a bond and provide more ethical wealth to promote the GDI from the perspective of concepts and ideas.

2. CHINA AND EUROPE SHOULD ADHERE TO THE PRINCIPLES OF THE UN CHARTER AND ACTIVELY BUILD A PARTNERSHIP OF GLOBAL GOVERNANCE

China-EU partnership of global governance will help in responding to global challenges and ensure the effective implementation of the GDI. Facing globalization and profound changes unseen in a century, new global issues keep emerging as countries around the world come closer. Therefore, the UN and other international organizations are playing even greater roles in global governance. As major economies, China and the EU have carried out a series of cooperation in implementing the UN 2030 Agenda for Sustainable Development, coping with climate change, releasing carbon neutrality and other areas. China and Europe should cooperate and contribute to the building of a fair and just global governance system for win-win outcomes. The rapid warming of US-EU relations and the ongoing

21. Sun, Y., "Internal needs, interferences and top agendas for China and the EU to enhance cooperation in the post-pandemic era", *Contemporary World*, 2020, pp. 50-57.

fermentation of the Russia-Ukraine crisis have brought about a sudden change in the international security situation and the European security landscape, posing new challenges to China-EU cooperation in the global governance system. Therefore, China and Europe should, under the premise of staying committed to the purposes and principles of the UN Charter, uphold true multilateralism, firmly oppose hegemonism and build a multi-polar global order and security pattern. As President Xi Jinping pointed out at the 76th session of the UN General Assembly, "In the world, there is only one international system, that is the international system with the United Nations at its core. There is only one international order, that is the international order underpinned by international law. And there is only one set of rules, that is the basic norms governing international relations underpinned by the purposes and principles of the UN Charter"[22].

3. EXPLORING NEW COOPERATION MODEL BETWEEN TWO MAJOR MARKETS OF CHINA AND THE EU BY INTEGRATING WITH CHINA'S "DUAL CIRCULATION" PARADIGM

The building of China-EU global partnership for development should serve our mutual benefits and be based on our common interests. China is the biggest developing country and emerging economy, while the EU is the biggest group of developed countries, making both of us important polars in the international community[23]. As two major economies of the three economies in the world, deepening China-EU cooperation will definitely boost the world economy and global development. However, the EU's increasing suspicion and guard towards China bring negative impacts on the implementation of the GDI. Therefore, China and Europe should actively explore new cooperation models between our two major markets, which will further expand the complementary roles of each other and lead to win-win outcomes.

China and the EU both need to adjust to new pressure brought by the spread of the COVID-19 pandemic and the intensifying of the Russia-Ukraine conflict. As the European economy has taken several shocks, it has become a paramount mission to revive the economy and upgrade energy

22. China Daily, *Chinese delegates: stand ready to safeguard the UN-centered international system and order with other countries*, 2021, retrieved from *https://cn.chinadaily.com.cn/a/202110/29/WS617b01eba3107be4979f5641.html* on 27/09/2023.
23. Ministry of Commerce of China, *China-EU Trade and Economic Relations in* Numbers, 2020, retrieved from *http://chinawto.mofcom.gov.cn/article/e/r/202203/20220303295730.shtml* on 28/09/2023.

mix for the sustainable development of the European single market. China strikes a balance between pandemic response and economic development and continues to deepen the supply-side structural reform. Therefore, China fully leveraged the advantages as a huge market and its domestic needs and fostered a new development paradigm in which domestic and foreign markets boost each other, with the domestic market as the mainstay, stimulating both domestic and foreign markets. Upholding the principle of openness, cooperation and mutual benefits, the EU should connect their own strategies with China's "dual circulation" and further integrate China's market with markets of EU member states through the major market of the Europe, so as to further unleash the opportunities and potential of China and Europe markets. For that reason, the EU should consider to re-open and implement the China-EU Comprehensive Agreement on Investment. Only by making the China-EU trade and investment market more open, can we find a new model which both markets can benefit from.

4. CHINA AND THE EU SHOULD BUILD A COMPREHENSIVE PARTNERSHIP FOR INNOVATIVE COOPERATION TO IMPLEMENT THE INNOVATION-ORIENTED DEVELOPMENT PHILOSOPHY

The innovation-oriented development philosophy stands among the six actions proposed by the GDI. In an era of digital technology, China and the EU should build a comprehensive partnership for innovative cooperation to deepen innovative cooperation, which means that China and the EU should upgrade the partnership for innovative cooperation and start more partnerships for innovative cooperation between China and the EU's member states.

Pursuing technological innovation and innovation in social institutions in China-EU comprehensive innovative partnership will offer massive productivity for global development. Science brings productivity. China's technological advances, innovation in the socialist system with Chinese characteristics and new philosophies and rules, such as the BRI and the GDI, provide important driving force for socio-economic development. Europe is the birthplace of industrial revolution and a pioneer in global technological revolution. Scientific innovation in Europe can not only be found in science and technology, but also in social governance, environment governance, climate change response and other areas. New innovative development philosophies proposed by Europe not only have boosted Europe's global scientific competitiveness, but also have driven the global development. As two major forces in scientific innovation, China and Europe have gained much progress in years of cooperation on science and technology. Our cooperation mechanisms on this front are being continuously improved, and our scientific cooperation has become closer. According to the statistics on May 3, 2022 from the Eurostat, in terms of partners out of the EU: In 2021, the EU imported most of its high-tech products from China (38% of total extra-EU imports), followed by the United States (19%) and Switzerland (8%). The largest category of high-tech products imported from China was electronics used for telecommunications, while for the United States and Switzerland, these categories were high-tech products used for aerospace and pharmaceuticals, respectively[24].

However, to date, China-EU partnership of science and technology has yet to be upgraded to comprehensive innovative partnership. Among European countries, China has a close innovative partnership with the UK, Switzerland, German and so on, but when it comes to other countries, innovative cooperation with China is just part of bilateral technological cooperation. Therefore, China and Europe should work together to implement the GDI, and build a comprehensive innovative partnership that fits closely with the current China-EU cooperation. With the power of innovation, the two sides can provide solutions for the implementation of the GDI.

5. BUILDING A SYNERGY OF CHINA AND EU STRATEGIES

China and the EU are pioneers and practitioners in promoting global development. European integration has become a paradigm for regional economic development in the world, driving the establishment of regional integration mechanism and organizations. China has been resolutely advancing reform and opening up and exploring a development path of socialism with Chinese characteristics that suits China's national conditions. After decades of development, China and the EU have become two major economies of the three biggest economies in the world, and made new headway in global poverty reduction, international aid and other areas.

It was mentioned in *Poverty Alleviation: China's Experience and Contribution*, first published by the State Council on April 6th, 2021, that China had secured a comprehensive victory in the fight against poverty, completed the eradication of extreme poverty — the first target of the UN 2030 Agenda for

24. China Chamber of Commerce to the E. U., *38% of total extra-EU imports came from China*, 2022, retrieved from *https://mp.weixin.qq.com/s/NFsFzvq_4PRLb4hH3MiaKQ* on 28/09/2023.

Sustainable Development — 10 years ahead of schedule, thus significantly reducing poverty-striken population in the world. As the biggest developing country in the world, China has achieved rapid development in parallel with massive poverty alleviation, and economic transformation in parallel with the eradication of absolute poverty, and has fully achieved the goal of eliminating extreme poverty as scheduled. In terms of international aid, China has been offering grants to underdeveloped countries and regions since the 1950s. According to China's third white paper: from 2013 to 2018, China has been providing assistance for 20 regional and international multilateral organizations and 122 countries, stretching across countries from Asia, Africa, Oceania, Latin America, and Europe. As the European Integration deepens and expands, the EU's assistance has not only been provided to new EU member states in central and eastern Europe, but also to countries in Africa, Asia, and Latin America gradually. There are broad prospects for China-EU cooperation on assisting the development of the Third-Party Market.

In the future, by deeply integrating strategies from both sides, the BRI (2013) and the GDI (2021) proposed by China will be able to connect with the European Green Deal (2019) and the Global Gateway (2021) proposed by the EU. Based on technological strength and socio-economic development advantages of China and the EU, the two sides can promote global sustainable development together in areas including green development, digitization, climate change response, energy, public health, education, research and other areas.

The GDI will serve as important guiding principles and the cooperation foundation for China and the EU to build the global development partnership. Facing new situations, the two sides should stick to the principle of putting development first and continue to explore new mechanisms and modes for China-EU cooperation. Based on the new philosophies from the GDI, such as opening wider, innovation-oriented development, inclusiveness, cooperation and win-win outcomes, China and the EU are bound to play more active leading roles in promoting world economic growth, innovation-driven development, and green cooperation.

Quo Vadis Global Governance? Assessing China and EU Relations in the New Global Economic Order

TOM PEGRAM & JULIA KREIENKAMP[1]
University College London (UCL)

I. INTRODUCTION: A NEW GLOBAL ECONOMIC ORDER?

The concept of global governance first gained prominence in academic and policy debates in the 1990s. Unprecedented levels of global interdependence after the Cold War ushered in a new era of multilateral collaboration under the leadership of the United States (US). From the outset, global governance served as both an analytical framework and a political programme, seen by many as 'a way of organizing international politics in a more inclusive and consensual manner'[2]. Liberalism provided a powerful normative framework for the post-Cold War world order, prompting Fukuyama to declare the 'end of history'[3]. Today, the liberal international order is widely seen as in crisis. In light of growing multipolarity, diverging interests and staggering levels of global inequality, old and new lines of contestation have (re) emerged. With intergovernmental organisations gridlocked across policy domains, public trust in these institutions is eroding and global governance is increasingly perceived as an elite project that benefits the few, not the many[4]. Populist leaders around the world have seized on these concerns, most notably

1. Dr Tom Pegram holds a Ph.D. in Politics from Nuffield College, University of Oxford. He is an Associate Professor in Global Governance at the Department of Political Science/School of Public Policy, University College London (UCL), where he is also the Deputy Director of the UCL Global Governance Institute. Julia Kreienkamp is a research fellow at the UCL Global Governance Institute.
2. Barnett, M. and Duval, R., "Introduction: Power in Global Governance" in Barnett, M. and Duval R. (eds.), *Power in Global Governance*, Cambridge: Cambridge University Press, 2004, p. 5.
3. Fukuyama, F., "The End of History?" in *The National Interest*, n. 16, 1989, pp. 3-18.
4. Hale, T., Held, D. and Young, K., *Gridlock: Why Global Cooperation is Failing when We Need It Most*, Cambridge: Polity Press, 2013; Kahler, M., "Global Governance: Three

US President Donald Trump, who has repeatedly questioned the value of multilateral organisations and likened global governance to 'control and domination'[5].

Global power structures are also in flux. Even before Trump's ascent to power and the shift towards 'America First', US global leadership was waning as a consequence of deep structural changes in the global economy[6]. Indeed, global economic governance has undergone profound reform in recent years, with the aftershocks of the 2008 global financial crash still reverberating through major international organisations and far beyond. Observers are scrambling to understand the contours of both the familiar and the novel in an unsettled global economic order, placing particular attention on the changing balance of power between advanced and emerging economies, as well as public and private sources of authority[7]. Signs of global economic disorder are particularly visible in the faltering architecture of economic governance, with the multilateral trade regime rendered inoperative by contestation, and efforts to hold accountable global private market actors and the social forces of unfettered globalisation falling short[8].

Against a backdrop of US retreat from its role as hegemonic stabiliser, the European Union (EU) —the world's most advanced experiment in governance beyond the nation-state— is grappling with a number of internal challenges that may weaken support for the European project as a whole. Nevertheless, the European Commission is actively manoeuvring to respond to a new global economic governance landscape. A recent think piece by the European Commission's Director- General for Economic and Financial Affairs calls upon the EU to shift focus away from "winning the war" —i. e. responding to the 2008 crisis— to "winning the peace"—i. e. overcoming the

Futures" in *International Studies Review*, vol. 20, n. 2, 2018, pp. 239-246; Zürn, M., *A Theory of Global Governance*, Oxford: Oxford University Press, 2018.

5. Trump, D., *Remarks by President Trump to the 73rd Session of the United Nations General Assembly*, The White House, 25 September 2018, retrieved from *https://www.whitehouse.gov/ briefings-statements/remarks-president-trump-73rd-session- united-nations-general-assembly- new-york-ny/*
6. Acharya, A., *The End of American World Order*, Cambridge: Polity Press, 2014.
7. Drezner, D. W., "Counter-Hegemonic Strategies in the Global Economy" in *Security Studies*, vol. 28, n. 3, 2019, pp. 505-531.
8. Shaffer, G., "A Tragedy in the Making? The Decline of Law and the Return of Power in International Trade Relations" in *Yale Journal of International Law*, 2018, retrieved from *https://cpb-us- w2.wpmucdn. com/campuspress.yale.edu/dist/8/1581/files/2018/12/Shaffer_YJIL-Symposium_A-Tragedy-in-the-Making_12.08.18-1zx9zvv.pdf*; Mattli, W., *Darkness by Design. The Hidden Power in Global Capital Markets*, Princeton, NJ: Princeton University Press, 2019.

legacy of the crisis and creating conditions for strong, sustainable, balanced and more inclusive growth'[9]. However, reflective of growing geopolitical turbulence, Europe has also dramatically sharpened its political stance on China's trade practices. The careful formulation of China as a 'strategic partner' in the 2016 EU strategy on China has been replaced in its 2019 EU-China strategic outlook by the much more forceful designation of 'economic competitor' and 'systemic rival'[10].

For its part, China increasingly appears to view US retreat as an opportunity to assert its role in global economic governance. Observers have identified the 2008 crisis as a notable inflection point for Chinese ambitions for economic statecraft as a key plank of its foreign policy[11]. Strategically, China under the leadership of President Xi Jinping has privileged participation in the informal intergovernmental mechanisms of the G20 over engagement with key Western- dominated organisations, such as the International Monetary Fund (IMF), the World Trade Organization (WTO) and the World Bank. This likely reflects longstanding Chinese discontent over the terms of its membership within the WTO in particular, as well as a preference for the more representative and open institutional design of the G20[12]. On the plus side, the rise of China and other emerging markets has significantly broadened participation in global economic governance, but it has also made cooperation more difficult. Despite reassurances from Chinese officials that Western powers have 'nothing to worry about, as China has been a big beneficiary of the current system and global governance architecture'[13], for

9. Buti, M., *The New Global Economic Governance: Can Europe Help Win the Peace?*, European Commission, 2017, retrieved from *https://ec.europa.eu/info/sites/info/files/economy-finance/marco-buti-the-new-global-economic-governance.pdf*
10. European Commission, *Elements for a New EU Strategy on China*, Joint Communication to the European Parliament and the Council, 2016, retrieved from *http://eeas.europa.eu/archives/docs/ china/docs/joint_communication_to_the_european_parliament_and_the_council_-_elements_for_a_new_eu_strategy_on_china.pdf*; European Commission, *EU-China — A Strategic Outlook*, Joint Communication to the European Parliament, the European Council and the Council, 2019, retrieved from *https://ec.europa.eu/ commission/sites/beta-political/files/communication-eu-china-a- strategic-outlook.pdf*
11. Wong, A., *China's Economic Statecraft under Xi Jinping*, Washington, DC: Brookings, 2019, retrieved from *https://www.brookings.edu/articles/chinas-economic-statecraft- under-xi-jinping/*
12. He, A., *The Dragon's Footprints. China in the Global Economic Governance System under the G20 Framework*, Waterloo, ON: Centre for International Governance Innovation, 2016.
13. Yafei, H., China's New Role in Global Governance, *China-US Focus*, 14 September 2018, retrieved from *https://www.chinausfocus.com/foreign-policy/chinas-new-role-in- global-governance*

many observers, recent events are reconfiguring 'the global as a realm of disputes and confrontation, rather than one driven primarily by interest alignment within multilateral state forums'[14].

While the great powers retain primacy in economic diplomacy, power and authority in global economic governance is clearly no longer the preserve of states. A growing number of market actors are now involved in global economic policy-making and delivery. This phenomenon is particularly prominent in the field of 'megaregulation', augured in by the defunct Trans-Pacific Partnership (TPP) and finally realised in the Japan-led Comprehensive and Progressive Agreement for Trans-Pacific Partnership (CPTPP), among other ambitious interstate and transregional economic ordering schemes[15].

Such megaregulatory economic projects have also mobilised significant civil society opposition amidst allegations of corporate capture and elite governance. To understand the internal dynamics of global economic governance, it is not only necessary to incorporate non-state actors, but also to 'disaggregate' the state, with different domestic agencies participating quasi-independently in the politics of negotiating and implementing globally defined economic goals[16]. This has opened up space for new forms of collaboration between heterogeneous actors —organising governance in less formal, less legalised, more 'networked' ways— but it has also revealed new areas of contestation as authority becomes more diffused and it is increasingly difficult to say who exercises economic power, how and over whom.

Rapid change is a hallmark of global economic governance. Global governance scholars have an important role to play in stepping back from the dizzying speed of real-world developments to try and take stock of the situation at hand. At a time when the major economic organisations are beset by geopolitics and economic nationalism, close scrutiny of major structural dynamics is important if we are to begin to decipher clues as to global economic governance futures. This paper offers some modest reflections in this direction, focusing in particular on the interrelationships of two of the major players in global economic governance: China and the EU. It builds upon the discussions of a workshop, hosted jointly by University College London (UCL)'s Global Governance Institute, UCL Laws and CEU San Pablo University Madrid on 22 March 2019. Funded by a Jean Monnet Network

14. Coen, D. and Pegram, T., "Wanted: A Third Generation of Global Governance Research" in *Governance*, vol. 28, n. 4, 2015, pp. 417-420, p. 419.
15. Kingsbury, B. et al., *Megaregulation Contested. Global Economic Ordering After TPP*, Oxford: Oxford University Press, 2019.
16. Slaughter, A.-M., *A New World Order*, Princeton, NJ: Princeton University Press, 2004.

grant, it brought together a multidisciplinary group of scholars from the EU and China to discuss global economic governance and regulation across issue areas spanning trade facilitation, investment, competition, tax and environmental concerns.

The study of China-EU economic governance offers a valuable sightline onto areas of innovation for a new generation of global governance scholarship. In particular, by framing key organisations and initiatives as sites of intervention and contestation, scholars can shed light on the endogenous causes of conflicts and struggles as functions of international organisations themselves, as opposed to 'seeing global politics as an epiphenomenon of struggles between independent units'[17]. We evidence this through showcasing two key domains of China-EU economic relations:

(1) China and the EU in the WTO and (2) the Belt and Road Initiative and Chinese foreign direct investments (FDI) in Europe. Puncturing the cooperation bias which permeated much first-generation global governance scholarship is an important first step to arriving at an appreciation of the *politics* of 'making' global governance and the distributive struggles involved, jettisoning linear accounts of changing global power dynamics. It also invites observers to take seriously conflict over norms, values, ideas and identities — issues that global governance scholars have too often shied away from. Finally, such an effort can shed light on some of the practical challenges of global policy-making and delivery in the 21st century and the pressing question of 'what works?'

COMING INTO VIEW: A THIRD GENERATION OF GLOBAL GOVERNANCE SCHOLARSHIP

If global governance research is to make sense of the full complexities of global public policy making and implementation, it must advance debate across disciplinary, theoretical and issue- specific silos. Against this background, Coen and Pegram have called for a 'third generation of global governance scholarship'[18]. Whereas a first generation of global governance researchers, grounded primarily in the liberal institutionalist tradition of international relations (IR) theory, has focused almost exclusively on interstate cooperation through formal multilateral structures, a second generation of scholars, spanning IR, public policy, international

17. Zürn, M., *A Theory of Global Governance, op. cit.*
18. Coen, D. and Pegram, T, "Wanted: A Third Generation of Global Governance Research", *op. cit.*; Coen, D. and Pegram, T., "Towards a Third Generation of Global Governance

law and other disciplines, has investigated the emergence of new actors, institutions and mechanisms in a rapidly changing, increasingly complex global governance landscape. An emergent third generation of global governance research has much to gain from accelerating a convergence across this pluralist body of research to develop a more comprehensive understanding of what is causing blockage in global governance and, crucially, to devise 'coherent and realistic solutions to global public policy challenges'[19].

If global governance research is to make sense of the full complexities of global public policy making and implementation, it must advance debate across disciplinary, theoretical and issue- specific silos. Against this background, Coen and Pegram have called for a 'third generation of global governance scholarship'[20]. Whereas a first generation of global governance researchers, grounded primarily in the liberal institutionalist tradition of international relations (IR) theory, has focused almost exclusively on interstate cooperation through formal multilateral structures, a second generation of scholars, spanning IR, public policy, international law and other disciplines, has investigated the emergence of new actors, institutions and mechanisms in a rapidly changing, increasingly complex global governance landscape. An emergent third generation of global governance research has much to gain from accelerating a convergence across this pluralist body of research to develop a more comprehensive understanding of what is causing blockage in global governance and, crucially, to devise 'coherent and realistic solutions to global public policy challenges'[21].

Arguably, one of the most pressing tasks for this new generation of researchers is to move decisively beyond the understanding of global governance as a consensual problem- solving exercise and think more seriously about the sources, dynamics and effects of contestation. Importantly, explanations must go beyond simplistic juxtapositions of 'global vs. national interests' or 'status quo vs. revisionist states', focusing instead on the complex power

---

Scholarship" in *Global Policy*, vol. 9, n. 1, 2018, pp. 107-113.

19. Coen, D. and Pegram, T., "Towards a Third Generation of Global Governance Scholarship", *op. cit.*, p. 109.
20. Coen, D. and Pegram, T, "Wanted: A Third Generation of Global Governance Research", *op. cit.*; Coen, D. and Pegram, T., "Towards a Third Generation of Global Governance Scholarship" in *Global Policy*, vol. 9, n. 1, 2018, pp. 107-113.
21. Coen, D. and Pegram, T., "Towards a Third Generation of Global Governance Scholarship", *op. cit.*, p. 109.

dynamics that are embedded in thick interdependencies. As Zürn has argued 'world politics is now embedded in a normative and institutional structure that contains hierarchies and power inequalities'[22]. This has produced distributional struggles —raising questions of 'who gets what, when, how'[23]— but also normative conflict over legitimacy, accountability and the thorny issue of how we arrive at transnational conceptions of the 'public good' and 'good governance'. In this endeavour, it is also important to not lose sight of world history. If scholars wish to understand the underlying causes of contestation within the global system, it will be imperative to describe and explain systematically how power dynamics have changed over time, and within specific historical contexts[24].

ore attention should also be paid to the drivers of contestation and resistance at the domestic level, the complicated relationship between 'rule-makers' and 'rule-takers', and the local actors and institutions that facilitate or impede the implementation of globally defined rules, norms, policies and goals. Simply put, notwithstanding the density of multilateral structures with independent capabilities, direct enforcement has often been elusive to global governance arrangements, especially those directed by international organisations. Adaptive responses by policy agents to regulatory failure are apparent across public goods domains, perhaps best exemplified by the Paris climate agreement's bottom-up 'catalytic' approach to environmental governance[25]. A shift beyond state-driven, top-down efforts to negotiate 'global deals' is also apparent in the scholarship, with researchers turning their attention to the promise and pitfalls of efforts to organise governance in less formal, less hierarchical, and less centralised ways[26]. While scholarship is making important advances in elucidating arenas for experimentation in the shadow of interstate hierarchy, we still lack in-depth and systematic insights into how global regulatory arrangements connect to the realities of domestic implementation.

22. Zürn, M., *A Theory of Global Governance*, *op. cit.*, p. 1.
23. Lasswell, H. D., *Politics: Who Gets What, When How*, New York: Meridian Books, 1958.
24. Murphy, C. N., *International Organization and Industrial Change: Global Governance since 1850*, Cambridge: Polity Press, 1994.
25. Hale, T., "Climate Change: From Gridlock to Catalyst" in Hale, T. and Held, D. (eds.), *Beyond Gridlock*, Cambridge: Polity Press, 2017.
26. Kahler, M., "Networked Politics: Agency, Power and Governance" in Kahler, M. (ed.), *Networked Politics: Agency, Power and Governance*, Ithaca, NY: Cornell University Press, 2009.

As Coen and Pegram suggest, a promising starting point for advancing a more pluralist debate on these issues is the intellectual convergence that is already underway across IR, European Public Policy, and international law[27]. Whereas IR's long-standing concern with power is key to understanding conflict and distributional struggles in global politics, an international law perspective allows us to rethink normative concepts such as legitimacy and accountability and their application beyond the nation-state. In turn, scholarship on European Public Policy can offer practice-oriented insights on the politics of implementation in multi-level systems. Going forward, global governance has a lot to gain from integrating more disciplinary perspectives, such as political economy, psychology or historical sociology[28]. On a theoretical level, a third generation of global governance should strive to integrate both liberal- functionalist and critical scholarship, with the former focusing on the immediate need to resolve collective action problems and the latter drawing attention to questions of legitimacy and the distributional effects of power asymmetries. In addition, insights from constructivist scholarship can help us make sense of how shifting norms, ideas, values and discourses can prompt change in global governance. Finally, and importantly, global governance research should strive to become more global itself, making room for plural voices, experiences and perspectives, including those from the non-West[29].

II. CHINA AND THE EU: WHOSE GLOBAL GOVERNANCE?

At the end of March 2019, Chinese President Xi Jinping met with French President Emmanuel Macron, German Chancellor Angela Merkel and EU Commission President Jean-Claude Juncker in Paris[30]. They issued a joint call

27. Coen, D. and Pegram, T, "Wanted: A Third Generation of Global Governance Research", *op. cit.*
28. Haufler, V., "Producing Global Governance in the Global Factory: Markets, Politics, and Regulation" in *Global Policy*, vol. 9, n. 1, 2018, pp. 114-120; Buzan, B. and Lawson, G., *The Global Transformation: History, Modernity and the Making of International Relations*, Cambridge: Cambridge University Press, 2015; Go, J. and Lawson, G., "Introduction: For a Global Historical Sociology" in Go, J. and Lawson, G. (eds.), *Global Historical Sociology*. Cambridge: Cambridge University Press, 2017.
29. Acharya, A., *Understanding the Emerging Multiplex World Order*, interview with Professor Amitav Acharya. UCL Global Governance Institute, 2019, retrieved from *https://www.ucl.ac.uk/global-governance/news/2019/jul/understanding-emerging- multiplex-world-order*
30. France24, *Xi Jinping in France: Full press conference with Xi, Macron, Merkel and Juncker*, 2019, retrieved from *https://www.france24.com/en/video/20190326-xi-jinping-france-watch-full-press-conference-with-xi-macron-merkel-juncker*

for stronger global governance, emphasising common ground and points for convergence. Macron suggested that both the EU and China have an important role to play in defending multilateral cooperation and that their partnership should be 'exemplary' across issue areas such as climate change, security and trade.

Only two weeks earlier, the European Commission had published a Joint Communication that made headlines because it portrayed China not just as a partner but also as a 'systemic rival promoting alternative models of governance'. The report maintained that 'China's engagement in favour of multilateralism is sometimes selective and based on a different understanding of the rules-based international order' and suggested that the EU adopts a more robust, assertive and principled approach towards China[31].

Similarly, 'China sees the EU both as an ally and as an opponent in its drive for reforms of the existing international system'[32]. The EU is generally seen as a partner in China's quest for more representation in global governance institutions and a greater diversification of power in the international system. At the same time, China remains suspicious of the EU's values-based engagement model and its efforts to upload its own normative preferences onto the global level[33].

Thus, while Europe and China have both positioned themselves as defenders of global governance, multilateralism, and 'an open, balanced, and inclusive global economy' it appears that they are not always talking about the same thing[34]. While the EU's approach to global governance is based on an explicit mission to promote human rights, democracy and the rule of law worldwide, China maintains that equity, sovereignty and non-interference are the overriding guiding principles of international relations[35]. Therefore, Delage and Abad suggest that 'whereas the EU is committed to the promotion of *multilateralism*, what China is really interested in is [the promotion of] *multipolarity*'[36].

31. European Commission, *EU-China — A Strategic Outlook, op. cit.*, pp. 1-2.
32. Christiansen, T., Kirchner, E. and Wissenbach, U., *The European Union and China*, London: Red Globe Press, 2018.
33. Crookes, P. I., "Resetting EU — China relations from a values-based to an interests-based engagement" in *International Politics*, vol. 50, n. 5, 2013, pp. 639-663.
34. European Council, *EU-China Summit Joint Statement*. Brussels, 9 April 2019, retrieved from *https://www.consilium.europa.eu/media/39020/euchina-joint-statement- 9april2019.pdf*
35. Pan, Z., "Sovereignty in China-EU Relations: The Conceptual Gaps in China-EU Relations" in Pan, Z. (ed.), *Conceptual Gaps in China-EU Relations: Global Governance, Human Rights and Strategic Partnerships*, London: Palgrave Macmillan, 2012.
36. Delage, F. and Abad, G., "China's Foreign Policy: A European Perspective" in Beneyto, J. M., Song, X. and Ding, C. (eds.), *China and the European Union: Future Direction*, CEU

1. CHINA'S ROLE IN GLOBAL GOVERNANCE: RULE-TAKER OR RULE-MAKER?

The rise of China has captured the attention of policy-makers, researchers, investors and the general public for more than three decades. Much of the early debate has focused on whether China and the other BRICS countries (Brazil, Russia, India, China and South Africa) would accept the existing global order or attempt to overthrow it. Some saw in China a "new 'Prussian' threat", posing a fundamental challenge to the status quo[37]. Others maintained that China could be socialised into the existing international regime as a 'responsible stakeholder' on the basis of 'shared interests *and* shared values'[38]. Today, it has become increasingly clear that there is no linear logic to the rise of China and other emerging states. In the words of veteran Chinese diplomat Fu Ying, 'China has neither the intention nor ability to overturn the existing order'[39]. At the same time, China has maintained its own normative preferences with regard to global governance, challenging the notion that China could be integrated into the international system through a one- directional socialisation process[40].

Initially, China played only a limited role in global governance. Up until the late 1970s, Maoist China remained isolated from the mainstream international order, positioning itself as a revolutionary power that opposed 'United States imperialism and its lackeys'[41]. Under Deng Xiaoping, China gradually became more integrated into the international order, in particular in the economic and financial realm. However, as Kim has argued, its approach to global governance was 'distinctively system-maintaining and

Ediciones. Madrid: CEU San Pablo University, 2013, p. 5, retrieved from *http://www.idee.ceu.es/Portals/0/Publicaciones/ Ebook%20nº%207.pdf* [emphasis added].

37. Cooper, A. F. and Alexandroff, A. S., "Introduction" in Alexandroff, A. S. and Cooper, A. F. (eds.), *Rising States, Rising Institutions. Challenges for Global Governance*. Washington, DC: Brookings Institution Press, 2010, p. 5.
38. Zoellick, R. B. *Whither China: From Membership to Responsibility? Remarks to the National Committee on U.S.-China Relations*, New York, 21 September 2005, retrieved from *https://2001- 2009.state.gov/s/d/former/zoellick/rem/53682.htm* [emphasis added].
39. Ying, F., *Under the Same Roof: China's View of Global Order*, Huffington Post, 11 November 2015, retrieved from *http://bit.ly/30ToTRQ*
40. Hurrell, A. and Loke, B., *Emerging Powers and Global Order: Much Ado About Nothing?*, PRIMO Working Paper n. 14, Hamburg: PRIMO (Power and Region in a Multipolar Order), University of Hamburg, 2017, retrieved from *https://ore.exeter.ac.uk/repository/handle/10871/33430*
41. Mao, T., *Text of Mao's Statement Urging World Revolution Against U.S. 21 May 1970*, New York Times Archive, 1970, retrieved from *https://www.nytimes.com/1970/05/21/archives/text-of-maos- statement-urging-world- revolution-against-us.html*

system-exploiting'[42]. Thus, rather than attempting to upset or transform the exiting international system, China was interested in system stability to support its internal reforms aimed at building a strong domestic order and modernising its economy[43]. After the Cold War, China's interactions with the rest of the world were guided largely by Deng Xiaoping's 1990 '24-Character Strategy' which, among other things, called for China to hide its capacities, bide its time, maintain a low profile and never claim leadership[44].

More recently, however, China —now the world's second largest economy by nominal GDP— has become a more proactive, ambitious and confident player in global affairs and in particular in global economic governance. It has adopted a dual strategy of *reform from within*, pushing for a greater influence in existing Western-dominated international institutions, and *reform from outside*, setting up new governance structures, some of which may pose a direct challenge to those already in existence[45]. For example, the establishment of the China-led Asian Infrastructure Investment Bank (AIIB) has raised concerns in the US and Japan, who view it as a rival to lenders such as the IMF, the World Bank and the Asian Development Bank (ADB). However, China insists that the AIIB is designed to complement and not upend the current global economic governance architecture and, significantly, the UK and other European countries have chosen to join the AIIB despite pressure from the US not to do so[46].

2. THE EU'S ROLE IN GLOBAL GOVERNANCE: A LEADER BY EXAMPLE?

For many years, the EU has been considered a remarkably successful model in multilevel and multistakeholder governance and 'the most advanced model for international cooperation'[47]. The EU self- identifies as

42. Kim, S. S., "Thinking Globally in Post-Mao China", *Journal of Peace Research*, vol. 27, n. 2, Special Issue on the Challenge of Global Policy, 1990, pp. 191-209, p. 193.
43. Chen, Z., "China, the European Union and the Fragile World Order" in *Journal of Common Market Studies*, vol. 54, n. 4, 2016, pp. 775-792.
44. Quoting Deng Xiaoping from Song, X. and Huang, W., "China and the Global Political Economy" in Beneyto, J. M., Song, X. and Ding, C. (eds.), *China and the European Union: Future Directions*, CEU Ediciones. Madrid: CEU San Pablo University, 2013, retrieved from *http://www.idee.ceu.es/Portals/0/Publicaciones/Ebook%20nº%207.pdf*
45. Chen, Z., "China, the European Union and the Fragile World Order", *op. cit.*
46. Yang, H., "The Asian Infrastructure Investment Bank and Status-Seeking: China's Foray into Global Economic Governance", *Chinese Political Science Review*, vol. 1, n. 4, 2016, pp. 754-778.
47. Moravcsik, A., "The European Constitutional Settlement" in Meunier, S. and McNamara, K. R. (eds.), *Making History: European Integration and Institutional Change at Fifty*, Oxford: Oxford University Press, 2007.

a normative leader and shaper of the rules-based international order[48]. The 2007 Treaty of Lisbon has enshrined this ambition into EU primary law, with Article 21 of the Treaty on European Union stating that EU's external actions should be 'guided by the principles which have inspired its own creation, development and enlargement, and which it seeks to advance in the wider world: democracy, the rule of law, the universality and indivisibility of human rights and fundamental freedoms, respect for human dignity, the principles of equality and solidarity, and respect for the principles of the United Nations Charter and international law'[49].

The EU can also be viewed as an 'experimental laboratory' for global governance[50]. The EU's supranational governance framework has produced a number of legal, institutional and procedural innovations, some of which have found their way into the global governance architecture. However, the ability of the EU to act as rules-shaper in the global governance system remains contested. In the mid-2000s, some saw in Europe an emerging superpower, both in material and normative terms, offering a compelling alternative to the American dream and a better model for collaboration to tackle today's most pressing global public policy challenges[51]. Others argued that Europe's soft power approach to foreign policy and its emphasis on international law and multilateralism stemmed from a position of relative weakness rather than strength[52].

Today, the role of the EU in global governance is still characterised by contradictions. One the one hand, it enjoys considerable influence on the global stage and is recognised as a consistent promoter of multilateralism and a 'leader by example' in issue areas such as climate change and human rights. With the advent of Trump, the EU is seen by many as the principle defender of the rules-based international order[53]. On the other hand, the EU's

48. Larik, J., "Shaping the International Order as an EU Objective" in Kochenov, D. and Amtenbrink, F. (eds.), *The European Union's Shaping of the International Legal Order*. Cambridge: Cambridge University Press, 2013.
49. Van Vooren, B., Blockmans, S. and Wouters, J., "The Legal Dimension of Global Governance: What Role for the European Union? An Introduction" in Van Vooren, B., Blockmans, S. and Wouters, J. (eds.), *The EU's Role in Global Governance: The Legal Dimension*. Oxford: Oxford University Press, 2013.
50. Christiansen, T., "The European Union and Global Governance" in Triandafyllidou, A. (ed.), *Global Governance from Regional Perspectives: A Critical View*, Oxford: Oxford University Press, 2017.
51. McCormick, J., *The European Superpower*, London/Basingstoke: Palgrave Macmillan, 2007.
52. Kagan, R., "Power and Weakness", *Policy Review*, n. 113, 2002, pp. 3-28.
53. Dworkin, A. and Leonard, M., *Can Europe Save the World Order?*, ECFR Policy Brief. London: European Council on Foreign Relations, 2018, retrieved from *https://www.ecfr.eu/publications/ summary/can_europe_save_the_world_order*

global 'actorness' appears to have decreased in light of changing external opportunity structures as well as the internal divisions laid bare by the European debt crisis, the refugee crisis and the Brexit vote[54]. The surge in far-right populist parties and movements across Europe is also casting doubts on the future global role of the EU as it risks undermining the very values on which the European project was founded and which it seeks to promote globally, prompting some to prophesise 'the end of Europe'[55].

3. NEGOTIATING GLOBAL GOVERNANCE: ZONES OF AGREEMENT AND CONTESTATION

The concept of global governance has received increased attention in academic and policy discussions in China since the turn of the century[56]. Chinese and Western scholars share a number of common views on global governance, including, most fundamentally, that it is necessary to address pressing global problems. However, they often disagree on the question of what makes global governance effective and/or legitimate, juxtaposing values such as 'harmony, inclusiveness and respect for differences' with Western values of democracy, freedom, and universal human rights[57]. China's interpretation of global governance has also found expression in policy slogans, notably the vision of a 'harmonious world', first put forward by Hu Jintao and later incorporated into Xi Jinping's 'Chinese dream'.

However, as Nordin reminds us, the values and experiences that inform different notions of global governance are also contested *within* policy communities: 'Just as "democracy" means different things to different people, discussions of "harmony" represent a diversity of opinion'[58]. A static

54. Bretherton, C. and Vogler, J., "A global actor past its peak?", *International Relations*, vol. 27, n. 3, 2013, pp. 375-90.
55. Kirchick, J. *The End of Europe: Dictators, Demagogues, and the Coming Dark Age*. New Haven, CT: Yale University Press, 2017.
56. Zang, L., *Global Governance: How Fine, How Fast, and How Far? — A Perspective of China*, Global Policy Projects, 2011, retrieved from *https://www.globalpolicyjournal.com/projects/global-audit/global-governance-how-fine- how-fast-and-how-far-perspective-china*; Wang, H. and Rosenau, J. N., "China and Global Governance", *Asian Perspective*, vol. 33, n. 3, 2009, pp. 5-39; Florini, A., "Rising Asian Powers and Changing Global Governance", *International Studies Review*, vo. 13, n. 1, 2011, pp. 24-33.
57. Jinping, X., *Working Together to Forge a New Partnership of Win-win Cooperation and Create a Community of Shared Future for Mankind*, Embassy of the People's Republic of China in the United Kingdom of Great Britain and Northern Ireland, 2015, retrieved from *http://www.chinese-embassy. org.uk/eng/zgyw/t1305051.htm*
58. Nordin, A., "Futures beyond 'the West'? Autoimmunity in China's Harmonious World", *Review of International Studies*, n. 42, 2016, pp. 156-177, p. 164.

perspective on contestation cannot explain how both China and the EU are constantly renegotiating their role in and interpretation of global governance in a complex and messy world. As China seeks a more proactive role in global governance, it must confront contradictions in its own grand strategy and accept that its ability to shape global —and even regional— governance remains constrained[59].The EU, on the other hand, has to come to terms with the fact that the promotion of its own model is no longer supported by a global trend towards deeper integration. Maybe most importantly, it has to confront its own illiberal backlash which threatens European identity and unity at a time when it is needed more than ever to sustain the EU's role as a global rules-shaper.

III. CONTESTATION IN GLOBAL ECONOMIC GOVERNANCE: CHINA AND THE EU

Many of the tensions discussed above also play out in the arena of global economic governance and the bilateral economic relations between the EU and China. The two powers have developed strong economic ties: The EU is China's biggest trading partner, while China is the EU's second-biggest trading partner behind the US. In 2018, China accounted for about a fifth of EU goods imports and more than a tenth of its exports[60]. Thus, there is significant scope for collaboration on global economic governance based on shared interests. Yet, this is also a realm of contestation triggered by the shifting of geopolitical tectonic plates. As one senior EU official recently reflected: "It has finally sunk in... While we were absorbed in our own crises for 10 years, the GDP of China soared and Trump was elected. We entered a different game"[61]. Significant differences in the economic systems of China and the EU limit opportunities for collaboration and are at the root of many disputes between the two countries. Some of these conflicts also reflect more fundamental disagreement about normative priorities and differing views on how economic governance and regulation should be done.

For global governance scholarship this illustrates the need to take seriously different sources of contestation. This is not to suggest that

59. Buzan, B., "The Logic and Contradictions of 'Peaceful Rise/Development' as China's Grand Strategy", *The Chinese Journal of International Politics*, vol. 7, n. 4, 2014, pp. 381-420; Summers, T., "Thinking Inside the Box: China and Global/Regional Governance", *Rising Powers Quarterly*, vol. 1, n. 1, 2016, pp. 23-31.

60. Peel, M., Hornby, L. and Sanderson, R., "European foreign policy: a new realism on China", *Financial Times*, 20 March 2019, retrieved from *https://www.ft.com/content/d7145792-4743-11e9-b168-96a37d002cd3*

61. Quote fromunnamed EU official in Peel, M., Hornby, L. and Sanderson, R., "European foreign policy: a new realism on China", *op. cit.*

material interests and normative preferences can be neatly separated but that the complex interactions between identities, interests, and norms are key to understand the role of China and the EU in global economic governance. Importantly, these identities, interests, and norms are formed and negotiated through both domestic and international processes. The dynamics of contestation between China and the EU in the area of global economic governance also point to the need of thinking across issue area boundaries. Economic governance is not a distinct game and the interactions between China and the EU in this area often raise a host of related problems in issue areas such as security, human rights and the environment. At the same time, as US and China relations deteriorate, raising the very real possibility of a balkanisation of the internet and related IT standards, the EU is uniquely positioned to serve as a mediating (and moderating) influence on both parties[62].

As China and the EU renegotiate their economic relationship, they also need to rethink their own growth models. In the EU, the euro crisis has laid bare significant disparities between member states which some view as the direct result of the 'technocratic attempt to promote a single [...] export growth model strategy, built around ordoliberal ideas of rules-based fiscal governance and cost-based competitiveness'[63]. China, meanwhile, seeks to respond to slowing economic growth by shifting from an investment and export-driven 'global factory' growth model towards a more sustainable model based on innovation and consumption. This has important implications for Europe, which has traditionally viewed China as a source of labour- intensive manufactured products and a market for European high-end goods and services. As a result, new distributional conflicts have emerged and 'reciprocity' has become a key concern for the EU as it seeks a level playing field for European businesses in areas such as trade, investment or intellectual property.

The below discusses two areas of economic governance that see increased contestation between the EU and China but also offer opportunities for further collaboration: the World Trade Organization (WTO) and China's Belt and Road initiative (BRI).

62. The Economist, "China has designs on Europe. Here is how Europe should respond", *The Economist*, 4 October 2018, retrieved from *https://www.economist.com/leaders/2018/10/04/china- has-designs-on-europe-here-is-how-europe-should-respond*

63. Johnston, A. and Regan, A., "Introduction: Is the European Union Capable of Integrating Diverse Models of Capitalism?", *New Political Economy*, vol. 23, n. 2, 2018, pp. 145-159, p. 155.

1. CHINA AND THE EU IN THE WORLD TRADE ORGANIZATION (WTO)

The WTO is the most important rule-making, monitoring and dispute resolution body in global trade and a central pillar of the liberal international order. In light of the rise of China and other emerging economies, it has also become 'a key site of global power struggles'[64]. While the WTO has been quicker than other institutions — such as the IMF or the World Bank — to adapt its governance structures to the new multipolar realities, this has left the system prone to deadlock[65].The difficulty to overcome longstanding divisions along North-South lines has been demonstrated most sharply by the breakdown of the Doha Development Round, which came to a permanent impasse in 2008.

The WTO is facing a range of other challenges as well. Due to the persistent deadlock of multilateral talks, it has struggled to keep pace with the digitalisation of the global economy, the emergence of global value chains, and the growing need to reconcile trade objectives with other goals such as environmental protection[66]. This has prompted states to revert to regional and bilateral negotiations, leaving the global trade governance landscape increasingly fragmented. The radical shift towards protectionism in US trade policy threatens to undermine the WTO even further. By blocking the appointment of new appellate judges, Trump has taken particular aim at the dispute settlement system, which he accuses of an anti- American bias. This could leave 'one of the major success stories of the WTO' in paralysis for years[67].

Both China and the EU have been alarmed by these developments. In a clear rebuke to Trump, the joint statement of the 2019 EU-China summit highlights the WTO as a shared priority, stating that '[t]he EU and China firmly support the rules-based multilateral trading system with the WTO at its core, fight against unilateralism and protectionism, and commit to complying with WTO rules'[68]. Brussels and Beijing have agreed to work

64. Hopewell, K., "The BRICS — Merely a Fable? Emerging Power Alliances in Global Trade Governance", *International Affairs*, vol. 93, n. 6, 2017, pp. 1377-1396, p. 1381.
65. Narlikar, A., "New Powers in the Club: The Challenges of Global Trade Governance", *International Affairs*, vol. 86, n. 3, 2010, pp. 717-728.
66. Woolcock, S., *WTO Rules OK? Not Anymore*. Brexit Blog, London School of Economics and Political Science, 2019, retrieved from *https://blogs.lse.ac.uk/brexit/2019/05/24/ wto-rules-ok-not-any-more/*
67. Klasen, A., "Trade: Gridlock and Resilience" in Hale, T. and Held, D. (eds.), *Beyond Gridlock*. Cambridge: Polity Press, 2017, p. 73.
68. European External Action Service, *Joint Statement of the 21st EU-China Summit*, Delegation of the European Union to China, 2019, retrieved from *https://eeas.europa.eu/*

together to advance WTO reform and address the crisis of the dispute settlement system, including through a joint working group. However, while China and the EU share an interest in a stable multilateral system, finding common ground on specific reform proposals will be much more difficult. On critical issues, such as subsidies for state- owned enterprises and forced technology transfers, the EU is firmly aligned with the US. Meanwhile, China has made clear that it will not accept any reforms that amount to 'a tailor-made straitjacket of trade rules to constrain China's development'[69].

Another issue that looms large because of its practical, political and symbolic implications is China's status within the WTO. China joined the WTO in 2001, after a long and arduous negotiation process. Although it was allowed to join as a developing country —a status that normally comes with special rights and preferential treatment— it had to accept a number of 'extraordinary concessions'[70]. These included a unique sunset clause that allowed other WTO members to treat China as a non-market economy (NME) in anti- dumping proceedings during a 15-year transition period, giving them greater scope when imposing tariffs on imports from China. At the time, there was a widespread expectation among Western negotiators that China would gradually develop into a fully liberalised market economy. However, these expectations have not been met and China's particular brand of state capitalism continues to pose a number of challenges to the global trade regime. Differing legal interpretations of China's accession protocol have contributed to the politicisation of the issue. The EU and the US, fearing an influx of under-priced goods, have refused to grant China market economy status after the 15-year transition period lapsed in December 2016. China's efforts to appeal this decision at the WTO have been unsuccessful[71].

The debate on China's status at the WTO is also tied up with wider questions of China's identity —or, rather, *identities*— and its position in the

---

delegations/china_ en/60836/Joint%20statement%20of%20the%2 021st%20EU-China%20 summit

69. Miles, T., "China will propose WTO reforms, but don't try to trap us: Beijing's WTO envoy", *Reuters*, 19 November 2018, retrieved from *https://www.reuters.com/article/us-usa-trade-wto-china/china-will-propose-wto-reforms-but-dont-try-to-trap-us-beijings-wto-envoy-idUSKCN1NO20J*
70. Scott, J. and Wilkinson, R., "China as a System Preserving Power in the WTO" in Lesage, D. and Van de Graaf, T. (eds.), *Rising Powers and Multilateral Institutions*. Basingstoke: Palgrave Macmillan, 2015, p. 204.
71. Miles, T., "China pulls WTO suit over claim to be a market economy", *Reuters*, 17 June 2019, retrieved from *https://www.reuters.com/article/us-usa-china-wto-eu/china-pulls-wto-suit-over-claim-to-be-a-market-economy-idUSKCN1TI10A*

international order. Chinese media and officials have repeatedly stressed the symbolic importance of market economy status as a recognition that the West engages with China on equal terms, 'the way a friend treats another friend'[72]. At the same, China is unwilling to give up its identity as a developing country, which has long constituted a key component of its foreign policy, even though its interests often differ from most developing countries[73]. In the eyes of the US and the EU, China has been leveraging its status as 'the world's largest developing economy' strategically to strengthen its voice in global governance through South-South coalitions while also securing benefits and avoiding taking on unwanted responsibilities. The current US administration has taken a particularly strong stance, arguing that China has benefited from WTO membership 'to the detriment of its trading partners' by resisting further liberalisation of its economic system and refusing to give up its status as a developing country[74]. While the EU takes a less zero-sum approach and acknowledges that China hasmade progress in reforming key parts of its economy, it agrees that 'China can no longer be regarded as a developing country' and maintains that WTO rules must be reformed 'to ensure a level playing field and eliminate unfair practices deployed by China'[75].

Given the conflicting interpretations of China's identity and positioning in the WTO, it is difficult to pin down its overall role in global trade governance. China's economic structure raises a number of unique legal and political issues, leading some to conclude that 'the rise of China presents a major challenge to the multilateral trade regime'[76]. However, China's behaviour since joining the WTO has not been consistent with that of a power-hungry 'international scofflaw'[77]. In fact, Scott and Wilkinson find that, during its

72. Quote of Wen Jiaboa in Burnay, M. and Wouters, J., "The EU and China in the WTO: What Contribution to the International Rule of Law? Reflections in Light of the Raw Materials and Rare Earths Disputes" in Wang, J. and Song, W. (eds.), *China, the European Union, and the International Politics of Global Governance*. New York: Palgrave Macmillan, 2016, p. 131.
73. Pu, X., "Controversial Identity of a Rising China", *The Chinese Journal of International Politics*, vol. 10, n. 2, 2017, pp. 131-149.
74. United States Trade Representative, "2018 Report to Congress on China's WTO Compliance", *Office of the United States Trade Representative*, February 2019, retrieved from *https://ustr.gov/sites/ default/files/2018-USTR-Report-to-Congress-on- China%27s-WTO-Compliance.pdf*
75. European Commission, "EU-China — A Strategic Outlook", *op. cit.*, p. 1 and 6.
76. Wu, M., "The China, Inc. Challenge to Global Trade Governance", *Harvard International Law Journal*, vol. 57, n. 2, 2016, pp, 261-324.
77. Webster, T., "China's Implementation of WTO Decisions" in Toohey, L., Picker, C. B., and Greenacre (eds.), *China in the International Economic Order. New Directions and Changing Paradigms*. Cambridge: Cambridge University Press, 2015, p. 98.

first decade of WTO membership, China 'has consistently demonstrated a stubborn commitment to the preservation of the status quo'[78]. Webster shows that China has a strong record of implementing WTO rulings, even compared to the EU, which has delayed or resisted compliance in a number of disputes[79]. Although China is becoming a more self-confident and assertive player, it has a strong stake in maintaining the system, leaving ample room for cooperation with the EU, in particular in light of Trump's repeated attacks against the WTO.

2. THE BELT AND ROAD INITIATIVE AND CHINESE FDI IN EUROPE

Since it was first announced in 2013, China's Belt and Road initiative (BRI) has garnered widespread attention around the world. Xi Jinping has hailed BRI as a 'new model of win-win cooperation' that promises to forge 'a big family of harmonious co-existence' by scaling up connectivity on a trans-continental scale[80]. Outside of China, BRI has been greeted with a mix of excitement, suspicion, and confusion. Conceived as a contemporary re-imagination of the historic Silk Road, BRI is a massive infrastructure investment scheme across Eurasia, made up of two components: an overland route (the 'belt') and a maritime route (the 'road') that together connect China with more than 70 countries across Asia, Europe, and Africa. Although estimates on total investments vary considerably, it is widely expected that BRI will cost more than 1 trillion USD[81]. Projects supported under BRI range from the construction of ports, roads and railways to the development of power plants, pipelines or fibre-optic connections. Flagship initiatives in Europe include the upgrade of the Piraeus port in Greece and the refurbishment of the Budapest-Belgrade railway. Many EU members are also indirectly engaging with BRI through participation in the AIIB, which is not an official BRI institution but key to financing projects under the initiative[82].

78. Scott, J. and Wilkinson, R., "China as a System Preserving Power in the WTO", *op. cit.*, p. 214.
79. Webster, T., "China's Implementation of WTO Decisions", *op. cit.*
80. Jinping, X., Full text of President Xi's speech at opening of Belt and Road fórum, *Xinhua*, 14 May 2017, retrieved from *http://www.xinhuanet.com/english/2017-05/14/c_136282982.htm*
81. Chatzky, A. and McBride, J., *China's Massive Belt and Road Initiative*. CFR Backgrounder. New York: Council on Foreign Relations, 2019, retrieved from *https://www.cfr.org/backgrounder/chinas-massive-belt-and-road-initiative*
82. Wang, X. and Ruet, J., *One Belt One Road and the Reconguration of China-EU Relations*, CEPN Working Paper N.º 2017-04. Paris: Centre d'Économie de l'Université Paris-Nord, 2017, retrieved from *https://hal.archives-ouvertes.fr/hal-01499020/document*

BRI has become a centrepiece of China's foreign policy but its exact meaning remains elusive and contemplates that 'BRI may be the most talked about and least defined buzzword of this decade'[83]. There remains substantial disagreement about the initiative's scope, ambition and conceptual boundaries within both Chinese and Western scholarly, policy and media discourses. Some see BRI primarily as a regional investment strategy that is largely a reflection of domestic concerns, in particular the need to ensure continued economic growth through capital exports and the development of new external markets. Others maintain that BRI is a new grand strategy for China's rise that promotes an alternative model of global governance, directly challenging the existing liberal international order[84]. Although the extent and intent of BRI remains ambiguous, it is clear that it has both material and normative elements, with 'connectivity' referring not just to the 'hardware' of physical infrastructure but also to the 'software' of the ideas, norms and rules that shape the global order[85].

In the EU, engagement with BRI varies significantly between and within member states and sectors[86]. While some see it as a potential threat to European competitiveness, security, identity and internal cohesion, others have embraced the initiative enthusiastically. To the consternation of some, the Czech president, Milos Zeman, has declared his country's ambition to be China's "unsinkable aircraft-carrier" in Europe[87]. Italy has become the first G7 country to formally endorse the BRI global investment drive, provoking rebukes from Washington and Brussels[88]. The EU as a bloc has taken a cautious approach. It

83. Ang, Y. Y., "Demystifying Belt and Road. The Struggle to Define China's "Project of the Century"", *Foreign Affairs,* 2019, retrieved from *https://www.foreignaffairs.com/articles/china/2019-05-22/ demystifying-belt-and-road.*

84. Reeves, J., "Origins, Intentions, and Security Implications of Xi Jinping's Belt and Road Initiative" in Ganguly, S., Scobell, A. and Liow, J. C. (eds.), *The Routledge Handbook of Asian Security Studies.* London: Routledge, 2018.

85. Callahan, W. A., "China's 'Asia Dream: The Belt Road Initiative and the New Regional Order'". *Asia Journal of Comparative Politics,* vol. 1, n. 3, 2016, pp. 226-243; Dave, B. and Kobayashi, Y., "China's Silk Road Economic Belt Initiative in Central Asia: Economic and Security Implications", *Asia Europe Journal,* vol. 16, 2018, pp. 267-281.

86. Wang, X. and Ruet, J., *One Belt One Road and the Reconguration of China-EU Relations, op. cit.*

87. Quote of Milos Zeman in Barboza, D., Santora, M. and Stevenson, A., "China Seeks Influence in Europe, One Business Deal at a Time", *New York Times,* 12 August 2018, retrieved from *https://www.nytimes.com/2018/08/12/business/china-influence-europe-czech-republic.html*

88. Ghiglione, D., Sevastopulo, D., Peel, M. and Hornby, L., "Italy set to formally endorse China's Belt and Road Initiative", *Financial Times,* 6 March 2019, retrieved from *https://www.ft.com/content/17f91d24-3f60-11e9-b896-fe36ec32aece*

has sought to increase dialogue and cooperation, including through the EU-China Connectivity Platform which aims to strengthen synergies between BRI and European connectivity initiatives such as the Trans- European Transport Network policy[89]. At the same time, it has repeatedly voiced concern over the lack of guarantees on transparency, sustainability and fair competition for BRI projects[90]. The Budapest-Belgrade railway, for example, came under scrutiny by the European Commission for failing to comply with EU tender regulations, reinforcing concerns that BRI could dilute European standards and pose a challenge to the EU's rule-setting power[91].

The discussion on BRI also feeds into broader concerns about the growing presence of Chinese companies and investments in Europe, in particularly in the years following the financial crisis, which saw Chinese FDI jump from 700 million EUR in 2008 to 35 billion EUR in 2016[92]. While investments have traditionally targeted countries such as the UK, Germany and France, more recently, China has shown an increasing interest in Eastern, Central and Southern European countries[93]. An important vehicle in this regard is the 16+1 cooperation framework which aims to strengthen China's linkages with 11 EU member states in Central and Eastern Europe and five Western Balkan states.

China's engagement with the 16+1 group and states such as Greece or Italy has raised concerns in Brussels, with some accusing China of 'debt trapping' targeted states and deploying 'divide and rule' tactics to weaken European cohesion. The fact that, in recent years, Hungary and Greece have refused to support some EU statements on critical issues, such as China's human rights record or the South China Sea dispute, has reinforced these fears[94]. China's ambitious international investment drive also throws into

89. European Council, *EU-China Summit Joint Statement, op. cit.*
90. Rolland, N., "Beijing's Response to the Belt and Road Initiative's 'Pushback': A Story of Assessment and Adaptation", *Asian Affairs*, vol. 50, n. 2, 2019, pp. 216-235.
91. Kynge, J., Beesley, A. and Byrne, A., "EU sets collision course with China over 'Silk Road' rail Project", *The Financial Times*, 20 February 2017, retrieved from *https://www.ft.com/content/003bad14-f52f-11e6-95ee-f14e55513608*
92. Hanemann, T. and Huotari, M., *EU-China FDI: Working Towards Reciprocity in Investment Relations*, MERICS Papers on China, Berlin: Rhodium Group and Mercator Institute for China Studies, 2018, retrieved from *https://www.merics.org/sites/default/files/2018-08/180723_MERICS-COFDI- Update_final.pdf*
93. Wang, X. and Ruet, J., *One Belt One Road and the Reconguration of China-EU Relations, op. cit.*
94. Benner, T. and Weidenfeld, J., "Europe, don't let China divide and conquer", *Politico*, 19 March 2018, retrieved from *https://www.politico.eu/article/europe-china-divide-and-conquer/*

sharp relief the lacklustre performance of the European Investment Bank (EIB) and the European Bank of Reconstruction and Development (EBRD) in jump-starting research and development within and beyond the union. Observers criticise the EU for being overly focused on reducing deficits, including in countries such as Germany which have ample scope to expand investment[95]. Such criticism chimes with the sentiment still expressed among some Eastern and Central European members that they remain 'second class' EU countries[96]. The EU still appears to be reluctant to mobilise the kind of resources that may be required to help 'win the peace'[97].

Assuming a defensive posture, growing unease over Chinese FDI in Europe and its political, economic and security implications has led the EU to adopt counter measures such as the new framework for FDI screening which entered into force in April 2018 and establishes an EU-wide system to enable member states and the Commission 'to exchange information and raise concerns related to specific investments'[98]. While in principle not targeted at a specific country, the mechanism is widely seen as directed against China and it is estimated that over 80% of Chinese M&A transactions in Europe could fall under it[99]. Interestingly, BRI also seems to have prompted the EU to recalibrate its own vision of connectivity. In September 2018, the EU released a joint communication that provides building blocks for a new strategy on connecting Europe and Asia. Although the document does not mention BRI, its promotion of a European brand of 'sustainable, comprehensive and rules-based connectivity' appears to be directly juxtaposed to the Chinese vision of connectivity under BRI[100].

---

95. Financial Times Editorial Board, "The EU should not slide into protectionism towards China", *Financial Times*, 8 April 2019, retrieved from *https://www.ft.com/content/688348c4-59f4-11e9-9dde-7aedca0a081a*
96. Zalan, E., "Eastern Europe warns against EU 'disintegration'", *EUObserver*, 2 March 2017, retrieved from https: / /euobserver.com / news / 137089
97. Buti, M., *The New Global Economic Governance: Can Europe Help Win the Peace?*, European Commission, 2017, retrieved from *https://ec.europa.eu/info/sites/info/files/economy-finance/marco-buti-the- new-global-economic-governance.pdf*
98. European Commission, *EU foreign investment screening regulation enters into force.* European Commission Press Office, 2019, retrieved from *europa.eu/rapid/press- release_IP-19-2088_en.htm*
99. Hanemann, T., Huotari, M. and Kratz, A., *Chinese FDI in Europe: 2018 Trends and Impact of New Screening Policies*, MERICS Papers on China. Berlin: Rhodium Group and Mercator Institute for China Studies, 2019, retrieved from *https://www.merics.org/sites/default/files/2019-03/190311_MERICS-Rhodium%20Group_COFDI-Update_2019.pdf*
100. European Commission, *Connecting Europe and Asia — Building blocks for an EU Strategy*, Joint Communication to the European Parliament, the Council, the European Economic and Social Committee, the Committee of the Regions and the European Investment

For global governance scholars, BRI raises a number of broader questions: Is BRI 'changing the rules of globalization' or is it old wine in new bottles?[101] Is it indicative of a broader shift towards mega-regionalism or mega-regulation? How is BRI tied up in China's identity and normative agenda? What are its implications for European identity and actorness on the global stage? What does *connectivity* actually mean and can it be usefully theorised in global governance? Evidently, these questions cannot be addressed without looking at both the 'hardware' (material) and the 'software' (normative) dimensions of BRI.

3. DISCUSSION

Contestation between China and the EU in global economic governance plays out in a variety of complex ways. The discussion about China's status in theWTO, for example, has not just practical but also important legal, symbolic and political dimensions and it epitomises China's multiple, and sometimes conflicting, interests and identities in global economic governance. Meanwhile, the difficulties of the EU to find a common response to BRI reflects its own internal divisions as well as a substantial amount of confusion about China's ultimate agenda.

As the case studies above suggest, static and binary accounts of China's role as either 'revisionist' or 'status- quo' fail to capture the more complex ways in which China engages with an evolving global order[102]. As China (re-)negotiates its place in global economic governance, it takes on different roles —as rule-taker, rule-shaker and, increasingly, rule-maker— opening up new areas for contestation as well as opportunities for collaboration. China's participation in the WTO suggests that it has indeed been socialised into the multilateral trading system but not necessarily as expected: It has largely embraced and complied with existing procedures and rules but without fully liberalising its economy, leading some to argue that 'China has been

Bank, 2018, retrieved from *https://eeas.europa.eu/sites/eeas/files/joint_communication_-_connecting_europe_and_asia_-_ building_blocks_for_an_eu_strategy_2018-09-19.pdf*

101. Zhang, W., Alon, I. and Lattemann, C., *China's Belt and Road Initiative. Changing the Rules of Globalization*, London: Palgrave Macmillan, 2018.
102. Hurrell, A. and Loke, B., *Emerging Powers and Global Order: Much Ado About Nothing?*, PRIMO Working Paper No. 14, Hamburg: PRIMO (Power and Region in a Multipolar Order), University of Hamburg, 2017, retrieved from *https://ore.exeter.ac.uk/repository/handle/10871/33430*; Hameiri, S. and Zeng, J., "State Transformation and China's Engagement in Global Governance: the Case of Nuclear Technologies", *The Pacific Review*, 2019, pp. 1-31.

undermining the principles of open trade even while observing the letter of the law'[103].

BRI provides a fascinating example of how China is increasingly reshaping global economic governance 'from the outside', shifting the discourse from how established powers such as the EU are socialising China into the international community to how 'China is changing us'[104]. As the EU takes a more self- confident and assertive stance towards China, this could sharpen internal divisions even further —or it could strengthen European identity and provide more clarity on the EU's own role in global economic governance.

IV. CONCLUSION: *QUO VADIS* GLOBAL GOVERNANCE?

Global governance scholarship has been criticised by some for '[assuming] globality where there is none' and 'portraying efforts at transboundary regulation as essentially "post-political"'[105]. In a practical sense, the growing engagement of China and other emerging states in global governance has made it more global — the rules of the game are no longer decided by an exclusive club of Western countries. But it has also highlighted the parallel existence of multiple 'globalities', exposing different views on what the global is and how it should be managed. In light of these differences, deciding collective goals and rules is not (and never was) an apolitical, consensual exercise.

It is important to clarify that while contestation is an inherent part of global governance, it does not necessitate conflict. The relationship between China and the EU in global economic governance is driven by both divergent and overlapping interests and goals. In some cases, further cooperation might be stymied by mistrust and misunderstanding rather than conflicting priorities. In other cases, contestation might be driven by norms, values, cultural differences and diverging definitions of global governance.

103. McBride, J. and Chatzky, A., *Is 'Made in China 2025' a Threat to Global Trade?*, CFR Backgrounder, New York: Council on Foreign Relations, 2019, retrieved from *https://www.cfr.org/backgrounder/ made-china-2025-threat-global-trade*

104. Quote of Michael Clauss, German ambassador to the EU in Valero, J., "German ambassador to the EU: 'China is changing us'", *Euractiv*, 12 July 2019, retrieved from *https://www.euractiv.com/section/economy-jobs/news/german-ambassador-to-the-eu-china-is-changing-us/*

105. Dingwerth, K. and Pattberg, P., "How Global and Why Governance? Blind Spots and Ambivalences of the Global Governance Concept", *International Studies Review*, vol. 12, n. 4, 2010, pp. 696-719, p. 702.

Understanding the sources, dynamics and effects of contestation is key to developing global governance solutions that are seen as more legitimate and are more effective in the sense that they motivate compliance and do 'not encounter too much resistance'[106]. Thus, a concern for contestation responds directly to the pressing challenge which global governance must respond to: how to accelerate learning from what works to facilitate collective action on global public goods challenges at unprecedented scale?

Going forward, global governance scholars have much to gain from developing a better understanding of what drives contestation and resistance to global governance solutions on the domestic level. The rise of national-populist, anti-globalist parties and movements in the EU and elsewhere has prompted researchers to pay more attention to what global governance looks like 'from the perspective of those on the bottom'[107]. This ontological shift is to be welcomed. However, it does beg the question as to why mainstream IR scholarship for so long has arbitrarily segmented the international from the domestic, hampering efforts to engage questions of multi-level governance and compliance. In China, domestic resistance to its growing global engagement is less pronounced and more difficult to assess but not inconsequential. For example, as Rolland notes, there is evidence of growing unease about BRI and its economic risks among some public intellectuals in China[108].

As national decision-making authority has become increasingly fragmented, domestic contestation may also arise between different state agencies that engage in negotiating global goals and policies as well as between national level policy makers and the 'street level bureaucrats' who ultimately implement these policies and who often have a substantial degree of discretion in the execution of their work[109]. In the multilevel governance system of the EU, these dynamics have long been acknowledged. China, however, has traditionally been seen as a unitary actor with a centralised, hierarchical and authoritarian political architecture that leaves little room for internal contestation. Recent scholarship has challenged that view,

106. Acharya, A., *Understanding the Emerging Multiplex World Order*, Interview with Professor Amitav Acharya. UCL Global Governance Institute, 2019, retrieved from *https://www.ucl.ac.uk/global-governance/news/2019/jul/understanding-emerging-multiplex-world-order*
107. Hurd, I., "Legitimacy and contestation in global governance: Revisiting the folk theory of international institutions", *The Review of International Organizations*, 2018, pp. 1-13.
108. Rolland, N., "Beijing's Response to the Belt and Road Initiative's 'Pushback' [...]", *op. cit.*
109. Lipsky, *Street-level Bureaucracy: Dilemmas of the Individual in Public Services*, New York: Russell Sage Foundation, 1980.

arguing that 'the uneven transformation — fragmentation, decentralisation and internationalisation — of state apparatuses' in China has resulted in conflict and coordination problems between different domestic agencies, with implications for global governance[110]. As Hurrell urges us, we must take 'the power of the global' seriously[111]. Grappling more fully with a globalised governance reality directs our attention to perhaps *the* crucial site of intervention, contestation and compliance: where supranational regulatory structures intersect with power relations within recipient states and societies.

110. Hameiri, S. and Zeng, J., "State Transformation and China's Engagement [...]", *op. cit.*, p. 3.
111. Hurrell, A., *Can the Study of Global Order Be De-centred?*, PRIMO Working Paper n. 2, Hamburg: PRIMO (Power and Region in a Multipolar Order), University of Hamburg, 2015, retrieved from *http://www.primo-itn.eu/PRIMO/wp-content/uploads/2015/07/WorkingPaper-2_Andrew- Hurrell.pdf*

European Union and China relations: Between a Strategic Autonomy Based on Values and a Necessary Global Agenda of Shared Interests

CARLOS URIARTE SÁNCHEZ
Lecturer of Constitutional Law, Faculty of Law and Political Science, Rey Juan Carlos University of Madrid

I. INTRODUCTION

The European Union-China´s diplomatic relations were formally settled in 1975. Following the violent crushing of the Tiananmen Square protests by military forces in 1989, which provoked the suspension of all type of diplomatic relations. The EU did not recover relations until 1994, however, the arms embargo it imposed in 1989 remains in place.

The growing economic and geopolitical interdependence between the EU and China is reflected in the **joint EU-China 2020 Strategic Agenda for Cooperation**. China is an essential economic partner and key partner cooperating on global issues, whether The EU remains China's biggest trading partner, while China is the EU's second largest trading partner.

China is an economic competitor and even a systemic rival with its rising political influence reshaping international governance structures. China's Silk Road initiatives are reaching every corner of the globe, promoting globalization with Chinese characteristics.

The EU's approach towards China was set out in a Strategy adopted in 2016 and updated in March 2019 in a Joint Communication of the European Commission and the High Representative. The balance of challenges and opportunities presented by China has shifted over time. For the EU, China is simultaneously (in different policy areas) a cooperation partner, a negotiation partner, an economic competitor, and a systemic rival. The EU pursues realistic, effective, and coherent engagement with China, based on European values and interests.

The 22nd EU-China Summit on June 22nd, 2020, held by videoconference, was overshadowed by the continuing COVID-19 crisis and by growing disagreements and serious strains on bilateral relations.

China firmly opposes any outside 'interference' in its internal affairs, including on human rights. During the 22nd EU-China Summit in June 2020, the EU underlined its expectation that the next Human Rights Dialogue will take place in China once the COVID-19 restrictions have been eased. However, a landmark agreement protecting European Geographical Indications was signed on September 14th, 2020, guaranteeing a high level of protection.

Additionally, on December 30t, 2020, EU and China announced the accomplishment of a long-awaited EU-China Comprehensive Agreement on Investment (EU-China CAI), in a move to open more investment opportunities between both economies. The political agreement must be ratified by the European Parliament.

We will analyze how the European Union is developing a policy towards China based on values and interests. For this we will analyze the different milestones and documents mentioned above. We will see some of the difficulties faced by these relationships and we will highlight some of the fields in which the development of these relationships is more necessary today than ever. Still the field of cooperation is vast and without renouncing our principles and values: dialogue, respect, and mutual knowledge, but also the rule of law must guide our common future.

II. EU-CHINA STRATEGIC RELATION

The strategic partnership with China has evolved into a complex relationship. China is a fundamental economic partner and a key associate who cooperates in the most important global issues as climate change, the global economic recovery, the pandemics, the threats to regional security and the digital legislation and rules.

China is an economic competitor and even a potential rival because of its growing political influence why is reconfiguring international governance structures. Initiatives related to China's Silk Road are reaching every corner of the world and thus promoting globalization with Chinese characteristics, such as non-transparent procurement and Chinese labour standards and debt policies. China aspires to become the world leader in high-tech industries and digital technologies, particularly artificial intelligence and 5G. It has its own investigative capacity, but often uses cyber-espionage to access technologies, as Parliament noted in a set of *memorandums* in its Resolution of 12 March 2019, with a particular concern on security threats related to China's growing technological presence in the environment of the Union, and additionally, possible actions to counteract Chinese influence in the area. The People's Republic of China has systematically developed thereto influence strategies through disinformation campaigns.

Also, with the rise of China's political and economic powers and military capability, the country has been violating Taiwan's waters and airspace, as well as building artificial land and building military facilities in the South China Sea, ignoring the 2016 Permanent Court of Arbitration ruling.

The twenty-second EU-China Summit, held on June 22nd, 2020, via online conference, was overshadowed by the persistent COVID-19 crisis that originated rising disagreements and serious tensions in bilateral relations. The European Union, however, has among its priorities to call on China in order to put pression on the Asian power to take greater responsibility for addressing global challenges through the rules-based international order, the promotion of international peace and security, and adherence to international standards. Leaders stressed that the substantive debate on new digital technologies must be paired with respect for human rights and data protection. The Union also raised unresolved issues in relation to cybersecurity and misinformation. In the context of the COVID-19 pandemic, the Union reiterated the shared responsibility for participating in global initiatives to stop the spread of the virus and promote research on treatments and vaccines and stressed the need for solidarity to address the consequences in developing countries, in particular with regard to debt relief.

At the end of the Summit, President Michel and President Von der Leyen noted with particular emphasis the lack of sufficient progress, imbalances as well as the lack of reciprocity in different areas, particularly in the trade and investment relationship that the European members suffer when connecting with the Asian market.

Negotiations are still ongoing with a view to a comprehensive and ambitious bilateral investment agreement, the *Comprehensive Agreement on Investment*, aimed at establishing a level playing field for businesses, providing new market opportunities to protect investors and their investments, and by then making it possible for both sides to produce broader initiatives. The objective remains to reach political agreement by the end of 2020, but the European Union believes that China is not enough ambitious yet. But more importantly for the EU is to reach an accord in which China would compromise itself to make real and sustainable commitments over time, specially concerning the behaviour of public enterprises, the transparency of subsidies and the issue of forced transfers of technology, that in the recent years have been under suspect of sensible information theft. The EU has concluded that solutions are needed to face China's overwhelming capacity to monopoly certain strategic sectors, even if there are no ongoing negotiations on these issues. For example, in the steel and metals sectors; and with respect to high technology in particular, where the Xi Jinping administration has become the leading supplier and the main producer of these type of components at global level, due to the relocation of production chain since the early years of the XXI century, that is executed almost entirely in the Chinese factories.

Nevertheless, China has surpassed the European Union in terms of active population and also with the constant growth of its annual GDP which in 2019 reached the figure of $14.4 Billion in 2019 representing the 16% of the world total, compared to the $18.7 Billion generated by the Euro Zone in that same year which represents the 21% of the world total GDP according to official statistics. In addition, among the members of the UN Security Council are China, France, and Great Britain, despite the rupture caused by the *Brexit*, still considered an important European actor. However, and done the proactivity to negotiate and establish diplomatic relations, we perceive a tangible approaching of the postures, despite the fact that both China and the EU are important poles in terms of economy, and international standing.

Nowadays, in pure commercial and financial terms, the European Union remains China's main trading partner, while China is the Union's second largest trading partner, as confirmed by data provided on the European Parliament official site[1]. This body ensures that trade in goods between the Union and China worth more than EUR 1.5 billion per day. In 2019, the EU made exports to China Worthing EUR 198 billion and China introduced imports in the European market with value of EUR 362 billion, representing for the Union a huge trade deficit that must be monitored. Although each year the forecasts expressed by the senior representatives of both economic powers augur an increase in trade, as well as an increase in the total value of trade, stressing the importance of maintaining good diplomatic relations between

1. Soutullo, J., Cantell, S., Gazzina, S., *Asia Oriental. Fichas temáticas sobre la Unión Europea*, European Parliament Official Site (2020), retrieved from *https://www.europarl.europa.eu/factsheets/es/sheet/182/asia-oriental. Spanish language.*

the European Union and its most important partner from the Far East. That is the importance of the Euro-Chinese negotiations, in order to define the conditions for trade which subjects the union to the claims of the Asian giant, which still fails to comply with many aspects of the Free Trade Agreements.

III. EU-CHINA CONNECTIONS

In the political scenario, the EU-China connections date back to 1975 when the first diplomatic relations were established, and since that point the relations and agreements in a multitude of issues have been constant. A prove of it is the increasing development of agreements which had the beginning with the creation of the EU-China Comprehensive Strategic Partnership in 2003 in particular, deepening a broad contact which has led to a cooperation in a wide range of areas. This initiative led to the creation of more than 70 consultation and dialogue mechanisms covering areas such as politics, economics, trade, culture, science and technology, energy, environment, among many others.

At an event organized by the Chinese Chair in Spain, titled *INTERNATIONAL DEBATE: "China and the Western countries face each other: Rivalry or Cooperation"*[2] on October 21st, 2020, where the Minister Counsellor of the Embassy of the People's Republic of China in Spain, Yao Fei gave a speech in which outstands the conciliatory nature of the negotiations between the two crucial players within global policy. He expressed that, following this aim of dialogue, many contacts have been registered with fluency during these past years in the high spheres. To add some examples of this tendency: in September 2020, the virtual meeting of leaders from China Germany and the European Union took place, sending positive signals of a deeper EU-China cooperate on, and also developing a Comprehensive Strategic Partnership most influential in the post-pandemic era.

In accordance with the words of the Minister Counsellor, both sides have reaffirmed concluding the investment agreement negotiations, thus contributing to the economic recovery after the health crisis. Both sides have agreed to establish high-level dialogues on environmental, climate and digital issues, with a view to establishing a China-EU and the China-EU Digital Cooperation Association. The priority objectives for both administrations can be resumed in the following statements:

---

2. Conclusions from the International Debate: "China y Occidente frente a frente: rivalidad o cooperación", Cátedra China with The International Schiller Institute, 21 October 2020. More information *at https://shoutout.wix.com/so/c0NKhPDCf?cid=00000000-0000-0000-0000-000000000000#/main*

1) China and the European Union must jointly combat the pandemic, strengthen cooperation in the supply of health products, vaccines and medicines development and manufacturing, support the World Health Organization and develop a multilateral cooperation with the African continent in the face of the pandemic.

2) China and the EU must move forward together in economic revitalization, recover the exchange of people correctly, facilitate the movement of goods and maintain the stability of international industry and securities chains.

3) China must together defend justice, the world order, and the free trade system, intensify communication and coordination in important regional and international affairs, with a view to implementing multilateralism.

IV. INTERNATIONAL SPHERE CONTEXT

China and the US are on the international board, but both advocates of multilateralism, economic globalization and trade liberalization, support reforms within the UN, which they must play a greater role in international governance. opposing the capricious use of force. attach paramount importance to climate change, poverty eradication, counterterrorism, defence of public health security, and the achievement of the UN's 2030 Sustainable Development Agenda. Strengthening international cooperation between China and the EU promotes resolving many important issues, defending the peace and stability of the world, and fostering common development and prosperity.

— The EU watches China from a rising scepticism:

However, not everything is simple in this relationship: in March 2019, in the report on the *strategic perspective of the EU-China relationship*, the European body defined China as a partner to cooperate and negotiate, but at the same time an economic competitor in the pursuit of technological leadership and a systemic rival that promotes alternative models of governance. The EU should not get caught up in the bipolarity seen as it approaches China, as many diplomatic experts point out. *"We have recently learned that the EU and the US are preparing a dialogue on policy towards China. We all hope that this dialogue with a sensible and correct manner in behalf China and not the other way around"*, Yao Fei declared. According to the opinion of some analysts, the adjustment of policy towards China has highlighted the European Union's concern at China's rapid growth, a growing competitiveness both economic and technological, although we must not forget that the Chinese model also presents values and a democratic system totally at the same time as that of the West.

— Chinese approach to the political dialogue EU-China:

But How China sees its relationship with the EU? In Words of the aforementioned Minister Counsellor, Yao Fei, *"in China's view, the perspective of being a partner and a rival at the same time are contradictory, as it is impossible to be partners and at the same time to be rivals. It is understandable that there are competitions and different opinions among the partners, but the differences must be properly resolved on the principle of mutual respect. both sides must adhere to peaceful coexistence, openness, cooperation, multilateralism and dialogue".*

Having all these concepts in mind, we all share the idea that the world of today is experiencing profound and complex changes, and the great multilateral institutions have been anticipating it and acting accordingly to establish more connections. Therefore, as well as important actors do in a multipolar world, the EU and China share responsibility for ***promoting peace, prosperity, and sustainable development*** in their spheres of influence, exercising their role of the most influential elements, geo-strategically speaking. They have agreed to continue consolidating and developing the strategic partnership to the benefit of both sides, based on the principles of equality, respect and trust promoted by the European Parliament. The EU, also reaffirms its respect for China's sovereignty and territorial integrity, trying to make relations closer. On its part, China is committed with the support to EU integration.

In that perspective, both sides jointly adopted the previously mentioned **EU-China 2020 Strategic Agenda for Cooperation**[3] published in 2013 in charge of the Delegation of the European Union to China. On this important document both representatives compromised to fully implement the *Strategic Agenda for Cooperation* through their annual Summit, which has the aim of providing strategic guidance to their relationship; through the three pillars directly addressed in the Summit:

- The annual High Level Strategic Dialogue.
- The annual High Level Economic and Trade Dialogue.
- And the bi-annual People-to-People Dialogue.

3. European Union, *EU-China 2020 Strategic Agenda for Cooperation*, Delegation of the European Union to the People's Republic of China (2013). Retrieved from *https://eeas.europa.eu/archives/docs/china/docs/eu-china_2020_strategic_agenda_en.pdf*

According to this strategic agenda, and with the aim of bringing positions closer, this *Agenda for Cooperation* was settled to be negotiated through regular meetings of counterparts and through their broad range of sectoral dialogues. Furthermore, the two sides in demonstration of their willpower to share perspectives, showed themselves committed to promote the EU-China Comprehensive strategic Partnership in the next decade.

Another aspect that both actors share is their common desire and will to protect, a common idea that both executives are decided to promote. The first pillar of this agenda is therefore achieve continental ***peace and security***, something that stands in strong contrast to the pressures that the government chaired by Xi Jinping has exerted in recent years, installing military structures and deploying a large number of naval military capability in Southeast Asia in order to maintain the peace of the area, although in all forums is perceived that its alleged intention is to ensure its presence in the area, challenging the traditional US presence in the area.

On the Strategic Plan outstands the importance of cultural diversity, that we can agree is growing rapidly, within an information society which is fast emerging, and this is a fact well-known by the governments specially referring to the capacity of controlling and monitoring the opinions of entire societies. However, the opinion of the European Union institutions is that countries are increasingly interdependent, with their interests more closely intertwined than ever before. On the other hand, the world is still far from being completely peaceful, due to economic interests and states that are still in a process of development, politically and social. With the spread of SARS-CoV-2 in the hole globe, a global financial crisis has had a far-reaching impact in every country, affecting all societies and living standards. Consequently, the imbalance in global development has widened. International and local conflicts keep breaking out worldwide. Conventional and non-conventional security issues are interwoven. However, peace, development, cooperation, and mutual benefit have become the trend of the times. And promoting multilateralism remains crucial to ensure effective, coordinated, and coherent responses to pressing global challenges. As important actors in a multipolar world, the EU and China have committed to enhance dialogue and coordination at bilateral, and intercontinental levels, to meet regional and global challenges together, but also work to make the international order and system fairer and equitable.

The second objective to overcome is the achievement of ***prosperity***, a theory that China has applied with prolific success since the deep reforms of Deng Xiaoping initiated in 1978, among which were included the de-collectivization of agriculture, China's opening up to foreign investors, and licensing to start private enterprises[4]. Executing a policy that also developed the shot down of the market abroad, especially in the field of exports. A long journey that only in recent decades has changed a mainly rural society into a technological and productive giant that is already beginning to put into check the hegemony of the United States, as we mentioned previously. Since 1980 to the present day, China is the country with the highest economic growth in the world with an average annual 10% increase with no stop, even in the last year of pandemic, with the restrictive measures applied by the Communist Party the crisis was rapidly controlled and that supposed an increasing of around a 5% of the economy when the rest of the countries were combatting the virus and trying to maintain themselves afloat.

But returning to the present momentum, the purpose of every proper government on Earth is the achievement of prosperity (with the exception of those countries governed by the military forces where the only aim is to subjugate their people to obtain benefits). And this predisposition is obviously applicable to the European Union and China, the reaching of general wealth that permits an increasing of investment, which would suppose the improvement of the economy and retroactively the achievement of wealth by the citizens. Said this, both economic powers desire to collaborate with the objective of mutual prosperity: according to the **EU-China 2020 Strategic Agenda for Cooperation:**

> *"EU and China enjoy one of the world's biggest and most dynamic trading relationships. Their trade and investment exchanges have become a major engine driving their respective economic development and innovation. Both sides share responsibility for ensuring that their economies remain key drivers for global economic growth and providing prosperity for all. They are committed to build a world economy where all countries enjoy development and innovation, interconnected growth, interests converging, and firmly safeguarding and developing an open world economy. In that perspective, they are determined to enhance further their trade and investment relationship towards 2020 in a spirit of mutual benefit, by promoting open, transparent markets and a level-playing field".*

Following this line, there are many initiatives to achieve this aim, characterised by a set of topics to collaborate in, passing through *Trade & Investment, Industry & Information, Agriculture, or Transport & Infrastructure.*

4. Asociación para el Progreso de la Dirección (APD), *Evolución de la economía china: viaje al pasado para entender el presente,* Redacción APD, 14 March 2018. Retrieved from *https://www.apd.es/evolucion-economia-china-viaje-al-pasado-para-entender-el-presente/*

Furthermore, the third pillar of this collaboration is the ***sustainable development issue***, a matter in which the European Union has focused its attention concerning the high emissions per year produced by China, being a fundamental aspect of the Strategic Agenda which the continental forum has shown repeatedly its concern. According to the previous quoted ***2020 Agenda for Cooperation:*** "the EU and China face the common task of achieving innovative, inclusive and sustainable development. Addressing climate change, protecting the environment, promoting transparent international energy markets, and facilitating resource-efficient, far-reaching, socially inclusive and low-carbon development policies are high on the international action list". To contribute for the consecution of these perspectives of future, both executives are firmly engaged in the project of promote *emerging green sectors* which could contribute to sustainable growth of the global economy and also in the creation of new business opportunities for Chinese and European companies. The sustainable philosophy is a must in the European Agenda for the next decades, as well as a compromise acquired by the international community in the signing of the *2030 Sustainable Development Goals* in the Addis Abeba Convention, as we previously pointed out.

In consequence, the *"green growth"* should therefore become a key area of strategic and practical EU-China cooperation as it supposes an important quote of the negotiations between the two parties. The EU and China are committed to continue promoting cooperation on the environmental flagship initiatives developed respectively by China and the EU, with a view of maximising the mutual synergies between China's ecological civilization and the European Union's resource efficiency agenda. Both sides agree, in accordance with the compromises ratified, that innovation has an important contribution to make for the achievement of sustainable development, but also is important the perspective of an effective protection of Intellectual Property Rights, as it is crucial to support the effective development and also the deployment of innovative solutions which come essentially from emerging industries that are more than ever calling for social attention. In addition, in order to ensure sustainable development, a number of important social challenges need to be addressed, including social security and health care, high and quality employment and demographic ageing.

V. CURRENT SCENARIO AFTER COVID

China strongly opposes to any external "interference" on its domestic affairs, including human rights. During the twenty-second EU-China

Summit in June 2020, the European Union underlined its expectation that the forthcoming human rights dialogue will take place in China when COVID-19 restrictions would be relaxed in consequence to the overcoming of the pandemic crisis.

European Parliament is deeply concerned about the human rights situation in China, which has drawn the attention in a negative manner, because of the serious human rights violations committed by China, in particular arbitrary detention, labour camps, the death penalty that is still in force, problems related to freedoms of expression and association, forced abortions, and repressive policies in the Special Administrative Region of Hong Kong that we have observed during recent years with a political and military influence increasing every year, also concerning the interventions in Tibet and Xinjiang; with cases like the controversial death of *Li Wenliang* by the 7th February 2020. Essentially threatening the freedom that the citizens of these cities have enjoyed during the last decades, but specially worrying is the question of Hong Kong which plays an especially important role at the financial and of course commercial level in connecting many markets worldwide, moving tons of merchandise every year. And this ability to connect Southeast Asia is what China desperately craves, knowing that incorporating this strategic centre could be the ultimate move to achieve the role of world economic leader, which over the past few years is seen from different areas of international diplomacy as increasingly close and possible.

The European Parliament condemned China's suppression of political opposition and pro-democracy activists in Hong Kong (on its the National Security Act of the People's Republic of China for Hong Kong and the need for the Union to defend Hong Kong's high degree of autonomy[5]). Parliament has also expressed concern about Xinjiang in its Resolution of 19 December 2019 about the controversy generated around the situation of the Uighurs people in China and Tibet in its Resolution of 18 April 2019 on China, in particular the situation of religious and ethnic minorities.

In addition, the European Union is more than ever concerned about the Chinese citizens' demands for effective political reforms and in this manner has also condemned the treatment of various activists and human rights defenders.

---

5. European Parliament, *European Parliament resolution of 19 June 2020 on the PRC national security law for Hong Kong and the need for the EU to defend Kong Kong's high degree of autonomy (2020/2665(RSP))*. Retrieved from *https://www.europarl.europa.eu/doceo/document/TA-9-2020-0174_EN.html*

On this matter must be noted that the huge growth of Chinese power on multiple fronts (including technological, increasingly important) makes the imbalance even more scourge and obvious that the times when China could be treated as a developing country or condescending to the internal difficulties in its long-time advances should have gone down in history. Its expansive international policy in Asia and other continents (Africa, Latin America, among other areas) increases the importance of competitive distortions and maintaining the same playing field globally.

Nevertheless, considering all these differences between both executives, that understand and apply a contrary (mainly) civil legislation, are open to negotiation with conciliatory moves that suggest a friendly whether fruitful collaboration. The EU and China have become highly interdependent as a result these set of programs, being the most recent the one published the past 30 December in Brussels named the *Key elements of the EU-China Comprehensive Agreement on Investment,* a multilateral agreement which brought many controversy specially from the Washington Administration who were newly elected since the final tally of results of 13 November elections, that gave the head of state to the figure of Joe Biden, and this decision from Europe and China of agreeing an important project on investment was criticised from the North American Government as it leaved them aside, not waiting to the presidential inauguration on 20 January 2021.

This desire of the European Union to establish relations is also reflected on its strong interest in preserving multilateral relations with all its trade and geostrategic partners, maintaining a conciliatory and friendly character, in search of a mutual cooperation that is for sure beneficial for all parties. We have observed over the past few years how during the Trump administration all proposed agreements were systematically denied, and not only that, but also caused great tensions within the Union the protectionist attitude of the former president who decided to increase tariffs on foreign products, affecting European companies, and thus violating all treaties on international trade, a country that represents the EU's largest trading partner with exports in 2020 of $384,435 billion value. With the results of the new election, they have resulted in the election of Joe Robinette Biden Jr. as the new head of state. This could also help in the rapprochement with China as both positions have come substantially close. Is evident that Europe's priority now is to reach agreements with China that could favour the exchange of goods and services, as well as to ensure that the Asian country respects existing trade rules regarding free trade, the possibility of entry for European companies into the Chinese market, as well as the fight against unfair competition elements such as dumping.

VI. CONCLUSIONS

Done the previous facts, the near future of negotiations between the European Union, the world's biggest trading partner without forgetting its role as one of the most influential international actors, and in the other hand China, the world's biggest trading supplier and the major economic power in the next years, appears to be fructiferous considering the good relation between the representants of both international *role-players*, expressing on many occasions their will to negotiate, collaborate and trade but always with the proper conditions, a premise that the EU maintains inalterable, and fulfilling the compromises formalized in the different global forums. Some of them are the 2020 Strategic Plan that represents for sure a turning point in the relations and that will also determine the politics deployed by both actors in the next decades, also the European Commission, launched on March 12nd, 2019 its Joint Communication with a strategic perspective towards the relations with the Asian superpower, among other communications that express the desire from the EU and China to have a common responsibility for the advancing in global development.

We can all understand that it is logical for China to differ from the Union, due to differences in fields as important as their history, culture, traditions, and political and economic systems. But differences are not an obstacle, at least for the moment, for both sides to address global challenges together and achieve their further development.

The Central Asian Region: Between the BRI and the EU Connectivity Strategy

ANTONIO ALONSO MARCOS[1]
PhD on International Relations. Lecturer at San Pablo CEU University of Madrid

I. INTRODUCTION

In 2007, the EU approved a Strategy for Central Asia, which was renewed and refurbished in 2019 —with a two-years delay, as a new one was supposed to be adopted in 2017—. Meanwhile, the Chinese government adopted a new strategy to connect Chinese products with international markets by building terrestrial and maritime infrastructures. That strategy was announced for first time in Kazakhstan in 2013, highlighting the importance of that region for the then so-called One Belt One Road (OBOR) initiative, which was renamed as Belt and Road Initiative (BRI) in 2016.

Few years later, once began the New EU Strategy for Central Asia implementation, the EU institutions and member states realized that Chinese counterpart was changing the global market rules, leaving EU standards at a clear disadvantage. They also realized that the "Connecting Europe and Asia — Building blocks for an EU Strategy – Council conclusions, 13097/18" —adopted in October 2018—, it was almost outdated as the so

1. Antonio Alonso Marcos is a Senior Lecturer at the Universidad San Pablo CEU since 2007. The author holds a BA degree on Political Science and a PhD on the topic "The Islamist movement 'Hizb ut Tahrir' (HT) in Central Asia: a challenge to security and stability (1995-2007)". He is author of some books and articles on Islamism and Central Asia (post-soviet space), but also on issues regarding Contemporary History, International Relations and Security Studies. He participated as electoral observer, both as independent or under OSCE mandate, in Kazakhstan, Uzbekistan and Armenia. Antonio Alonso has done research under the Spanish Ministries of Defense and Foreign Affairs, apart from participating in research groups in UNISCI and CESEDEN. He is also foreign supervisor of some Central Asian PhD students and deliver seminars and conferences in institutions in Uzbekistan, Kazakhstan and Tajikistan.

called "EU Strategy on Connecting Europe and Asia" had been surpassed by the new situation created by the BRI.

A priori, both strategies are full of advantages for Central Asian countries because two external actors help them to break their endemic problem: they are landlocked countries, isolated from the rest of the global trade routes —and global markets, consequently—. Other foreign powers play a crucial role in the region, which needs to be taken into account in the analysis[2].

On the other hand, there are also some disadvantages in that cooperation. Not only the "debt trap", but also the way the Chinese government negotiated those agreements —bilaterally and on cheaper conditions— generated big concerns both in Brussels and in the EU member states capitals. What is behind the EU optimistic and confident attitude towards the Chinese strategy? How is the EU dealing with the problems created by the clash between those three different strategies —the Chinese BRI and the EU for Central Asia and Connecting Europe and Asia— and the Chinese *modus operandi* in Central Asia? What rules were implemented in Central Asia in terms of global governance, especially in the fields of investment, competition and market regulation? What role are the international institutions and forums born due to these strategies playing? What kind of conclusions can we deduce from the decisions adopted by Central Asian rulers?

II. A NATURAL COOPERATION

The geographical situation of this region between Europe and Asia makes it essential for the connectivity between the two continents. Since prehistorical times, nomadic peoples moved from one side to another crossing these territories; it is useful to remind that in Central Asia it is possible to find hostile landscapes —such as deserts and steppes—, but also human-friendly territories like fertile valleys, rivers and mountains full of forests.

Some centuries later, the Persians and the Greeks, crossed Eurasia from the West to the East, and even Nestorian missionaries got the current territory of China. Oriental peoples came to this region in their way to Europe, too. Mongols and Chinese emperors planted their seeds, left their heritage in these territories. I Their concept of border, demarcation or limit was completely different to ours; even nowadays, European concept of border is not exactly the same as the Central Asian one.

2. See Ministerio de Defensa de España, "Asia Central: de pivote a encrucijada", *Cuaderno de Estrategia IEEE*, N. 216 (2023), retrieved from *https://www.ieee.es/publicaciones-new/cuadernos-de-estrategia/2022/Cuaderno_216.html*

Of course, there were not only wars, but also trade. Samarkand and the cities created along the Silk Road are vivid witnesses of that. Their inhabitants were tolerant people, as they received influence form many cultural backgrounds; they were also multilingual, as they needed to exchange products. It is possible to affirm that the cooperation between the West and the East in that region is something completely natural, almost inscribed genetically in those peoples.

As stated in several documents, EU and China share common interests in Central Asian region: mainly, energy and security. They want to have a kind of cultural influence in the region, although avoiding the appearance of a neo-colonial power and keeping the prestige of "equal partners". Apart from having shared interests, the EU perception on Chinese presence in this region is problematic from Brusselian point of view: there is a lack of transparency, industrial policies and non-tariff measures discriminate against foreign companies, and Chinese government exercise a strong government intervention in the economy[3].

As seen in other free trade agreements, EU is worried about the lack of competence and the use —and abuse— of subsidies, as it makes the prices go down. This is valid not only for products, but also for tenders. Is possible to affirm that there is fair competition environment in Central Asia? Is possible to say that Chinese and European partners are competing under similar conditions? Are the Chinese playing with any kind of advantages such as the participation of state-owned companies or state-subsidize companies? Is there any link with the "debt trap" or with the fact that China is a debt holder of these countries' national debt[4]? Following a 2018 report, Tajikistan and Kyrgyzstan were the most vulnerable countries to this debt-trap[5]. It seems the situation remains the same or even has been worsened[6].

3. See Directorate-General for Trade of the European Commission, "EU trade relations with China. Facts, figures and latest developments", retrieved from *https://policy.trade.ec.europa.eu/eu-trade-relationships-country-and-region/countries-and-regions/china_en#:~:text=While%20China%20has%20made%20progress,government%20intervention%20in%20the%20economy*

4. See Buchholz, K., "The Countries Most in Debt to China", *Statista* (2023), retrieved from *https://www.statista.com/chart/19642/external-loan-debt-to-china-by-country/*

5. See Center for Global Development, "Examining the Debt Implications of the Belt and Road Initiative from a Policy Perspective", *CGD Policy Paper*, N. 121 (2018), retrieved from *https://www.cgdev.org/sites/default/files/examining-debt-implications-belt-and-road-initiative-policy-perspective.pdf*. See also Standish, R., "China's Belt and Road Grapples with Mounting Debt Crisis, Impacting Central Asia, Pakistan, and Beyond", *Radio Free Europe/Radio- Liberty* (2022), retrieved from *https://www.rferl.org/a/china-debt-crisis-belt-road-initiative-kyrgyzstan-pakistan-/31970756.html*

6. See Bhutia, S., "Data show Kyrgyzstan weathering debt load", *Eurasianet* (2019), retrieved from *https://eurasianet.org/data-show-kyrgyzstan-weathering-debt-load*. See also "Republic

On the other hand, while dealing with China, the EU —both EU institutions and Member States— try to be polite, avoiding talking about delicate issues and highlighting the progress made in several fields and calling to a deeper cooperation. What is behind the EU optimistic and confident attitude towards the Chinese strategy? Reading the last statements delivered by European leaders, it is possible to find sentences full of hope and respect there, due to the current global situation: the search of Russian isolation, because the Ukrainian war; the acknowledgement that China is the —next or current?— first economy in the world; the fear of an escalation of tensions with the USA for Taiwan; the necessity to re-establish the pre-pandemic consumption scheme.

III. THE NEW INTERNATIONAL FRAMEWORK

For a better understanding about the competition between China and the EU in Central Asia, it is necessary to consider some facts and drivers working in that region.

First and foremost, it is crucial to realize that these states gained their independence from the Soviet Union when it collapsed in 1991. Consequently, it is crucial to analyse the current Russian influence in that region. They are five countries, with five different developments of that relationship. Russia tried not to lose its influence there, although some countries felt better and safer far from Moscow; that goal was impossible in the case of Tajikistan, but accomplished completely in Turkmenistan —mainly, due to its neutrality policy—. The war in Ukraine has triggered some feelings and fears in the neighbouring countries, and while Tajikistan cannot avoid the Russian partnership —Tajik immigration to Russia, and the subsequent remittances, Russian market, security of their border, among other reasons—, Uzbekistan and Kazakhstan saw how thousands of Russians crossed their borders and established there —escaping from forced recruitment—, or receive thousands of tourists from the Russian Federation, and declared fear of further Russian invasions[7].

---

of Tajikistan: Staff Report for the 2022 Article IV Consultation — Debt Sustainability Analysis", International Monetary Fund (2023), retrieved from *https://www.elibrary.imf.org/view/journals/002/2023/125/article-A003-eN.xml?rskey=PH4ZgB&result=10*

7. As a kind of contradiction, all the five Central Asian leaders participated in 2023 in Moscow at the 9th of May celebration, the Victory Day, when Former Soviet Union countries commemorate the victory over Nazism in 1945. Only Armenia and Belarus joined them at this celebration, while the other seven former members of the Red Amy

Second, the declining of the USA as a global player and the emergence of China as a global supplier of goods and buyer of raw materials —sources of energy, included—. This picture can be seen also here, in Central Asia, where USA is demanding some changes in their legislation and policies —focusing on Human Rights—, while acknowledging the terrible mistake made in Afghanistan, not because the handing down of the power on the hands of the Taliban —something agreed and signed officially in 2020, and materialized in August 2021[8]—, but because the chaotic Western countries withdrawal. Only a small fistful of embassies remained open and not stormed in those days in Kabul, Russian and Chinese among them.

The emergency of China is undeniable. It has maintained a GDP interannual growth no lower than 6% during the first two decades of this century, while the highest was in 2006 (12.7%), moving from 1.3 billion euro in 2000 to 17.1 billion euro in 2022. Obviously, the impact of coronavirus was big (2.1% in 2020), as it was the Ukrainian war (3% in 2022). The last has interrupted the flow of goods from China to the European market; it is not a problem of lack of energy —now China is buying Russian hydrocarbons, even cheaper than before—, but a disruption in the supply chains and at the supply-demand dynamic.

The military expenditure is another indicator to check the growing influence and power of the People's Republic of China. According to the SIPRI, China spent 22,237 M US$ in 2000[9], while spent 291,958 M US$ in 2022. Even more interesting is checking the global military expenditure: the three big (56%) are USA (39%), China (13%) and Russia (3.9%), all of them permanent members of the UN Security Council and nuclear powers. To give more global context about the military expenditure:

> World military spending grew for the eighth consecutive year in 2022 to an all-time high of $2240 billion. By far the sharpest rise in spending (+13 per cent) was seen in Europe and was largely accounted for by Russian and Ukrainian spending. However, military aid to Ukraine and concerns about a heightened threat from Russia strongly influenced many other states' spending decisions, as did tensions in East Asia. [...] China remained the world's second largest military spender, allocating an estimated $292 billion in 2022. This was 4.2 per

avoided to be there or even prohibited to their population to celebrate it in their home countries —even if they were descendants of veterans—.

8. See United States of America, "Joint Declaration between the Islamic Republic of Afghanistan and the United States of America for Bringing Peace to Afghanistan", retrieved from *https://www.state.gov/wp-content/uploads/2020/02/02.29.20-US-Afghanistan-Joint-DeclaratioN.pdf*
9. Current US$. See *https://www.sipri.org/databases/milex*

cent more than in 2021 and 63 per cent more than in 2013. China's military expenditure has increased for 28 consecutive years[10].

Since the 1990's, China is gaining the first position as an important economic player[11]; accordingly, it is called to play a similar role as a global security provider[12]. Therefore, it needs to increase the military expenditure. Besides that, although some reports talked about the deficient quality of Chinese armament two decades ago, nowadays, the situation is completely different, and even the USA Pentagon recognized its superiority[13].

Although the USA has repeated several times that China is not a threat but a strategic competitor[14], the threat of the Thucydides trap is still active[15] and NATO is used to deter China[16] so that it cannot follow the path of

10. See Stockholm International Peace Research Institute, "World military expenditure reaches new record high as European spending surges", *SIPRI for the media* (2023), retrieved from *https://www.sipri.org/media/press-release/2023/world-military-expenditure-reaches-new-record-high-european-spending-surges#:~:text=World%20military%20spending%20grew%20for,time%20high%20of%20%242240%20billioN. See also Tian, Nan & alia: "Trends in World Military Expenditure", SIPRI, 2022, at https://www.sipri.org/sites/default/files/2023-04/2304_fs_milex_2022.pdf*. See also Tian, N. *et al.*, "Trends in World Military Expenditure, 2022", *SIPRI Fact Sheet* (2022), retrieved from *https://www.sipri.org/sites/default/files/2023-04/2304_fs_milex_2022.pdf*
11. "In the 1990's, China has the fastest growing economy in the world". See Kristof, N. D., "China Sees 'Market-Leninism' as Way to Future", *The New York Times* (1993), retrieved from *https://www.nytimes.com/1993/09/06/world/china-sees-market-leninism-as-way-to-future.html*. Picked up on Hung, M. and Herman, F., "China in Central Asia: Harmonizing Mackinder's Heartland", Education About Asia, Vol. 18, N. 3 (2013), retrieved from *https://www.asianstudies.org/publications/eaa/archives/china-in-central-asia-harmonizing-mackinders-heartland/*
12. In the last years, Chinese diplomacy has been involved in solving several longstanding conflicts in Africa and the Middle East, apart from offering a 12-Points Peace Roadmap for Ukraine.
13. See Ziezulewicz, G., "Pentagon: Yes, we are still lagging behind China's hypersonics", *Navy Times* (2023), retrieved from *https://www.navytimes.com/news/your-navy/2023/04/18/pentagon-yes-we-are-still-lagging-behind-chinas-hypersonics/*
14. For the USA, China is not a democracy and it is not in the path to transform into one of them: "Many non-democracies join the world's democracies in forswearing these behaviours. Unfortunately, Russia and the People's Republic of China (PRC) do not". See The White House, "National Security Strategy" (October 2022), retrieved from *https://www.whitehouse.gov/wp-content/uploads/2022/10/Biden-Harris-Administrations-National-Security-Strategy-10.2022.pdf*, p. 8.
15. See Allison, G., *Destined for War: can America and China escape Thucydides' Trap?*, Scribe, Melbourne 2018.
16. "Strategic competitors and potential adversaries are investing in technologies that could restrict our access and freedom to operate in space, degrade our space capabilities, target our civilian and military infrastructure, impair our defence and harm our

Russia[17] —its strategic partner, especially since 4th February 2022—. The EU, following these statements, also declared China as a partner, an economic competitor, but also as a systemic rival as the PRC has different principles and ideas over democracy and Human Rights[18].

Thirdly, the impact of the pandemic was catastrophic for Central Asian economies, too. It evidenced the extreme dependency on foreign trade, mainly imports of goods. In 2020, the GDP growth was really low: Kazakhstan (-2.6%), Kyrgyzstan (-8.6%), Tajikistan (4.4%), Turkmenistan (-2.9%), and Uzbekistan (2.0%). Once the gates of China have been reopened, a wave of hope flooded the region, as the January 2022 virtual summit and the off-line summit in Xian (18-19 May 2023)[19].

Because of the landscape described before, the world is witnessing the end of US hegemonial unipolarity and the beginning of a new multilateralism: while Western countries insist on using new expression —"rules based global order"—, the BRICS countries still employ the expression "International Law". The main difference among those two expressions is that the International

---

security". The term "strategic competitor" is used three times and is a euphemism to avoid the word "China" and "PRC" (used in total 10 times in 11 pages). See North Atlantic Treaty Organization, "NATO 2022 Strategic Concept", *NATO Summit* (June 2022), retrieved from *https://www.nato.int/nato_static_fl2014/assets/pdf/2022/6/pdf/290622-strategic-concept.pdf*

17. "Russia and the PRC pose different challenges. Russia poses an immediate threat to the free and open international system, recklessly flouting the basic laws of the international order today, as its brutal war of aggression against Ukraine has shown. The PRC, by contrast, is the only competitor with both the intent to reshape the international order and, increasingly, the economic, diplomatic, military, and technological power to advance that objective". See The White House, "National Security Strategy", *op. cit.*, pp. 8 and 23.
18. "China is, simultaneously, in different policy areas, a cooperation partner with whom the EU has closely aligned objectives, a negotiating partner with whom the EU needs to find a balance of interests, an economic competitor in the pursuit of technological leadership, and a systemic rival promoting alternative models of governance". See European Union, "Joint Communication to the European Parliament, the European Council and the Council EU-China — A strategic outlook", JOIN/2019/5 final, EUR-Lex (2019), retrieved from *https://eur-lex.europa.eu/legal-content/EN/ALL/?uri=CELEX%3A52019JC0005*, p. 1.
19. See Standish, R., "Visa-Free Travel, Investment, And Summits As 'New Era Of Cooperation' For China And Central Asia Is Heralded", *RadioFreeEurope/RadioLiberty* (2023), retrieved from *https://www.rferl.org/a/china-central-asia-visa-free-travel-investment/32405178.html*. Arziev, F., "After a decade of BRI, China-Central Asia Summit to start new chapter", *UZ Daily* (2023), retrieved from *https://www.uzdaily.uz/en/post/81011*

Law refers to the norms adopted by the international community at the United Nations and the other "global order" has been imposed by Western countries alone. The WTO rules are a vivid expression of that.

It seems the world is entering into a new phase and the rules of past decades are about to expire, starting from the unilateral sanctions adopted by some countries —USA, EU, South Korea, Switzerland, among others— against some Russian assets, and the diversion of those Russian frozen assets to Ukrainian budget. This topic is really interesting, as it endangers the trust and confidence needed to invest in another countries, or to buy US dollars or euro —or sovereign debt in those currencies—. Who is going to invest in Western countries? Who is going to trust on them? How can financial institutions assure foreign investors that their money, accounts, assets are going to be respected and not intervened, only in case they are involved in criminal allegations and only after a fair trial? If Chinese, Russian, Indian businesspeople are not going to invest in Western countries, maybe they will decide to do it in Central Asia.

Here it is possible to see a self-fulfilling prophecy: EU offers Central Asian countries a wide range of fields to cooperate and to invest, offering a non-exclusive partnership, but as a reaction to the Ukrainian war the EU is sanctioning Central Asian tycoons and companies, and warning Central Asian governments about circumventing EU sanctions against Russia[20], thus creating a kind of bipolar globalization with mutually exclusive spheres.

For better or worse, the Ukrainian war is triggering a set of dynamics that will endure for some decades[21]. And it seems that Chinese Government speakers lost their fear to speak aloud against the USA and criticize its foreign policy, pointing out their double standard discourse. In addition, there is a clear gambit to substitute the US dollar for the Chinese yuan in international

20. David O'Sullivan, the EU Envoy on Sanctions, visited Turkey, Uzbekistan and Kazakhstan by the end of April 2023. See Moens, B., Kijewski, L. and Lynch, S., "EU targets Central Asia in drive to stop sanctioned goods reaching Russia", *Politico* (2023), retrieved from *https://www.politico.eu/article/eu-aims-central-asia-sanction-circumvention-russia-war/*

21. For example, the Russian natural resources (hydrocarbons included) which cannot be sold to Western markets (European Union, USA, UK, but also Australia, Republic of Korea and Japan), now are sold to Asian and African markets, sold at a generous discount. This is one of the explanations for the increase of exchanges between Russia and China. See Devonshire-Ellis, C., "China, Russia Trade Turnover Grew 38.7% in Q1 2023", *China Briefing* (2023), retrieved from *https://www.china-briefing.com/news/china-russia-trade-turnover-grew-38-7-in-q1-2023/*. See also Black, J. S. and Morrison, A. J., "The Strategic Challenges of Decoupling", *The Magazine* (2021), retrieved from *https://hbr.org/2021/05/the-strategic-challenges-of-decoupling*

payments; once the American currency is overthrown as the most used for the international exchanges, what could happen to the US dollar? What would be its real value? Will it be accepted everywhere at any time forever?

IV. THE ROLE OF CHINA IN CENTRAL ASIA

Since 1991, the China's role in Central Asia has evolved from a good —passive and quiet— neighbour to a main investor, trade partner and security provider. Besides, China invests a huge amount of money to promote their culture and language, granting full scholarships to students from those countries every year.

The main pillars of the Chinese role in Central Asia are trade, the investment in infrastructures and national debt, and security. Commercial exchanges between them are completely normal, as they are neighbours and there were no big conflicts among them, which usually interrupts the continuous flow of human relations —such as a war, like in Nagorno-Karabakh—. In the last 25 years, the trade turnover between China and these countries has increased considerably. Besides, the Ukrainian war had another secondary effect —or collateral damage—: Russia's *Polymetal* abandoned the London Stock Exchange and moved to Astana Exchange, probably signalling a new dynamic and trend[22]. Furthermore, the interest of China on this region is not only the region itself, but they conceive Kazakhstan and Kyrgyzstan as the main gate to the Eurasian Economic Union (EAEU) —the free trade bloc that also includes Armenia, Belarus, and Russia—, although it is not so clear whether they have the intention to use this tool to circumvent the unilaterally-imposed Western sanctions or not. On the other hand, the Western countries' attitudes and decisions can be perceived as counterproductive and inconvenient for the rules based global order, more specifically regarding the freezing and confiscation of Russian assets; if they can use those assets freely, who is going to invest money in those countries? Who is going to send money to the banks established there?

What is undeniable is the fast growth of trade volume between China and Central Asia, as pointed out by Julien Vercueil:

> Since 2000, China's share in trade has grown rapidly and by now, China is Turkmenistan's first client (more than 80% of the latter's exports goes

22. See "Central Asian Stock Exchanges Preferred Over London", *Silk Road Briefing* (2023), retrieved from *https://www.silkroadbriefing.com/news/2023/05/11/central-asian-stock-exchanges-preferred-over-london/*

to China, being composed almost exclusively of natural gas), and the first supplier of Kyrgyzstan, Tajikistan (between 30 and 40% of its imports) and Uzbekistan (around one-fourth)[23].

Up to date, Kazakhstan is the most preferred Central Asian country for Chinese trade and investment. In 2021, the trade turnover was US$ 25.25 billion (17.6% higher than in 2020, maybe because the lockdown), and US$$ 31.2 billion in 2022[24]. China exported goods to Kazakhstan worth of US$ 13.98 billion, while China imported from Kazakhstan goods for US$ 11.27 billion. Kazakhstan exported to China agricultural products, oil (US$ 4.1 billion), gas (US$ 1.2 billion), copper ores and concentrates (US$ 2.04 billion), uranium and nuclear fuel (US$ 817 million), among other natural resources. On the other hand, Kazakhstan imported from China appliances and equipment worth US$ 6.1 billion; textiles and footwear for US$ 1.5 billion. Also imported 3.5 million car tires, 12,500 passenger cars, almost 3,000 tractors, 2,800 thousand trucks, over 200,000 motorcycles and almost half a million bicycles. Most of that cargo left China using the Alashankou and Khorgos border crossings. In 2022, 12,000 cargos crossed the border —around 33 per day—, while the total amount of cargo could reach 24.5 million tons in 2023, being 30 million tons the goal by 2025.

China is an energy-hungry country. It receives regularly Kazakh gas, but it was reduced from 13 bcm in 2021 to 5.5 bcm in 2022. It is important to note that Kazakhstan is transforming its energetic mix, increasing its dependency on its own gas, consequently reducing its gas exports; besides, Kazakhstan use one third of its gas to support the current flow rate of oil wells —using the gas-injection wells technique—. China demands uranium from Kazakhstan, too. That is why they created a joint venture, the Ulba TVS (51% owned by NAC Kazatomprom, 49% by China Nuclear Energy Corporation, CGNPC), to supply regularly fuel for Chinese nuclear power plants since 2021. They foresee to export around 200 tons per year by 2024.

Between 2005-2019, the largest investors in Kazakhstan were the Netherlands, the United States, Switzerland, and China. The investment

23. See Vercueil, J., "Taming the Bear while Riding the Dragon? Central Asia confronts Russian and Chinese economic influences", *Revue de la Régulation*, N. 24 (2018), retrieved from *https://journals.openeditioN.org/regulation/13626*

24. See Avdaliani, E., "China's 2023 Trade and Investment with Kazakhstan: Development Trends", *Silk Road Briefing* (2023), retrieved from *https://www.silkroadbriefing.com/news/2023/02/20/chinas-2023-trade-and-investment-with-kazakhstan-development-trends/#:~:text=China's%20exports%20to%20Kazakhstan%20reached,staggering%20US%24%2431.2%20billion*

in Kazakhstan was US$ 960 million in 2020, US$ 1.85 billion in 2021, and US$ 996 million in 2022 —half of which came in the Q4—, being US$ 18.9 billion only in extraction (mainly oil and gas) and manufacturing. Since 2005, China invested US$ 44.5 billion in real state, debt instruments and capital of companies, both in cash and in other forms.

Regarding Kyrgyzstan, China is its largest trade partner[25] and a very important investor, where "Foreign direct investment in Kyrgyzstan is mainly concentrated in mining and other extractive sectors"[26].

Regarding Tajikistan, China is searching for a wider cooperation with it, in energy issues and security-defense sector[27], while settling old disputes related to border delimitation. When both parts agreed the settlement in 2011, the then Chinese Foreign Ministry spokesman, Hong Lei, said that the dispute was solved "according to universally recognised norms of international law through equal consultations"[28]. Important to note that in the last decade, China built some new highways and railways, developed several hydropower projects, apart from the Presidential Palace and the Istiklol Complex in Dushanbe[29].

Turkmenistan is also open to do business with China, mainly in the energy sector[30], but also investing in ambitious infrastructures such as the

25. "According to the National Statistic Committee of the Kyrgyz Republic, in 2016 the foreign trade between two countries turnover amounted to 1.563 billion US$. Export from Kyrgyzstan to China, in particular, amounted to 80 million US$, import — 1.483 billion US$. The volume of trade in 2017 amounted to 1.597 billion US$. Export was 97.5 million US dollars, import — 1.500 billion US$. The flow of foreign direct investments from China to Kyrgyzstan in 2016 made up to 301,303 million US$, in 2017 — 303,025 million US$". See Ministry of Foreign Affairs of China, "Trade and Economic Cooperation", retrieved from *https://mfa.gov.kg/en/dm/Embassy-of-the-Kyrgyz-Republic-in-the-Peoples-Republic-of-China/Menu---Foreign-/--uslugi/Trade-and-Economic-Cooperation/RC*
26. See Schulz, D., "China-Kyrgyzstan Relations", *Caspian Policy Center* (2022), retrieved from *https://www.caspianpolicy.org/research/security-and-politics-program-spp/china-kyrgyzstan-relations#_ednref9*
27. See Lew, L., "Why China is funding a base in Tajikistan", *South China Morning Post* (2021), retrieved from *https://www.scmp.com/news/china/diplomacy/article/3155133/why-china-funding-base-tajikistan*
28. See "Tajikistan cedes land to China", *BBC News*, 13 January 2011, retrieved from *https://www.bbc.com/news/world-asia-pacific-12180567*
29. See Syundyukova, N., "China has begun to build new buildings of government and parliament in Dushanbe", *The Qazaq Times* (2018), retrieved from *https://qazaqtimes.com/en/article/49121*
30. See Iwaszczuk, Natalia; Wolak, Jacek and Iwaszczuk, Aleksander: "Turkmenistan's Gas Sector Development Scenarios Based on Econometric and SWOT Analysis", *Energies*, (May 2021), 14(10), retrieved from *https://www.mdpi.com/1996-1073/14/10/2740.*

Turkmenbashi International Seaport on the Caspian[31]. According to the United Nations COMTRADE database on international trade, China exports to Turkmenistan was US$ 867.64 million in 2022, where the most important products were: machinery, nuclear reactors, boilers (US$ 190.60 M), electrical, electronic equipment (US$ 117.05 M), articles of iron or steel (US$ 70.41 M), vehicles other than railway, tramway (US$ 57.61 M), and rubbers (US$ 44.60 M)[32]. On the other hand, China was the 17th customer/supplier to Turkmenistan, with a value of US$ 7.61 M in 2000 (last data available)[33], while Turkmenistan exported US$ 4.79 B to China in 2021: petroleum and gas (US$ 4.74 B), ethylene polymers (US$ 9.95 M), and other vegetable products (US$ 7.09 M). As conclusion, from 1995 to 2021, Turkmenistan to China increased trade at an annualized rate of 29.5%, from US$ 5.79 M to US$ 4.79 B[34]. as a result, China became the first destination for Turkmen products (66%), followed by Turkey (9.23%), Uzbekistan (8.76%) and Georgia (2.85%).

Finally, China (13.2%) was the fourth destination for Uzbek exports, following Switzerland (16.4%), United Kingdom (12.8%) and Russia (11.6%)[35]. In 2021, Uzbekistan exported US$ 1.94 B to China: non-retail pure cotton yarn (US$ 595 M), petroleum gas (US$ 581 M), and refined copper (US$ 226 M), increasing the annual rate of trade by 14%, from US$ 63.9 M in 1995 to US$ 1.94 B in 2021[36]. Uzbekistan, the double-landlocked Central Asian country, is one of the main focus of Chinese investment and its support is highly appreciated in the diplomatic and political field[37], apart from signing several agreements and build important infrastructures[38].

---

31. See Devonshire-Ellis, C., "Turkmenbashi's Caspian Window and the Turkmenistan Belt and Road", *Silk Road Briefing* (2018), retrieved from *https://www.silkroadbriefing.com/news/2018/07/04/turkmenbashis-caspian-window-turkmenistan-belt-road/*. On the other hand, the Ashgabat Olympic Village was built between 2010-2017 by a Turkish company. See "Turkey's Polimeks Insaat to build Olympic Village in Ashgabat", *Azer News*, 2 October 2013, retrieved from *https://www.azernews.az/region/60195.html*
32. See Trading Economics, "China Exports to Turkmenistan", retrieved from *https://tradingeconomics.com/china/exports/turkmenistan*
33. See Trading Economics, "Turkmenistan Exports by Country", retrieved from *https://tradingeconomics.com/turkmenistan/exports-by-country*
34. See Observatory of Economic Complexity, "Turkmenistan-China Trade", retrieved from *https://oec.world/en/profile/bilateral-country/tkm/partner/chn*
35. See Observatory of Economic Complexity, "Country Profile: Uzbekistan", retrieved from *https://oec.world/en/profile/country/uzb*
36. See Observatory of Economic Complexity, "Uzbekistan-China Trade", retrieved from *https://oec.world/en/profile/bilateral-country/uzb/partner/chn*
37. See Shah, M., "China-Central Asia relations at the start of a new chapter", *UZ Daily* (2023) Available at *https://www.uzdaily.uz/en/post/81008*
38. See "Chinese company to build Olympic village in Uzbekistan", *Eurasiante*, 10 November 2022, retrieved from *https://eurasianet.org/chinese-company-to-build-olympic-village-in-uzbekistan*

Regarding the BRI projects and the debt, it's useful to offer a wider outlook:

> China is not only a key trade and investment partner but also an important source of loans. For instance, 45% of Kyrgyzstan's external borrowing (worth $1.7 billion) is from China, along with 52% of Tajikistan's foreign debt ($1.2 billion). Despite the situation in other Central Asian countries being better, the indicator remains high. In particular, Turkmenistan owes China the equivalent of 16.9% of its GDP, Uzbekistan — 16%, and Kazakhstan — 6.5%. The countries of Central Asia, in particular Tajikistan and Kyrgyzstan, have difficulties with paying the debts back[39].

The construction of new infrastructures, in the framework of BRI, is attracting Chinese investment in Kazakhstan: two railway border crossings, a cross-border cooperation center, several dry ports, and five oil and gas pipelines. The Lianyungang seaport on China's east coast is used by Kazakhstan, concentrating the business from Shanghai and the provinces of Jiangsu and Zhejiang.

In 2021, the Kyrgyzstan´s debt was around US$ 5 B, being the 85.44% external debt and the 14.4% domestic. US$1,8 B owed to Export-Import Bank of China because the construction of some BRI projects. This amount means that the debt in 2021 reached 59.47% of Kyrgyzstan GDP, a 8.18 percentage point fall from 2020, when it was 67.65% of GDP[40].

The impact of COVID-19 caused several problems over the Kyrgyz economy[41] and the ability to face its financial duties. Some of those investments went to the Jetim-Too iron-ore mine and the reconstruction of Bishkek's main power plant. According to John Hillman, the director of the Reconnecting Asia Project at the Center for Strategic and International Studies, "Examples of asset seizures have been extremely rare". Hillman also warned about the situation in Kyrgyzstan, as President Sadyr Japarov knows that if they don't pay in time, they will have to pay with properties: "But I think this is a lesson on the risks of doing business with China. This is what happens when you have a lack of transparency around lending"[42].

39. See Khitakhunov, A., "Economic Cooperation between Central Asia and China", *Eurasian Research Institute*, retrieved from *https://www.eurasian-research.org/publication/economic-cooperation-between-central-asia-and-china/*
40. See "Kyrgyzstan National Debt", Expansion, retrieved from *https://countryeconomy.com/national-debt/kyrgyzstan*
41. The Chinese restrictions due to covid-19 affected all the Central Asian economies. See Khitakhunov, A., "Economic Cooperation between Central Asia and China", *op. cit.*
42. See Standish, R., "How Will Kyrgyzstan Repay Its Huge Debts to China?", *Radio Free Europe/Radio Liberty* (2021), retrieved from *https://www.rferl.org/a/how-will-kyrgyzstan-repay-its-huge-debts-to-china-/31124848.html*

Regarding the security, defense and military sectors, it is necessary to highlight the relationship established through the SCO. China initiated the Shanghai Forum, first to solve the border issues which were still problematic ten years after gaining their independence. Later, they focused their efforts to fight against the so called three evils: terrorism, separatism (or "splittism") and religious extremism. Now, the Shanghai Cooperation Organization (SCO) is conceived as a regional security organization, and step by step is being transformed into a true military coalition to fight against regional threats[43].

The SCO members hold military drills annually since 2002[44]. The "Peace Mission 2021" counter-terrorism military exercise took place in Orenburg (Russia) in September 2021[45], and the Joint Anti-Terrorist Exercise (JATE) 2021 was held in the northwestern Khyber-Pakhtunkhwa province (Pakistan), where Pakistani and Chinese troops "practiced various drills as part of the Joint Counter Terrorism Operations from planning to conduct; including Cordon & Search, Compound Clearance, Close Quarter Battle, Rappelling from Helicopter, Explosive Handling and Medical Evacuation"[46]. In October 2022 they held anti-terror exercises in India, the "Manesar Anti-Terror 2022" under the framework of the SCO Regional Anti-Terrorist Structure (RATS)[47]. Besides, Russia and China participated in 2022 at the Russia's quadrennial military exercises known as *Vostok* (East), with "units from China, India, Laos, Mongolia, Nicaragua and Syria, and around 50,000 personnel"[48].

43. The SCO future is not clear, as the close cooperation between China and India, or India and Pakistan, or Pakistan and Iran, is considered as highly problematic. Anyway, what today seems impossible, maybe tomorrow will be completely accepted as normal; when a foreign or external enemy appears, everything is plausible.
44. See State Council Information Office (SCIO) of China, "A quick guide to SCO and its military cooperation", *CGTN* (2018), retrieved from *http://english.scio.gov.cn/infographics/2018-06/05/content_51673238.htm*
45. See Negi, M., "Peace Mission-2021: India takes part in SCO joint military exercise in Russia", *India Today*, 15 September 2021, retrieved from *https://www.indiatoday.in/india/story/peace-mission-2021-indian-army-sco-joint-military-exercise-russia-1853099-2021-09-15*
46. See "First-ever military exercise conducted in Pakistan under Shanghai Cooperation Organization concludes", *Arab News Pakistan*, 4 October 2021, retrieved from *https://www.arabnews.pk/node/1941441/pakistan*
47. See "SCO anti-terror exercise hosted by India concludes", *India Today*, 13 October 2022, retrieved from *https://www.indiatoday.in/india/story/sco-manesar-multilateral-joint-anti-terror-exercise-hosted-by-india-concludes-2285073-2022-10-13*
48. See Ferris, E. and Nouwens, V., "Russia's Vostok 2022 Military Drills: Not Size or Tanks, but Context", *RUSI* (2022), retrieved from *https://rusi.org/explore-our-research/publications/commentary/russias-vostok-2022-military-drills-not-size-or-tanks-context*

This kind of exercises are negotiated and prepared in previous meetings, where diplomacy is deploying its tools and rules; it is important to note that it is really difficult to accommodate so different "languages" —manners, interests, codes— such as Russian, Chinese, Kazakh, and the others. The next counter-terror drills —the so-called Peace Mission 2023— were held in Russia's Central Military District in the Chelyabinsk Region in the Urals in August. Important to note that Chelyabinsk is a bordering region Northern Kazakhstan; if some Kazakhs were worried about their fate, as they feared a Russian invasion, now they can be in panic[49]. Although Kazakhs are aware that the Russian-led coalition forces of the CSTO saved President Kasim-Jomart Tokayev from that horrible insurrectional episode in January 2022, they are not sure about what happened really there and who organised it; they don't have a clear idea whether that was something originated from inside —with some Nazarbayev relatives and loyalists as main perpetrators— or they received foreign aid, or even was orchestrated by a/some foreign powers —Russia itself, maybe USA, why not the UK; they are open to almost any possibility, even conspirationist—.

Another important issue regarding Chinese cooperation on defence issues in Central Asia is the military sector. China is not only a machinery provider for civil purposes, but also a military one.

The field of Defence Industry is highly competitive globally. One of the key issues is who is the provider. In Europe, where most of the countries are NATO members, the provider comes from the USA —100% American companies or joint ventures—, but in Central Asia the situation is completely different. According to their traditional neutrality —as in Turkmenistan case— or multivectorial foreign policy —Kazakhstan and Uzbekistan— they cannot rely upon only one partner and must find a balance of influence and diversify their expenses. Regarding China, it is the second largest provider of military equipment to those countries, while Russia keeps its first position —for how long?—.

49. "Duma member Konstantin Zatulin warned of potential 'territorial issues' in Kazakhstan's northern provinces after President Tokayev refused to recognise Russia-occupied areas in Ukraine". See Altynbayev, K., "Russian lawmaker floats idea of Ukraine-style invasion of Kazakhstan", *Central Asia News*, 24 June 2022, retrieved from *https://central.asia-news.com/en_GB/articles/cnmi_ca/features/2022/06/24/feature-02*. See also Dumoulin, M. "Steppe change: How Russia's war on Ukraine is reshaping Kazakhstan", *European Council on Foreign Relations*, Policy Brief, 13 April 2023, retrieved from *https://ecfr.eu/publication/steppe-change-how-russias-war-on-ukraine-is-reshaping-kazakhstan/*. See also Matussek, T., "How Kazakhstan changed in light of the Russian invasion of Ukraine", *Euroactiv* (2023), retrieved from *https://www.euractiv.com/section/central-asia/opinion/how-kazakhstan-changed-in-light-of-the-russian-invasion-of-ukraine/*

Turkmenistan and Uzbekistan are the most dependent, as they received more than 20% of their arms from Beijing since 2013[50]. China provided *Wing Loong-1* drones to Kazakhstan, Turkmenistan and Uzbekistan —also the models the CH-3, CH-4, CH-5—, and gifted thirty *Jiefang J6* heavy-duty trucks and 30 large-load trailers worthing US$ 3.2 M to Kazakhstan[51] in 2015 and more than US$ 30 M to upgrade the Kyrgyz weapons; China Ordnance Industry Group Corporation Limited donated military equipment —mainly armoured carriers and VP11 patrol vehicles— to Tajikistan in 2018. Turkmenistan received surface missiles, *QW-2 Vanguard 2* man-portable air defence systems modelled on Russian *9K38 Igla 2018*, and mobile radars. Between 2015 and 2020, China sold 18% of the region's arms. In addition, China built its first military facilities in the region in Tajikistan's Pamir Mountains in 2016[52]. In 2018, Kazakhstan bought eight Chinese *Y-8* transport airplanes, based on the Russian *Antonov An-12*. In November 2019, Uzbekistan tested two Chinese FD-2000 medium-range air-defence system or transport erector launchers (TELs) on a target drone, with support from command-and-control assets and a HT-233 target-acquisition radar[53].

Could the growing Chinese influence be considered as a threat by Russia, as Central Asia is "its backyard"? Some authors believe that as long as Russia needs China to break their isolation from the rest of the world —mainly due to the Ukrainian war—, Russia will resist any temptation to break their relationship and will allow China to do whatever in Central Asia, at expenses of reducing their own influence —maybe losing tenders and business, too—; other authors understand that Central Asia is the limit and Russia will prevent China to increase its influence in the region[54].

---

50. See US Congress Foreign Affairs Committee, "China Regional Snapshot: Central Asia", 25 October 2022, retrieved from *https://foreignaffairs.house.gov/china-snapshot-project-central-asia-2/*
51. See Jardine, B. and Lemon, E., "Kennan Cable N. 52: In Russia's Shadow: China's Rising Security Presence in Central Asia", *Kennan Cable*, N. 52 (2020), retrieved from *https://www.wilsoncenter.org/publication/kennan-cable-no-52-russias-shadow-chinas-rising-security-presence-central-asia*
52. *Ibid*.
53. See Cranny-Evans, S., "Uzbekistan conducts first FD-2000 air-defence test", *Janes*, 22 November 2019, retrieved from *https://www.janes.com/defence-news/news-detail/uzbekistan-conducts-first-fd-2000-air-defence-test#:~:text=The%20FD%2D2000%20is%20the,countermeasures%20or%20anti%2Dradiation%20missiles*
54. "The China — Kyrgyzstan — Uzbekistan (CKU) railway, which will provide a key alternative to the Russian route, is an example of how China is expanding its power at the expense of Russia. Russia's indifference and the ineffectiveness of the Collective Security Treaty Organization (CSTO) during the fierce border conflict between Tajikistan and Kyrgyzstan discredited the Kremlin's role as a regional sheriff.

Finally, it is necessary to pay attention to the BRI corridors which dynamize the Chinese economy —and Central Asian too—. The two main projects are the New Eurasian Landbridge and the China-Central Asia-West Asia Corridor (CCAWEC), but also the New International Land-Sea Trade Corridor (ILSTC). While the two first come from China and finish their route in Europe, crossing Central Asia, the ILSTC starts in Alashankou (in the Western China region of Xinjiang) and finishes in Chongqing (Eastern China) to connect with Singapore and ASEAN countries. Obviously, that transforms Alashankou into a hub in both directions from Eastern China to Western Europe[55].

The CCAWEC —also known as the Middle Corridor (MC)[56]— starts from Xinjiang and reaches the Persian Gulf, the Mediterranean coast and the Arabian Peninsula, and provides an alternative land route between China and Europe, avoiding Russian territory. Besides, the Central Asia Natural Gas Pipeline is China's first cross-border gas pipeline, starting from the border of Turkmenistan and Uzbekistan in the west, passes through central Uzbekistan and southern Kazakhstan, and enters through Xinjiang Horgos Port. There are three pipelines —A, B and C—, while another fourth (D) is still under construction[57]. These lines are connected to the second and third lines of the West-East Gas Pipeline through the Khorgos gas compression first station, and the estimation is that Central Asian gas will satisfy the 20% of Chinese needs[58]. However, this corridor it is not only a matter of energy, but also there is connectivity in terms of roads and railroads, linking all the

---

Kyrgyzstan's refusal to participate in joint CSTO exercises, called 'Indestructible Brotherhood-2022', provided further evidence of Moscow's declining reputation in Central Asia". See Sharifli, Y., "China's Dominance in Central Asia: Myth or Reality?", *RUSI* (2023), retrieved from *https://rusi.org/explore-our-research/publications/commentary/chinas-dominance-central-asia-myth-or-reality*

55. See Hui, Z., Nan, Y., and Siying, Z., "International land-sea trade corridor for sustainable transportation: A review of recent literature", *Cleaner Logistics and Supply Chain*, Vol. 6 (2023), retrieved from *https://www.sciencedirect.com/science/article/pii/S2772390922000622*

56. See Khan, M., "BRI & role of Middle Corridors & forces of hegemony", *Azernews* (2023), retrieved from *https://www.azernews.az/region/206994.html*

57. The D Line will connect the Fluxing gas field in Turkmenistan with China. See Ministry of Foreign Affairs of China, "Xi Jinping and Turkmen President Gurbanguly Berdymukhamedov Jointly Attend the Inauguration Ceremony of First-Phase Construction of Fuxing Gas Field" (2013), retrieved from *https://www.fmprc.gov.cn/mfa_eng/topics_665678/3755_666062/2013zt/xjpfwzysiesgjtfhshzzfh_665686/201309/t20130906_707024.html*

58. See "The China-Central Asia-West Asia Economic Corridor has achieved results", *Seetao* (2023), retrieved from *https://www.seetao.com/details/200014.html*

main Central Asian cities[59], apart from some border crossing points, such as the new Bakhty border crossing in China's Western Xinjiang Province and the Dostyk railway station, near the Kazakh-Chinese border[60].

The New Eurasian Landbridge is a railway to Europe via Kazakhstan, Russia, Belarus, and Poland. The main problem in this route is the gauge of the trains, as the former Soviet railways had —and still have— a different gauge, so they need to change gauges when they enter in Kazakhstan and, again, after leaving Belarus and before entering Poland. Again, the Ukrainian war has disrupted and interrupted the continuous flow of cargos from China to Europe. To be more precise, freight trains link Chongqing to Duisburg, Chengdu to Lodz, Yiwu to Madrid, Wuhan to Hamburg, and Wuhan to Lyon.

Besides, the China-Kyrgyzstan-Uzbekistan railway project started in August 2022. This project is complementary to the Southern passage of the New Eurasian Land Bridge, and it is estimated to cut the journey from China to Europe and the Middle East by 900 Km and saving seven to eight days of travel time, thus boosting trade and economic exchanges in Eurasia[61].

V. TWO STRATEGIES, DIFFERENT VIEWS?

The EU was a main investor in the area since the very beginning of its independence. For more than 30 years, its goals, interests and principles in the region didn't change drastically but they were more or less the same. In November 1994, European Commission established in Alma Ata, its first Delegation in the region, while other delegations were opened much later Kyrgyzstan (2010), Tajikistan (2010) and Uzbekistan (2012). EU money flowed to the region in the form of humanitarian aid initially through ECHO, the Humanitarian Aid Office of the European Commission created in 1992.

In 1995, the European Commission established its main priorities for the region in the document COM (1995) 206 final, which are very similar to

---

59. See Nedopil, C., Krechetova, V. and Kryuchkov V., "Strengthening capacity for operationalizing sustainable transport connectivity along the China-Central Asia-West Asia Economic Corridor to achieve the 2030 Agenda", *United Nations Economic and Social Commission for Asia and the Pacific (ESCAP) Study Report 2022*, retrieved from *https://www.unescap.org/kp/2022/strengthening-capacity-operationalizing-sustainable-transport-connectivity-along-china*
60. See Avdaliani, E., "China's 2023 Trade and Investment with Kazakhstan: Development Trends", *op. cit.*
61. See "Feasibility study of China-Kyrgyzstan-Uzbekistan railway project kicks off: NDRC", *Global Times* (2022), retrieved from *https://www.globaltimes.cn/page/202208/1272073.shtml*

those promoted by the current New EU Strategy for Central Asia (2019): 1) support the development of democratic, representative and broad-based institutions; 2) reduce the chances of conflict; 3) continue promoting the economic reform process; and 4) improve your own financial security. Later, that instrument was combined with the TACIS technical assistance program (Technical Assistance to the Commonwealth of Independent States). Under this program, 16 M ECU[62] were budgeted for Turkmenistan. For Tajikistan, an additional 3.6 M ECU was budgeted; 35 M ECU for Uzbekistan; 20 M ECU for Kyrgyzstan; and more than 60 M ECU for Kazakhstan. In addition, the Communities granted the Former Soviet Union republics a loan (which they then had to repay) of 1,250 M ECU, of which 55 M were authorized to Kazakhstan, 32 to Kyrgyzstan, 55 to Tajikistan, 49 to Turkmenistan and 129 to Uzbekistan.

The TACIS program was replaced by the Development Cooperation Instrument (DCI), the Financing Instrument for Development Cooperation — DCI (2007-2013). The priorities for this DCI, both nationally and regionally, were established by the Regional Strategy Paper for Assistance to Central Asia for the period 2007-13. Among them were: promoting sustainable development, promoting stability and security, and fostering closer regional cooperation both between the countries of the region and with the EU.

The EU assistance to the CA countries amounted to 1,132 M € (1991-2004), of which 516 M correspond to the TACIS Program. For the period 2000-2006, TACIS took 3,138 M € from the community budget. In 1999 came into force the Partnership and Cooperation Agreement (PCA) for Kazakhstan, Kyrgyzstan and Uzbekistan. In 2010 for Tajikistan. For Turkmenistan they agreed an "Interim Agreement on Trade and Commercial Affairs between the European Community, the European Coal and Steel Community and the European Atomic Energy Community, on the one hand, and Turkmenistan" (2011, not yet in force).

In 2007 they adopted the EU Strategy for CA, whose guiding principles were equal dialogue, transparency and result orientation: "The EU has a strong interest in a peaceful, democratic and economically prosperous Central Asia"[63]. The aim of this strategy relies on the EU security strategy outlined by Javier Solana when he was "Mr. PESC". His conception about the

62. Euro did not exist in the 1990's, but another currency was used. The ECU was a basket-currency, a mix of several European currencies.
63. See Council of the European Union, "The EU and Central Asia: strategy for a New Partnership" (2007), retrieved from *https://data.consilium.europa.eu/doc/document/ST-10113-2007-INIT/en/pdf*, p. 4.

neighbourhood is that repeated by Josep Borrell —maybe not with the most appropriate comparison—, when he explained that the European Union is a peaceful and ordered garden, while the surrounding territories are a jungle[64].

The EU self-conception is explained in several documents every year and can be summarize as a messianic idea where EU is a more civilized region, based upon Human Rights, Liberal Democracy and Free Market economy, and we should export those ideas to other regions and implement them there. The main difference with a kind of new colonisation is that we cannot impose by force these ideas, but they should be accepted freely by the rest of the countries. EU uses its 400 million consumers market as an economic leverage[65], as a precondition to establish or continue trade relationships. Just a reminder: trade policy with third countries is an EU exclusive competence, so the member states cannot legislate on that issue nor conclude agreements. It is a powerful tool in the hands of the EU.

In 2016, the EU reviewed its security strategy and approved the EU Global Strategy, where this idea of "principled pragmatism" is pivotal:

> We will engage in a practical and principled way, sharing global responsibilities with our partners and contributing to their strengths. We have learnt the lesson: my neighbour's and my partner's weaknesses are my own weaknesses. So, we will invest in win-win solutions, and move beyond the illusion that international politics can be a zero-sum game[66].

After the adoption of the EU Strategy for CA (2007), the EU negotiated several Enhanced Partnership and Cooperation Agreement (EPCA): EPCA with Kazakhstan (signed in 2016) and EPCA with Kyrgyzstan (signed in 2019), while the EPCA with Uzbekistan and Tajikistan are being still negotiated, and with Turkmenistan there is only a proposal.

The EU developed some programs in different areas such as:

- Education: TEMPUS, ERASMUS Mundus Partnership, and the Central Asia Research and Education Network (CAREN).

64. See Liboreiro, J., "Josep Borrell apologises for controversial 'garden vs jungle' metaphor but defends speech", *Euronews* (2022), retrieved from *https://www.euronews.com/my-europe/2022/10/19/josep-borrell-apologises-for-controversial-garden-vs-jungle-metaphor-but-stands-his-ground*
65. This is the main goal with the trade agreements, the Partnership and Cooperation Agreement (PCA) and EPCA (Enhanced, new generation), and the Generalised Scheme of Preferences (GSP) or GSP+.
66. See European Union, "Shared Vision, Common Action: A Stronger Europe", *A Global Strategy for the European Union's Foreign and Security Policy* (2016), retrieved from *https://www.eeas.europa.eu/sites/default/files/eugs_review_web_0.pdf*, p. 4.

- Energy: Interstate Oil and Gas Transportation to Europe (INOGATE).
- Security Borders: Programme on Border Management in Central Asia (BOMCA).
- Environment: Promoting Integrated Water Resources Management and Fostering Transboundary Dialogue in Central Asia and the Regional Environmental Program for Central Asia (EURECA).
- Transport: the Transport Corridor Europe-Caucasus-Asia (TRACECA)[67].

In 2019, the EU adopted a New Strategy for CA, and also the multi-annual budget 2020-2027 for development aid for the region. The New Strategy:

> aims to forge a stronger, modern, and non-exclusive partnership with the countries of Central Asia so that the region develops as a sustainable, more resilient, prosperous, and closely interconnected economic and political space. It will build upon the lessons learnt from EU engagement in the region, take into consideration other relevant strategies including the Global Strategy for the EU's Foreign and Security Policy, the New European Consensus on Development, the EU Strategy on Connecting Europe and Asia and EU Strategy on Afghanistan, and be guided by the UN 2030 Agenda for Sustainable Development[68].

Following this spirit, Ambassador Peter Burian, the then EU Special Representative for CA stated:

> Our approach to the region is that we want to develop a stronger, more modern, and non- exclusive partnership with the region, which does not leave our partners with binary choices between us or somebody else. We very clearly stress this, and we continue stressing it when we present our strategy to our partners, but also to other actors and players in the region, including Russia[69].

---

67. This ambitious program was created for transport in 1993 to connect China with Europe through the Black Sea, the Caucasus, the Caspian Sea and Central Asia. Currently this project has been surpassed by the Chinese BRI.
68. See European Union, "Joint Communication to the European Parliament and the Council — The EU and Central Asia: New Opportunities for a Stronger Partnership", JOIN(2019) 9 final, EUR-Lex (2019), retrieved from *https://eur-lex.europa.eu/legal-content/en/TXT/?uri=CELEX:52019JC0009*, p. 1.
69. See Heinecke, S., "EU-Central Asia Relations: New Opportunities for A Stronger Partnership? Interview With Peter Burian", *EUCACIS in Brief*, N. 9 (2019), retrieved from *https://www.cife.eu/Ressources/FCK/EUCACIS%20in%20Brief%20No%209_final.pdf*, p. 7.

Besides, the Working Party on Eastern Europe and Central Asia (COEST) plays an essential role in following up —and watching— the progress of third countries in political reforms, economic liberalisation and human rights:

> The common values underpinning our democratic and societal models are the foundation of European freedom, security and prosperity. The rule of law, with its crucial role in all our democracies, is a key guarantor that these values are well protected; it must be fully respected by all Member States and the EU[70].

EU members and institutions lobby for constitutional changes to adapt internal political life into more democratic systems, with real freedom of the press, freedom of expression, division of powers, multi-political party system, stronger Parliaments —which paradoxically means weaker Governments and also more unstable political regimes—, and the elimination of the child and forced labour, among other steps.

VI. CONCLUSIONS

The world has changed after the covid-19 and the Ukrainian war. The world will be no longer as we met before those crises. In 2022, two fundamental documents on security issues were published: the EU Strategic Compass and the new NATO Strategic Concept, both describing Russia as a threat and China as a challenge[71]. It is useful —and maybe scary— to remind that some years ago, EU and NATO described Russia as a challenge. In this new scenario, can EU and China share common interests in a win-win game in Central Asia? Are they exclusive partners? Can they cooperate?

On the other hand, BRI infrastructures are smashing the CA traditional isolation. Besides, China is perceived as a trustable partner, non an intruder, as non-interference in internal affairs is Chinese golden rule, and this is highly appreciated in CA.

On 30 December 2020, the EU and China concluded in principle the negotiations on the Comprehensive Agreement on Investment (CAI) to create a better balance in the EU-China trade relationship, as "the EU has traditionally been much more open than China to foreign investment", and "the CAI aims to address this lack of balance". There was high concern at the EU institutions about the unbalanced relationship between Brussels

70. See European Council, "A new strategic agenda 2019-2024" (2019), retrieved from *https://www.consilium.europa.eu/media/39914/a-new-strategic-agenda-2019-2024.pdf*, p. 3.
71. It is important to note that most EU countries are NATO member states.

and Beijing. After the Ukrainian invasion, those concerns are growing and growing. A clearer, transparent dialogue it is needed when talking about the rules governing the relation with these Central Asian countries.

Since the beginning of the 21st century second decade, it seems that the global scenario is changing drastically. Central Asia was an area where it was possible to find a balance of power between all the powers interested in the region, but the current situation indicates that maybe that time has passed away and a new era is starting, where Russia is regaining its influence in the region, China is becoming increasingly important, and the USA and EU are playing a lower role.

At the end of the day, it is easier for Central Asian authorities to deal with only one country following the format C5+1 —with USA, or China, India, Russia—, than with 27 Ambassadors, plus several EU Delegates, plus Brussels authorities.

Some questions still remain and need further answer. How is EU dealing with the problems created by the clash between those three different strategies —the Chinese BRI and the EU for Central Asia and Connecting Europe and Asia— and *modus operandi* in Central Asia? What rules were implemented in Central Asia in terms of global governance, especially in the fields of investment and competition and market regulation? What role are playing international institutions and forums born due to these strategies? What kind of conclusions can we deduce from the decisions adopted by Central Asian rulers?

China and Russia's Disinformation Strategy in Latin America and the European Union's Response

MARTA HERNÁNDEZ RUIZ
Lecturer of International Relations at Universidad Loyola Andalucía

I. INTRODUCTION

Disinformation has become a significant technique of social destabilisation in modern international relations. Countries perceive digital communication as a way not only to interact with their own public opinion, but also with other states' ones. This reality offers numerous opportunities for the strengthening of cultural ties among societies, but also for polarising the public opinion in conflicts.

Disinformation can be defined as "false or misleading content that is spread with an intention to deceive or secure economic or political gain, and which may cause public harm"[1]. It differs from misinformation in that it is "false or misleading content shared without harmful intent though the effects can be still harmful" to public opinion[2]. In other words, the difference between the two terms lies in the intentionality: while in the former there is an intention to destabilise public opinion, in the latter there is a lie with no intention of causing harm, although it may do so. In this paper, we will focus on the EU's response to Chinese and Russian disinformation, introducing a case study of the role of these actors in a key region for the EU: Latin America.

1. European Commission, *Tackling online disinformation*, 2023, retrieved from *https://digital-strategy.ec.europa.eu/en/policies/online-disinformation* on 1 June 2023.
2. European Commission, *online disinformation*, *op. cit.*

II. THE EU'S FIGHT AGAINST DISINFORMATION: A STRATEGY FOCUSED ON RUSSIA AND CHINA

1. BACKGROUND AND DEVELOPMENT OF THE STRATEGY

In recent years, EU countries have increasingly drawn attention to the interference of external actors using disinformation to destabilise their societies. Campaigns emanating from Russia and, to a lesser extent, China, have been of particular concern within the EU. They realized that propaganda campaigns organized from these countries were not only focused on European countries: they had an international scale and were coordinated. Even the same Russian-driven narratives could be seen in different contexts or conflicts[3]. According to a US State Department study, several Russian accounts posted very similar messages in different Latin American countries at the same time, within 90 minutes of each other[4].

These propaganda campaigns relied on the use of social networks for mass dissemination. According to the study *Russian propaganda on social media during the 2022 invasion of Ukraine*, a Russian organisation known as the Internet Research Agency (IRA) launched a coordinated campaign on social networks during the Crimea conflict in 2014, the Brexit referendum in the United Kingdom and the French presidential elections in 2017[5]. In other words, the EU is dealing with orchestrated and coordinated propaganda campaigns.

Faced with this, the European Union's strategy against disinformation has sought to respond to the actions of Russia and, secondarily, China, particularly by observing the activity of the Russian media RT and Sputnik News. For this reason, in 2015 the European External Action Service and the European Council set up the East Stratcom Service, dedicated to detecting false content coming from these countries and disproving it. Therefore, the first actions of the strategy had a reactive approach.

As the months went by, the EU decided to diversify the strategy, integrating the *Code of Good Practices*, which involved key technology companies and social networks. In addition, the *Action Plan against Disinformation* was published,

---

3. Geissler, D., Bär, D, Pröllochs, N., Feuerriegel, S., "Russian propaganda on social media during the 2022 invasion of Ukraine" in *arXiv:2211.04154*, Cornell University, 2023, p. 4
4. Hobbs, C. and Torreblanca, J. I., "La Alianza Digital UE-ALC: Cómo hacer que Europa vuelva a escena", *European Council on Foreign Relations*, 2022, retrieved from *https://ecfr.eu/madrid/publication/la-alianza-digital-ue-alc-como-hacer-que-europa-vuelva-a-escena/* on 1 June 2023.
5. Geissler, D., Bär, D, Pröllochs, N. and Feuerriegel, S., "Russian propaganda on social [...]", *op. cit.*, p. 4.

which had the merit of identifying the priority lines to be followed. The document emphasised the importance of improving coordination between Member States, in particular through the Early Warning Mechanisms, as well as the organization of campaigns to increase social resilience and media literacy among citizens.

Currently, the strategy is still being developed and new internal actions have been announced, such as a Proposal for a *Directive on foreign influence* or a Proposal for a *Regulation to establish a common framework for media services in the internal market*, focused on the media field at European level and integrating not only the disinformation processes, but also some characteristics of misinformation ones.

2. CHINA'S GROWING IMPORTANCE FOR THE EUROPEAN STRATEGY

The EUvsDisinfo website, which is focused on debunking propaganda campaigns coming from Russia and which, as mentioned above, particularly observes RT and Sputnik News campaigns, started to adopt a more proactive strategy against content from China. Such a move became visible thanks to the development of several actions, mainly the creation of a specific team dedicated to China, working in coordination with the EEAS China division[6], and the publication of reports on the Ukrainian war in Chinese. The aim of the latter action is to show another point of view to the Chinese audience, with information "based on facts to help raise awareness of the disinformation surrounding the war in Ukraine"[7]. Previously, the EUvsDisinfo portal had already highlighted "the alignment between pro-Kremlin sources and state-affiliated Chinese sources (...) For example on COVID-19, or on human rights violations in Xinjiang, Afghanistan and Ukraine. It has also covered China's messages about Russia's military aggression against Ukraine"[8].

The identification of China as a source of foreign interference grew in the context of the pandemic. The European Commission published a report on disinformation that stated:

> "In the EU, in its neighbourhood and globally, foreign actors, for example Russia and China, have launched targeted influence operations and

6. Tidey, A., "La Unión Europea comienza a desmentir también en chino noticias falsas sobre la guerra de Ucrania", *Euronews*, 2022, retrieved from *https://es.euronews.com/my-europe/2022/05/06/la-union-europea-comienza-a-desmentir-tambien-en-chino-noticias-falsas-sobre-la-guerra-de-* on 1 June 2023.
7. Tidey, A., "La Unión Europea comienza a desmentir también [...]", *op. cit.*
8. Tidey, A., "La Unión Europea comienza a desmentir también [...]", *op. cit.*

> disinformation campaigns around the coronavirus to undermine democratic debate, exacerbate social polarisation and enhance their own image in the context of the coronavirus. The best response is to denounce these attempts, to identify those responsible and, for our part, to tell the truth as soon and as often as possible. The European Commission, the European Parliament and the European External Action Service are working to identify and raise awareness of the disinformation surrounding the virus"[9].

Researcher Ivana Karaskova, founder of MapInfluenceEU, explained to Euronews that "the EU has gradually realised, during the COVID-19 pandemic and the war in Ukraine, that not only Russia, but also China, have been targeting the European public with anti-system messages for years"[10]. It is therefore a strategy that requires a more holistic approach to include the particularities of both actors, which sometimes act in a coordinated manner. Karaskova explains that "China has been tapping into Russian channels in Europe for quite some time, so any measures targeting pro-Kremlin disinformation sites will also have side effects in China"[11].

III. RUSSIA AND CHINA'S PROPAGANDA STRATEGY IN LATIN AMERICA

1. AN APPROACH TO CHINA AND RUSSIA'S GEOPOLITICAL INFLUENCE IN THE REGION

The geopolitical influence of both actors in the region is unequal: China has positioned itself strategically, while Russia, however, has a more complicated situation.

China is the largest trading partner of Brazil, Chile, Peru, Uruguay and Argentina, and has free trade agreements with Chile, Costa Rica and Peru[12]. Total trade has increased from almost $18.000 million in 2002 to $318.000 million in 2020. In the same year, China's imports from the region amounted to $168.000 million, and exports were $150.000 million[13].

---

9. European Commission, "Lucha contra la desinformación", 2023, retrieved from *https://commission.europa.eu/strategy-and-policy/coronavirus-response/fighting-disinformation_es* on 1 June 2023.
10. Tidey, A., "La Unión Europea comienza a desmentir también [...]", op. *cit.*
11. Tidey, A., "La Unión Europea comienza a desmentir también [...]", *op. cit.*
12. Zapata, S., "Auge chino (y caída rusa) en América Latina", *Política Exterior*, 2022, retrieved from https://www.politicaexterior.com/auge-chino-y-caida-rusa-en-america-latina/ on 1 June 2023.
13. Zapata, S., "Auge chino (y caída rusa) en América Latina", *op. cit.*

It is important to mention the Belt and Road initiative, of which 20 Latin American countries are members, including the region's three largest economies, Brazil, Mexico and Argentina[14].

In the financial sphere, the China Development Bank and the Export-Import Bank of China are leaders in financing the region[15]. Between 2005 and 2020, loans amounted to more than $137.000 million, with Venezuela, Brazil, Ecuador and Argentina being the main recipients. Likewise, Chinese investments in the region amounted to $140.000 million between 2005 and 2021[16].

All these measures correspond to *hard power* influencing actions, but China is also cultivating its *soft power*. It has 41 Confucius Institutes, dedicated to teaching Chinese language and culture, in 23 countries in the region[17].

These actions also have repercussions from a diplomatic point of view: "only eight countries in Latin America and the Caribbean recognise Taiwan. Panama, the Dominican Republic and El Salvador switched recognition to the People's Republic of China between 2017 and 2018, and Nicaragua did so in December 2021"[18].

When the COVID-19 pandemic started, China also took a leading role: "it became the world's leading producer of vaccines and the main supplier to the low- and middle-income country market, displacing the US and the EU in that role"[19]. By May 2023, China had shipped 165 million doses of the vaccine to Latin America, helping to strengthen its image of generosity and effectiveness in the context of the fight against the pandemic[20]. However, it is worth noting that much of the vaccine shipment was sold at an affordable price, but China did not donate most of these doses. Shortly thereafter, both the US and the EU also began shipping doses to the region. "By the end of 2021, the US had donated 53 million doses to Latin America, the EU had donated 11.5 million, while China had donated 5 million"[21].

14. Manzano, C., "Nuevas oportunidades para América Latina", *Instituto Español de Estudios Estratégicos*, 2023, retrieved from *https://www.ieee.es/en/Galerias/fichero/docs_analisis/2023/DIEEEA47_2023_CRIMAN_Latinoamerica.pdf* on 1 July 2023, p. 13.
15. Zapata, S., "Auge chino (y caída rusa) en América Latina", *op. cit.*
16. Zapata, S., "Auge chino (y caída rusa) en América Latina", *op. cit.*
17. Manzano, C., "Nuevas oportunidades para América Latina", *op. cit.*, p. 13.
18. Zapata, S., "Auge chino (y caída rusa) en América Latina", *op. cit.*
19. Zapata, S., "Auge chino (y caída rusa) en América Latina", *op. cit.*
20. Manzano, C., "Nuevas oportunidades para América Latina", *op. cit.*, p. 14.
21. Manzano, C., "Nuevas oportunidades para América Latina", *op. cit.*, p. 14.

It is difficult for China to win the 'image battle'. The clear geostrategic advantage that China has is not translated into attraction for the public opinion. Confidence in the Chinese government fell from 47% to 38% in most Latin American countries after the coronavirus, except in Haiti and Peru[22].

Russia, for its part, has a very strategic relationship with Cuba and Venezuela. It is the leading emitter of tourists to Cuba and the Dominican Republic. "With Caracas, [Russia] has more than 20 bilateral agreements on military cooperation, exchange of personnel and training. […] The relationship has expanded to other areas of influence, with trade, investment and humanitarian aid being the most important connections"[23].

Venezuela receives economic, financial and military aid from Russia. This has resulted in initiatives such as the military exercises organized by Russia, China, Iran and Venezuela on Venezuelan territory as part of the International Army Games initiative in July 2022[24].

However, from an economic point of view, Russia's presence in Latin America is not as significant as China's, the United States's or the EU's one[25]. For this reason, and as we will see in this paper, Russia uses propaganda and disinformation mechanisms to increase its influence in the region.

2. RUSSIA AND CHINA'S INFORMATION INTEREST IN LATIN AMERICA

During the last years, Russia has decided to advance on the geopolitical chessboard by consolidating synergies and alliances.

Latin America presents a linguistic attraction for China and Russia: it is part of the Spanish-language communication market, in which there are 496 million people who speak Spanish as their first language, distributed not only in Spain and Latin America, but also in the United States (62 million)[26]. The fact-checking centre Maldita.es explains that, for this reason, it is "a very interesting market for disinformation. The same narratives that are created for Latin America have an impact in the United States and Spain, and through Spain, in Europe"[27].

22. Manzano, C., "Nuevas oportunidades para América Latina", *op. cit.*, p. 14.
23. Zapata, S., "Auge chino (y caída rusa) en América Latina", *op. cit.*
24. Manzano, C., "Nuevas oportunidades para América Latina", *op. cit.*, p. 15.
25. Manzano, C., "Nuevas oportunidades para América Latina", *op. cit.*, p. 16.
26. Kahn, G., "Bloqueada en Occidente, la propaganda rusa prospera en español en TV y redes sociales", *Reuters Institute, University of Oxford*, 2023, retrieved from *https://reutersinstitute.politics.ox.ac.uk/es/news/bloqueada-en-occidente-la-propaganda-rusa-prospera-en-espanol-en-tv-y-redes-sociales* on 1 June 2023.
27. Kahn, G., "Bloqueada en Occidente, la propaganda rusa […]", *op. cit.*

Accessing to the Latin American media sector requires first understanding the political situation of these countries, which is different to Europe and North America:

> "98% of Western European and North American countries enjoy liberal democracy (protection of individual rights, checks and balances and freedom of expression) and 2% electoral democracy (free elections, freedom of expression and access to public office). In Latin America it is very different, only 4% have liberal democracy, 84% have varying degrees of electoral democracy, 12% are on the way to being autocracies, in some cases reaching authoritarianism. Government decisions are more transparent in democratic systems, while autocracies are also defined by a lack of access to information"[28].

In this context, it is important to reflect on how detrimental the interference of disinformation is for public opinion. Carla Hobbs and José Ignacio Torreblanca state:

> "In Colombia, disinformation reportedly contributed to a significant increase, between 2018 and 2022, in public concern about alleged presidential election fraud. In Brazil, social media helped spread unfounded claims by President Jair Bolsonaro that the country's electronic voting system was vulnerable to fraud. This helps explain why a third of the electorate say they do not trust the electoral system 'at all' and only a quarter say they trust it 'a lot'. In this environment, increasingly polarised and permeable to hate speech, the number of politically motivated violent incidents increased by 23% in the country between 2020 and 2022"[29].

These authors explain that the case of Colombia is very striking in terms of disinformation, having suffered some 50,000 cyber-attacks attributed to Russia and Venezuela during the 2022 legislative elections[30].

3. RUSSIA AND CHINA'S INFORMATION POSITIONING IN THE REGION BEFORE THE WAR IN UKRAINE: THE COVID-19 PANDEMIC AND THE PREPARATION OF THE WAR

For **China**, Latin America became a relevant region in terms of media during the COVID-19 pandemic. As the pandemic started in China, it was important for this country to manage its image in the international public opinion, especially in the regions where it had more influence. According to the

28. Amado Suárez, A., "Politización de la desinformación en contextos de información devaluada. El caso Latinoamérica" in *Revista Internacional de Comunicación y Desarrollo*, vol. 4, n. 17, 2022 p. 4.
29. Hobbs, C. and Torreblanca, J. I., "La Alianza Digital UE-ALC [...]", *op. cit.*
30. Hobbs, C. and Torreblanca, J. I., "La Alianza Digital UE-ALC [...]", *op. cit.*

study *Medición del impacto de la información falsa, la desinformación y la propaganda en América Latina*, carried out by Global Americans, China's communicative influence in the region at the media level was structured through its main official media: the Xinhua news agency, the People's Online newspaper, CGTN television and China Radio International[31]. The study analysed the content promoted by these media and found that the narrative was centred on denying that COVID-19 was originated in China and that it was not spread through a cover-up by the authorities; on the other hand, China promoted the image of being the world's largest donor of medical supplies[32].

When it came to the production of vaccines, the Chinese discursive strategy also placed special emphasis on this, stressing the success of the Chinese management model, presenting Chinese vaccines in a positive light and Western vaccines in a negative one[33]. The following text was published in China Radio International (CRI): "Although the Chinese vaccine has been promoted and highly recognised in many countries, the Western media simply turned a blind eye; on the contrary, they deliberately belittle or even discredit the Chinese vaccine and politicise it". The reason for this would be to "maximise the profits of their own vaccines on the international market" and to use "vaccines as a tool to maintain hegemony"[34].

The strategy of confrontation with Western countries has been widely used by the Chinese media in Latin America, also in areas where the Western image is consolidated, such as the protection of human rights. The study includes the following statement from the official Chinese media:

> "In the face of the slander of some Western anti-China forces, China's remarkable achievements in human rights are the most powerful counterattack. Over the past 100 years, the CCP has successfully embarked on a path of human rights development that is adapted to China's national conditions. This fully proves that the definition of human rights should not be monopolised by the West"[35].

As we will see in the case of Russia, China also conducted its messages through specific profiles and influencers, who added credibility due to their

31. Global Americans, "Medición del impacto de la información falsa, la desinformación y la propaganda en América Latina", *Global Americans*, 2021, retrieved from *https://theglobalamericans.org/wp-content/uploads/2021/11/2021.11.03-Global-Americans_Reporte-Desinformacion.pdf* on 1 July 2023, p. 199.
32. Global Americans, "Medición del impacto de la información falsa [...]", *op. cit.*, p. 201.
33. Global Americans, "Medición del impacto de la información falsa [...]", *op. cit.*, p. 210.
34. Global Americans, "Medición del impacto de la información falsa [...]", *op. cit.*, p. 213.
35. Global Americans, "Medición del impacto de la información falsa [...]", *op. cit.*, p. 225.

direct interaction with the public. The aforementioned study identified 54 users in the three countries analysed (Argentina, Chile and Peru), of which 23 were institutional accounts and 31 were private users[36] — they added up to 662,478 followers[37]-. The study says:

> "Apart from the two recurrent approaches, i. e. presenting China as a great economic power and describing its role in the management of the pandemic, there is an inclination to disseminate official narratives: those presenting the Communist Party as the architect of all China's achievements, its alleged success in alleviating extreme poverty, or showing Beijing as a reference in the developing world thanks to its cooperation, donations and aid"[38].

Finally, it is important to briefly mention the case of the social network Tik Tok.

Tik Tok is Chinese-owned, and grew internationally during the COVID-19 pandemic, consolidating itself in those months of isolation in Latin America. Its popularity was remarkable, achieving record download figures during the second quarter of 2020: it was downloaded 315 million times in the App Store and Google Play Store applications[39]. In Ecuador, Tik Tok obtained 10 million users (with 17.77 million inhabitants)[40].

In the case of **Russia**, it is necessary to highlight the importance of RT en Español and Sputnik News in Russia's communication strategy abroad, although they are not the only actors involved, as we will see below. However, to study the period prior to the outbreak of the war, we will focus on the role of these media outlets as the main catalysts of the Russian narrative for Latin American public opinion.

RT en Español is a media outlet whose mission is to promote narratives close to the Russian position at the international level and operates mainly through its website and social networks. Sputnik News, on the other hand, is a communication agency that provides news to international media, so its main target audience is the media themselves, as it aims to become a source of information for them. RT was founded in 2005 with the objective of

36. Global Americans, "Medición del impacto de la información falsa [...]", *op. cit.*, p. 227.
37. Global Americans, "Medición del impacto de la información falsa [...]", *op. cit.*, p. 227.
38. Global Americans, "Medición del impacto de la información falsa [...]", *op. cit.*, p. 229.
39. Cabrera-Espín, S., Vaca-Tapia, A. and Mendoza, N., "Análisis de la red social TikTok como medio de divulgación científica para luchar contra la desinformación. Estudio de caso: Comunidad Andina" in *Journal of Science Communication — América Latina*, vol. 6, n. 1, 2023, p. 2
40. Cabrera-Espín, S., Vaca-Tapia, A. and Mendoza, N., "Análisis de la red social TikTok [...]", *op. cit.*, p. 3.

promoting a different view of Russian politics in the world. However, shortly afterwards it decided to change its editorial line and prioritised national issues of interest in the countries where it operates, while promoting the Kremlin's strategic interests[41]. This means that RT and Sputnik inform about national issues affecting the countries where they operate in a consistent way with Russian foreign policy interests, rather than trying to provide only Russia-related content.

RT's director, Margarita Simonyan, said that Russia needs these media for the same reasons it needs a Ministry of Defence. They have the task of "creating an audience and turning it into a captive audience, to be called upon later at critical moments"[42]. The success of RT's Spanish version is undeniable, outshining versions in other languages, including English, Arabic, German and French[43].

RT en Español is particularly successful in Mexico, Venezuela, Argentina and Colombia, countries that constitute the 50% of the visitors to its website[44]. It is important to highlight the growth in Venezuela. Its audience grew to 14.33% in June 2020 (a drastic increase compared to January 2018, when it was 9.8%[45]). Venezuelans also constitute the 15% of RT en Español's followers on Twitter[46]. On Facebook, the Spanish version of RT en Español is so relevant that it became more popular than the English version. In July 2020, it had a difference of 10 million likes and followers compared to it (it has more capacity for interaction with the public and, therefore, more engagement).

In conclusion, the integration of these media into the news routines of the Latin American public opinion did not begin with the war in Ukraine; it increased notably during the COVID-19 pandemic, whose news coverage was widely followed in Latin America through RT. In June 2020, RT en Español reached 14.6 million "likes" on Facebook, consolidating a 96% growth compared to February[47].

---

41. Sastre, D. G., "Auge y caída de Russia Today (RT), la Fox de Putin", *epe*, 2022, retrieved from *https://www.epe.es/es/internacional/20220313/auge-caida-russia-today-rt-13365134* on 1 June 2023.
42. Hobbs, C. and Torreblanca, J. I., "La Alianza Digital UE-ALC [...]", *op. cit.*
43. Kahn, G., "Bloqueada en Occidente, la propaganda rusa [...]", *op. cit.*
44. DFRLab, *A glimpse into RT's Latin American audience*, 2020, retrieved from *https://medium.com/dfrlab/a-glimpse-into-rts-latin-american-audience-487d52bed507* on 1 June 2023.
45. DFRLab, *A glimpse into RT's Latin American audience*, *op. cit.*
46. DFRLab, *A glimpse into RT's Latin American audience*, *op. cit.*
47. DFRLab, *A glimpse into RT's Latin American audience*, *op. cit.*

For Vladimir Rouvinski, associate professor at the Universidad Icesi in Colombia, there are three reasons that explain why RT achieved such success during its coverage of the pandemic in Latin America: the absence of media outside the Western world in Latin America that provide different visions of current affairs; a strong anti-US sentiment in the region — since the most successful media conglomerates at the international level are those that come from the United States — and, finally, the lack of knowledge of the reality in Russia today[48]. For these reasons, the alternative voices promoted by RT and Sputnik became consolidated during the pandemic. As Carla Hobbs and José Ignacio Torreblanca explain, based on a study by the United Nations Development Programme[49], "a large part of the online disinformers promoting supposedly miraculous therapies or sowing mistrust towards authorities in general and vaccines in particular were located in countries outside the region, such as Russia and China"[50].

RT and Sputnik identified the narratives and interpretative frameworks they needed to promote to become mainstream sources of information for public opinion. Moreover, it is worth noting the support they received from some Latin American leaders. DW published the following Adriana Amado's words, Director of Infociudadana:

> "There were cases, such as that of Cristina Fernández de Kirchner when she was president, who preferably accepted interviews from Russia Today or Telesur, and not from other media in her own country (...). Thus, the Russian media in Latin America have had the approval of the sources of power and many colleagues to legitimise their informative role, as if they were traditional or professional media"[51].

This government support is also noticeable in Venezuela:

> "Russia has the greatest reach among the population in Venezuela, thanks to the support in social networks to Putin, promoted by the Maduro government. That support is translated into disinformation distributed by VTV, the Venezuelan state channel, which justifies and minimises Russia's

48. Kahn, G., "Bloqueada en Occidente, la propaganda rusa [...]", *op. cit.*
49. United Nations Development Programme, "Exploring COVID-19 online debates and information pollution in Latin America and the Caribbean", *Constella*, 2021, retrieved from *https://constellaintelligence.com/wp-content/uploads/2022/03/220316-Information-Pollution-LAC-UNDP-Constella.pdf* on 1 June 2023.
50. Hobbs, C. and Torreblanca, J. I., "La Alianza Digital UE-ALC [...]", *op. cit.*
51. Ospina-Valencia, J., "Los medios rusos en América Latina: cuando la invasión choca con la ilusión", *DW.com*, 2022, retrieved from *https://www.dw.com/es/los-medios-rusos-en-am%C3%A9rica-latina-cuando-la-invasi%C3%B3n-choca-con-la-ilusi%C3%B3n/a-61311270* on 1 June 2023.

invasion of Ukraine, saying that, after all, the United States has done the same throughout its modern history"[52].

We can therefore assert that the Russian media have been positioning themselves in the region since their creation, but the key moment of their rise was the coronavirus pandemic. From February 2020 to June 2020, the first months of the pandemic, the most repeated words in these media point to an argumentative framework centred on the United States and on presenting Russia as an alternative to the US position. The most repeated words, according to a study by the Atlantic Council's Digital Forensics Research Lab, were: "US", "president", "Washington", "Donald Trump", "government", "Russia" and "Venezuela"[53].

These data are consistent with the analysis made by Iria Puyosa, senior researcher at DFRLab, for the Reuter Institute: "The common thread of RT's communication in the region is the questioning of US imperialism"[54]. She continues: "part of the Russian strategy is to blame any social problems on Western countries and to present a narrative which defend that Putin is a 'global leader who brings stability and progress' and that he is able to create a new world order in which the Global South has a seat at the table"[55]. For Rouvinski, this success is due to the fact that RT en Español and Sputnik Mundo have differentiated themselves from other foreign news media (DW Español, France 24 Español, BBC or CNN), because they focused on creating critical content against the US and the West[56].

According to another DFRLab empirical study carried out between 1 December 2021 and 14 February 2022, it was possible to conclude that public opinion was premeditatedly prepared to justify the war that began on 24 February. Specifically, ten narratives aimed at presenting the attack on Ukraine as an armed action in response to a prior provocation were identified[57]:

— Ukrainian border guards shoot Belarusian migrants (1 December 2021). A video appeared on several private Facebook pages showing images of five armed people shooting dead about 20 people.

52. Ospina-Valencia, J., "Los medios rusos en América Latina: cuando la invasión [...]", *op. cit.*
53. DFRLab, *A glimpse into RT's Latin American audience, op. cit.*
54. Kahn, G., "Bloqueada en Occidente, la propaganda rusa [...]", *op. cit.*
55. Kahn, G., "Bloqueada en Occidente, la propaganda rusa [...]", *op. cit.*
56. Kahn, G., "Bloqueada en Occidente, la propaganda rusa [...]", *op. cit.*
57. DFRLab, *How ten false flag narratives were promoted by pro-Kremlin media*, 2022, retrieved from *https://medium.com/dfrlab/how-ten-false-flag-narratives-were-promoted-by-pro-kremlin-media-c67e786c6085* on 1 June 2023.

Commentators claimed that the footage showed Ukrainian border forces shooting at refugees fleeing Belarus. One account even claimed that Ukrainian President Volodymyr Zelensky issued the order because he had received it from abroad[58].

— US companies prepare biochemical weapons in Ukraine (21 December 2021). Russian Defence Minister Sergei Shoigu claimed that private US military companies were preparing biochemical components to provoke a fight in eastern Ukraine. The leader of DNR (the self-proclaimed Donetsk People's Republic), Denis Pushilin, stated that Donetsk's water supply was poisoned. Pentagon press secretary John F. Kirby denied the allegations during a press conference the same day[59].

— Ukraine prepares a plan to attack the Donbas (1 February 2022). The deputy head of the DNR militia, Eduard Basurin, stated that the General Staff of the Armed Forces of Ukraine completed its plan to invade the Donbas. He stated that the plan would be presented by the leader of the Armed Forces of Ukraine and then sent for approval by the National Security and Defence Council[60].

— Ukrainian special services planted a bomb in an administrative building in Donetsk (1 February 2022). The DNR Defence Ministry reported that the security services prevented a terrorist act of the Ukrainian special forces to bomb an administrative building in Donetsk[61].

— Ukraine is preparing a massive military mobilisation (3 February 2022). Russian-funded media claimed that Ukraine was preventing men of military service age from leaving the country. They also reported that enlistment offices would be preparing lists of citizens subject to mobilisation, implying that the decision to go to war was made. The Ukrainian government's Centre for Strategic Communication denied the claim and called it a provocation[62].

— Ukrainian armed forces launched a massive artillery attack on Donetsk (5 February 2022). The pro-Kremlin media outlet

58. DFRLab, *How ten false flag narratives were promoted by pro-Kremlin media, op. cit.*
59. DFRLab, *How ten false flag narratives were promoted by pro-Kremlin media, op. cit.*
60. DFRLab, *How ten false flag narratives were promoted by pro-Kremlin media, op. cit.*
61. DFRLab, *How ten false flag narratives were promoted by pro-Kremlin media, op. cit.*
62. DFRLab, *How ten false flag narratives were promoted by pro-Kremlin media, op. cit.*

Moskovskiy Komsomolets reported that Ukrainian forces began a massive shelling of Donetsk, including artillery, mortars and grenade launchers. The fact-checker Polygraph.info argued that it was strange that either side could have carried out a massive artillery shelling, as only 38 explosions were recorded in the Donetsk region over a 48-hour period[63].

— Polish mercenaries arrive in Donbas to organise terrorist acts (7 February 2022). On 7 February, the DNR claimed that two groups of Polish mercenaries had appeared in the Ukrainian-controlled areas of the Donbas. They alleged that the mercenaries were working with Ukrainian forces to carry out terrorist acts and sabotage the self-proclaimed republics[64].

— Ukraine deployed S-300 anti-aircraft missiles near the Donbas (11 February 2022). DNR's Eduard Basurin claimed that Ukraine deployed S-300 anti-aircraft missile systems in Kramatorsk. Multiple Russian media amplified the message, adding that such systems could be dangerous to Russian airliners near the border, reiterating the claim that Ukraine shot down the MH-17 airliner rather than Russia[65].

— Explosion in Donetsk (12 February 2022). RT quoted unnamed local media sources as reporting an explosion on 12 February in Donetsk. Citing DNR's Denis Pushilin, RT Director Margarita Simonyan confirmed that the explosion had taken place on the Ukrainian side of the conflict line, but added that RT correspondents in Donetsk did not hear any explosion. Meanwhile, Pushilin maintained that the situation was under control and that the explosion on Ukrainian-controlled territory could have been a provocation against the DPR. The Ukrainian Forces issued a statement which said that Ukrainian troops were following the ceasefire and did not carry out any shelling. RT simultaneously confirmed and denied the explosion[66].

— Ukrainian nationalists prepare saboteurs to carry out terrorist attacks in Donbas (14 February 2022). The LNR (self-proclaimed Lugansk People's Republic) claimed that Ukraine had created a secret network of saboteurs to carry out terrorist acts and sabotage

63. DFRLab, *How ten false flag narratives were promoted by pro-Kremlin media, op. cit.*
64. DFRLab, *How ten false flag narratives were promoted by pro-Kremlin media, op. cit.*
65. DFRLab, *How ten false flag narratives were promoted by pro-Kremlin media, op. cit.*
66. DFRLab, *How ten false flag narratives were promoted by pro-Kremlin media, op. cit.*

of infrastructure facilities in the Donbas region in cooperation with the Ukrainian security services[67].

For this analysis, DFRLab selected ten Kremlin-controlled and pro-Kremlin Russian media outlets and examined how many of them covered the above narratives. At least six out of the ten narratives were covered by all ten media outlets[68], indicating significant communicative orchestration. It also empirically tested, during the study period, the significant influence these narratives had. Stories about the phantom explosion in Donetsk were the most popular, reaching more than 440000 views, followed by stories about Polish mercenaries, which garnered more than 345000 views on media websites and Telegram. Stories about US mercenaries deploying biochemical weapons got more than 2800 interactions on different platforms, followed by stories about the phantom explosion in Donetsk, which accumulated more than 520 interactions[69].

4. RUSSIAN AND CHINESE PROPAGANDA STRATEGY IN LATIN AMERICA DURING THE UKRAINIAN WAR

4.1. Western Blockade of RT and Sputnik and the Pivot to Latin America

Following the outbreak of the Ukrainian war, the European Union, the United States, the United Kingdom and Canada, among other countries, decided to ban RT and Sputnik News from broadcasting in their territories, for "systematic manipulation of information and disinformation by the Kremlin"[70]. This action was part of the EU's decision to support Ukraine in the face of Russia's violation of international law. It was also a clear step forward in the EU's anti-disinformation strategy. Several important media companies, such as Meta, blocked RT and Sputnik content on their networks in these territories. YouTube decided to block all state-funded Russian media globally[71].

Following the invasion, social media companies tried to promote policies to reduce the impact of Russian-sponsored content. They focused mainly on advertising and demonetising their accounts. Twitter tried to go further

67. DFRLab, *How ten false flag narratives were promoted by pro-Kremlin media, op. cit.*
68. DFRLab, *How ten false flag narratives were promoted by pro-Kremlin media, op. cit.*
69. DFRLab, *How ten false flag narratives were promoted by pro-Kremlin media, op. cit.*
70. Kahn, G., "Bloqueada en Occidente, la propaganda rusa [...]", *op. cit.*
71. Kahn, G., "Bloqueada en Occidente, la propaganda rusa [...]", *op. cit.*

and demonetised war-related search terms, preventing ads from appearing (Twitter banned ads from RT and Sputnik since 2017, and those appearing on Russian state-sponsored news sites since 2019)[72]. In addition, after the outbreak of the war, Facebook started to globally demote (i. e. penalise such content in the search algorithm, indexing the results worse) the content of Russian state media pages. Twitter added tags to tweets containing links to Russian state-backed media websites. In April 2022, Twitter announced that it would not extend or recommend government accounts of states that limit access to information in their countries and are involved in interstate armed conflicts, starting with Russia[73].

4.2. Main Narratives Promoted

Since the Ukraine War, according to Jessica Brandt and Valerie Wirtschafter, the storylines of the Russian propaganda campaign have focused on three thematic axes: a framing of Ukrainians as "Nazis and aggressors, particularly in regions where Russia was trying to consolidate its power"[74]; a presentation of any information or opinion contrary to the war with Ukraine as disinformation; and a constant criticism of Western sanctions[75]. Puyosa agrees with part of this diagnosis, although with some differences; for her, the three main messages have been that Ukraine posed a threat to Russia as a puppet of NATO and the US; that Ukraine was a Nazi regime; and that Russia had to wage this "anti-imperialist" war against Europe and the US'[76]. Consistent with this, during the first weeks of the war, it was common to read headlines on the front page of RT en Español such as the following: "'Thanks for the victory!' Mariupol residents thank Putin for liberating the city" or "Russia: US tries to divert attention from responsibility for Nord Stream sabotage with cheap hoaxes"[77].

According to a study made by Foreign Policy, two narratives were particularly prominent in Russian state-backed messages from the beginning of the war: on the one hand, the invasion of Ukraine was necessary to counter the growing threat of Nazi influence in Kiev, and on the other, Western

72. Brandt, J. and Wirtschafter, *Working the Western Hemisphere. How Russia spreads propaganda about Ukraine in Latin America and the impact of platform responses*, Foreign Policy at Brookings, 2022, p. 13.
73. Brandt, J. and Wirtschafter, *Working the Western Hemisphere. How Russia [...], op. cit.*, p. 13.
74. Brandt, J. and Wirtschafter, *Working the Western Hemisphere. How Russia [...], op. cit.*, p. 3.
75. Brandt, J. and Wirtschafter, *Working the Western Hemisphere. How Russia [...], op. cit.*, p. 3.
76. Kahn, G., "Bloqueada en Occidente, la propaganda rusa [...]", *op. cit.*
77. Kahn, G., "Bloqueada en Occidente, la propaganda rusa [...]", *op. cit.*

sanctions were responsible for the growing economic difficulties in Latin America and around the world[78].

The authors agree in highlighting the framing of the "Nazi" threat. This is also supported by empirical studies; the term 'Nazi' was among the most used terms, with almost 2,000 references, throughout the eight-month period analysed in the Foreign Policy study[79]. The constituent publications collectively accounted for 8% of the total number of interactions focused on content about the Ukrainian war, indicating a certain attraction and impact on public opinion.

This study provides an even more relevant result: from a rhetorical point of view, Russia used the narrative that there were 'Nazis' in the Ukrainian government as a pretext for attack. The data obtained showed that the word "Nazi" appears mostly ex post facto, after the conflict started. Specifically, 81% out of the 2000 references mentioned emerged after the conflict began[80].

Other popular publications related to this narrative emphasised that the US and European countries were ignoring the rise of Nazis in Kiev because they saw them as allies in opposing Russia as well[81]. Although the primary target audience was Eastern European public opinion, Latin American countries may also have been receptive, being more sensitive to such issues, since "after the end of World War II, several Latin American countries, including Argentina and Brazil, were among the most popular destinations for Nazis fleeing prosecution for war crimes"[82].

Source: DFRLab, *RT and Sputnik in Spanish boosted by Russian embassy tweets and suspicious accounts*, 2022, retrieved from *https://medium.com/dfrlab/rt-and-sputnik-in-spanish-boosted-by-russian-embassy-tweets-and-suspicious-accounts-3a24dcd7cf57* on 1 June 2023.

The authors also agree that the response to sanctions was one of the most relevant narratives, and according to the Foreign Policy study, it became the second most popular topic. Whether characterising sanctions as unjustified or blaming them for global economic difficulties, they were alluded to in the publications they analysed almost 4,500 times[83].

The issue of sanctions first entered the Russian media agenda in early December 2021, when Putin, in a video that garnered nearly 24,000 interactions

78. Brandt, J. and Wirtschafter, *Working the Western Hemisphere. How Russia [...], op. cit.*, p. 17.
79. Brandt, J. and Wirtschafter, *Working the Western Hemisphere. How Russia [...], op. cit.*, p. 17.
80. Brandt, J. and Wirtschafter, *Working the Western Hemisphere. How Russia [...], op. cit.*, p. 17.
81. Brandt, J. and Wirtschafter, *Working the Western Hemisphere. How Russia [...], op. cit.*, p. 18.
82. Brandt, J. and Wirtschafter, *Working the Western Hemisphere. How Russia [...], op. cit.*, p. 18.
83. Brandt, J. y Wirtschafter (2022), *Working the Western Hemisphere*... op. cit., p. 19

counted as of 25 June 2022, warned the United States and the European Union about the consequences of imposing sanctions on Russia[84]. As Western sanctions escalated in the early days of the invasion, the Kremlin's rhetoric shifted to the argument that these sanctions were causing global economic hardship, impacting fuel prices and food shortages. This narrative had a major impact in Latin America, where public opinion appears to be against providing financial support to Ukraine (given the domestic economic crisis) or paying more for fuel[85].

According to Carla Hobbs and José Ignacio Torreblanca, Russia emphasised in its narrative that "global food supply problems and inflationary pressure linked to high energy prices are a consequence of Western sanctions and not the Russian invasion"[86].

In an analysis developed by the fact-checking centre Chequeado, they found that, during the first six months of the conflict, there were four very recurrent Russian disinformation techniques[87]:

— Videos and photos of fake military actions. Images from earlier conflicts were promoted as if they were happening at the time[88]. In some cases, images involving Russia and Ukraine were not even used. Videos from conflicts such as the Syrian war[89] in 2018 or in Gaza[90] in 2021 were detected. More extremely, images from videogames were presented as videos of the conflict[91].

84. Brandt, J. y Wirtschafter (2022), *Working the Western Hemisphere*... op. cit., p. 20.
85. Brandt, J. and Wirtschafter, *Working the Western Hemisphere. How Russia [...], op. cit.*, p. 20.
86. Hobbs, C. and Torreblanca, J. I., "La Alianza Digital UE-ALC [...]", *op. cit.*
87. Sohr, O., "A un año del inicio de la Guerra en Ucrania, cuáles fueron las desinformaciones más comunes", *Chequeado*, 2023, retrieved from *https://chequeado.com/ultimas-noticias/a-un-ano-del-inicio-de-la-guerra-en-ucrania-cuales-fueron-las-desinformaciones-mas-comunes/* on 1 June 2023.
88. Corral, I., "No, la foto de la pelea entre soldados ucranianos y rusos no es actual sino de 2014", *Chequeado*, 2022, retrieved from *https://chequeado.com/el-explicador/no-la-foto-de-la-pelea-entre-soldados-ucranianos-y-rusos-no-es-actual-sino-de-2014/* on 1 June 2023.
89. Corral, I., "No, la imagen de la niña ensangrentada no corresponde al conflicto en Ucrania sino a la guerra en Siria", *Chequeado*, 2022, retrieved from https://chequeado.com/el-explicador/no-la-imagen-de-la-nina-ensangrentada-no-corresponde-al-conflicto-en-ucrania-sino-a-la-guerra-en-siria/ on 1 June 2023.
90. Corral, I., "No, este video no corresponde a la guerra en Ucrania sino a un ataque en Gaza en 2021", *Chequeado*, 2022, retrieved from *https://chequeado.com/verificacionfb/no-este-video-no-corresponde-a-la-guerra-en-ucrania-sino-a-un-ataque-en-gaza-en-2021/* on 1 June 2023; Gardel, L., "Este bombardeo no ocurrió en Ucrania, sino en Gaza, y es de 2021", *Chequeado*, 2022, retrieved from *https://chequeado.com/el-explicador/este-bombardeo-no-ocurrio-en-ucrania-sino-en-gaza-y-es-de-2021/* on 1 June 2023.
91. Corti, D., "No, el video de un avión que esquiva disparos no muestra un ataque en Ucrania, es un videojuego", *Chequeado*, 2022, retrieved from *https://chequeado.*

— Images of victims that were not current, were not taken during the conflict or were not real. Images of victims from other times or places were used, which elicited emotional responses and therefore easily went viral[92]. Even images from films were used[93].

— Content to cast doubt on the existence of the war, and to present it as a Western construct[94]. There was a lot of content denying the war or its magnitude. For example, videos of protests were used, in which protesters lay down in body bags against climate change. While using this video they argued that the presumed dead of the Ukrainian war were not real dead, as movements were seen inside the bags and therefore they were alive[95]. This video, which was also used during the COVID-19 pandemic, was particularly viral in Argentina. Another example was the use of images from a music video to prove that the deaths were staged filming[96].

— The use of images to support the Ukrainian government's association with Nazism[97]. Zelenski was accused of using Nazi symbology[98] or the head of the Ukrainian police[99].

com/verificacionfb/no-el-video-de-un-avion-que-esquiva-disparos-no-muestra-un-ataque-en-ucrania-es-un-videojuego/ on 1 June 2023.

92. Sohr, O., "A un año del inicio de la Guerra en Ucrania [...]", *op. cit.*
93. Corral, I., "No, la imagen de la niña llorando en el piso no corresponde al conflicto bélico entre Ucrania y Rusia", *Chequeado*, 2022, retrieved from *https://chequeado.com/el-explicador/no-la-imagen-de-la-nina-llorando-en-el-piso-no-corresponde-al-conflicto-belico-entre-ucrania-y-rusia/* on 1 June 2023.
94. Sohr, O., "A un año del inicio de la Guerra en Ucrania [...]", *op. cit.*
95. Giménez, J., "No, el video que muestra a un supuesto cadáver levantándose no está relacionado con la guerra en Ucrania ni con el coronavirus", *Chequeado*, 2022, retrieved from *https://chequeado.com/el-explicador/no-el-video-que-muestra-a-un-supuesto-cadaver-levantandose-no-esta-relacionado-con-la-guerra-en-ucrania-ni-con-el-coronavirus/* on 1 June 2023.
96. Corral, I., "No, el video de un hombre fumando en una bolsa mortuoria no corresponde a la guerra en Ucrania sino que es una ficción", *Chequeado*, 2022, retrieved from *https://chequeado.com/verificacionfb/no-el-video-de-un-hombre-fumando-en-una-bolsa-mortuoria-no-corresponde-a-la-guerra-en-ucrania-sino-que-es-una-ficcion/* on 1 June 2023.
97. Sohr, O., "A un año del inicio de la Guerra en Ucrania [...]", *op. cit.*
98. Corral, I., "Es falso que Zelensky vistió una remera con un símbolo vinculado al nazismo ante el Congreso de EEUU", *Chequeado*, 2022, retrieved from *https://chequeado.com/verificacionfb/es-falso-que-zelensky-vistio-una-remera-con-un-simbolo-vinculado-al-nazismo-ante-el-congreso-de-eeuu/* on 1 June 2023.
99. Corral, I., "No, el neonazi Artem Bonov no es el jefe de la policía de Kiev en Ucrania", *Chequeado*, 2022, retrieved from *https://chequeado.com/verificacionfb/no-el-neonazi-artem-bonov-no-es-el-jefe-de-la-policia-de-kiev-en-ucrania/* on 1 June 2023.

As the weeks progressed, the propaganda and diplomatic effort took effect. In March, five Latin American governments (Bolivia, Cuba, El Salvador, Nicaragua and Venezuela) abstained or refused to participate in the UN vote condemning Russia's actions in Ukraine[100]. According to the study *Russian propaganda on social media during the 2022 invasion of Ukraine*:

> "The accumulation of messages on the day of the UN vote on Resolution ES-11/1 gives rise to concerns that countries that abstained from the UN voting were targeted by Russian propaganda efforts. Strikingly, many likely bots that spread pro-Russian messages were creates shortly before the UN vote, which indicates an intentional and planned manipulation of public opinion on Twitter as part of a Russian propaganda campaign"[101].

In April, following reports on Bucha, Mexico and Brazil abstained in the vote on the resolution proposing to suspend Russia from the Human Rights Council. That month, RT en Español was the third most shared Spanish-language account for information on Russia's invasion of Ukraine[102].

In May 2022, current president Lula da Silva stated that Zelensky was "as responsible as Putin for the war"[103]. And this image became increasingly consolidated. According to Oliver Stuenkel's analysis, "many Latin American voters believe NATO is as much responsible for the war as Russia"[104].

Russian platforms experienced a clear spike in content volume right after the invasion of Ukraine. It was more pronounced on Twitter than on Facebook. During this time, the Russian government intensified the narrative that the attack was justified because there was an existential threat. "Moscow argued that the Ukrainian government, led by drug addicts and neo-Nazis, was committing genocide against Russian speakers in the east of the country"[105]. The means used to reach such a high level of message implementation is discussed below.

5. ANALYSIS OF THE MEANS USED IN PROPAGANDA CAMPAIGNS

5.1. RT and Sputnik on Social Networks

RT had traditionally — before the war — focused on social networking sites (SNS) to disseminate content, especially on YouTube, with RT's English-

100. Brandt, J. and Wirtschafter, *Working the Western Hemisphere. How Russia […], op. cit.*, p. 3.
101. Geissler, D., Bär, D, Pröllochs, N. and Feuerriegel, S., "Russian propaganda on social […]", *op. cit.*, p. 25.
102. Brandt, J. and Wirtschafter, *Working the Western Hemisphere. How Russia […], op. cit.*, p. 3.
103. Brandt, J. and Wirtschafter, *Working the Western Hemisphere. How Russia […], op. cit.*, p. 3.
104. Brandt, J. and Wirtschafter, *Working the Western Hemisphere. How Russia […], op. cit.*, p. 3.
105. Brandt, J. and Wirtschafter, *Working the Western Hemisphere. How Russia […], op. cit.*, p. 8.

language channel achieving a better position than CNN and BBC. However, since YouTube removed RT and Sputnik from the platform in March 2022, they switched to linking their content directly to their websites or apps, rather than linking to videos posted on YouTube[106]. In other words, they rely directly on their websites to link social media content and interact with public opinion.

According to a study on RT and Sputnik News' website and app influence on public opinion, it is not easy for these media to influence the citizens with these resources, as they did not reach more than 5% of the digital population of the 21 countries they analysed in the months leading up to the war in Ukraine, between 2019 and 2021 (Germany, Mexico, United States, Spain, France, Argentina, United Kingdom, Canada, Australia, Italy, Colombia, Norway, Ireland, Singapore, Chile, Finland, India, Malaysia, Hong Kong, Brazil, Japan)[107]. In these months, the use of YouTube videos was highly favourable to them. However, in the face of the aforementioned vetoes, they linked their content directly to their websites and applications in their strategy in Latin America.

However, by the time the Ukrainian war came along, RT had achieved such a high degree of credibility in Latin American public opinion during its coverage of the pandemic that, with less communication effort and less social media resources, RT achieved a greater impact among its Spanish-language readers (who, due to the blockades, were mainly located in Latin America). As DW reports, in the words of Joseph Bodnar, an analyst at the Alliance for Securing Democracy: "While in the first six months of the Russian war in Ukraine only 14% of all social networks content from Russian state media and diplomats was published in Spanish, it generated 37% of all retweets and 25% of all likes"[108]. RT en Español had more than twice as many followers on Facebook as the English-language version in 2022[109].

106. Kling, J., Toepfl, F., Thurman, N. and Fletcher, R., "Mapping the website and mobile app audiences of Russia's foreign communication outlets, RT and Sputnik, across 21 countries" in *Harvard Kennedy School Misinformation Review*, 2022, retrieved from *https://misinforeview.hks.harvard.edu/article/mapping-the-website-and-mobile-app-audiences-of-russias-foreign-communication-outlets-rt-and-sputnik-across-21-countries/* on 1 June 2023.

107. Kling, J., Toepfl, F., Thurman, N. and Fletcher, R., "Mapping the website and mobile app audiences of Russia's [...]", *op. cit.*

108. Traeder, V., "Medios rusos en América Latina: Muchos países son caldo de cultivo para la desinformación", *DW*, 2022, retrieved from *https://www.dw.com/es/medios-rusos-en-am%C3%A9rica-latina-muchos-pa%C3%ADses-son-caldo-de-cultivo-para-la-desinformaci%C3%B3n/a-62972978* on 1 June 2023.

109. DFRLab, "RT and Sputnik in Spanish boosted by Russian embassy tweets and suspicious accounts", 2022, retrieved from *https://medium.com/dfrlab/rt-and-sputnik-in-spanish-boosted-by-russian-embassy-tweets-and-suspicious-accounts-3a24ded7ef57* on 1 June 2023.

Overall, RT en Español was, according to 2022 data, the third most shared domain on Twitter for Spanish-language content about the war, while Sputnik News was among the top 15[110]. This takes on special relevance if we consider that Sputnik is a news agency, and its main mission is to provide other media with content, instead of interacting directly with public opinion. RT currently employs 200 Spanish-speaking staff and has bureaus in Caracas, Havana and Buenos Aires[111].

Continuing with the analysis of the dimension that RT acquired in Latin America at the time of the outbreak of the war, it is worth noting that, two out of the five most retweeted Russian public media accounts on Twitter between 2021 and 2022 were Spanish-language accounts (@ActualidadRT and @RTUltimaHora). In that period, RT en Español's Twitter account (@ActualidadRT) had more followers than its primary English-language account (@RT_com) and was retweeted twice as often[112].

However, despite its popularity, an empirical study made by Medium found that a significant proportion of retweets received by RT en Español and Sputnik News come from accounts suspected of not having authentic activity (so-called bot farms). "The fact that RT en Español is the third most-shared outlet on Twitter in the Ukraine war conversation in Spanish is primarily due to the number of retweets, of which a large proportion have been posted by such suspicious accounts"[113].

Another study, called *Russian propaganda on social media during the 2022 invasion of Ukraine*, analysed in depth the impact that these bots had on the coverage of the war, using the so-called Botometer tool. They focused on Twitter between February and July 2022. Their most prominent result was that 20.28% of accounts using the hashtags #istandwithrussia, #standwithrussia, #standwithputin and #standwithputin were categorised as bots[114]. Furthermore, they proved that there was a clear increase in the creation of new bots on 24 February 2022, the day the war started. "Pro-Russian messages have been spread on Twitter disproportionately through likely bots, which interacted in highly-connected retweet networks. The retweet networks showed distinctive clusters in countries that are of key interest for Russian politics [...] and thus suggest a coordinated effort"[115].

110. DFRLab, "RT and Sputnik in Spanish boosted by Russian embassy [...]", *op. cit.*
111. DFRLab, "RT and Sputnik in Spanish boosted by Russian embassy [...]", *op. cit.*
112. Brandt, J. and Wirtschafter, *Working the Western Hemisphere. How Russia [...], op. cit.* p. 3.
113. DFRLab, "RT and Sputnik in Spanish boosted by Russian embassy [...]", *op. cit.*
114. Geissler, D., Bär, D, Pröllochs, N. and Feuerriegel, S., "Russian propaganda on social [...]", *op. cit.*, pp. 12-13.
115. Geissler, D., Bär, D, Pröllochs, N. and Feuerriegel, S., "Russian propaganda on social [...]", *op. cit.*, p. 25

5.2. Russian Official Profiles as Key Players in the Strategy

It is worth mentioning the success of the embassies in disseminating Russian government messages. The Spanish account of the Russian Ministry of Foreign Affairs (@mae_russia) is retweeted more frequently than the Russian one (@MID_rf), even though the latter tweets five times more[116]. Therefore, we perceive the same dynamic that we identified previously: with less effort, Spanish accounts obtain better engagement thanks to the positioning in the public sphere that they achieved during the pandemic.

The Twitter accounts of the Russian embassies were also very active during the pandemic, amplifying the RT and Sputnik's content. Especially important was the activity of Russian embassies in some Latin American countries, such as Argentina, Cuba, Ecuador, Guatemala, Mexico, Panama, Peru and Uruguay, as well as the Russian embassy in Spain[117]. And not only the embassy accounts, but also the Russian ambassador to Venezuela and the Spanish-language account of the Russian Ministry of Foreign Affairs, who also replicated content from these media[118].

For expert Vladimir Rouvinski, this diplomatic effort must be understood in the light of the importance that Latin America acquired due to its proximity to the United States. "The Russian government's information strategy has to diminish the influence of the United States and the influence of Western values associated with Washington or Europe here in Latin America"[119].

Moreover, according to another DFRLab study, Russian embassies in Latin America and Spain have been used as main amplifiers of Russian media rhetoric[120]. The involvement of embassies is important, according to Puyosa, as a way of getting local media to report from the Russian perspective, as they are regular sources for these media, which have their own audience and credibility. In this way, "they reach people who do not follow these media and who only get their news from their usual newspaper and TV channel"[121].

Russian state-backed accounts targeting Latin American audiences have sought to garner support for Russia through the aforementioned techniques. According to the Foreign Policy at Brookings study, among most successful publications were those showing videos of Russian President Vladimir Putin

116. Brandt, J. and Wirtschafter, *Working the Western Hemisphere. How Russia [...]*, *op. cit.*, p. 3
117. DFRLab, "RT and Sputnik in Spanish boosted by Russian embassy [...]", *op. cit.*
118. DFRLab, "RT and Sputnik in Spanish boosted by Russian embassy [...]", *op. cit.*
119. Kahn, G., "Bloqueada en Occidente, la propaganda rusa [...]", *op. cit.*
120. Kahn, G., "Bloqueada en Occidente, la propaganda rusa [...]", *op. cit.*
121. Kahn, G., "Bloqueada en Occidente, la propaganda rusa [...]", *op. cit.*

and Foreign Minister Sergey Lavrov warning against NATO expansion, indicating that the invasion was a response to genocide against part of its population[122]. It was also emphasised that the Russian media blackout was a fabricated excuse to end any hint of uncomfortable storytelling by journalists who challenged Western narratives[123]. Another popularised publication used the early fighting in the Donetsk region to justify a full-scale Russian invasion, blaming Ukraine for the violence[124].

Meanwhile, Medium's analysis complements the previous study by indicating that Russian diplomatic accounts mostly shared content related to the possible use of biological weapons by Ukraine, the critical contents in pro-western media that they considered 'disinformation', and the justification of the invasion, mainly through anti-NATO narratives and the plan to "demilitarise and denazify" Ukraine[125]. "Russian diplomatic accounts also play an important role in the online conversation, as they have mainly spread false claims and conspiracies by amplifying narratives from Kremlin media outlets"[126].

Source: DFRLab, *RT and Sputnik in Spanish boosted by Russian embassy tweets and suspicious accounts*, 2022, retrieved from *https://medium.com/dfrlab/rt-and-sputnik-in-spanish-boosted-by-russian-embassy-tweets-and-suspicious-accounts-3a24ded7ef57* on 1 June 2023.

122. Brandt, J. and Wirtschafter, *Working the Western Hemisphere. How Russia [...], op. cit.*, p. 17
123. Brandt, J. and Wirtschafter, *Working the Western Hemisphere. How Russia [...], op. cit.*, p. 17
124. Brandt, J. and Wirtschafter, *Working the Western Hemisphere. How Russia [...], op. cit.*, p. 17
125. DFRLab, "RT and Sputnik in Spanish boosted by Russian embassy [...]", *op. cit.*
126. DFRLab, "RT and Sputnik in Spanish boosted by Russian embassy [...]", *op. cit.*

5.3. Dissemination Through Messaging Channels: the Case of Telegram

The propaganda strategy is not only structured on the basis of RT en Español, Sputnik Mundo and diplomatic accounts. According to a study by Olivia Sohr, in the first months of the war, disinformation circulated through Facebook, Instagram, TikTok, Telegram and WhatsApp as the main channels[127]. Particularly relevant seems to be the case of Telegram, with global newsgroups, which the factchecking centres point out as sources of structured disinformation. Factcheckers of Maldita.es explain: "We had located the groups that were disinforming especially on the issue of COVID and vaccines. When Russia invaded Ukraine, those groups — all of them — turned and started to support the Russian invasion"[128].

Medium conducted a study of 56 pro-Kremlin Telegram channels, divided into three networks of accounts, which are dedicated to disseminating pro-Kremlin content to users around the world. They observed them from 24 February 2022 to 17 January 2023[129]. The research assessed the language and found that the channels used both machine and human translations. In addition, when analysing the open-source code, they found that one of the three main networks (Surf Noise, Info Defense and Node of Time) was associated with the NVP ROKOT volunteer military training programme[130].

They further proved that the three networks of accounts were connected to each other through forwarded posts. In addition, they found that the amplification efforts were stronger in Russian, German, Italian and Spanish[131].

Particularly interesting is the conclusion about the sources they used. They mainly used similar pro-Kremlin channels, official accounts, such as that of Maria Zakharova, spokesperson of the Russian Foreign Ministry, the pro-Kremlin agency TASS, RT director Margarita Simonyan, the head of the Donetsk People's Republic Denis Pushilin, Russian blogger Semyon Pegov and former Russian President Dmitry Medvedev[132].

---

127. Kahn, G., "Bloqueada en Occidente, la propaganda rusa [...]", *op. cit.*
128. Kahn, G., "Bloqueada en Occidente, la propaganda rusa [...]", *op. cit.*
129. DFRLab, *Networks of pro-Kremlin Telegram channels spread disinformation at a global scale*, 2023, retrieved from *https://medium.com/dfrlab/networks-of-pro-kremlin-telegram-channels-spread-disinformation-at-a-global-scale-af4e319bd51e* on 1 June 2023.
130. DFRLab, *Networks of pro-Kremlin Telegram channels [...], op. cit.*
131. DFRLab, *Networks of pro-Kremlin Telegram channels [...], op. cit.*
132. DFRLab, *Networks of pro-Kremlin Telegram channels [...], op. cit.*

Regarding the thematic areas, the priorities previously identified were maintained. It is noteworthy that the word 'Nazi' was used 404 times in the period under study[133].

5.4. Using Influencers to Add Credibility to the Message

Another technique used to add credibility to the above-mentioned arguments was the choice of credible interlocutors for public opinion in the country where the strategy was developed. Russia made concerted efforts with independent journalists to spread the message.

According to the Foreign Policy at Brookings study, two out of the 15 most retweeted accounts supported by or belonging to Russia belonged to accounts of government or diplomatic entities (@embajadarusaes, @mfa_russia), three to RT or Sputnik employees (@senderov_rt, @ javiercarrasco, and @aliananieves) and one to an RT en Español-affiliated media outlet (@ahilesvainfo). The rest were influencers: two are or were affiliated with Western English-language alternative media, including Grayzone and MintPress, frequently cited by Kremlin media; and seven were independent Spanish-language journalists (two from Latin America and five from Spain).

These influencers regularly tweeted anti-Western views on different topics, with content that Russian media-affiliated journalists shared more commonly than Russian diplomatic accounts[134]. They did not have a massive degree of influence, but they prove that Russia tried to have a loudspeaker for its messages, while adding credibility as the message did not come from governmental sources. This strategy has been used extensively to reach US, European and Latin-American audiences. Social networks cannot label their content as coming from government accounts because this would set a precedent difficult to handle in terms of freedom of expression[135].

According to an investigation by El Confidencial cited by the Reuter Institute, Spanish YouTubers Rubén Gisbert and Liu Sivaya travelled to the Russian-controlled area of Donbas to film from there. This zone is off-limits to most Western media, and Russian authorisation and escorts are required to enter it[136].

They are influencers who share pro-Russian narratives, and even the Russian embassy in Spain broadcasts their content. In the case of Sivaya, her

133. DFRLab, *Networks of pro-Kremlin Telegram channels [...], op. cit.*
134. Brandt, J. and Wirtschafter, *Working the Western Hemisphere. How Russia [...], op. cit.*, p. 15.
135. Brandt, J. and Wirtschafter, *Working the Western Hemisphere. How Russia [...], op. cit.*, p. 15.
136. Kahn, G., "Bloqueada en Occidente, la propaganda rusa [...]", *op. cit.*

YouTube channel has 200,000 subscribers, and her coverage from Mariupol, describing the city as "liberated" and "reborn", stands out[137]. Gisbert has a channel with 476,000 subscribers and used to appear on RT to criticise Western coverage of the war[138].

Russia also uses local influencers in Latin America, who have credibility in regional environments. As Puyosa explains, Russia is "disseminating news using local influencers: people who are YouTubers, who have a popular TV news channel, who have more than 100,000 followers on Twitter (...). These people are working together with Russia"[139].

We previously mentioned the media outlet Ahí les Va, which defines itself as independent, but is affiliated with RT en Español. It regularly retweets RT en Español posts, promotes its video content, and defends it from online critics. The media established a new Twitter account in April 2022, shortly after the social network imposed new restrictions on Russian-backed accounts[140].

The popularity of Ahí les Va is due to Inna Afinogenova, who is well known by RT in Latin America. She covers international events and emphasises the particularities and incongruities of some Latin American leaders[141]. According to Adriana Amado, director of Infociudadana, in declarations to DW, "this type of media is very effective in relativising the information of the professional media. Inna Afinogenova works in a genre that is very popular in conspiracy groups, which usually lead with 'they don't want to tell you about this'"[142]. DW also includes the analysis of expert Morales, Professor of Social Communication at the Javeriana University in Colombia, who explains that "her followers do not necessarily believe in what she is saying, although they find in her a reformulated product of something that is also very common in Latin America: cause or militant journalism"[143].

The verification centre Maldita.es concludes: "It is much more effective to spread disinformation narratives through influencers who have

137. Kahn, G., "Bloqueada en Occidente, la propaganda rusa [...]", *op. cit.*
138. Kahn, G., "Bloqueada en Occidente, la propaganda rusa [...]", *op. cit.*
139. Kahn, G., "Bloqueada en Occidente, la propaganda rusa [...]", *op. cit.*
140. Brandt, J. and Wirtschafter, *Working the Western Hemisphere. How Russia [...], op. cit.*, p. 16.
141. Ospina-Valencia, J., "Los medios rusos en América Latina: cuando la invasión [...]", *op. cit.*
142. Ospina-Valencia, J., "Los medios rusos en América Latina: cuando la invasión [...]", *op. cit.*
143. Ospina-Valencia, J., "Los medios rusos en América Latina: cuando la invasión [...]", *op. cit.*

created their own communities and who serve as viralisers of hoaxes and manipulations"[144].

6. THE CONTRAST WITH CHINA'S INFORMATION STRATEGY

China's strategy has not been particularly proactive in terms of disseminating disinformation about the Ukrainian war in Latin America, although it shares dissemination networks with Russia and allows the Russian propaganda to be effective in those countries where it has influence. Nicolás de Pedro, researcher at the Institute for Statecraft, explains: "there is an exchange of narratives, which mutually amplify each other and multiply their reach because both China and Russia share them"[145].

China's information networks are aimed at proactively asserting its foreign policy interests; in the case of Latin America, it is especially interested in a better understanding of its model of country and in creating sympathy among its citizens, who do not fully understand its economic system, as Juan Pablo Cardenal explains[146]. For Cardenal, "China is trying to monopolise the discourse on the current China and present itself as friendly"[147].

Latin American countries are currently among the most strategic ones in the world in terms of information for China. The China Index, which studies China's influence in more than 80 countries, evaluates its influence in the field of the media -among other aspects-. It shows that the third most influential country in the world is Peru, followed by other Latin American countries such as Panama and Venezuela (20th place), and Argentina (35th)[148].

Thus, Russia is characterised by its pro-activeness in the war narrative, while China allows this strategy to be effective in public opinion in the countries where it has influence. However, from a proactive point of view, China focused on its own narrative to continue presenting the country in positive terms, as "supportive, compassionate and collaborative"[149].

144. Kahn, G., "Bloqueada en Occidente, la propaganda rusa [...]", *op. cit.*
145. Guevara, T., "Redes de desinformación chinas y rusas penetran en Latinoamérica", *Voz de América*, 2023, retrieved from *https://www.vozdeamerica.com/a/redes-de-desinformacion-china-y-rusas-penetran-en-latinoamerica-expertos/7067324.html* on 1 July 2023.
146. Guevara, T., "Redes de desinformación chinas y rusas penetran en Latinoamérica", *op. cit.*
147. Guevara, T., "Redes de desinformación chinas y rusas penetran en Latinoamérica", *op. cit.*
148. Alberro, H., "China y sus mentiras propagandísticas en América Latina", *Expediente Abierto*, 2023, retrieved from *https://www.expedienteabierto.org/china-y-sus-mentiras-propagandisticas-en-america-latina* on 1 July 2023.
149. Alberro, H., "China y sus mentiras propagandísticas en América Latina", *op. cit.*

IV. THE EUROPEAN UNION AND ITS FIGHT AGAINST DISINFORMATION IN LATIN AMERICA

The European Union has developed several actions that prioritise closer relations with Latin America from a multidisciplinary perspective. Through the Global Gateway strategy, it plans to allocate 3.4 billion euros in the framework of relations with LAC countries[150]. The European Fund for Sustainable Development Plus is also expected to mobilise 135 billion euros in strategic sectors for the achievement of the Global Gateway[151].

The EU points to China (due to its economic pre-eminence and its information synergies with Russia) and Russia (less successful economically, but stronger in terms of political influence on public opinion) as its main rivals in the region[152]. It is worth noting that RT's launch in the region came shortly after Russia concluded economic and security agreements with Cuba, Argentina, Brazil and Nicaragua in 2014. Later, RT opened offices in Buenos Aires, Caracas, Havana, Los Angeles, Madrid, Managua and Miami[153].

Despite attempts to reach the public opinion in the region, citizens have traditionally been closer to the EU. A July 2021 survey of ten countries in the region revealed that between the 17% and the 19% had a favourable opinion of Russia and China, compared to 43% of people that had it of Germany, the only European country included in the survey. The EU was also highlighted as a global champion of human rights (58%), the fight against poverty and inequality (5%) and the promotion of peace (56%)[154].

Therefore, Hobbs and Torreblanca conclude that "while Chinese engagement may be economically attractive, most countries in the region want to reform their education, health and public administration systems in line with European rather than Chinese objectives and align their environmental and social inclusion policies with European rather than Chinese ones"[155].

In relation to the issues identified in this paper, it is important to mention other initiatives such as the EU debate on a Declaration on Digital Rights and Principles[156], the joint work on digital ethics[157], and the proposal to

150. Hobbs, C. and Torreblanca, J. I., "La Alianza Digital UE-ALC [...]", *op. cit.*
151. Hobbs, C. and Torreblanca, J. I., "La Alianza Digital UE-ALC [...]", *op. cit.*
152. Hobbs, C. and Torreblanca, J. I., "La Alianza Digital UE-ALC [...]", *op. cit.*
153. Hobbs, C. and Torreblanca, J. I., "La Alianza Digital UE-ALC [...]", *op. cit.*
154. Hobbs, C. and Torreblanca, J. I., "La Alianza Digital UE-ALC [...]", *op. cit.*
155. Hobbs, C. and Torreblanca, J. I., "La Alianza Digital UE-ALC [...]", *op. cit.*
156. European Commission, *Declaración sobre los principios y derechos digitales europeos*, 2022, retrieved from *https://digital-strategy.ec.europa.eu/es/library/declaration-european-digital-rights-and-principles* on 1 June 2023.
157. Hobbs, C. and Torreblanca, J. I., "La Alianza Digital UE-ALC [...]", *op. cit.*

cooperate to fight disinformation and foreign interference together, especially in electoral processes, which could imply more EU election observation missions focused on disinformation. Hobbs and Torreblanca also note that disinformation training for other election monitoring bodies and capacity building programmes should be encouraged, with the aim of helping both regional governments and civil society actors to jointly address the issue[158].

In early 2023, in the framework of the Spanish Presidency of the Council of the EU, two new collaborative projects to fight disinformation were also announced: a project focused on preventing disinformation and increasing legal protection for independent journalists in Panama, Costa Rica, Dominican Republic and Ecuador[159], and the initiative "Democracy", which, according to the Spanish Minister of Foreign Affairs, European Union and Cooperation, José Manuel Albares, will focus on defending freedom of expression, while promoting "good practices in the use of social networks against disinformation and hate speech"[160].

V. PROPOSALS FOR THE FUTURE

According to Olivia Sohr, it is necessary a deeper understanding of the phenomenon of disinformation, being able to identify the fake stories that generate interest and why people believe in them[161]. The public must know the tools they need to use in order to identify fake photos or videos. She thinks that the problem will be worse in the future, because of the images generated by artificial intelligence[162]. Citizens "must know what to look for, whether it is the hands, whether it is the eyes, whether it is the metadata that comes with the image [...] to be able to differentiate what is real from what is not"[163].

Rouvinski and Puyosa highlight awareness-raising and education, rather than banning Russian media, as the best long-term strategy. They think that if citizens understand why the Russian media do what they do, it will be more difficult to manipulate them with circumstantial data[164].

158. Hobbs, C. and Torreblanca, J. I., "La Alianza Digital UE-ALC [...]", *op. cit.*
159. De León, Ana, "la UE y España anuncian dos proyectos contra la desinformación en Latinoamérica", *Euroefe*, 2023, retrieved from *https://euroefe.euractiv.es/section/latinoamerica/news/la-ue-y-espana-anuncian-dos-proyectos-contra-la-desinformacion-en-latinoamerica/* on 1 June 2023.
160. De León, Ana, "la UE y España anuncian dos proyectos contra la desinformación en Latinoamérica", *op. cit.*
161. Kahn, G., "Bloqueada en Occidente, la propaganda rusa [...]", *op. cit.*
162. Kahn, G., "Bloqueada en Occidente, la propaganda rusa [...]", *op. cit.*
163. Kahn, G., "Bloqueada en Occidente, la propaganda rusa [...]", *op. cit.*
164. Kahn, G., "Bloqueada en Occidente, la propaganda rusa [...]", *op. cit.*

According to the Foreign Policy study, to counter the disinformation strategy analysed in Latin America, the West should resist the temptation to refute everything it is accused of by disinformation networks. Thus, "they should focus on highlighting the tools and tactics that Russia employs (e. g. whataboutism and conspiracy theories)"[165].

Diplomats "can also use truthful messaging to go on the offensive; they can highlight Russia's corrupt, clandestine, and coercive activities in Latin America, including its use of private security contractors and illicit commercial deals to prop up illiberal leaders, as well as Russia's repressive behaviour at home. Doing so may help dampen the attractiveness of Russia's messaging"[166].

The study *Russian propaganda on social media during the 2022 invasion of Ukraine* concludes that without significant efforts by social media platforms to curb the spread of disinformation, propaganda can be disseminated widely and virally[167]. They also suggest focusing on reducing the influence of bots, although this requires further research to be achieved. Finally, they recommend monitoring propaganda campaigns that seek to destabilise public opinion, while fighting against the proliferation of online propaganda with counter-messaging or verification.

VI. CONCLUSIONS

Latin America has become a central region for the European interests. It is also a strategic area for China, which has grown in importance and influence in recent years, and for Russia, which is trying to gain public support in this region. Latin America is also very attractive for China and Russia because it is part of the Spanish-language communication market, where 496 million people speak Spanish as their first language.

For China, the Latin American region became strategic from an information point of view during the COVID-19 pandemic. As the pandemic started in China, it prioritised to manage its image in the international public opinion. Its narratives focused on denying that COVID-19 was originated in China and that it was spread by a cover-up by the authorities, while trying to reinforce the Chinese image of being a global donor of health supplies. When the vaccines arrived, a strategy of confrontation with Western countries

165. Brandt, J. and Wirtschafter, *Working the Western Hemisphere. How Russia […], op. cit.*, p. 22.
166. Brandt, J. and Wirtschafter, *Working the Western Hemisphere. How Russia […], op. cit.*, p. 22.
167. Geissler, D., Bär, D, Pröllochs, N. and Feuerriegel, S., "Russian propaganda on social […]", *op. cit.*, p. 27.

was detected in the Chinese media in Latin America, also in fields in which the Western image is consolidated, such as the protection of human rights.

After the Ukraine war began, China's strategy was not proactive in terms of disseminating content about this topic in Latin America, although it allowed Russia to effectively spread its message in those countries where China had influence. China's information media were aimed at asserting its foreign policy interests; in this case, they focused on reinforcing citizens' perception of its model of country.

In the case of Russia, it is necessary to highlight the importance of RT en Español and Sputnik News in Russia's outward propaganda strategy. The integration of these media into the information routines of the Latin American public opinion increased during the COVID-19 pandemic, whose news coverage was widely followed through RT. This was possible because of the lack of knowledge of the population about Russia and the absence of other alternative media, far from the US perspectives -part of the population had a strong anti-US sentiment-.

This paper demonstrates that the Russian propaganda campaign has been orchestrated and coordinated to present the war as a reactive measure to a previous provocation. And once the war began, there was a constant framing of Ukrainians as "Nazis and aggressors", presenting any opinion or perspective contrary to the Russian one as disinformation. Russia also emphasised that this was an "anti-imperialist" war, which could lead to some public sympathy with Russia, since, as we have already mentioned, part of the citizens had a strong anti-United States sentiment. Finally, Russia claimed that Western sanctions were the cause of Latin America's and the world's economic difficulties. All of this was combined with visual resources, often from other moments or conflicts, to add credibility to the messages and interact with the most emotional part of public opinion.

In addition to RT and Sputnik News, a comprehensive communication strategy was developed to convey these storylines. Bots were used to position and give visibility to the main messages on social networks. These actions were coordinated with the embassies and official profiles in social networks, and they also included external influencers into the strategy, which added more credibility to messages. They also disseminated the contents using the main messaging channels, such as TikTok, WhatsApp and Telegram — especially the latter, where mass networks were created to promote the main storylines.

The European Union is aware of the importance Latin America has for its geostrategic interests. For this reason, it is developing several initiatives to recover its position in the region and to fight against disinformation. Through the Global Gateway strategy, the EU plans to mobilize important funds to improve its cooperation with LAC countries. The EU also announced the debate on a Declaration on Digital Rights and Principles, the collaboration on digital ethics and the joint initiative to fight disinformation and foreign interference.

In addition, in early 2023, in the framework of the Spanish Presidency of the Council of the EU, two new collaborative projects to fight disinformation were announced: a project against disinformation and focused on the legal protection of independent journalists in Panama, Costa Rica, Dominican Republic and Ecuador, and the project 'Democracy', which will focus on the defence of freedom of expression.

This paper demonstrated the importance of disinformation in Latin America and the risks of polarising the public opinion. The EU must take an active role to regain its influence in the region and work with Latin American countries to fight against the foreign interference. This should be done at the macro level, with some of the initiatives mentioned above, but also through media literacy, because citizens must be able to distinguish the main features of fake news and be less vulnerable to disinformation attacks.

II. TRADE, INVESTMENTS, COMPETITION & MARKET REGULATION

The Future of the WTO and EU-China Trade Relations

ALLAN F. TATHAM
PhD in Law from the Faculty of Law of Leiden University (The Netherlands)
Lecturer of European Law, Faculty of Law, San Pablo CEU University

I. INTRODUCTION

The twentieth anniversary of the accession of the People's Republic of China ("PRC" or "China") to the World Trade Organization ("WTO" or "Organization") in December 2021[1] has come to be seen in a much broader context of evolving relations that have been impacted on variously by alterations of approaches in US[2] and EU[3] trade policies, the stalled ratification of the EU-China Comprehensive Agreement on Investment ("CAI")[4], the disruption in supply chains accentuated by the global Covid pandemic[5] and the current war in Ukraine[6] with the notion of "de-coupling" or "de-risking"

1. See the earlier contributions in Gao, H., Lewis, D. (eds.), *China's Participation in the WTO*, London: Cameron May, 2006.
2. On US attitudes to PRC membership, both before and after its accession, as well as continuing American confrontation in trade matters generally with the PRC, see Mavroidis, P. C., Sapir, A., *China and the WTO: Why Multilateralism Still Matters*, Princeton (NJ) and Oxford: Princeton University Press, 2021.
3. Burnay, M., Wouters, J., "The EU and China in the WTO: What Contribution to the International Rule of Law? Reflections in Light of the *Raw Materials* and *Rare Earths* Disputes", in Wang, J., Song, W. (eds.), *China, the European Union, and the International Politics of Global Governance*, Basingstoke: Palgrave Macmillan 2016, chap. 6, pp. 115-135.
4. Chaisse, J., Burnay, M., "Introduction — CAI's Contribution to International Investment Law: European, Chinese, and Global Perspectives", in *The Journal of World Investment & Trade*, vol. 23, n. 4, 2022, pp. 497-520.
5. Shih, W. C., "Global Supply Chains in a Post-Pandemic World: Companies Need to Make Their Networks More Resilient. Here's How", *Harvard Business Review*, vol. 98, n. 5, 2020, pp. 82-89.
6. Livingstone, D., "Chinese supply chains could tip the balance in Ukraine", Expert Comment, *Chatham House (Online)*, 29 March 2023, retrieved from *www.chathamhouse.org/2023/03/chinese-supply-chains-could-tip-balance-ukraine*

from overreliance or overdependence on Chinese goods[7]. To this mix may be added such topical issues of climate change and the digital economy, with the concomitant and sustained rise in popular fears associated with data protection, cyber security and artificial intelligence[8].

With these extensive concerns in mind — coupled with the fears of a looming trade war — as forming the backdrop to this paper, it may seem rather challenging to speak of EU-China relations, even of potential co-operation, in the WTO either as a way to progress already considered issues or to evolve the process for reform of the Organization itself. The possibility of joint initiatives between the PRC and the EU has been made even more fraught, especially since the Union caused profound disappointment in the PRC in 2019 when the EU referred (in a policy document) to China being a "systemic rival" that promoted alternative systems of governance[9] .While the Union may come to rue the public use of such a direct and pointed description of its relation or partnership with China[10], the multipolar world in which we live will still require collaboration between the PRC and the EU in order successfully to address the challenges facing humankind.

One of the arenas where such cooperation may bear some fruit is, somewhat surprisingly, the WTO. Needless to say, the Organization is experiencing various crosswinds at this time but still manages to provide a diplomatic forum for discussion beyond the limelight of posturing on (potential) trade wars. In seeking to move the WTO forward in order to reflect the reality of international trade in present-day circumstances, the EU and the PRC may together hold the key to unlocking future (more focused)

7. Schaus M., Lannoo, K., "The EU's aim to de-risk itself from China is risky... yet necessary", *CEPS Commentary (Online)*, 7 September 2023, retrieved from *www.ceps.eu/the-eus-aim-to-de-risk-itself-from-china-is-risky-yet-necessary/*
8. See, e.g., Girard, B., "The Real Danger of China's National Intelligence Law", *The Diplomat (Online)*, 23 February 2019, retrieved from *thediplomat.com/2019/02/the-real-danger-of-chinas-national-intelligence-law/*; McCarthy, S., "Will China's revised cybersecurity rules put foreign firms at risk of losing their secrets?", *South China Morning Post (Online)*, 13 October 2019, retrieved from *www.scmp.com/news/china/diplomacy/article/3032649/will-chinas-revised-cybersecurity-law-put-foreign-firms-risk?campaign=3032649&module=perpetual_scroll_0&pgtype=article*; and Sheehan, M. "China's AI Regulations and How They Get Made", *Working Paper*, Carnegie Endowment for International Peace, Washington DC, 2023, retrieved from *carnegieendowment.org/files/202307-Sheehan_Chinese%20AI%20gov.pdf*
9. European Commission and Vice President/High Representative of the Union for Foreign Affairs and Security Policy, "EU-China — A strategic outlook", Joint Communication, 12 March 2019, JOIN(2019) 5 final, p. 1.
10. On the partnership in general, see Michalski, A., Pan. Z., *Unlikely Partners? China, the European Union and the Forging of a Strategic Partnership*, Singapore: Palgrave MacMillan, 2017.

negotiations on discrete issues that could build further confidence in a renewed WTO, more relevant for the third decade of the 21st century.

In order to appreciate the ongoing possibilities of cooperation, this work will look at the past, present and possible future of bilateral relations between China and the EU within the overall context of the WTO. It will accordingly aim to provide a very short overview of past relations between the EU and China in the context of the latter's accession to the WTO in 2001, before turning to look at their continued working relations despite the emergence of the current malaise in relations. The work will proceed to look at some examples of Sino-European cooperation that have occurred, despite the present dip in the intensity of relations, and will then conclude with a discussion as to how China and the EU might create openings for their further working together in the WTO, especially in the context of the present reform proposals.

II. THE PAST — THE PROCESS OF PRC ACCESSION TO THE WTO: MISPLACED EUPHORIA?

1. EU ENGAGEMENT WITH CHINA IN WTO ACCESSION NEGOTIATIONS

With its dependence on the free flow of trade across the globe, the EU's continuing commitment to upholding the rules-based international order and to supporting effective multilateral trade governance[11], centred on the WTO, ultimately allowed it steadily to emerge as a counterweight to the influence of the USA during the lengthy negotiations for China's accession to the WTO (1986-2001)[12]. In these international trade negotiations, the EU was motivated by both strong geoeconomic as well as mercantilist considerations, particularly its interest in maximising its wealth relative to other powers[13]. As the European Commission noted at that time:[14] "In order for European

11. European Commission, Communication "Trade Policy Review — An Open, Sustainable and Assertive Trade Policy", COM(2021) 66 final, pp. 8-9.
12. See, generally, Ching, C., Ching, H. Y., *Handbook on China's WTO Accession and Its Impacts*, Singapore and London: World Scientific Publishing, 2003; Gertler, J. L., "What China's WTO Accession is all about", in Bhattasali, D., Li, S., Martin, W. (eds.), *China and the WTO Accession, Policy Reform, and Poverty Reduction Strategies*, Washington DC and Oxford: World Bank and Oxford University Press, 2004, chap. 2, pp. 21-28; Wang, L. (ed.), *China's WTO Accession Reassessed*, Abingdon: Routledge, 2015.
13. Zimmermann, H., "Realist Power Europe? The EU in the Negotiations about China's and Russia's WTO Accession", *Journal of Common Market Studies*, vol. 45, n. 4, 2007, pp. 813-832, at pp. 813-814.
14. European Commission, Communication "A Long Term Policy for China-Europe Relations", at pp. 4-5: COM(1995) 279 final.

industry to be globally competitive we must be present on the world's most dynamic markets... An active role for EU business in China, where US and Japanese competition is already fierce, is essential".

When China started to open up to global commerce in 1978, it became clear that the main thrust of its policy — in international trade terms — was resurrecting its erstwhile membership of GATT. Having applied for membership in 1986, it soon became clear that the most important arenas for negotiations would be those with the USA and the EU. However, whereas the US-Chinese talks were beset by a high degree of mutual mistrust, together with domestic resistance (at times, both commercial and popular) and political division in the USA, the EU instead presented a much more united position throughout the subsequent WTO accession negotiations[15]. Moreover, it was not subjected to the pushback experienced in the USA and, publicly at least wary of how its allies could still take advantage of any continuing discord on its part with China[16], the European Commission needed rather to encourage EU companies to "take the plunge" and invest in the PRC[17]: "EU companies are being less dynamic than their competitor in the Chinese market — and are hence missing opportunities. This could not only have negative implications for future trade, but also weaken the EU's global competitiveness".

Through its whole conceptual approach[18] to the PRC's WTO accession negotiations (compared to that adopted by the USA) and its progressive positioning as a 'bridge' between those two parties, the EU was able to put its well-honed trade diplomacy skills to good use in progressing the talks in a positive direction. Its stance was considerably aided by the emergence of a European Commission with a stronger voice in international trade negotiations[19], following the completion of the Single Market that had thereby ensured the EU rise as the world's then largest trading bloc.

Ultimately[20], the EU has to receive credit for easing political tensions and for defusing at least the rhetoric over one of the major sticking points in the

15. Zimmermann, *op. cit.*, note 13, at pp. 820-821.
16. Möller, K., "Diplomatic Relations and Mutual Strategic Perceptions: China and the EU", China Quarterly, vol. 169, n. 2, 2002, pp. 10-32, at p. 17.
17. Commission, *op. cit.*, note 14, para. C.1, at pp. 8-9.
18. Zimmermann, *op. cit.*, note 13, at p. 823.
19. See, generally, Meunier, S., *Trading Voices: The European Union in International Commercial Negotiations*, Princeton (NJ): Princeton University Press, 2007.
20. Eglin, M., "China's Entry into the WTO with a Little Help from the EU", *International Affairs*, vol. 73, n. 3, 1997, pp. 489-509, at pp. 493-494.

negotiations, viz., that of China's status as a developing country under the terms of the WTO[21].

In fact, in supporting China's accession to the WTO[22], the EU was well aware of its unique position compared to other states that wished to accede at that time[23]:

In the first place, in political terms, China was put in a class of its own, characterised by a highly centralised and relatively closed system.

Secondly, in economic terms, China was one of the largest and most rapidly growing markets in the world. The negotiating advantage China derived from this position was the attraction to others of its market and the price WTO Members and companies were prepared to pay in order to gain secure access to it. It therefore came as no surprise that large, multinational manufacturers in France, Germany, Italy, Spain and the United Kingdom were particularly desirous of obtaining a large slice of the Chinese market for their exports. Accordingly, they lobbied their governments hard to support China's WTO accession through the EU.

Thirdly, from an administrative perspective, China's huge territory posed a problem of implementing and enforcing a uniform trade policy that was consistent with WTO rules. Setting nationwide technical standards and regulations and ensuring their even enforcement across the whole country were together seen as a sine qua non for China's WTO accession. Differences across Chinese regions would have constructed enormous trade barriers (e.g., to entry on the different regional markets) to the detriment of producers and consumers alike.

However, at the bottom of all these matters, China's real difference lay in the fact that it had already become a formidable trade power in record time while remaining firmly outside the multilateral trading system. As such, the WTO and its Members could not fail to acknowledge that the PRC had been and would increasingly become one of the major contributors to the forces driving the globalisation of economic, trade and financial activities.

Recognising the opportunities and possible difficulties that China could bring as it exerted its influence and caused momentous shifts in the global

21. *Ibid.*, at pp. 501-505.
22. For an analysis of the process, see Gao, H., "China's Participation in the WTO: A Lawyer's Perspective", *Singapore Year Book of International Law*, vol. 11, 2007, pp. 1-34, esp. pp. 1-17.
23. Eglin, *op. cit.*, note 20, at pp. 506-507.

trading system, the EU considered it important as well as prudent that China would become a WTO Member and thus an active participant in the rules-based international trade order. Initially, as an applicant, China would be clearly a "norm-taker". Nevertheless, its vital role and growing strength on the international scene would ensure that its actorness in the corridors of power in the WTO would soon allow it to emerge as a "norm-maker"[24].

Thus, with one eye on the future, the EU became a strong though realistic supporter of China's accession to the WTO. Such entry was eventually achieved, as may be recalled, after lengthy negotiations and strict commitments on the part of China, on 11 December 2001.

2. CHINESE ENGAGEMENT IN THE WTO AFTER ACCESSION

The gradual and successful Chinese engagement in the institutions of the WTO at all levels, from their ambassadors in the General Council to their experts in the technical committees and subcommittees, has been one of the achievements of its accession to the Organization[25]. Ensuring the training and preparedness of individuals to make a contribution in the interests of the PRC from the start of membership — coupled with an openness to socialisation in these institutions as a means of consolidating the Chinese voice in the WTO over time — has allowed the PRC to overcome many reservations of WTO Members intimated during the accession negotiations.

Part of the problem for WTO Members had been in their critical view (supported by commentators) of the Chinese approach to international law in general and its enforcement in particular[26]. Reservations were voiced as to the likely Chinese attitude to the compulsory adjudicative WTO system in the form of its dispute settlement mechanism, including the establishment of ad hoc panels and the final appeal on questions of law to the permanent Appellate Body. These reservations revolved around China's traditional

24. Gao, H., "China's ascent in global trade governance: from rule taker to rule shaker and, maybe rule maker?", in Deere Birkbeck, C. (ed.), *Making Global Trade Governance Work for Development: Perspectives and Priorities from Developing Countries*, Cambridge: Cambridge University Press, 2011, chap. 6, pp. 153-180.

25. Hsieh, P. L., "China's Development of International Economic Law and WTO Legal Capacity Building", *Journal of International Economic Law*, vol. 13, n. 4, 2010, pp. 997-1036.

26. See, in general, Hanqin, X., "Chinese Contemporary Perspectives on International Law: History, Culture and International Law", *Collected Courses of the Hague Academy of International Law*, Leiden and The Hague: Brill and The Hague Academy of Internal Law, 2012, vol. 355.

mistrust of international adjudication[27] including (i) Chinese perceptions of international law as a threat to the primacy of their state sovereignty (together with such principles as non-intervention and territorial integrity)[28]; (ii) the cultural/historic Chinese approach to resolving disputes, with Confucianism promoting harmony through (informal) mediation (as well as negotiations and conciliation) rather than litigation through the rival legalism approach[29]; and (iii) Chinese concerns over the impartiality and independence of international courts[30] that they considered as biased and dominated by the West[31].

Nevertheless, over the years of its membership, the PRC has come to be perceived as a more active and willing participant, thereby throwing into relief its usual position in other international organisations and dispute settlement mechanisms[32]. With international trade disputes entailing no loss of territorial sovereignty and only indirectly smacking of intervention domestically (through necessary legal amendments or new laws or the disapplication of WTO-inconsistent practices)[33], the PRC has taken both a cost-benefit attitude to the WTO system as a whole as well as one which acknowledges a bias in favour of socialisation as a means of projecting Chinese interests in the WTO institutional universe[34].

27. Harpaz, M. D., "China and International Tribunals: Onward from the WTO", in Toohey, L., Picker, C. B., Greenacre, J. (eds.), *China in the International Economic Order: New Directions and Changing Paradigms*, Cambridge: Cambridge University Press, 2015, chap. 4, pp. 43-61, at p. 47.
28. Carlson, A., "More Than Just Saying No: China's Evolving Approach to Sovereignty and Intervention since Tiananmen", in Johnston A. I., Ross, R. S. (eds.), *New Directions in the Study of China's Foreign Policy*, Stanford (CA): Stanford University Press, 2006, pp. 217-241; and Muller, W., "China's Sovereignty in International Law: From Historical Grievance to Pragmatic Tool", *China-EU Law Journal*, vol. 1, nos. 3-4, 2013, pp. 35-59.
29. Pan, J., "Chinese Philosophy and International Law", *Asian Journal of International Law*, vol. 1, n. 2, 2011, pp. 233-248; and Picker, C. B., "China's Legal Cultural Relationship in International Economic Law: Multiple and Conflicting Paradigms," in Toohey, Picker, Greenacre, op. cit., note 27, chap. 5, pp. 62-76, at pp. 66-70.
30. Posner, E. A., Yoo, J., "International Law and the Rise of China", *Chicago Journal of International Law*, vol. 7, n. 1, 2006, pp. 1-15, at pp. 9-14.
31. Hsieh, *op. cit.*, note 25, at p. 1001.
32. Ngangjoh Hodu, Y., Zhang, Q., *The Political Economy of WTO Implementation and China's Approach to Litigation in the WTO*, Cheltenham: Edward Elgar, 2016, chap. 7, s.v. "China and the WTO dispute settlement system", pp. 108-193.
33. Potter, P. B., "China's Performance on International Treaties on Trade and Human Rights", in Lo, C., Li, N. N. T., Lin, T. (eds.), *Legal Thoughts between the East and the West in the Multilevel Legal Order: A Liber Amicorum in Honour of Professor Herbert Han-Pao Ma*, Singapore: Springer Nature, 2016, chap. 14, pp. 217-238, at pp. 219-224.
34. Harpaz, *op. cit.*, note 27, at pp. 43-45 and 58-60.

China's story in the WTO in the years following accession has thus been one of evolution[35], particularly in its use of the dispute settlement process and its increasing willingness to bring actions before panels and the Appellate Body[36]. This process was executed over a number of years, reinforced by training and development of a cadre of Chinese international trade experts to represent the PRC in WTO proceedings[37]. Such positive engagement — reflected in its conducting business across many of the WTO institutions — and its position as a global trade power has also led to China successfully nominating two members of the Appellate Body: Mme. Zhang Yuejiao (2008-2016); and Mme. Zhao Hong (2016-2020). In this sense, the PRC and USA both came to obtain, *de facto*, the right to a permanent seat on the Appellate Body[38].

Nevertheless, while this engagement deepened[39], concerns were raised by some commentators as to China's willingness to implement the findings in panel and Appellate Body reports[40]. However, research also found that China was in practice more compliant in observing the decisions in international trade matters that went against it than in any other sphere of international law[41]. Moreover, through its socialisation in the WTO system, the PRC was able to game that system in the same way as the USA and the EU, and so developed the tools and behaviour necessary to delay (permanently) implementation of WTO panel or AB reports that went against it[42].

35. In this, the PRC has been aided by a new approach to use the WTO rules more effectively with the support of public-private networks: Luo, Y., "Engaging the Private Sector: EU-China Trade Disputes Under the Shadow of WTO Law?", *European Law Journal*, vol. 13, n. 6, 2007, pp. 800-817.
36. Ji, W., Huang, C., "China's Experience in Dealing with WTO Dispute Settlement: A Chinese Perspective", *Journal of World Trade*, vol. 45, n. 1, 2011, pp. 1-37.
37. Hsieh, *op. cit.*, note 25.
38. Moynihan, H., "China's Evolving Approach to International Dispute Settlement", *International Law Program: Briefing Paper*, March 2017, The Royal Institute of International Affairs, Chatham House, London, p. 6, retrieved from *www.chathamhouse.org/sites/default/files/publications/research/2017-03-29-chinas-evolving-approach-international-dispute-settlement-moynihan-final.pdf*
39. According to Moynihan, *ibid.*, at p. 7, in the WTO dispute settlement mechanism, the PRC has become one of the top five respondents in proceedings, one of the top 10 initiators of such proceedings and one of the top five third-party interveners in disputes at Geneva.
40. See, in general, pre-WTO accession, Feinerman, J. V., "Chinese Participation in the International Legal Order: Rogue Elephant or Team Player?", *China Quarterly*, vol. 141, 1995, pp. 186-210.
41. Webster, T., "China's Implementation of WTO Decisions," in Toohey, Picker & Greenacre, *op. cit.*, note 27, chap. 7, pp. 98-111.
42. *Ibid.*, at pp. 101-102

III. THE PRESENT — STILL POSSIBLE TO WORK TOGETHER?

1. CHANGING LANDSCAPE

Fast forward to the present and we can see the political and economic landscape has been, perhaps fundamentally, redrawn[43]. No longer are international trade matters capable of being strictly "divorced" from geostrategic and global security concerns (at least with respect to the EU[44], the US perspective in contrast having almost always linked them) or the evolving politics of international relations in a multipolar world[45]. One example of this being the series of disputes at the WTO between the EU (and other WTO Members) and the PRC over the latter's response — in international trade terms — over Lithuania's stance as regards the nature of its relations with the Separate Customs Territory of Taiwan, Penghu, Kinmen and Matsu ("Chinese Taipei")[46].

The three economic powers of the USA, the PRC and the EU continue to dominate the operations of the WTO in particular and international trade relations in general[47]. This has however been undermined in more recent years between, on the one hand, the USA under former President Donald Trump and his effectively launching a trade war against China[48] as well as undermining the role of the WTO and, on the other, the rapidly emerging "wolf warrior diplomacy" of China and its impact on challenging prior perceptions of its conduct of international relations[49]. Moreover, the

43. Geeraerts, G., (2013). "The changing global context of China-EU relations", *China International Studies*, vol. 42, 2013, pp. 53-69; and Li, M., "China-EU Relations: Strategic Partnership at a Crossroads", *China: An International Journal*, vol. 7, n. 2, 2009, pp. 227-254.

44. See the contributions in Kirchner, E. J., Christiansen, Th., Dorussen, H. (eds)., *Security relations between China and the European Union from convergence to cooperation?*, Cambridge: Cambridge University Press, 2016.

45. Geeraerts, G., "China, the EU, and the new multipolarity", *European Review*, vol. 19, 2011, pp. 57 67.

46. *China — Measures concerning Trade in Goods and Services — Request for the establishment of a panel by the European Union* (9 December 2022), WT/DS610/8. The relevant panel was established on 27 January 2023 and composed on 18 April 2023.

47. Hoekman, B., Wolfe, R., "Reforming the World Trade Organization: Practitioner Perspectives from China, the EU, and the US", *China & World Economy*, vol. 29, n. 4, 2021, pp. 1-34.

48. Fetzer, T., Schwarz, C., "Tariffs and Politics: Evidence from Trump's Trade Wars", *The Economic Journal*, vol. 131, n. 636, 2021, pp. 1717-1741.

49. While the naming of this more assertive projection of Chinese foreign policy is not universally welcomed, the epithet has stuck: Zhu, Z., "Interpreting China's 'Wolf-Warrior Diplomacy': What explains the sharper tone to China's overseas conduct recently?", *The Diplomat (Online)*, 15 May 2020, retrieved from *thediplomat.com/2020/05/*

dislocation of supply chains during the recent pandemic have fed into the EU's growing security concerns (now exacerbated by the Ukraine war) and have, in turn, undermined to some extent the serious maintenance of its former role of "bridge" between the USA and China.

2. CONTINUING VIABILITY OF EU-PRC CO-OPERATION IN THE WTO

These emerging challenges of ideology, values and systems between China (representing the new world order) and the USA (as the champion of the old Bretton Woods system and its institutions) have naturally had a severe impact on EU-China cooperation in the WTO bodies. To this must be added side note on the fall-out from Brexit. Nevertheless, the picture remains mixed on this key trade relationship with the EU.

What has helped keep EU-China relations on a steady keel has been the existence of institutional systems that allow for collaboration between these two partners, either exclusively or within a broader multilateral context.

2.1. EU-PRC Bilateral Frameworks for Collaboration

On the one hand, China and the EU have developed — over several decades — an unparalleled and dense network of highly-structured bilateral dialogues[50], institutionalised spaces that permit discussion and exchange as well as further socialisation[51]. At the pinnacle of this huge "dialogue architecture" is the annual EU-China summit that brings together policymakers from both strategic partners[52]. The ambit of the dialogues is broad[53] and they are built around three pillars, viz., political, economic

interpreting-chinas-wolf-warrior-diplomacy/; and Xiaolin, D., Liu, Y., "The Rise and Fall of China's Wolf Warrior Diplomacy", The Diplomat (Online), 22 September 2023, retrieved from *thediplomat.com/2023/09/the-rise-and-fall-of-chinas-wolf-warrior-diplomacy/*

50. Fanoulis, E., Song, W., "Cooperation between the EU and China: A post-liberal governmentality approach", *Review of International Studies*, vol. 48, n. 2, 2022, pp. 346-363.
51. Christiansen, Th., "A liberal institutionalist perspective on EU-China relations", in Wang, Song, *op. cit.*, note 3, pp. 29-50, at p. 41.
52. *Ibid.*
53. Geeraerts, G., "The EU-China Partnership: Balancing Between Divergence and Convergence," paper presented at the Final International Conference and Researchers' Workshop "A New Dimension in Asia-Europe Relations: Exploring EU's Global Actorness and Strategic Partnership in Asia", Jean Monnet Network NEAR Project, 21-23 March 2019, Korea University, Seoul, at p. 9, retrieved from *www.researchgate.net/publication/332263267_The_EU-China_Partnership_Balancing_Between_Divergence_and_Convergence*

and social relations, each of which is headed by a particular bilateral high-level dialogue ("HLD"): the High-Level Strategic Dialogue (set up in 2010); the High-Level Economic and Trade Dialogue (2007); and the High-Level People-to-People Dialogue (2012)[54]. These together with other HLDs form the framework of a more extensive eco-system of sub-dialogues and focused working groups of experts from the European External Action Service, the European Commission and relevant line ministries from China[55].

Although these platforms are deliberative in nature rather than decisional, they allow such policymakers a space for mutual exchange of views, for forming an understanding of different positions and for addressing potential problems[56]. The nature of these dialogues thus fits well with the approach taken by Chinese diplomacy, and the long-held Confucian way of resolving problems. By moulding these arenas of deliberation and potential reciprocal (long-term) socialisation for officials from both partners[57], they have provided themselves with a structure that may well be resilient enough to withstand the storms of disputes and frictions that arise in any bilateral relations, although which have become more serious over recent times[58]. While differences between the two parties are always going to remain due to their very natures and identities[59], nevertheless this eco-system of dialogues provides the necessary space for both of them to achieve general agreement on a series of strategic matters while simultaneously permitting some degree of deviation[60].

Of particular relevance for the present discussion are, first, the High-Level Economic and Trade Dialogue; secondly, the three High-Level Dialogues in the sector of maritime affairs and fisheries, namely on Ocean Affairs, on Fisheries and on Law of the Sea and Polar Affairs; and, lastly, the High-Level Digital Dialogue. While these dialogues occur annually, further work is continued throughout the year between the relevant officials from both partners.

In trade matters, the High-Level Economic and Trade Dialogue is co-chaired by a Vice-Premier from the PRC and a Vice President of the European

54. Liu, H, Breslin, S., "Shaping the agenda jointly? China and the EU in the G20", in Wang, Song, *op. cit.*, note 3, pp. 95-113.
55. Christiansen, *op. cit.*, note 52, at p. 41.
56. *Ibid.*, at p. 42.
57. Geeraerts, *op. cit.*, note 54, at pp. 10-11.
58. *Ibid.*, at p. 43.
59. Gross, E., Jian, J., "Conceptual Gaps on Global Governance between China and the EU," in Pan, Z. (ed.), *Conceptual Gaps in China-EU Relations: Global Governance, Human Rights and Strategic Partnerships*, Basingstoke: Palgrave Macmillan, 2012, pp. 202-215.
60. Terhalle, M., "Reciprocal socialization: Rising powers and the West", *International Studies Perspectives*, vol. 12, 2011, pp. 341-361.

Commission representing the EU. The EU's trade policy towards China is set out in the EU-China 2020 Strategic Agenda for Cooperation[61] and in the EU-China Strategy of 2016[62], later updated by Commission in its 2019 Communication "EU-China — A Strategic Outlook"[63]. To these documents must be added the EU-China trade and economic priorities reiterated at the annual EU-China Summits that, in 2019 at the 21st summit, stated:[64]

> The EU and China firmly support the rules-based multilateral trading system with the WTO at its core, fight against unilateralism and protectionism, and commit to complying with WTO rules.
>
> The two sides reaffirm their joint commitment to co-operate on WTO reform to ensure its continued relevance and allow it to address global trade challenges....
>
> The two sides welcome the work so far in the EU-China Joint Working Group on WTO reform. Both sides also agreed to continue working to resolve the crisis in the WTO Appellate Body and build convergence on other areas of WTO reform.

The work of the three HLDs on maritime affairs and fisheries is complemented by regular meetings of the EU-China Working Group on Illegal, Unreported and Unregulated ("IUU") fishing matters. They are guided[65] in their work by the 2018 bilateral Blue Partnership for the Oceans[66] that seeks to improve cooperation aiming at better ocean governance, sustainable fisheries, and a thriving maritime economy between the EU and

---

61. European External Action Service, 'EU-China 2020 Strategic Agenda for Cooperation', 2013, retrieved *from eeas.europa.eu/sites/eeas/files/20131123.pdf*
62. European Commission and Vice President/High Representative for Foreign Affairs and Security Policy, "Elements for a New EU Strategy on China", Joint Communication, 22 June 2016, JOIN 30 final (2019), p. 1; and Council of the European Union, "EU Strategy on China", Council Conclusions, 11252/16, Brussels, 18 July 2016, p. 2, retrieved from *data.consilium.europa.eu/doc/document/ST-11252-2016-INIT/en/pdf*
63. European Commission and VP/HR, "EU-China — A strategic outlook", *op. cit.*, note 9.
64. EU-China, "Joint statement of the 21st EU-China summit", 10 April 2019, para. 13, retrieved from *www.eeas.europa.eu/node/60836_en*
65. Raftopoulos, M., Nissen, A., "EU and China's strategic partnership on the Blue Economy: Challenges and Opportunities", in Li, X. (ed.), *China-EU Relations in a New Era of Global Transformation*, Basingstoke: Routledge, 2021, chap. 12, pp. 209-227.
66. EU-China, Declaration on the establishment of a Blue Partnership for the Oceans: towards better ocean governance, sustainable fisheries and a thriving maritime economy between the European Union and the People's Republic of China, 16 July 2018, Beijing, retrieved from *demaribus.files.wordpress.com/2018/07/eu-china-blue-partnership.pdf*

China. In fisheries issues[67], the Partnership speaks of cooperation to prevent unregulated commercial fishing in the high seas areas and to promote sustainable fisheries governance, policies and management as well as to strengthen effective systems of control, inspection and enforcement. It also seeks promotion of the initiatives of the Food and Agriculture Organization of the United Nations and of relevant Regional Fisheries Management Organisations (of which both the PRC and the EU are parties) aimed at fighting IUU fishing activities and exchanging information relating to fishing vessels suspected of such activities together with conducting necessary follow-up cooperation, in accordance with applicable international law, to effectively combat IUU fishing, including through the already mentioned EU-China Working Group on IUU fishing matters.

Lastly, the High-Level Digital Dialogue (established in 2020)[68] serves to identify priorities in the digital transformation of both the EU's and China's economies, including areas where concrete progress is possible as well as allow for discussion where there are differences in approach. The EU's position is based on the Commission's 2021 Communication on the Digital Compass that translates the Union's ambitions in the sector for the next "digital" decade into clear, concrete targets. Laying down a European way for the digital decade because digital transformation poses global challenges, the EU seeks simultaneously to promote its positive and human-centred digital agenda internationally. In view of the sector's increasing importance to both economies, this HLD covers a broad range of issues including digital policies, innovation and standardisation as well as strategic cooperation.

Linked to this Digital HLD is the annual dialogue[69], launched in 2009, on policy regarding information and communications technologies that the Commission's Directorate General for Communication Networks, Content and Technology conducts with the PRC's Ministry of Industry and Information Technology. Since 2012, the European Commission and EEAS have co-chaired the EU-China Cyber Taskforce with the PRC Ministries of Industry and Information Technology and of Foreign Affairs which taskforce has as its objective the enhancing of mutual exchanges on cyber issues. Recent discussions have emphasised their common interest in developing the digital economy and maintaining a peaceful and stable cyberspace,

67. *Ibid.*, point (3), at p. 5.
68. European Commission, "EU-China: Commission and China hold first High-level Digital Dialogue," *Press Release*, IP/20/1600, 10 September 2020, retrieved from *ec.europa.eu/commission/presscorner/detail/fr/ip_20_1600*
69. *Ibid.*

agreeing to uphold multilateralism and address challenges in a collective manner. Both the PRC and the EU further underlined the importance in maintaining an open and non-discriminatory environment for all businesses, and in the fact that internet governance was to be promoted as based on principles of openness and inclusiveness[70].

2.2. EU and PRC Participation in Negotiations for WTO Reform

On the other hand, the PRC and the EU have also opened up other arenas of communication, discussion and socialisation in respect of their approaches to the reform of the WTO — both in bilateral co-ordination of their positions as well as in the practical expression of their shared commitments through participation in plurilateral negotiations within the overall WTO context, that seek to help keep the Organization in the forward direction of evolution to meet the challenges of the 21st century.

A) EU-China Working Group on WTO Reform

As already indicated, the PRC and the EU are equally committed to WTO reform to the extent that they have already established a joint Working Group on that matter. Proposed at the 20th EU-China Summit in July 2018 in order to help the WTO meet new challenges[71], the first joint vice-ministerial meeting of the EU-China Working Group on WTO Reform[72] was held in Beijing in October that year. Since then, regular meetings have provided an arena for discussion of common interest although these are outweighed by the many differences in their aims for WTO reform.

As has been argued[73], "both the EU and China have an immediate and urgent interest in maintaining the WTO to ensure the predictability and stability of the multilateral trading order, and the [Appellate Body] concerns the survival of the WTO". On this general question, both the PRC and the EU face off against the USA. The EU and China are also in agreement that

---

70. Ministry of Foreign Affairs of the PRC, "The 8th Meeting of China-EU Cyber Taskforce was Held," 26 November 2021, retrieved from *www.fmprc.gov.cn/eng./wjb_663304/zzjg_663340/jks_665232/jkxw_665234/202111/t20211126_10453799.html*
71. European External Action Service, Joint Statement of the 20th EU-China Summit, Beijing, 17 July 2018, retrieved from *www.eeas.europa.eu/node/48424_en*
72. Ministry of Commerce (PRC) ("MOFCOM"), "The First Meeting of China-EU Vice-Ministerial Level Joint Working Group for WTO Reform", 11 October 2018, retrieved from *english.mofcom.gov.cn/article/newsrelease/significantnews/201810/20181002794775.shtml*
73. Chen, D., "Convergence in Name, Divergence in Substance: A Comparison of the EU and China's WTO Reform Proposals", *EU-China Observer*, n. 3.19, pp. 4-8, at p. 5, retrieved from *www.coleurope.eu/sites/default/files/research-paper/eu-china_observer_issue319_0.pdf*

negotiations on new areas in trade ought be included on the reform agenda, such as e-commerce and small and medium enterprises (SMEs), which will be discussed presently. In addition, with respect to improvement in the operational efficiency of some WTO committees, both partners see the need to improve the compliance of notification but retain different emphases in this respect[74]. These mark the present core areas of limited agreement between the PRC and the EU while differences still admittedly remain[75] as set out in their individual reform proposals for the WTO[76].

B) Plurilateral Approaches to WTO Reform

Given the breakdown in the operation of the AB (due to US intransigence in appointing new members or extending the mandate of others caused by a failure to address American concerns with respect to the functioning of the AB) together with the complete loss of momentum in the Doha Round and the failure of the multilateral approach to create the necessary consensus to produce tangible results, the EU and China (among other WTO Members) have tried to continue to progress the creation of international trade rules in certain areas of common concern through a plurilateral approach. In this respect, they mark a return to the practice under the original GATT regime from 1947. The move to plurilateral negotiations is only a partial (and, one daresay, temporary) solution to concluding agreements with the consensus of all WTO Members[77]. Thus while plurilateral approaches cannot be regarded as a panacea for the present WTO impasses, they nevertheless offer a mechanism for the larger trading powers to cooperate without having to engage in interminable multilateral negotiations[78]. Two issues will be shortly considered here, viz., the improved use of WTO deliberative bodies and the issue of Joint Statement Initiatives.

74. *Ibid.*
75. *Ibid.*
76. *Cfr.* EU, European Commission, "WTO modernisation: Introduction to future EU proposals", *Concept Paper*, 18 September 2018, retrieved from *trade.ec.europa.eu/doclib/docs/2018/september/tradoc_157331.pdf*; and European Commission, *Reforming the WTO: Towards a Sustainable and Effective Multilateral Trading System*, Luxembourg: EU Publications Office, 2021, retrieved from *knowledge4policy.ec.europa.eu/sites/default/files/NG0221300ENN.en_.pdf*; and PRC, Ministry of Commerce of the People's Republic of China, China's Position Paper on WTO Reform, Beijing, 20 December 2018, retrieved from *lt.china-office.gov.cn/eng/xwdt/201811/t20181128_2710643.htm*; and WTO General Council, *China's Proposal on WTO Reform — Communication from China* (13 May 2019), WT/GC/W773, retrieved from *docs.wto.org/dol2fe/Pages/SS/directdoc.aspx?filename=q:/WT/GC/W773.pdf&Open=True.*
77. Hoekman, Wolfe, *op. cit.*, note 47, at p. 9.
78. Hoekman, B., Sabel, C., "Plurilateral Cooperation as an Alternative to Trade Agreements: Innovating One Domain at a Time", *Global Policy*, vol. 12, suppl. 3, 2021, pp. 49-60, at pp. 57-58.

a) Improved Use of WTO Deliberative Bodies

As intimated earlier, the many different WTO technical committees and councils represent an important professional network of deliberative bodies within the Organization that are able to discuss emerging problems and to address "specific trade concerns" raised by WTO Members attempting to clarify already adopted national measures[79]. By discussing these concerns within the context of a WTO committee[80], a WTO Member may modify or even withdraw a measure having negative consequences for trade with other Members without their having the need to initiate proceedings under the dispute settlement mechanism. The most effective WTO bodies in addressing these trade concerns are the Technical Barriers to Trade Committee and the Sanitary and Phytosanitary Measures Committee although use of this option has begun to increase in many other such bodies.

In order to improve the use of the possibilities offered by the General Council and committee meetings to discuss and resolve Members' concerns regarding trade-related domestic measures, the EU — supported by 19 other Members including the PRC — made a proposal to furnish all such bodies with horizontal procedural guidelines[81]. This proposal commenced by determining timelines for the presentation of convening documents and further arrangements respecting the meetings of the bodies concerned with the aim of making more efficient use of the committees' time. Such aim was also shared by the PRC[82]. The EU's proposal also advocated for the submission of written questions and answers to such meetings thereby increasing transparency[83] for other Members[84].

79. Wolfe, R., "Reforming WTO conflict management: Why and how to improve the use of 'specific trade concerns'", *Journal of International Economic Law*, vol. 23, n. 4, 2020, pp. 817-839.
80. Hoekman, Wolfe, *op. cit.*, note 47, at pp. 18-19.
81. WTO, "Procedural guidelines for WTO councils and committees addressing trade concerns — Draft General Council decision — Communication from Albania; Australia; Canada; China; European Union; Hong Kong, China; Iceland; Republic of Korea; Republic of Moldova; New Zealand; North Macedonia; Norway; Panama; Qatar; Singapore; Switzerland; the Separate Customs Territory of Taiwan, Penghu, Kinmen and Matsu; Thailand; Turkey; and Ukraine", WT/GC/W/777/Rev.5, 20 February 2020, retrieved from *docs.wto.org/dol2fe/Pages/FE_Search/FE_S_S009-DP.aspx?language=E&CatalogueIdList=261432*
82. See the PRC's own reform papers in this respect, *op. cit.*, note 76.
83. Wolfe, R., 2018, "Is World Trade Organization Information Good Enough? How a Systematic Reflection by Members on Transparency Could Promote Institutional Learning", 16 July 2018, Bertelsmann Stiftung, Gütersloh, retrieved from *www.bertelsmann-stiftung.de/de/publikationen/publikation/did/is-world-trade-organization-information-good-enough*
84. For a fuller discussion of the EU's proposal, see Hoekman, Wolfe, *op. cit.*, note 47, at pp. 19-20.

More recently[85], the EU has followed up this proposal with another that calls for a reinvigorated deliberative function for the WTO bodies and committees, going beyond essential procedural requirements and looking at further ways to improve the mode and delivery of such function. This might even lead to its acting as a potential bridge towards possible rule-making where WTO Members — having already identified the relevant issues and the best ways to deal with them through due deliberation — could then consider this an appropriate way forward[86]. The EU thus sees the objectives and means under such a reinvigorated deliberative function as a way to[87]:

- improve the understanding of new trade policy challenges through the sharing of information, including background analysis and research by the WTO Secretariat;
- identify best practices and the sharing of experiences through the increased use of informal meetings, thematic sessions, enhanced cross-committee coordination and joint sessions to leverage in-house expertise;
- develop non-binding instruments, such as non-binding principles, guidelines and recommendations, to facilitate the implementation of existing trade agreements, to assist developing countries in such implementation or to respond to new global trade policy challenges....

The EU's proposal's novel approach, as mentioned earlier, accordingly considers the need to assess the scope for convergence on issues not yet sufficiently addressed by the WTO and to consider elements for a response, including the possibility, where appropriate, of rule-making.

b) Joint Statement Initiatives

At the 11th Ministerial Conference in December 2017[88], like-minded groups of WTO members issued so-called "Joint Statement Initiatives" ("JSIs") on advancing discussions on e-commerce, on developing a

85. WTO General Council, *Reinforcing the Deliberative Function of the WTO to Respond to Global Trade Policy Challenges — Communication from the European Union* (22 February 2023), WT/GC/W/864, retrieved from *docs.wto.org/dol2fe/Pages/SS/directdoc.aspx?filename=q:/WT/GC/W864.pdf&Open=True*
86. *Ibid.*, paras. 6-7, at 2.
87. *Ibid.*, para. 8, p. 2.
88. WTO, 11th Ministerial Conference, Buenos Aires, 10-13 December 2017, retrieved from *www.wto.org/english/thewto_e/minist_e/mc11_e/mc11_e.htm*

multilateral framework on investment facilitation, on launching a working group on micro, small and medium-sized enterprises ("MSMEs") and on advancing ongoing talks on domestic regulation in services trade.

The groups remain open to all WTO members and are being conducted on a plurilateral basis in order to utilise the opportunities offered by the rules-based international trading system[89]. Although these initiatives include a cross-section of the WTO membership, their legality (beyond being considered as informal discussions among a group of WTO Members) has been challenged by the WTO due to the lack of consensus[90] in which approach commentators have also added their voices[91]. The EU participates in all four of these JSI groups while the PRC was an initiating co-sponsor of three of them and became a member of the fourth group — on e-commerce — soon after deliberations had started[92].

Of interest to the present discussion are e-commerce JSI talks involving more than 80 WTO members and focusing on a combination of trade restrictive policies such as regulation of cross-border data flows and data localisation requirements and digital trade facilitation — issues like electronic signatures, e-invoicing, electronic payment for cross-border transactions, and consumer protection.

In view of their standing bilateral formations of the Digital HLD, the annual dialogue on information and communications technologies and the cyber taskforce, this JSI has again brought together EU and Chinese experts this time in a broader global trade context. It may be that practices and understandings come to within the PRC-EU bilateral context will strengthen both the participation and even the coordination of positions of the PRC and the EU in this (and other) JSIs.

2.3. Successes from EU-PRC Interactions in Dialogues and Working Groups

This background of socialised learning and discussion has contributed to a more understanding approach of working together for both EU and Chinese

89. Hoekman, Wolfe, *op. cit.*, note 47, at p. 9.
90. WTO General Council, *The Legal Status of 'Joint Statement Initiatives' and their Negotiated Outcomes — Communication from India and South Africa* (19 February 2012), WT/GC/W/819, retrieved from *docs.wto.org/dol2fe/Pages/SS/directdoc.aspx?filename=q:/WT/GC/W819.pdf&Open=True*
91. Kelsey, J., "The Illegitimacy of Joint Statement Initiatives and Their Systemic Implications for the WTO", *Journal of International Economic Law*, vol. 25, 2022, pp. 2-24.
92. Hoekman, Wolfe, *op. cit.*, note 47, at p. 10.

officials. It has already produced results and may induce further evolution of the relationship, whether on a bilateral or in a broader multilateral basis. With WTO reform a top of the agenda item for both China and the Union, previous positive experience of collaboration in one area may spillover into a related or less related policy area.

For example, the EU and the PRC (among other Members) worked well together to set up the new, temporary dispute resolution mechanism to replace the now moribund Appellate Body[93]. In reality, the cooperation between China and the EU was pivotal in securing the setting up and proper functioning of the so-called Multi-Party Interim Appeal Arbitration Arrangement ("MPIA")[94]. Part of the reason for China's support in this matter — already flagged as a common interest with the EU in their Working Group on WTO Reform — was that it represented an attempt on its part to signal to the world that, unlike the USA, it aimed to play a constructive and stabilising role in the global trade regime (despite its noted aversion to international courts and tribunals)[95].

In addition, EU-China cooperation was evident in the final negotiations that led to the conclusion of the "Geneva package" at the 12th Ministerial Conference on 12-17 July 2022, securing ten agreements, declarations and decisions in total. Of particular interest to both the EU and China was the Agreement on Fisheries Subsidies. While this had been subject to many years of negotiations, a number of issues — e.g., on IUUs — had already formed part of the discussions at the HLDs on maritime affairs and fisheries between the EU-China. In fact, the two sides had established their own Working Group on IUU fishing matters and had recently agreed to the Blue Partnership for the Oceans. Thus, having worked together bilaterally on these issues, both the PRC and the EU were able to concentrate more of their efforts on outstanding issues within a more conducive atmosphere to their successful resolution.

These also appear to be a confirmation of the Chinese approach to negotiating priorities and tactics with respect to WTO reforms. As has been noted[96], the PRC

93. Hoekman, B., Mavroidis, P. C., "To AB or not to AB? Dispute settlement in WTO reform", *Journal of International Economic Law*, vol. 23, n. 3, 2020, pp. 1-20.
94. Caffarena, A., Gabusi, G., "Europe-China and the Third Way: steering order in times of change. Evidence from the AIIB and WTO reform", in Li, X. (ed.), *China-EU relations in a new era of global transformation*, Abingdon: Routledge, 2022, chap. 2, pp. 19-36.
95. Basedow, J. R., "The EU, China and the WTO", Transatlantic Dialogue on China, *Royal United Services Institute (Online)*, 10 November 2021, retrieved from *www.rusi.org/explore-our-research/projects/transatlantic-dialogue-china/eu-china-and-wto*
96. Ghosal Singh, A., "China's Evolving Strategy for WTO Reforms", *The Diplomat (Online)*, 31 July 2019, retrieved from *thediplomat.com/2019/07/chinas-evolving-strategy-for-wto-reforms/*

has adopted an "early fruits" strategy according to which WTO Members ought initially to seek common ground to resolve pressing problems while reserving determination of their differences on principled issues until later. WTO Members would thereby avoid repeating the failure of the Doha Round. The PRC thus rejected the US attitude (supported, in the main, by the EU and Japan) of giving priority to the issues of its greatest concerns, e.g., government subsidies, state-owned enterprises, competition neutrality, compulsory technology transfer, and improvement intellectual property rights' protection.

Instead, the Chinese narrative focused primarily on reforms related to transparency and mundane work that, while relatively less controversial, could produce bear fruit in the short term. In view of the PRC proposals to reform the WTO[97], then, the Chinese identified as primary areas that could produce favourable results much earlier than the developed Members' priorities included AB reform, fisheries subsidies, e-commerce, and investment facilitation[98]. From the earlier discussion and analysis of the JSIs, MPIA and Agreement on Fisheries Subsidies, the PRC has successfully managed to charter this course in WTO reform negotiations, with the active collaboration of the EU in these circumstances. In so doing, the Chinese approach has gained traction — not just with the EU but with other Members — and has (at least for now) put the WTO back on track in a forward direction for reform.

IV. THE FUTURE — THE UNDISCOVERED COUNTRY

Given the current tense situation, how then could the EU and China constructively re-engage in the WTO, if that re-engagement is needed to reset international trade relations between these two Members? The omens are not necessarily very positive at this time where — at a minimum — a gradual de-coupling is foreseen of the PRC from the EU on China's own terms (even within the sphere of international trade) and — at a maximum — the potential outbreak of a trade war as a prelude to further re-ordering of the global economy.

However, despite this gloomy prognosis, a reset may still be on the cards in the mid-term if relations — although currently frosty — can be maintained and even reinvigorated. The possibilities, perhaps even the contours of a roadmap for further cooperation between the EU and China, have already been sketched out.

97. See PRC reform proposals, *op. cit.*, note 76.
98. Ghosal Singh, *op. cit.*, note 96.

As regards getting the WTO Appellate Body operational again, there is no better guidance than that contained in the valedictory or farewell speech of the last member of that august Body, Prof. Dr. Hong Zhao. In her presentation[99], she called inter alia for the restoration of the Appellate Body, taking into consideration issues raised by the various Members; the improvement of the implementation of dispute settlement reports; the strengthening of panel proceedings; the ability of Members to litigate in their mother tongue; and the ultimate establishment of a World Trade Court as first envisaged in the original (non-ratified) treaty for the International Trade Organization in 1948.

In respect of the WTO generally, the MC12 Outcome Document (adopted at the 12th Ministerial Conference referred to above) proposes an agenda on reform and renewal of the WTO, including trade in services, developing countries, women's economic empowerment and environmental challenges. In their approaches on these areas, negotiators from China and the EU could easily coalesce and develop joint proposals. At the same time, it would need to be admitted that the issues, e.g., of China's market economy status and self-designated developing country status, of industrial subsidies, of state-owned enterprises and of the general matter of transparency, would continue to remain areas of disagreement.

Even the idea of reforming the WTO bodies themselves, setting deadlines for decisions in them and the many committees and sub-committees could play to the strengths of Chinese trade diplomacy and long-held principles of Confucian philosophy in aiming to establish harmony and so being able to solve problems before needing to engage in the dispute settlement mechanism.

For these reforms to go forward and bear fruit will need not only enhanced cooperation in the WTO between the EU and China but also hopefully with the USA in the established triangular trade diplomacy, not forgetting other major trading countries and groups. In this latter respect, the advent of a stronger role for Africa in international trade — heralded by the African Comprehensive Free Trade Agreement[100] — may presage a more decisive role for the African Union in the WTO.

99. Zhao, H, "Equal Justice under the Treaty — A Farewell Speech", Farewell speech of Appellate Body member Prof. Dr. Hong Zhao, 20 November 2020, Graduate Institute, Geneva, retrieved from *www.wto.org/english/tratop_e/dispu_e/farwellspeechhzhao_e.htm#:~:text=The%20world%20needs%20healing%2C%20and,to%20the%20164%20WTO%20Members*

100. Haram Acyl, F. "African Union Priorities at the WTO", in Low, P., Osakwe, C., Oshikawa, M. (eds.), *African Perspectives on Trade and the WTO: Domestic Reforms,*

However, only with movement on both sides will the necessary preconditions of an EU-China partnership in the WTO in particular and in international trade in general start to re-emerge. Confirmation of trade as one of the two pillars of EU-China cooperation (together with the climate crisis) underlines its importance as the two WTO Members continue to forge ahead in their potential future collaboration, based on their already dense network of dialogue and discussion.

V. CONCLUSION

EU-China relations, both before and after WTO accession, have been governed by a realistic understanding of each party's role in the global trading system and the rules-based order provided by the WTO.

Despite the current geostrategic tensions, EU and Chinese officials and experts still work together at all levels within the context of both the bilateral arrangements of the EU and the multilateral or, more recently, plurilateral arrangements of the WTO, forging and developing the operation of the various agreements.

At a higher level, the EU and China can use these opportunities to reset relations by collaborating on plans to reform and renew the WTO, particularly the dispute settlement mechanism through the various HLDs as well as their Working Group on WTO Reform. Such processes have the potential to reinforce more harmonious relations which have underscored the Chinese diplomatic approach for centuries, at least within the context of international trade that seems to touch much less markedly on the basic tenets of PRC sovereignty and non-interference.

After all, as it appears from this work, it is somehow more straightforward for the EU and China to agree on general principles such as the depoliticisation of trade disputes compared to the other issues creating imbalances in their relations. In a real sense, then, the PRC and the EU may be able to build on this more circumscribed partnership for the future, thereby replicating their already functioning co-operation in other fields like climate change, biodiversity, and the environment[101].

Structural Transformation and Global Economic Integration, Cambridge: Cambridge University Press, 2016, chap. 2, pp. 15-17.

101. See, e.g., EU-China, "EU and China Partnership on Climate Change", MEMO/05/298, 2 September 2005, Brussels, retrieved from *climate.ec.europa.eu/system/files/2016-11/joint_declaration_ch_eu_en.pdf*

The Competition Law Global Governance Dilemma and the EU-China Relationship[1*]

JERÓNIMO MAILLO GONZÁLEZ-ORÚS & MIGUEL VERDEGUER SEGARRA[2]
Lecturers at San Pablo CEU University of Madrid

I. GENERAL REMARKS

As cross-border operations between global market players attempt to expand their businesses abroad and grow internationally by entering unknown new markets, rules governing Competition law remain purely national. The European Union (EU) provides an exception to this since its legal framework, which is regional, has been conformed through the progressive conferral of powers by its Member states on the Union. It is not quite common to see such a high degree of harmonisation on Competition law matters in other jurisdictions. What is more, the EU is constantly seeking further harmonisation. Let us take for instance its wish to further align national legislations on the limitation periods in damages actions on occasion of the review of the Damages Directive[3].

Whereas in the EU it is to be found a legal model where European national regimes are driven by a shared supranational authority to match certain common standards, it might be argued that the rest of jurisdictions worldwide do not embrace such a kind of "hard harmonisation". In fact, Competition law around the world is, by and large, fashioned in a way

1. * A first draft of this paper was published in Revista General de Derecho Europeo, n. 56, 2022. The paper was nominated for the Antitrust Writing Awards by Concurrence.
2. Dr Maillo is a Full Professor of EU & International Public Law, as well as Jean Monnet Chair at Universidad San Pablo-CEU (CEU Universities). Dr Miguel Verdeguer holds a PhD in Law from the Universidad San Pablo-CEU (CEU Universities). He is a Professor of EU Law at Universidad San Pablo-CEU (CEU Universities) and Professor of EU Economics at EDEM Escuela de Empresarios.
3. Barennes, M., Deferme, D., and Verhulst, M. "Limitation Periods in Competition Law Damages in the EU: Are further clarification and harmonization needed?" in *Concurrences*, n. 92716, 2020, pp. 1-30.

that solely responds to the specific needs posed by each individual country. However, the lack of convergence may refrain these countries from facing effectively cross-border issues. The point made by some scholars is that global problems need global solutions and the increasing number of domestic legislations on Competition law does not seem to be the answer if these are not accompanied by the appropriate toolbox for harmonisation[4]. The rapid growth of divergent Antitrust regimes in every corner of the planet is unmistakable but the major difficulty in setting globalized benchmark standards for Competition law issues is unquestionable too[5].

As Professor David J. Gerber once claimed with regards to Competition law convergence with Asian countries: "convergence is a central topic because it represents what is widely considered to be the only currently viable strategy for global Competition law development"[6].

The internationalization phenomenon brings new global challenges for jurisdictions around the globe as they lack the necessary tools to come to grips with anticompetitive effects stemming from cross-border operations. National Competition Authorities can only intervene if there are significant effects on their territories, if followed the "effects doctrine", as the US has traditionally done and as the EU seems to be moving forward especially after the prominent *Intel vs Commission II* case[7]. The "effects doctrine" has been used in a manner that enables the authority to liberally assert jurisdiction over foreign operators[8]. Nonetheless, such a doctrine only enables countries to stretch their powers beyond their boundaries whenever effects have an impact inside their territories but it does not straighten out all the questions arising from extraterritoriality and the lack of harmonisation. In addition, when two or more countries claim to have jurisdiction to evaluate the same

4. Foster, S., "While America Slept: The Harmonization of Competition Laws based upon the European Union Model" in *Emory International Law Review*, vol. 15, 2001, pp. 467-519.
5. Hamner, K. J., "The Globalization of Law: International Merger Control and Competition Law in the United States, the European Union, Latin America and China" in *Journal of Transnational Law and Policy*, vol. 11, n. 2, 2002, pp. 385-205.
6. Gerber, D., "Asia and global competition law convergence" in Dowdle, M. W. (ed.), Gillespie, J. (ed.) and Maher, I. (ed.), *Asian Capitalism and The Regulation of Competition: Towards a Regulatory Geography of Global Competition Law*, Cambridge University Press, 2013, pp. 36-52, p. 36.
7. Behrens, P., "The extraterritorial reach of EU competition law revisited: The "effects doctrine" before the ECJ" in *Discussion Paper, Europa-Kolleg Hamburg, Institute for European Integration*, n. 3/16, Hamburg, 2016.
8. Alford, R. P., "The Extraterritorial Application of Antitrust Laws: The United States and European Community Approaches" in *Virginia Journal of International Law*, vol. 33, n. 1, pp. 1-50.

issue there is an obvious risk of divergent outcomes[9]. This observation brought to the Merger Control arena is not particularly new at all. Opposing conclusions by different authorities is one of the greatest concerns of those advocating for harmonisation. Let us take for instance the landmark *GE/ Honeywell* case in which the U. S. Department of Justice (DOJ) and the European Commission collided head-on in their respective decisions[10]. The fallout from the case gave food for thought about the need to enhance international harmonisation of Competition law.

However, and no matter how tight a domestic jurisdiction clings to the aforementioned doctrine, that its possibilities to pursue investigations, collect evidence and of course to enforce sanctions in other territories are scant. This leads to inefficiencies in the world markets. Inefficiencies that are prone to affect developing countries to a greater extent than developed countries either because Competition law does not exist in the former or because they lack solid Competition authorities or good enforcement mechanisms.

Against this backdrop and as pointed out by Professor Frédéric Jenny: "Firms are thus in a position to engage, with impunity, in transnational anticompetitive practices that contradict the trade liberalization efforts of governments"[11]. Undertakings take advantage of the lack of a coherent and all-encompassing worldwide set of rules to knowingly shape their behaviour and build up their acquisitions in a manner that facilitates them the way to avert the jurisdictional scope of many jurisdictions that oppose their interests. This problem is clearly accentuated in digital markets. The staggering spread of digital activities by a few operators is not being matched effectively by the adoption of appropriate legal tools adjusted to the idiosyncrasies of such activities. Digital platforms operate globally in a fast-evolving way and at a very fast pace. This phenomenon has taken enforcers aback who have seen how their Competition rules are unfit to deal with the new digital reality. Ex-post scrutiny of digital platforms' behaviour proves insufficient in the face of the new challenges and because of it a number of ex-ante regulatory tools are to arise around the globe in a near future[12]. Hence, alongside the already

9. Horner, N., "Unilateral Effects and the EC Merger Regulation — How The Commission Had its Cake and Ate it Too" in *Hanse Law Review*, vol. 2, n. 1, 2006, pp. 23-43, p. 41.
10. Leigh, D., "The GE/Honeywell merger controversy and the path to analytical convergence in international merger assessment: A critical commentary" in *Liverpool Law Review*, vol. 24, n. 1, 2002, pp. 89-107.
11. Jenny, F., "Competition Law and Policy: Global Governance Issues" in *World Competition, Kluwer Law International*, vol. 26, n. 4, 2003, pp. 609-624, p. 609.
12. For the EU case, see among others, Petit, N., "The Proposed Digital Markets Act (DMA): A Legal and Policy Review" in *Journal of European Competition Law and Practice*, vol. 12, n. 7, 2021, pp. 529-541.

existing divergent Competition law regimes it will be highly likely to observe differing regulatory instruments. The tech giant Google, who dominates the Internet searching, is currently facing nearly nineteen Antitrust probes around the world. And most of them are based on the same grounds. Such a plurality of proceedings translates into a real burden on Competition authorities. This may be of especial interest for developing jurisdictions that might well prefer waiting for a third authority to render the final outcome of its investigation and thus save time and economic resources to invest in other pressing issues. Aside from the digital agenda, public interest goals are also presenting themselves as imperative for Competition law to act on them. The fight against climate change calls for global action and notwithstanding the secondary role of Competition policy in this arena it is convenient to gather as many efforts as possible to contribute to this major cause[13].

Divergent regimes nourish legal uncertainty ultimately[14]. That is why "the debate over harmonisation or internationalization often centres around the prospects for adopting a workable worldwide antitrust standard that would reduce the burdensome costs of legal uncertainty occasioned by divergent local standards"[15]. Thus, it stands to reason that in order to shed some light on such a state of uncertainty it is in everyone's best interest to establish a level playing field for all actors in a globalized market. The question is how this can be achieved and how far differing Competition laws can be brought together to follow a common path. Scholars, practitioners, and public authorities have long pursued the answer to this question by bringing forward a series of insights that could eventually allay the 'Competition law dilemma of Global Governance'. Amongst the main contributions it could be highlighted the following:

II. UNILATERALISM

This stream of thought is merely based on the reliance on those jurisdictions whose Competition authorities have a long and solid experience in dealing with Competition law issues, such as that of the US and the EU jurisdiction. And because of it, it is in the interest of both the US and the EU

13. Holmes, S., Middelschulte, D., and Snoep, M. (eds), *Competition Law, Climate Change and Environmental Sustainability*, Concurrences, 2021.
14. Damro, C. and Terrence, G., "Transatlantic Merger Relations: The Pursuit of Cooperation and Convergence" in *Journal of European Integration*, vol. 34, n. 6, 2012, pp. 643-661.
15. Manne, G. A. and Weinberger, S., "International Signals: The political dimension of international competition law" in *The Antitrust Bulletin*, vol. 57, n. 3, 2012, pp. 485-561, p. 488.

to encourage and advocate for the spread of their respective systems in the form of advice and technical assistance to countries on how to implement their Competition laws[16]. The extension of US and EU Competition regimes may be implemented from two approaches:

The first approach or mechanism relates to the unilateral extraterritorial application of their respective legislations under the scope of the above mentioned "effects doctrine". Aside from domestic implementation of Antitrust Law, the US has traditionally also applied it abroad, namely because in its view "mere territorial enforcement fails to protect US consumers and producers who are the victims of foreign cartels"[17]. Seen from a different angle, "to fail to enforce US Antitrust Law extraterritorially is unfair to producers in the United States who have to comply with US Antitrust Law"[18]. The US originated this doctrine in the aftermath of WWII on occasion of the prominent ALCOA case in which Judge Learned Hand decided to render illegal agreements negotiated by foreign undertakings and concluded in foreign territories but whose effects reached the US market[19]. It is true that only if it has effects on US commerce that were direct, substantial and reasonably foreseeable[20]. This case law was codified later in the Foreign Trade Antitrust Improvements Act of 1982, which stated that the Sherman Act and the FTC Acts "shall not apply to conduct involving trade or commerce (other than import trade or import commerce) with foreign nations unless...(1) such conduct has a direct, substantial and reasonably foreseeable effect" on US commerce or on US exporters, and (2) such effect give rises to an antitrust claim[21]. This doctrine evolved with the case-law and did it not without some controversy[22]. Some authors yearn for a more flexible or cautious approach to the effects doctrine that would take into consideration international comity[23]. The bottom line is that, with the effects doctrine, there seems to be no limit (or at least very reduced limit) for the enforcer to apply

16. Rivers, R. D., "General Electric/Honeywell Merger: European Commission Antitrust Decision Strikes a Sour Note" in *ILSA Journal of international and Comparative Law*, vol. 9, 2003, pp. 525-539.
17. Rosenthal, D. E. and Nicolaides, P., "Harmonizing Antitrust: The Less Effective Way to Promote International Competition, Global Competition Policy" in Graham, E. M. (ed.) and Richardson, D. J. (ed.), *Global Competition Policy*, 1997, pp. 355-383, p. 372.
18. *Ibid.*
19. *United States v. Alcoa*, 148 F.2d 416 (2d Cir. 1945).
20. *Hartford Fire Insur. v. California*, 509 U. S. 764, 796 (1993); Matsushita Elec. Industrial Co. V. Zenith Radio Corp., 475 U. S. 574, 582, n. 6 (1986).
21. 15 U. S. C. 6.ª, 45(a)(3).
22. Raymond, J. M., "A New Look at the Jurisdiction in ALCOA" in *The American Journal of International Law*, vol. 61, n. 2, 1967, pp. 558-570.
23. Alford, R. P., "The Extraterritorial application of Antitrust Laws: A Postcript on Hartford Fire Insurance Co. v California" in *Virginia Journal of International Law*, vol. 34, 1993, pp. 213-231.

domestic Competition rules to foreign undertakings even when these are not present in the forum at the time of the anticompetitive behavior. That is why commentators point to the need for a more cautious approach and some sort of multijurisdictional convergence on the effects doctrine that safeguards negative comity considerations. Negative comity entails the deference of a domestic Court or agency towards third countries in order to prevent international disputes and thus preserve sound relations between jurisdictions as a sign of respect. As laid down by the OECD, "negative comity may be described as the principle that a country should (i) notify other countries when its enforcement proceedings may have an effect on their important interests, and (ii) give full and sympathetic consideration to possible ways of fulfilling its enforcement needs without harming those interests"[24]. Some US cases point out to a multi-balancing test to weigh the substantial effects in the US with the interests of foreign nations[25]. The only limits were given in the landmark *Hartford Fire case* which set out that international comity cannot restrain the effects doctrine but for where a foreign law mandates conduct that a US law forbids, or where the observance of the US law violates foreign law[26].

Over time the EU did likewise and eventually accepted the "effects doctrine"[27]. And so gradually did other jurisdictions[28]. Recent studies conducted by the United Nations Conference on Trade and Development (UNCTAD) show the progressive embracement of extraterritoriality by many jurisdictions[29]. Although the most developed jurisdictions took the lead in the extraterritorial

24. OECD Report, Positive Comity, 1999, p. 18, available at *https://www.oecd.org/daf/competition/prosecutionandlawenforcement/2752161.pdf*. In contrast, positive comity is defined in the same text, p. 17, as "the principle that a country should (1) give full and sympathetic consideration to another country's request that it open or expand a law enforcement proceeding in order to remedy conduct in its territory that is substantially and adversely affecting another country's interests, and (2) take whatever remedial action it deems appropriate on a voluntary basis and in considering its legitimate interests."
25. *Timberlane Lumber v. Bank of America*, 549 F.2d 597, 611-15 (9th Cir. 1976); *Mannington Mills v. Congoleum Corp.*, 595 F 2d 1287, 1297 (3d Circ. 1979); *Empagram*, 542 U. S. 155.
26. *Hartford Fire Insurance Co. v California*, 113 S Ct 2891. Comity does not imply the non-application of US Antitrust Law merely because the extraterritorial conduct is legal in the foreign nation but where the foreign law "actually compels that conduct". See, in this sense, Elhauge, E., *United States Antitrust Law and Economics*, 3rd ed., Thomson Reuters Foundation Press, 2018, pp. 50-51.
27. Case T-102/96, Gencor Ltd v Commission of the European Communities, ECLI:EU:T:1999:65. More recently, Case C-413/14 P Intel v. Commission, EU:C:2017:632.
28. Gerber, D. J., "The Extraterritorial Application of the German Antitrust Laws" in *American Journal of International Law*, vol. 77, 1983, pp. 756-783.
29. UNCTAD's Report: Developing Countries' Experience with Extraterritoriality in Competition Law, UNCTAD/DITC/CPLP/2021/3, December 2021, pp. 1-14.

application of Competition law, most developing countries seem to be following the same path[30]. The effects doctrine has helped developing countries not only to protect their respective markets but also to "develop capacity in dealing with transnational businesses"[31]. Nonetheless, this practice does not fix any multijurisdictional problem as it simply allows countries to stretch their jurisdictional scope beyond their borders. The UNCTAD's research pinpoints a series of shortcomings in transnational enforcement, in particular:[32]

— *Procedural rules, especially relating to service of process;*

— *Collection and sharing of evidence;*

— *Dealing with non-compliance/non-cooperation during investigations;*

— *Absence or insufficiency of existing international instruments regarding enforcement;*

— *Enforcement/execution of rendered decisions/judgments (inclusive collection of any imposed fines).*

Thus, it can be derived that far from harmonising laws, the "effects doctrine" is only useful in order to catch anticompetitive behavior that would otherwise escape from being scrutinized. The whole conundrum of Competition law global governance is not at all untangled by means of the spread of this doctrine throughout new jurisdictions. International coordination mechanisms should be placed in service to eliminate jurisdictional conflicts. Some voices argue that an international treaty on extraterritorial application of Competition law would do the trick[33]. However, it must be acknowledged the difficulty in attaining such an ambitious goal. Furthermore, unilateralism provides few incentives for most of the States to coordinate and resolve jurisdictional conflicts and therefore is not likely to inspire widespread confidence[34].

All these reasons suggest that unilateralism is not the right path -for sure not sufficient- and also that deeper and alternative international cooperation mechanisms should lay the groundwork first before an international treaty on the matter could be adopted.

30. *Ibid.*
31. *Ibid.*, p. 11.
32. *Ibid.*, pp. 9-10
33. Taylor, M. D., *International Competition Law: A New Dimension For the WTO?*, Cambridge University Press, 2006, pp. 1-520.
34. Gerber, D. J., *Global Competition. Law, Markets and Globalization*, Oxford University Press, 2010, p. 342.

Unilateralism can also be sought as some sort of "soft harmonisation" but in principle with no need to issue guidance or recommendations. This second approach will be examined below under the corresponding section on "soft harmonisation".

III. HARD HARMONISATION: INTEGRATIONIST APPROACH

The second possibility would consist of the creation of a supranational enforcement authority. This seems to be unrealistic, but the theory is not new. The most resounding proposal took place in the late 1990s when the EU suggested that the then recently created World Trade Organization (WTO) could also be used as a worldwide platform for Competition purposes. In fact, a Working Group on Competition law, created at the very core of the WTO, effectively raised the issue of Competition law as well as that related to the many hurdles that enforcement could encounter in the face of international violations of domestic rules on Competition. The Working Group of Competition law, aware of the challenges posed by extraterritoriality, was keen to push for harmonisation of legislations. As Professor Eleanor M. Fox highlights, the 1990s was a time when the open-minded outlook on the world of most countries made them less prejudiced to "search for a more coherent treatment of problems with a global dimension"[35]. It was clear that those obstacles to trade that were being lifted by the General Agreement on Tariffs and Trade (GATT) could not be replaced by private ones as a result of not dealing with Competition law issues, such as international cartels or transnational abuse of dominance. Thus, public and private restraints could no longer be understood isolated in the same manner as it must be accepted the somewhat supplementary goals of International Trade law and Competition law as hinted by the WTO. Nonetheless, attempts by the WTO at deepening Competition law convergence reached stalemate[36]. Difficulties for making the world's largest trade organization the hub of reference for the international community of Competition law were particularly hard to overcome. These difficulties may be listed as follows:

First, the creation of a single Competition body would have needed to be accompanied by a compulsory legal instrument with binding force

35. Fox, E. M., "Toward World Antitrust and Market Access" in *The American Journal of International Law*, vol. 91, n. 1, 1997, p.8.

36. Djelic, M-L. and Kleiner, T., "The International Competition Network: Moving towards transnational governance" in Djelic, M. (ed.) and Sahlin-Andersson, K. (ed.), *Transnational Governance: Institutional Dynamics of Regulation*, Cambridge University Press, 2006, pp. 287-307.

so as to be enforced by the supranational entity. As a matter of fact, there got to be a genuine proposal for a common Competition legal framework intended to set a range of legal standards to be commonly adopted by all those jurisdictions wishing to adhere to the legal agreement. However, the Draft Antitrust Code, as named by the group of scholars who took part in its drafting, lacked clarity, and provided the hypothetical common Antitrust authority with a too broad scope of action that could potentially be frowned upon by Competition authorities around the world[37].

Second, emerging jurisdiction were wary of an eventual common Competition policy. Many developing jurisdictions considered that developed jurisdictions could make use of a mandatory legal instrument just for their own good, and all that to the detriment of the firms belonging to the younger jurisdictions.

Third, throughout the 1990s the WTO barely had a background of convergence or cooperation between countries in Competition law issues. If that had been the case, tighter interjurisdictional relations would have contributed to laying the foundations for backing the WTO as a common international authority. That feature is to be sharply contrasted against the Competition law backdrop observed today at a worldwide level. Now, there already exists a solid background of soft convergence that may, if necessary, pave the way for the attainment of a hypothetical hard convergence scenario.

Fourth, a leading jurisdiction such as that of the US had already expressed its opposition to the EU's proposal of enhancing the powers of the WTO in Competition law issues. Over the years the US has shown a more proactive and flexible attitude towards Antitrust international cooperation, although still far from conferring jurisdictional powers to a third authority.

Fifth, and as mentioned at the beginning of the paper the increasing number of major global challenges, such as climate change and the digitalization of the economy, are more than ever calling for common action to crack down on them.

Sixth, it shall not be overlooked that the set of Competition rules of any jurisdiction responds to the particular features of the economic policy followed in a given country. Whether liberal or interventionist, jurisdictions around the world adopt different standards in accordance with their respective needs and interests. Welfare standards may vary from country

37. Gifford, D. J., "The Draft International Antitrust Code Proposed at Munich: Good Intentions Gone Awry" in *Minnesota Journal of Global Trade*, vol. 6, n. 1, 1997, pp. 1-66.

to country. China, for instance, has traditionally advocated for an industrial policy that could facilitate the creation of "National Champions" capable of competing in the international arena against the most powerful companies[38]. This stand originally taken by China has been for a long time in stark contrast with the principles that the EU preserves. However, China has steadily leaned towards a more flexible approach to European Competition Law[39]. This topic shall be addressed in the last point of the paper.

Perhaps, there are other ways less extreme for seeking convergence in a hard way. Although its classification as "hard" or "soft" would be conditional upon the content of the provisions, it should be reckoned that multilateral and bilateral agreements, especially those to be concluded between jurisdictions pertaining to the same region or geographically close to one another, may give rise to a more feasible form of hard harmonisation. It is easier to come to terms on Competition policy issues under this type of agreements as countries of the same region share more immediate economic interests. These agreements also deliver other advantages as they can easily include in their wording anti-dumping provisions that help counter predatory pricing[40]. Historically, bilateral agreements on Competition law have successfully been concluded: US and Germany (1976), Australia and New Zealand (1994), EU and Canada (1999), US and Brazil (1999) amongst others. "Game theory demonstrates that without international agreements or international mechanisms, the world (or a regional trade block) will end up in a mutually harmful situation featuring little regulation and lax enforcement of cross-border anti-competitive behavior"[41].

Although there exist a few examples of regional organizations that have adopted a Competition law regime, such as ASEAN and CARICOM, the EU definitely provides the best example of regional integration. At the very outset of the European integration process, the Treaty of Rome already contained Competition law provisions in order to ensure the effectiveness of the envisaged common market. The European lawmaker understood that the elimination of public barriers to trade between Member States could not be inhibited by the establishment of private ones. The European Commission subsequently became the central Competition authority whereas the

38. Bush, N., "Constraints on convergence in Chinese antitrust" in *The Antitrust Bulletin*, vol. 54, n. 1, Spring, 2009, pp. 87-155.
39. Deffains, B., D'ormesson, O., and Perroud, T., "Competition Policy and Industrial Policy: for a reform of European Law" in *Foundation Robert Schuman*, 2020, pp. 1- 47.
40. Passman, B. R., "Multilateral Rules on Competition Policy: an overview of the debate" in *ECLAC — SERIE Comercio Internacional*, n. 4, 1999, pp. 1-55.
41. *Ibid.*, p. 25.

European Court of Justice became the reviewing body to deal with appeals on the decisions of the Commission.

And when it comes to the EU's relations with third countries, whenever the European Commission approves or adopts a Free Trade Area Agreement, it usually includes a chapter on Competition Law or at least some provisions[42]. By doing so the EU is promoting Competition Law in other jurisdictions. This is like the instance provided by the North America Free Trade Agreement (NAFTA) between the US, Canada, and Mexico. Although not in an exhaustive manner, the NAFTA set out a couple of provisions aimed at encouraging cooperation between these three countries in order to improve conditions of fair competition in the free trade area. In particular, the agreement provides that Canada, Mexico and the U. S. would each "adopt or maintain measures to proscribe anticompetitive business conduct"[43]. The limited scope of the Antitrust provisions under the NAFTA was namely due to the lack of a Competition Law regime in Mexico and the clear disparities existing between the Canadian Antitrust regime and that of the US[44].

It must be said though that these free trade agreements, either concluded by the EU or the US, are hardly considered as hard harmonisation measures on the grounds of the cooperative nature of the provisions laid down in them, which are closer to a soft approach to global governance. These provisions are shaped as statements of intent and, in consequence, when not going beyond the mere commitment to information exchange between Competition authorities they should not, at least in principle, be considered as hard harmonisation measures. In contrast, the inclusion of a mutual recognition clause in the agreement would do represent an ambitious step towards harmonisation as it would formally imply the domestic observation of a decision delivered by the enforcer from a third jurisdiction. Mutual recognition goes a step further from informally reaching a common decision over a common issue as it occurred on occasion of the *booking.com* case where the French, Italian, and Swedish Competition authorities agreed on the commitments to be adopted by the infringing undertaking[45].

This may be useful in terms of time-management and resourcing, especially for those jurisdictions less experienced. In terms of cost-effectiveness, plenty

42. Kotigala, M. I., *Analysing competition related issues in Free Trade Agreements with emphasis on the Competition Chapter of the Trans-Pacific Partnership, Research Gate*, 2016, pp. 1-34.
43. Article 1501 of NAFTA.
44. Collins, K. M., "Harmonizing the Antitrust Laws of NAFTA Signatories" in *Loyola of Los Angeles International and Comparative Law*, vol. 17, n. 157, 1994, pp. 157-196.
45. Vidalon, D., *France, Sweden, Italy accept booking.com antitrust proposals*, Thomson Reuters, 2015, p. 1.

of advantages may stem from mutual recognition whenever the economic benefits outweigh the economic costs of performing multiple investigations over a given issue that affects the same market players. Mutual recognition thus would not only be in the best interests of Competition authorities but also of private actors. The minimization of legal, administrative and timing burdens would foster effective enforcement. The promotion of sound competition law and enforcement globally improves "global resource allocation", and this can be better observed when companies need to notify a merger in a plurality of jurisdictions and wait for an outcome to be reached in all of them[46]. Although in other cases undertakings might be reluctant to further harmonisation as they may feel that their information is more exposed with a greater risk of being investigated[47].

The drafting of a mutual recognition clause can be approached in two ways: a) Enabling the evaluating jurisdiction (normally the most experienced) to additionally take into consideration the specific features of the ceding jurisdiction in order to deliver a customized decision to the market needs of the latter. This option entails a higher burden for the evaluating jurisdiction as it would need extra work to deliver two decisions: or b) Accepting a single decision as a common answer to both the evaluating and the ceding jurisdiction. The controversy here, even though this second option would maximize the benefits of mutual recognition in terms of cost-effectiveness, lies in the lower adaptability of the decision to the special market circumstances of the jurisdiction recipient of the foreign decision.

Despite the prospective enhancement of global enforcement of Competition law, it is safe to say that there are considerable difficulties in seeing a widespread acceptance of mutual recognition as a leading principle of Competition law global governance. The difficulties for mutual recognition can be shown by looking at an EU case. It is revealing that, even in a more cohesive context as the EU, automatic mutual recognition of decisions of National Competition Authorities or courts of other Member States could not be imposed. The Antitrust Damages Directive[48] laid down that national final infringement decisions are irrefutably binding for the

46. OECD/ICN, *Joint Report on International Enforcement Co-operation, Directorate for Financial and Enterprise Affairs Competition Committee*, Working Party n. 3 on Co-operation and Enforcement, 11 November 2020, pp. 1-278, point 133
47. *Ibid.*, point 135.
48. European Parliament and Council Directive 2014/104/EU on certain rules governing actions for damages under national law for infringements of the competition law provisions of the Member States and of the European Union, [2014] OJ L 349/1 (hereinafter Antitrust Damages Directive).

damages court[49] but final decisions taken in other Member States are only *prima facie* evidence of the infringement[50]. If this is the most ambitious solution that could be adopted in the EU in relation to infringement decisions enforcing the same common provisions (article 101 and 102 TFEU), thinking of automatic mutual recognition at global level does not seem realistic. However, this EU technique of using decisions taken in other Member States as *prima facie* evidence might well be an easier path to take.

Furthermore, we should not forget the current global context. The resurgence of nationalisms raises serious doubts about governments formally committing to the acceptance of foreign decisions as if they were of their own making. Even in the heart of the EU the prohibition of the proposed acquisition of Alstom by Siemens, leading companies in Europe in the supply of railway signaling systems and high-speed trains, reignited the debate over the inclusion of industrial policies into Competition policy[51]. On the top of it, the debate over the progressive consideration of public interest goals in Competition law enforcement can backfire if certain global goals are not embraced by everyone as their own. This remark must be emphasized when at a worldwide level it is not yet clear whether public interest goals should be included in the Competition review and, by extension, assessed by a non-competition authority.

Because of all the contingencies that hard harmonisation entails it might be wiser to rule out a full implementation of these "hard" measures. It may be claimed, with almost total certainty, that achieving a global framework for Competition Law capable of striking a balance between every country's needs and meet the demands of each differing economic policy is rather overoptimistic, not to say utopian. Jurisdictions around the world would continue to turn a deaf ear to any proposal of a hypothetical global Competition law whose rules remained binding in the face of their own national interests. Therefore, voluntary and non-binding harmonisation may be viewed as the most appealing alternative to any attempt at globally supranationalising Competition law. The key thus lies in co-operation and not in integration, at least for the time being.

49. Article 9.1 of the Antitust Damages Directive says: "an infringement of competition law found by a final decision of a national competition authority or by a review court is deemed to be irrefutably established for the purposes of an action for damages brought before their national courts".
50. Article 9.2 of the Antitrust Damages Directive.
51. Case M.8677 — Siemens/Alstom, C(2019) 921, 6 February 2019.

IV. SOFT HARMONISATION: COOPERATIONIST APPROACH

As explained at the outset of this article, the proliferation of emerging regimes on Competition law puzzled observers around the world who have intended to come up with the least-worst option to Global Governance issues. As claimed above, hard harmonisation measures do not seem to be the answer to the dilemma since national interests are rather intertwined with the Competition policy adopted in every country Extraterritorial application of Competition Law is of a complementary nature and thus does not represent the key to addressing global challenges brought by Competition. In 1995, on occasion of the 22nd Annual Conference on International Antitrust Law and Policy held at Fordham University, Mr. Robert Pitofsky claimed that there is no jurisdiction capable of securing the advantages of markets "beyond its own borders by means of unilateral antitrust enforcement"[52]. He followed on to acknowledge that "the increased globalization of the world's economy has led to much interest in cooperation, convergence, and harmonisation"[53]. Hence, if hard harmonisation measures are constantly declined as they clash head-on with national interests and the extraterritorial application of Competition law solely helps lay the groundwork for a partial solution, *which other options remain up for grabs?*

Soft-harmonisation measures seem to be the most reasonable solution to the dilemma since they better balance global challenges with local circumstances. Non-binding rules blend with the particularities of emerging jurisdictions as guidelines and recommendations are shaped in accordance with the target jurisdiction's needs[54].

Voluntary rules would subsequently replace a hypothetical international code on Competition and the mentioned supranational enforcement authority with a voluntary informal platform aimed at bringing consensus in Competition law matters. In this manner no country would be liable to confer powers on any international organism and they would subsequently keep their powers within their boundaries to legislate and enforce the law as they wish. Materially speaking, no mandatory legal instrument would be adopted, guidelines, recommendations or a set of best practices would

52. Robert Pitofsky at Fordham Corporate Law Institute 22nd Annual Conference on International Antitrust Law and Policy, Fordham University Law School, 26 October 1995.
53. *Ibid.*
54. Cheng, T. K., "Convergence and Its Discontents: A Reconsideration of the Merits of Convergence of Global Competition Law" in *Chicago Journal of International Law*, 2012, vol. 12 n. 2, p. 433-490.

be issued instead. Only by flexible and tailor-made measures it is possible "to achieve sensible convergence, one that reduces global divergences of Competition law without neglecting local circumstances"[55].

Instead of creating a supranational sovereign authority, it is deemed more appropriate to set up, or better yet, make use of a common platform for Competition law that transcends the individuality of a state. Such a platform would be made up of a group of individuals with a wealth of knowledge and broad experience in the subject matter. On account of their expertise, they would issue recommendations or guidelines aimed to the platform's members in response to a stated request from any of them. Or even on its own initiative, the group of experts should be entitled to issue statements of advice for voluntary adherence by the members. While the WTO's contribution to the international landscape of Competition has been rather limited other international organizations have been doing their bit, to a greater or lesser extent, to enhance international cooperation on Competition issues, namely the International Competition Network (ICN), the Organization for Economic Cooperation and Development (OECD), the United Nations Conference on Trade and Development (UNCTAD) and the World Bank:

Despite the importance of all these organizations on the international stage, it is actually the ICN the one that best embodies the encouragement for convergence on Competition law amongst jurisdictions. "The organization's efforts have yielded important contributions to the development of widely accepted international Competition policy norms, and its annual meeting has become perhaps the single most important annual gathering of Competition agency leaders"[56]. With 135 members, the ICN provides practical advice to Antitrust agencies around the world, either from developed or developing countries, on policy issues of common concern for Antitrust and Merger Control enforcement both from a substantive and a procedural perspective.

The reality shows that competition agencies are now working and cooperating within this informal network. The network is not just comprised of competition authorities but also of non-governmental actors, such as academics, economists, or lawyers. Most of its activities are open to both competition authorities and non-governmental actors, but some activities are only for competition agencies. The network is extremely flexible, very

55. *Ibid.*, p. 450.
56. Hollman, H. M. and Kovacic, W. E., "The International Competition Network: Its Past, Current and Future Role" in *Minnesota Journal of International Law*, vol. 20, n. 2, 2011, pp. 274-323, p. 275.

practical, project oriented and runs on working groups with specific targets[57]. It issues non-binding acts, just recommendations, best practices, training materials for the competition authorities. It has been rather successful on pushing forward soft convergence and more effectiveness on the enforcement of Competition law in different jurisdictions. It has reduced the risks of conflict between different competition authorities and for sure improved soft convergence, while at the same time it has maintained flexibility and full respect for diversity. It is up to each competition agency whether or not to stick to the recommendations on best practices. Notwithstanding the freedom of every domestic agency, it must be noted that there is a mechanism of peer pressure between competition agencies in such a way that they closely monitor each other's adherence to the recommendations issued by the network and their consistency with the stand taken by them at the panels held at the core of it[58].

Hence, the ICN is really helping build consensus and at the same time push forward soft convergence through this peer pressure mechanism.

Last but not least, it is noteworthy how the ICN evaluates the state of convergence of the diverse Competition systems by means of regular periodical reports that detect whether or not soft convergence is growing.

Highly significant is also the role played by the OECD. Since 1961 the OECD, through its Competition law and Policy Committee, has been playing an increasingly active role in Competition law issues. Even though compliance with its numerous recommendations, both on Antitrust and Merger Control, remains fully voluntary. Aside from its recommendations, it is also worth highlighting OECD's statistics on Competition for each Member country, country reviews, best practice roundtables and specific reports on particular areas of Competition. Considering the increasing role played by economics in the formulation, enforcement and analysis of Competition policy, it must be said that the OECD is a strong advocate for the application of this discipline as a tool to improve global enforcement.

It is worth highlighting the fact that the ICN along with the OECD have recently issued the first Joint Report on International Enforcement Co-operation which outlines key aspects of the on-going state of international

57. Bode, M. and Budzinki, O., "Competing Ways Towards International Antitrust: the WTO versus the ICN" in *Marburg Papers on Economics*, n. 3, 2005, pp. 1-33.

58. Budzinki, O., *The International Competition Network as an international merger control institution, International Institutions and Multinational Enterprises: Global Players-Global Markets*, Edward Elgard Publishing, 2004, pp. 1-27.

enforcement co-operation between Competition authorities[59]. From it, it can be derived that notwithstanding persistent barriers to international enforcement, it can actually be observed a significant increase of enforcement cooperation between authorities regardless of their size and experience[60]. Furthermore, regional enforcement co-operation is presented as the most important form of interagency co-operation[61].

Like the OECD, UNCTAD recognizes that Competition problems have a cross-border component that must be tackled globally. UNCTAD has to report to the United Nations Secretariat as part of the UN, in consequence it stands to reason that whereas the OECD has a greater tendency to comment on Competition in developed countries, the UNCTAD is more oriented towards achieving a level playing field for all business in developing countries[62]. It is to be highlighted the failed Competition code that UNCTAD also tried to promote. (United Nations Set of Multilaterally Agreed Equitable Principles and Rules for the Control of Restrictive Business Practices -1980).

Finally, the World Bank, alongside the other major international institution, its Washington neighbor the International Monetary Fund (IMF), promoted trade liberalization and globalization in its early origins[63]. They even conditioned loans to countries in need of economic aid upon the development by the borrowers of laws that would foster Competition[64].

In addition to making use of a common international platform, the leading jurisdictions, i. e. that of the US and the EU's, are called to play a significant role in the development of Competition at a worldwide level. In the face of the rampant proliferation of emerging jurisdictions on Competition law, the legislation of the US and that of the EU have inevitably become an outright reference for all those regimes who want to emulate the wording of their consolidated legal texts and established practice[65]. In this sense, with no need to issue guidance or recommendations, the US and the EU may be soft harmonising Competition policy beyond their own borders.

59. OECD/ICN, *Joint Report on International Enforcement Co-operation, Directorate for Financial and Enterprise Affairs Competition Committee, op. cit.*
60. *Ibid.*, p. 20.
61. *Ibid.*
62. Malinauskaite, J., "Harmonisation of Competition Law in the Context of Globalisation" in *European Business Law Review*, 2010, pp. 369-397.
63. The Washington Consensus.
64. ABA Int'l Divergence Report.
65. Kovacic, W. E., "Merger Enforcement in Transition: Antitrust controls on acquisitions in emerging economies" in *Cincinnati Law Review*, vol. 66, n. 4, 1998, pp. 1075-1112.

The EU has traditionally been more open to seek harmonisation. The "global reach" of EU law beyond their borders has been unquestionable for many[66]. Although the US has traditionally remained hesitant to harmonisation, it is needless to say that it has an interest in making its Competition policy the model to be followed by new jurisdictions. "Of course, US antitrust law provided the model for the core triad of modern competition law that has been universally adopted around the world". In fact, there are conflicting interests between the US and the EU to make their respective jurisdictions the best reference for the lawmakers of brand-new regimes. Emerging jurisdictions are in position to weigh pros and cons of each regime and subsequently fit into their own regimes those features that deem most appropriate in accordance with the characteristics of their markets. Jurisdictions around the world have been seeking some sort of soft convergence in the interpretation of its decisions when supporting them with arguments stemming from the EU. This has been the case of India. For instance, by aligning their concept of "enterprise" with that of "undertaking" envisaged in EU law. A part of the scholarly claims that, even at a private level, multinational companies are also interested in extending the EU rule to govern their global operations.

Considering the role model played by the US and the EU jurisdictions, it may be claimed that the greater the coordination that there is between their respective agencies the greater the chances for soft convergence will also be globally. In fact, throughout the past decades it can be observed greater cooperation between these two jurisdictions which has led them to gradually match some standards. After all, in many ways the inception of EU Competition law was influenced by the more experienced US Antitrust Law. And on both sides of the Atlantic it is conducted "a Competition policy which is based on sound economics and which has the protection of consumer interest as its primary concern". Let's take for instance the joint issuance of the "Best Practices on Cooperation in Merger Investigations" which sets forth an advisory framework for interagency cooperation in the field of Merger Control[67]. The text elaborates on the first set of Best Practices of 2002 by drawing on the experience gathered throughout the investigations in many cases in which the agencies cooperated pursuant to the 1991 US/EU Cooperation Agreement. Upon learning of a merger that seems to require review in both the US and the EU, agencies are compelled to contact each other immediately to facilitate

66. Monti, G., "The Global Reach of EU Competition Law", in Cremona, M. and Scott, J., *EU Law Beyond EU Borders The Extraterritorial Reach of EU Law*, Oxford University Press, 2019, pp. 174-196.

67. US-EU Merger Working Group: Best Practices on Cooperation in Merger Investigations, 2014, pp. 1-6.

information to each other, increase the transparency of the reviewing process and subsequently minimize the risk of divergent decisions. And more recently the issuance of a "Joint Technology Competition Policy Dialogue" focused on developing common approaches and strengthening the cooperation on competition policy and enforcement in the technology sector[68].

Thus, considering the consolidated Competition practice in the US and the EU, it seems sensible to claim that the increasing interagency cooperation between their authorities will gradually benefit, in a soft way, global governance of Competition law. It must be noted though that their strengths in terms of influence over the international landscape should always be balanced in such a way that no authority (and or government) would be enticed to replace global interests with domestic ones. That could easily undermine neutrality in the development of global governance of Competition law when self-interests are at stake. The exclusive leadership in the field by a single jurisdiction should be taken off the table as a permanent solution to resolve the dilemma. The success of a a global competition law strategy will rest on fixing common objectives, based on shared views, and on its capacity to maintain durable commitments to these common objectives[69].)

V. SOFT CONVERGENCE BETWEEN THE EU AND CHINA

In the race between the US and the EU to promote their Competition law, it might be stated that the EU won when it came to the advocacy of its legal framework in China. As tariff and non-tariff barriers were being torn down globally, undertakings started to increasingly engage in cross-border trade and face the consequent challenges posed by divergent jurisdictions. Observing the central role that Competition law had being playing in the economy of both sides of the Atlantic, China did not want to fall behind and thus had to design a Competition system suitable to the needs of the country. The stronger advocacy for the market self-correcting mechanisms observed in the US seemed to be key for China to leaning towards the EU's regime[70].

The 2004 accession of former communist countries to the EU may have also been a contributing factor for China to use EU Competition law as a

68. Inaugural Joint Statement between the European Commission, the United States Department of Justice Antitrust Division and the United States Federal Trade Commission, Washington, 7 December 2021.
69. Gerber, D. J., *Global Competition. Law, Markets and Globalization*, Oxford University Press, 2010, p. 344.
70. Li, G., *Revisiting China's Competition Law and Its Interaction with Intellectual Property Rights*, Nomos Verlagsgesellschaft, 2018, pp. 36- 46, p. 37.

model[71]. Materially speaking the Chinese law is modeled on that of the EU, "but here again the Competition Authority's embeddedness in the central bureaucracy and its social market economy principles leads to variations in application"[72].

Differences between the blocs are beyond obviousness: the welfare standards used by the agencies, the interference of political factors in decision-making, the economic policy to be followed by implementing rules on Competition and the degree of transparency detected in the Merger Control decision process[73]. Notwithstanding their differences, the relationship between the EU and China has grown ever since[74]. In parallel, the latter years have revealed a larger European mistrust on Chinese activities in Europe and an increased will of laying down stricter controls. Take for instance the recent proposal for an International Procurement Instrument (IPI) that would introduce measures limiting the access to open EU public procurement tenders of non-EU companies from countries that do not offer similar access to EU companies[75]. Or the recent Commission's proposal on foreign subsidies, which is also an instrument, whose dimension is clearly framed to answer to the Chinese behavior in competition matters[76]. Or the new screening of foreign direct investment (FDI) in Europe for security or public order concerns[77]. Although the Regulation clearly establishes the

71. *Ibid.*, p. 38.
72. Gerber, D. J., *Competition Law and Antitrust: A Global Guide*, Oxford University Press, 2020. pp. 1-190, p. 124.
73. Sokol, D., "Merger Control under China's Anti-Monopoly Law", in *New York University Journal of Law and Business*, vol. 10, n. 1, 2013, pp. 1-36; Maillo, J., "Understanding China's Competition Law and Policy: Merger Control as a Case Study" in *Serie Política de la Competencia, Instituto Universitario de Estdudios Europeos*, Universidad CEU San Pablo, Working Paper 30/2011, retrieved from *https://repositorioinstitucional.ceu.es/bitstream/10637/3488/1/understanding_maillo_2011.pdf*.
74. EU China Comprehensive Agreement on Investment: The Agreement in Principle, 30 December 2020, pp. 1-5. However, the future of the agreement is blocked in the European Parliament due to human rights conflict and sanctions.
75. Draft on the proposal for a regulation of the European Parliament and of the Council on the access of third-country goods and services to the Union's internal market in public procurement and procedures supporting negotiations on access of Union goods and services to the public procurement markets of third countries (COM(2016)0034 –C9-0018/2016 –2012/0060(COD)), pp. 1-61.
76. European Commission, *White Paper on levelling the playing field as regards foreign subsidies*, COM(2020) 253 final, 2020. See as well the follow up: Proposal for a Regulation of The European Parliament and of the Council on foreign subsidies distorting the internal market, COM(2021) 223 final.
77. Regulation 2019/452 was finally adopted, establishing a framework for the supervision of FDI in the Union, OJ L79 1/1. See Maillo, J., "New screening of foreign direct

principle of non-discrimination between third countries[78] and, therefore, is not aimed at investments from any specific country, it is evident that one of the main triggers of the new mechanism has been the exponential increase in direct investments in Europe from emerging economies and especially from China[79]. Therefore, it seems that the EU is trying to solve is concerns about China's activities in Europe more by new trade defence instruments than by a change of its competition rules. Interestingly, however, some of these new trade defense instruments are inspired and use a logic, concepts and tools familiar to competition rules. It is yet to be seen how these new instruments will work and which will be their effects, in particular whether they will be enough to eliminate the concerns of unlevel playing field and public security of Europeans. It would also be interesting to see whether they would favour further cooperation and convergence of competition law enforcement between China and the EU.

At a steady pace the two blocs have taken 'soft' steps towards convergence by establishing permanent mechanisms of consultation in Competition law. Amid international trade tensions both, the EU and China, can benefit from sharing a common path for understanding[80].

To understand the state of play, it is deemed important to trace down this common path from a brief overview of the evolution of the EU's approach to extraterritoriality to the evolution of the Chinese Competition law regime:

---

investment (FDI) in Europe: a first step towards a new paradigm?" in *Spanish Yearbook of International Law*, n. 24, 2020, pp. 180-209.

78. Article 3.2 of the Regulation: "Rules and procedures related to screening mechanisms [...] shall be transparent and not discriminate between third countries".

79. See, among others, Schaake, M., "Comment of a Member of the European Parliament" in Bourgeois, J. (ed), *EU Framework for Foreign Direct Investment Control*, Wolters Kluwer, 2020, pp. 99-101, or J. Bourgeois, J. and Malathouni, E., "The EU regulation on Screening Foreign Direct Investment: Another Piece of the Puzzle", in Bourgeois, J. (ed), *EU Framework for Foreign Direct Investment Control*, Wolters Kluwer, 2020, pp. 169-191, at p. 170: "The regulation comes largely as a response to the lack of reciprocity faced by EU investors abroad and mainly in China". See also European Commission, Staff Working Document on Foreign Direct Investment in the EU, Following up on the Commission Communication "Welcoming Foreign Direct Investment while Protecting Essential Interests" of 13 September 2017, SWD (2019) 108 final, 13 march 2019, at p. 67.

80. Geeraerts, G., "The EU China Partnership: Balancing Between Divergence and Convergence". Paper presented at the Final International Conference and Researchers' Workshop "A New Dimension in Asia-Europe Relations: Exploring EU's Global Actorness and Strategic Partnership in Asia", Korea University, 2019, pp. 1-20.

1. EVOLUTION OF THE EU'S APPROACH TO EXTRATERRITORIALITY AND OTHER CONTRIBUTIONS TO COMPETITION LAW GLOBAL GOVERNANCE

The EU has traditionally played an important role in the development of Competition law beyond their borders, namely from the unilateralist approach to soft convergence. It has traditionally investigated and prosecuted foreign Antitrust practices that were either implemented within the EU's territory or that had effects within it.

The European Commission practice on the extraterritorial application of EU Competition law has evolved throughout history. Three different approaches have been adopted to address this matter, the last of which resemblances that of the US, namely[81]:

i. Firstly, the "single economic entity doctrine" was applicable to determine the extraterritorial application of EU Competition rules[82]. According to this doctrine, a parent company and its subsidiaries are regarded as the same company and subsequently anticompetitive conduct from a company located in a third country could be scrutinized under the scope of the Commission provided that such a company had a subsidiary inside the EU's territory[83].

ii. Secondly, the European Commission went a step further in the extraterritorial application of EU Competition rules by embracing the so-called "implementation doctrine" which advocates for the application of EU Competition law whenever the conduct is implemented in the EU's territory and regardless of where that conduct was conceived for the very first time. Even though the conduct took place in a third country[84].

iii. Thirdly, the Commission followed in the steps of the US by adopting the "effects doctrine"[85]. Although similar to the implementation

81. "Roundtable on Cartel Jurisdiction issues, including the effects doctrine", Working Party n. 3 on Co-operation and Enforcement, DAF/COMP/WP3/WD(2008)93, 21 October 2008.

82. Case C-882/19, Sumal SL vs Mercedes Benz Trucks España SL [2001] ECLI:EU:C:2021:800 (Sumal).

83. Case 48/69 Imperial Chemical Industries Ltd v Commission [1972] ECLI:EU:C:1972:70 (Dyestuffs).

84. Case 89/85 Ahlström Osakeyhtiö and others v Commission [1994] ECLI:EU:C:1994:12 (Wood Pulp).

85. Case T-102/96, Gencor and, more recently Case C-413/14 P Intel, both *supra* note 25.

doctrine, the "effects doctrine" covers more scenarios in order to apply Competition rules extraterritorially. This doctrine claims that any anticompetitive conduct taking place in a third country could eventually be brought under the EU jurisdiction if effects arising from that conduct occur within the EU territory.

As pointed out earlier in this paper, in addition to the extraterritorial application of its legal framework on Competition, the EU has typically encouraged the thought of creating Competition law rules within the WTO. And it has also been very active both in the OECD and within the ICN. In particular, the European Commission plays a very important role within the ICN, with very significant contributions and leadership within the group. EU lawyers and economists are by far more involved in the network than any other group of professionals from any other jurisdiction altogether with those from the US.

On the top of it, the EU has signed more than 85 international agreements dealing with Competition issues, some of them, around 25, are to be found in Free Trade Area Agreements where there is a chapter on Competition. That is the case of the agreement recently signed with New Zealand, whose Chapter 15 is fully devoted to Competition policy[86].

On other occasions the European Union prefers concluding specific agreements on competition to having just a Chapter within a larger agreement on different topics. This is the case of the EU and China, where there is a dedicated agreement on Competition Law issues with special support of the EU to the development of Competition law in China.

Furthermore, the EU is an excellent example of a very advanced and intense cooperation between different national competition authorities and national courts with regard to the enforcement of competition rules, and the harmonisation of EU's and Member States' competition rules. Arguably, due to the high degree of integration in the EU in this field, many of the cooperation mechanisms and solutions cannot be easily transplanted to a global governance context or even to other regional contexts. However, they may provide ideas and tools for those wishing to intensify their cooperation in the future (also for global governance), even if they may have to be adjusted to the different contexts.

In sum, all this is strong evidence of the contributions and impetus that the EU has been giving to Global Governance on Competition law,

86. EU-New Zealand Free Trade Agreement, 9 July 2023.

probably more than any other region in the world has ever done. For that goal, the EU has used different mechanisms: by extraterritoriality (with international comity), by promoting hard harmonisation at both bilateral and multilateral level to the extent that is possible and by actively advocating for soft harmonisation and convergence Moreover, its rich internal experience of advanced and intense cooperation may also be valuable, although very likely will require adjustments to the different contexts.

2. EVOLUTION OF THE CHINESE COMPETITION LAW REGIME AND ITS INTERNATIONAL DIMENSION

China adopted the Antimonopoly Law of the People's Republic of China (AML) in 2007 which came into force the following year. It is generally thought that the tight control exercised by the state in the private sector of its economy through a numerous range of state-owned enterprises held the country back from adopting earlier a legal framework on Competition law[87]. And, by extension, it also refrained the country from reproducing a more similar model to a Western-style pre-existing Antitrust law[88]. Outwardly, China could take as a reference either the US or the EU jurisdiction[89].

Internally, the drafting process of the AML grew in complexity when it came across with a plurality of laws that governed different aspects to be addressed from a Competition law perspective. There was therefore a need to rip apart some pre-existing domestic laws in China and conceive the first Chinese Competition law. Clearly, the fact that China became a member of the WTO provided the necessary impetus to the AML's drafting[90]. Especially if taking into account that the adoption of a Competition law toolkit is considered as a must in order for the jurisdiction in question to satisfy the internal rules governing the WTO[91].

87. Emch, A. and Stallibrass, S., *The Chinese Anti-Monopoly Law: The First Five Years*, Wolter Kluwer, 2013.

88. Zheng, W., "Transplanting Antitrust in China: Economic Transition, Market Structure and State Control", in *University of Pennsylvania Journal of International Law*, vol. 32, n. 2, 2010, pp. 643-721.

89. Gerber, D. J., "Constructing Competition Law in China: The Potential Value of European and U. S. Experience" in *Washington University Global Studies Law Review*, vol. 3, 2004, pp. 315-331.

90. Harris, H. S. JR., "The Making of an Antitrust Law: The Pending Anti-Monopoly Law of the People's Republic of China" in *Chicago Journal of International Law*, vol. 7, n. 1, 2006, pp. 169-229.

91. *Ibid.*

Since its inception China's Competition law has clearly shown signs for the extraterritorial application of its legal instrument. As a matter of fact, China is already playing a major role in Merger Control, because international mergers are being nowadays notified to the Chinese competition authority. Therefore, it has the possibility of blocking international mergers when these have effects on the Chinese markets. Let us take for instance the intended and failed acquisition of *Huiyuan Juice* by *Coca-Cola* which would have been the largest-ever buyout of a Chinese company by a foreign rival[92]. The blocking of the operation was considered by many as vivid signs of the reminiscent protectionism of China, which far from a western-style liberal approach, is still embedded in its Merger Control system[93]. The decision in the prominent *Coca-Cola* case might be interpreted as a warning sign for foreign investors to refrain themselves from putting money into the Chinese market[94]. The first years of enforcement left strong concerns about the neutrality of Chinese merger control with suspicions of strict supervision being applied mainly to foreign operations and not to domestic ones. This distrust was based on the fact that many of the problematic cases decided were either foreign-to-foreign transactions or projected acquisitions by foreign companies of Chinese businesses; (b) the doubts about whether State-owned enterprises and sectoral Chinese companies have to notify and whether compliance with this notification obligation was being effectively supervised and enforced; (c) the possibility for the Chinese competition authorities to consider not only competition concerns but also issues such as the "development of the national economy" or "national (economic) security". Although the Chinese authorities defend their neutrality and made efforts to reduce these concerns, complaints continued[95]. For instance, harsh antitrust remedies have been imposed on offshore merger transactions and aggressive interventions in business practices have taken place, leading to enforcement differences with Western economies and complaints by foreign operators of protectionism, unequal treatment and lack of due process[96].

---

92. Huang, X. Y., "Huiyuan's Acquisition by Coca-Cola in PRC — Case Analysis" in *Journal of Economics, Business and Management*, vol. 3, n. 2, 2015, pp. 271-275.
93. Hemphill, T. A. and White G. O., "China's National Champions: The Evolution of a National Industrial Policy — Or a New Era of Economic Protectionism?" in *Thunderbird International Business Review*, vol. 55, n. 2, 2013, pp. 193-212.
94. Davis, B., "China's Anti-Monopoly Law: Protectionism or a Great Leap Forward?" in *Boston College International and Comparative Law Review*, vol. 33, 2010, pp. 305-321.
95. Maillo, J., "Understanding China's Competition Law and Policy: Merger Control as a Case Study", *op. cit.*, pp. 23-29.
96. Zhang, A. H., *Chinese Antitrust Exceptionlism: How the rise of China challenges global regulation*, Oxford University Press, 2021, pp. 2-3.

To these intrinsic competition law differences in the design of competition rules and above all on their enforcement, it must be added a non-favourable political climate. The long-standing political strain between the US and China clearly have not helped pave the way for convergence. Tensions that have distinctly been transferred to actors in the market. Do not forget the allegedly arbitrary decision from the US Administration to ban Chinese app *Tik Tok* in an attempt at addressing national security concerns in the view of the former President of the US[97]. No matter the final outcome of this fallout that there is no denying that this sort of decisions contribute to polarizing jurisdictions' positions on Global Governance of Competition law. This phenomenon is what some scholars call "Geoeconomic Competition"[98]. The AML, thus, "emerges as a powerful economic weapon allowing the Chinese. authority to exercise extraterritorial jurisdiction over foreign multinationals"[99]. The AML provides that "this Law shall apply to the monopolistic conducts in economic activities within the territory of the People's Republic of China; this Law shall apply to the monopolistic conducts outside the territory of the People's Republic of China that has the effect of eliminating or restricting competition on the domestic market of China"[100].

Thus, taking roots in the effects doctrine, even though when there is hardly a link with the Chinese market, China is able to scrutinize the behavioral or structural conduct of firms[101]. A sector from the academia insists to underline that the AML has been increasingly weaponized at the service of China in the midst of the so-called 'Sino-US (trade) war'[102]. Within the "wide discretionary power" China may aggressively use the AML, namely[103]:

a. to impose hefty sanctions on infringing firms;

b. to delay the approval of mergers and acquisitions;

c. to impose strict behavioral remedies.

Just take for instance the landmark Qualcomm/NXP case that the EU cleared once the Commission allayed its doubts over interoperability

97. Executive Order on Addressing the Threat Posed by TikTok, White House, Presidential Actions, August 6, 2020.
98. Gertz, G. and Evers, M., "Geoeconomic Competition: Will State Capitalism Win?" in *The Washington Quarterly*, 2020, pp. 117-136.
99. Zhang, A. H., *Chinese Antitrust Exceptionlism [...]", op. cit.*, p. 214.
100. Article 2 of the Antimonopoly Law of the People's Republic of China.
101. See Zhang, A. H., *Chinese Antitrust Exceptionlism [...]", op. cit.*, p. 217.
102. *Ibid.*, p. 203.
103. *Ibid.*, p. 218.

issues[104]. Qualcomm is a US leading manufacturer of chips for smartphones. Qualcomm notified in nine jurisdictions its intention to purchase NXP which was devoted to the manufacture of semiconductors. Rapid and streamlined procedures were conducted by all the jurisdictions but for the Chinese. China stretched its investigation and allegedly withheld the completion of the transaction. The delay was seen by many as unnecessary and as a politized decision. This case thus represents a good instance of the wide discretionary powers of China and how it can leverage its AML into a trade tool that foreign operators may need to be wary of.

The trade war, transferred today mainly to the digital sector, gives food for thought about whether it is appropriate for Competition authorities to exert their jurisdictional powers over matters that are embedded in the Chinese domains[105]. Maybe the too lax interpretation given to comity and extraterritorial application of Competition law have created between these two concepts a tug of war that would need for clarification. The use of multilateral fora at this point may prove useful. In any event, China has not yet step forward in the international fora in Competition matters. It is not formally present neither in the ICN nor in the OECD, but curiously enough China acceded to cooperate with the latter. It is not that easy to come across the underlying reason that motivated China to stay clear of the ICN. It might be that they do not need global cooperation that much because China is having bilateral cooperation with both the EU and the US authorities on Competition, or that the Chinese competition authorities prefer to wait to be more developed, with more resources and experience, before entering this international fora..

It is not clear though if, by remaining outside the framework of the ICN, China is putting a break on the promotion of worldwide competition convergence. Whenever China decides to enter the network it will likely want to take a leading role that could influence the perspectives of developing countries and nations in which competition law is less developed. Therefore, although its entry should be promoted and welcome, it is yet to be seen whether it will favour convergence.

China also makes use of soft convergence mechanisms to strengthen enforcement cooperation on Competition Law. Evidence of that are the

104. Case M.8306 Qualcomm / NXP Semiconductors.
105. Bu, Q., "Respectful Consideration, but Not Deference: Chinese Sovereign Amici in the US Supreme Court Vitamin C Judgment" in *Journal of European Competition Law and Practice*, vol. 11, n. 5-6, 2020, pp. 274-286.

Chapters devoted to Competition found in the Free Trade Agreements concluded with third countries[106]. Over more than twenty agreements of this type have come into effect and there are ten currently under negotiation.

China and Australia signed a Memorandum of Understanding to show their commitment to and cooperate in competition enforcement, consumer protection as well as regulation of on-line goods transactions and related services[107]. A few years later, in 2015, the same parties agreed to a Free Trade Area Agreement which represented a further stage in the process of cooperation, setting out more practical detail on how the respective authorities will work together within the framework of Competition law, namely through[108]: a) the exchange of information; b) notification; c) coordination of cross-border enforcement matters and the exchange of views in cases which are subject to the common review of both Parties; and d) technical cooperation.

To cite another meaningful Free Trade Agreement in terms of China's commitment to broadening the application of Competition law worldwide, there's the China-Korea agreement. Both jurisdictions literally commit to "preventing the benefits of trade liberalization from being undermined and to promoting economic efficiency and consumer welfare"[109].

In sum, Chinese antitrust seems to be quite different to the traditional one of Western economies. Although the design of the Chinese Law, at first sight, may look similar, a detailed examination of the Law already shows relevant distinctive features. More importantly, enforcement is very conditioned, among other factors, by the different Chinese context, its State-led economy, the importance of State Owned Enterprises, the major political influence of the public authorities even in private businesses, the role of local public authorities and the past of the institutions entrusted with its enforcement. Moreover, it is still rather recent and immature. All these factors limit the current degree of convergence. Regarding its international dimension, extraterritoriality was applied since the very beginning and seems to be

106. *http://fta.mofcom.gov.cn/topic/enswiss.shtml*

107. Memorandum of Understanding on Cooperation between the State Administration for Industry and Commerce of the People's Republic of China and the Australian Competition and Consumer Commission, September 2012, pp 1-3, article 2.

108. Free Trade Area Agreement between the Government of Australia and the Government of the People's of the Republic of China of 17th June 2015, Article 16.7. (2).

109. Free Trade Area Agreement between the Government of the People's of the Republic of China and the Government of the Republic of Korea of June 2015, Chapter 14, Article 14.1.

-at least sometimes- wider (less limited on international comity) than as understood in Western economies. The participation of Chinese authorities in international antitrust fora and its role is still very limited, The Chinese contribution to global governance in the field is scarce, although no doubt may have a great potential in the future.

3. STATE OF PLAY OF EU-CHINA RELATIONS ON COMPETITION

Since late 2003, even long before the enactment of the Chinese Law on Competition, the EU opted for the establishment of a permanent institutionalized dialogue with China where respect with one another has proven to be paramount and where support and technical assistance have been the key drivers for the development of the Chinese legislation on Competition[110]. The Declaration signed by the European Commission and the Chinese Ministry of Commerce acknowledged that "Competition policy is an important factor in ensuring consumer welfare and it should provide for a level playing field and legal certainty to the business community in the market"[111]. So did the EU when Mario Monti, the Commissioner for Competition at that time, managed to seal the historic partnership agreement with China[112].

The EU-China Strategic Partnership of 2003 paved the way for further cooperation in such a way that the two blocs agreed to schedule subsequent annual meetings in their agendas. A couple of years later and as a result of the talks held throughout the Summit, the European Union and China created the so-called "Competition Policy Dialogue"[113]. On account of it, the Directorate General for Competition of the European Commission and the Ministry of Commerce of China (MOFCOM) signed the Terms of Reference of the EU-China Competition Policy Dialogue[114]. This Policy Dialogue consisted of a permanent consultation mechanism that would legitimize each party to approach each other in order to raise questions of relevance on Competition law issues. Additionally, it laid down the foundations for the establishment of a technical cooperation between the EU and China.

Under the Presidency of Manuel Barroso, the EU reviewed its strategic partnership with China on occasion of the 15th EU-China Summit. In it, the

110. Declaration on the start of a dialogue on Competition by the EU and China of 24 November 2003, pp. 1.

111. *Ibid.*

112. European Commission, Commissioner Monti launches Competition dialogue with China, Press Release IP/03/1587, Brussels, 24 November 2003.

113. Wu, Q., "EU — China Competition Dialogue: A New Step in the Internationalisation of EU Competition Law?" in *European Law Journal*, vol. 12, n. 3, 2012, pp. 461-477.

114. Terms of Reference of the EU-China Competition Policy Dialogue, 06 May 2004, pp.1-2.

leaders on both sides conveyed valuable comments on the path mutually traced years ago for Antitrust cooperation purposes[115] Following the talks, both parties reached a common understanding of their willingne.ss to continue to deepen their bilateral relations on Competition Policy[116].

Pursuant to the meeting, a Memorandum was signed envisaging exchanges of views on Competition law in a soft harmonising kind of way. In particular, on the following points[117]:

(a) *Exchange of views on developments in competition legislation and on their experience in the enforcement of this legislation;*

(b) *Exchange of experiences on the enhancement of the operation of the Sides' competition authorities;*

(c) *Exchange of views with respect to multilateral competition initiatives;*

(d) *Exchange of experiences on competition advocacy including on raising awareness of companies and the wider public of competition and antimonopoly legislation.*

(e) *Exchange of views and experiences regarding a coordinated approach to technical cooperation between the EU and China in the area of competition law.*

Far from turning into an authentic bilateral deal, the Memorandum followed suit with the terms of Reference of the EU-China Competition Policy Dialogue adopted in 2004 in a more political way. Since then, the successive Commissioners for Competition have held constructive talks with China in search of a continuum of soft-convergence mechanisms with the Asian country. Mario Monti, Neelie Kroes, Joaquin Almunia and Margrethe Vestager have regularly met the Ministers responsible for Anti-Monopoly Law enforcement in China. Not long ago, Vestager held talks with Liu He, Vice Premier of China, on the progressive digitalization of the economy and on how communication technologies are becoming a key factor to creating value in terms of trade.

115. Joint Press Communiqué 15th EU-China Summit, Towards a stronger EU-China Comprehensive Strategic Partnership, Brussels, 20 September 2012, point. 12.
116. Memorandum of Understanding on Cooperation in the area of anti-monopoly law between on the one side the European Commission (Directorate-General for Competition) and on the other side The National Development and Reform Commission (NDRC) and The State Administration for Industry and Commerce of the People's Republic of China, 20 September 2012, pp. 1-3.
117. *Ibid*, point 2.1.

Since the EU is China's biggest trading partner and China is the EU's second-biggest trading partner, it is crucial for both to create common paths of convergence to maintain the sound economic relations between them. As Vestager put it after the Digital Dialogue: "The EU and China will both play a role in defining how global technological developments will go forward. The dialogue is therefore necessary to foster cooperation, but also to address divergences we have, like on reciprocity, data protection and fundamental rights"[118].

As with China, similar cooperation remains open to other Asian jurisdictions on the part of the EU. In fact, a larger EU program fostered by DG COMP at the European Commission was set in motion with a view at maintaining an effective dialogue on Competition law issues with Asian jurisdictions[119]. Amongst those jurisdictions included in the program it may be found, besides China: India, Japan, and South Korea. And in addition to them, the ASEAN Member States: Brunei Darussalam, Cambodia, Indonesia, Lao PDR, Malaysia, Myanmar, Philippines, Singapore, Thailand, and Vietnam.

This project has subsequently represented a major achievement for Competition law through the implementation of a soft convergence technique that bridges the gap left on Global Governance issues by the EU and Asian jurisdictions. Running from 2018 to 2020, the Project sought to promote a regulatory level playing field for the mutual benefit of all the jurisdictions involved. In order to attain such an ambitious goal, the European Commission set in motion a series of summer courses on Competition law for officials of the different National Competition Authorities, a range of lectures held in the participating countries and delivered by DG COMP officials, and internal training aimed at officials from the Asian Competition Authorities and hosted by the European Commission itself.

VI. CONCLUSION

The sharp increase of Antitrust regimes poses new challenges for jurisdictions around the globe as they lack the necessary tools to come to grips with anticompetitive effects arising from cross-border operations. The possibilities for competition authorities to pursue investigations, collect evidence and of course to enforce sanctions in other territories are

118. European Commission, EU-China: Commission and China hold first High-level Digital Dialogue, European Commission's Press Release, 10 September 2020, Brussels, IP/20/1600.
119. *https://competitioncooperation.eu/about-the-project/*

scant. This inevitably triggers inefficiencies to every market affected by cross-border operations. An issue that is not precisely easy to address since Competition policy is customized by each sovereign state pursuant to their political interests and the needs stemming from their macroeconomics figures. Against this backdrop, the legislation of the US and that of the EU are unavoidably reference for emerging jurisdictions. Fact that compels these two jurisdictions to also attempt to align their policies. The issuance of "Best Practices Guidelines" allays some of the doubts that the whole Competition law Dilemma of Global Governance brings to the fore.

Hard-harmonisation measures, such as the adoption of a common authority empowered to mandatorily fine-tune the legal instruments of every domestic legislation seems to be quite stringent. Plus, this approach may forego the distinctive features of each domestic macroeconomic environment and thus disrupt their interests in favour of those of others. Because of it, soft-harmonisation may be viewed as the most appealing alternative to any attempt of global governance of Competition law. The key thus lies in co-operation and not in integration, at least for the time being. A co-operation based on the adoption of voluntary instruments such as guidelines, recommendations or even a set of best practices. The ICN and the OECD are the platforms best suited to do such a commendable job. This has recently been observed on occasion of the issuance of their first Joint Report on International Enforcement Co-operation.

Notwithstanding the benefits from the use of Multilateral Fora, also bilateral co-operation on the part of the US and the EU towards third countries is expected. The relation that the EU and China have been growing together for the past two decades sets a solid illustration of this approach. Despite the highly governmental intervention traditionally observed in China, the country has been keen to follow the EU's advice and shape in consequence a proper Antimonopoly Law, although with some distinctive features. Technical assistance provided by the EU to Chinese authorities continues to be very relevant for a correct enforcement of the Law and a good and convergent understanding of its goals. However, the different context and conceptions of China and Western economies has made this convergence difficult in practice up to now. A mutual understanding between the two blocs may well play a relevant role for current Competition law challenges, such as that posed by Digitalization. While the contributions of the EU to competition law global governance are numerous, the role of China is still very limited. It is desirable that China gets more involved in international fora, in particular the ICN.

Player or Board Game? In Search of Europe's Strategic Autonomy: The Need of a Common Digital Strategy of the European Union Towards the People's Republic of China

LORETO MACHÉS BLÁZQUEZ
Consultant for Energy & Utilities, PwC Spain

I. INTRODUCTION

In June 2016 former HR/VP, Federica Mogherini, presented the European Global Strategy (EUGS) which replaced the European Security Strategy of 2003. The new doctrine addresses the security and defence approach of the Union and its Member States in order to protect its civilians, engage in cooperation with third countries and organisations and positively respond to threats. Moreover, it puts the main focus in achieving the strategic autonomy of the EU, which becomes a guiding objective in the development of future actions. This Strategy comes as a much-needed response towards a series of external challenges and events such as the economic crisis of 2008, the refugee crisis, social integration concerns, terrorist attacks or the surge of armed conflicts in certain regions of the world, that have shaken the Union's security and stability. In addition, the document is presented shortly after the result of the Brexit referendum, notifying the departure of Great Britain from the EU in the following years. Therefore, it becomes clear that the Union has to rethink its own Agenda and start acting consciously in order to promote a common direction.

Besides the difficulties and obstacles, these episodes have triggered community initiatives and doctrines in numerous affairs as to pursue a more united and stronger Europe. This is clearly visible in the six objectives set out by the current European Commission for 2019-2024, which address issues that are vital to guarantee the proper progress of the Union and consolidate it as a major power with strategic autonomy. One of the priorities is *"a Europe fit for the digital age"*, focused on delivering a digital strategy in order to adapt European countries for a new generation of technologies. This is a very significant approach for one simple reason, the future will go hand in hand with digitalisation. Even though it cannot be precisely predicted how fast technology will evolve or the scope of influence it might reach, the reality shows that the defence and security, economic, social, and political spheres cannot be conceived without digital or technological tools. It is therefore unquestionable that the Union has to take action in this realm and strengthen its position towards the outside world. More precisely in its own digital strategy towards China, which, as a major economic power and its ongoing rivalry with the United States, will have a considerable influence in the future evolution of global affairs. Taking this into consideration, it is of significant interest for the Union to have a united and precise approach towards a country that is already in the playing field seeking its position. The EU has to decide whether it just wants to remain silent or participate.

The purpose of this paper is to analyse the European Union's digital strategy concerning today's most important rising technological giant, the People's Republic of China (PRC). This country has developed over the last years a number of initiatives regarding digitalisation such as the New Digital Silk Road (DSR) or Made in China 2025, which have and will have a world-wide impact, including the EU and its Member States. Furthermore, it also generates an open confrontation with the United States as the main rival, dividing the countries, including Europeans, between two technological powers and their disputes in the search of a hegemonic position. In this sense, the European Union needs to review its own digital strategy in relation to China, which already knows the advantages of dividing the Union and addressing Member States individually in an attempt to reach agreements faster and easier than dealing with a united EU. It is visible that the PRC has a clear mind of what it wants and what it wants to pursue, the EU might however still have to transform its words into action or strong strategies.

The aim is to provide, an analysis of four possible scenarios *—board game*, *referee player* and *hybrid—* that will depend on the type of strategy the Union might choose, highlighting what the possible combinations are between them and what strengths and opportunities each of them offer. This will be based on the previous analysis of eight internal and external drivers, which play an important role in building the EU's approach towards China.

II. THE EU'S DIGITAL STRATEGY

The European Union is widely known by scholars for being a normative actor. The Union has developed over the years a singular personality that is described by professor Anu Bradford in her book *The Brussels Effect*[1], as the ability of being an influential superpower that shapes the world in its image. The academic highlights how the EU has been able to promulgate regulations that influence the international business environment and elevate standards at a global level. This has led to the Europeanization of several important elements of international trade, shaping policy areas in consumer health, data privacy and protection, antitrust, online hate speech, or environmental protection among others. Furthermore, "The Brussels Effect shows how the EU has acquired such power, why multinational companies use EU standards as global standards, and why the EU's role as the world's regulator is likely to outlive its gradual economic decline, extending the EU's influence long into the future"[2].

Regarding the digital arena, the Union started to take measures concerning information and technology since 2002, as to create a common European data space. These first policies were aimed at exchanging good practices, data collection between the private-public sector and facilitating the information re-use in the public sector. In 2014 the European Commission takes a step beyond and introduces the first measures to ease the development of a data-agile economy with policies, communications, and initiatives such as[3]:

- European Data Portal (2015)
- Digitising European Industry (2016)
- General Data Protection Regulation (2016)
- Building a European Data Economy (2017)
- Towards a common European data space (2018)
- Regulation on the free flow of non-personal data (applicable 28 May 2019)

---

1. Bradford, A., *The Brussels Effect: How the European Union Rules the World*, New York: Oxford University Press, 2020.
2. Wang-Inverson, J., "Anu Bradford. The Brussels Effect: How The European Union Rules The World", *BrusselsEffect*, 2020, retrieved from *https://www.brusselseffect.com/* on 27/3/2021.
3. European Commission, "Data policies and legislation — Timeline", *European Commission*, 2020, retrieved from *https://ec.europa.eu/digital-single-market/en/data-policies-and-legislation-timeline* on 30/3/2021.

- Directive on open data and the re-use of public sector information (2019)
- Cybersecurity Act (2019)
- Data Strategy (2020)
- White Paper on Artificial Intelligence (2020)

The von der Leyen Commission, which took office on 1 December 2019 outlines a total of six priorities that will guide the work of the Institution for the years 2019 to 2024. The second objective holds the title of *a Europe fit for the digital age*, aiming at developing policies as to prepare European countries, businesses and citizens to fit the new digital era and aim at Europe's digital sovereignty. All together with the prime target of reaching a climate-neutral Europe by 2050.

The Commission has divided the digital objective in two spectrums: (i) Europe's Digital Decade, and (ii) Shaping Europe's Digital Future[4]. The first focuses on the vision for Europe's digital transformation by 2030 centring around four cardinal target points: (1) skills, (2) secure and sustainable digital infrastructures, (3) digital transformation of businesses, and (4) digitalisation of public services. These areas will be assisted through the implementation of digital rights and principles for Europeans, including[5]:

- targets and key milestones
- a robust joint governance structure including a traffic light monitoring system to identify successes and gaps
- multi-country projects combining investments from the EU, Member States and the private sector

The second approach is based on three main pillars as to guarantee that Europe seizes the opportunity to give individuals, companies and governments the control over the digital transformation. These are: (1) technology that works for the people, (2) a fair and competitive digital

4. European Commission, "A Europe fit for the digital age. Empowering people with a new generation of technologies. Introduction", *European Commission*, 2021, retrieved from *https://ec.europa.eu/info/strategy/priorities-2019-2024/europe-fit-digital-age_en* on 15/4/2021.
5. European Commission, "Europe's Digital Decade: digital targets for 2030", *European Commission*, 2021, retrieved from *https://ec.europa.eu/info/strategy/priorities-2019-2024/europe-fit-digital-age/europes-digital-decade-digital-targets-2030_en* on 15/4/2021, p. 1.

economy, and (3) an open, democratic and sustainable society[6]. Furthermore, as a whole, the Union aims at becoming a global role model of a digital economy, supporting developing economies in their digital transitioning, and developing digital standards that will be promoted internationally[7].

In February 2020, the Commission started a couple of initiatives under the first two pillars: a white paper on artificial intelligence (AI) and a European data strategy, in addition, the Revision of the Security of Network and Information Systems Directive is also scheduled for 2020[8]. Moreover, it also introduced the Digital Services Act package, which "encompass a single set of new rules applicable across the whole EU to create a safer and more open digital space"[9]. The two legislative proposals to upgrade the rules of digital services in the EU are, the Digital Services Act (DSA) and the Digital Markets Act (DMA). The core aims of both are[10]:

- to create a safer digital space in which the fundamental rights of all users of digital services are protected;
- to establish a level playing field to foster innovation, growth, and competitiveness, both in the European Single Market and globally.

Regarding the Industry and SMEs, the Commission seeks to support the transformation towards a green and digital economy and, in the single market, to lay out the most regular obstacles faced by consumers and businesses and propose measures for better application of single market rules[11].

The Commission Work Programme of 2020 outlines 21 legislative and non-legislative actions for the *a Europe fit for the digital age* objective, with the Commission having adopted for the moment seven of the initiatives[12].

---

6. European Commission, "Shaping Europe's digital future", *European Commission*, 2021, retrieved from *https://ec.europa.eu/info/strategy/priorities-2019-2024/europe-fit-digital-age/shaping-europe-digital-future_en* on 15/4/2021.
7. European Commission, "Shaping Europe's digital future", *op. cit.*
8. Bassot, E., "The von der Leyen Commission's six priorities: State of play in autumn 2020", *EPRS European Parliamentary Research Service*, 2020, retrieved from *https://www.europarl.europa.eu/RegData/etudes/BRIE/2020/652053/EPRS_BRI(2020)652053_EN.pdf* on 15/4/2021.
9. European Commission, "The Digital Services Act package", *European Commission*, 2021, p.1, retrieved from *https://digital-strategy.ec.europa.eu/en/policies/digital-services-act-package* on 15/4/2021.
10. European Commission, "The Digital Services Act package", *op. cit.*, p. 1.
11. Bassot, E., "The von der Leyen Commission's six priorities: State of [...]", *op. cit.*
12. European Commission, "Commission Work Programme 2020. A Union that strives for more. Annexes to the Communication from the Commission to the European

For its part, the European Council introduces in its new strategic agenda 2019-2024 a total of four priorities. Regarding the second aim, developing a strong and vibrant economic base, the digital component is very much present. It highlights the importance of the digital transformation and the need to ensure the digital sovereignty of Europe, with a common policy that embodies the European values and way of life. Furthermore, aspects as: artificial intelligence, infrastructure, connectivity services, data, regulation, or investment need to be addressed and worked by the Union[13].

As it can be seen, the new agenda and objectives of both Institutions highlight the need of the European Union to achieve its digital sovereignty and obtain its fair share of this development through the establishment of norms and standards that reflect the Union's values. The digital transformation is a reality, and it will have a far-reaching impact on the economic, political, and social spheres. In this regard, the EU strongly bets for creating initiatives within its internal market, but that ultimately will have a possible effect as a guiding model in the rest of the global market. This notion is portrayed in the essay collection *La soberanía digital de Europa*[14] by the several authors, however, they also demand a more active role, creating European digital providers and services for not having to depend on Chinese or American ones.

III. THE IMPACT OF CHINA'S DIGITAL STRATEGY IN THE EU

The singularity of the EU-China relation is the fact that there is no true consistent communitarian strategy towards the Asian country, even less in the digital realm. This is accentuated by the notion that the European Union is, for the moment, an actor lacking technological autonomy. This has put the EU between a rock and a hard place, with both the United States and China pressing the Union to either veto or include Huawei in its 5G networks. Moreover, under the Trump presidency, the US even threatened the EU and

---

Parliament, the Council, the European Economic and Social Committee and The Committee of the Regions", *European Commission*, 2020, retrieved from *https://ec.europa.eu/info/sites/default/files/cwp-2020-publication_en.pdf* on 10/4/2021.

13. Arauzo Azofra, "A new strategic agenda 2019-2024", *European Council and Council of the European Union*, 2019, retrieved from *https://www.consilium.europa.eu/en/press/press-releases/2019/06/20/a-new-strategic-agenda-2019-2024/* on 17/4/2021.

14. Hobbs, C. and Torreblanca, J. I. (eds.), *La soberanía digital de Europa. De regulador a superpotencia en la era de la rivalidad entre Estados Unidos y China*, Madrid: Los libros de la Catarata, 2020.

its Member States with retaliation in intelligence or defence cooperation if they did not block the Chinese company, while China threatened with economic measures if they did it[15].

As Member States have their own relations with the two powers, each country handles the situation in a different manner, but besides the differences, the common element is that all of them consider the United States to be its most important ally, while they take advantage of the benefits generated from a closer economic relation with China. Although European governments are diverting the focus of attention from the final decision on whether to use or not the Chinese supplier, as a means to avoid a geopolitical confrontation, the reality is that the majority of Member States are not vetoing Huawei. Moreover, several countries already had Huawei networks of other generations installed in their telecommunications systems for decades, as it is the case of Germany, the United Kingdom or Spain[16].

In addition, Beijing has relied on bilateral relations with European states directly, emphasising its own interests and ignoring the Union's regulations. In this sense, the country uses the well-known strategy of *divide et impera* or divide and conquer, while introducing its state capitalism to strategically invest and divide the market. Using therefore, a different approach in each Member State. Furthermore, the introduction of the Belt and Road Initiative, the Digital Strategy, or the Cooperation between China and Central and Eastern European Countries known as 16+1 (China-CEEC) has further divided the European Union's states, making it difficult to reach common grounds[17].

The Made in China 2025 and China Standards 2035 strategies also indicate the PRC's intention to globally influence in the digital realm and its rules of the game. Not having a common united digital stand towards the Asian country brings the EU to a very weak position and hinders its objective of achieving strategic autonomy. Even if the Union has elaborated the EU Coordinated Risk Assessment of the Cybersecurity of 5G, the EU-China 2020 Strategic Agenda for Cooperation and the EU-China a Strategic Outlook 2019, that address the more problematic points, these strategies do not close a common policy towards Beijing. At the moment, one of the

15. Gacho Carmona, I., "La Unión Europea frente al ascenso de China como potencia tecnológica: el caso del 5G", *Documento de opinión: Instituto Español de Estudios Estratégicos*, 2020, retrieved from *http://www.ieee.es/Galerias/fichero/docs_opinion/2020/DIEEEO23_2020ISAGAC_5G.pdf* on 23/4/2021.
16. *Ibidem.*
17. *Ibidem.*

most important statements is included in the las mentioned document, in which it is outlined that[18]:

> China is, simultaneously, in different policy areas, a cooperation partner with whom the EU has closely aligned objectives, a negotiating partner with whom the EU needs to find a balance of interests, an economic competitor in the pursuit of technological leadership, and a systemic rival promoting alternative models of governance. This requires a flexible and pragmatic whole-of-EU approach enabling a principled defence of interests and values.

As it is stated in the last sentence, the Union needs a whole-EU approach, and it needs it in different areas, including the digital realm. Furthermore, it is indispensable to clarify whether it wants to consolidate itself as a normative power, as it seems it is doing with the digital objective of the Commission, and if it therefore wants to simply aim at representing the game board for the US and China or if it also wants to take part in the game.

Esteban and Otero Iglesias[19] outline three main positions of EU Member States towards the PRC. Firstly, countries like France and Germany advocate for a more assertive shift in EU policy towards China, as they are concerned about the geostrategic implications of China's rise and call for the creation of "European champions". Secondly, Nordic countries and the Netherlands share the preoccupation of the first but oppose a public intervention in the economy as a means to confront competition with China. Lastly, countries of southern and eastern Europe with greater financial difficulties, support closer economic ties with Beijing and its investment and financing. However, even the most critical States still defend political and economic ties with the PRC.

China's pursuing for technological leadership is evident, and the Union has already addressed it. Nonetheless, as Hobbs and Torreblanca[20] highlight, a common and clear EU digital strategy is needed if it wants to consolidate its power and take advantage of the new technological revolution. According to the authors it has to decide whether it wants to consolidate its referee position

---

18. European Commission (2019). "Joint Communication to the European Parliament, the European Council and the Council, of 12 March 2019, by the High Representative of the Union for Foreign Affairs and Security Policy on 'EU-China a strategic outlook'", *European Commission*, 2019, retrieved from *https://eur-lex.europa.eu/legal-content/EN/TXT/PDF/?uri=CELEX:52019JC0005* on 27/3/2021, p. 1.
19. Esteban, M. and Otero Iglesias, M., "La política europea frente al desafío chino", *Real Instituto Elcano*, 2019, retrieved from *http://www.realinstitutoelcano.org/wps/wcm/connect/cdf58e1c-979b-4208-a098-81256d160247/Comentario-Esteban-OteroIglesias-politica-europea-frente-al-desafio-chino.pdf?MOD=AJPERES&CACHEID=cdf58e1c-979b-4208-a098-81256d160247* on 20/4/2021.
20. Hobbs, C. and Torreblanca, J. I. (eds.), *La soberanía digital de Europa [...], op. cit.*

or solely serve as the game board for others. Moreover, a straightforward digital agenda towards China would allow the EU to become a possible player or achieve a combination status with the previous roles.

IV. ANALYSIS

The analysis is divided in two parts. The first section consists of the analysis of two groups of drivers, internal and external, with four subdivisions each. The second section provides the analysis of four possible scenarios -*board game*, *referee*, *player*, and *hybrid*- that result from the previous study of the eight drivers and their respective impacts. In this case, the scenarios will be studied using three characteristics -description, analysis of drivers' influence, and advantages vs difficulties. Lastly, in a separate segment a comparative analysis will draw the implications of the four scenarios, offering possible considerations and predictions.

1. PART I: DRIVERS

Drivers are guiding forces that determine the evolution of the main subject matter. They are composed by a series of variables that include events, documents, positions, or approaches among many others. For this specific study, the relevant data has been reorganized in two sets of drivers, internal and external, as to better portray and draw relations to the possible future scenarios. Moreover, they have been chosen from the contextualization and state of the art sections regarding their important influence in addressing Europe's strategic autonomy and outlining the need of building a Union's digital approach towards China.

1.1. Thesis

The effect of the COVID-19 crisis has foresighted the start of a new decade as a mainly digital one. Nowadays it is unconceivable to think about the social, economic, and political arena without the use of digital and technological tools. The private and professional spheres are all influenced by new technologies and current events have strongly speeded-up its reach. Although it is still unknown how exactly these mechanisms will change and impact the course of action of States and individuals, the reality is that the future will undoubtably be digital. This idea has not gone unnoticed by the European Union, which under the new von der Leyen Commission 2019-2024 has included the objective of *a Europe fit for the digital age*. Nonetheless, if the EU wants to consolidate itself as a strong actor, a series of aspects need to be tackled.

In order to achieve its objectives of the Global Strategy 2016 (EUGS) and pursue strategic autonomy, the Union has to address various agendas, including the digital one. In this sense, it has to decide where it wants to lead and how it wants to lead in this field: as a game board, a referee, a player or a combination of them. This decision will also depend on the strategy towards China and the country's digital advancement.

1.2. Framing

Data shows that the People's Republic of China will become the country with the highest percentage of GDP allocated to investment in research, development, and innovation. Furthermore, during the last decade, Beijing has launched and even re-launched a number of strategies -BRI, DSR, Made in China 2025, and China Standards 2035- that have strong links with digital components, mostly the three last ones. This shows that the Asian country has a clear view of what it wants and, at least, certain methods of how it wants to achieve it.

In addition, China's advancement in the digital realm has triggered a confrontation with the United States, which sees its hegemony and interests disrupted by the interference of the PRC in many parts of the world, including European countries. In this regard, the EU cannot accept to be the board game of the United States and China.

This undoubtedly forces the Union to review its own strategy towards the Asian country in these matters and start moving forward with a single voice in digital affairs, which, as an important component of the economy, will be indispensable in the future.

1.3. Drivers

The division of drivers in internal and external depends on whether the driving force comes from within the European Union or from the outside of its borders respectively. This distinction allows to better size the influencing forces regarding the Union's digital strategy towards China and its digital autonomy.

Figure 1 depicts a table with the final composition of the selected drivers. All of them are further divided in a series of points that will be studied and analysed in the corresponding section through the use of four characteristics, as shown in Figure 2, including their type of trend or impact, displayed in Figure 3, towards the four possible scenarios.

INTERNAL DRIVERS	EXTERNAL DRIVERS
STRATEGIC AUTONOMY	US-CHINA RIVALRY
EU DIGITAL INITIATIVES	CHINA'S TECH GIANTS
APPROACH TO CHINA	CHINA'S STRATEGY IN THE EU
MEMBER STATES	COVID-19

Figure 1: Internal and External Drivers
Source: Own elaboration

TREND/IMPACT
POSITIVE-NEGATIVE
STRONG-WEAK
NEUTRAL

Figure 2: Driver's Trend/Impact Towards Scenarios
Source: Own elaboration

A) Internal Drivers

Regarding driving forces coming from within the European Union a total of four elements can be identified. These will be studied and analysed below.

a) Strategic Autonomy

Strategic Autonomy is not a new concept in the European Union's agenda. It has been addressed over a period of time by both the Union itself and figures of the Member States. This concept is important in the sense that, for the EU to be able to be a political and economic union that acts as a global player, it has to be autonomous.

A total of two aspects can be analysed when addressing Strategic Autonomy. On the one hand, the EU-Global Strategy of 2016 and, on the other hand, more recent statements of political leaders in European Institutions, reports and works, already introduced in the contextualization section, which describe new forms of autonomy.

b) EU Digital Initiatives

The European Union has not ignored the relevance of including digital rules in its legal framework. Moreover, it has proven to be indispensable in order to guarantee the protection of the Internal Market, the Union's businesses and its citizens. At the beginning, the majority of norms were mostly directed at securing the treatment of information and its flow between the EU Institutions and then between the private-public sectors. As of 2014 the European Commission starts to address the objective of developing a data-agile economy introducing more ambitious and far-reaching policies, initiatives and communications.

For the purpose of the study, two timelines can be differentiated. The first period expands from 2016 to 2019 and englobes a series of mechanisms focused on regulating and protecting the management of data that have already been put into practice. The second period refers to the new set of rules introduced by the new legislature from 2020 to 2024 which is starting to be implemented and with some acts still being under voting.

c) Approach to China

A total of four documents can be analysed when addressing the Approach to China implemented by the Union. These are in chronological order the EU-China 2020 Strategic Agenda for Cooperation, the 2016 Strategy on China, EU-China a Strategic Outlook 2019, and the EU-China Comprehensive Agreement on Investment (CAI). The singularity of all of them is that even if they incorporate commitments and principles, none of them actually close a common European policy towards the PRC.

d) Member States

It is clear that China is a strategic partner for the European Union and that for the benefit of all it has to seek mutual understanding and cooperation. This is clearly sought through the numerous documents that have been published over the years since official relations between both actors started in 1975. Nonetheless, even now the Union lacks a common consistent community strategy towards the PRC, not to mention in the digital realm, and Member States continue to have their own relations with the country. Fact that hampers the capacity of the Union to act with a single strong voice and be treated as an autonomous actor.

B) External Drivers

Regarding driving forces coming from outside of the European Union a total of four elements can be identified. These will be studied and analysed below.

a) US-China Rivalry

When the Trump Administration took office in 2017, it marked the beginning of a new area of international relations. The most powerful democracy in the world welcomed a government that soon implemented its personal vision of foreign relations and how the United States would act from that moment on towards the rest of the world.

This direction was no other than Donald Trump's campaign slogan *America First*. According to this idea, it was time to put the prosperity of the country back to the centre of the political agenda and strengthen the country both internally and externally. It abandoned the notion of embodying the good Samaritan, helping others without receiving anything in return. External actions were welcomed as long as the US would see a high benefit when offering its contribution.

This new foreign approach has clashed with Beijing's turn in foreign policy under Xi Jinping who introduced the "China Dream" policy with the aim of modernizing the country and gain international influence.

Even if the relationship between both countries has always been turbulent and not without difficulty, the ambitions of these two leaders have only added fuel to the situation. Moreover, now under the Biden Presidency there is no strong indicator for a change beyond the instauration of a more correct diplomatic relationship.

b) China's Tech Giants

It is not without a reason that this Thesis addresses a digital strategy of the Union specifically towards the PRC. The country has already become the second most powerful world economy and it is heading to lead the digital race against the United States.

Moreover, the Union's change in paradigm under the Strategic Outlook 2019 notes that it is very conscious about the digital intentions of the Asian country. The future is digital and those who own, control, and set the rules for technologies will undoubtedly gain power and decision-making influence. It has become clear that strategic autonomy is closely linked with digital capacity.

c) China's Strategy in the EU

The initiation of the EU-China relations and diplomatic recognition started in 1975, leading to a period of partnership that can be divided into four stages until today.

With the taking into office of President Xi Jinping, the Asian country declares its favourable stance towards the European integration process and demands a more transparent, fair, and trusted partnership. Since then, its interest regarding the opportunities of the European Internal Market have only grown, starting a strong approach towards the region.

d) COVID-19

The pandemic caught the entire world by surprise. From one day to the other a considerable amount of the global population was not allowed to go outside and had no other option than to stay at home in isolation. This aspect triggered once more the importance of digital tools, which became indispensable for 'staying connected' to the outside world. Activities like studying, working, grocery shopping, social communication, or social entertainment that already had a digital component were now forced to only provide services and goods through technological tools, and its demand skyrocketed during the strongest periods of restrictions. Although it has been a temporary effect, it has opened the door for innovation that will guide the future of economies.

2. PART II: SCENARIOS

Following the study of the eight internal and external drivers, its respective trends towards the four scenarios will be closer examined in the following section.

This part of the analysis will use Fulton's Model K handout for building scenarios. Firstly, the thesis of the study will be presented, followed by the individual analysis of the scenarios under three characteristics. Lastly, in a separated section with a comparative analysis, the implications, considerations, and the predictions will be portrayed.

2.1. Thesis

The European Union needs to know how it wants to participate in the digital future. More precisely, it needs to think where it can be leading in this realm and what it is willing to do. The core sole of the Union are its values, principles, and democratic spirit, providing its citizens with a secure, safe, and prosperous territory.

The EU has now the opportunity to build a digital future that is fit for Europeans and that the Union itself is fit to provide for. Striving for strategic autonomy means to take a stronger action towards internal and external affairs, englobing all the necessary agendas beyond traditional security.

Having this in mind, the EU finds itself under the option of engaging in four possible scenarios concerning the digital sphere: *game board, referee, player, or hybrid*.

2.2. Scenarios

This Final Thesis works with the four possible scenarios that result from the combination of the previous studied internal and external drivers. Depending on the delivery of decisions from Member States and lastly the Union, the future engagement in digital and technological matters can take a more active or a more passive form.

Figure 4 depicts a table with the final composition of the future scenarios and figure 5 includes the three characteristics that will be employed to analyse them.

Board Game	Referee	Player	Hybrid

Figure 4: Scenarios
Source: Own elaboration

CHARACTERISTICS
DESCRIPTION
ANALYSIS OF DRIVERS' TREND ON SCENARIOS
ADVANTAGES VS. DIFFICULTIES

Figure 5: Analysis of Scenarios Through Characteristics
Source: Own elaboration

A) Game Board

Characteristics

a) Description

The *game board* scenario implies that the Union's territory is used as a playing field by technology-leading actors, who compete in spreading their power and influence.

The EU zone, comprised by 27 Member States and hosting over 400 million citizens in a unique Internal Market, is seen as an important gold mine for tech champions and their respective States that wish to generate profit in a non-autonomous digital block.

At this point, there is no doubt that the future will be digital, and China will soon become the highest allocator of GDP on investment in innovation and research in new technologies, in order to be prepared for this new era and achieve the leading position.

This unequal strength and wealth of states has triggered disparities in the digital realm, with only a few countries in Asia and North America counting with international powerful tech giants that are revolutionising the market. This means that only a short number of actors will play, while the rest will serve as a game board for the moves and tricks of the players.

Even if the Union has introduced the aim of carrying out a process of modernisation of the economic, political, and social structures, including a green and digital transformation, it has not been able to implement a common digital strategy. Beyond the formulation of certain standards, EU Institutions have not been capable to push for an active role in financing, developing, and innovating in the fields of new technologies due to differences between the Member States.

This absence of union has put the EU in a weak position, which has seen its objective of achieving strategic autonomy wrecked and with a lacking internationally strong competitive digital market. As a consequence, China, aiming to spread its digital influence, will focus on expanding within the Union's territory. Following, the US will try to stop this and guarantee its own impact. All this leads to a situation in which the EU is left at the mercy of digital powers that use its territory as their board game.

b) Analysis of Driver's Trend on Scenarios

The impact towards the *board game* scenario of the eight internal and external drivers, previously introduced in the first analysis section, are represented in Figure 6.

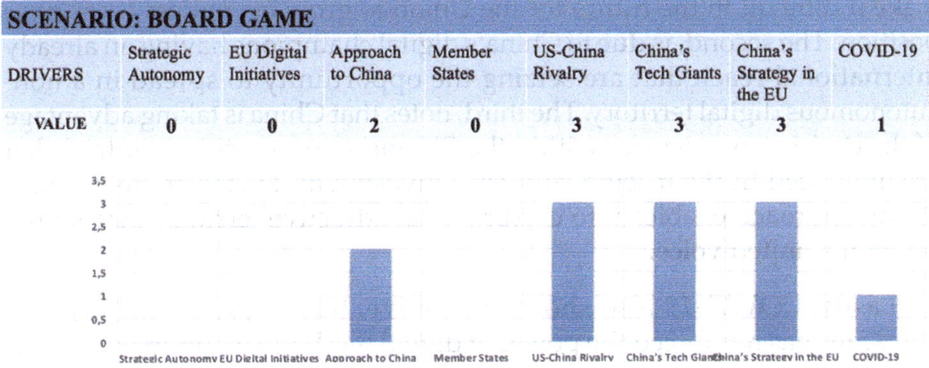

SCENARIO: BOARD GAME								
DRIVERS	Strategic Autonomy	EU Digital Initiatives	Approach to China	Member States	US-China Rivalry	China's Tech Giants	China's Strategy in the EU	COVID-19
VALUE	0	0	2	0	3	3	3	1

Figure 6: Board Game
Source: Own elaboration

The first thing to note is that no driver, either external or internal, has a negative influence on the *game board* scenario. This is because the analysed forces have a more positive impact on its fulfilment.

The second aspect to bear in mind is that it is the only case in which three drivers have a neutral effect on the scenario. *Strategic autonomy, EU digital initiatives* and *Member States* positions do not pose a positive or negative tendency towards the likeliness of the Union to serve as a playing field. This is because, despite the internal drivers promoting respectively the objective of strategic autonomy and the normative digital future objective that enforces the Brussels Effect, this does not affect the capacity of the Union to stop or promote a digital race within its territory. Moreover, the different postures of Member States regarding China do not influence this either.

The resting internal driver, the Union's *approach to China,* has a considerable positive effect (+2) for this scenario. This is because the last important reports relating to the relationship with the PRC have not included a digital strategy towards the state. The Union empathises that China is no longer a developing country and that it is heading towards a digital leadership. Nonetheless, it does not include a common objective of how to engage or confront the country, leaving more chance to the EU to serve as the playing field for China's digital race.

Moving on to the external drivers, it stands out that the *US-China rivalry, China's tech giants* and *China's strategy in the EU,* all strongly affect (+3) the realisation of this scenario. The first driver shows that the US and China are leading countries in the digital realm and their influence and power will make it difficult in the future for the Union to grow beyond its *board game* position. The second, is due to China's digital champions having an already international reach that are seizing the opportunity to spread in a non-autonomous digital territory. The third, notes that China is taking advantage of the division of postures within the EU, targeting specific countries that are interested in the foreign country's investment. Furthermore, China's strong approach enables it to expand in an attractive territory that cannot act with a united voice.

Lastly, *COVID-19* also shows a positive, but weak, trend (+1). The pandemic has reinforced the power of digital mechanisms, moreover, it has outlined the notion that the future will be digital and only the best players win the game. This can trigger a stronger competition between China and the US, with the EU caught in the middle.

c) Advantages vs. Difficulties

Regarding the *board game* scenario there are a series of advantages and disadvantages for the European Union.

Even if in this specific case the advantages seem to be less favourable, they are not less important. This does not mean however that it is desirable for the EU. First of all, it would imply the easiest future scenario to be achieved because it accounts for actually not needing to take any action at all. This means that it is already taking place, being the last strong example of it the Huawei dispute of 2018 in which the US threatened European countries with sanctions if they did not abandon the Chinese networks.

Secondly, the Union does not have to change its direction. It can continue with its previous agenda and take things one step at a time, not having to rush into desperate political dialogue to reach a common ground between Member States. Accepting to be the playing field of others is not negative as long as the Union makes its values and norms to be respected.

Thirdly, it gives the EU the opportunity to sit down and think if it wants to continue like this or better change its condition. By letting others assume the digital leadership, it can observe where it can gain strength and be prepared before reaching the time it thinks it is ready to participate.

Lastly, this scenario does not imply the inevitable disintegration of the EU.

Concerning the disadvantageous aspects, these are more damaging for the prosperous and desired future of the EU. Firstly, it means that the Union has not been able to pursue its objective of strategic autonomy. Moreover, it is not autonomous in the digital realm, and it is dependent on the demands and timelines of leading actors.

As a second point, it represents a step backwards. Not being able to develop a common digital agenda that has a strategy towards China, the future leading actor in this field, leads to a weakening of the Union as an international and regional actor. Furthermore, it seems that Member States are not concerned of the Union's future and its future wellbeing.

Thirdly, it would lead to a greater polarisation of Member States' positions towards China. This dispute will mostly confront those countries that demand a stronger autonomous European action with digital champions against those countries that are more interested in attracting Chinese investment.

Fourthly, the longer this scenario is in place, the more difficult it will become to change the situation. How the digital realm will evolve is unpredictable, but one thing is for sure, it will develop, and it will develop fast. Not keeping track of new technologies' research, innovation and investment will be very costly for the EU as a whole, loosing market opportunities.

Lastly, it has a direct negative effect on European citizens who are losing opportunities of prosperity and growth in their professional and private lives.

B) Referee

Characteristics

a) Description

The *referee* scenario implies that the Union continues to consolidate its position as a regulatory superpower, establishing digital and technological standards that influence the international market environment.

The European Union is widely known for its commitment to play by the rules of the game, dedicating its efforts to establish a consistent set of norms with the protection of citizens' rights and freedoms as the guiding principle.

This notion is described under the term of Brussels Effect that has allowed the EU to Europeanise important elements of international trade, shaping policy areas in consumer health, data privacy and protection, online hate speech or environmental protection, and now, on digital standards.

The international spread of the Union's legal methodology model has made it acquire a powerful position, enabling it to extend its normative influence long into the digital future.

Even if the EU is not a player in the digital race as such that holds technological power, it has come together to set the rules of the game. This gives the Union a powerful position in the sense that it decides and controls how foreign digital actors can operate on European territory, a major targeted market.

b) Analysis of Driver's Trend on Scenarios

The impact towards the *referee* scenario of the eight internal and external drivers, previously introduced in the first analysis section, are represented in Figure 7.

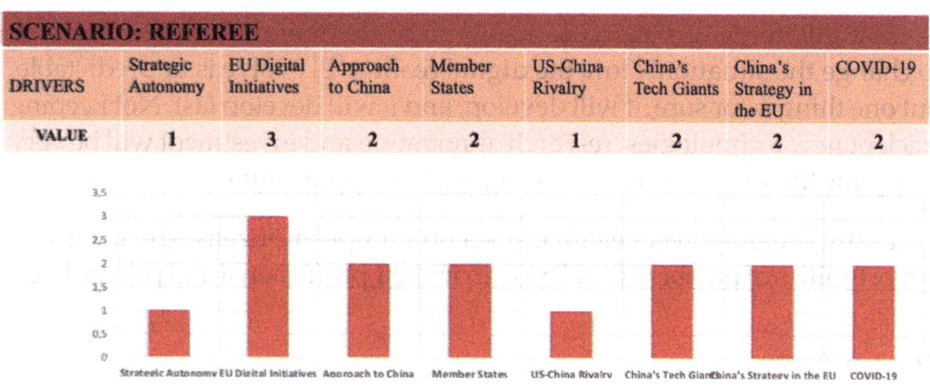

SCENARIO: REFEREE								
DRIVERS	Strategic Autonomy	EU Digital Initiatives	Approach to China	Member States	US-China Rivalry	China's Tech Giants	China's Strategy in the EU	COVID-19
VALUE	1	3	2	2	1	2	2	2

Figure 7: Referee
Source: Own elaboration

The first thing to note is that no driver, either external or internal, has a negative influence on the *referee* scenario. This is because all the analysed forces have a positive impact on its fulfilment.

Regarding the internal drivers, these can be classified in three groups of positive strength from less to more impact. The first are the *strategic autonomy* and the *approach to China* (+1). On the one side, the objective of the EUGS 2016 that sets strategic autonomy as the guiding principle of the Union's action, contributes to the role of the Union in the digital realm, which is a major component to seek autonomy. This is more appreciable in the Union's normative power that has already been recognised in the international sphere. On the other side, the documents addressing the relationship towards China include digital initiatives that aim at establishing standards and principles that are set to serve as global models. However, the lack of a strategic digital agenda as such, that directs the Union makes them have a less of a stronger impact.

Secondly are the positions of *Member States* (+2). EU-States are favourable with the Union setting a normative structure for new technologies that is aimed at protecting citizens from predatory market practices.

The third strongest posture are the *EU digital initiatives* (+3). The timeline of the EU digital actions shows its major involvement in normative aspects. The Union considers itself as a normative power and it has applied this task in the digital realm. Furthermore, the *a Europe fit for the digital age* objective of the current Commission continues this path by introducing initiatives aiming at protecting the Internal Market, European citizen and European businesses under the implementation of the core EU values. This shows a clear aspect reinforcing and further developing the Brussels Effect.

Concerning the external drivers, only the *US-China rivalry* has a less strong positive impact (+1). The confrontation between the two digital actors leaves the Union in a weak competitive position with the only defensive action the enforcement of standards that lack a common digital strategy.

The resting drivers, *China's tech giants, China's strategy in the EU* and *COVID-19* have a considerable strong positive impact (+2). The advancement of China's digital champions in the EU territory, the divide and conquer approach implemented by China in the EU, and the Next Generation EU plan including a digital transition aim, strengthen the current normative approach of the EU in technologies. Although, the Union still has to develop a digital agenda, the confirmation of the fact that the future will be digital enhances the need of protecting European values.

c) Advantages vs. Difficulties

Regarding the *referee* scenario there are a series of advantages and disadvantages for the European Union.

The advantages of this position imply, first of all, the consolidation of the Brussels' effect in the digital realm. The EU is already known as a normative power, but by expanding its regulatory influence into the whole technological world, it enters into a new level of power. Furthermore, the recognition of these norms by international actors, leads to a shape in business relations, giving the Union international prestige for its capacity to change and influence policy areas.

Secondly, as the future will be digital, the Union has converted itself in the editor of the rules of the game by which the world will follow. Even if it is not an active player, the EU assures its influence and participation by designing how technologies can affect the lives of citizens and how the technological market can operate. In other words, it controls the evolution of the EU itself and impacts that of other important territories.

Fourthly, it allows the Union to adopt a strong common position towards the outside world. The elaboration of normative digital rules puts Member States into one boat, defending the values and principles of the European Union. It strengthens the EU as an international actor.

Lastly, this scenario contributes to the achievement of strategic autonomy in the sense that it does not allow others to tell the EU how it has to behave, what it should do and what it should not.

Concerning the disadvantages that this scenario presents, the first to highlight is the notion that it is only a temporary solution. What will happen afterwards? The establishing of norms is a one-single action, the EU only has to target the specific activity, analyse it, and set the rule. It does not define the digital tool itself, only its possible reach. This has a time-limited power once the norm has been introduced. The Union is working on already elaborated digital mechanisms, instead of developing ones.

Secondly, the recognition of being a powerful normative digital actor does not mean that the Union is an autonomous actor itself. Setting the rules does not make you a participant of the game, only an observer. Not being able to actively participate hinders the proper achievement of strategic autonomy because the EU is still dependant on digital aspects from foreign powers.

Lastly, the referee does not win the game. It only observes the match from an outside perspective but does not get to hold the trophy.

C) *Player*

Characteristics

a) Description

The *player* scenario implies that the Union is participating as an active actor in the digital future.

The European Union has come together as a whole and decided to take the relevant steps as to set common objectives, actions, and purposes in new technologies.

Member States have realised the need for common action in the technological and digital realm, being conscious that none of them can act alone and actually succeed. In this sense, major compromise and consensus has been reach in order to lift the Union as a digital actor capable to compete in the international sphere.

This united stand gives the EU a strong position, which supports objective of achieving strategic autonomy as a reachable reality. Moreover, the European territory will be on the same page when dealing with foreign intervention, like China's interest in spreading its influence in the region.

It is an idyllic situation in which the EU has finally reached a powerful digital position.

b) Analysis of Driver's Trend on Scenarios

The impact towards the *player* scenario of the eight internal and external drivers, previously introduced in the first analysis section, are represented in Figure 8.

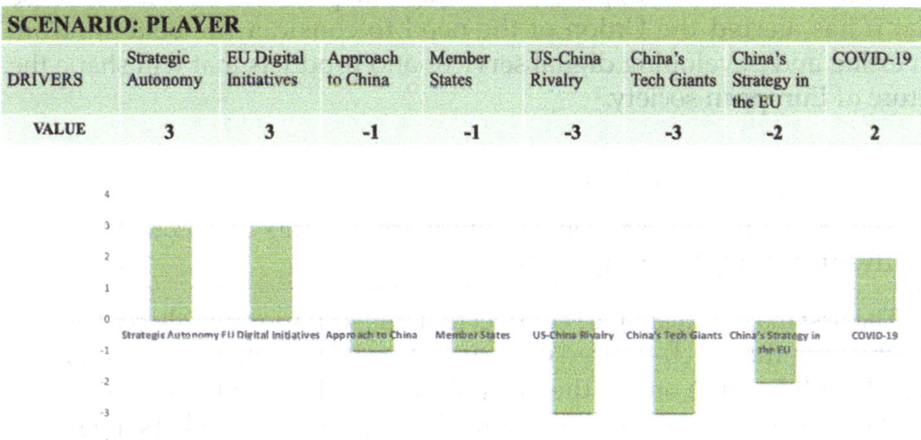

SCENARIO: PLAYER								
DRIVERS	Strategic Autonomy	EU Digital Initiatives	Approach to China	Member States	US-China Rivalry	China's Tech Giants	China's Strategy in the EU	COVID-19
VALUE	3	3	-1	-1	-3	-3	-2	2

Figure 8: Player
Source: Own elaboration

The singular aspect of this table is that only two internal drivers have a weak negative trend, while three external drivers present a considerable, or more, negative impact on the fulfilment of the scenario. In fact, it is the only one with negative impacts.

Concerning the internal drivers, these can be divided in two groups, one positive and one negative. The first is composed by the *strategic autonomy* and the *EU digital initiatives* (+3). Autonomy implies to not only set standards and guidelines but having the capacity to act as well with one's own digital champions. In addition, if these standards are introduced properly, gaining the capacity to influence, and set global rules respected by other important technological powers gives the EU an active role.

The second group, *approach to China* and *Member Sates' position*, negatively influence this scenario (-1). None of the analysed documents indicates a commitment to further engage in a digital agenda that enables the Union to strengthen its position and compete as a major player. And not all Member States are positive to support a more competitive and autonomous Union, although supporters of it can soften this tendency.

Moving on to the external drivers, three pose a negative influence, *US-China rivalry*, *China's tech giants* (-3), and *China's strategy in the EU* (-2). All of them show the leadership of China and the US in the digital arena and the Union's lacking capacity to become a player that competes in the digital realm.

Lastly, *COVID-19* (+2) poses a considerable positive effect in the sense that it has alerted the Union of the need to consider the benefits from investing and developing digital services and products that will shape the future of European society.

c) Advantages vs. Difficulties

Regarding the *player* scenario there are a series of advantages and disadvantages for the European Union.

The first major advantage is the fact that this scenario strongly contributes to achieving the much-desired objective of strategic autonomy. The digital agenda will become one of the most important fields in the future. Being autonomous in this realm means to not having to rely on others' mercy. In this sense, the Union will be strong as a whole, not needing to depend on foreign actors for its own development and deciding on its own how to design the future for Europeans.

Secondly, it positions the European Union as a strong actor with a united voice. The Union has been pushed to serve as a single actor in the digital realm, representing the Member States as a whole. This gives the Union a seat at the negotiation table in the international sphere. Moreover, it can participate in the design of the digital future and confront those which go against the wellbeing of Europeans.

Lastly, being an active player that engages in innovation, research, and investment of new technologies, contributes to the growth of the European economic strength. It allows for the proper modernisation of the Internal Market and the social sphere. Citizens are given the opportunity to enjoy a prosperous future within the EU, characterised by wellbeing.

Concerning the disadvantages, the most latent one is the fact that it is the most complex scenario to be achieved. It is very difficult to put together the different positions of 27 Member States into agreeing to convert the Union in a digital actor. In fact, countries would be reticent as how too much 'influence' and 'power' allow the EU to have in this realm, and therefore loose the opportunity to be a digital actor themselves.

Secondly, timely speaking, the EU cannot convert itself from one day to the other into an actor capable of competing against international superpowers.

Thirdly, it would suppose a completely new change in its foreign affairs relations. At the moment, the Union has been mostly perceived as a diplomatic actor, with now completely independent powers. Engaging in the digital race would mean to compete against the United States and China, being more challenging the last one. This implies to know what moves exactly to make, and the EU is new in this game.

Finally, by opening the possibility of becoming a digital actor, where is to draw the line of generating possible European tech giants? Can this lead to a weakening of the Internal Market's essence? The major problem would be to lose track of European values and standards.

D) Hybrid

Characteristics

a) Description

The *hybrid* scenario implies that the Union presents a combination of the previous three scenarios: *board game*, *referee*, and *player* with a lower intensity in all cases.

The first possible combination is that the European Union maintains a *board game* and a *referee* position. In this regard, the Union continues to be an attractive playing field for digital leaders, but it enforces its normative power over digital standards. This allows for a protection of the European territory, while still allowing foreign investment and contribution. Moreover, the Brussels' effect is also reinforced.

The second possible combination is a mix of all three, *board game, referee, and player*. Here, Member States are eager to contribute for the Union's development and introduce aims, objectives and actions as to not only serve as the playing field and a rule-maker, but to participate in the game as well. The degree of the respective scenarios is reduced, but it represents a will to move together in the same direction.

A third combination is the *referee* and *player* option. In this case, the Union is capable to develop and not serve as the playing field for the rest of actors. Moreover, instead of only assuming its normative strength it pushes to reinforce its influence by also participating in the game.

A last option is to serve as a *board game* and as a *player*. The Union decides to leave on one side its regulatory power and focus on serving as a playing field, attracting foreign investment, and participating in the game as well.

b) Analysis of Driver's Trend on Scenarios

The impact towards the *hybrid* scenario of the eight internal and external drivers, previously introduced in the first analysis section, are represented in Figure 9.

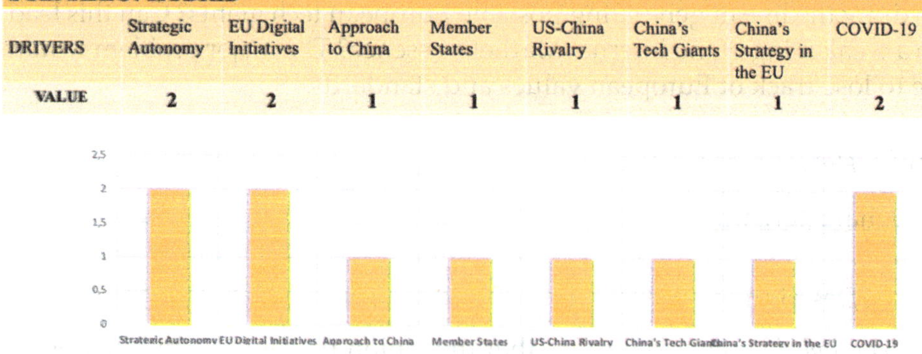

SCENARIO: HYBRID								
DRIVERS	Strategic Autonomy	EU Digital Initiatives	Approach to China	Member States	US-China Rivalry	China's Tech Giants	China's Strategy in the EU	COVID-19
VALUE	2	2	1	1	1	1	1	2

Figure 9: Hybrid
Source: Own elaboration

The notorious element of this table is that all drivers have a positive effect on the scenario. In fact, it is a smooth influence, with the majority having a +1 trend, followed by +2. This shows that it is the scenario with the most stable impact by the drivers.

Of the internal drivers, *strategic autonomy* and the *EU digital initiatives* are the ones to pose a more positive effect, while of the external drivers it is the impact of *COVID-19*. This is because all three are more prone to allow for a combination of the three scenarios, *game board*, *referee*, and *player*. The influence of the resting drivers will set the type of combination. This means, as to what extend it will be a combination of the three or only of two scenarios.

c) Advantages vs. Difficulties

Regarding the *hybrid* scenario there are a series of advantages and disadvantages for the European Union.

The first important advantage is the fact that it is the best option regarding the current reality. This means, on the one hand, that it is easier for the Union to achieve a combination because it does not imply to fully develop each of the individual scenarios, but to find a balance between them. This also allows Member States to still have different opinions and postures but engage at a certain degree in further development. On the other hand, the Union has already presented certain elements of the scenarios, being the *board game* and *referee* the most prominent ones. Further strengthening and comminating them will be a fast and achievable target.

The second advantage is the opportunity to carry out a step-by-step approach. Not jumping directly into one single role, allows the Union to discover its potential in different areas. The objective is not to fully convert into one solid position bur rather engage in a variety of activities of the three scenarios that are indispensable for the EU to develop as an autonomous actor. Objectives need time to organise and to be fulfilled, engaging in different areas gives the chance to address all the components instead of just one part of it.

The third advantageous point is the possibility it offers to bring Member States back together. In order to be able for the Union to move on, certain chapters need to be closed first. Addressing the needs of Member States and taking their considerations into account is best accomplished by not forcing a strong position in the digital realm, but by introducing little aims and objectives. This generates a period of dialogue and reflection, time in which more pro-active Member States can show the doubtful, the importance of having a solid and active digital agenda.

Lastly, it strengthens the Union as a whole and opens a window of opportunity to engage into more action and heading towards strategic autonomy.

Concerning the disadvantages, the less favourable aspect of this scenario is that it is more difficult to find a balance of the combinations. How much *board game* is better with a *referee* position, and with a *player* role? It is a blurred line that does not allow to settle a specific agenda.

Secondly, engaging in several roles without committing to fully develop them, leads to a weak digital strategy. Decisions and objectives can be too vague and confusing, achieving therefore not a real strong policy direction.

Lastly, a *hybrid* scenario can lead to a two speed-Europe. A group of Member States would incline towards more action and commitment, while another group would support a slower and more cautious approach. These differences in ideas lead to differences in milestone settings, making it more difficult to move forward all together at the same pace.

2.3. Comparative Analysis

After having analysed the scenarios individually, this section will provide for a comparative study as to what are the considerations to bear in mind, what are the possible implications, and which are the predictions.

Figure 10 shows the totality of drivers' trends towards the four scenarios. When adding all the points, the scenario that has the more positive quantity is the *referee*, followed by *board game*, *hybrid*, and lastly with a negative figure, the *player* scenario. This does not represent a sequence of the preferred outcome for the EU, but the strength by which the drivers impact on the future possible outcomes.

COMPARISON								
	DRIVERS							
SCENARIO	Strategic Autonomy	EU Digital Initiatives	Approach to China	Member States	US-China Rivalry	China's Tech Giants	China's Strategy in the EU	COVID-19
Board Game	0	0	2	0	3	3	3	1
Referee	1	3	2	2	1	2	2	2
Player	3	3	-1	-1	-3	-3	-2	2
Hybrid	2	2	1	1	1	1	1	2

RANGE OF VALUES		
Impact of drivers	Positive	+
	Negative	-
	Stronger	3
	Weaker	1
	Neutral	0

Figure 10: Comparison
ource: Own elaboration

A) Considerations

Certain elements need to be addressed to identify the possible implications of the drivers on the fulfilment of the respective scenarios.

It is important to highlight that the positive influence on a scenario is achieved by what that driver stands for and how the Union has addressed it. This does not mean however, that the driver has been fully completed or that it is static. Having this in mind, the following table can be elaborated:

- *Strategic autonomy (1)*: introduced by EUGS 2016 and reaffirmed by European Institutions and authorities. However, there is still a need to fix a more precise strategy that includes the different agendas (digital, health, environmental ...)
- *EU digital initiatives (2)*: strongly supported by the EU institutions, lastly under the *a Europe fit for the digital age* priority introducing new technologies. Nonetheless, it has to be far more ambitious.
- *Approach to China (3)*: the EU has several documents discussing the relationship but there is no common strategy towards the Asian country. It has not been fully discussed to introduce it.
- *Member States (4)*: there is a lacking common posture towards China, involving different interests and ambitions. There has not been an express commitment to find a stronger united front.
- *US-China rivalry (5)*: is a reality that affects the European Union.
- *China's tech giants (6)*: have an international impact and influence, far beyond the capacity of European ones.
- *China's strategy in the EU (7)*: seeks to divide and conquer in a territory that lacks a common approach and autonomy.
- *COVID-19 (8)*: has shown the need to prepare for the digital future.

B) Implications

The previous considerations show the differences that can be drawn between the impact of internal and external drivers and what each group implies for the scenarios. It is crucial to note that one thing is the trend they have on the future, and another thing the probability of the driver itself to be accomplished.

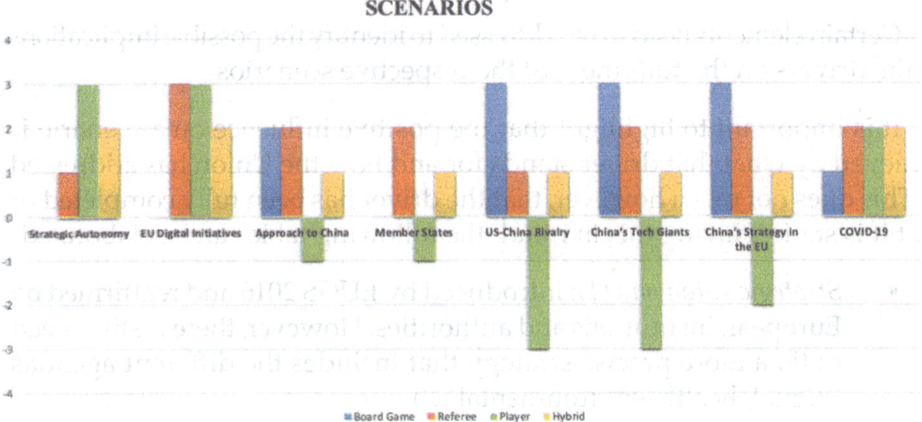

Figure 11: Comparison of Driver's Trends on Scenarios
Source: Own elaboration

On the one hand, internal drivers represent indispensable factors for the EU: heading towards strategic autonomy, having a strong set of digital initiatives, establishing a united strategy on digital terms towards China, and enjoying a common position towards the country. Nonetheless, the analysed data shows more commitment to develop the first and second drivers, while the third and fourth note less intention and more division. Therefore, the first two will influence more the *player* and *hybrid* forms, with the other two influencing more the *referee* and *hybrid*.

On the other hand, external drivers represent an exterior reality that is occurring and that marks the need for a common digital action by the Union. The first three reflect the Union's lack of autonomy and strength, influencing more the *board game* scenario, but also the *referee*, that implies a response of the Union to defend itself. The last one, *COVID-19*, has been the call for attention, influencing all scenarios.

The combination of all the drivers indicates that the *referee* scenario, has the strongest influence. This is because the normative power of the Union is already wide-spread, and it is not new in the digital realm. This leads to a higher probability for its consolidation, and what is known as the Brussels Effect. The second more influenced future is the *game board* position. The lacking digital strategy towards China, a diffuse position towards the country and the, at the moment, lacking autonomy, combined with the external events, punish the Union to serve as playing field for others advancement. The third most influenced scenario is the *hybrid* form, that pushes for a combination of the three, while the last position is given to the *player*. Building upon the previous facts, at the present time, the forces of the drivers do not allow for a consolidation of the Union to serve as an active digital actor that confronts China.

C) Predictions

Once the implications have been studied, the predictions and the feasibility of the results need to be measured.

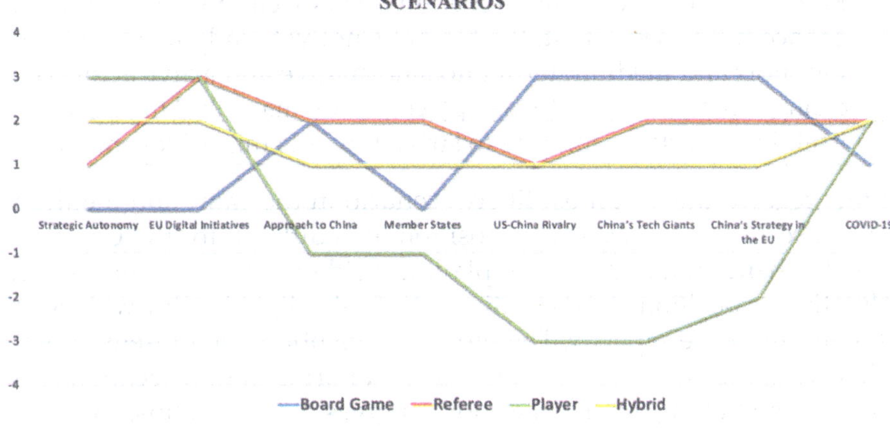

Figure 12: Comparison of Scenarios
Source: Own elaboration

Taking into consideration the obtained information, the scenario that demonstrates a positive, linear, and constant trend is the *hybrid* form. This is because regarding the drivers, no scenario can be present on its own, elements of the others will somehow appear or are already in place (see figure 12).

The previous analysis indicates the following predictions of the *hybrid* combinations including the impact over time:

- *Board game + referee*. Highest probability. As it has been shown, the *referee* and the *board game* scenarios are the most influenced by drivers, being already present in a certain degree. In a short and medium term, however, there is a space of opportunity and willingness for the Union to continue strengthening its normative position in the digital realm.
- *Board game + referee + player*. Intermediate probability. In the medium term it is feasible to incorporate to the previous roles, little objectives

and actions that allow the Union to assume a more active position. It does not imply however a strong autonomous position, but the beginning to start a new direction that can gain feasibility in the long term.

- *Board game + player*. Low probability. This combination offers a low likelihood because the Union itself is a normative power and abandoning this role would imply to abandon the mere essence of the EU.

- *Referee + player*. Very low probability. This scenario has the lowest chance in the sense that, the Union is not yet ready to advance in the short and medium term into a normative and active actor. The changes that first need to take place are too many and the EU finds itself in an early position as to strive towards this achievement.

In this regard, the first most likely scenario in the short and medium term is the *board game + referee* composition. It is difficult for the Union to completely abandon its position of playing field overnight. Nonetheless, consolidating its position of a normative actor in the digital realm, will mean a far higher influence capacity. Therefore, this combination presents a first step. Allowing the EU to settle standards and norms in new technologies can lead to a global impact. Furthermore, it gives the Union time to better organise what it wants and address the needs and thoughts of the different positions of Member States.

Afterwards, as a continuation of the previous, in the medium term the next possible scenario is the grouping of all the three. It implies the incorporation of elements that seek to put the EU in a player position, while the presence of the first two scenarios allows for a balance of ambitions and capabilities. It represents a second step towards the consolidation of a digital strategy and a common approach towards China. The Union has to strive to achieve this scenario and include, little by little, objectives, aims and goals towards digital action. It does not mean that the EU will become a major actor in this field, but it represents the beginning of a new agenda in which the Union can find its role and competitive position. Furthermore, it permits to take things step by step, advancing more in certain technological areas than others depending on the circumstances. But ultimately, it opens the opportunity to seek strategic autonomy, more EU.

The third probable scenario, only in the long term and highly ambitious, is the *referee + player*. Over time, under the proper amount of solidarity between Member States and the enough desire to push the Union forward as an autonomous actor, the EU can overcome its position of playing field and acquire a normative and player role. It is the ultimately goal as to be able to reach strategic autonomy and strengthen the Union as an international powerful actor. This is the desired scenario for the long future, and the aim it has to strive for. Even if it will undoubtedly take a lot of time, if the EU wants to survive in the digital future and continue growing, it has no other option.

The *game board + player* combination is very unlikely in the sense that the EU is itself a normative power and it is not going to stop. Therefore, it is not considered in the study.

As it can be seen, the transition from one scenario to the other is not only dependent on time, but also on the capacity of the EU to reach a common ground and be able to move together. The future is Europe, a stronger Europe. It is about time that Member States take this into consideration and start building solidarity between them as to pursue a strong digital territory that is fit for European citizens and businesses and protects them from Chinese and further foreign intervention. Something that can only be achieved through a strong digital Europe.

V. CONCLUSIONS

The results of this final Thesis lead towards the establishment of the following conclusions.

The world crisis generated by the COVID-19 pandemic has brought to light, more than ever, the key role of technology in today's world. Furthermore, it has contributed to reaffirm the notion that the future will be digital.

This leads to the fact that those actors who are capable of consolidating a strong position in this realm will have a position of power and influence in the international sphere.

The People's Republic of China is very much aware of it and has started in the last years to investing heavily in digitalisation. Moreover, it will soon become the country with the highest percentage of GDP allocated to investment in research, development, and innovation of new technologies.

The race for technological leadership has strongly confronted the United States and the People's Republic of China, conditioning the rest of countries to position themselves with one or another actor if they lack their own digital means and resources.

The Union itself has been subject to external pressures, noting that its territory is being used as a playing field for the digital advancement of foreign more powerful international actors.

These events show that it is about time for the Union to review its approach towards China in the digital realm and decide whether it wants to serve as a *game board*, *referee*, *player* or a *hybrid* combination.

The analysed eight internal and external drivers, impact differently the probability of the four possible future scenarios.

The objective of strategic autonomy introduced in the EUGS 2016 and supported by European and political authorities is the leading principle of the Union's direction. Its proper achievement would imply to include a precise digital agenda, among other fields, that will lead the EU to serve as a strong autonomous actor. In this regard, it is indispensable that Member States come together for this purpose and agree on a common stand towards the relationship with China. Elements that for the moment are only feasible in the long term and under solidarity between all.

The digital initiatives of the Union are a clear example of its normative power. Furthermore, the protection of the individual and the respect for European values are at the core, embodying the essence and persona of the EU. The protection of data and information has been completed by the introduction of regulations for new technologies, more precisely under the new *a Europe fit for the digital age* priority. This indicates the EU strong approach towards standards, which under more ambitious steps can lead to a consolidation of the Brussels Effect and therefore, the strengthening of the Union.

The EU's approach towards China includes documents that discuss the relationship between both actors, including the mentioning of digital components, notwithstanding, no common European strategy has been established.

The Member States have a lacking common posture towards China, having different groups of interests and ambitions. This puts the Union in a weak position, not being strong and autonomous to defend a united stand.

The US-China rivalry, and the international reach of China's tech giants have a negative impact on the Union's capacity to compete, demonstrating its lacking strength in this realm.

China's strategy in the European Union indicates that the Asian country knows very well what it wants and what it needs to do in order to achieve it. By dividing and conquering it assures to influence the targeted countries. While it becomes evident that the EU has still to address what it wants to achieve.

COVID-19 has shown the need to prepare for the digital future and has triggered several aims to incentive digital transition in the European territory.

When adding all the points that the eight drivers have on each of the four scenarios, the future outcome that counts with the highest positive number is the *referee*, followed by *board game*, *hybrid*, and lastly with a negative figure, the *player* scenario. This does not represent however a sequence of the preferred outcome for the EU, but the strength by which the drivers impact on the future possible scenarios.

Regarding predictions, the only scenario that demonstrates a positive, linear, and constant trend is the *hybrid* form with a series of combinations. No scenario can be fully present on its own as elements of the others will somehow appear or are already in place.

In the short medium term, the highest probability is occupied by the *board game + referee* union. These two scenarios are the most influenced by drivers, being already present in a certain degree.

With an intermediate probability the composition of all, *board game + referee + player*, can be found. In the medium term it is possible to include little objectives and actions that allow the Union to assume a more active position, without yet becoming a full player.

The lowest probability is presented under the *referee + player* combination. Under the current circumstances, even in the long term it is difficult for the Union to introduce the changes that first need to take place as to achieve this outcome.

The Union has to consolidate over a period of time the *board game + referee* scenario, and then strive to achieve the combination of all three. In order for the Union to develop as an international actor, it has to consolidate strategic autonomy, and this is not possible without being a player in the digital realm.

The future of the Union depends on the commitment and solidarity of Member States to engage in the medium term in a more united, normative, and active scenario in the digital arena.

It is time for Europe to take its destiny into its own hands.

E-Commerce, Consumers' Guarantees In European Union International Private Law Regulations And Their Counterbalancing External Legal Effects Regarding Partnerships Towards The People's Republic Of China

ENRIQUE MANUEL PUERTA DOMÍNGUEZ

PhD in Law from the University of Alcalá de Henares (Madrid, Spain). Lecturer at CEU Fernando III University in Sevilla and University of Huelva (Spain)

ID ORCID https://orcid.org/0000-0003-1816-5703

I. EU DIRECTIVES AND REGULATIONS INVOLVED IN E-COMMERCE AND THEIR EXTERNAL IMPACT BEYOND EUROPEAN BOUNDARIES

Since its early days, in which it attracted special doctrinal interest as a phenomenon, of course legal, but certainly economic and business[1], the unstoppable phenomenon of online purchases has increased exponentially[2], and with this it has become clear that there is still a large lack of homogeneous and fully integrated Regulations capable of responding, not only from the material legal point of view, but also from the procedural, to the eventual litigations that may occur in case of dissatisfaction of the consumer, who is manly a home-localized subject. We have been progressively discovering

1. See Chan, H. et al., *E-Commerce: fundamentals and applications*, Wiley, Chichester, 2001; Damanpour, F. and Damanpour, J. A., "E-business e-commerce evolution: perspective and strategy", *Managerial Finance*, Vol. 27, n. 7 (2001), pp. 16-33. And later Laudon, K. C. and Traver, C. G., *E-commerce: business, technology, society*, Pearson Prentice Hall, New Jersey, 2007.
2. Revealing statistics are released every year in this regard. For the European case we find those that are sent annually. Check Ecommerce Europe and Euro Commerce for retail & wholesale, "European E-Commerce Report 2022", Amsterdam University of Applied Sciences & Ecommerce Europe (2022), retrieved from *www.ecommerce-europe.eu/wp-content/uploads/2022/06/CMI2022_FullVersion_LIGHT_v2.pdf*

even greater possibilities for the expansion of electronic commerce, but in case of dissatisfaction we have not found that justice to end those differences is anywhere near as close as a click away as in the first case. The impact of e-commerce differs from one kind of goods to another. The sensation of risks linked to Internet commerce has been present in the doctrine since the first steps of this economic modality[3]. However, we do find that the financial risks also vary by category and our results are very similar to those of previous research. However, attitudes towards electronic commerce have gone from the idea of risk to the idea of utility, understood as diverse attitudes of consumers that deserve their specific treatment[4]. Therefore, items such as books, music, travel, and apparel are strongly affected by perceived risk. However, products such as housewares and health and beauty products are less impacted by risk, and there is even no significant effect of risk on sports equipment and auto products.

There is logically a dual game or contrasts between the attitude of e-consumers towards electronic commerce, which move between risk and trust[5]. But in every case, if consumers' protecting provisions are different or very divergent among international partners, it risks turning e-commerce into an unsafe hazard, not to say that consumers, as the weaker party, may feel uncertain the prospect of filing legal actions against the product manufacturer in case of unsatisfied expectations. Anyway, such a wide range of matters must be accurately defined.

We must recall that this our contribution should not deal with material law framed in what is known as Consumer Protection Policy, which has been of interest to the EU for so long. This is meant to be an aspect of integration law that has been significantly successful in achieving the European Internal Market, and in which the Directives have played the most prominent role

---

3. Bhatnagar, A., Misra, S. & Ragav Rao, H., "On risk, convenience, and Internet shopping behavior" in *Communications of the ACM*, Vol. 43, n. 11 (2000), pp. 98-105.
4. We find this approach both in Western and Chinese authors. We quote: Henderson, R. and Divett, M. J., "Perceived usefulness, ease of use and electronic supermarket use" in *International Journal of Human-Computer Studies*, Vol. 59, n. 3 (2003), pp. 383-395; Liu, X. and Wei, K. K., "An empirical study of product differences in consumer E-commerce adoption behavior" in *Electronic Commerce Research and Applications*, Vol. 2, n. 3 (2003), pp. 229-239.
5. Fang, Y. et al., "Trust, satisfaction, and online repurchase intention: the moderating role of perceived effectiveness of e-commerce institutional mechanisms", *Mis Quarterly* Vol. 38, n. 2 (2014), pp. 407-427; Giovanis, A. N. and Athanasopoulou, P., "Gaining customer loyalty in the e-tailing marketplace: the role of e-service quality, e-satisfaction and e-trust", *International Journal of Technology Marketing* Vol. 9, n. 3 (2014), pp. 288-304.

among the instruments of Secondary law (Regulations and Directives taking their legal basis from the constitutive EU-Treaties). The Regulation of electronic commerce is therefore at the heart of Directive 2000/31 of the European Parliament and of the Council of June 8, 2000, on certain legal aspects of information society services, and in particular electronic commerce, in the internal market, which sets out the rules relating to the requirements on the establishment and information of information society service providers, as well as on the liability of intermediary providers. The normative process does not stop advancing.

E-commerce affects thus a variety of areas of economic life which are not covered by the said Directive, such as games of chance, questions relating to agreements or practices governed by cartel law and taxation (see art. 1.5 of the Electronic Commerce Directive, on the purpose and scope of that Directive). Similarly, copyright, and related rights, trademark rights, consumer protection and personal data protection fall within the domain of e-commerce but are governed by a set of special Directives and Regulations[6].

6. Concerning Directives, we find for instance:
a)- Council Directive 93/13/EEC of 5 April 1993 on unfair terms in consumer contracts, OJ L 095, 21/04/1993, pp. 29-34.
b)- Directive 1999/34/EC of the European Parliament and of the Council of 10 May 1999 amending Council Directive 85/374/EEC on the approximation of the laws, regulations and administrative provisions of the Member States concerning liability for defective products, OJ L 141, 04/06/1999, pp. 20-21.
c)- Directive 1999/44/EC of the European Parliament and of the Council of 25 May 1999 on certain aspects of the sale of consumer goods and associated guarantees, OJ L 171, 07/07/1999, pp. 12-16.
d)- Directive 98/6/EC of the European Parliament and of the Council of 16 February 1998 on consumer protection in the indication of the prices of products offered to consumers, OJ L 080, 18/03/1998, pp. 27-31.
e)- Directive 2005/29/EC of the European Parliament and of the Council of 11 May 2005 concerning unfair business-to-consumer commercial practices in the internal market and amending Council Directive 84/450/EEC, Directives 97/7/EC, 98/27/EC and 2002/65/EC of the European Parliament and of the Council and Regulation (EC) No 2006/2004 of the European Parliament and of the Council ('Unfair Commercial Practices Directive'), OJ L 149, 11/06/2005, pp. 22-39.
f)- Directive 2006/114/EC of the European Parliament and of the Council of 12 December 2006 concerning misleading and comparative advertising, OJ L 376, 27/12/2006, p. 21-27.
g)- Directive 2009/22/EC of the European Parliament and of the Council of 23 April 2009 on injunctions for the protection of consumers' interests, OJ L 110, 01/05/2009, pp. 30-33.
h)- Directive 2011/83/EU of the European Parliament and of the Council of 25 October 2011 on consumer rights, amending Council Directive 93/13/EEC and Directive

What is just being stated affects another area, also assumed by European integration, but much more recent, complex and under construction, which is the one that includes the widely developed domain since the turn of this century of European Union International Private Law (EU-PRIL from now on) , built through a notorious number of Regulations adopted with the beginning of this century to the present[7]. We traditionally define EU-PRIL as a specific branch of Law, with a national and international presence, and lately with a marked role in charge of the EU, whose purpose is to organize the factual assumptions of a private nature that present foreign or foreign elements with respect to the territory or population of the State in which the claim takes place, and that have elements of connection with territories or populations from other countries. All questions that arise related to EU-PRIL respond in reality to those that correspond to who will apply the Law (competent judicial court), which Law will be applied to resolve the matter raised and what is the effectiveness, for the legal system forensic, of the realities and manifestations created in the system of another country through resolutions or actions of its authorities (jurisdictional or of another type).

These range of problems are resolved through rules on applicable law, on competent jurisdiction and through both procedural and substantive rules relating to the recognition and enforcement of foreign documents and resolutions. This is where the usual distinction between EU-PRIL and International Civil Procedure Law comes from. Well, all these facets are of

1999/44/EC of the European Parliament and of the Council and repealing Council Directive 85/577/EEC and Directive 97/7/EC of the European Parliament and of the Council, OJ L 304, 22/11/2011, pp. 64-88.

i)- Directive (EU) 2019/2161 of the European Parliament and of the Council of 27 November 2019 amending Council Directive 93/13/EEC and Directives 98/6/EC, 2005/29/EC and 2011/83/EU of the European Parliament and of the Council as regards the better enforcement and modernisation of Union consumer protection rules, OJ L 328, 18/12/2019, pp. 7-50.

Other crucial instruments regarding e-transactions show the form of Regulations, such as:

a)- Regulation (EU) No 910/2014 of the European Parliament and of the Council of 23 July 2014 on electronic identification and trust services for electronic transactions in the internal market and repealing Directive 1999/93/EC, OJ L 257, 28/08/2014, pp. 73-91.

b)- Regulation (EU) 2016/679 of the European Parliament and of the Council of 27 April 2016 on the protection of natural persons with regard to the processing of personal data and on the free movement of such data, and repealing Directive 95/46/EC (General Data Protection Regulation), OJ L 119, 04/05/2016, pp. 1-88.

7. For a quick introduction to EU-PRIL aims and essence, see Bogdan, M., *Concise Introduction to EU Private International Law*, European Law Publishing, Groningen 2006.

interest to the EU from an integration point of view, but with the sui generis specificities that we are going to expose, which must be compared from the plaintiffs' positions as eventual purchasers of defective products via internet in countries other than the one they are located in. In a nutshell, we will dedicate this contribution to make accessible to our Chinese partners the entire set of Regulations that concern the security of transnational electronic commerce from the EU perspective, always in accordance with balanced, procedural frameworks.

Up to three Regulations are applicable a priori, the first being a generic procedural Regulation, 1215/2012 (known as Brussels I bis) of the European Parliament and of the Council, of December 12, 2012, regarding jurisdiction recognition and execution of judicial resolutions in civil and commercial matters (which replaces and absorbs its predecessor, Regulation 44/2001-Brussels I- through a consolidated text), while those that determine the conflict Regulations (material or substantial Law) applicable from the perspective of the EU-PRIL are two, Regulation (known as Rome II) 864/2007 of the Council, of July 11, 2007, regarding the Law applicable to non-contractual obligations, and the Regulation (known as Rome I) 593/2008 of the Council, of June 17, 2008, regarding the Law applicable to contractual obligations. We recall that denominations such "Brussels" or "Rome" are related to the fact that the EU considers such instruments to bring cause in their predecessors, the Brussels and Rome Conventions, born in a conventional context prior to the adoption of the currently integrated EU-PRIL existing. Thus, since the entry into force of the Amsterdam Treaty on May 1, 1999, the matters regulated by the Brussels Convention of September 27, 1968, became part of EU policies, in accordance with art. 61, letter c), and to art. 65 of the EC Treaty. Therefore, the 1968 Brussels Convention became a Regulation, its mechanisms were modernized on the basis of integration, and the recognition and enforcement system became more agile and effective, with a first version known as the Brussels I Regulation. 44/2001, to later reach the current Brussels I bis. In addition, it must be understood that the relationship is so close between Conventions and Regulations that scientific and forensic doctrine are unanimous in considering that the jurisprudence on both conventions can be extrapolated *mutatis mutandis*, and in terms of *acquis communautaire* (EU case Law & institutional practices), to current EU-PRIL Regulations.

Previous concerns are related to the essential procedural aspects in the private order, while the second collects the two fields of the obligations in the private sector (contractual and non-contractual); This initially leads to the problem of whether or not there is a contract between the vendor and the purchaser of the defective product on the Internet, and consequently there is doubt as to whether one Regulation or another should apply. That is why we will dedicate this contribution to delimiting the applicative and instrumental scopes of the three Regulations mentioned just above, always from the point of view of the consumer and purchaser on the internet of products that are possibly defective, or that in any other way disappoint the expectations that motivated their buys.

Both kind of provisions, Directives and Regulations, being properly enforced within the member States respective legal orders, have not only internal effects, but also external, providing consumers both EU nationals and EU- established with a wide range of strong guarantees towards e-commerce providers; this goes equally no matter if an e-commerce vendor or provider is established outside the EU boundaries. Interesting conclusions can be extracted from two pronouncements that once concerned the trading giant Amazon in the course preliminary rulings raised before the CJEU and answered in 2016 and 2019. We will dedicate a detailed interest to them, along with other rulings quoted of our present contribution.

II. MAIN, GENERIC ASPECTS ADOPTED BY THE EUROPEAN E-COMMERCE LEGAL PROVISIONS; RANGE AND SCOPE OF DIRECTIVE 2000/31

The material body concerning as such electronic commerce within the EU is the cited Directive 2000/31 Europe of the fifteen and, beyond, many countries bound by cooperation agreements with the European Union, have a common legal framework for the development of online services, which should facilitate the development of what is commonly called the "information society". This legal framework only constitutes a minimum base, which leaves many questions open; it should be largely supplemented by various national provisions. Moreover, under the principle of subsidiarity, only certain specific issues raising problems for the internal market are addressed. If there is harmonization, it is altogether both limited (points left to the Member States) and minimal (on the points discussed).

Focusing then our analysis on Directive 2000/31, we must consider that it therefore leaves room for initiatives by the Member States, and potentially for the creation of future divergences, which can however be corrected during the reviews of the Directive provided for in art. 21. In every circumstance, the other quoted Directives, as protecting consumers' rights in many other provisions may fill up the gaps, as they can work either in a standard o an electronic commerce context. Once all this considered, the objective stated by the Directive (in art. 1.1) is "to contribute to the proper functioning of the internal market by ensuring the free movement of information society services". It intends to regulate only what is strictly necessary for the proper functioning of the borderless market. In addition to this objective, the Directive intends to guarantee a high level of protection of the objectives of general interest, particularly affecting consumers, which is reflected in particular in the provision that the Directive is "without prejudice to the level of protection, in particular with regard to public health and consumer interests established by EU instruments and national implementing legislation" (art. 1, 3). According to the designers of the Directive, consumer protection and information measures will not endanger the development of online services, but, on the contrary, strengthen the consumer's confidence and therefore the rise of online services.

It is by reducing the risks of illegal activities (see the rules on the liability of intermediaries and the rules providing for effective control of the Member State where the company is established), by imposing obligations of information and transparency to operators, by clarifying the will of consumers in the event of the conclusion of a contract and by guaranteeing better means of redress (through the encouragement codes of conduct and the use of dispute resolution mechanisms) that consumer confidence should be enhanced. In conclusion, among the matters most typically affecting the Directive would be the protection of various essential aspects concerning e-commerce, such as:

a) consumer's position;

b) personal data;

c) copyright;

d) advertising standards;

e) competition standards;

f) taxation and fiscal aspects.

Nevertheless, other certain matters concerning e-commerce would in particular fall outside the scope of the Directive to be intended for the Regulations of EU-PRIL, in concrete terms, their main subjects concern in particular aspects such as the contractual relationship between the parties, aspects of jurisdictional competence and applicable law (that is, aspects of EU-PRIL). Both Amazon rulings that we are about to comment will concern, the first (issued in 2016) the aspects of judicial jurisdiction and applicable law (that is to say, matters affecting the EU-PRIL), while the second judgment (from 2019) deals about consumer protection in a joint application of EU-PRIL Regulations with Directive 2000/31.

It must be considered that this Directive of 2000 already has a distant horizon and leaves many open questions. These are complemented, as we have had the opportunity to see, by various additional provisions that take the form of Directives, and some of them even replaced by Regulations. Besides, the Directive leaves room for initiatives by the Member States and, potentially, for the creation of future divergences, which however can be corrected during the revisions of the Directive provided for in art. 21. Furthermore, by virtue of the principle of subsidiarity, only certain specific issues that pose problems for the internal market are addressed. If there is harmonization, it is both limited (factors left to the Member States) and minimal (in the most disputed aspects). In this way, the Internet commerce Directive, with so much time elapsed and despite some important tweaks, is always affected by the risk of being outdated.

III. THE BRUSSELS I BIS GENERAL PROCEDURAL REGULATION CONCERNING ITS USE FOR ACTIONS FILED BY ONLINE CONSUMERS

This is the first step of the logical legal process that must be clarified, since the acquirer (or in any case his legal advisor) must be perfectly clear about which jurisdiction has to be the first and foremost competent to deal with a possible claim or litigation. , in matters related to jurisdictional assistance with other external courts, as well as in the way in which the various judicial pronouncements that may exist in the case may be enforceable (all of this against the supplier of the disputed good that causes consumer dissatisfaction). Let us bear in mind that the Rome I and II Regulations lack aspects of procedural relevance; therefore, they only have the Brussels I bis Regulation as a reference in this field. This instrument must therefore be analyzed from the specific problem of its use by the consumer or Internet user. From this peculiar point of view there are many specifications, both in the text of the provision itself and in the jurisprudence developed by the CJEU. It was already considered in its day that the previous Regulation 44/2001 Brussels I in its art. 15 had already accepted the jurisdictional clause (which is particularly valid for contracts concluded on the Internet), since the merchant internationalizes the contract to the extent that he directs his activities to the consumer's country of residence. For this reason, the trader will bear the risk of being sued in the country of habitual residence of the consumer.

We must know from the outset that the scope of subjective application of the Brussels I bis Regulation is articulated as a normal guideline, establishing the defendant's domicile as the competent jurisdiction. This is regardless of the latter's nationality, as the action is favored by having the defendant domiciled in a Member State participating in the Regulation. Such main competence mechanism is included in art. 4.1 a). According to such precept: "Except for the provisions of this Regulation, persons domiciled in a Member State shall be subject, whatever their nationality, to the jurisdictional bodies of that State". The Brussels I bis Regulation therefore places the General jurisdiction in the State in which the defendant has his domicile, being more suitable e for contexts of a commercial nature compared to the judiciary identified with that of the common residence of the defendant (present in other EU-PRIL Regulations). Assuming this, it will be the internal procedural regulations on competence for the matter and the territory of the State of said domicile to which it corresponds to individualize the Judge that is specifically competent in accordance with the general principles.

On the contrary, placing the domicile of the defendant (the internet supply company) as a main should be precisely detrimental to the consumer. For this reason, together with the defendant's domicile main jurisdiction, the Brussels I bis Regulation articulates in its art. 7 a series of subsidiary options of special jurisdictional competence (also called concurrent, alternative or optional) that overlap the aforementioned general clause of the defendant's domicile or the registered office, and that, in derogation of that same common jurisdictional pattern, no they are limited to individualizing the Member State of the Judge, but also directly designate the territorially competent Judge (without the need to apply the rules on nationals regulating internal jurisdiction). The jurisdictional competence is thus distributed among the Judges of several EU Member States in the perspective of the Single European Judicial Space of Freedom, Security and Justice. The Brussels I bis Regulation in its art. 7.1 synthesizes and restructures them according to the matter, affecting each of the institutes or singular figures to which they refer. Thus, in short, we find: 1)- In contractual matters, the Judge of the place in which the obligation claimed in court has been or must be fulfilled is competent; consequently, if the purchasers of products on the Internet arise issues, for example, related to the crime of fraud, it must be considered that by means of this Regulation, actions for compensation for damages filed before criminal jurisdictions by way of liability are included in civil matters[8].

Even despite these guidelines, the doubts regarding the accessibility of justice in the case of a consumer confined to his place of residence who tried to start legal procedures due to a defective product or that did not meet the expectations he had when he bought it online. Thus, there are special assumptions of exclusive jurisdiction that, in a guaranteeing sense for the plaintiff, will play out without considering the fact that the defendant is domiciled in a Member State of the EU. It is in this field where the actions filed by consumers enter significantly, so that the Brussels I bis Regulation in its art. 18 makes it possible for the domicile of the consumer, as the initiator of the action, to be the one that determines jurisdiction in case of litigation[9].

Another precept to be quoted is art. 25 of the Brussels I bis Regulation, by virtue of which the jurisdiction clause may refer generically to the authority or judicial power of a Member State as a whole, without specifying a specific judicial body. In such a case, the material and territorially competent Judge will be individualized in accordance with what is determined by the internal provisions related to jurisdictional competence. And even the choice of the competent jurisdiction in charge of the parties may be valid, even when the designated Judge does not present any connection with that of such Member State. Said choice must be expressly stated prior to the emergence of the possible controversy between the parties, and always in accordance

8. This reasoning is due to European jurisprudential contribution, as it happens for instance in CJEU Case C-523/14, *Aannemingsbedrijf Aertssen NV, and Aertssen Terrassements SA v VSB Machineverhuur BV, Van Sommeren Bestrating BV, and Jos van Sommeren*, 22.10.2015, ECLI:EU:C:2015:722 (TJCE,2019,273), relapsed in interpretation of the preceding Regulation Brussels I 44/2001, as well as various others that will be cited below. And 2)- in matters of intentional and negligent civil offenses, the Judge of the place where the harmful event has occurred or may occur (understood as the place where the damage occurs, or as the place where the event generating the harmful event has been verified is competent according to art. 7.2).

9. Indeed, the art. 18 that resolves the issue very evenly from the point of view of jurisdictional competence in the field of consumer protection in its three paragraphs as follows: "1. The action brought by a consumer against the other contracting party may be brought before the courts of the Member State in which said party is domiciled or, regardless of the domicile of the other party before the court of the place where the consumer is domiciled. 2. The action brought against the consumer by the other contracting party may only be brought before the courts of the Member State in which the consumer is domiciled. 3. This article shall not affect the right to file a counterclaim before the jurisdictional body hearing the initial claim in accordance with this section".

with one of the following modalities: 1)- in writing or orally, with written confirmation (letter a, in connection with 25.2); In this sense, the written form includes any contacts through electronic means that allows a lasting record of the clause, in which scope we will see below that the CJEU makes the acceptance procedure of the general conditions of the contract fall by clicking on the website of the seller; 2)- in a form admitted by the practices that the parties have established between themselves (letter b); and 3)- in international trade, in any form admitted by widespread use in the sector in which the parties operate (letter c, thinking of documentary and similar credit modalities).

In addition, another passage that comes into play in the context chosen for our analysis is art. 62, which also establishes how the pattern of general jurisdictional competence based on the *Forum rei* (Law of the place where the disputed thing is located) should be understood; For this purpose, the following qualification rules are deployed: 1)- to establish whether a party is domiciled in the territory of the Member State where the Judge against whom the claim is filed is located, the Judge must first evaluate his or her own jurisdiction upon receipt ; and 2)- if, on the contrary, any party turns out not to be domiciled in the Member State before whose Judges the claim is filed, the Judge hearing the matter will apply the Law of that last State to rule that that party is domiciled in that other State.

It has been also widely discussed whether the pre-stamped indication that appears on the sales invoices accompanied by the corresponding payment, as a clause of adhesion relative to the competent jurisdiction and without any protest, could be valid as a valid element for the purposes of determining the jurisdiction. In this regard there was a certain jurisprudential uncertainty, although initially hostile to this practice. Thus: 1)- Certain jurisprudence in some Member States, such as Italy, understood that the choice of the competent court requires the consent of both parties present in the contract, since the unilateral indication of the competent jurisdiction contained in the invoices not only does not reflect the requirement in writing of the current Brussels I bis Regulation in its art. 25.1 a). Nor would it comply with the considerations of letter b) of the same precept, as a form expressly admitted between the parties, nor with respect to letter c), that is, as behavior corresponding to commercial uses generally admitted. 2)- More concisely, the CJEU jurisprudence considered the requirement of the written form fulfilled in these cases of the pre-stamped indication on the sales invoices when the competent court election clause by the parties concerned (*optio Fori*) was contained, in addition to such invoices, in previous documents, such as confirmations of orders prior to payment, notions that can be extrapolated to the present moment as *acquis communautaire*, given that such pronouncements fell essentially in the context prior to that of the Brussels I and I bis Regulations of the Brussels Convention of 1968[10]. This physical over-printing can be estimated to currently occur in electronic format when filling out the different purchase forms and registering on online sales pages.

The adequacy of the European jurisprudence existing until then for the needs of the growing distance trade was put to the test, as another dimension of the problem in question began to arise around new concerns; It was speculated whether the requirement of the written form was respected, even when the competent court election clause was only included in the general conditions of the contract held by at least one of the contracting parties. Faced with such questions, the supreme EU Court ratified the validity of the *optio Fori* contained in the general conditions of the contract, but only when: first, said contract contained an express indication with reference to said circumstance; second, if it had been reliably made known to the other contracting party; and third and not least, if the designated jurisdictional seat coincides with a city of a Member State[11]. Around the same time and in a similar situation, (only raised exactly in the field of internet business) the supreme jurisdictional body of the Union[12].

We must also know that art. 26 of the Brussels I bis Regulation provides for the tacit acceptance of jurisdiction in cases in which the defendant does not appear in court before the Judge of a Member State to formulate an objection of incompetence (as arbitrated in the terms and conditions of the *Lex Fori*), unless the incompetence refers to matters for which an exclusive

10. CJEU Case C-106/95, *Mainschiffahrts-Genossenschaft eG (MSG) v es Gravières Rhénanes, SARL*, 20.02.1997, ECLI:EU:C:1997:70 (TJCE 1997,35).

11. Which guarantees legal certainty by virtue of the ELSJ, CJEU Case C-222/15, *H☒szig Kft. v Alstom Power Thermal Services*, 07.07.2016, ECLI:EU:C:2016:525 (TJCE 2016,273).

12. In such sense, CJEU Case C-322/14, *Jaouad El Majdoub v CarsOnTheWeb.Deutschland GmbH*, 21.05.2015, ECLI:EU:C:2015:334 (TJCE 2015,196), clarified that also the procedure known as click wrapping (which is perfected by clicking the textual hyperlink by which the contracting party consents to the conditions by viewing, conserving and printing the business conditions, when it contains a competent court election clause) is valid as an electronic communication that allows a lasting record, and therefore, is equivalent to the written form of art. 25.1 a) and 25.2 of the current Brussels I bis Regulation. Consequently, unless the parties have established it differently, the individual Judge with the jurisdiction extension agreement becomes the only one competent to hear the case; the *optio iudicis* therefore deactivates the other patterns of jurisdictional competence contemplated by the Brussels I bis Regulation (with the exception of the exclusive competences set forth in art. 24).

attribution is foreseen according to art. 24 of the Regulation (given that such so-said exclusive powers admit no exclusion). If the defendant appears in person and does not question jurisdiction, the Judge will not be able to correct it *ex officio* even when the dispute concerns a contract that contains an *optio Fori* by the Judge of a third country[13]. On the contrary, the conduct of the defendant who appears in court to present an objection for lack of jurisdiction does not constitute a form of tacit acceptance. It is discussed here whether the tacit acceptance can at least dispense with the applicability requirement of the Regulation consisting of the defendant being domiciled in the territory of the EU; the general feeling excludes this possibility, arguing that, unlike the spirit that informs the arts. 24 (exclusive powers), and 25 (express cases of determination of the competent jurisdiction in charge of the parties) art. 26 on the tacit acceptance of jurisdiction does not apply to those cases in respect of which art. 6.1 admits a derogation to said principle.

In short, the Brussels I bis Regulation establishes that in the matters for which mandatory powers are foreseen, the Judge may declare jurisdiction in the event of tacit acceptance of its jurisdiction, that is, after having previously verified that the defendant had been informed in sufficient way of his right to file an objection of incompetence before said jurisdictional body, and he would have also been aware of the consequences of his appearance, or conversely, of his absence in court (art. 26.2). Therefore, the procedural movements of the supplying company as defendant must be considered, since they have a significant impact; however, we believe that the attractive and specialized procedural force of art. 18 of the Brussels I Regulation exercises its domain in the European framework over all these peculiarities for the benefit of the consumer or acquiring user in this case by online means.

IV. ROME I AND ROME II REGULATIONS IN THEIR BENEFITS FOR ONLINE CONSUMERS

Starting with the first of these instruments, we will say that the matter addressed by the Rome I Regulation encompasses all contractual obligations in situations involving conflicts of applicable law, or that in any case are connected with a State other than the State in which the claim is raised, even when it is not a member of the EU[14]. Such is the rule of universal

13. CJEU Case C-175/15, *Taser International Inc. v SC Gate 4 Business SRL and Cristian Mircea Anastasiu*, 17.03.2016, ECLI:EU:C:2016:176 (TJCE 2016,47).

14. For a general survey Lando, O. and Nielsen, P. A., "The Rome I Proposal", *Journal of Private International Law*, Vol. 3 (2007), pp. 48-51; Leible, S., *Rome I Regulation: The Law applicable to contractual Obligations in Europe*, Munich, Beck (2009).

application of art. 2 of the Regulation, by which: "The law designated by this Regulation shall apply, even if it is not that of a Member State". On the point just mentioned, it is worth questioning whether it would be possible for the parties to stipulate that the contract be governed by a Law that does not present any relationship with the factual assumption; the answer must be positive, but with limitations. The art. 3 of the Rome I Regulation is applied *erga omnes*, what means that legal provisions from third or extra EU countries may take place. Such provision enables a wide autonomy to the parties, establishing that the choice of Law linked with a choice of a foreign Court is free, always excepting the general rule that this implies an inadmissible lack of protection for the consumer.

Such a choice is not, however, without limits. The conflictive normative discipline established by the Rome I Regulation is based on a successive concurrence of connection points, the first of which is determined by the free choice of applicable Law of art. 3[15]. In such provision we read: "1. The contract will be governed by the law chosen by the parties. This choice must be expressly stated or unequivocally result from the terms of the contract or the circumstances of the case. By this choice, the parties may designate the law applicable to all or only part of the contract. 2. The parties may, at any time, agree that the contract be governed by a law other than the one that governed it previously, both by virtue of a previous choice made in accordance with any provisions contained in these Regulations. Any modification related to the determination of the applicable law as consequence to the conclusion of the contract, will not affect the formal validity of the contract for the purposes of art. 11 and will not affect the rights of third parties. 3. When all other relevant elements of the situation are located at the time of the election in a country other than the one whose law is chosen, the choice of the parties shall not prevent the application of the provisions of the law of that other country that cannot be excluded by agreement. 4. Where all other relevant elements of the situation at the time of the choice are located in one or more Member States, the choice by the parties of a law other than that of a Member State shall be without prejudice to the application of the provisions of EU law, if any, as applied in the Member State where de claim appears, which cannot be excluded by agreement. 5. The existence and validity of the consent of the parties regarding the choice of the applicable law shall be governed by the provisions established in arts. 10, 11 and 13". Such a system constitutes,

15. Gillies, L., "Choice-of-Law Rules for Electronic Consumer Contracts: Replacement of the Rome Convention by the Rome I Regulation", *Journal of Private International Law*, Vol. 3 (2007), p. 87; Tang, Z., "Parties' Choice of Law in E-Consumer Contracts", *Journal of Private International Law*, Vol. 3 (2007), p. 111.

according to Recital 11, one of the cornerstones of the system prescribed by the Regulation, according to which: "The freedom of the parties to choose the applicable law must constitute one of the keys to the system of rules of conflict of laws in matter of contractual obligations".

Consequently, the contracting parties know a wide freedom in the choice of the applicable Law (they can also limit the choice to a single part of the contract, as well as modify it during the term of the contract (arts. 3.1 and 3.2), provided that: 1)- said option is exercised expressly, or where appropriate; 2)- is reasonably certain based on the clauses of the contract or the circumstances arising from it. To prevent abuses that could derive from the fact of subtracting from the home Law that would govern a completely internal factual assumption, art. 3.3 specifies that, if all the other data or factual elements refer to a single country, the choice of law that is proposed cannot have the effect of excluding the applicability of the regulations, that precisely the legal system of such country does not admits derogation by contractual means (for example, those provisions considered mandatory). The Regulation is therefore based on the guideline of freedom of choice contemplated in art. 3, and only if this is not possible are determined in art. 4 conflicting guidelines as far to determine the applicable law in the absence of choice. The precept expresses: "1. This Regulation shall not affect the application of international conventions to which one or more Member States are a party at the time of the adoption of this Regulation and which regulate conflicts of laws in matters of contractual obligations. 2. However, regarding the relations between Member States, this Regulation shall take precedence over agreements concluded exclusively between two or more Member States to the extent that said agreements deal with the matters regulated by it". This article pretends to provide with the most of legal protection conferred to e-consumers, particularly when there is an absence of choice[16]. In that sense art. 4.4 declares: "When the applicable law cannot be determined in accordance with paragraphs 1 or 2, the contract will be governed by the law of the country with which it has the closest links".

Jurisprudentially with respect to this art. 4 and the notion of the closest link, it has been considered that, if a part of the contract is separable from the rest and has a closer relationship with a different country, the Law of this other nation may apply; however, the EU Court considers this eventuality as exceptional, so that the aforementioned technique of distinction or separation is only appropriate if the portion of the contract in question can

16. Tang. Z, "Law applicable in the Absence of Choice — The New Article 4 of Rome I Regulation" in *Modern Law Review*, MLR Vol. 71, n. 5 (2008), pp. 785-800.

be assessed autonomously in relation to the rest of the contract, and not as a mere appendix of this[17].

Considering now in more detail the Rome II Regulation, its subsidiary value applicable in commercial relations perfected through the network must be recalled. In any case, although the commercial relationship over the Internet must be understood substantially as contractual, the configuration of the Rome II Regulation makes it possible that it does not have to be ruled out from the outset when it comes to playing a decisive role in the online commercial exchanges that we analyze here. Initially, it is necessary to rely on the close interrelationships that the Rome II Regulation knows with other European legal provisions that, without being properly EU-PRIL, do have a very significant impact on it by sharing the same field of action; we refer to Directive 85/374 on the approximation of the laws of the Member States on liability for damage caused by defective products. The Directive considers the manufacturer of the finished product or one of its components, as well as the producer of the material, to be responsible for the damage caused by the defective product, even when he presents himself as a producer by placing his own name or brand on the product or preparation. For products not originating in the EU, similar responsibility is provided for by the importer, regardless of whether said import is for sale or other various forms of distribution. The Directive introduces a modality of strict liability, which the producer can only avoid by offering the corresponding exculpatory evidence.

As a start, the liability between direct contracting parties that could arise from the defects of the thing sold would not fall under the factual assumption of non-contractual damage for products, since it falls under the Law governing the contractual relations (*Lex contractus*); however, non-contractual liability for product damages can be combined with contractual liability in the (apparently rare) cases of a direct sale operated from producer to consumer in which the existence of a prior contractual relationship is obviated. Consequently, non-contractual liability for products would have been introduced by the EU system to overcome the intrinsic limits that determine that mere contractual protection is insufficient. In this regard, it should be noted that the Directive builds its legal regime with respect to limited assumptions, focused on the objective moment of the conduct or adjusted on the causal link; In this way, this EU standard of harmonization of the laws of the Member States would exercise an essential influence in

17. CJEU Case C-133/08, *Intercontainer Interfrigo SC (ICF) v Balkenende Oosthuizen BV, and MIC Operations BV*, 06.10.2009, ECLI:EU:C:2009:617 (TJCE 2009,313).

practice when it comes to identifying the competent jurisdictions in the field of product liability.

The art. 5 of the Rome II Regulation (without prejudice to art. 4.2) provides a meticulous conflict regulation regarding liability for damages caused by defective products, built through a series of successive connection points; however, other options must be ruled out. Previously, it would be necessary to consider giving an opportunity to the Law chosen between the parties, which in fact can only happen when there is a direct contract between the producer and the affected party in the terms seen above, and apart from the conditions of art. 14 on freedom of choice, already studied. Failing that, it would be necessary to resort to the Law of the common country of habitual residence of the presumed responsible party and the injured party at the time in which the damage was verified. If the options just referred to do not report procedural utility, said art. 5 displays certain complementary mechanisms that must not be neglected. By virtue of said precept, it reads: "The law applicable to the non-contractual obligation that arises in the event of damage caused by a product may be : a) the law of the country in which the injured person had his habitual residence at the time of occurrence. the damage, if the product was marketed in said country, or, failing that; b) the law of the country in which the product was purchased, if the product was marketed in said country, or, failing that; c) the law of the country in which the damage occurred, if the product was marketed in that country. However, the applicable law shall be that of the country in which the person whose liability is alleged has his habitual residence if he could not reasonably foresee the marketing of the product or a product of the same type in the country whose law is applicable in accordance with the letters a), b) or c). 2. If from all the circumstances it appears that the harmful event has manifestly closer links with another country other than the one indicated in section 1, the law of this other country will apply. A manifestly closer link with another country could be based on a pre-existing relationship between the parties, such as a contract, which is closely linked to the harmful event in question".

As can be appreciated from the reading of the precept, the described connections allow individualizing the Law in accordance with which the injured party may file his action for compensation, always on the condition that such applicable rule may be foreseeable or known by the producer (we find here the reason why reference is made, as a safeguard clause, to the place of residence of the producer and to the circumstances of the commercialization expressed at the end of the first three options). Surely this rule reflects the presence of Member States within the EU where important production companies dedicated to export are located. On the other hand, as we talk now about liability for products, other provisions would apply, in the case of the common rules of arts. 15 to 22. In particular, the one in art. 17, which assesses about the conduct of the alleged cause of the damage, the safety and conduct standards in force at the time, as well as the place where the occurrence of the harmful event is verified. And it must of course be indicated that any conflict rule of a national nature in this regard that remains formally in force is directly suppressed because of the entry into force of the Regulation.

With reference to this specialized assumption of non-contractual liability for damages caused by defective products, certain conclusions can be drawn regarding jurisdictional competence, for which we must refer again to the Brussels I bis Regulation, in particular points 2 and 3 of its art. 7 (specificities with respect to the common rule of the jurisdiction corresponding to the defendant) and without excluding the use of other passages of greater specialization (for example, the action of the injured party against the insurer of the civil liability of the deceased of art. 13.2). What is most interesting is to address specific competent jurisdictions of points 2 and 3 of art. 7, cited above of the Brussels I bis Regulation in its play with Rome II, weighing its procedural impact for the issue that now concerns us. Consequently: 1)- in matters of civil wrongdoing, considering competent the Judge of the place in which the harmful event has occurred or has presumably been able to occur supposes a novelty that has constituted a significant improvement for consumers affected by said defects or damages with respect to the previous regulation of a conventional nature of non-integration, by giving space to the possibility of taking substantiated actions in relation to the danger that can be deduced, even in advance to avoid, precisely, the materialization of that; and 2) — even in the case of an action for compensation or compensation for damages, or restitution for illegal or criminal abduction, the Judge before whom the criminal action is brought may use the dynamics of the Rome II Regulation in regard to civil action in such contexts of the patrimonial responsibility born of the crime. This also has very interesting guarantee applications when Internet commerce presents its worst face of fraud or fraud (although it must be considered that determining the exact entity and location of the fraudsters seems almost an impossible mission, since it is precisely from the first point where falsehoods begin, an element that is significantly facilitated in the Internet medium).

We will have to consider that the possible specific application of provisions fixing the jurisdictional competence corresponding to that of the place of occurrence of the harmful event are obviously very numerous, and cannot be examined except casuistically, or at least, with respect to particularized factual assumptions. Such an examination therefore operates with a weight that falls significantly on procedural issues of jurisdictional competence such as those addressed above. In the case of damage resulting from defective goods, the place of the generating event coincides with the place of manufacture of the product, while the place where the damage is detected (*locus damni*) coincides with the place where the affected things are found; it is there precisely where the injured party can summon the manufacturer with which he has no contractual relationship. As a secondary option, the seller may be sued by the consumer in application of the guarantees provided for the sold products[18], in interpretation of the previous Brussels I Regulation. Finally, another important aspect that must be determined in the peculiar context of internet commerce concerns the place where the damage occurred. Such an aspect has also played as mean for determining jurisdictional competence and has long been of interest to the work of the High European Court. In some of its pronouncements, EU jurisprudence has confirmed that the place where the initial damage is verified is coincident with the location where the product is used for its appropriate purposes in a relevant manner.

In some factual assumption raised, such place coincided with the establishment in which the purchaser had produced a fertilizer with a defective component, not resulting in significant change that the delivery of said problematic compound had been verified in a different place[19].

V. REVISITING THE CJEU AMAZON RULINGS

Starting by the CJEU of July 28, 2016, *Amazon I*, C-191/15, it mainly deals with questions concerning both applicable Law and jurisdictional competence. The company Amazon EU SRL, established in Luxembourg, carried out electronic sales of goods to consumers established in different Member States. In the main proceedings, the Austrian association for the defense of consumer interests (*Verein für Konsumenteninformation*) had brought an action for injunction, based on Directive 2009/22, and alleging that the contractual clauses used by Amazon were contrary legal prohibitions or best practices. Seized by the Austrian association, the *Oberster Gerichtshof* (Supreme Court, Austria) sought to know whether a clause appearing in the

18. CJEU Case C-45/13, *Andreas Kainz v Pantherwerke AG*, 16.01.2014, ECLI:EU:C:2014:7 (TJCE 2014,4).
19. These nuances can be appreciated in the CJEU Case C-189/08, *Zuid-Chemie BV v Philippo's Mineralenfabriek NV/SA*, 16.07.2009, ECLI:EU:C:2009:475 (TJCE 2009,224).

general conditions of sale of a contract concluded electronically between a professional and a consumer, according to which the law of the Member State of the registered office of this professional governs this contract, is abusive within the meaning of art. 3.1 of Directive 93/13. Furthermore, the *Oberster Gerichtshof* wondered whether the processing of personal data by a company is subject, pursuant to art. 4.1 a) of Directive 95/46, to the law of the Member State to which that undertaking directs its activities.

According to the Court, the Rome I and Rome II Regulations must be interpreted as meaning that the law applicable to such an action for injunction must be determined in accordance with art. 6.1 of the Rome II Regulation, since the infringements to the legal order result from the use of unfair terms. On the other hand, the law applicable to the assessment of the contractual term in question must be determined pursuant to the Rome I Regulation, whether this assessment is carried out in the context of an individual action or in that of a collective action. However, it follows from art. 6.2 of the Rome I Regulation that the choice of applicable law is without prejudice to the application of the mandatory provisions provided for by the law of the country where the consumers whose interests are defended in the means of an injunction. These provisions may include those transposing Directive 93/13, whenever they ensure a higher level of protection for e-consumers[20].

On the other hand, the CJEU of July 10, 2019, *Amazon II*, C-649/17 is more focused on what affects consumer protection. The Amazon EU SRL provokes in this controversy, that the Federal Union of German Consumer Centers and Associations (hereinafter the "Federal Union") had brought before a regional court an action for cessation of Amazon EU's practices in display of the information appearing on its website www.amazon.de and allowing the consumer to contact this company. That judicial office having dismissed that appeal, the Federal Union appealed to a higher regional court, which was also dismissed. As a result, the Federal Union brought an appeal for Revision before the referring judicial instance, the *Bundesgerichtshof* (Federal Court of Justice, Germany). The request for a preliminary ruling concerned the interpretation of art. 6.1, specially as regards its letter c), of Directive 2011/83. First, the Court recalled that the possibility for the consumer to contact the trader quickly and to communicate with him effectively, as provided for in that provision, is of fundamental importance for the safeguarding and effective implementation of consumer rights and particularly the right of withdrawal whose terms and conditions of exercise are indicated in arts. 9 to 16 of this Directive. However, in interpreting that provision, a fair balance

20. Points 59 and 60.

should be struck between a high level of consumer protection and business competitiveness, as set out in art. 4 of Directive 2011/83, while respecting the freedom of enterprise of the entrepreneur, as enshrined in the Charter of Fundamental Rights of the European Union[21].

The CJEU held that it is for the national court to assess whether, including all the circumstances in which the consumer contacts the trader via a website and in particular the presentation and functionality of this site, communication means made available to this consumer by this trader enable the consumer to contact the trader quickly and reach him effectively, in accordance with art. 6.1 c) of the Directive 2011/83[22]. In this regard, the CJEU underlined that an unconditional obligation to make available to the consumer, in all circumstances, a telephone number, or even to set up a telephone or fax line, or to create a new e-mail address for allowing consumers to contact the trader seems disproportionate[23]. The CJEU therefore ruled that the term "when available" in art. 6.1 c) of Directive 2011/83 should be interpreted as meaning that they refer to cases where the trader has a telephone or fax number and does not use them solely for purposes other than contact with consumers. Failing this, this provision does not require him to inform the consumer of this telephone number, or even to set up a telephone or fax line, or to create a new electronic address to allow consumers to contact him[24].

In a second phase, while examining whether that trader may, in circumstances such as those in the main proceedings, use means of communication which are not mentioned in art. 6.1 c) of Directive 2011/83, such as an instant messaging or telephone reminder system, the Court ruled that art. 6.1 c) of Directive 2011/83 must be interpreted as meaning that, Although this provision requires the trader to make available to the consumer such communication channels capable of satisfying the criteria of direct and effective connection, it does not preclude the said trader from providing means useful as to get in touch other than those listed in that provision for the purpose of satisfying those criteria[25].

---

21. Hereinafter the "Charter", points 41 and 44.
22. Point 47.
23. Point 48.
24. Points 51 to 53.
25. Points 52 and 53.

VI. CONCLUSIONS

We would finally remark that the system described, despite its complexity and clearly improvable nature (especially for the sake of a future codifying system through a single body in charge of the EU, can lay the foundations for a Private International Law based on integration) serves in order to provide a versatility and proximity comparable to the mere fact of acquiring goods online, with the immediacy and simplicity that this involves. That same idea of what is accessible and useful must be within the reach of the consumer in the current context of the pandemic, in which online bound relationships are so much reinforced; all this stating once again the integrative legal system as the only feasible and realistic way to face populism and dispersion that irresponsibly try to lead us into backward movement and discord. And it is the actors of the world of Law who must further enhance their work of assisting the Internet consumer through undoubtedly agile, and effective instruments in the face of the challenges posed by the immense virtual ocean of e-commercial transactions.

As far as Europe is concerned, the national Law applicable to electronic commerce, whether by way of contractual or non-contractual liability, will be harmonized under normal conditions by the various Directives, knowing the consumer protection in terms of regulatory choices that are imposed from the outside. The same conditions come with respect to the competent jurisdiction, so that the choice of such jurisdiction is generally excluded as a consumer who must be protected, while avoiding the existence of disparities between the competent jurisdiction and the regulations, potentially strange, that said judicial instance is inclined to apply. The relocation of variables of space and time in electronic commerce therefore deserves, from the point of view of the protective regulations of the European Union, an even more detailed and committed commitment, which every future partner in electronic commerce (China as well) has to weigh and consider. Anyway, it is to be hoped that this context should be seriously assumed by future telemarketers of electronic commerce in relations between the EU and China, not as a unilateral imposition, but as a fruitful exchange in terms of legal certainty for de benefit of e-consumers.

EU Disputes on IP Anti-Suit Injunctions in China: Extraterritoriality, Innovation and Selective Adaptation of the Trips Agreement

EMILIO RAMOS CALZÓN

PhD in Chinese Law, School of Oriental and African Studies, University of London. Lawyer

I. INTRODUCTION

It is not very common for the European Union (EU) to exercise jurisdiction extraterritoriality as opposed to what J. Scott called territorial extension in domains such as climate change, environment, maritime transport, air transport, and financial services regulation[1]. While it is beyond the scope of this chapter the study of extraterritoriality vis-à-vis territorial extension in EU Law, it seems that the term extraterritoriality is a contested concept[2]. In fact, it can be regarded as an Essentially Contested Concept. Precisely, W. B. Gallie who coined the expression Essentially Contested Concepts (ECCs), defined them as those which are impossible, by means "of a rational-logical argument to resolve the disagreement about their meaning and whatever meaning is attached to them is contingent on substantive normative assumptions"[3].

1. Scott, J. "Extraterritoriality and Territorial Extension in EU Law" in *American Journal of Comparative Law*, vol. 62, n. 1, 2014, p. 96. Territorial extension applies in scenarios when "the application of a measure is triggered by a territorial connection but in applying the measure the regulator is required, as a matter of law, to take into account conduct or circumstances abroad".
2. *Ibid.*, p. 89. The term extraterritorial is used in the literature particularly by George Steiner, *Extraterritorial: essays on literature and the linguistic revolution*, Atheneum, 1971. It refers, according to Steiner, to "other languages, and their ideas involved, a consequence of a certain "apatricity"".
3. Gallie, W. B., "Essentially Contested Concepts", in *Proceedings of the Aristotelian Society*, vol. 56, 1956, p. 168. Hurley, following Gallie, refined the idea of ECCs as "appraisive and applicable to objects of an internally complex character that may be described in various ways by altering one´s view of the significance of descriptions of their

At the first glance, the common characteristic of extraterritoriality is the exercise by a state of a prescriptive conduct beyond its boundaries[4]. It is claimed that there must be not only a note of prescription but also that the conduct is to have an impact abroad in accordance with Public International Law and, particularly, international comity[5]. International comity refers, following the US Ninth Circuit case *E. & J. Gallo Winery v. Andina Licores S. A.*, to "the recognition which one nation allows within its territory to the legislative, executive or judicial acts of another nation, having due regard both to international duty and convenience, and to the rights of its own citizens, or other persons who are under the protections of its laws"[6]. This opens the doors to additional forms of the exercise of extraterritorial jurisdiction, not only through prescription, but also by way of i) adjudication, when deciding competing claims beyond the State´s boundaries; and ii) enforcement of a court decision[7].

In addition to prescription, the chapter will treat extraterritoriality in connection to these latter forms of exercise linked to anti-suit injunctions (hereinafter ASIs). Hence, we will look at the disputes raised by the EU around ASIs involving the People´s Republic of China (hereinafter PRC) as a result of a selective outlook of The Agreement on Trade-Related Aspects of Intellectual Property Rights (hereinafter the TRIPs Agreement or TRIPs)

component features. Hurley S., *Natural Reasons*, Oxford, 1989, pp. 46-47. The following conditions are to be met according to Hurley:

i) The contested concept is evaluative in the sense that it implies something valuable.
ii) It is an abstract concept.
iii) The nature of the concept must be internally complex.
iv) The concept is open textured since there are no sharp boundaries.
v) It is not clear whether the meaning chosen is, inter alia, the best, the right or the most worthy

4. According to the Max Planck Encyclopedia of Public International Law [MPEPIL] 'Extraterritoriality' and 'extraterritorial jurisdiction' refer to "the competence of a State to make, apply and enforce rules of conduct in respect of persons, property or events beyond its territory", retrieved from *https://opil.ouplaw.com/display/10.1093/law:epil/9780199231690/law-9780199231690-e1040*
This inevitably mirrors territorial jurisdiction in the sense that, according to para. 402 (1) of The Restatement (Third) of Foreign Law of the United States, it confers authority on a state to prescribe laws with respect to the status of persons, or interests of things, present within its territory.
5. *Ibid.*
6. E. & J. Gallo Winery v Andina Licores S. A. 446 f.3d 984, 991 (9th Circuit 2006). See Contreras, J., "Anti-suit Injunctions in Global FRAND Litigation: The Case For Judicial Restraint" in *Journal of Intellectual Property and Entertainment Law*, vol. 11, n. 1, 2021, p. 174.
7. *Ibid.*

as per the Communication from the EU to China requesting information pursuant to Article 63.3 TRIPs. In other words, the goal of the present chapter is to see as to whether the prescriptive reach of the TRIPs Agreement is flexible enough to accommodate the innovation policies of the PRC in view of the adjudication and enforcement accounts resulting from ASIs endorsed in the field of the mobile industry in the various proceedings in which such injunctions have been applied in recent years by Chinese courts in an extraterritorial way. It is argued that there could be not only adjudication and enforcement but a prescriptive action of the judges in China in line with a different understanding of international comity in view of the flexibilities endorsed in the TRIPs Agreement allowing for technology transfer.

What was described as *"the EU's aversion to extraterritoriality"*[8], has no counterpart in China since it has been generally performed through adjudication and enforcement[9], allegedly consistent with international comity according to the Supreme People´s Court guiding case Huawei v. Conversant. Thus, this chapter intends to clarify such exercise in the light of the Communication from the EU to China by focussing on ASIs and FRAND rates (fair, reasonable and non-discriminatory) of the standards-essential patents of the mobile industry implementing specific innovation policies of the PRC.

The chapter comprises five parts. Part I looks at extraterritoriality by exploring ASIs, linked to standards-essential patents and FRAND royalties in the mobile industry. Part II reviews, inter alia, the legal framework on which anti-suit injunctions are based in China. In addition, it refers to international comity. Part III examines arguments of policy underlying collective innovation goals in China by reference to the quantification of royalties and the extent to which this could impact on innovation. Part IV deals with selective adaptation and flexibilities in the TRIPS Agreement. Part V engages in the analysis of the request for consultations as a result of Article 63.3 TRIPs made by the European Union to the PRC on 18 February 2022 with regard to the measures adversely affecting the protection and enforcement of intellectual property rights as far as anti-suit injunctions and the TRIPS Agreement are concerned. It looks at the different approaches towards extraterritoriality applied in relation to ASIs/FRAND royalties by looking at adjudication and enforcement in view of the selective adaptation and flexibilities of the TRIPs Agreement which could reshape international comity in a prescriptive manner. Part IV ends with some conclusions.

8. *Ibid*, p. 94 95
9. It refers to the EU, regardless of EU Members.

II. EXTRATERRITORIALITY: ANTI-SUIT INJUNCTIONS, STANDARDS-ESSENTIAL PATENTS AND FRAND ROYALTIES

According to Jorge L. Contreras, an anti-suit injunction is "an interlocutory *in personam* remedy issued by a court in one jurisdiction to prohibit a litigant from initiating or continuing parallel litigation in another jurisdiction"[10]. ASIs have been widely used in various jurisdictions on disputes related to patents covering the so-called "standards-essential patents" (hereinafter "SEPs")[11].

Generally Kroeber defined standards as the ways in which "systems and products from different producers can function together"[12]. He suggested that explicit and implicit government policies on standards and intellectual property rights (IPRs) support the entire innovation policy in China[13]. Thus, whilst explicit government policies are based on intellectual property rights protection of proprietary standards that ensure systems and products from different makers can work together; implicit innovation policies have a totally different approach with regard to IPRs and proprietary standards. In this respect, he pointed out that protection of IPRs "has long been seen as a constraint on technology diffusion because it makes products more expensive. And proprietary standards, on the other hand, are increasingly seen as a potential way for China to strengthen the market position of domestic firms and reduce the influence of foreign ones"[14], while seeking to open international markets. The ways in which proprietary standards incorporate domestic patents reflect those indigenous innovation policies endorsed, inter alia, in the National Medium-and-Long Term Plan for the Development of Science and Technology (hereinafter the MLP) (in place between 2006-2020 during the major Chinese ASIs cases to which the EU Communication refers). This document provided that the State has to "establish a platform to service standards, support and speed up the transformation of advanced foreign standards into domestic standards, and give key support to enterprises that promote the formation of technological standards with ourselves as the dominant factor through re-innovation".

The conflict arises when standards and IPRs overlap in cases where a standard, broadly used by the industry, contains some kind of patent to make

10. Contreras, J., "Anti-suit Injunctions in Global FRAND Litigation […]", *op. cit.*, p. 174.
11. *Ibid.*, p. 172
12. *Ibid.*, p. 44
13. Kroeber, A., "China's push to innovate in information technology" in *Innovation with Chinese Characteristics: High-Tech Research in China*, 2007, p. 44.
14. *Ibid.*

it workable[15]. As a result of being proprietary, it involves the payment of a fee to the patent holders. And this is the case with SEPs particularly used in the context of the mobile industry which requires licenses to exploit patents incorporating 3G, 4G and 5G proprietary standards while ensuring that the terms of the licenses are to be "fair, reasonable and non-discriminatory" ("FRAND").

Arguably, the use of ASIs for SEPs/FRAND purposes encourage the promotion of indigenous innovation. In fact, there seems to be a relationship between both in achieving this aim. While it was suggested that proprietary standards were implemented in China as "a narrow IPR regime which can be made to benefit only domestic and not foreign firms"[16]; the policies underlying SEPs in the mobile industry looks towards a more globalized approach.

In this context, the Chinese government encourages domestic companies to foster core technologies able to turn into proprietary international standards from which they can obtain royalties[17]. Before this happens, however, there must be a reverse process through which Chinese companies are due to pay royalties meeting what they consider the most favorable FRAND test.

Thus, some problematic issues arise when royalties do not seem to comply with one party´s expectations leading to a sort of a jurisdictional race in order to find the more convenient *forum* to determine the best FRAND rates[18]. Hence, the importance of ASIs as a spearhead used to challenge prices significantly higher compared to those adopted in courts of the People's Republic of China and more in line with the expected FRAND rates of the plaintiff (usually a Chinese company).

To achieve this goal, courts in China over the past years, and with the guidance of the Supreme People´s Court, have been accommodating the Civil Procedural Law (hereinafter CPL) to make global -and thus extraterritorial- the setting of the FRAND rates in SEPs disputes to the extent that such patents endorsing proprietary standards (3G, 4G, 5G) have a worldwide impact involving, at the same time, multinationals of the mobile industry. Due to the contractual nature of the disputes, extraterritoriality is more akin to the twofold modes of its exercise through adjudication and enforcement that ASIs provide[19]. This is to say that the prohibition imposed by a Chinese

15. *Ibid.*, p. 45
16. *Ibid.*
17. *Ibid.*, p. 63
18. Contreras, J., "Anti-suit Injunctions in Global FRAND Litigation [...]", *op. cit.*, p. 174.
19. Scott, J. "Extraterritoriality and Territorial Extension in EU Law", *op. cit.*

court when issuing ASIs refraining litigants from commencing or carrying on proceedings in third countries jurisdictions, essentially implies not only the adjudication practice, but interim enforcement measures of the courts decisions as well. To carry out this prohibition, the CPL enables courts to impose daily penalties, in a cumulative manner, often reaching the maximum allowed by this procedural Law.

III. LEGAL BASIS AND JUDICIAL REFERENCE OF ANTI-SUIT INJUNCTIONS: WIDENING THE SCOPE OF ARTICLE 100 OF THE CIVIL PROCEDURAL LAW. INTERNATIONAL COMITY

The legal reference on which ASIs is based is Article 100 of the CPL (2017 amendment) which allows a Chinese court to issue an interim measure in order to preserve certain conduct, as follows:

> "For a case where, for the conduct of a party or for other reasons, it may be difficult to execute a judgment or any other damage may be caused to a party, a people's court may, upon application of the opposing party, issue a ruling on preservation of the party's property, order certain conduct of the party or prohibit the party from certain conduct; and if no party applies, the people's court may, when necessary, issue a ruling to take a preservative measure. A people's court may order the applicant to provide security for taking a preservative measure and, if the applicant fails to provide security, shall issue a ruling to dismiss the application. After accepting an application, a people's court must, if the circumstances are urgent, issue a ruling within 48 hours; and if it rules to take a preservative measure, the measure shall be executed immediately".

The problem should not be the internal impact of "the conduct of a party" to which the interim measure refers, but the exercise of jurisdiction over the foreign conduct of non-Chinese nationals in a third jurisdiction, even when the non-national is also resident or established in the PRC and the dispute relates to a global licence over patents in a SEPs/FRAND contractual scenario. The landmark decision of the Supreme People´s Court of August 28, 2020 in the well-known case Huawei v. Conversant interpreted Article 100 CPL giving leeway to grant ASIs in such a context, by explicitly saying that "before this Court renders the final judgment in the three pending cases, Conversant Wireless Licensing GmbH will not seek enforcement of the first instance judgment of the Düsseldorf District Court of the Federal Republic of Germany of August 27, 2020".

The basic facts of the case are the following. Huawei brought an action on 25 Jan 2018 before the Jiangsu Nanjing Intermediate Court seeking to determine FRAND rates on 2G, 3G, 4G SEPs owned by Conversant. Conversely, Conversant asked for a counteraction before the Düsseldorf Court, Germany, on 20 April 2018 claiming that Huawei had infringed the same type of SEPs. On 16 Sept 2019, the Chinese court set a FRAND rate much lower for the SEPs portfolio compared to the judgment that the Düsseldorf Court took on 27 Aug 2020. The former decision was appealed before the Supreme People´s Court on 18 Nov 2019. As said, on 27 Aug 2020, the German Court found Huawei liable for infringement and likewise fixing a much higher FRAND rate up to 18.3 times compared to that granted by the Chinese court. Huawei applied to the Supreme People´s Court for an ASI seeking to avoid the enforcement of the Dusseldorf court judgment. The Supreme People´s Court issued the ASI having in mind the following:

— such enforcement would have a negative impact on the case pending in Chinese court;

— it prevents irreparable harm to Huawei;

— the measure would not significantly damage to Conversant compared to the damage that Huawei would have if the ASI is no issued;

— the ASI will not have an impact on public interest and international comity.

Huawei v. Conversant is considered one of the "guiding case" in this area of law. According to FaFa (2010) No. 51 of Provisions of the Supreme People's Court Concerning Work on Guiding Cases, promulgated by the SPC, "People's courts at all levels should refer to the Guiding Cases released by the Supreme People's Court when adjudicating similar cases"[20]. The 2019-2023 Five-Year Plan for the reform of People's Courts has strengthened the guiding case system by encouraging the reporting, selection, publication and evaluation of cases.

In the absence of the doctrine of the binding precedent, and with the purpose of avoiding the disparity of outcomes in similar cases, the Judicial Interpretations of the Supreme People's Court play a major role in that they

20. First Guiding Case on Intellectual Property. As Finder pointed out, before that, in practice, however, even non-Guiding Cases were used as a source of reference, establishing "a type of soft precedent frequently used by Chinese legal professionals in a variety of ways, with the intellectual property courts taking the lead. Senior judges involved are careful to distinguish China's case law system from the Anglo-American precedential system". Finder, S., "China's Evolving Case Law System In Practice" in *Tsinghua China Law Review*, vol. 9, n. 2, 2017, p. 1.

not only provide guidance, for example, in the application of intellectual property laws and regulations, but also include exhaustive provisions to the extent, according to Clark, that they "are more akin to legislation and generally interpreted by the courts as such"[21]. The Judicial Interpretation issued by the Supreme People´s Court with regard to ASIs, namely "Supreme People´s Court´s Provisions on Several Issues Concerning the Application of Law in Examining Act Preservation Cases in Intellectual Property Disputes" (approved by the 1755th conference of the judicial committee of the Supreme People´s Court on 23 November 2018 -Fa Shi 2018 No 21) offer additional guidelines to the extent that the Request for Consultations made by European Union to China on 22 February 2022 in the ambit of Disputes Settlement mechanism of the WTO in relation to the worldwide use of ASIs, considers it as one of the legal instruments "through which China imposes and administers these (ASIs) measures"[22].

Importantly, the decision, with regard to the international comity states the following:

> "When considering the factor of international comity, a court can examine the time sequence of case acceptance, whether the case jurisdiction is appropriate, whether the impact on the trial and judgment of extraterritorial courts is moderate, etc. In terms of the time of acceptance, the court of first instance accepted the three cases in January 2018, and the Court of Düsseldorf accepted the related German lawsuit in April 2018. The three cases were accepted first. Meanwhile, to prohibit Conversant from applying for enforcement of the Düsseldorf court's relevant judgment before the issuance of final judgment in these three cases neither affects the subsequent trial on the German case nor detract from the legal validity of the German judgment, only suspending the enforcement of it, and the impact on Düsseldorf court trial and the judgment is within a moderate extent".

This shows that the comity, such as extraterritoriality as it was mentioned earlier, is an Essentially Contested Concept. Actually, comity was generally considered an "elusive concept" like beauty, which is sometimes "in the eye of the beholder," as the decision on ASIs of the US First Circuit in the *Quaack* case noted[23]. In this American case, it was also mentioned that such interim measure can be justified when it safeguards important national policies[24], which could be applied to innovation policies too.

21. Clark, D., *Patent Litigation in China*, Oxford: Oxford University Press, 2011, p. 9.
22. WT/DS611/1 IP/D/43 G/L1427
23. The US First Circuit case Quaack v. Klynveld Peat Marwick Goerdeler 361 F 3d at 18-19. *Loc. cit.* Daniel Tan, D., "Anti-Suit Injunctions and the Vexing Problem of Comity" in *Virginia Journal of International Law*, vol. 45, n. 2, 2005, pp. 283-356.
24. *Ibid.*

IV. CHINESE INNOVATION POLICIES IN RELATION TO ASIS AND DISSUASIVE PENALTIES

This part examines as to whether the use of ASIs vis-à-vis proprietary standards encourage the promotion of indigenous innovation when imposing penalties to the party who does not voluntarily accept the interim measure to be implemented in the jurisdiction abroad, as in Huawei v. Conversant.

In effect, in Huawei v. Conversant, the Supreme People´s Court imposed the maximum amount allowed by Article 115 CPL, that is, one million yuan per day in a cumulative manner, an amount sufficiently dissuasive for the defendant. Article 115 reads as follows:

> "The amount of a fine on an individual shall not be more than 100,000 yuan. The amount of a fine on an entity shall not be less than 50,000 yuan but not be more than 1 million yuan".

This recalls the use that has been generally made of economic measures in China to promote indigenous innovation in various distinctive ways, in particular damages in patent infringement cases. Thus, the so-called statutory damages as the last of the possible options of the former Article 65 of the Patent Law gave ample discretion to Chinese Courts when granting damages between RMB 10,000 to 1,000,000 (nowadays up to a maximum of 5,000,000 RMB after the fourth amendment). Actually, the amounts usually granted were generally very low compared to the fine imposed in antitrust cases[25]. This last resort offered by the former Article 65 of the Patent Law was the most commonly applied by courts in China over the past years to the extent that judges in 99% of patent infringement cases involving damages awarded statutory compensation; whereas only 1% of the decisions took patentee's actual losses as the basis for the calculation of compensation[26]. In

25. Cohen argued that the average of damages -and based on a sample of 511 cases collected by CIELA between the years 2006 and 2013- were around 419,366 RMB (70,000 US dollars) which is about 1/10,0000 of the fine imposed on an antitrust cases, such as the Qualcom case. In this respect, he concluded that this disproportionality between antitrust damages and patent damages showed an aggressive antitrust enforcement in China that could disincentive licensing in contrast to an IP system fundamentally weak that can favor the free-riding phenomenon. Qualcomm announced on 9 February 2015 that reached a resolution with China's National Development and Reform Commission (NDRC) regarding the NDRC's investigation of Qualcomm under China's Antimonopoly Law (AML). The NDRC has issued an Administrative Sanction Decision finding that Qualcomm has violated the AML. See Cohen, M., "*IPR Abuse and Refusals to License*", 2016, retrieved from *https://chinaipr.com/2016/03/13/ipr-abuse-and-refusals-to-license/*

26. Ningxin, H. et al. "Empirical Studies on the Effectiveness of the Patent Infringement Compensation Mechanism", in *Scientific Research and Management*, vol. 4, 2012. More

the case of ASIs, there is a dual approach that combines penalties to dissuade the defendant of a potential breach of the mandate and low FRAND rates to facilitate the absorption of foreign technology endorsed in SEPs.

Kong coined the term "gradualism" to describe the adaptation of IPRs protection standards to the level of technological development and their enforcement through the judicial system but with the guidance of the Chinese Communist Party[27]. Similarly, the term gradualism enlightens the various ways in which China has fashioned indigenous innovation in the eyes of collective innovation goals articulated in the MLP and the Plan Made in China 2025. It is arguable that Chinese IP polices appear to be a key element in how IPRs are protected in accordance with the level of innovation that the country demands, in line with the MLP and other national IP strategy documents which shed light to many of the provisions of patents[28]. Mutatis mutandis, this is equally applicable to the ASIs measures of enforcement and adjudication whilst acknowledging FRAND low rates that help Chinese companies to increase their innovative capacity in the mobile industry. The MLP (in place until 2020, overlapping the major Chinese ASIs cases that the EU refers in its communication) defined indigenous innovation as "enhancing original innovation, integrated innovation, and re-innovation based on assimilation and absorption of imported technology, in order improve our national innovation capability" while calling for "restricting blind and duplicative technology importation". Such statements were crucial in that they described the principal goals of the MLP underpinning China´s national patent law strategy. As it can be inferred, indigenous innovation, according to the MLP, encompasses three types of innovation while highlighting the importance of the assimilation and absorption of foreign technology. These assumptions are extensible to the mobile sector. The need of absorption in the mobile industry is reflected gradually in the three stages of the 3G, 4G and 5G standards.

---

recently, there is a tendency to award damages based on actual losses of the patent holder while the amounts are significantly increased, particularly since the fourth amendment of the Patent Law was in force since June 1st, 2021. This amendment introduced a presumption relying on the claims and the evidence presented by the plaintiff in case the defendant would not cooperate in the submission of the account books and materials related to the act of infringement in order to determine the actual losses of the plaintiff

27. Kong, Q., "The Political Economy of the Intellectual Property Regime-Building in China: Evidence From the Evolution of the Chinese Patent Regime" in Global Business & Development Law Journal, vol. 21, n. 1, 2008, p. 114.

28. Ramos Calzón, E., *Patentes e Innovación en China: cómo se fraguó jurídicamente el cambio tecnológico*, Editorial Aranzadi/Thomson Reuters, 2022.

In the case of the 3G standard, the Chinese government's attempt to make TD-SCDMA the exclusive standard was not very welcome by Chinese companies since they preferred mobile international standards instead as a way of expanding their business abroad while maintaining the position in the national market[29]. Likewise, 4G has its own standard in China, the so-called TD-LTE system which has been used -to some extent- by some mobile operators outside China, such as Sprint in the US and Soft Bank in Japan and even in India led, in this case, by Qualcomm and its local partners[30]. Notwithstanding, Chinese mobile phone manufacturers like Huawei and ZTE require 4G standards widely accepted in the rest of the world, in particular the FDD-LTE standard. It explains the use of ASIs seeking to adjust the transfer price in FRAND terms for both 3G and 4G SEPs. This led to the current 5G stage much more proactive in that China has positioned itself with its own 5G standards internationally to the extent that Huawei has contributed to widespread its standards competing with Ericsson and Nokia. Still, the real impact of Huawei´s technology largely depends on the innovative value of its patents, which caused some legal conflicts with Nokia[31], and, at the end of the day, needed the absorption of foreign technology via ASIs. Additionally, ASIs were employed to deter Ericsson from licensing 5G SEPs in the below case Samsung v Ericsson dealt by the Wuhan Intermediate People's Court.

Such three stages are reflected in the five ASIs cases collected in the Communication from the EU to China requesting information pursuant to Article 63.3 TRIPs. The commonalities of all cases are the determination of FRAND rates of SEPs through ASIs with an extraterritorial impact. To avoid unnecessary repetitions, reference is made to the facts of the cases endorsed in the Communication, except for some details below. In addition to the Supreme People´s Court decision -Huawei v Conversant- that served as a guiding case for Intermediate People's Courts to outline ASIs in such a way, the following are the cases mentioned in the EU Communication:

i) *Xiaomi v InterDigital — Wuhan Intermediate People's Court (3G, 4G) (2020)*

The aim of the ASI, inter alia, was to avoid irreparable damage, understanding that this does not violate the legitimate interests of the other party.

29. Kroeber, A., "China's push to innovate in information technology", *op. cit.*, p. 65.
30. Bischoff, P., "*How deliberately crippling its 4G rollout will help China bust a global monopoly and make billions*", 2014, retrieved from *https://www.techinasia.com/china-telco-protectionism-4g-mobile-unicom-telecom-td-lte*
31. Dano, M., "*Study: Huawei was the biggest contributor to 5G standards*", 2020, retrieved from *https://www.lightreading.com/5g/study-huawei-was-the-biggest-contributor-to-5g-standards/d/d-id/758279*

ii) *ZTE v Conversant — Shenzhen Intermediate People's Court (4G) (2018-20)*

As a result of the ASI, Conversant reached a FRAND agreement between the two parties. On November 2, 2020, ZTE withdrew its petition from the Shenzhen Intermediate Court, prior to Conversant's withdrawal of the lawsuit made before the Düsseldorf Court against ZTE.

iii) *OPPO v Sharp — Shenzhen Intermediate People's Court (3G, 4G) (2020-21)*

OPPO requested the Shenzhen Intermediate People's Court to take various measures to implement a prohibition addressed to Sharp and its subsidiaries to prevent:

— the request, in turn, of permanent or provisional measures or other similar protection measures in third countries, with clearly extraterritorial purposes (anti-anti suit injunctions AASIs);

— the filling of lawsuits for infringement of SEPs patents against OPPO with regard to 3G and 4G standards.

iv) *Samsung v Ericsson — Wuhan Intermediate People's Court* (4G, 5G) (2020-21)

The Wuhan Intermediate People's Court agreed to issue an ASI with the following measures prohibiting Ericsson from requesting:

— an injunction against Samsung regarding its 4G and 5G patents before any other court inside or outside of China (AASI);

— the enforcement of pre-existing resolutions related to licenses in third countries;

— to ask any other court, inside or outside China, to order Samsung to withdraw its ASI application.

V. SELECTIVE ADAPTATION AND FLEXIBILITIES IN THE TRIPS AGREEMENT

TRIPs provisions were very often viewed as "externally dictated transplants"[32] and the outside coercion used in their implementation[33], in

32. Miller, J. M., "A Typology of Legal Transplants: Using Sociology, Legal History and Argentine Examples to Explain the Transplant Process" in *The American Journal of Comparative Law*, vol. 51, n. 4, 2003, p. 847. See in this regard Shi, W., "Globalization and Indigenization: Legal Transplant of a Universal Trips Regime in a Multicultural World" in *American Business Law Journal*, vol. 47, n. 3, 2010.

33. Foster N. H. D., "Company Law Theory in Comparative Perspective: England and France" in *The American Journal of Comparative Law*, vol. 48, n. 4, 2000, p. 612 et seq.

countries with a legal background and values in conflict with WTO's goals. It recalls Watson's theory of legal transplants[34], and echoes Twining's ideas about cultures or social orders that are never impermeable or sealed-off, but subject to the influence of outside forces evolving into sub-systems which interact with other referents in very dynamic and complex ways[35]. It is interesting to see that in literature, for instance, it was introduced the term "contact zones", coined by Pratt, "as those semiotic spaces in which the local meets the global and new realities are produced"[36].

Generally, WTO economic liberalism pursues the lifting of market restrictions and trade barriers together with the protection of private property (in particular IPRs) by fostering the enactment of specific laws at domestic level incorporating such goals. The addressee then has to formally accept this bulk of economic liberal reforms whilst, in the case of China, constitutionally applying other competing values such as those underpinning the socialist market economy where the public property is the benchmark[37]. This is what more generally D. Dicke called dualism as opposed to monism since the incorporation by the recipient of a specific system of laws clashes with domestic values[38].

Potter in his 2007 paper "China and the International Legal System: Challenges of Participation" explained, under the perspective of the selective adaptation analysis, the responses given by China to international obligations derived from the TRIPs Agreement, in particular. Thus, Potter after examining

34. Watson, A., *Legal Transplants: An Approach to Comparative Law,* London: University of Georgia Press, 1993, p. 21.
35. Twining, W., *Globalisation and Legal Theory*, Cambridge: Cambridge University Press, 2000, p. 85.
36. Pratt, M. L., *"Arts of the Contact Zone"* in *Profession*, 1991, pp. 33-40.
37. Expressly, Article 6 of the current Constitution of the PRC provides that "The basis of the socialist economic system of the People's Republic of China is socialist public ownership of the means of production, namely, ownership by the whole people and collective ownership by the working people". Adopted at the Fifth Session of the Fifth National People's Congress and promulgated for implementation by the Announcement of the National People's Congress on December 4, 1982. Amended in accordance with the Amendments to the Constitution of the People's Republic of China adopted respectively at the First Session of the Seventh National People's Congress on April 12, 1988, the First Session of the Eighth National People's Congress on March 29, 1993, the Second Session of the Ninth National People's Congress on March 15, 1999 and the Second Session of the Tenth National People's Congress on March 14th, 2004, retrieved from *http://www.npc.gov.cn/englishnpc/Constitution/node_2825.htm*
38. Dicke, D., "Public International Law a New Economic Order" in Sarcevic, P. (ed.) and Van Houtte, H. (ed), *Legal Issues in international Trade*, 1990, p. 23.

the institutional capacity and the legal culture in relation to China´s law reform, concluded that selective adaptation helps to explain how compliance with international norms remains contextualized to domestic conditions and local imperatives[39]. Generally, selective adaptation is defined by reference to the variations experienced domestically in the reception of international legal standards by an interpretative community. He argued that the Chinese recipient interpretative community tends to adjust WTO standards for domestic application in accordance with its own normative perceptions[40].

Yu, Contreras and Yang pointed out that Chinese ASIs are legal transplants borrowed from other jurisdictions, particularly the US, by selectively adapting the interim measure enabling China to lead the development of global SEP standards[41]. Some issues are raised in view of the selective adaptation of ASIs. Firstly, to what extent such adjustment is consistent with the adaptative endorsement of TRIPs Agreement in the eyes of the flexibilities contained therein which potentially would allow to accommodate the innovation policies of the PRC and eventually facilitate the technology transfer. Subsequently, whether the role that Chinese courts is playing as regards ASIs reshapes international comity through prescription in view of the adjudication and enforcement accounts resulting from ASIs applied by these courts in an extraterritorial way. Thislatter query will be addressed towards the end of the chapter.

Selective adaptation undoubtedly mirrors flexibilities in the TRIPs Agreement. Such flexibilities enable China, as a WTO Member, to explicitly incorporate innovation policy goals according to its patent law implementation strategy following the landmark decision *US-India Mailbox*[42]. Thus, WTO Members are free to implement public policies on development regardless of the economic expectations of foreign patentees, as long as such policies comply with TRIPS standards[43].According to Reichman, the mentioned *US-India Mailbox* decision enables countries to freely endorse their own IP laws and policies not specifically harmonized by the set of TRIPs standards[44], strengthening consequently the residual faculties of the

39. Potter, P., "China and the International Legal System: Challenges of Participation" in *The China Quarterly*, vol. 191, 2007, pp. 699-715.
40. *Ibid.*
41. Yu, P. K, et al., "Transplanting Anti-Suit Injunctions" in *American University Law Review*, vol. 71, 2022, p. 1537.
42. Appellate Body, WT0 doc. WT/D550/AB/R 19 December 1997 (97-5539)
43. *Ibid.*
44. Reichman, J. H., "Securing Compliance with the TRIPS Agreement after US V India" in *Journal of International Economic Law*, vol. 1, 1998, pp. 585-601.

states within the reserved powers of Article XX (d) GATT 1994[45]. except for the so-called black letter rules contained in the TRIPs Agreement[46].

Article 1.1 TRIPs also states that "Members shall be free to determine the appropriate method of implementing the provisions of this Agreement within their own legal system and practice" requiring, in accordance with the Appellate Body in the referred *US-India Mailbox* decision, to "provide a sound legal basis" of implementation[47], although this is not the same however as self-certification of compliance with TRIPS obligations[48].

TRIPs in-built flexibilities let WTO Members implement the Agreement in such a way that contributes to the social and economic welfare and to a balance of rights and obligations as per Article 8 TRIPs. So, the issue of technology transfer in the TRIPs Agreement turns crucial in view of the flexibilities by pondering the intellectual property standards of protection that WTO members must incorporate in their domestic laws[49]. In this regard, Article 7 TRIPs provides that "the protection and enforcement of intellectual property rights should contribute to the promotion of technological innovation and to the transfer and dissemination of technology, to the mutual advantage of producers and users of technological knowledge and in a manner conducive to social and economic welfare, and to a balance of rights and obligations". In fact, as Matthews pointed out, patents can hamper development if they only pay attention to the inventive process and the avoidance of the free-riding problem as there is a need to achieve a balance between "rewarding inventors and safeguarding the public domain for a wider public good"[50].

---

45. Article XX (d) GATT 1994 says that "(...) nothing in this Agreement shall be construed to prevent the adoption or enforcement by any contracting party of measures: d) necessary to secure compliance with laws or regulations which are not inconsistent with the provisions of this Agreement, including those relating to customs enforcement, the enforcement of monopolies operated under paragraph 4 of Article II and Article XVII, the protection of patents, trademarks and copyrights, and the prevention of deceptive practices".
46. Reichman, J. H., "Securing Compliance with the TRIPS Agreement after US V India", *op. cit.*, p. 596.
47. India — Patent Protection for Pharmaceutical and Chemical Agricultural Products, Report of the Appellate Body, 19 December 1997, WT/DS50/AB/R, para.70
48. The UNCTAD-ICTSD Project on IPRs and Sustainable Development 2005.
49. Reichman, J. H., "Universal Minimum Standards of Intellectual Property Protection Under the TRIPS Component of the WTO Agreement" in *International Lawyer*, vol. 29, n. 2, p. 345.
50. Matthews, D., "Patents in the Global Economy" in *School of Law. Legal Studies Research Paper*, n. 73, 2010, p. 1.

VI. THE REQUEST FOR CONSULTATIONS MADE BY THE EUROPEAN UNION TO CHINA IN THE AMBIT OF DISPUTES SETTLEMENT MECHANISM OF THE WTO IN RELATION TO THE WORLDWIDE USE OF ASIS[51]

While Article 27 of the Brussels Convention on the jurisdiction and the recognition and enforcement of judgements in civil and commercial matters forbids the ASI mechanism[52] (prohibition confirmed by the Court of Justice of the European Union as it interferes with the jurisdiction of a foreign court)[53]; the EU should have considered in its request for consultations made to China on 22 February 2022 that ASIs could have challenged the selective adaptation of the TRIPs Agreement beyond its flexibilities in the context of disputes settlement mechanism of the WTO in relation to the worldwide impact of ASIs. However, this was not the case. Neither did the 8 June 2023 document submitted by the EU entitled "The First Written Submission before the Panel,"[54] even though it refers to Article 7 TRIPs generally.

The EU alleged in the Request a breach of Articles 63(1) and 63(3) TRIPs together with a violation, inter alia, of the following provisions:

— Articles 28 granting exclusive rights to the patent holder.

— Article 41 since China's measures would create barriers to legitimate trade avoiding safeguards of the abuse of enforcement procedures.

— Article 44 because China's measures prevent, or seek to prevent, the judicial authorities of the other Members from ordering a party to desist from an infringement at the request of patent owners involved in patent litigation in China.

The Request and the subsequent Consultations to China may have opposite interpretations which, at the end of the day, may be complementary if we look at ASIs with a dual approach depending on China´s stage of development. While it could be argued that China still needs of the foreign

51. WT/DS611/1 IP/D/43 G/L1427

52. Article 27 of the Brussels Convention (Regulation 1215/2015) it was interpreted in the sense that once a procedure has commenced in a court of any EU Member State, all other EU courts must deny jurisdiction over parallel actions the EU. See Bonadio, E., and Lucchi, N., "Antisuit Injunctions in SEP Disputes and the Recent EU's WTO/ TRIPS Case Against China" in Journal of World Intellectual Property, 2023, p. 4.

53. CJEU Case C-159/02, *Gregory Paul Turner v Felix Fareed Ismail Grovit*, 27.04.2004, ECLI:EU:C:2004:228.

54. DS611

technology which would require giving weight to Articles 7 and 8 of the TRIPs Agreement; ASIs can be regarded as an efficient tool to increase China´s level of technology allowing the absorption of foreign technology by paying low royalties rates and enabling re-innovation and co-innovation processes as the MLP demands. The injunction can be also considered an extraterritorial instrument to apply Chinese Law, not only procedurally but in a substantive and a prescriptive way[55], by incorporating those TRIPS flexibilities fostering technology transfer with an impact in international comity.

So, whereas Article 7 (Objectives) and Article 8 (Principles) of the TRIPs Agreement are key tools of interpretation of the Agreement with regard to the protection and enforcement of intellectual property rights as this *should* contribute to the promotion of technological innovation and to the transfer and dissemination of technology allowing Members to take measures to promote the public interest in sectors of vital importance, inter alia, to their technological development; the scope of Articles 7 and 8 is to be seen in relation to Article 32 of the Vienna Convention on the Law of Treaties which demands avoiding "results which are manifestly absurd or unreasonable". This enlightens their interpretation from the perspective of customary rules of public international law (where their codification in the Convention is acknowledged by the GATT/WTO jurisprudence). On the other hand, Article 31 of the Vienna Convention provides that "a treaty is to be interpreted in good faith in accordance with the ordinary meaning to be given to the terms of the treaty in their context and in the light of its object and purpose".

In *United States — Section 211 Omnibus Appropriations Act of 1998,* the Panel claimed that "Article 7 of the TRIPS Agreement states that one of the objectives is that "[t]he protection and enforcement of intellectual property rights should contribute...to a balance of rights and obligations". We consider this expression to be a form of the good faith principle"[56]. Thus, the principle of good faith seems to work along with the objective of weighing rights and obligations when Member states seek to protect and enforce IPRs.

55. For example, in Microsoft v Motorola the ASI awarded was linked to a dispute in the US considered a dispositive in nature over a German matter concerning a breach of contract and a related infringement. Contreras, J. L., "It's Anti-Suit Injunctions All The Way Down — The Strange New Realities of International Litigation Over Standards-Essential Patents" in *IP Litigator*, vol. 26, n. 4, 2020, p. 1-7.

56. US — s211 (n 8) [8.57]

The *Omnibus* decision is also important because, as Slade pointed out, the Panel not only looked at Article 7 as a tool to implement the "good faith" as a general principle of international law, but also as a way of "balancing of rights and obligations, that up to this point have been conspicuously absent from the reasoning of the WTO tribunals"[57].

It seems to be clear that Articles 7 and 8 of the TRIPs Agreement play a key role in promoting innovation. Likewise, Article 30 of the Agreement makes provision for exceptions to the rights conferred as opposed to Article 28 which gives patentees exclusive rights over their inventions. According to Article 30, the exceptions "do not unreasonably conflict with a normal exploitation of the patent and do not unreasonably prejudice the legitimate interests of the patent owner, taking account of the legitimate interests of third parties".

Nevertheless, Articles 7 and 8 TRIPs are not always viewed as operative provisions, according to Correa[58]. In *Canada — Patent Protection of Pharmaceutical Products,* the Panel alleged that these provisions only had to be "borne in mind" in the context of Article 30 TRIPs dealing with exceptions to patent rights overruling Canada's allegation. Canada argued that Articles 7 and 8 were part of a more general legal and policy approach where the exceptions of Article 30 TRIPs had to be interpreted[59]. Rather than examining which interests deserve more attention other than of the patentee's (for example the public interest) in view of the object and purpose of the Agreement; the Panel grounded its decision on the effect that the exemption of Article 30 TRIPs had on the patent holder[60] while ignoring other interpretative recourses offered by such provisions that would have led to assess "how much society might gain, from a given exception"[61].

In a similar way, "The First Written Submission before the Panel" of 8 June 2023 refers to the Article 7 TRIPs, in the light of the objectives contained therein, by saying that:

57. Slade, A., "Good faith and the TRIPS Agreement: putting flesh in the bones of the TRIPS 'objectives'" in *The International and Comparative Law Quarterly,* vol. 63, n. 2, 2014, pp. 353-383.

58. Correa, C., "Can TRIPs Foster Technology Transfer?" in Maskus, K. (ed.), Reichman, J. H. (ed.), *International Public Goods and Transfer of Technology Under a Globalized Intellectual Property Regime,* Cambridge: Cambridge University Press, 2005, p. 234.

59. *Canada-Patent Protection of Pharmaceutical Products* WT/DS114/R 7.26

60. Okediji, R., "Public Welfare and the Role of the WTO: Reconsidering the TRIPs Agreement", in *Emory International Law Review,* n. 17, 2003, p. 819.

61. Howse, R., "The Canadian Generic Medicines Panel. A Dangerous Precedent in Dangerous Times" in *The Journal of World Intellectual Property,* vol. 3, n. 4, 2000.

> "the obligation of WTO Members to give effect to Article 28.1 of the TRIPS Agreement is not limited to ensuring that patent owners enjoy in their respective territories the exclusive rights conferred by that provision. Members should also refrain from adopting or applying measures that restrict, or seek to restrict, the exercise by patent owners of their exclusive rights in the territories of other Members, in so far as those measures disrupt the carefully balanced system of protection and enforcement of patents laid down in the TRIPS Agreement".

And it concludes the following:

> "the European Union considers that China's anti-suit injunction policy in SEP litigation constitutes, "as such", a severe restriction on the exercise of the rights of the patent owners outwith China and is inconsistent with China's obligations under Article 1.1, first sentence, of the TRIPS Agreement, in conjunction with Article 28.1 of the TRIPS Agreement".

Therefore, neither the Report nor the First Written Submission put forward any substantial argument as for the TRIPs flexibilities in connection with Article 28.1 and 30 of the Agreement, despite mentioning Article 7.

Before, the Panel in *Canada-Patent Protection of Pharmaceutical Products* commenting Article 30 TRIPs clarified that only when the level of interference involves "a small diminution of the right in question"[62] (first condition) and does not "detract significantly from the economic return anticipated from a patent's grant of market exclusivity"[63] (second condition), can be regarded as an acceptable interfering[64]. Likewise, "legitimate interests" of both the patent holder and third parties in Article 30 TRIPs (third condition) are to be interpreted as "interests that are 'justifiable' in the sense that they are supported by relevant public policies or other social norms" seeking a balance between both parties[65]. Nevertheless, for legitimate purposes, it is arguable that judges in China have looked at the referred innovation policies of the MLP underpinning China´s national patent law strategy by outweighing the interests in conflict and therefore favoring the petitioner of the ASI measure. As Endicott argued, the duty of resolution applies even "when the various incommensurable requirements of good judicial decision-making conflict with each other"[66].

62. *Canada-Patent Protection of Pharmaceutical Products* WT/DS114/R, para. 7.30.
63. *Ibid.*, para. 7.55.
64. Torremans, P., "Substantive law issues in Europe a decade after of TRIPs" in *Intellectual property and TRIPS compliance in China: Chinese and European perspectives*, London: Edward Elgar Publishing, 1998, p. 39.
65. *Canada-Patent Protection of Pharmaceutical Products* WT/DS114/R, para. 7.69.
66. Endicott, T., *Vagueness in Law*, Oxford: Oxford University Press, 2000, p. 198.

However, as Piraino pointed out:

> "balancing tests are ill-suited to determine the extraterritorial application (...). These types of tests do not operate well in practice and become problematic for judges. Courts cannot properly judge and *balance* the political factors inherent in balancing tests. Further, these balancing tests-which do not represent rules of international law- have not adequately addressed the comity concerns raised by foreign nations"[67].

By contrast, in Huawei v. Conversant, the Supreme People´s Court examined whether the international comity covers such measure, as follows:

> "(...) to prohibit Conversant from applying for enforcement of the Düsseldorf court's relevant judgment before the issuance of final judgment in these three cases neither affects the subsequent trial on the German case nor detract from the legal validity of the German judgment, only suspending the enforcement of it, and the impact on Düsseldorf court trial and the judgment is within a moderate extent".

Comity is understood in view of the low and temporary impact that ASIs cause. Comity —and extraterritoriality—, in a prescriptive way, can also be seen from the perspective as to how ASIs rely on TRIPs flexibilities promoting technology transfer. Correa in his paper "Can TRIPs Foster Technology Transfer?"[68] tried to answer this question by enumerating some of the ways through which the TRIPs Agreement —and its flexibilities— arguably promotes technology transfer. Here, are the most relevant applicable, in my view, to FRAND cases and eventually to ASIs measures:

i) Article 8.2 allows for measures intended to impede practices which adversely affect the international transfer of technology, for instance, unreasonably high royalties, impeding FRAND rates.

ii) This mirrors the content of Article 40.1 TRIPs which sets out that licensing practices restraining competition "may have adverse effects on trade and impede the transfer and dissemination of technology" Both Articles 8.2 and 40.1 differ each other in that the former does not include dissemination whereas the latter only refers to impediments and not to measures that may adversely affect the transfer of technology[69]. In addition, paragraph 2 of Article 40, dealing with the case-by-case assessment of restrictive practices,

67. Piraino, S. D., "A Prescription for Excess: Using Prescriptive Comity to Limit the Extraterritorial Reach of the Sherman Act" in *Hofstra Law Review*, vol. 40, n. 4, 2012.
68. Correa, C., "Can TRIPs Foster Technology Transfer?", *op. cit*.
69. *Ibid*., p. 236.

has a rather limited scope[70]. In effect, Article 40.2 focuses solely on some of the possible cases that may involve an abuse of IPRs with an adverse impact on competition such as exclusive grant back provisions and coercive package licensing[71]. However, the provision ignores other potential grounds based on the evaluation of limitations on development, beyond national policies in the field of competition, as suggested by the proposal of International Code of Conduct on TT under the UNCTAD[72]. In any case, the consultation system provided by paragraph 3 of Article 40 leaves ample leeway "to the full freedom of ultimate decision of either Member" to solve conflicts in connection with the issues of Article 40. The whole point ii) undoubtedly applies to FRAND rates and ASIs measures.

iii) Correa interpreted "refusal to deal" as an "autonomous" ground within Article 31(b) seen as "the refusal to a voluntary licence as a pre-condition for granting compulsory licences". This wider interpretation could lead to consider ASIs, in my view, as a measure to facilitate "quasi compulsory licensing" since, and following Correra, the merits of Article 31 to grant compulsory licences are not totally limited.

There are various interpretations as regards ASIs. On the one hand, Piraino made an interesting point in relation to the extraterritorial impact of the Sherman Act for antitrust conducts abroad. While applying laws extraterritorially depended upon the comity of nations, "if the conduct is regulated under a comprehensive regulatory scheme, a court should decline to exercise extraterritorially in order to respect that nation's right to regulate its own industries". [73] Yu, Contreras and Yang suggested that Chinese ASIs aim at protecting their own jurisdiction and judicial sovereignty[74].

On the other hand, Bonadio and Lucchi conclude, by summing up different academic opinions, that Chinese ASIs are considered a tool for preventing and reducing the abuse of parallel litigation, and from this viewpoint, ASIs could be deemed as an instrument which allows Chinese courts to make reciprocal arrangements to reinforce and not disturbing international comity; while giving the opportunity to a foreign court to "symmetrically comply with a legally granted Chinese ASI and its refusal

70. *Ibid.*
71. *Ibid.*
72. *Ibid.*
73. Endicott, T., *Vagueness in Law, op. cit.*
74. Yu, P. K, *et al.*, "Transplanting Anti-Suit Injunctions", *op. cit.*, pp. 1537-1618.

to issue a 'neutralising' an anti suit-injuction (AASI), again can promote international comity"[75].

From a different perspective, the extraterritorial effect of ASIs issued by Chinese Courts echoes TRIPs flexibilities allowing for the transfer of technology when calculating FRAND rates for SEPs whilst not disturbing comity since it is arguable that ASIs appear to be consistent with both internal regulations and, inter alia, Articles 8.2 and 40.1 of the TRIPs Agreement.

In the light of the above, it seems that ASIs could reshape comity in such a way that the addressee of the injunction in another jurisdiction would have to accept the measure since it comes from international law. By issuing ASIs, Chinese courts not only adjudicate and try to enforce the remedy extraterritoriality, but also invite for an application of the flexibilities endorsed in the TRIPs Agreement in a prescriptive manner mirroring, if accepts so, the prescriptive comity of the addressed jurisdiction.

VII. CONCLUSIONS

Having in mind that other jurisdictions such as US have issued ASIs for SEPs claims, it is not easy to arrive, according to Bonadio and Lucchi, what will be the decision of the WTO Panel further to the EU request for Consultations to China[76]. Beyond considering ASIs either as a threat to jurisdictional independence of the destination country or a practical vehicle reflecting the judicial autonomy of the country granting ASIs[77]; certainly the role to be played in this regard by the TRIPs flexibilities is crucial in that could foster the transfer of technology through the procedural extraterritorial tool that ASIs mean.

Nevertheless, a first conclusion, following Correa and Maskus, is that the flexibilities do not always help to promote the transfer of technology, except with regard to the access to medicines in non-producing developing countries, particularly after the Doha Declaration on TRIPs and Public Health and the incorporation of Article 31 bis TRIPs[78]. Apart from the role in the context of health issues, Articles 7 and 8 TRIPs seek to strike a balance between

75. Bonadio, E., and Lucchi, N., "Antisuit Injunctions in SEP Disputes and the Recent EU's WTO/TRIPS Case Against China" *op. cit.*

76. *Ibid.*

77. *Ibid.*

78. Matthews, D., "TRIPS Flexibilities and Access to Medicines in Developing Countries: The Problem with Technical Assistance and Free Trade Agreements" in *European Intellectual Property Review*, vol. 28, n. 11, 2005, pp. 420-427, p. 425.

IPRs protection and the promotion of the social and economic welfare more broadly[79]. In this process, Articles 7 and 8 are to be regarded key tools in the interpretation of public. interest flexibilities by giving a development outlook to TRIPs while offering policy space to member states[80]. This entails to interpreter the Agreement in a holistic manner, according to Article 31.1 of the Vienna Convention, by giving meaning and effect to all the terms of a treaty[81], whilst avoiding results manifestly "absurd or unreasonable" in reaching the objective, inter alia, of technology transfer. In this scenario, it is noteworthy that WTO Members are free to define as to how to implement IPR obligations as long as minimum standards set out in TRIPs are met by subsequently allowing them to endorse innovation policies in the context of the patent law implementation strategy in line with the landmark decision *US-India Mailbox*[82].

Although the term public interest is an essentially contested concept (ECC) (like extraterritoriality and comity, as seen); public interest mirrors, in the light of Articles 7 and 8 TRIPs, a public conception of IP[83]. In effect, these provisions appear to depict intellectual property in that way since the protection and enforcement of IPRs have necessarily to contribute to the promotion of public interest in order to foster technological innovation and the transfer and dissemination of technology of Member States, safeguarding therefore the public domain for a wider public good[84].

The patents linked to proprietary standards are essential (SEPs) and the FRAND rates, by definition, are to be fixed fairly and reasonably. Fair and reasonable are vague standards in that they "seem to presuppose a standard but not to set one" leaving an ample grade of discretion in setting the standing[85]. In this scenario of uncertainty, while fixing a sensible rate, it is arguable thathe prescriptive reach of the TRIPs Agreement is flexible enough to accommodate the innovation policies of the PRC demanding the transfer and dissemination of technology as per Articles 7, 8, 40 and 31 TRIPs as generally discussed.

79. The UNCTAD-ICTSD Project on IPRs and Sustainable Development 2005
80. Slade, A., "Articles 7 and 8 of the TRIPS Agreement: A Force for Convergence within the International IP System" in *Journal of International Property Law*, vol. 14, n. 6, 2011, pp. 413-440.
81. US — s211 (n 8) [8.57], p. 19.
82. Appellate Body, WT0 doc. WT/D550/AB/R 19 December 1997 (97-5539)
83. Piraino, S. D., "A Prescription for Excess: Using Prescriptive [...]", *op. cit.*
84. Matthews, D., "Patents in the Global Economy", *op. cit.*
85. Endicott, T., *Vagueness in Law*, Oxford: Oxford University Press, 2000, p. 49.

Although Articles 7 and 8 TRIPs are not always interpreted as operative provisions according to *Canada — Patent Protection of Pharmaceutical Products,* when approaching the exceptions of the exclusive patent rights as per Article 30 TRIPs[86]. there is room enough to consider that China is taking the TRIPs Agreement in such a manner that helps not only to reinforce[87] but also to reshape international comity. Subsequently, ASIs granted by Chinese courts with an extraterritorial impact, not only adjudicate and enforce the interim measure, but also spread a plausible interpretation of TRIPs in the eyes of its in-built-flexibilities in a prescriptive way that favors accordingly a prescriptive comity in the addressed final jurisdiction.

The First Written Submission of the European Union presented before the Panel on 8 June 2023 does nor clarify as to what extent TRIPs flexibilities could operate in the context of ASIs. It confirms that "the European Union further requests, pursuant to Article 19.1 of the DSU, that the Panel recommends that China bring its measures into conformity with the TRIPS Agreement and the Protocol on the Accession of the People's Republic of China".

86. Piraino, S. D., "A Prescription for Excess: Using Prescriptive [...]", *op. cit.*, p. 234.
87. Yu, P. K, et al., "Transplanting Anti-Suit Injunctions", *op. cit.*

III. CLIMATE CHANGE & TAXATION

Construction of EU and China's Blue Partnership for Oceans: Challenges & Opportunities

YOULIN ZHAO
Université catholique de Louvain

I. INTRODUCTION

The 2030 Agenda for Sustainable Development was established by the United Nations in 2015. This 15-year global framework focuses on a comprehensive set of 17 Sustainable Development Goals (SDGs)[1]. SDG 14 focuses on the preservation and responsible utilization of our seas and marine resources. Furthermore, the 2030 Agenda promotes the creation of international partnership as a primary objective to facilitate the achievement of other goals (SDG 17)[2], notably SDG 14, which focuses on the sustainable development of oceans and seas.

During the 20th EU-China Summit on July 16, 2018, China and the EU signed a distinctive maritime partnership agreement, *blue partnership*[3]. The two dominant marine economies globally will collaborate in multiple areas, including the development of a sustainable blue economy and the advancement of sustainable fisheries governance. Furthermore, they will collaboratively tackle issues such as climate change, preventing illegal fishing, and safeguarding the maritime ecological environment[4]. In order to

1. United Nations, Transforming our world: the 2030 Agenda for Sustainable Development, UN, September 2015, retrieved from *https://sdgs.un.org/2030agenda*
2. Singh, G. G. *et al.*, "A rapid assessment of co-benefits and trade-offs among Sustainable Development Goals" in *Marine Policy*, vol. 93, 2018, pp. 223-224.
3. Declaration on the establishment of a Blue Partnership for the Oceans: towards better ocean governance, sustainable fisheries and a thriving maritime economy between the European Union and the People's Republic of China, 16 July 2018, retrieved from *https://sdg.iisd.org/news/eu-china-sign-ocean-partnership/* on 10 March 2022.
4. European Commission, EU and China sign landmark partnership on oceans, 2018, retrieved from *https://ec.europa.eu/newsroom/mare/items/631485* on 11 March 2022.

accomplish the United Nations' 2030 Agenda for Sustainable Development, the European Union (EU) and China have forged a pioneering maritime partnership, making them the first countries or regions to establish such a collaboration[5].

The EU-China Blue Partnership aims to fulfill the obligations of the 2030 Agenda for Sustainable Development. Specifically, Sustainable Development Goal (SDG) 14 aims to preserve and responsibly utilize the oceans, seas, and marine resources to achieve sustainable development, along with other interconnected SDGs. The Sustainable Development Goals aim to eradicate problems that affect society and the environment. Out of all the goals, Sustainable Development Goal 14 is supported by 10 ambitious and specific objectives[6]. For instance, the goals include preventing and significantly reducing marine pollution (14.1); addressing the impacts of ocean acidification (14.3); prohibiting overfishing, illegal, unreported and unreported fishing and destructive fishing practices (14.4); protecting at least 10% of coastal and Marine areas (14.5); developing research capabilities and marine technology transfer (14.A).

The EU and China have been diligently collaborating at both the domestic and global levels to effectively execute the 2030 Agenda and the *Blue Partnership*[7]. It has been a span of six years since the agreement was made, during which there have been both advancements and deficiencies. The writers of this article identify existing deficiencies in both policy and operational aspects and suggest a set of specific measures to rectify them. Both the EU and China should evaluate their existing accomplishments and make necessary adjustments and advancements in order to attain their respective objectives.

5. European Commission, EU and China join forces to improve international ocean governance, 10 September 2019, retrieved from https://ec.europa.eu/oceans-and-fisheries/news/eu-and-china-join-forces-improve-international-ocean-governance-2019-09-10_en on 11 March 2022.
6. United Nationals, Sustainable development goals, *SDGs Transform Our World 2030*, 2015, p. 20.
7. European Parliament, *Europe's approach to implementing the Sustainable Development Goals: good practices and the way forward*, 1 February 2019, p. 6; Yu, S. *et al.*, "Adoption and implementation of sustainable development goals (SDGs) in China — Agenda 2030" in *Sustainability*, vol. 12, 2020, pp. 1-3.

II. DEVELOPMENT OF THE EU-CHINA BLUE PARTNERSHIP AND THE PRIORITY AREAS OF COOPERATION

1. KEY BILATERAL INSTRUMENTS RELATED TO BLUE PARTNERSHIP BETWEEN THE EU AND CHINA

In 2003, EU and China forged a comprehensive strategic partnership, enhancing collaboration across diverse domains like economy, science and technology, politics, and culture[8]. In a 2003 policy document, the EU emphasized that China and the EU, as strategic partners, share a growing interest in collaborating to uphold and advance sustainable development, peace, and stability[9]. Both parties have achieved consistent advancements in their collaboration on maritime affairs, with a particular focus on safeguarding the ecological integrity of the Earth and the marine environment, which are shared concerns. Since 2009, the EU has sought to enhance its dominant position in global governance by bolstering multilateral cooperation grounded in binding international rules. The European Union considers the BRICS countries, particularly China, to be both strategic partners and competitors within the global governance system and the liberal order. The EU aims to foster mutual growth in sustainable development alongside the BRICS countries and other emerging economies. The EU's ability to assume a worldwide leadership role and enhance its international influence in the areas of climate change and environmental protection heavily relies on China's support and collaboration[10]. Without China's involvement, achieving these goals would be challenging for the EU.

In 2010, the Chinese government and the European Commission entered into an agreement known as the Memorandum of Understanding on Establishing a High-Level Dialogue on an Integrated Approach to Maritime Affairs. This agreement resulted in a mutual understanding between the two parties to enhance cooperation in maritime policy[11]. Following the signing of the Memorandum of Understanding, a biennial high-level discourse on a comprehensive approach to ocean affairs commenced since 2013.

8. People's Daily Online, *Wen stresses importance of developing EU-China comprehensive strategic partnership*, 7 May 2004, retrieved from *https://www.mfa.gov.cn/ce/cenz//eng/xw/t94877.htm* on 23 April 2022.
9. European Commission, *A maturing partnership — shared interests and challenges in EU-China relations*, Commission policy paper, COM(2003) 533 final, 2003, p. 1.
10. European Parliament, *Report on the EU foreign policy towards the BRICS and other emerging powers: objectives and strategies*, 2011/2111(INI), 2012, p. 4.
11. Xing, L. (ed.), *China-EU Relations in a New Era of Global Transformatio*, Routledge, 2021, pp. 1-10.

Throughout these discussions, the extent and structure of collaboration continued to broaden[12]. The China-EU 2020 Strategic Cooperation Agenda focuses on and highlights collaboration in the maritime domain. The agenda mandates both parties to enhance exchanges and collaboration in various domains, including integrated ocean management, marine spatial planning, ocean knowledge, ocean observation and surveillance, ocean science and technology research and development, ocean economic development, and ocean energy utilization[13].

In 2018, *EU-China Ocean Blue Partnership: Achieving Better Ocean Governance, Sustainable Fisheries and a Prosperous Ocean Economy* was signed by both parties. This agreement is widely seen as a significant achievement in the field of international ocean governance. The world's two greatest economies have formed a marine cooperation framework for the first time. This framework is built on the principles of equality, respect, and trust, with the goal of enhancing collaboration and achieving mutual benefit and win-win outcomes. The primary objective of the Blue Partnership is to enhance ocean governance, with a specific focus on establishing a sustainable blue economy and attaining the marine environmental conservation targets outlined in the Paris Agreement and the 2030 Agenda, particularly Sustainable Development Goal 14. While the Blue Partnership is not legally enforceable, it presents a valuable opportunity for both sides to improve their global influence and credibility by harnessing substantial economic and environmental benefits. It is noted that the ultimate success of a partnership is on the capacity of both sides to consistently align their actions with their stated principles[14].

2. KEY AREAS OF COOPERATION IN THE EU-CHINA BLUE PARTNERSHIP

2.1. Maritime and Blue Economy

China has always prioritized collaboration with the European Union in the field of port economy and associated maritime sectors. The bilateral commerce volume between China and the European Union surpassed

12. Ministry of Foreign Affairs of People's Republic of China, China's relationship with the EU, October 2020 retrieved from *https://www.fmprc.gov.cn/web/wjb_673085/zzjg_673183/xos_673625/dqzz_673633/oumeng/gx_673639/* on 23 April 2022.
13. Delegation of the European Union to the People's Republic of China, EU-China 2020 Strategic Agenda for Cooperation, 23 November 2013, p. 13.
14. World Wildlife Fund , *All life on Earth depends on our oceans* , retrieved April 24, 2022, from *https://www.wwf.eu/what_we_do/oceans/*.

US$682 billion in 2018, with 60% of this amount being accomplished by maritime transportation[15]. In the last ten years, Chinese private and state-owned enterprises have obtained ownership shares in seaports located in several nations such as Belgium, Germany, Greece, Italy, France, and Spain[16]. The 2020 negotiations about the EU-China Investment Agreement have established standards and possibilities for economic investment cooperation between EU and China in port-related activities. According to the agreement, the 27 member states of the European Union collaborate with China based on standardized cooperation criteria. This reduces the investment expenses for Chinese companies, eliminates obstacles to investment, and facilitates enhanced port trade cooperation between China and the EU. China has reciprocated by pledging to support EU investment in global maritime services. European enterprises will achieve assurance and reliability in their operations across the sectors encompassed, including the eradication of discriminatory practices against foreign companies[17].

Currently, collaboration between China and EU in port operations primarily occurs through the purchase of ownership stakes in European ports by Chinese commercial companies and state-owned enterprises. The primary investors in these joint ventures are COSCO Shipping Ports and China Merchants Ports, both of which are state-owned corporations[18]. COSCO possesses minority interests in container terminals located in Antwerp, Belgium, Las Palmas, Spain, and Rotterdam, the Netherlands,

---

15. Mission of People's Republic of China to European Union, *Speech by Ambassador Zhang Ming at the Closing Ceremony of the First China-EU Blue Partnership Forum*, 7 September 2019, retrieved from https: / / www.mfa.gov.cn / ce / cebe / / chn / stxw / t1695408.htm on 26 April 2022.
16. European Network for Corporate Observatories, *The Corporate Silk Road: A new era of (e-) infrastructure in Europe? COSCO in the port of Zeebrugge*, p. 3; Container News, *COSCO buys 35% stake in Hamburg container terminal*, 21 September 2021, retrieved from *https://container-news.com/cosco-buys-35-stake-in-hamburg-container-terminal/* on 26 April 2022; National Development and Reform Commission (NDRC) People's Republic of China, *Greece's Piraeus port vitalized under BRI cooperation*, 30 December 2021, retrieved from *https://en.ndrc.gov.cn/news/mediarusources/202112/t20211231_1311182.html* on 26 April 2022; German Marshall Fund of the United States, *The Security Implications of Chinese Infrastructure Investment in Europe*, 2021, p. 12; Brussels Diplomatic, *Vado Port: the future of China-Europe relationship*, 19 November 2019, retrieved from *https://brusselsdiplomatic.com/2019/11/19/vado-port-the-future-of-china-europe-relationship/* on 26 April 2022.
17. European Commission, *China and EU reach agreement in principle on investment*, 30 December 2020, p. 2.
18. Ganyi, Z., *Lessons in Hindsight: the Impact of China's European Port Acquisition Strategy*, 7 May 2019, retrieved from *https://market-insights.upply.com/en/lessons-in-hindsight-the-impact-of-chinas-european-port-acquisition-strategy* on 27 April 2022.

within the European Union. COSCO holds majority stakes in container ports located in Piraeus (Greece), Valencia (Spain), Vadoligur Port (Italy), and Zeebrugge (Belgium)[19]. The Piraeus Port project has emerged as a prominent endeavor for China and Greece to collaboratively enhance the port economy as part of the "One Belt, One Road" strategy. Since acquiring the Piraeus Port concession in 2008, COSCO Group has consistently made substantial concession payments to the Greek government on an annual basis, while also generating a significant number of employment opportunities for the local population. The Chinese stakeholders have significantly enhanced and converted the loading and unloading machinery at the Port of Piraeus, resulting in a thorough enhancement of operational efficiency. This facilitates the expansion of Chinese exports to Europe and neighboring regions, concurrently augmenting the import of European goods into China. The Port of Pireas has emerged as a central point for the eastern Mediterranean region as part of the 21st Century Maritime Silk Road Initiative[20].

Since its adoption in 2018, the Blue Partnership has facilitated the steady growth of China-EU port collaboration. This collaboration primarily focuses on two key areas: port economics and port infrastructure. Over time, it has expanded to encompass other domains, including blue economic cooperation. There is ongoing discussion on the meaning of the blue economy[21]. More precisely, the blue economy exhibits the following distinct features: First, the blue economy encompasses both established and growing marine businesses, but it must align with Sustainable Development Goal 14, which emphasizes the preservation and sustainable utilization of oceans and marine resources. Second, the blue economy is a direct result of the green economy concept. The green economy, as discussed at the Rio 20 Summit discussions, refers to the transition of the economic development paradigm towards a sustainable economy. The international world commonly views the blue economy as a sustainable economic model that is well-suited for the growth and conservation of oceans and coastal regions[22]. Third, blue economy is a strategic framework that aims to foster the growth of the marine industry, achieve ecological, economic, and social advantages from

19. Van der Putten, F. P., "European Seaports and Chinese Strategic Influence" in *Clingendael*, vol. 3, 2019, p. 5.
20. Embassy of the People's Republic of China in the Hellenic Republic, *Sino-Greek cooperation in Piraeus Harbour bears fruit*, 11 August 2016, retrieved from *http://gr.chineseembassy.org/chn/ztlm1/zyblafsgxm/t1388538.htm* on 24 May 2020.
21. Wenbo, L. and Xinyi, M., "Maritime Silk Road Port Cooperation Boosts the EU-China Blue Partnership" in *Belt and Road Report*, 2021, pp. 108-111.
22. UNEP, Green Economy in a Blue World, 2012, p. 7.

the marine ecosystem, and incorporate the ecosystem-based management model as the core of decision-making process for industrial and community development.

Since 2012, the blue economy has transitioned into the phase of practical implementation and exploration. Both the European Union and China are dedicated to the advancement of the blue economy[23]. The collaboration between China and the European Union on the carbon trading system serves as a notable illustration of success. Between 2014 and 2020, the European Commission collaborated extensively with China on two consecutive three-year initiatives aimed at assisting in the development and execution of China's carbon trading system. The programs also establish a forum for policy discourse between the European Commission and the Chinese Ministry of Ecology and Environment. At the 2018 China-EU Summit, the EU and China signed a memorandum of understanding to further expand cooperation on carbon emissions trading. The Memorandum of Understanding (MoU) establishes a strong foundation for engaging in policy discussions, as well as fostering additional collaboration through other means, such as jointly conducted workshops and symposiums[24]. The EU's Carbon Border Adjustment Mechanism (CBAM) is expected to serve as a "external incentive" to promote the development of China's national Emission Trading System (ETS)[25].

Moreover, China and the EU can utilize and organize marine science in order to attain a blue economy that is both sustainable and fair. Marine science data play a crucial role in enhancing the understanding of ocean users, their responsibilities and ambitions. Thus far, the development of the blue economy has primarily relied on economic and ecological research[26]. In 2020, China and the EU initiated collaborative initiatives centred on marine data exchange and diplomacy under the framework of the China-EU Blue Partnership. These projects include the EU-China Marine Data Network Partnership (EMOD-PACE) and the China-EU Marine Data Network Partnership (CEMDNET). In January 2021, the two parties signed *a memorandum of understanding (MoU) between the European Ocean Observation and Data Network (EMODnet) and the*

23. Duchâtel, M. and Duplaix, A. S., "Blue China: Navigating the maritime silk road to Europe" in *Policy Brief*, vol. 3, 2018, pp. 10.
24. European Commission, "*International carbon markets can play a key role in cost-effectively reducing global greenhouse gas emissions*", retrieved May 5, 2022, from https://ec.europa.eu/clima/policies/ets/markets_zh.
25. Ivano di Carlo (ed.) EU — China relations at a crossroads, Vol. II: Decoding complexity, mitigating risk, *published under the EU & China Think-Tank Exchanges project* , p. 53.
26. United Nations, *Promoting and strengthening a sustainable ocean economy* , 2021, p. 32.

*Chinese National Oceanic Data and Information Service (NMDIS).*The primary objective of these initiatives is to advance international ocean governance and assist the EU and China in fulfilling their worldwide obligations by enhancing the accessibility and quality of marine data products[27].

2.2. Biodiversity Beyond National Jurisdiction

With the establishment of the Blue Partnership, the EU and China reached a consensus on cooperating to deal with the challenges of marine biological diversity in areas beyond national jurisdiction. For instance, they would make efforts together to elaborate the text of an international legally binding instrument under UNCLOS on the conservation and sustainable use of marine biological diversity of areas beyond national jurisdiction (BBNJ), as well as to support academic research and exchange of views on BBNJ-related views. After years of consultation and negotiation, the United Nations General Assembly adopted A/RES/69/292 resolution in June 2015, determining for the formulation of an international legally binding agreement on the issue in relation to marine biodiversity beyond national jurisdiction consistent with UNCLOS[28].

The EU and China have agreed to collaborate through the Blue Partnership to tackle issues related to marine biodiversity in areas beyond national jurisdiction. For instance, the two parties have collaborated to create a legally binding global instrument concerning the protection and sustainable utilization of marine biodiversity in regions that are beyond national jurisdiction (BBNJ). This effort will align with the United Nations Convention on the Law of the Sea. Additionally, the parties will promote scholarly research and facilitate the exchange of viewpoints related to BBNJ. In June 2015, the United Nations General Assembly adopted resolution A/RES/69/292 after extensive consultations and negotiations. This resolution decided to create a legally binding treaty on marine biological diversity in areas beyond national jurisdiction in accordance with the UNCLOS[29].

---

27. *Memorandum of Understanding between* EMODnet and National Ocean Data and Information Service, EMODnet (EU) and NMDIS (China) , p. 4.
28. United Nations General Assembly, *Recommendations of the Ad Hoc Open-ended Informal Working Group to study issues relating to the conservation and sustainable use of marine biological diversity beyond areas of national jurisdiction to the sixty-ninth session of the General Assembly*, 23 January 2015, retrieved from http://www.un.org/Depts/los/biodiversityworkinggroup/documents/AHWG_9_recommendations.pdf on 1 May 2022.
29. United Nations General Assembly, *Recommendations of the Ad Hoc Open-ended Informal Working Group to Study the Conservation and Sustainable Use of Marine Biological Diversity Beyond Areas of National Jurisdiction to the General Assembly at its sixty-ninth session,*

At the Preparatory Committee meeting, the EU and China strongly and unanimously advocated for the creation of a new legal instrument. Both parties also endorsed the substance of the new instrument on Biodiversity Beyond National Jurisdiction (BBNJ). However, there were still divergent interests on several specific matters. China's stance on the negotiations regarding marine biodiversity beyond national jurisdiction mostly centers around topics like as marine genetic resources, marine environmental impact assessment, marine protected areas, and marine technology transfer[30]. An essential aspect of the negotiations revolves around the precise delineation of marine genetic resources. China supports the idea that "marine genetic resources should be classified as the human heritage of mankind". China contends that the "first come, first served" principle, which some countries support, may result in detrimental exploitation of marine genetic resources in areas beyond national jurisdiction. This could potentially lead to conflicts between nations for plundring marine resources[31]. China favors the concept of "common heritage of mankind" as a more equitable approach in terms of exploitation of maritime resources. China's recommendations for the marine environmental impact assessment method prioritize three key elements: "equity", "transparency", and "collaboration". China's environmental impact assessment technology is less advanced than that of industrialized countries. Therefore, China advised to employ a constantly updated blacklist to establish the parameters and criteria for evaluation in order to ensure transparency[32]. China's level of engagement with the establishment of marine protected areas (MPAs) in areas beyond national authority is comparatively lower than that of the European Union (EU). China aims to utilize marine protected areas as a means of managing and safeguarding marine biodiversity in the region. This approach also seeks to establish the status of natural resources in the Area Beyond National Jurisdiction (ABNJ) as the common heritage of mankind, thereby restricting the exclusive exploitation of resources in the region by developed countries[33].

23 January 2015, 2022 Retrieved May 1, 2018, from http://www.un.org/Depts/los/biodiversityworkinggroup/documents/AHWG_9_recommendations.pdf.

30. Qu Yongbo, Peng Zemin: "Marine Rights Management and China's Practice", *Economic Daily Press* , 2015, pp. 90-118.

31. Tladi, D., "The common heritage of mankind and the proposed treaty on biodiversity in areas beyond national jurisdiction. The choice between pragmatism and sustainability" in Yearbook of international environmental law, vol. 25, 2014, pp. 5.

32. United Nations, "*Second week of drafting conference on marine biological diversity treaty opens, delegates focus on how the instrument will address environmental impact assessment issues*" , retrieved May 3, 2022 *https://www.un.org/press/en/2018/ sea2081.doc.htm.*

33. IISD, *Summary of the First Session of the Preparatory Committee on Marine Biodiversity Beyond Areas of National Jurisdiction: 28 March to 8 April 2016* , 11 April 2016, 5 May

From the onset of the discussions, the EU has been the primary advocate for the advancement of BBNJ agreement, known as the Internationally Legally Binding BBNJ Agreement (ILBA). During the sessions of the Working Group on the High Seas and Contiguous Zones and the Preparatory Committee, the European Union acknowledged the importance of tackling marine ecological interconnections. The EU occupies a position that lies between the conflicting concepts of freedom of the high seas and the common heritage of mankind (CHM). Its objective is to garner the endorsement of developing countries in order to establish new legally binding regulations on marine biodiversity beyond national jurisdiction. The meeting also concurred that an exclusively "first come, first served" methodology for marine genetic resources is unsuitable[34]. Furthermore, the European Union has actively contributed to the establishment of systems for assessing the environmental impact of marine activities and the creation of protected areas in regions that are not within the jurisdiction of any one country. Given the EU's extensive expertise in environmental regulation and mastery of modern environmental protection technology, the establishment of a marine environmental impact assessment process aligns with its environmental and economic goals. Hence, the European Union favors the establishment of a thorough and efficient process for assessing the environmental impact within the BBNJ agreement[35]. Simultaneously, the European Union suggests the creation of a broader array of marine protected areas globally, with the aim of protecting regions that fall outside of national jurisdiction and implementing full governance of the marine ecosystem[36].

Following the creation of the EU-China Blue Partnership in 2018, the collaboration between the European Union and China on BBNJ has experienced a notable increase in speed. The 21st China-EU Summit, held

2022 Retrieved *at https://enb.iisd.org/vol25/enb25106e.html*

34. Wright, G., Rochette, J., Gjerde, K., and Seeger, I., "The long and winding road: negotiating a treaty for the conservation and sustainable use of marine biodiversity in areas beyond national jurisdiction" in *IDDRI* , 2018 , pp. 1.
35. European Union, *Development of an international legally binding instrument under the United Nations Convention on the Law of the Sea on the conservation and sustainable use of marine biological diversity beyond areas of national jurisdiction (BBNJ process), Environmental* Impact Assessment of the European Union and its Member States Written Submission, February 15, 2017, Retrieved May 6, 2022, from https://www.un.org/depts/los/biodiversity/prepcom_files/rolling_comp/EU_Written_Submission_on_Environmental_Assessments.pdf.
36. Pentz, B., Klenk, N., Ogle, S., and Fisher, JA, "Can regional fisheries management organizations (RFMOs) manage resources effectively during climate change?" in *Marine Policy* , vol. 92, 2018 , pp.2.

in April 2019, released a joint statement announcing the establishment of the Antarctic Marine Protected Area. This initiative serves as a collaborative effort between China and the EU to effectively implement the Blue Partnership[37]. During the Fourth EU-China High Level Environment and Climate Dialogue in 2023, both parties expressed their dedication to collaborating on maritime protection, emphasizing the principles of equality and mutual benefit. China will act upon the implementation agreement of the United Nations Convention on the Law of the Sea once it is implemented. Efforts to conserve and responsibly utilize marine biodiversity in regions beyond national jurisdiction (BBNJ) are progressing by enhancing communication and coordination about the ratification and implementation of relevant treaties. Both parties reiterated their dedication to advancing the safeguarding of Antarctic marine living resources in accordance with the Convention for the Conservation of Antarctic Marine Living Resources. They also continued deliberations on the establishment of a comprehensive network of marine protected areas in the waters surrounding Antarctica[38].

2.3. Climate Change

The EU and China have established a longstanding partnership in addressing climate change and have mutually pledged to enhance collaborative endeavors in this regard. The EU's China policy document in 2003 categorized the collaboration between the two parties in the realm of climate change within the context of "enhancing the multilateral system and collectively addressing global environmental challenges"[39]. This has transitioned the task of tackling climate change from unilateral EU assistance to global collaboration. The China-EU Joint Statement on Climate Change, established in 2005, marked a significant advancement in climate collaboration between China and the European Union, signifying a noteworthy milestone in their partnership. The China-EU Joint Statement on Climate Change conversation and Cooperation, published in 2010, created a platform for ministerial conversation between China and the EU on climate

37. Mission of the People's Republic of China to the European Union, "Joint Statement *on the 21st EU -China Summit"* , April 10, 2019, retrieved May 8, 2022, from http: / / w w w. chinamission.be / chn / ssht / t165283420190515shtml / t1663739.htm.

38. Delegation of European Union to the People's Republic of China, Joint Press Release following the Fourth EU-China High Level Environment and Climate Dialogue, 24 July 2023, available at 9 February 2024 from *https://www.eeas.europa.eu/delegations / china/joint-press-release-following-fourth-eu-china-high-level-environment-and-climate-dialogue_en?s=166.*

39. European Commission, *"A mature partnership — common interests and challenges in the EU-China relationship "*, COM(2003) 533 final, 2003, p. 12.

change. This mechanism aims to facilitate practical cooperation and the exchange of perspectives between the two parties. This indicates that the collaboration between China and the European Union on climate issues has progressed to the stage of institutionalization, thereby establishing institutional assurances for their joint efforts on climate matters. This was verified in the 2010 Joint Statement and further emphasized in the 2015 Joint Statement and the 2018 Leaders' Statement[40].

The Paris Agreement was adopted by all parties during the 21st United Nations Climate Change Conference held in Paris on December 12, 2015. Notably, the Paris Agreement came into effect a just 11 months after it was signed. China and the EU adhere to the Paris Agreement established inside the United Nations Framework Convention on Climate Change and strive to enhance the execution of the United Nations Framework Convention on Climate Change. Both parties are signatories of the Paris Agreement. The China-EU climate change collaboration received a significant boost in spring 2017 following the announcement by the US administration, led by Donald Trump, to withdraw from the Paris Agreement. China, the EU, and Canada promptly reacted to the statement by endeavoring to establish a fresh alliance in order to preserve the accord[41]. They restated their dedication to the pact and resolved to enhance collaboration on climate change and renewable energy[42]. The 2018 Katowice Conference of the states played a pivotal role in shaping the future of global climate politics, as participating states engaged in discussions to establish a practical set of guidelines for implementing the Paris Agreement.

China and EU collaborate under the *Blue Partnership* to tackle climate change issues relating to the ocean. Both parties have agreed to collaborate in order to effectively execute the Paris Agreement in areas pertaining to climate change and oceans. The European Commission declared a *climate*

40. European Commission, "*Climate Action in the EU-China Cooperation Area*", retrieved 27 April 2022 from https://ec.europa.eu/clima/eu-action/international-action-climate-change/cooperation-non- eu-countries-regions/china_en.
41. Gurol, J. and Starkmann, A., "New partners for the planet? The role of the EU and China in international climate governance from a role theory perspective " , in *JCMS* , Volume 59, 2021, pp. 518- pp. 520; Dröge, S. and Rattani, V., " International climate policy leadership after COP23: The EU must resume its leading role, but cannot do so alone "in *SWP Comment* , 2018, pp. 1-3.
42. European Commission, "*EU and China strengthen cooperation on climate change and clean energy* ", 2018, retrieved April 29, 2022 https://ec.europa.eu/clima/news-your-voice/news/eu-and- china-step-cooperation-climate-change-and-clean-energy-2018-07-16_en.

law in March 2020, which obligates the 27 EU countries to achieve a complete elimination of net greenhouse gas emissions by the year 2050. Half a year later, Chinese President Xi Jinping made a commitment that China would achieve carbon neutrality by the year 2060. Both comments are considered crucial in the worldwide effort to combat climate change[43]. The EU's initiative is referred to as the *European Green Deal*. The strategy effectively reduces the EU's dependence on fossil fuels and levies tariffs on imports from nations with substantial greenhouse gas emissions. China's climate strategy centers around implementing an emissions trading system for domestic companies, so establishing the largest carbon market worldwide and substantially augmenting China's portion of global emissions[44]. During the April 2022 EU-China summit, the parties entered into an administrative agreement for the period of 2021-2024. This arrangement aims to facilitate joint research projects in two agreed-upon areas of focus: Food, Agriculture, and Biotechnology, as well as Climate Change and Biodiversity. Projects conducted through administrative arrangements will contribute to the advancement of important EU objectives, such as the mitigation of climate change impacts[45]. During the 24th EU-China Summit in 2023, leaders expressed their support for sustained collaboration on climate change and the environment. The EU emphasized the importance of both the EU and China taking the lead in global endeavors to decrease greenhouse gas emissions, including at the ongoing 28th Conference of the Parties. The European Union recognized the recent advancements made in the spread of renewable energy and China's commitment to addressing methane emissions. The European Union emphasized the imperative for all nations to promptly intensify their efforts to address climate change. Additionally, they urged China to participate in the worldwide initiative to treble renewable energy capacity and double energy efficiency by 2030, as well as the Global Methane Commitment[46].

---

43. EU External Action Service, *China's carbon neutrality in 2060: a potential climate game-changer* , 23 October 2020, retrieved 28 April 2022 from *https://www.eeas.europa.eu/eeas/china Retrieved on -carbon-neutrality-2060-possible-game-changer-climate_en.*
44. "Nature, China's Net Zero Goal", April 5, 2022, Retrieved April 28, 2022, from *https://www.nature.com/articles/d41586-022-00802-3.*
45. European Commission, "EU and China have signed administrative arrangements to support cooperation", retrieved 5 May 2022 from *https://ec.europa.eu/info/news/eu-and-china-have-signed-administrative-arrangement -support-cooperation-2022-apr-26_en.*
46. European Council, 24th EU-China Summit: engaging to promote our values and defend our interests, 7 December 2023, available at 9 February 2024 from *https://www.consilium.europa.eu/en/press/press-releases/2023 /12/07/24th-eu-china-summit-engaging-to-promote-our-values-and-defend-our-interests/.*

III. OBSTACLES AND CHALLENGES FACED BY THE EU AND CHINA FOR THE CONSTRUCTION OF BLUE PARTNERSHIP

1. THERE ARE STILL DEFICIENCIES IN CHINA'S OCEAN AWARENESS AND DOMESTIC OCEAN GOVERNANCE EXPERIENCE

Throughout history, the social activities of Chinese people have been mostly influenced by the agricultural economy prevalent in the mainland. Conversely, the maritime economy has never had substantial importance. The ancient Chinese dynasties consistently depended on agriculture as the foundation of their political authority, establishing an ideological notion that prioritized land over the sea[47]. Prior to the Ming Dynasty, the ancient Chinese dynasties exhibited a rather lenient stance towards the advancement of the maritime domain around China. Prior to the 15th century, marine operations were constrained and mostly focused on coastal regions of the respective countries. There were no maritime routes connecting Asia to other continents, such as Africa and Latin America. From 1405 to 1433, during the Ming Dynasty, Zheng He, a renowned Chinese navigator, commanded a massive fleet on seven consecutive extensive expeditions across the Western Pacific and various countries and regions in the Indian Ocean. Nevertheless, Zheng He's expeditions to the West were primarily driven by political motives. Specifically, the Ming Dynasty aimed to foster and enhance amicable relations with neighboring and global nations by showcasing China's affluence and power, with the ultimate goal of securing lasting peace. Hence, the primary objective of Zheng He's missions was not to foster economic growth and trade via navigation[48]. China's sea power awareness significantly declined during the early Ming Dynasty as a result of the implementation of the maritime prohibition policy by the Ming and Qing dynasties in the mid-15th century.

The rapid development of China's shipping industry began only after the establishment of New China in 1949. The initiation of the reform and opening up policy in 1978 encouraged China's coastal towns to capitalize on their advantageous proximity to global trade routes in order to actively foster the growth of China's maritime trade[49]. In 2012, China put out a proposal to

47. Xu, L., "Chinese traditional marine culture philosophy" in China's *Ethnic Groups* , 2005, pp. 5.
48. Ding, J., Shi, CJ, and Weintrit, A., "An Important Waypoint on Passage of Navigation History : Zheng He's Voyages to the West" , *International Journal of Navigation and Maritime Transport Safety* , 2007, pp. 285-292.
49. Quan, Y. and Zhou, P. Academic *Star Library: "Maritime Rights Management and Chinese Practice"* , Economic Daily Press, 2015, pp. 1-10.

establish a maritime power and advance ocean development at a national strategic level in order to protect and defend maritime rights and interests.

Europe is a continent that is heavily influenced by the sea. In terms of both coastline length and overall area, Europe surpasses all other continents in terms of its proximity to the ocean. Marine culture has consistently influenced Europe, and its marine activities align with its civilization[50]. The economies of Europe, West Africa, and the New World were intricately interconnected through commerce and immigration over several historical periods[51], such as the ancient Greek and Roman civilizations in the Mediterranean and the European expansion in the Atlantic from 1500 to 1800. The worldwide trade and imperial development of Spain, Portugal, the Netherlands, and the United Kingdom were all predicated on maritime activities. Following World War II, European nations and the European Union actively engaged in the development of a contemporary legal framework for marine affairs, drawing upon the United Nations Convention on the Law of the Sea. All Member States of the European Union have ratified the Convention and are committed to guaranteeing the European Community's right to join the Convention[52]. The EU Common Fisheries Policy made significant progress following the transfer of fisheries responsibilities from member states to the EC. The EC played a leading role in the discussions of the United Nations Fish Stocks Agreement (FSA) in 1995 and 1996. The agreement was signed in the specified year[53]. The European Commission's influence is evident in numerous significant clauses of the Fish Stocks Agreement. Currently, the Convention and its related agreements have been ratified by twenty-seven Member States and the European Union. Hence, the European Union holds a significant position and exerts influence in the domains of marine resources, economic endeavors, marine conservation and governance, as well as the development and enforcement of the legal framework pertaining to international law of the sea.

50. Blume, D., & Brennecke, C. , *Europe* and *the Sea* , München , 2018 , pp. 1.
51. Fusaro, M., & Polónia, A. (Eds.). *Maritime history as global history* , Liverpool University Press, 2017, pp. 5-9.
52. Long, R. "The European Union and Law of the Sea Convention at the age of 30, *The International Journal of Marine and Coastal Law*" , vol. 27, 2012, pp. 711-712; Myron Nordquist (eds), United *Nations Convention on the Law of the Sea 1982*. Volume IA Commentary, Brill, 1985, pp: *Volume IA Commentary* , Brill Press, 1985, pp. 201-210.
53. Council of the European Union, Decision 98/414 of 8 June 1998, OJ L/189/14 of 3 July 1998.

2. THERE ARE STILL PROBLEMS IN THE INTERFACE AND IMPLEMENTATION OF MARITIME COOPERATION BETWEEN THE EU AND CHINA

2.1. Possible Power Conflict Between EU and Member States Over Maritime Cooperation with China

Multiple actors participate in the process of setting the agenda, formulating policies, making decisions, and implementing actions related to EU international ocean governance[54]. Regarding the EU, the majority of agreements concerning international ocean governance, with the exception of marine living resource conservation, are mixed accords that involve shared competencies between the EU and its member states. Hence, the European Union possesses a twofold representation in the process of negotiating these foreign agreements. Article 218 of the Treaty on the Functioning of the European Union (TFEU) states that the European Commission serves as a representative for matters that fall under the exclusive jurisdiction of the EU. Conversely, items that are still the duty of the Member States, such as financial affairs or matters not governed by EU directives or rules, are deliberated by the Council Presidency[55]. The chairmanship of the Council is rotated among member nations every six months, with three member states co-chairing each session. During instances involving conflicts of interest, each representative endeavors to maximize their own advantage. Consequently, the recommendations and viewpoints of certain member states may be disregarded and rejected if a sense of collegiality cannot be achieved.

Member states possess numerous competences in areas that have not been completely delegated to the European Union. Regarding maritime cooperation, member nations maintain jurisdiction over sectors such as agriculture and fisheries (except the safeguarding of marine living resources), environment, energy, and industry. China has formed several marine collaborations with member states of the European Union, and the *Blue Partnership* between China and Portugal serves as a representative instance. China and Portugal signed the *Concept Document and Joint Action Plan Framework for the Blue Partnership between the Portuguese Ministry of Oceanography and the State Oceanic Administration of China* on November 3, 2017. Portugal has become the inaugural European Union member state to officially create a blue cooperation with China. Both

54. Dany, C., "Politicization of humanitarian aid in the European Union" in *European Foreign Affairs Review* , vol. 20, 2015 , pp. 5.
55. Costa, O. (ed.) and Jørgensen, KE (ed.) , *The influence of international institutions on the EU: when multilateralism hits Brussels* , Palgrave Macmillan, 2012, 20-27.

parties aim to enhance innovation and development in the areas of blue economy, deep-sea research, marine biotechnology, and marine renewable energy development[56]. Furthermore, in 2012, China and Central and Eastern European countries forged a formalized collaborative alliance with the aim of fostering economic and investment ties between China and the 16 nations in Central and Eastern Europe. China perceives this action as a mutually beneficial collaboration for both China and the relevant European Union nations. European think tanks have proposed the perspective that China is implementing a firm and strategic approach of "divide and rule" with the intention of advancing China's interests while disadvantaging Europe[57].

The EU's susceptibility to "political anxiety" may be heightened by China's collaboration with member states and sub-regions. The EU's apprehension primarily stems from two factors: firstly, the EU is concerned that China's collaboration with its member states could impact the EU's influence in China-EU ties, diminish its sway over member states, and perhaps encroach onto EU competences. This will impede the European Union's ability to establish a cohesive approach towards China, so weakening the EU's unity in negotiations with China and its consensus on decisions concerning China. In 2017, the German Foreign Minister Gabriel stated that China had steadily transformed European political life. Furthermore, he explicitly emphasized Greece's desire to ensure that the progress of the Piraeus port construction remains unaffected by any strained relations with China. He interpreted this as an indication that China had the potential to effectively fragment Europe[58]. Conversely, the European Union is concerned that the collaboration between China and its member states would diminish its appeal to those member states. If the "17+1" cooperation mechanism established by China and Central and Eastern European countries adequately considers the maritime interests of the member states, there is a risk that the Central and Eastern European countries may distance themselves from the European Union as a consequence of their collaboration with China. This could result in European fragmentation and the inability to achieve a cohesive maritime policy[59]. The

56. Sheng Gao, Y., "*China and Portugal formally establish blue partnership*", *China Daily, 2020, retrieved from http://www.chinadaily.com.cn/cndy/2017-11* on May 10, 2022 Retrieve */07/content_34217802.htm*.

57. Garlick, J., "China's Economic Diplomacy in Central and Eastern Europe: *Eurasian Studies*" , Volume 71 , 2019, Pages 1390-1414.

58. Cetinic, O. and Rising, D., *German foreign minister says European unity key to future*, 30 August 2017, retrieved from *https://apnews.com/article/9fd0d5c4edd645d384b722bcb7dd0c63* on 13 May 2022.

59. Turcsanyi, R., "Central and Eastern Europe's Courtship with China: Trojan Horse within the EU?" in*European Institute for Ansian Studies*, 2014, pp.1-6.

presence of multi-national and multi-level political actors within the EU may introduce uncertainties in promoting the EU-China Blue Partnership.

2.2. Administrative Arrangements of China

As for the stipulations of China's Treaty Conclusion Procedure Law, China has the authority to enter into treaties and agreements with foreign nations under three designations: (1) the People's Republic of China; (2) the government of the People's Republic of China; (3) various governmental departments of the People's Republic of China. Nevertheless, in reality, due to the absence of explicit regulations regarding the extent of authority for each ministry, there can arise circumstances where numerous departments possess the administrative capability to engage in agreements with other nations on same subjects[60]. The Ministry of Natural Resources and the Ministry of Agriculture and Rural matters of the People's Republic of China have been given the authority to establish a *Blue Partnership* with the European Commission regarding comprehensive marine matters. The European Commission in Brussels is presently engaged in negotiations with the Chinese Ministry of Science and Technology over a collaborative roadmap for future cooperation in science, technology, and innovation (STI) between China and Europe. This includes a specific focus on maritime science and technology. Various ministries in China may possess divergent interests and priorities[61]. Conflicts may arise when different ministries make decisions that involve balancing environmental protection with economic and technological development, particularly in the area of renewable energy technologies. These technologies are becoming increasingly important in fostering collaboration between the two parties. Hence, in the event that EU representatives engage in negotiations with other ministries over the same issue, conflicting accords may be attained. Practically, there can be instances where various Chinese ministries and commissions engage in competition to negotiate with the EU about areas of interest, and subsequently evade responsibility when it comes to shouldering obligations. The presence of conflicting interests within ministries and commissions in China will hinder the establishment of a cohesive stance and complicate communication between the European Union and China.

---

60. Ministry of Foreign Affairs of the People's Republic of China, "*Law on the Procedure for the Conclusion of Treaties*" , December 28 , 1990, retrieved on May 16, 2022 *https://www.fmprc.gov.cn/web/wjb_673085/zfxxgk_674865/zcfg/fl/200403* /t20040304_9276665.shtml.
61. Delegation of the European Union to the People's Republic of China, "*Relationship with EU Research and Innovation*" , 14 September 2021, accessed 18 May 2022 from https://www.eeas.europa.eu/china/research-innovation_en? Search on s=166.

3. THE INTERFERENCE AND INFLUENCE OF THIRD COUNTRIES ON EU-CHINA COOPERATION

The concept of the balance of power is a longstanding and essential principle in the field of international relations theory. According to this theory, the existence of imbalances and concentrations in military and material capabilities among the major countries is monitored and corrected to maintain equilibrium and assure the survival of these powers in the international system[62]. In his article, Hakan Edström posited that the determining entities in the current international order are the exclusive superpower, the United States (US), the emerging potential superpower, China, and the other major powers, namely the European Union (EU), Russia, and the United Kingdom (UK)[63]. In this scenario, the European Union and China have the strongest motivation to evaluate the influence of the United States[64].

The United States is a current dominant power with a single pole of influence. In 2017, the former President Trump announced his intention to advance a strategy of power equilibrium that would be advantageous to the United States and its allies. Simultaneously, the former president underscored his belief that the distribution of responsibilities between the United States and its allies was inequitable. Consequently, he held the belief that conventional alliances were a suitable means to promote U.S. objectives[65]. The United States and the European Union continue to possess the most robust foundation for a strong and intimate partnership, across the Atlantic. They possess a common political structure, mutual ideals, and profound cultural and religious connections. Significantly, both parties have established NATO and other collaborative frameworks to address their individual security and economic interests. Upon assuming office, Biden declared a shift in the United States' global approach from unilateralism and protectionism, as seen during the tenure of previous President Trump. The new policy entails enhancing collaboration with allies and "like-minded

62. Oxford Bibliographies, *Balance of Power Theory*, 2019, retrieved from https://www.oxfordbibliographies.com/view/document/obo-9780199743292/obo-9780199743292-0083.xml on 20 May 2022.
63. Edström, H. and Westberg, J., "The alignment strategies of great powers: Managing power asymmetries and structural changes in the international system" in *Comparative Strategy*, vol. 41, 2022, pp. 97-119.
64. Zhenqiang, P., *The US-Europe-China Triangle in an Increasingly Multipolar World*, Konrad Adenauer Stiftung, 2006, pp. 1-32.
65. The President of the United States: "*National Security Strategy* ,"Trump White House Archives, 2017, pp. 1-9 ; U. S. National Intelligence Council: "*Global Trends: The Paradox of Progress* ,"COSIMO Report, 2017.

partners" and reverting to a multilateral approach. Amidst significant shifts in U.S. domestic politics and foreign policy, the EU published *EU-US: A New Transatlantic Agenda for Global Change* in late 2020. This document also emphasizes the need to enhance transatlantic policy coordination with regards to China[66]. The United States also expressed a favorable response to the ideas put out by the European Union. The EU and US have established the EU-US Trade and Technology Council to collaboratively address significant trade and technology matters[67]. The United States and Europe want to enhance their competitiveness against China in the economic, trade, and technology domains through the reinforcement of policy cooperation.

Since 2014, Russia has made the decision to enhance and broaden its practical collaboration with China, aiming to elevate the Russia-China comprehensive strategic cooperative partnership to a more advanced stage. This decision is based on the fact that Russia considers China as a crucial and enduring strategic ally. China and Russia maintain a strong and extensive partnership in various domains such as politics, economics, trade, culture, and more. China and Russia have been dedicated to identifying a practical convergence point between the Silk Road Economic Belt project and the Eurasian Economic Union, particularly in the Eurasian continent. This convergence aims to enhance the economic integration of Asia and Europe, while also creating a favorable opportunity for cooperation between the European Union and China[68]. However, it is undeniable that Russia has emerged as a formidable rival to the European Union. While Russia and China primarily concentrate on maritime cooperation in Northeast Asia and the Arctic, the relationship between Russia and Europe continues to worsen due to the outbreak of the war in Ukraine[69]. Consequently, the relations between China, the EU, and Russia will form an unsteady triangle dynamic, potentially hindering EU-China maritime collaboration.

The competition and collaboration within the triangle interaction involved in the creation of the Eurasian transport corridor can be used as an example. The Eurasian Transport Corridor seeks to establish a transportation

66. European Commission, EU-US: European Commission, EU-US: A new transatlantic agenda for global change , 2020, p. 2.
67. European Commission, "Digital in the EU-US Trade and Technology Council", retrieved 25 May 2022 from *https://digital-strategy.ec.europa.eu/en/policies/trade-and-technology-council* Retrieve.
68. Libman, A., "Linking the Silk road economic belt and the Eurasian Economic Union: Mission impossible?" in *Caucasus International*, vol. 6, pp. 41-45.
69. Cheng, M., "The Ukraine Crisis: Causes, Conundrum and Consequences" in *Journal of Social and Political Sciences*, vol. 5, 2022, pp. 96-108.

network connecting Eurasia, the Pacific Ocean, and the Atlantic Ocean, with the ultimate goal of achieving economic unification across the region. It can be seen as a contemporary iteration of the historic Silk Road. Russia now holds a monopoly over the present Eurasian transport pattern, as all the existing transport corridors with sufficient capacity must pass through Russia. Consequently, China, the European Union, and Central Asian countries are seeking to establish alternative routes for the future Eurasian transport corridor, with the aim of diversifying the transportation system in Eurasia and avoiding reliance on Russia[70]. In contrast, Russia is evidently dissatisfied with the collaboration between the European Union and China in this particular domain. Russia upholds its supremacy over the Eurasian rail network by endorsing its own predominantly controlled railways, such as the "north-south" international transport corridor stretching from Saint Petersburg to Mumbai. Russia is obstructing the diversification of railway link between China and Europe. The failure of the China-Kyrgyzstan-Uzbekistan railway project can be attributed, in part, to the influence of Russia[71].

IV. RECOMMENDATIONS ON THE CONSTRUCTION OF THE EU-CHINA BLUE PARTNERSHIP

1. CHINA AND THE EU NEED TO DRAW EXPERIENCE FROM EACH OTHER IN OCEAN GOVERNANCE

EU countries, being traditional maritime powers, possess a rich history of ocean governance. Consequently, the EU wields significant influence in both the theoretical advancement and practical implementation of international ocean governance[72]. China's extensive coastline has had significant environmental repercussions as a result of the rapid industrialization and urbanization that began in the 1970s[73]. The European Union has the ability and actively assumes a position of leadership by implementing maritime environmental policies.

70. Bu, S., "China-EU-Russia Trilateral Relations: A Possibility Analysis" in *Reform and opening up*, vol. 19, 2014, pp. 43-45.
71. Russia has expressed support for the construction of Russian-Kazakhstan-Uzbekistan railway, which is competing with China-Kyrgyzstan-Uzbekistan railway. Russia to support Kyrgyzstan in joining Customs Union, trend news agency, 26 September 2013, retrieved from *https://en.trend.az/casia/kyrgyzstan/2194810.html* on 25 May 2022.
72. Ronan L., "The EU and the law of the sea convention at the age of 30" in *The International Journal of Marine and Coastal Law*, vol. 27, 2012, pp. 711-713.
73. Chen, S. and Uitto, J. I., "Governing marine and coastal environment in China: building local government capacity through international cooperation" in *China environment series*, vol. 6, 2003, pp. 67-68.

This leadership extends to both internal and foreign contexts, encompassing the economic, social, and environmental aspects, as well as considering the passage of time in the pursuit of sustainable development[74]. Considering this, China can benefit from the extensive regional expertise of the EU. The EU's successful experience is rooted on its emphasis on maritime environmental protection and the effective utilization of policy and management measures.

The implementation of EU maritime policy relies on three key tools: the European Network for Maritime Surveillance, Maritime Spatial Planning and Integrated Coastal Zone Management, and Marine Data and Information. Marine surveillance plays a crucial role in ensuring the safety and security of marine environments, particularly in addressing concerns such as unlawful immigration, illicit, unreported, and unregulated fishing, and safeguarding the environment[75]. Consequently, the European Union has established numerous methods to oversee marine activities, particularly those related to ships, such as automatic ship identification systems and ship traffic management systems. Due to the fragmentation of these systems, which are managed by various bodies, efforts have been made at both the international and EU levels to establish connections between the existing decentralized systems. In February 2008, the European Commission granted approval for the creation of a European border surveillance system[76]. This system integrates the current EU surveillance system with the pertinent systems of member states, establishing a public platform for sharing information within the marine industry. Furthermore, the European Union plans to utilize space technology for the purpose of border monitoring. One notable example is the European Galileo system, which offers a sophisticated technological framework for the development of satellite-based sea surveillance applications[77]. Maritime spatial planning(MSP) is a public management process that involves analyzing and adapting human activities in maritime areas to meet ecological, economic, and social goals for the marine environment. The MSP Directive was enacted by the European Union in 2014. In accordance with the provisions of this directive, member states are

74. Carpenter, A., "The EU and marine environmental policy: a leader in protecting the marine environment?" in *Journal of Contemporary European Research*, vol. 8, 2012, pp. 249-263.
75. Siemers, H., "A European Integrated Maritime Policy: An Innovative Approach to Policy-Making", in Chircop, A. (ed.), Coffen-Smout, S. (ed.) and McConnell, M. L. (ed.), *Ocean Yearbook*, vol. 23, 2009, pp. 201-244.
76. Commission of the European Communities, *Examining the Creation of a European Border Surveillance System*, February 2008, p. 2.
77. European Space Agency, *The Ambitions of Europe in Space*, retrieved from *http://www.esa.int/About_Us/Welcome_to_ESA/The_ambitions_of_Europe_in_space* on 28 May 2022.

required to thoroughly assess current human activities, the interplay between land and sea, and the optimal management strategy when developing plans, and enhance collaboration with other member states[78]. Over the last two decades, European Union member states have diligently executed marine spatial planning policies, successfully implementing or experimenting with marine spatial planning in their various maritime areas and coastal zones, resulting in positive environmental and social outcomes. The Netherlands, Belgium, Germany, and the United Kingdom have sequentially accomplished the planning and zoning of sea area exploitation inside their national seas[79].

In addition, the European Commission considers accurate data and information to be a crucial component of the EU's integrated maritime research program, particularly for efficient spatial planning and thorough marine surveillance[80]. In 2010, the European Commission suggested that EU countries utilize the European Marine Observation and Data Network (EMODnet) as a means to exchange data and enhance the utilization of scientific information[81]. In 2019, a data management strategy for marine litter was created at the European level as part of the current EMODnet network. The plan aims to gather, standardize, and make available standardized data sets and data products. These resources can be used to assess marine litter on a pan-European level[82].

The other way around, the EU can also gain insight from China's expertise in global collaboration over ocean governance. The purpose of China's plan to collaboratively construct the "21st Century Maritime Silk Road" is to facilitate marine connectivity and practical collaboration across many sectors. This initiative aims to foster the growth of the blue economy, bolster cultural exchanges related to maritime affairs, and collectively improve the well-being of the ocean[83]. In June 2017, China's National Development and Reform

78. European Commission, *Proposal for a Directive of the European Parliament and of the Council Establishing a Framework for Maritime Spatial Planning and Integrated Coastal Management*, COM(2013) final, 2013.
79. Ma, R. and Li, J., "How Should the Effectiveness of Marine Functional Zoning in China Be Evaluated? Taking Wenzhou Marine Functional Zoning as an Example" in *Land*, vol. 11, pp. 267-269.
80. European Commission, Blue Paper, 2007, p. 5-6.
81. European Commission, *Marine Knowledge 2020, Marine Data and Observation for Smart and Sustainable Growth*, COM (2010) 461 final, 2010.
82. European Marine Observation and Data Network (EMODnet), *New maps show the extent of marine litter in European seas*, 24 March 2019, retrieved from *https://emodnet.ec.europa.eu/en/new-maps-show-extent-marine-litter-european-seas* on 29 May 2022.
83. China Daily, "Gathering '*blue power'" to build a community with a shared future for mankind*, May 3, 2022, retrieved from *http://cn.chinadiplomacy.org.cn/2022-05/03/ on May 30, 2022 Retrieved on content_78198885.shtml.*

Commission and State Oceanic Administration published the *Vision for Maritime Cooperation under the One Belt, One Road Initiative*. This document outlines China's intention to enhance its strategic partnership with countries along the 21st Century Maritime Silk Road and actively foster practical collaboration across various sectors. Collaborate to collectively establish seamless, secure, and effective marine routes, jointly advance the establishment of maritime cooperation platforms, and together foster blue alliances[84]. Hence, European Union member states have the opportunity to participate in China's Maritime Silk Road as a catalyst for economic expansion and prosperity. This collaboration would also foster innovation by capitalizing on China's substantial investments in industry and R&D, resulting in reciprocal advantages.

Meanwhile, China is actively delivering marine public services and products to different countries to the extent of its capabilities. The Chinese State Oceanic Administration has recently coordinated the establishment of a regional marine monitoring network and security service system in areas covered by the "One Belt and One Road" program. Currently, numerous developing countries and least developed countries, especially small island countries worldwide face the predicament of inadequate governance capabilities as they grapple with the resolution of oceanic issues. China annually establishes government-funded marine scholarships and conducts diverse training programs to cultivate numerous skilled individuals in the field of marine sciences for developing nations. The Chinese government has facilitated the enhancement of maritime governance capacities in developing nations through the coordination of collaborative scientific expeditions and the establishment of shared scientific research facilities[85].

2. THE TWO SIDES NEED TO STRENGTHEN THE BLUE PARTNERSHIP BASED ON THE PRINCIPLE OF EQUALITY AND WIN-WIN

The Blue Partnership Agreement between the EU and China establishes a mutual agreement to foster collaboration based on the principles of equality, respect, and trust, with the objective of achieving mutually advantageous outcomes. Hence, both parties should engage in maritime collaboration with a focus on fairness and reciprocal advantages. The EU perceives itself as a prominent figure in global leadership regarding international maritime

84. State Council of the People's Republic of China, "*Vision for Maritime Cooperation under the Belt and Road Initiative*", June 20, 2017, p. 1.
85. Dekun, H. and Yu, J., "China's Ocean View in the New Era and Its Influence on International Ocean Governance" in *Research in International Issues*, 2021, pp. 73-88.

policy[86]. The EU is progressively marginalizing and excluding China in the domains of economy, commerce, and science and technology, perceiving China as a formidable rival[87]. The EU's strategy involves increasing the threshold and implementing legislative barriers in order to effectively exclude China from the European market[88].

The EU holds a prominent position globally in the domain of maritime research and technology. Nevertheless, the EU must not employ this as a justification to stifle and marginalize the progress of other nations in this domain. If the European Union solidifies its monopoly by engaging in unfair competition, it would hinder the progress of establishing a fair, equitable, and rational world order[89]. The collaboration between the EU and China in the domain of climate change is a progressive and visionary illustration. The EU recognizes that in order to enhance its global impact on the matter of climate change, it requires the backing of China. Both parties endeavor to sustain collaboration and engage in policy discourse over this matter. Both actors have expressed their determination to enforce the Paris Agreement and collaborate on addressing climate change. However, it should be noted that there may still be differing opinions and varied expectations. An instance of this may be seen in the European Union's recent restated demand for China to significantly and expeditiously reduce emissions. This implies that the European Union lacks confidence in China's ability to fulfill its commitments and assertions[90].

3. CHINA AND THE EU NEED TO ACTIVELY BROADEN THE AREAS OF MARITIME COOPERATION

While bilateral cooperation on maritime security has been limited, it has gained significant importance in the security policy agendas of both the EU

86. Kadfak, A. and Antonova, A. "Sustainable Networks: Modes of governance in the EU's external fisheries policy relations under the IUU Regulation in Thailand and the SFPA with Senegal" in *Marine Policy*, vol. 132, 2021, pp. 1-2.
87. European Commission and HR/VP contribution to the European Council, JOIN(2019) 5 final, EU-China — A strategic outlook, 12 March 2019, p. 1.
88. European Commission, *EU strengthens protection against economic coercion*, 8 December 2021, retrieved from *https://ec.europa.eu/commission/presscorner/detail/en/ip_21_6642* on 2 June 2022.
89. Hsiung, J. (ed.), *Twenty-first century world order and the Asia Pacific: value change, exigencies, and power realignment*, Springer, 2001, pp. 1-10.
90. Gurol, J. and Starkmann, A., "New partners for the planet? The European Union and China in International climate governance from a role-theoretical perspective" in *Journal of Common Market Studies*, vol. 59, 2021, pp. 518-531.

and China[91]. Both actors seek to bolster their stature as international security entities in order to elevate their reputation and influence. Maritime security cooperation, which has yet to reach its maximum potential, is emerging as a vital domain as it has the ability to foster mutual comprehension and confidence. Collaborative efforts addressing a low-risk matter, such as anti-piracy, have the potential to serve as a means for the European Union and China to establish collaboration in the field of maritime security. When discussing maritime security in relation to anti-piracy, the EU and China primarily focus on the Gulf of Aden (GoA)[92]. Substantial bilateral mechanisms have been established since 2008. The issue of combating piracy was addressed at a high-level meeting in 2014, where Chinese President Xi Jinping and President of the European Council Herman Van Rompuy discussed the advantages of military collaboration in the Gulf of Aden. Furthermore, at their Blue Partnership Forum for the Oceans in 2019, all parties reached a consensus to intensify efforts in enhancing global ocean governance and maritime security.

EU and China largely collaborate through the EU's Operation Atalanta, also known as EU NAVFOR Task Force 465. This operation was created in December 2008 by the EU Council Joint Action 2008/749/CFSP. In addition, European Union troops and Chinese People's Liberation Army forces are collaborating under the comprehensive CGPCS framework to alleviate political tensions in the Gulf of Aden, the Bab al-Mandab Strait, and the Strait of Hormuz, with a primary emphasis on providing escort services for commerce vessels[93]. Therefore, both the European Union and China have significant stakes in addressing piracy in the Gulf of Aden. Both parties must enhance collaboration in the field of anti-piracy, since it is vital and holds great promise.

Other than that, China and the EU have the potential to integrate deep-sea mining collaboration inside the structure of the *Blue Partnership*. Currently, China is actively engaged in and making significant contributions to the affairs concerning the international seabed area. Chinese businesses of significance have also emerged as "trailblazing investors" in the pursuit of

91. Grault, L. B. C. and Ferreira-Pereira, L. C., *Maritime Cooperation in the European Union-China Relations and the 21st Century Maritime Silk Road: What is at Stake?. The Belt and Road Initiative*, Palgrave Macmillan, 2020, pp. 255-256.
92. Gurol, J., *EU — China Relations on Maritime Security and Anti-Piracy. The EU — China Security Paradox*, Bristol University Press, 2022, pp. 87-90.
93. Gippner, O., "Antipiracy and unusual coalitions in the Indian Ocean region: China's changing role and confidence building with India" in *Journal of Current Chinese Affairs*, vol. 45, 2016, pp. 107-110.

polymetallic nodules resources in the international seabed region. China has acquired four exclusive exploration mining zones in this particular region[94]. The EU is a leading entity in the exploration and development of deep-sea resources. Germany, France, and Belgium, as EU member states, have acquired permits from the International Seabed Authority for the purpose of deep-sea mining exploration. Projects such as BlueMining, MIDAS, and PharmaSea have made specific contributions to the development of a dynamic and essential scientific community, positioning the EU as a leader in deep-sea exploration and exploitation[95].

4. BOTH SIDES COULD FORMULATE TOP-LEVEL DESIGN AND IMPLEMENT IT THROUGH CONCRETE PROJECTS

4.1. Both Sides Need to Strengthen Cooperation in Marine Science and Technology Innovation

Green technology has consistently had a prominent role globally. In 2020, the European Commission allocated more than €2 billion to fund 140 significant transportation projects. Within the marine sector, particular emphasis was placed on supporting short-sea-shipping initiatives that utilize alternative fuels and implementing on-shore power supply systems in ports to reduce emissions from ships while they are docked[96]. The Horizon 2020 initiative of the European Union prioritized research and development in innovative areas such as low carbon technologies, climate change adaptation, circular economy, digitization, and the transformation of European industry and services. The Horizon Europe initiative, scheduled to run from 2021 to 2027, aims to allocate a proposed budget of €100 billion to enhance intellectual assistance for sustainable development in Europe. China places significant emphasis on and actively invests in the domain of marine research and technology. China's capacity for autonomous innovation in this sector has consistently grown in recent years, leading to a notable enhancement in industrialization. Several pivotal technologies

---

94. Zou, K., "State Practice in Deep Seabed Mining: The Case of the People's Republic of China" in *Sustainable Ocean Resource Governance*, 2018, pp. 185-203.

95. Rademaekers, K. *et al.*, *Deep-seabed Exploitation-Tackling economic, environmental and societal challenges*, European Parliament Research Service (IP/G/STOA/FWC/2013-001/Lot3/C4), 2015, retrieved from *https://www.europarl.europa.eu/RegData/etudes/STUD/2015/547401/EPRS_STU(2015)547401_EN.pdf.* on 6 May 2022.

96. European Commission, *Boosting the EU's Green Recovery: EU invests over €2 billion in 140 key transport projects to jump-start the economy*, 16 July 2020, retrieved from *https://ec.europa.eu/commission/presscorner/detail/en/IP_20_1336* on 5 June 2022.

and significant initiatives pertaining to the oceans have achieved significant advancements, hence broadening China's opportunities for the exploration and utilization of the sea.

The comparative analysis reveals that the European Union prioritizes research and development in energy-saving technologies, emission reduction, and environmental protection. In contrast, China places emphasis on the research and development of technology in the exploration and usage of marine space. Therefore, it is probable that the two parties will enhance each other's capabilities in the realm of sustainable marine science and technology. Facilitating the interchange of marine technology between the EU and China at the governmental level is an effective means of promoting collaboration. China has the potential to utilize its technological capabilities in the exploration of marine resources and space. In return, it may seek environmental protection technologies from the European Union. Private entities, including enterprises from China and the European Union, have the ability to enter into project contracts to engage in the trade or transfer of environmentally friendly technologies at rates that are just and reasonable. The collaboration between EU and Chinese enterprises on marine technology has shown to be beneficial through the implementation of offshore Wind Energy exchange. During the November 2019 conference organized by WindEurope, a European Wind Energy Association, companies from Europe and China participated and demonstrated their eagerness to collaborate in the expanding offshore wind energy sector. Chinese entrepreneurs are certain that by incorporating European technology and equipment into their operations, they can significantly increase offshore wind energy production[97]. Currently, there is a widespread agreement and universal effort globally to achieve energy transformation, with offshore wind power being recognized as the future of energy. In the future, China and Europe can enhance their cooperation in this field by mutually acquiring knowledge from one another, resulting in mutually beneficial outcomes.

4.2. China and the EU Need to Strengthen Cooperation on Polar Affairs

During the third round of the China-EU Dialogue on the Law of the Sea and Polar Affairs in November 2020, China and the EU engaged in a comprehensive discussion regarding Arctic policy and Antarctic marine protected areas. Both parties reached an agreement to enhance their collaboration and exchanges

97. Koivisto, M. and Sørensen, P., "North Sea region energy system towards 2050: Integrated offshore grid and sector coupling drive offshore wind power installations" in *Wind Energy Science*, vol. 5, 2020, pp. 1705-1712.

in the fields of law of the sea and polar affairs[98]. Both parties pledged in the 2018 Blue Partnership agreement and the 2019 EU-China agreement to collaborate on the construction of marine protected zones in the Antarctic Ocean. China's level of involvement in the construction of Marine Protected Areas (MPAs) in Antarctica is not as extensive as that of the European Union. China primarily utilizes MPAs as a management tool to safeguard marine biodiversity and establish the status of natural resources in Areas Beyond National Jurisdiction (ABNJ) as a common heritage of mankind. This approach aims to prevent developed nations from exclusively exploiting marine resources in these areas. However, it is worth acknowledging that all parties are committed to preserving and protecting marine resources in the Antarctic regions. During the 8th EU-China Ministerial Environment Policy Dialogue in April 2021, China was urged to join the coalition of nations that endorse the establishment of new extensive Marine Protected Areas in the Southern Ocean[99]. Although the EU can assert its moral superiority on environmental matters, it would be prudent to refrain from assuming a leadership role or adopting a missionary-like approach, considering China's significant global influence. Hence, the European Union may effectively capitalize on the increasing global momentum to endorse Marine Protected Areas (MPAs) and leverage diplomatic channels to secure China's consent for the establishment of three further Marine Protected Areas in the Southern Ocean[100].

Regarding Arctic matters, both China and the EU, as non-Arctic nations and international organizations, have similar interests, policy stances, and identities in Arctic governance[101]. Given the current state of affairs, where the international cooperation mechanism and governance model for Arctic affairs have been mostly settled, it is challenging for China and the EU to make significant progress as non-regional participants[102]. But it is

98. Chinese Ministry of Foreign Affairs, *China and EU hold third round of dialogue on law of the sea and polar affairs*, 23 November 2020, retrieved from *https://www.fmprc.gov.cn/web/wjb_673085/zzjg_673183/tyfls_674667/xwlb_674669/202011/t20201123_7671169.shtml* on 6 June 2022.

99. European Commission, *EU and China step up cooperation on biodiversity ahead of COP 15*, 27 April 2021, retrieved from *https://environment.ec.europa.eu/news/eu-and-china-step-cooperation-biodiversity-ahead-cop-15-2021-04-27_en* on 8 June 2022.

100. Liu, N. and Brooks, C. M., "China's changing position towards marine protected areas in the Southern Ocean: Implications for future Antarctic governance" in *Marine Policy*, vol. 94, 2018, pp. 189-195.

101. Shaohua, Y. and Xueyi, L., "European Union and Global Governance" in *Social Science Literature Press*, 2020, pp. 50-54.

102. Sheng, E. L., "Extra-Regional Players in the Arctic: EU, China, Japan, Singapore, and South Korea" in *Arctic Opportunities and Challenges*, 2022, p. 115-120.

noteworthy that by participating in the annual Arctic Circle Conference held in Reykjavik, Iceland, non-Arctic countries, organizations or other players can declare their Arctic policies, introduce plans to develop Arctic interests, and conduct extensive exchanges. Hence, it is anticipated that China and the EU would engage in further exchanges and collaboration on international platforms, such as the aforementioned Conference, in the coming times.

4.3. Both sides should strengthen cooperation to promote the implementation and implementation of the BBNJ Agreement

After five years of negotiations, the Treaty on Biodiversity Beyond National Jurisdiction (BBNJ) was adopted on June 19, 2023. The EU and China should strengthen the coordination in order to broaden consensus, narrow differences, foster synergy, and promote the implementation of a Biodiversity Beyond National Jurisdiction (BBNJ) agreement that further interests of both parties and those of the international community. The EU and China have worked together to establish a number of mechanisms to preserve biological diversity. For the sake of advancing the enforcement of the BBNJ agreement, it is recommended that the two parties rearrange existing channels and set up a comprehensive dialogue mechanism on marine biodiversity beyond national jurisdiction. The two parties can promote developing countries' capacity for conservation and sustainable use of BBNJ and the technological level through various forms of cooperation, such as actively providing public goods, building an international cooperation regime, and establishing an information-sharing platform. These efforts can lead to the expectation that many countries will strictly abide by the new BBNJ agreement.

V. CONCLUSIONS

With the rapid progress in ocean affairs, the existing global ocean governance structure, which relies on the UNCLOS, is facing growing challenges in effectively dealing with emerging oceanic concerns. It is widely recognized that no country can effectively tackle oceanic challenges in isolation. The current circumstances emphasize the significance of successfully executing global ocean governance by means of cooperative bilateral or multinational initiatives.

The Declaration on the Establishment of the Blue Partnership for the Oceans was signed by China and the European Union in July 2018. This event represents a significant milestone in the collaboration between the EU and China in maritime affairs. The creation of the Blue Partnership between

China and the EU is a practical endeavor for both parties to actively engage in global ocean governance regarding the following areas: (1) the blue economy and associated marine industries; (2) climate change; (3) the preservation and sustainable utilization of biodiversity beyond national boundaries; and (4) matters related to fisheries. The EU-China Blue Partnership encompasses various significant instruments. A comprehensive examination of the formulation process and the content of these instruments indicates the presence of numerous areas of consensus as well as diverging interests. It is evident that further efforts are required to complete the work at hand.

This paper specifically examines potential paths for building the EU-China Blue Partnership for Oceans. The construction of this Partnership must occur in the specified regions: In order to enhance their individual capacity for ocean governance, China and the EU should exchange their expertise in ocean governance. Furthermore, it is imperative for both sides to enhance their internal motivation towards achieving fair and mutually beneficial collaboration in marine affairs. Another crucial aspect is the crucial for the European Union and China to actively expand the scope of their collaboration in maritime affairs, encompassing domains such as marine security and deep-sea mining cooperation. Furthermore, the European Union and China have the potential to formulate comprehensive top-level designs that can be effectively executed through the corresponding pivotal projects.

Towards a Carbon Club? EU, ETS, and China's National ETS Searching for Compatibility

JUSTO CORTI VARELA

Vice-Dean for Quality and Teaching Innovation at the Faculty of Law, Universidad Nacional de Educación a Distancia (UNED, Spain). Associate Professor of International Public Law, Faculty of Law, UNED

I. INTRODUCTION

Economic transition towards a low-carbon economy is a common goal of international society. Since the Paris Agreement, climate policy tools and the rhythm of implementation depend on the compromise of each country. However, the use of market tools, including carbon taxes and emission trade systems (ETS) has become particularly popular because of its effectiveness and relatively little interference with free market rules.

However, this assumption, once the ETS increases in effectiveness and emission costs rise, problems with national production competitiveness emerge. The national nature of ETS clashes with the globalization of climate change and international trade. To address this problem, equalization instruments have been proposed, with one of the most important being the Carbon Border Adjustment Mechanism (CBAM). Its rationale is to apply to imported products similar rules that national producers are obliged to follow. This idea, even though it seems logical as a preliminary approach, produces complex problems, on the one hand, regarding the compatibility with International Trade Law (WTO Law) and, on the other hand, regarding how different ETS interact with each other when, although their design could be considered *prima facie* similar, in practice, they have different implementation mechanisms and practices.

To put this problem in context, we have chosen the two most important ETSs in force: the EU and the Chinese National one. Involving activities that produce 1.5 billion and 4.5 billion tonnes of CO2 emissions (tCO_2e) annually respectively, together they cover the vast majority of ETS activity worldwide[1]. Are they compatible enough to recognize each other allowances? Could they create a club where other ETS may find a model to follow? Would the EU CBAM, and particularly its exception to products coming from countries with other ETS, fulfil WTO regulations? In this chapter, we will try to find answers to these questions.

II. CARBON LEAKAGE: CLIMATE POLICY EFFECTIVENESS OR ECONOMIC COMPETITIVENESS?

Public regulation is never neutral. As with any market input, it produces expected and unexpected effects. Spillovers are frequent, and predicting players' reactions is a complicated task for regulators.

In this context, it is not unsurprising that domestic climate regulation could promote the relocation of high-emitting activities towards jurisdictions where the legal environment is less restrictive[2]. Additionally, thanks to free trade, goods, and services produced in such places end up being consumed in the places where regulation standards are higher. This side effect of more ambitious domestic climate policies has three main negative consequences. The first one is that the efforts made by some members of the international community do not result in a reduction of Greenhouse Gas (GHG) global emissions since they are diluted by mirror expansion of GHG emissions elsewhere. The second negative effect concerns local industry, particularly small and medium companies with small opportunities for relocation, which have no choice but to assume local higher costs meanwhile imported products, coming from multicentre companies, do not. Consequently, climate regulation may represent a reduction of competitiveness, economic concentration, and unemployment rise[3]. The third consequence is a result of

1. The following ETS are those established in Korea (580 tCO_2e), California (320 tCO_2e) and the UK (140 tCO_2e). Statista, "Coverage of largest emissions trading systems (ETS) worldwide as of 2022", 6 February 2023. Retrieved from: *https://www.statista.com/statistics/1315109/largest-ets-markets-by-coverage/*
2. Academics have distinguished two possible contents of carbon leakage. The first happens when the implementation of a climate policy (particularly carbon pricing) in one jurisdiction leads to increased emissions in other jurisdictions. The second one is the broader concept of global trade in embodied carbon, where carbon-intensive production tends to shift toward developing countries and return as imports to industrialized countries. Peters, G. P., Minx, J. C., Weber, C. L., Edenhofer, O., "Growth in emissions transfers via international trade from 1990 to 2008", *Proceedings of the National Academies of Science of the United States of America*, n. 108, 2011, pp. 8903-8908.
3. Carbone, J., Rivers, N., "The impacts of unilateral climate policy on competitiveness", *Review of Environmental Economics and Policy*, vol. 11, n. 1, 2017, pp. 24-42.

the previous one and affects the social support of climate transition. If the rich societies perceive that climate regulation benefits multinationals and affects negatively local jobs, social support for the climate transition, or at least for most ambitious initiatives, could be negatively affected[4].

Nonetheless, carbon leakage is not just a competitiveness issue for most advanced economies. If that were the case, any measure to tackle it could be understood as a quasi-protectionist measure against the spirit of the common but differentiated responsibilities and respective capabilities principle[5]. As per Görlach and Zelljadt analyze[6], climate regulation gaps go beyond carbon leakage, interfering in energy markets and technology innovation. Regarding the first one, strict climate regulation in central countries promotes a drop in fossil fuel international prices which, at the same time, incentivizes their consumption in the periphery. Concerning the second, if regulations promote expensive clean technologies only in advanced economies but admit imported products that do not, less wealthy economies would have no incentive to adopt these technologies, thereby increasing the traditional innovation gap North-South.

Although there was little evidence of carbon leakage in practice, both in general[7] and in intrafirm trade[8], energy-intensive sectors have obtained generous free allocations arguing the necessity of preventing it[9]. Over-

4. Falkner, R., "The Paris Agreement and the new logic of international climate politics", *International Affairs*, vol. 92, n. 5, 2016, pp. 1107-1125.
5. Venzke, I., Vidigal, G., "Are Unilateral Trade Measures in the Climate Crisis the End of Differentiated Responsibilities? The Case of the EU Carbon Border Adjustment Mechanism (CBAM)", in *Netherlands Yearbook of International Law 2020: Global Solidarity and Common but Differentiated Responsibilities,* The Hague: TMC Asser Press, 2022, pp. 187-225. For a study measuring the economic burden on developing countries *see*: Böhringer, C., Fischer, C., Rosendahl, K. E., "The global effects of subglobal climate policies", *The B. E. Journal of Economic Analysis & Policy,* vol. 10, n. 2, 2010, pp. 1-35.
6. Görlach, B., Zelljadt, E., "Forms and Channels of Carbon Leakage", *Climate Change 16/2018,* Report prepared for the German Environment Agency, 2018. Retrieved from: *https://www.umweltbundesamt.de/sites/default/files/medien/1410/publikationen/2018-06-21_climate-change_16-2018_carbon-leakage_2020_0.pdf*
7. Verde, S. F., "The impact of the EU emissions trading system on competitiveness and carbon leakage: The econometric evidence", *Journal of Economic Surveys,* vol. 34, n. 2, 2010, pp. 320-343.
8. Aus Dem Moore, N., Grozkurth, P., Themann, M., "Multinational corporations and the EU emissions trading system: The specter of asset erosion and creeping deindustrialization", *Journal of Environmental Economics and Management*, n. 94, 2019, pp. 1-26.
9. Naegele, H., Zaklan, A., "Does the EU ETS cause carbon leakage in European manufacturing?", *Journal of Environmental Economics and Management*, n. 93, 2019, pp. 125-147.

allocation of allowances could have maintained production activity in the EU, but it has not changed the tendency to redirect new investments to non-EU jurisdictions with environmentally lenient regulation[10].

In the current ETS trading phase (2021-2030), free allocation has been reduced dramatically, but it is maintained at 100% for sectors at the highest risk of relocating their production outside of the EU[11]. The reduction of allocation in other sectors, however, has resulted in carbon prices being now four times higher than they were previously[12]. Perhaps it is because this change in carbon pricing, or the substantial increase of energy prices is due to the war in Ukraine, the case is that the European energy-intensive industry has started to call for a reform to the system[13]. One possibility would be to outsource the most energy-intensive parts of the value chain to concentrate the transitional efforts on higher value-added links[14]. This would produce industry restructuring, higher unemployment rates in affected sectors (at least temporarily), and supply dependency. Possibly influenced by the dramatic effects of the disruptions in the supply chain during the COVID-19 pandemic, the European Commission does not envisage, for the moment, the externalization option but the full greening of the energy-intensive industry keeping the activity inside. The Green Deal Industrial Plan[15] is a clear example of this political option, which includes almost unlimited funding for the transformation of energy-intensive industries into net-zero energy ones (REPowerEU) and the creation of private-public investment initiatives in EU priority areas, many under risk of carbon leakage (InvestEU Programme). The transformation of facilities is important, but operational costs will be, higher. Consequently, the competitive problem of carbon leakage persists.

10. De Beule F, Schoubben F, Struyfs K., "The pollution haven effect and investment leakage: The case of the EU-ETS", *Economics Letters*, n. 215, 1 June 2022, p. 110536.
11. Commission Delegated Decision (EU) 2019/708 of 15 February 2019 *supplementing Directive 2003/87/EC of the European Parliament and of the Council concerning the determination of sectors and subsectors deemed at risk of carbon leakage for the period 2021 to 2030, C/2019/930*, Official Journal L 120, 8.5.2019, p. 20-26.
12. EMBER, "Carbon Price Tracker", *Sandbag Climate Campaign CIC*. Retrieved from: *https://ember-climate.org/data/data-tools/carbon-price-viewer/*
13. Financial Times, "Global CEOs urge G7 leaders to step up climate action", 26 June 2022. Retrieved from: *https://www.ft.com/content/8b118e44-a256-4aae-aaa0-464009276e56.*
14. Sgaravatti, G., Tagliapietra, S., Zachmann, G., "Adjusting to the energy shock: the right policies for European industry", *Bruegel Policy brief*, 17 May 2023. Retrieved from: *https://www.bruegel.org/policy-brief/adjusting-energy-shock-right-policies-european-industry*
15. Communication from the Commission to the European Parliament, the European Council, the Council, the European Economic and Social Committee and the Committee of the Regions, *A Green Deal Industrial Plan for the Net-Zero Age*, 1 February 2023, COM (2023) 62 final.

Although The Green Deal Industrial Plan includes a chapter on global cooperation and making trade work for the clean transition, it does not solve the carbon leakage competitive problem itself because it solely advocates the support of EU industry competitiveness through the application of traditional trade defence instruments against unfair trade practices (e. g., dumping and distortive subsidies).

Fit for 55 Package, adopted in 2023, finally tackled the issue with a new approach to carbon leakage: A Carbon Border Adjustment Mechanism[16].

III. CARBON BORDER ADJUSTMENT MECHANISMS: ECONOMIC RATIONALE AND TRADE LAW CONDITIONALITY

The imposition of a carbon price on carbon-intensive imports to ensure that all goods in the EU market are treated equally has been discussed in the academic literature for decades[17]. The rationale is that ETS (or a carbon tax) applied to domestic producers only benefits imports from places where such costs are not incorporated into the price. Consequently, consumers face inconsistent prices regarding the carbon content of the products they buy. Mechanisms of carbon border adjustment would solve such distortion by imposing a duty equivalent to the carbon price that domestic producers pay. Importation from trade partners where equivalent carbon prices have been paid would also obtain a benefit from such a mechanism, showing that it is not about protectionism. Hence, the border adjustment would complete the market mechanism of carbon pricing in an optimal economic way, and if similar rules are fixed by a sufficiently large group of states with high climate regulation standards, some major energy-intensive and trade-exposed producers may have sufficient incentive to adopt abatement targets, thus reducing the global cost of climate policies[18].

16. Regulation (EU) 2023/956 of the European Parliament and of the Council of 10 May 2023 *establishing a carbon border adjustment mechanism*, Official Journal L 130, 16.5.2023, p. 52-104.
17. For an updated overview of the literature *see*: Böhringer, C., Fischer, C., Rosendahl, K. E. and Rutherford, T. F., "Potential impacts and challenges of border carbon adjustments", *Nature Climate Change*, vol. 12, n. 1, 2022, pp. 22-29. Cosbey, A., Droege, S., Fischer, C. and Munnings, C., "Developing guidance for implementing border carbon adjustments: lessons, cautions, and research needs from the literature", *Review of Environmental Economics and Policy*, vol. 13, n. 1, 2019, pp. 3-22.
18. Böhringer, C., Carbone, J., Rutherford, T., "The strategic value of carbon tariffs", *American Economic Journal: Economic Policy*, vol. 8, n. 1, 2016, pp. 28-51.

In fact, it could be the case that effective sanctions would not be necessary; the simple threats of them could be enough, as happened with the Montreal Protocol for regulating the use of ozone-depleting substances[19]. Multi-sector and multi-region models show that CBAM reduces leakage from 14 to 8 percent[20]. However, CBAM would not eliminate leakage. As Markusen showed, tariffs interfere with trade dynamics, promoting new trade flows that escape to restriction, undoing partially expected effects of the measure[21]. Another practical problem concerns administrative costs related to monitoring and taxing target products. Carbon-intensive products normally involve complex global supply chains covering several jurisdictions and intrafirm trade. Only very standardised products with high carbon costs could be candidates for such a mechanism[22].

Despite all these issues, CBAM could be considered, in principle, economically sound. However, what about their international law consistency? To answer this question, international trade law shall be analysed first, and then, the implications from an international climate law perspective.

Regarding the first one, quite before the proposal for an EU CBAM, quite strong literature had discussed the compatibility of such mechanisms with WTO law[23]. These studies concluded that CBAM could be trade law compatible

19. Barrett, S., "Rethinking Climate Change Governance and Its Relationship to the World Trading System", *World Economy*, vol. 34, n. 11, 2011, pp. 1863-1882.
20. Branger, F., Quirion, P., "Climate policy and the 'carbon haven' effect", *Wiley Interdisciplinary Reviews: Climate Change*, n. 5, 2014, pp. 53-71.
21. Markusen, J., "International externalities and optimal tax structures", *Journal of International Economics*, n. 5, 1975, pp. 15-29.
22. Mehling, M., van Asselt, H., Das, K., Droege, S., Verkuijl C., "Designing border carbon adjustments for enhanced climate action", *American Journal of International Law*, vol. 113, n. 3, 2019, pp. 433-481.
23. Among others *see*: Goh, G., "The World Trade Organization, Kyoto and Energy Taxes at the Border", *Journal of World Trade*, n. 38, 2004, pp. 395-423; de Cendra, J., "Can Emissions Trading Schemes Be Coupled with Border Tax Adjustments? An Analysis Vis-à-Vis WTO Law", *Review of European Community & International Environmental Law*, n. 15, 2006, pp. 131-145; Das, K., "Can Border Carbon Adjustments Be WTO-Legal?", *Manchester Journal of International Economic Law*, n. 8, 2011, pp. 65-97; Holzer, K., *Carbon-Related Border Adjustment and WTO Law*, Edward Elgar, Cheltenham, 2014; Pauwelyn, J., "Carbon Leakage Measures and Border Tax Adjustments Under WTO Law", in Prevost, D., Van Calster, G., *Research Handbook on Environment, Health and the WTO* (eds.), Edward Elgar, Cheltenham, 2013, pp. 448-506; Tamiotti, L., "The Legal Interface Between Carbon Border Measures and Trade Rules", *Climate Policy*, n. 11, 2011, pp. 1202-1211. Trachtman, J., "WTO Law Constraints on Carbon Credit Mechanisms and Export Border Tax Adjustments", in Delimatsis P. (ed.), *Research Handbook on*

depending on the design of the measure and the way that GATT obligations and exceptions are understood[24]. Before analysing the characteristics of the EU model, it is worth briefly examining such GATT obligations and exceptions.

We assume that a CBAM is, essentially, a climate version of a Border Tax Adjustment (Art. II:2(a) GATT) which, intending to guarantee trade neutrality of domestic taxation, permits to impose domestic taxes and charges on imported products[25]. Art. III:2 GATT adds that imported goods "shall not be subject, directly or indirectly, to internal taxes or other internal charges of any kind in excess of those applied, directly or indirectly, to like domestic products". The Working Party never confirmed whether inputs used in the production process, including the energy consumed in the manufacturing process (and the related taxes), are included in the definition[26]. Neither the GATT nor the WTO dispute settlement mechanism have clarified the issue yet[27]. Emissions Trading Systems, like the EU-ETS, which require the purchase and surrender allowances, could also be understood as an internal regulation under Art. III:4 GATT[28]. As we will see in the following paragraphs, in both cases (either as a carbon tax under art. II:2(a) and/ or as an internal regulation under art. III:4 GATT), the likeness and the competitive/substitute tests apply.

If the Carbon Border Adjustment is understood as a border tax (Art. II.2(a) GATT), as we assumed previously, national treatment (art. III:2 GATT) and Most-Favoured Nation Treatment (art. I GATT) shall be applied.

Climate Change and Trade Law, Edward Elgar, Cheltenham, 2017, pp. 109-118. Pirlot A., *Environmental Border Tax Adjustments and International Trade Law. Fostering Environmental Protection*, Edward Elgar Cheltenham, 2017.

24. General Agreement on Tariffs and Trade, 30 October 1947, 61 Stat. A-11, 55 UNTS 194, as incorporated in General Agreement on Tariffs and Trade 1994, 15 April 1994, Marrakesh Agreement Establishing the World Trade Organization, Annex 1A, 1867 UNTS 187.
25. For a commentary *see* GATT, "Border Tax Adjustments", *Report of the Working Party*, L/3464, BISD 18S/97, 2 December 1970.
26. *Ibidem*, para. 14.
27. Only ones it was almost the case, in the GATT Panel Report, *U. S. — Superfund case, Taxes on Petroleum and Certain Imported Substances*, BISD 34S/136, 17 June 1987. The report agreed that taxes on substances used in the composition of the final product could be adjusted at the border, without distinguishing between substances physically present in the final product and those that had been exhausted in the production process. *See* Committee on Trade and Environment, "Taxes and Charges for Environmental Purposes — Border Tax Adjustment", WT/CTE/W/47, 2 May 1997, para. 70. For a commentary on the different positions in the literature *see* Holzer, *op. cit.*, p. 103.
28. de Cendra, *op. cit.*, pp. 135-136.

The likeness problem is central and, unfortunately, shall be considered an unsolved question when Process and Production Methods are involved[29]. To determine the likeness/unlikeness, the Report of the Working Party has given an open list of criteria[30] that could be extended by the caselaw on a case-by-case basis[31], assuming certain flexibility[32]. Among this list, only consumers' tastes and habits criterion seem to be candidates to make a distinction between two products that are physically equal excepting for their carbon footprint[33].

Always as a border tax, if the measure affects products that fail to pass the likeness test, they could, anyway, be considered WTO legal if they are "directly competitive or substitutable products" (art. III:2 GATT, second condition), which is much more flexible[34]. In fact, the Appellate Body has said that this situation "constitutes a competitive relationship between products

29. This is an old discussion in WTO Law that involve Environmental PPM but also other issues like the protection of human rights or labour conditions prevailing during the manufacturing process of imported products. *See* Howse, R., Regan, D., "The product/process distinction-an illusory basis for disciplining unilateralism in trade policy", *European Journal of International Law*, vol. 11, issue 2, 2000, pp.249-289; Hudec, R. E., "The Product-Process Doctrine in GATT/WTO Jurisprudence", in Bronckers M., Quick R (eds.), *New Directions in International Economic Law: Essays in Hounour of John H. Jackson*, Kluwer Law International, The Hague, 2000, p.187-217; Conrad, C. R., *Processes and production methods (PPMs) in WTO law: interfacing trade and social goals*, Cambridge University Press, 2011; Sifonios, D., *Environmental process and production methods (PPMs) in WTO law*, Cham: Springer, 2018.

30. The Report of the Working Party L/3464 (*op. cit.*, para 18) produced a list that includes, among others: products' properties, nature, and quality; products' end-uses in a given market; "consumers' tastes and habits," international classification of the products for tariff purposes.

31. Appellate Body Report, *European Communities — Measures Affecting Asbestos and Asbestos-Containing Products*, WT/DS135/AB/R, 5 April 2001, paras. 101, 109 and 120.

32. Appellate Body Report, *Japan — Taxes on Alcoholic Beverages*, WT/DS8/AB/R, WT/DS10/AB/R, WT/DS11/AB/R 22, 4 October 1996, paras. 19-21.

33. In *EC — Asbestos, op. cit.*, para. 146 the WTO Appellate Body suggested that consumer distinctions "are very likely to be shaped by the health risks associated with a product". The relation between carbon emissions (and climate change) are much more indirect that in the case of Asbestos. However, in another case a WTO Panel observed that consumer distinctions could be consequence of a "perceived difference" which would be, itself, a new multifactor window of unlikeness. Panel Report, *European Communities — Measures Affecting the Approval and Marketing of Biotech Products*, WT/DS291/ WT/DS292/ WT/DS293, 29 September 2006. para. 7.2411.

34. Appellate Body Report, *Korea — Taxes on Alcoholic Beverages*, WT/DS75/R, WT/DS84/R, 18 January 1999, para. 118. Appellate Body Report, *Japan — Alcoholic Beverages, op. cit.* para. 25. Appellate Body Report, *Canada — Certain Measures Affecting the Renewable Energy Generation Sector*, WT/DS412/AB/R, WT/DS426/AB/R, 6 May 2013, para. 5.63.

[that] may require consideration of inputs and processes of production used to produce the product"; thereby facilitating the legality of CBAMs[35].

On the other hand, if the adjustment is understood as internal regulation (Art. III:4 GATT), the likeness test is not exactly equal to the one applied regarding art. II:2(a)[36]. In this case, a "competitive relationship in the marketplace"[37] is essential, making it much more likely to distinguish among products with different footprints if such distinction is unrelated to the foreign origin of the product[38].

Regarding art. I:1 GATT (most-favored-nation treatment), similar rules on likeness apply[39]. Although initially denied[40], PPMs have finally been considered as an admissible criterion[41]. Nevertheless, in this case, challenges arise when the product is from a country that adopts a carbon emission reduction policy but whose measures are not recognized as equivalent to the one that imposes the border adjustment — a subject that is essential for answering the research question of this chapter[42]. We will revisit this matter at a later point.

In the case that the CBAM is considered a violation of WTO law, a general exception (art. XX GATT) could still be considered. Climate policy measures are not specifically mentioned among the exception clauses, however art. XX:b and art. XX:g, along with the requirements of the chapeau, are normally argued as possible justifications.

As usual, the possibilities of a successful application depend on the arguments used to justify the measure. Reducing carbon emissions[43] would fit

35. Appellate Body Report, *Canada — Renewable Energy Generation Sector*, *op. cit.*, para. 5.63.

36. "...the 'accordion' of 'likeness' stretches in a different way in Article III:4" *EC — Asbestos*, *op. cit.*, para. 98.

37. *Ibidem*, para. 103.

38. Panel Report *United States — Measures Affecting the Production and Sale of Clove Cigarettes*, WT/DS406/R, 2 September 2011, para. 7.268. Holzer, *op. cit.*, pp. 135-36.

39. Appellate Body Report, *United States — Measures Concerning the Importation, Marketing and Sale of Tuna and Tuna Products (Recourse to Article 21.5 of the DSU by Mexico)*, WT/DS381/AB/RW, 20 November 2015, para. 7.281.

40. Panel Report, *Indonesia — Certain Measures Affecting the Automobile Industry*, WT/DS54/R, WT/DS55/R, WT/DS59/R, WT/DS64/R, 2 July 1998, para. 14.143.

41. Panel Report, *Canada — Certain Measures Affecting the Automotive Industry*, WT/DS139/R, 11 Feb. 2000, para. 10.25. Benoit, C., "Picking Tariff Winners: Non-product Related PPMs and DSB Interpretations of Unconditionally Within Article I:1", *Georgetown Journal of International Law*, vol. 42, n. 2, 2011, pp. 583-604, p. 598.

42. Pauwelyn, *op. cit.*, p. 494.

43. Panel Report, *Brazil — Certain Measures Concerning Taxation and Charges*, WT/DS472/R, WT/DS497/R, 30 August 2017, para. 7.880.

in Art. XX:b, however safeguarding the competitiveness of energy-intensive industries, would not[44]. The *necessity* of the measure means that there shall be "a genuine relationship of ends and means"[45], that is to contribute to emission reductions, inter alia, by reducing the risk of carbon leakage[46], and regarding the proportionality, that there would not be "alternative measure that would achieve the same end and that is less restrictive of trade"[47]. Certainly, the free allocation of emission allowances is not a less restrictive measure as it does not contribute to the reduction of carbon emissions[48].

On the other hand, art. XX:g only applies if a safe climate could be understood as an "exhaustive natural resource", like clean air was[49]. A reasonable flexibility shall be included in the interpretation "in the light of contemporary concerns of the community of nations about the protection and conservation of the environment"[50], The corpus of climate treaties, the Paris Agreement in particular, is a strong support for the existence of such concerns[51]. The "reasonably related" condition that connects the measure and the expected result is much easier to fulfil than the "necessity" of Art. XX:b, so it does not represent a problem, in principle. Similarly, the "conjunction with restrictions on domestic production and consumption" exigence is weaker than the national treatment clause, permitting its use even when art. III GATT has been violated[52].

Now is the time for the *chapeau* of art. XX GATT. It does not concern the (climate) measure itself but rather how it is put into practice[53]. What

44. Tamiotti, *op. cit.*, pp. 1207-08; Pauwelyn, *op. cit.*, pp. 450-52; Holzer, *op. cit.*, p. 156.
45. Appellate Body Report, *Brazil — Measures Affecting Imports of Retreaded Tyres*, WT/DS332/AB/R, 3 December, 2007, para. 145.
46. Mehling *et. al.*, *op. cit.*
47. Appellate Body Report, *EC — Asbestos*, *op. cit.*, para. 172.
48. Rubini L., Jegou I., "Who'll Stop the Rain? Allocating Emissions Allowances for Free: Environmental Policy, Economics, and WTO Subsidy Law", *Transnational Environmental Law*, vol. 1, n. 2, 2012, pp. 325-354.
49. Panel Report, *United States — Standards for Reformulated and Conventional Gasoline*, WT/DS2/R, 20 May 1996, as modified by the Appellate Body Report, WT/DS2/AB/R, para. 6.37.
50. Appellate Body Report, *United States — Import Prohibition of Certain Shrimp and Shrimp Products*, WT/DS58/AB/R, 6 November 1998, para. 129.
51. Dobson, N., "The EU's Conditioning of the 'Extraterritorial' Carbon Footprint: A Call for an Integrated Approach in Trade Law Discourse", *Review of European, Comparative & International Environmental Law*, vol. 27, n. 1, 2018, pp. 75-89.
52. Like it happened in Appellate Body Report, *U. S. — Gasoline*, *op. cit.*, para. 21. Similarly; Appellate Body Report, *China — Measures Related to the Exportation of Rare Earths, Tungsten, and Molybdenum*, WT/DS431/AB/R, WT/DS432/AB/R, WT/DS433/AB/R, 7 August 2014, para. 5.134.
53. GATT Panel Report, *United States — Imports of Certain Automotive Spring Assemblies*, L/5333, BISD 30S/107, para. 56.

GATT wants is to guarantee that a formally justified measure would not be applied in a way that it could be considered an "arbitrary or unjustifiable discrimination, [n]or a disguised restriction to international trade".

In practice, it means that the process that executes the measure shall be transparent and predictable and that in such proceedings there would be opportunities for affected agents "to be heard, or to respond to any arguments"[54]. The real effects of the measure must correspond to the objectives of the measure, which formed the basis for justifying the exception (that is the arguments for fulfilling art. XX:b and/or XX:g)[55].

These requirements could have an important impact on the details of a CBAM implementation. For example, foreign producers may have enough time and "sufficient flexibility" to prove the carbon intensity of their products,[56] and in any analysis of the level of protection of their own regulation it must be taken "into account the specific conditions prevailing" in their countries[57]; third countries may have sufficient time (and receive technical assistance if necessary) to adapt their domestic regulation to be "comparable in effectiveness"[58] before imposing an effective economic burden[59]; countries that want to impose a CBAM may be engaged in "serious, across-the-board negotiations with the objective of concluding bilateral or multilateral agreements"[60], in this case, with the goal of reducing carbon emissions.

In order for the adjustment to not be deemed a "disguised restriction", it must effectively contribute, both in design and in practice, to reduce global

54. Appellate Body Report, *U. S. — Shrimp, op. cit.*, para. 180-181.

55. Appellate Body Report, *European Communities — Measures Prohibiting the Importation and Marketing of Seal Products*, WT/DS400/AB/R WT/DS401/AB/R, 22 May 2014, para. 5.318. Appellate Body Report, *Brazil—Retreaded Tyres, op. cit.*, para. 227.

56. Ismer, R., Neuhoff, K., "Border tax adjustment: a feasible way to support stringent emission trading", *European Journal of Law and Economics*. n. 24, 2007, pp. 137-164, p. 148.

57. Appellate Body Report, *United States — Import Prohibition of Certain Shrimp and Shrimp Products (art. 21.5)*, WT/DS58/AB/RW, 22 October 2001, para. 149.

58. *Ibidem*. para. 144. According to the Appellate Body, the measure should not be "an economic embargo to *require* other members to adopt essentially the same comprehensive regulatory program, to achieve a certain policy goal". On the other hand, the comparative analysis of the level of protection shall take "into consideration different conditions which may occur" in the two countries. Appellate Body Report, *U. S. — Shrimp, op. cit.*, para. 164.

59. Holzer, *op. cit.*, p. 173.

60. Appellate Body Report, *U. S. — Shrimp, op. cit.*, para. 166. Participating in Paris Agreement negotiations or, much more generally, in UNFCCC framework, could be enough. However, if the CBAM affects specifically two countries, probably a bilateral negotiation may be the only way to prove the good faith. Conf. Mehling *et. al., op. cit.*, p. 469.

emissions without pursuing another main objective[61]. It is insufficient for it to make only a marginal contribution to reducing carbon emissions while it has an important impact on other goals, such as improving local competitiveness.

Consequently, to pass the control of the *chapeau*, the application of a CBAM shall include an analysis of the implementation effectiveness of other countries' climate policy[62], a progression of these policies (e. g., as reported in their NDCs)[63], a comparison with their own policy (including effectiveness and progression) and, at the same time, an equalization of these variables with the principle of common but differentiated responsibilities and respective capabilities[64], the special and differential treatment of developing countries as recognized in WTO law[65], of least developed and small island developing states as recognized in Paris Agreement[66] and, in general, of the different levels of economic development[67]. Finally, to have both in design and in practice as the main objective of those argued for fitting art. XX:b and/or art. XX;g, and no other objectives such as the improvement of domestic industry competitiveness.

IV. THE EUROPEAN CARBON BORDER ADJUSTMENT MECHANISM (CBAM): FROM UNILATERAL ADJUSTMENT TO GLOBAL CLUBBING

On 16 May 2023, the definitive text of the CBAM Regulation was published in the Official Journal of the EU[68]. It has entered into force on

61. Appellate Body Report, *U. S. — Gasoline, op. cit.*, para. 25. Appellate Body Report, *U. S. — Shrimp (Article 21.5), op. cit.*, para. 5.142.
62. Pauwelyn, *op. cit.*, pp. 502-503.
63. Mehling *et. al.*, *op. cit.*, p. 469.
64. United Nations Framework Convention on Climate Change, New York, 9 May 1992, *UN Treaty Series*, n. 1771, p. 107, art. 3(1). Paris Agreement, Paris, 12 December 2015, *UN Treaty Series*, vol. 3156, p.79, art. 2(2). Hertel, M., "Climate-Change-Related Trade Measures and Article XX: Defining Discrimination in Light of the Principle of Common but Differentiated Responsibilities", *Journal of World Trade*, vol. 45, n. 3, 2011, pp. 653-678; Larbprasertporn, P., "The Interaction Between WTO Law and the Principle of Common but Differentiated Responsibilities in the Case of Climate-Related Border Tax Adjustments", *Goettingen Journal of International Law*, vol. 6, n. 1, 2014, pp. 645-670.
65. For example, Arts. XVIII, XXXVI, XXXVII, XXXVIII of GATT, of the preamble of Marrakesh Agreement, Annex IA, *UN Treaty Series*, n. 1867, p. 187.
66. Paris Agreement, *op. cit.*, arts. 4(6), 13(3). For a commentary *see* Rajamani, L., "Ambition and Differentiation in the 2015 Paris Agreement: Interpretative Possibilities and Underlying Politics", *International & Comparative Law Quarterly*, vol. 65, n. 2, 2016, pp. 493-514.
67. Pauwelyn, *op. cit.* pp. 503-504.
68. Regulation (EU) 2023/956 of the European Parliament and of the Council of 10 May 2023 *establishing a carbon border adjustment mechanism* (CBAM Regulation). OJ L 130,

1 October 2023, with payment obligations set to commence on 1 January 2026[69]. The CBAM Regulation covers specific goods with intensive energy consumption (iron and steel, cement, fertilizer, aluminium, electricity, and hydrogen)[70], but it is expected that gradually and before 2030, it will be expanded to all sectors covered by the EU ETS[71]. The CBAM, consequently, acts as a mirror of the EU ETS applied to imported products in the sectors covered by Directive 2003/87/EC.

According to the CBAM Regulation, declarants shall monitor and report CO2 equivalent emissions produced during the elaboration of the imported goods[72]. They must also purchase and surrender CBAM certificates to the extent their products caused greenhouse gas emissions during their production[73]. CBAM certificates will have a price linked to the price of the allowances used within the EU ETS[74]. Since free allocations of allowances for intensive energy sectors will continue until 2034, a correction mechanism has been designed to extend these free allocations to imports. Consequently, the economic impact of the CBAM is not expected to be, by the moment, very high[75]. However, the administrative burden to monitor and report CO2 equivalent emissions that is imposed on declarants has been in force since 1 October 2023. This requirement itself constitutes a trade restriction that needs justification[76].

16.5.2023, p. 52-104.

69. Art. 36.2b CBAM Regulation.
70. Annex I CBAM Regulation.
71. Whereas 67 Regulation.
72. Art. 6 CBAM Regulation.
73. Art. 22 CBAM Regulation.
74. Art. 21 CBAM Regulation.
75. In fact, according to current calculations, the two projection lines (the one referred to the reduction of free allowances and other one concerning to the increase of the price of CBAM equivalent rights) will cross each other in 2030, year when the economic effect of the mechanism will start to have an economic impact. *See* Statista, "Pathway of EU ETS free allowances phase-out and Carbon Border Adjustment Mechanism (CBAM) phase-in from 2025 to 2034", 25 July 2023. Retrieved from: *https://www.statista.com/statistics/1401673/eu-ets-free-allowance-cbam-pathway/*
76. If importers do not qualify as an authorised CBAM declarant, they can delegate the obligation to apply for authorisation to an indirect customs representative. In case that the importer is not established in the EU, the indirect customs representative must apply for the status of CBAM declarant by default. The declaration is made on annual basis the 31st of May of the following year and shall include information on the total quantity of each type of goods, total embedded emissions, total number of certificates to be surrendered, corresponding to the total embedded emissions, and copies of verification reports issued by accredited verifiers. CBAM Regulation, art. 5.

Information obligations during the "transitional period"[77] include data on quantity and type of goods, along with calculations on their embedded and indirect emissions[78]. In case of omissions or errors, EU member states can impose a penalty from 10 to 50 euros *per tonne* of unreported emissions depending on the relevance of the mistake and the degree of negligence of the reporting declarant[79].

To calculate embedded emissions, declarants shall use methods included in Annex IV of the Regulation and Annex III of the Implementing Regulation. However, until 31 December 2024, alternative methods may be used "if they lead to similar coverage and accuracy of emissions data compared to the methods listed"[80]. Following a similar approach, until 31 July 2024 default reference values may be reported if the reporting declarant lacks all the information for calculating actual embedded emissions[81]. Additionally, for complex goods, 20% of the total embedded emissions may be reported on estimations, adding even more flexibility to the reporting obligation[82].

To avoid suspicion of discrimination, CBAM is designed to be product-based rather than origin-based. There could be instances where the carbon price paid in the country of origin does not correspond to emissions produced in that same country but rather in a third one. However, a weak aspect is that it must be a price "effectively paid"[83], leaving out regulatory measures to reduce carbon emissions that do not involve explicit carbon pricing[84]. This element could be considered contrary to what the EU agreed upon in the international fora since it leaves out other alternatives to fight against climate change that are perfectly compatible with the Paris Agreement.

Even leaving out climate policies that do not represent an "effective payment" for carbon emissions, carbon pricing policies applied worldwide are

77. From 1 October 2023 until 31 December 2025. European Commission Implementing Regulation (EU) 2023/1773 of 17 August 2023 *laying down the rules for the application of Regulation (EU) 2023/956 of the European Parliament and of the Council as regards reporting obligations for the purposes of the carbon border adjustment mechanism during the transitional period* (CBAM Implementing Regulation). OJ 15.09.2023.
78. The report shall follow the form included in the annex I of the CBAM Implementing Regulation.
79. Art. 16.2 CBAM Implementing Regulation.
80. Art. 4.2 CBAM Implementing Regulation.
81. Art. 4.3 CBAM Implementing Regulation.
82. Art. 5 CBAM Implementing Regulation.
83. Art. 9.1 CBAM Regulation.
84. Delbeke J., Vis P., "How CBAM can become a steppingstone towards carbon pricing globally", *STG Policy Papers*, n. 2023/06, March 2023. Retrieved from: *https://cadmus.eui.eu/bitstream/handle/1814/75472/STG_PB_2023_06.pdf?sequence=1&isAllowed=y*

far from being a monolithic block. Different approaches include compulsory schemes with an absolute emission reduction target (like the EU ETS), Voluntary Carbon Markets based on credits generated in comparison to a baseline without any regulatory intervention (like the Chicago Carbon Exchange)[85], or nationwide systems combined with local initiatives (like Canada or China). Arguing the equivalence of payments among them will be a difficult task for declarants. Another difficulty is to determine what happens when the carbon price "is paid" by a reduction of emissions outside of the country of origin of the goods, something quite usual in many carbon pricing mechanisms[86].

Up to this extent, the CBAM seems to be a heavy bureaucracy machinery imposed unilaterally by the EU to importers (and to make matters worse, up to 2030 with almost no impact on carbon pricing). In fact, we can say that except in those cases where trade is intra-group (giving access to all the information about the product, suppliers, processes, and proceedings), and declarants are companies with sufficient expertise and experience in EU-ETS to make the calculations, declarants will face strong difficulties in fulfilling all the required information.

However, not everything is lost. The CBAM regulation includes a very important exclusion of applications that grant third countries' governments (and not companies) the possibility to avoid any negative effect of the CBAM on their exports, including administrative ones. If the good originated from a country covered by the EU ETS (for example EFTA members) or from a territory with an agreement with the Union that recognizes a full linking between the EU ETS and the emission trading system of that third country or territory (for example Switzerland)[87].

This is a real application of what is called "clubbing" or "coalition of the willing" in climate literature[88]. The CBAM would act as a *de facto* climate

85. Wessel G., de Boer R., "Voluntary Carbon Markets: Supervisory issues", *The Dutch Authority for the Financial Markets Occasional Paper*, 2023. Retrieved from: *https://www.afm.nl/~/profmedia/files/rapporten/2023/occasional-paper-handel-in-co2.pdf* It would be expected that minimum standards would be a pre-requisite of any recognition. For a brief analysis of these possible minimum standards *see*: ICVCM, "The Core Carbon Principles. Plus the Program-Level Assessment Framework and Assessment Procedure", *Integrity Council for the Voluntary Carbon Market*, 2022. Retrieved from: *https://icvcm.org/the-core-carbon-principles/*
86. La Hoz Theuer, S., Hall, M., Eden, A., Krause, E., Haug, C., De Clara, S., "Offset Use Across Emissions Trading Systems", *International Carbon Action Partnership*, Berlin, 2023. Retrieved from: *https://icapcarbonaction.com/en/publications/offset-use-across-emissions-trading-systems*
87. Art. 2.6 and Annex III CBAM Regulation.
88. Nordhaus W., "Climate clubs: overcoming free-riding in international climate policy", *American Economic Review*, vol. 105, n. 4, 2015, pp. 1339-1370. Keohane, N., Petsonk,

club[89] where entry conditions are not specified yet. These conditions will undoubtedly encompass equivalent carbon pricing mechanisms, but the degree of recognition of equivalence could be modulated by other conditions or compensations including much more ambitious trade agreements[90] or other types of cooperation in climate-related areas such as research and development, innovation, or industrial initiatives[91].

In fact, it could be said that a CBAM club has a double standard membership or a "club within the club"[92]. Golden membership is reserved for those countries with full links with the EU ETS. Products from these countries are directly excluded from the CBAM regulation and do not need to follow any requirements, including administrative ones[93]. However, there is a second level, or standard membership, for products that had paid for their emissions in a third country and are eligible for full or partial compensation for the payments to be made by the CBAM[94]. In this case, standard members still do need to declare emissions, provide evidence of the payments made, and they are subject to registration of installations in their countries of origin[95]. In essence, producing in a third country that belongs to this standard membership allows companies to reduce the number of CBAM certificates to be surrendered (direct costs), but not bureaucratic ones.

One challenge with the EU's climate club exception is that it requires other countries to adopt systems with fundamentally the same design as the EU's.[96] This idea echoes arguments presented in the *United States —*

A., and Hanafi, A., "Toward a club of carbon markets", *Climatic Change*, n. 144, 2017, pp. 81-95. Leal-Arkas, R., "Climate clubs and international trade across the European and International Landscape", *European Energy and Environmental Law Review*, vol. 29, n. 3, 2020, pp. 72-88. Stern, N. and Lankes, H. P., "Collaborating and Delivering on Climate Action through a Climate Club: An independent report to the G7", London School of Economics and Political Science, 2022.

89. Szulecki, K., Overland, I., Smith, I. D., "The European Union's CBAM as a de facto Climate Club: The Governance Challenges", *Frontiers in Climate*, n. 4, 2022, p. 942583.
90. Kuhn, T., Pestow, R., Zenker, A., "Formation of climate coalitions and preferential free trade: the case for participation linkage", *Environmental Economics and Policy Studies*, 2023.
91. Carraro, C., "Clubs, R&D, and Climate Finance: Incentives for Ambitious GHG Emission Reductions", *Brief 1/2017*, Fondazione Eni Enrico Mattei, 2017.
92. Mbengue, M. M., Cima, E., "'Clubbing in the Club': Could Climate-Related Trade Arrangements Set the Pace for Future Climate Cooperation?", *American Journal of International Law*, n. 116, 2022, pp. 219-224.
93. Art. 2.6 CBAM Regulation.
94. Art. 9 CBAM Regulation.
95. Art. 10 CBAM Regulation.
96. Vidigal, G., Venzke, I., "Of false conflicts and real challenges: trade agreements, climate clubs, and border adjustments.", *American Journal of International Law*, n. 116, 2022, pp. 202-207.

Shrimp[97] or in the *United States — Tuna II*[98]. According to this WTO case law, the EU CBAM call to "clubbing" by systems of monetary disincentives to emissions would be admissible only if there is no other system "comparable in effectiveness" to carbon pricing that achieves "essentially the same" policy objectives as the EU ETS. If this is not the case, the measure would not pass art. XX GATT *chapeau* standard and, therefore, could be declared arbitrary or unjustifiable discrimination.

The spirit of the Paris Agreement is to open climate strategies to any effective policy, not to a single one. Consequently, there could be numerous countries that fight climate change, but not necessarily through a carbon emission market. In case of a hypothetical WTO dispute over the CBAM, a pivotal question would arise: how to quantify other countries' regulatory disincentives, such as carbon taxes, assessing whether they fulfil the same objective of the EU's ETS to the same degree as the EU is allowed to demand[99]. That calculation is extremely difficult[100] and, contrary to the approach taken by the CBAM regulation, the burden of proof in WTO law lies with who claims an exception to general rules of free trade, that is the EU, and not on who trades, as per CBAM regulation requirements.

Touching back on the clubbing rationale of the CBAM, to contextualise the problem we need to ask ourselves who would be interested in meeting the membership requirements. According to UN COMTRADE figures, the primary exporters to the EU in the affected sectors and, consequently, candidates for EU CBAM club membership are: Norway, Russia, Iceland, China and Switzerland (for aluminium), Turkey, Colombia, Vietnam, Belarus, and Ukraine (for cement), Norway, Switzerland, Serbia, Russia, and Ukraine (for electricity), Russia Algeria, Egypt, Morocco, and Norway (for fertilizers); and China, Russia, Turkey, Ukraine, and India (for iron and steel)[101]. The four

97. Appellate Body Report, *U. S. — Shrimp, op. cit.*, para. 161. Appellate Body Report, *U. S. — Shrimp (Article 21.5), op. cit.*, para. 144.
98. Appellate Body Report, *United States — Measures Concerning the Importation, Marketing and Sale of Tuna and Tuna Products (Article 21.5 by Mexico)*, WT/DS381/AB/RW, 20 November 2015, para. 7.330.
99. Vidigal and Venzke, *op. cit.*
100. However, it could be not so difficult if an International Carbon Price Floor (ICPF) is implemented, as the International Monetary Fund proposed. Parry, I., Black, S., Roaf, J., "Proposal for an International Carbon Price Floor Among Large Emitters", *IMF Staff Climate Notes 2021/001*, International Monetary Fund, 2021. Even possible in theory, practical problems remain. On this regard *see* World Bank, *"State and Trends of Carbon Pricing 2019"*, Washington DC: World Bank, 2021. Retrieved from: *https://openknowledge.worldbank.org/handle/10986/31755.*
101. UN COMTRADE data base. Retrieved from: *https://comtradeplus.un.org/*

most concerned countries are Russia, China, and Turkey, in this order[102]. This data could be altered by the economic sanctions against Russia due to the war in Ukraine (from December 2022 steel, iron, and cement are included in the banned products), but it does not change the essence[103].

Some of these affected countries are already part of the EU ETS or an equivalent system (Norway, Iceland, Switzerland); in other words, they hold the golden membership to the club. Among the remaining three most affected countries, only China has developed a carbon market that monetizes carbon emissions. Neither Russia nor Turkey has equivalent initiatives[104]. In this sense, a comparison between EU ETS and China National ETS proves essential. Firstly, to clarify whether payments done in the latter qualify for art. 9 CBAM certificates reduction, i. e., a standard membership pass to the club. And secondly, to know which steps shall be followed, if ever possible, to achieve full recognition as an "equivalent system", i. e., the golden membership pass.

V. THE CHINESE NATIONAL ETS AND THE EU ETS: SIMILARITIES AND DIFFERENCES

In 2010 China mentioned for the first time its intention to use carbon trading to mitigate its growing emissions[105]. Carbon trading was included in the 12th Five-Year Plan (2011-2015)[106]. Soon after, a work plan for designing

102. Using data from 2021: UNCTAD, "EU should consider trade impacts of new climate change mechanism". Retrieved from: *https://unctad.org/news/eu-should-consider-trade-impacts-new-climate-change-mechanism*. For an analysis see: Smith, I. D., Overland, I., Szulecki, K., "The EU's CBAM and Its 'Significant Others': Three Perspectives on the Political Fallout from Europe's Unilateral Climate Policy Initiative", *Journal of Common Market Studies*, 2023.
103. European Council, "EU sanctions against Russia explained", last review 12 October 2023. Retrieved from: *https://www.consilium.europa.eu/en/policies/sanctions/restrictive-measures-against-russia-over-ukraine/sanctions-against-russia-explained/#sanctions*
104. Incipient initiatives were registered in 2023 for Russia and for Turkey, but it seems they are in their beginning. *See* ICAP, "Turkey" International Carbon Action Partnership, 2023. Retrieved from: *https://icapcarbonaction.com/en/ets/turkiye*; ICAP, "Russian Federation" International Carbon Action Partnership, 2023. Retrieved from: *https://icapcarbonaction.com/en/ets/russian-federation-sakhalin*
105. Decision of the State Council (China) on *Accelerating the Fostering and Development of Strategic Emerging Industries*, 10 October 2010. An unofficial translation into English is available. Retrieved from: *https://chinaenergyportal.org/wp-content/uploads/2017/01/Development-Strategic-Emerging-Industries.pdf*
106. Notice of the State Council on issuing the *Work Plan for Greenhouse Gas Emission Control during the 12th Five-Year Plan Period*, 1 December 2011. An unofficial translation into

and implementing pilot carbon trading markets was prepared and executed[107]. To facilitate exchange among pilot markets, basic regulation of trading was published in 2012[108] and 2014[109]. This initial regulatory framework would be the seed of the future Chinese National ETS.

Unlike the EU ETS, Chinese pilot markets operated on a voluntary basis. After 2015, carbon allowances co-existed with, and were almost replaced by, less transparent "Certified Emission Reductions" (CERs), a form of Clean Development Mechanism given to companies meeting reduction goals[110]. Target sectors were quite open and heterogeneous, including electrical power, steel, chemicals, petrochemicals, nonferrous metals, building materials, civil aviation, papermaking, and ceramics. Once a sector accepted to participate, companies were given a period to set reduction goals. If any of them failed to achieve objectives, they had to purchase CERs on the market. The idea was that pilot markets would serve as a tool for promoting the implementation of green technologies rather than punishing emitting sectors. However, CERs were not fully interchangeable. Due to differing provisions[111] within each pilot market; each market had diverse CER policies regarding market entry and different thresholds[112]. In 2016, it was clear that the main problem was the lack of standardization among sectors and markets[113]. Due to insufficient

English is available. Retrieved from: *http://english.cbcsd.org.cn/databases/database_energy/policies/Domestic/20130808/58943.shtml*

107. Pilot markets were located in Beijing, Tianjin, Shanghai, Chongqing, Hubei Province, Guangdong Province and Shenzhen. Notice of the National Development and Reform Commission on Issuing the *Carbon Emissions rights Trading Pilot Work*, 29 October 2011. No English version available. For a commentary *see*: Munnings C, Morgenstern RD, Wang Z, Liu X., "Assessing the design of three carbon trading pilot programs in China", *Energy Policy*, n. 96, 2016, pp. 688-699.
108. Notice of the National Development and Reform Commission on issuing the *Interim Measures for the Administration of Voluntary Greenhouse Gas Emission Reduction Transactions*, 13 June 2012. An unofficial translation into English is available Retrieved from: *https://www.lawinfochina.com/display.aspx?lib=law&id=10767&CGid=&EncodingName=gb2312.*
109. Notice of the National Development and Reform Commission on issuing the *Interim Measures for the Administration of Carbon Emission Permit Trading*, 10 December 2014. An unofficial translation into English is available. Retrieved from: *http://www.csrcare.com/Law/LawShowEn?id=35179.*
110. Li, L., Ye, F., Li, Y., Chang, C-T., "How will the Chinese Certified Emission Reduction scheme save cost for the national carbon trading system?", *Journal of Environmental Management*, n. 244, 2019, pp. 99-109.
111. Differences were related to the CER proportions allocated, project category, project source, method of reducing displacement output time, and offset limits.
112. Weng Q., Xu H., "A review of China's carbon trading market", *Renewable and Sustainable Energy Reviews*, n. 91, 2018, pp. 613-619.
113. In fact, the last too markets launched in Sichuan and Fujian in December 2016 (officially no pilots) were designed focussing on that issue, unfortunately with little success.

market liquidity, low carbon emissions price, and small trading volume, the NDRC suspended the application of CERs in March 2017[114].

The idea of a Chinese National ETS was launched in 2017, initially focusing on three sectors (electricity, cement, and aluminium electrolysis). Ultimately focusing solely on electricity due to the persisting challenges of obtaining accurate data for the other sectors[115].

China's national ETS commenced trading on the Shanghai Environment and Energy Exchange on 16 July 2021, covering over 40% of the country's carbon emissions, distributed in 2,162 companies from the electricity power sector, as well as captive power plants in other sectors. Allowances are freely allocated using benchmarks, and they are based on actual production levels. Compliance obligations are not yet harmonized as they vary among different types of power generation[116]. Standardization and simplification have been introduced through ministerial orders; however, the verification process is managed by provincial-level authorities[117]. In 2021, a general fraud involving the information provided by companies was discovered, casting doubt on all the data of the Chinese National ETS[118]. In response, new instructions were implemented, including a notice proposing to strengthen the supervision, management, and information disclosure of carbon emissions; to explore the enterprise carbon accounting system; and to regularly conduct enterprise carbon audits that may prevent carbon

Zhang, S., Jiang, K., Wang, L. *et al.*, "Do the performance and efficiency of China's carbon emission trading market change over time?", *Environmental Science and Pollution Research*, n. 27, 2020, pp. 33140-33160.

114. Huang, W., Wang, Q., Li, H., Fan, H., Qian, Y., Klemeš, J. J., "Review of recent progress of emission trading policy in China", *Journal of Cleaner Production*, n. 349, 2022, p. 131480.

115. Cao J., Ho, M. S., Jorgenson, D. W., Nielsen C. P., "China's emissions trading system and an ETS-carbon tax hybrid", *Energy Economics*, n. 81, 2019, pp. 741-753. Corti Varela, J., "El mercado chino de derechos de emisión", in Giles Carnero R. M. (ed.), *Desafíos de la Acción Jurídica Internacional y Europea frente al cambio climático*, 2018, pp. 73-85.

116. ICAP, "China National ETS", International Carbon Action Partnership, 2023. Retrieved from: *https://icapcarbonaction.com/system/files/ets_pdfs/icap-etsmap-factsheet-55.pdf*

117. These orders are produced by the Ministry of Ecology and Environment, for example, the "Work Plan on the Management of Enterprise Greenhouse Gas emissions Reporting and verification in 2022" and the "2022 Guidelines for Power Greenhouse Gas Emission Measurement and Reporting". For a commentary on these documents *see*: Hao H., Yang X., "China's Carbon Market in the Context of Carbon Neutrality: Legal and Policy Perspectives", *Sustainability* vol. 14, n. 18, 2018, p. 11399.

118. Yihe, X., "China vows zero tolerance on carbon emissions fraud", *Upstream*, 20 April 2022. Retrieved from: *https://www.upstreamonline.com/energy-transition/china-vows-zero-tolerance-on-carbon-emissions-fraud/2-1-1202527.*

data fraud. Additionally, a *Format Guidelines for Legal Disclosure of Enterprise Environmental Information* was distributed. These guidelines stipulate that when enterprises prepare annual and interim reports, the expression of relevant environmental issues should be true, accurate, and objective. There should be no misleading judgments and no exaggerated, fraudulent, misleading, inaccurate, or biased language[119]. Despite recommendations to authorities, no essential changes in monitoring, reporting, and verification regulations were implemented.

The Chinese Monitoring, Reporting, and Verification (MRV) system for carbon emissions data has been under construction since 2013. However, it was not until 2017, when the preparation of the national market started, that the Chinese government accelerated its development[120]. The MRV system is essential for the effective management of a complex structure such as an ETS. It involves the participation of different levels of public authorities, the corporate sector, and third-party verification companies, all integrated by laws and regulations, technical standards, and data reporting systems. If one level of the building fails, the whole system collapses. Unfortunately, according to *The National Measures for the Administration of Carbon Emission Trading*[121], a significant part of the data exchange still depends on the politized provincial-level Department of Ecology and Environment, as well as Municipal-level authorities. The first ones are responsible for overseeing the implementation of the ETS, including identifying covered entities, organizing MRV, hiring verifiers, calculating allowances, managing provincial registry accounts, overseeing compliance, and the submission of annual GHG emissions reports. The second ones are in charge of managing covered entities.[122]

119. Hao, H., Yang, X., *op. cit.*
120. Guoqiang, Q., Xiaoming, H., Yaning, J., "Constructing China's MRV System. Leveraging Finance for Green Policy Briefs", Paulson Institute, 2018. Retrieved from: *https://www.paulsoninstitute.org/wp-content/uploads/2018/09/MRV-Policy-Brief_Sm.pdf*
121. Order 19/2021 of the Ministry of Ecology and Environment of the People's Republic of China on *The National Measures for the Administration of Carbon Emission Trading*, ref. 14672/2021-00004. No English version available. Retrieved from: *https://www.mee.gov.cn/xxgk2018/xxgk/xxgk02/202101/t20210105_816131.html*. *See* also: Guidelines on Enterprise Greenhouse Gas Emissions Accounting and Reporting-Power Generation Facilities, issued on 15 March 2022. No English version available. Retrieved from: *https://www.mee.gov.cn/xxgk2018/xxgk/xxgk06/202112/W020211202787049808223.pdf*. For a commentary of both, *see* Hao/Yang, *op. cit.*
122. Notice 111/2022 of the Ministry of Ecology and Environment of the People's Republic of China *on the Key Tasks of the Management of Enterprises Greenhouse Gas Emission Reporting in 2022*. No English version available. Retrieved from: *https://www.mee.gov.cn/xxgk2018/xxgk/xxgk06/202203/t20220315_971468.html*

During the first year of the Chinese National ETS implementations, eighty-nine of the three hundred institutions, including ninety-four national quality test centers, violated MRV regulations[123]. Nine of these irregularities, including four national quality test centers, raised suspicions of providing false reports. Another nine, including two national quality test centers, were related to test results beyond their testing capabilities.[124]

The Chinese Central Government responded to these anomalies by issuing a joint notice of the People's Procuratorate, the Ministry of Public Security, and the Ministry of Ecology and the Environment on *Law-Violating Crimes of Dangerous Waste Abandoning and False Reporting of Automatic Monitoring Data on Key Pollution Units*[125]. The message was that MRV proceedings were fine but there were some rotten apples in the basket.

The criminalization of the monitoring included examinations of third-party monitoring institutions, comparing their monitoring reports by cross-checking, and the establishment of severe punishments for environmental crimes of providing false testing reports or distorted proof documents. This indicates that the data from third-party verification companies was not reliable. Finally, in 2022, at the National Carbon Market Construction Conference the Ministry of Ecology and Environment announced changes in the management of data quality by a daily quality-control mechanism for carbon market data[126], whose details are not available yet.

The MRV regulation is, precisely the main difference between the EU and the Chinese National ETS. It is true that the EU ETS covers many more sectors than the Chinese[127], but the percentage of emissions included is quite similar

123. Zuming, Z., "With the Proliferation of Fraudulent Testing Data, What will be the Focus of the Upcoming Annual Inspection Agency Supervision and Spot Check?", *The Paper*, 6 September 2022. Retrieved from: *www.thepaper.cn/newsDetail_forward_19788284.*
124. Shang, H., Tang, F. F., "The mechanisms and development of emissions-trading markets: A comparison of the European Union and China", in Song, L., Zhou Y. (eds.), *China's Transition to a New Phase of Development,* Canberra: The Australian National University, 2022, pp. 239-256.
125. Join notice of the People's Procuratorate, the Ministry of Public Security and the Ministry of Ecology and the Environment on *Law-Violating Crimes of Dangerous Waste Abandoning and False Reporting of Automatic Monitoring Data on Key Pollution Units,* 6 May 2022. No English version available. Retrieved from: *www.spp.gov.cn/xwfbh/wsfbt/202205/t20220506_556243.shtml#1*. For a commentary *see ibidem*.
126. Ministry of Ecology and Environment, "National Carbon Market Construction Work Conference Held in Beijing", *Shanghai Observer*, 16 July 2022. Retrieved from: *https://sghexport.shobserver.com/html/baijiahao/2022/07/16/799615.html*
127. Carbon dioxide (CO2) from electricity and heat generation, energy-intensive industry sectors (including oil refineries, steel works, and production of iron, aluminium, metals,

(around 40%). Both have free allocations and policies for the reduction of such rights to create incentives for reducing emissions. Additionally, since the *2015 EU-China joint statement on climate change*[128], the EU and China have collaborated with each other to create a *Platform for Policy Dialogue and Cooperation between the EU and China on Emissions Trading*[129]. This instrument should provide capacity building and training to support the Chinese Ministry of Ecology and Environment, in the development of the Chinese National ETS. All these efforts have not provided, up until now, a real coupling of EU and Chinese MRV regulations. Moreover, without a fine harmony of data collection, data processing, and similar supervision intensity in previous proceedings —a true common MRV regulation framework —art. 9, CBAM certificate reduction is highly unlikely to become a reality for Chinese products[130].

EU MRV regulation indeed has a quite long history and Rome was not built in a day. The first EU MRV regulation was passed in 2004[131]. For phase two of the EU ETC, improved MRV rules were introduced[132]. They included

---

cement, lime, glass, ceramics, pulp, paper, cardboard, acids and bulk organic chemicals), aviation (within the European Economic Area and departing flights to Switzerland and the United Kingdom), maritime transport (specifically 50% of emissions from voyages starting or ending outside of the EU and 100% of emissions from voyages between two EU ports and when ships are within EU ports); nitrous oxide (N2O) from production of nitric, adipic and glyoxylic acids and glyoxal; and perfluorocarbons (PFCs) from the production of aluminium. And from 2024, installations for the incineration of municipal waste above a certain threshold are also required to monitor and report their emissions in the EU ETS. And from 2027 the ETS 2 will include buildings, road transport and additional sectors. *See* Annex 1 of the Directive 2003/87/EC of the European Parliament and of the Council of 13 October 2003 *establishing a system for greenhouse gas emission allowance trading within the Union and amending Council Directive 96/61/EC*, consolidated version 2023. Retrieved from: *http://data.europa.eu/eli/dir/2003/87/2023-06-05.*

128. EU-China Joint Statement on Climate Change, 29 June 2015. Retrieved from: *https://www.consilium.europa.eu/media/23733/150629 eu-china-climate-statement-doc.pdf*

129. Memorandum of Understanding to Enhance Cooperation on Emissions Trading between the European Commission and the Ministry of Ecology and Environment of the People's Republic of China, 16 June 2018. Retrieved from: *https://climate.ec.europa.eu/system/files/2018-07/20180713_mou_en.pdf*

130. Farkaš, E., "The European Union Carbon Border Adjustment Mechanism: An Opportunity for Global Carbon Price Synchronization?", *Review of European & Transatlantic Affairs*, vol. 7, n. 1, 2023, pp. 35-57.

131. Commission Decision 2004/156/EC of 29 January 2004 *establishing guidelines for the monitoring and reporting of greenhouse gas emissions pursuant to Directive 2003/87/EC of the European Parliament and of the Council. Official Journal* L 59, 26.2.2004, p. 1-74.

132. Commission Decision 2007/589/EC of 18 July 2007 *establishing guidelines for the monitoring and reporting of greenhouse gas emissions pursuant to Directive 2003/87/EC of the European Parliament and of the Council. Official Journal* L 229, 31.8.2007, p. 1-85.

the submission of member countries' reports at the end of each cycle and their audit by an accredited MRV sector before March 31 of the subsequent year. Unlike the Chinese MRV regulation, the EU ETS has strict penalties on companies. Penalties amount to €100 per missing allowance, representing a fine equivalent to 100% of the value of the emissions omitted, according to current market prices[133].

In 2012[134] and 2018[135], new adaptations were introduced in the EU MRV regulation to make it compatible with the changes in the ETS mechanism. However, they do not alter the essence of the system. This system includes complex technical proceedings for the monitoring and reporting of greenhouse gas emissions and activity data: a monitoring plan[136] and monitoring development[137], data management, and control[138] made by each operator; and reporting requirements to be done by the operator to the national authority[139], verification by an independent entity (art. 6-43), accreditation of verifiers by a national accreditation body (art. 44-52) and the requisites of the national accreditation body (art. 53-69).

The complete framework of the EU MRV includes guidelines, templates, training handbooks, data models, and examples of reports, all of which contribute to a comprehensive and harmonized implementation[140]. No such

133. The penalty was fixed in article 16.3 of the ETS Directive in 2013 and it is increased in line with the European Index of Consumer Prices.

134. Commission Regulation (EU) No 601/2012 of 21 June 2012 *on the monitoring and reporting of greenhouse gas emissions pursuant to Directive 2003/87/EC of the European Parliament and of the Council. Official Journal* L 181, 12.7.2012, p. 30-104.

135. Commission Implementing Regulation (EU) 2018/2066 of 19 December 2018 *on the monitoring and reporting of greenhouse gas emissions pursuant to Directive 2003/87/EC of the European Parliament and of the Council and amending Commission Regulation (EU) No 601/2012. Official Journal* L 334, 31.12.2018, p. 1-93. Consolidated version (2022) could be retrieved from: *http://data.europa.eu/eli/reg_impl/2018/2066/oj*. See also Commission Implementing Regulation (EU) 2018/2067 of 19 December 2018 *on the verification of data and on the accreditation of verifiers pursuant to Directive 2003/87/EC of the European Parliament and of the Council, Official Journal* L 334, 31.12.2018, p. 94-134. Consolidated version (2022) could be retrieved from: *http://data.europa.eu/eli/reg_impl/2018/2067/2021-01-01*.

136. Regulation (EU) 2018/2066, art. 11-18. This includes Calculation-based methodology (Activity data, Calculation factors), and Measurement-based methodology.

137. Regulation (EU) 2018/2066, art. 19-50.

138. Regulation (EU) 2018/2066, art. 58-67.

139. Regulation (EU) 2018/2066, art. 68-73.

140. European Commission, "Monitoring, reporting and verification of EU ETS emissions", 2023. Retrieved from: *https://climate.ec.europa.eu/eu-action/eu-emissions-trading-system-eu-ets/monitoring-reporting-and-verification-eu-ets-emissions_en*

development and transparency are available on the Chinese side. In fact, there is not a single point that includes all the information on the Chinese MRV regulation, no official translations into languages other than Chinese[141], and the documents available seem to be much less detailed than those of the EU, leaving many factors to the discretion of application authorities.

Moreover, many important factors such as the quota allocation methods or quota settlement are decided by each Implementation Plan[142] (normally year by year), there is no clear cross-reference of the regulation available. Guidelines for monitoring, data management, reporting, and verification (and accreditation of verifiers) are not accessible on the internet. This lack of transparency is probably the reason why Chinese authorities have decided to follow a criminal law strategy (normally non-public trials) to fight infractions instead of a system of economic sanctions like the EU does, which involves a legal and economic argumentation to justify why the entity, or the verifier, has violated the ETS framework and how to improve it with better MRV regulations.

VI. CONCLUSIONS

The fight against climate change has focused, since the Kyoto Protocol, on the transition of our economies into low-carbon or, and more recently, into neutral-carbon economic structure. Given that major emitters were market economies, and that international trade operates primarily under free market rules, the most important proposals for promoting the transition included market tools for promoting the reduction of emissions without altering the free interaction of economic forces. In this sense, initially in the EU and then in other countries, ETS has been considered the main tool for the decarbonisation of market economies.

The domestic nature of ETS creates, however, interferences with imported products in open economies, with carbon leakage being probably the most important one of these interferences. The EU has decided to tackle the problem through a CBAM which, at the moment, only establishes an administrative burden on importers but, in the long term, will involve payments. However,

141. Unofficial translation of key regulation can be found at: *https://chinaenergyportal.org/*

142. Ministry of Ecology and Environment of the People's Republic of China, *Implementation Plan for the 2019-2020 national carbon emission trading quota setting and allocation (power generation industry)*, 30 December 2020. Unofficial English version available. Retrieved from: *https://chinaenergyportal.org/en/implementation-plan-for-the-2019-2020-national-carbon-emission-trading-quota-setting-and-allocation-power-generation-industry/*

the EU CBAM includes two exceptions: one for products from countries with ETS fully linked with the EU (EEA and Switzerland) to which neither administrative nor payment charges would apply. The other exception is for products coming from countries where an "effective payment" for emission has been made. In this latter case, administrative obligations are still applicable, but payments' ones can be reduced. The term "Effective payment" is the keyword since the idea of "effectivity" implies certain compatibility of climate policies at origin and the EU. These two exceptions would be the means by which the EU is promoting a "carbon club" with two levels of membership.

Focusing on China, its National ETS is not fully linked with the EU ETS, hence, it cannot enjoy the "golden membership" to the EU promoted carbon club. Regarding the "standard membership", although formally designed with the technical support of the EU, the Chinese National ETS still lacks transparency, particularly regarding data collection and data processing. Strong doubts remain on its MRV system, particularly on the effectiveness of persecution proceedings in case of fraud, which makes any payment there difficult to qualify as "effective" according to the EU CBAM regulation.

Indeed, payment obligations will not be economically significant until 2030, providing China with time to improve its MRV to fulfil EU standards. However, the lack of transparency of the Chinese National ETS does not seem to be the consequence of its immaturity, but it would be part of Chinese regulatory philosophy. In fact, it would be a constant in all of China's economic regulation that follows, probably, objectives of economic independence and full sovereignty in strategic economic sectors.

If this analysis is true, two paths would be available when payments start to negatively affect China's imports. Either the EU accepts Chinese standards, water down the effect of the CBAM; or China decides to fight initiating a trade dispute, probably under the WTO dispute settlement mechanism. And in this last case, unless the case law changes drastically, China has many chances to win.

A Study on China's Measures for the Decoupling of the Economic Growth and the Carbon Emission

RAO LEI[1] AND GAO MIN
School of economics, Sichuan University (China)

I. INTRODUCTION

China's economy has been developing at a continuously rate of the average annual growth rate of 9.36% since the economic reforms and open-door policies in 1978, which has become the fastest growing economy in the world. China's GDP in 1978 was 367.87 billion yuan, which accounted for 1.8% of the world economy[2], while in 2019, China's GDP has exceeded 99 trillion yuan, which is expected to account for more than 16% of the world economy[3]. However, since the foundation of China's national economy was weak and the economic development lagged far behind western developed countries at the time of 1978, China has started with the extensive economic growth mode based on the low level of technologies, resulting excessive energy consumption, causing the rapid increase of carbon dioxide emissions and environmental pollution from then on. As China has made considerable progress in the economic development and technologies, the awareness of energy saving and emission reduction has been gradually enhanced as well. At present, China is at a critical period of national economic development, accompanying with the reduction of the consumption of fossil energy and reducing carbon emissions.

---

1. School of economics, Sichuan University, No. 24, Section 1 South of first Ring Road, Chengdu 610065, Sichuan, China; Tel: +86 13568898658; E-mail: raoleiscu@163.com
2. National Bureau of Statistics of China, *The 23th of series reports on the achievements of economic and social development in the 70th anniversary of the founding of the People's Republic of China*, retrieved from *http://www.stats.gov.cn/*
3. The State Council Information Office of the People's Republic of China, *China's economy in 2019*, retrieved from *http://www.scio.gov.cn/*

As a big and responsible country, China has made a commitment to reduce carbon dioxide emissions per unit of GDP by 40% to 45% by 2020, based on the level of that in 2005, and has successfully fulfilled the commitment in advance. Then China has announced to reach the peak of CO_2 emissions at around 2030 and strive to achieve it even ahead of that time. Another commitment for 2030 is that the CO_2 emissions per unit of GDP in China is to be reduced by 60% to 65% than that in 2005[4]. Therefore, it is significant to study the causes and the measures for the decoupling of China's economic growth and carbon emissions to find out the more efficient measures for the further carbon reduction.

II. LITERATURE REVIEW

The current study on the relationship between economic growth and carbon emissions focuses on the following aspects: firstly, using economic analysis tools to study the law between carbon emissions and economic growth. Zhang has used environmental Kuznets curve (EKC) to analyse the relationship between per capita income and per capita CO_2 in the study of carbon emissions and economic growth in Beijing[5]. Via EKC hypothesis and the decoupling theory, Zhang *et al.* has found that the coordination of carbon emissions and economic growth between EU and other countries is very good, but in the developing countries, such as China and India, it needs to be strengthened[6]. Qi has analysed the fluctuation trend of the "expansion connection —weak decoupling— strong decoupling" between China's economic growth and carbon emissions by using the decoupling model[7].

Secondly, by summarizing empirical data, analysing empirically the relationship between economic growth and carbon emissions. Wang has analysed the relationship between energy consumption and economic growth in China, basing on the historical data from 1990 to 2007, and

4. The State Council Information Office of the People's Republic of China, *China's Energy Policy 2012*, retrieved from *http://www.scio.gov.cn/*
5. Zhang, L., "An Empirical Study on the relationship between carbon emission and economic growth in Beijing--Based on EKC and STIRPAT model" in *Technology economy*, vol. 32, n. 1, 2013, pp. 90-95.
6. Zhang, X., Luo, H. & Lv, L., "Analysis of coordination between carbon emission and economic growth" in *Journal of environmental engineering technology*, vol. 7, n. 4, 2017, pp. 517-524.
7. Qi, Y., "An analysis of the decoupling effect of China's regional economic growth and carbon emissions and the track of the shift of the center of gravity" in *Modern finance and Economics (Journal of Tianjin University of Finance and Economics)*, vol. 38, n. 5, 2018, pp. 17-29

has pointed out that at certain stages, the economic growth and energy consumption can be in absolute decoupling or in relative decoupling[8]. Peng *et al.* has analysed the relationship between carbon dioxide emissions and economic growth from a national or regional perspective, which shows a weak decoupling phenomenon in China then[9]. Schandl has assessed the decoupling potential of economic growth and environmental pressure in 13 countries and regions around the world and has found that OECD countries still have great potential to reduce carbon emissions and have little impact on economic growth[10].

As for the building of China's emission trading scheme (ETS), it is based on the experience of EU ETS with the typical mode of Cap and Trade. Wang & Chen has combed through the relevant policy development and the process of China's carbon market building[11]. He has analysed the market performance and the performance of each pilot carbon market. Tian & Xu has summarized the results of China's carbon trading pilot and has put forward relevant policy recommendations considering the existing problems[12]. Li *et al.* has compared the operation mechanism and current situation of emission trading market at home and abroad and has analysed the transaction volume and transaction volume of the seven major carbon emission trading pilot areas in China to found out the root cause of the slow development of carbon emission trading market[13]. Based on the development of global carbon market, Wang & Zao has analysed the research situation of carbon accounting, carbon quota and carbon pricing and has put forward corresponding countermeasures and suggestions for China's national carbon market construction according to the research results and gaps[14].

---

8. Wang, C., "Decoupling Analysis of China Economic Growth and Energy Consumption" in *China Population, Resources and Environment*, vol. 20, n. 3, 2010, pp. 35-37.
9. Peng, J., Huang, X., Zhong, T. & Zhao, Y., "Study on the decoupling of China's economic growth and energy carbon emissions" in *Resource science*, vol. 33, n. 4, 2011, pp. 626-633.
10. Schandl, H., "Decoupling global environmental pressure and economic growth: scenarios for energy use, materials use and carbon emissions" in *Journal of Cleaner Production*, vol. 132, n. 20, 2016, pp. 45-56.
11. Wang, K. & Chen, M., "Review and Prospect of China's carbon trading market" in Journal of Beijing Institute of Technology (Social Sciences Edition), vol. 20, n. 2, 2018, pp. 24-31.
12. Tian, C. & Xu, C., "Effectiveness analysis and policy suggestions of carbon trading pilot in China" in *Journal of North China University of Technology*, vol. 31, n. 1, 2019, pp. 7-14.
13. Li, Z., Zhang, X. & Dong, Y., "Research on the operation status, problems and Countermeasures of China's carbon emission trading market" in *Journal of ecological environment*, vol. 23, n. 11, 2014, pp. 1876-1882.
14. Wang, W. & Zhao, Y., "Global carbon market research and Its Enlightenment on China's carbon market construction" in Northeast Asia Forum, vol. 28, n. 2, 2019, pp. 97-112 & 128.

The above-mentioned literatures mainly analyse the relationship between economic growth and carbon emissions through empirical analysis, but few studies the reasons for the decoupling of economic growth and carbon emissions from the internal relationship among the economic growth, energy consumption and carbon emissions. Therefore, it is significant to take the coupling relationship between energy consumption and economic growth as the starting point so as to have further explanation for the policies and measures which make China's economic growth and carbon emission be decoupled through the reduction of carbon intensity.

III. THE DECOUPLING PROCESS OF CHINA'S ECONOMIC GROWTH AND CARBON EMISSION

China has become a middle-income country since 2012 and has become the world's second largest economy after the United States. As China's economic development continues, the quality and the efficiency of the economic development are taken into consideration with keen interest. For a couple of decades, China has been trying to find a green and low-carbon development mode consistent with the national conditions to decouple the economic growth from the carbon emissions. As the carbon emissions mainly depends on energy consumption structure and energy efficiency, on the premise of unchanged energy consumption structure, the larger energy consumption means the more carbon emission, and the higher the energy efficiency, the lower the carbon intensity. Therefore, China takes energy consumption as the breakthrough point and gradually realizing the decoupling of the carbon emissions from the economic growth by optimizing energy structure and improving energy efficiency.

1. THE DECOUPLING TURNING OF CHINA'S ECONOMIC GROWTH AND CARBON EMISSION

1.1. China's Economic Growth Coupling the Increasing Growth Rate of Energy Consumption

China's GDP has shown a rapid growth trend from 1978 (the beginning of the reforms) to 2019. In the period of the early stage of the reforms and opening-up, the economic growth has the priority and the extensive and high-speed growth is characterized by "high energy consumption and high pollution" which lead to various environmental problems. The growth of GDP means the increasing consumption of energy. The dual effects of industrialization and urbanization cause the energy consumption and carbon emission increasing rapidly, which make China become the world's top energy consumer and carbon dioxide emitter, accounting for nearly 30% of global emissions although China's per capita carbon emission is still at a low level[15].

It can be seen from Fig.1 that over the past 40 years, China's energy consumption has increased with the increase of economic aggregate, especially before 2008. Although China's economic development has made remarkable achievements, the rapid growth trend of energy consumption should be eased.

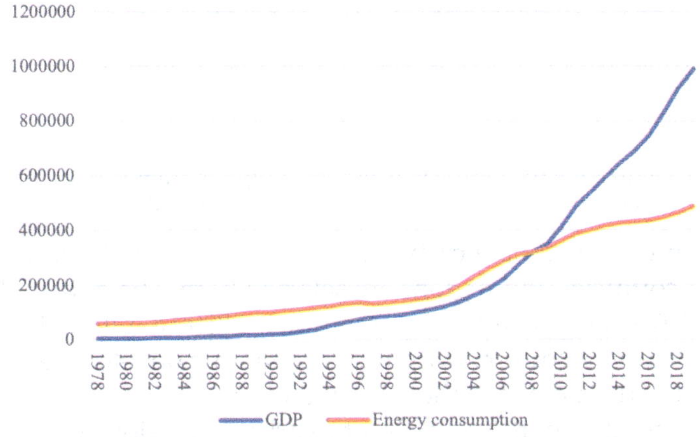

Figure 1. The trend of GDP growth and energy consumption growth in China 1978-2019
Data source: National Bureau of Statistics of China.

Fig. 2 shows that since 1978, with the development of China's industry and the advancement of urbanization, the total energy consumption has increased year by year and exceeded the total energy production in early 1990s. As China's economic growth has increased continuously together with that of the energy consumption, it brings about the increase of carbon emission since 1978.

Since 2000, due to the rising proportion of manufacture in the national economy, China's growth rate of energy consumption is much higher than that of energy production. Until the "12th Five Year Plan" period of 2011-2015, China has emphasized the transformation of energy development mode and the adjustment of energy structure as well, resulting in the slowdown of the growth rate of total energy consumption and total energy production, although the energy production and consumption have picked up a bit since 2017.

15. Shan, Y. *et al.*, "China CO2 emission accounts 1997-2015" in *Sci Data*, n. 5, 2018, retrieved from *https://doi.org/10.1038/sdata.2017.201*

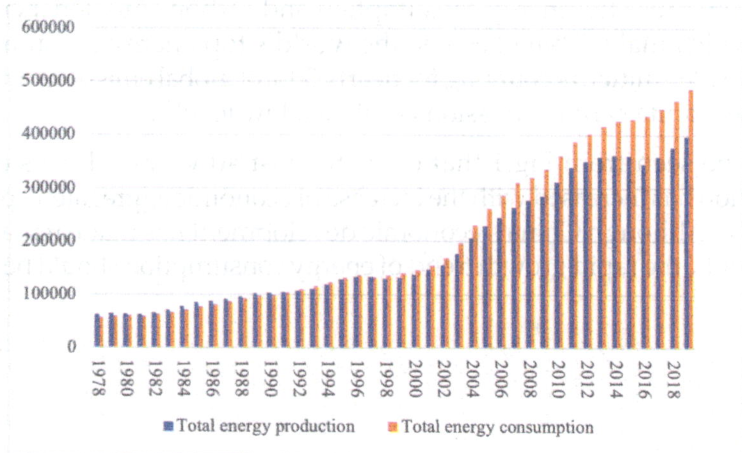

Figure 2. China's energy production and consumption from 1978 to 2019
Data source: National Bureau of Statistics of China.

The following is the global carbon emissions ranking (Table 1) in 2018. Only the top 7 countries and regions are selected here. The data in the table shows that in 2018, the global carbon emission is 33890.8 million tons, while China as a developing country with rapid economic development and the world's largest carbon emitter, the carbon emission is 9428.7 million tons, which accounts for 28% of the world's total carbon emission and is 1.8 times than that of the second ranked United States and 2.7 times than that of the third ranked EU. However, as for the per capita carbon emission, it is 6.7 tons in China, which is lower than that of the developed countries such as the US (14.6 tons), Japan (8.9 tons) and Germany (8.7 tons)[16].

Country	Total CO_2 emissions (Mt)	Proportion of global carbon emission (%)	CO_2 emissions per capita (t)
World	33890.8	1	4.4
China	9428.7	0.28	6.7
United States	5145.2	0.15	14.6
EU	3479.3	0.10	6.3
India	2479.1	0.07	1.6
Russia	1550.8	0.05	10.6
Japan	1148.4	0.02	8.9
Germany	725.7	0.02	8.7

Table 1 Ranking of global carbon emissions for 2018
Data source: BP Statistical Review of World Energy (2019)

16. Data source: BP Statistical Review of World Energy, 2019, retrieved from *https://www.bp.com/zh_cn/china/*

The main reason for the continuous increase of carbon emissions in China is the increase of the huge consumption of fossil energy. China is rich in coal but poor in oil and gas. Such characteristics of the natural resource endowments determine that the primary energy consumption structure is dominated by coal which may cause more emissions than oil and gas.

Since 1978, China's total carbon emissions show an overall upward trend, which are showed in Fig. 3. The carbon emissions before 1995 have showed a relatively uniform growth trend, but after 1995, they are more diverse. The carbon emissions from 1995 to 2018 can be divided into three dynamic stages: firstly, from 1995 to 2001, the total carbon emissions increase slowly from 3029 million tons to 3525 million tons, with a growth rate of only 16.37%; secondly, from 2002 to 2011, it is a period of a rapid growth from 3845 million tons to 8805 million tons, with a growth rate of 129%; thirdly, from 2012 to 2018, the growth rate slows down to 4.9% and the total carbon emissions just increase from 8991 million tons to 9428 million tons, and even with a slightly drop down in 2013[17].

The causes for the dynamic changes of the carbon emission are closely related to the development of China's economy and the macro-control of the government. Before 2000, China's economy had developed more slowly with less energy consumption increase and less carbon emission increase. Since the accession to WTO in 2001, China's economy has developed rapidly. The GDP has increased from 12 trillion yuan in 2002 to 47.2 trillion yuan in 2011[18]. As the economic growth mainly depends on the increase of the output value of the second industry, which causes a sharp increase of the energy consumption and then leads to a rocket-up in carbon emission.

The turning point of China's carbon emission comes as China's energy saving and emission reduction policies have been successively introduced in line with the "Common but Differentiated Responsibilities" for the emission reduction. Since 2011, China has started to carry out carbon emission pilots, to establish voluntary emission reduction mechanism, and to deploy comprehensively the key emission reduction plan. From then on, the carbon emissions have been controlled with a relatively stable growth trend.

17. Data source: BP Statistical Review of World Energy, 2019, retrieved from *https://www.bp.com/zh_cn/china/*
18. Data source: National Bureau of Statistics of China, retrieved from *http://www.stats.gov.cn/*

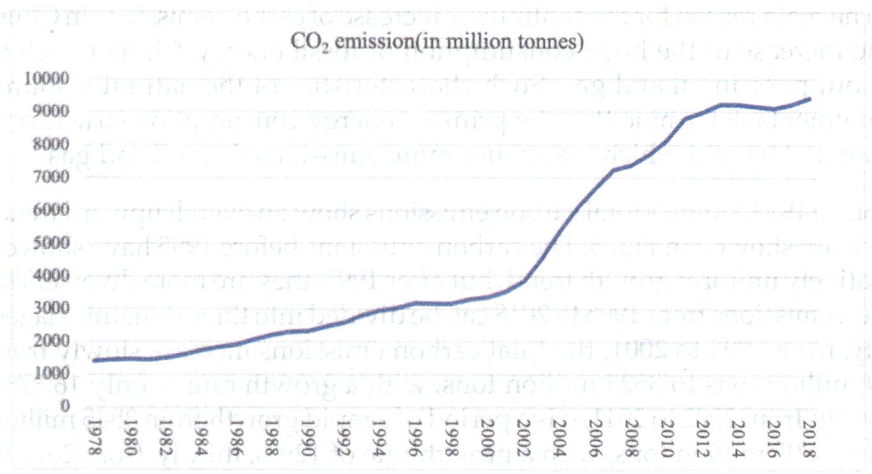

Figure 3. Total carbon emissions in China from 1978 to 2018
Data source: BP Statistical Review of World Energy (2019)

1.2. China's Economic Growth Coupling with the Slowdown Growth Rate of Energy Consumption

Energy is one of the basic elements of production, and the growth rate of energy consumption is often used as an important indicator to judge the economic situation. However, as the industrial structure and energy structure are constantly changing, the progress of science and technology and the improvement of energy efficiency result in the gradual decoupling of economic growth and energy consumption. As can be seen from Fig.4, in recent years, China's economic growth and energy consumption have achieved a slight decoupling. During the 11th Five Year Plan (2006-2010) and the 12th Five Year Plan (2011-2015), China has taken a variety of energy saving and emission reduction measures so that the growth rate of energy consumption has slowed down notably. With the adjustment of China's industrial structure and the transformation of economic growth mode, the energy consumption from 2013 has declined significantly.

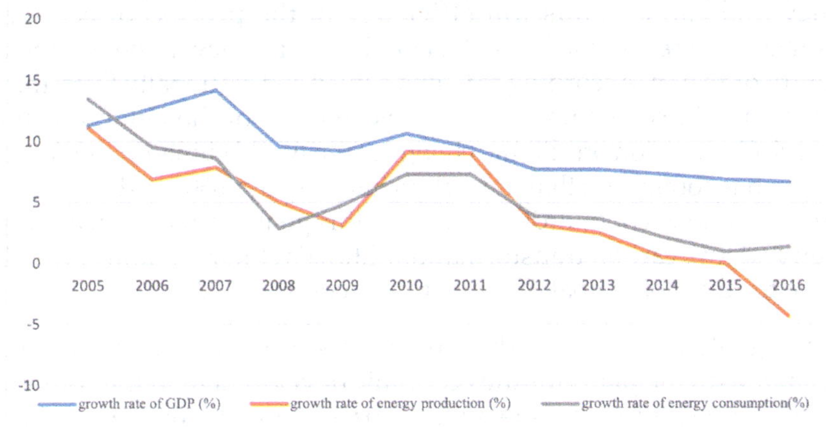

Figure 4. GDP growth rate and energy growth rate in China
Data source: National Bureau of Statistics of China.

It is shown in Fig. 4 that China keeps an increasing growth rate of GDP in the recent decades, but the energy production growth rate drops down obviously in recent years. Meanwhile, as the economic development goes hand in hand with the improvement of people's living standard, the demand for energy consumption also grows in China. However, due to the improvement of energy utilization, the carbon emission per unit GDP, in other words the carbon intensity, is continuously reduced. Although China's economic growth and energy consumption have not yet achieved a strong decoupling, as the increasing contribution of the tertiary industry in the proportion of GDP, the adjustment of the energy structure for less fossil fuels especially for less coal, and the improvement of energy efficiency, China is striving to peak the greenhouse gas emissions by 2030 or even earlier. The significant contribution of the decreasing carbon intensity is remarkable for China's low-carbon development.

2. THE CAUSES FOR THE DECOUPLING OF CHINA'S ECONOMIC GROWTH AND CARBON EMISSION

2.1. The Decrease of Carbon Intensity as the Most Apparent Cause

The most apparent cause for decoupling economic growth from carbon emissions in China is the decrease of carbon intensity which mainly due to the reduction of energy consumption and improvement of energy efficiency. The carbon emission intensity index, which reflects the resource utilization efficiency and carbon emission efficiency in the process of economic development, can reflect the level of technology efficiency in the production of a country or region. According to China's Intended Nationally Determined Contributions (INDC) submitted to the Secretariat of the United Nations Framework Convention on climate change at the world climate conference in 2015, China has committed that the carbon intensity by 2030 is to be 60%--65% lower than that in 2005. In order to achieve this goal, China has accelerated the green and low-carbon transformation. China's climate actions provide a solid base for the global goal of temperature control of 2.°C[19].

China's goal for reducing carbon intensity is clear and determined and it is correlated with the plans for the economic development in the country. It also shows China's efforts to cope with global governance of climate change and China's determination to improve the mode of economic development by reducing energy consumption, developing green economy, and taking on the sustainable development in the production and the low-carbon life style of the people.

Country	2014-2015	Country	2015-2016	Country	2016-2017	Country	2017-2018
World	-2.8%	**World**	-2.6%	**World**	-2.6%	**World**	-1.6%
China	-6.4%	**UK**	-7.7%	**China**	-5.2%	**Germany**	-6.5%
UK	-6.0%	**China**	-6.5%	**Mexico**	-5.0%	**Mexico**	-5.2%
US	-4.7%	**Mexico**	-4.6%	**Argentina**	-4.9%	**France**	-4.2%
South Africa	-4.5%	**Australia**	-3.8%	**UK**	-4.7%	**Italy**	-4.0%
Mexico	-4.4%	**Brazil**	-3.8%	**Brazil**	-4.5%	**Saudi Arabia**	-4.0%
Canada	-4.2%	**US**	-3.4%	**US**	-3.7%	**China**	-3.9%
Japan	-2.7%	**Japan**	-2.4%	**South Africa**	-3.6%	**EU**	-3.7%
Turkey	-2.6%	**Canada**	-2.1%	**Germany**	-2.8%	**Brazil**	-3.5%
India	-2.0%	**Russia**	-1.7%	**India**	-2.5%	**UK**	-3.5%
Korea	-1.4%	**EU**	-1.7%	**Australia**	-1.8%	**Japan**	-3.0%

Table 2 Global carbon intensity change in 2014-2018
Data source: Price Waterhouse Coopers

19. The State Council Information Office of the People's Republic of China, *Enhanced Actions on Climate Change: China's Intended Nationally Determined Contributions*, retrieved from *http://www.scio.gov.cn/*

Table 2 shows the data by PwC (Price Waterhouse Coopers) of the global carbon intensity changes in 2014-2018 as well as the top 10 countries in terms of carbon intensity reduction. From 2014 to 2015, as the global carbon emission intensity decreasing by 2.8%, China ranked first with a decline rate at 6.4%, and in the following two years, kept the rate at 6.5% and 5.2%. However, by 2017-2018, China dropped to the sixth place with the carbon intensity decreasing rate at 3.9%[20]. The decline of the decreasing rate for China's carbon intensity since 2017 is caused firstly by the smooth growth of the macro-economy in China which leads to the coal consumption growing continuously; secondly by the instability of alternative non fossil energy. Since the hydropower generation was affected by the fluctuation of incoming water, the power generation capacity was reduced by 4.2% in 2017, and at the same time, the instability of wind power generation led to an increase of 7.1% in thermal power generation and an increase in coal consumption of more than 70 million tons[21]; thirdly, by the declining trend of emissions, China's carbon emissions have been continuously in a fast-declining trend, but it would inevitably come across the bottleneck in the process of decline, because there are many factors which may influence the speed of carbon intensity decline so that it would be difficult to maintain the high-speed decline all the time; fourthly by the cyclical recovery of the global industrial production. Since the decline of energy intensity and carbon intensity can hardly be offset with the growth of population and that of the per capita income, especially in the year of 2017, hence the increase of carbon emissions; fifthly by the continuous promotion of energy saving and emission reduction in the previous years, which has been hindered for it is difficult to furtherly stimulate the reduction of carbon emissions with the measures already in use. Therefore, it is urgently demanded to have creative methodologies and innovative measures for further emission reduction in China.

2.2. The Energy Saving and Carbon Reduction Policies as the Most Important Cause

Since 1978, China's total carbon emissions have continuously increased, because China's economic development depends a lot on the manufacture which causes the increase of energy consumption. However, due to the policies and the measures for energy saving and emission reduction,

20. Price Waterhouse Coopers, *The Paris Agreement: a turning point? The low carbon economy index 2016-2019*, retrieved from *https://www.pwccn.com/*
21. Data source: National Bureau of Statistics of China, retrieved from *http://www.stats.gov.cn/*

China has made great improvement in decreasing the energy intensity and increasing the energy efficiency.

In November 1997, the first Energy Conservation Law of the People's Republic of China has been passed by the National People's Congress, which has been implemented since 1998. With the implementation of the law, a series of energy saving policies and regulations related to industry, construction, transportation, and end products have been issued later, promoting the overall improvement of energy saving and energy efficiency. In August 2004, China's National Development and Reform Commission and the General Administration of Quality Supervision have jointly formulated and issued the measures for the administration of energy efficiency labeling. From then on, China's energy efficiency labeling system has been established with a great significance to improve the energy efficiency for the energy consuming equipments and to improve the consumers' awareness of energy saving. In addition, energy saving and emission reduction are closely related to the implementation of the policies for industrial structure adjustment.

Because of implementing the policies to promote energy saving and emission reduction, China's energy efficiency, as an example, is getting more and more efficient and the energy intensity is getting lower and lower. As can be seen from Fig. 5, China's energy intensity has greatly decreased since 1990.

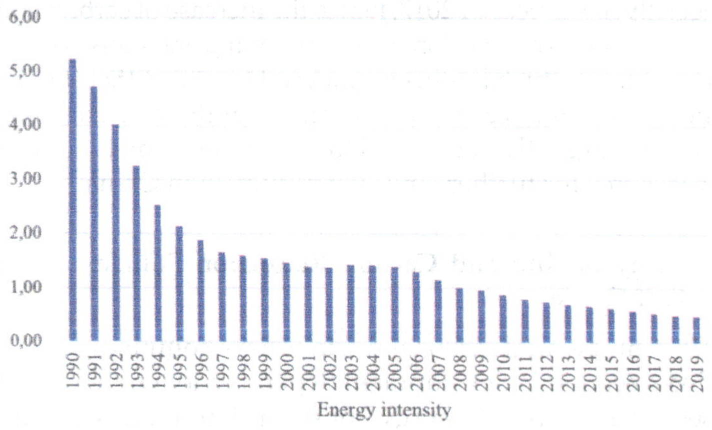

Figure 5. Trends of energy intensity in China from 1990 to 2019
Data source: National Bureau of Statistics of China.

IV. THE MEASURES FOR THE DECOUPLING BY DECREASING CARBON INTENSITY IN CHINA

The decrease of carbon intensity in China is the most apparent reason to achieve the goal for the decoupling of China's economic growth and carbon emissions, which mainly depends on the reduction of energy intensity, the improvement of energy productivity and energy efficiency. Therefore, it is significant to study the measures taken to reduce the carbon intensity in China from the perspectives of energy activities and carbon emission reduction.

1. THE MEASURES ON ENERGY-ACTIVITIES FOR THE DECREASE OF CARBON INTENSITY IN CHINA

1.1. Adjustment of Industrial Structure to Decrease Carbon Intensity

In the past 4 decades, China's rapid economic development is a coin with two sides, and the backward side shows a series of problems as the acceleration of resource consumption, pollution, and emission and so on. The problems are closely related to the characteristics of China's industrial structure — the continuously increase of manufacture which causes more energy and resource consumption. In recent decades, China's industrial structure has been constantly adjusted. An important feature as China's economy entering the "new normal" stage is to emphasize the importance of continuous optimization and upgrading of economic structure. In the 13th five-year plan released in 2015, the government's work has focused on transforming the mode of economic development, adjusting, and optimizing the industrial structure to achieve sustainable economic development.

As energy saving and emission reduction are closely related to economic development, which are inseparable from industrial restructuring and promoting the upgrading of the industrial structure, changing the mode of economic development have become the main theme of China's economic and social development. China has adopted the industrial restructuring measures include upgrading traditional industries, accelerating the development of emerging industries, closing backward production capacity, and reducing production in energy intensive industries. The increasing growth rate of tertiary industry, which exceeds the second industry from 2014 on[22], is a good way to show the decrease of the carbon intensity by adjusting the industrial structure in China.

22. Data source: National Bureau of Statistics of China, retrieved from *http://www.stats.gov.cn/*

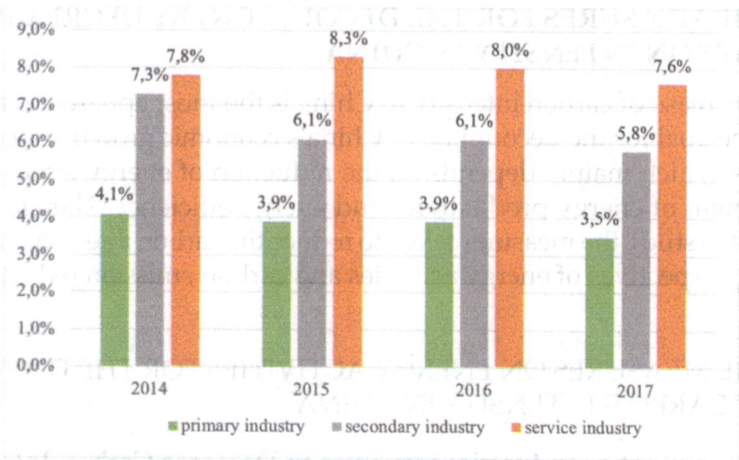

Figure 6. changes in the growth rate of the industries
Data source: China Statistical Yearbook 2015-2019

Fig.6 shows the development and changes of the industrial structure of China in 2014-2017. The first industry keeps at a lower growth rate and has a declining trend, and the second industry keeps at a higher growth rate as 7.3% in 2014 but declines to 5.8% in 2017. However, the service (or tertiary) industry has developed more rapidly, which surpasses the second industry for years. As the proportion of tertiary industry consists more in the GDP, China's industrial structure is to be greener, and the carbon intensity is decreasing[23].

1.2. Optimizing of Energy Structure to Decrease Carbon Intensity

The optimization of energy structure demands the reasonable proportion of all kinds of energy in the total energy consumption in which the proportion of fossil energy consumption should not be too large. It could be diverse for different countries with different economic conditions so that countries may optimize the energy structure in accordance with their own resources and technologies to effectively achieve energy saving and carbon emission reduction. At the background of low-carbon economy, China's measures for optimizing energy structure includes: imposing strict control over the growth of total energy consumption, especially that of coal and oil which are the high-carbon energy; promoting the clean utilization of fossil fuel and the development of non-fossil energy. In fig.7, it can be seen that China's total energy consumption is growing, and the coal dominates the biggest

23. Data source: National Bureau of Statistics of China, retrieved from *http://www.stats.gov.cn/*

proportion in the energy consumption structure. However, since 2013, China's total coal consumption has declined, and the proportion of coal consumption in the total energy consumption has declined, which makes the energy structure be optimized with the decrease of heavy emission by coal.

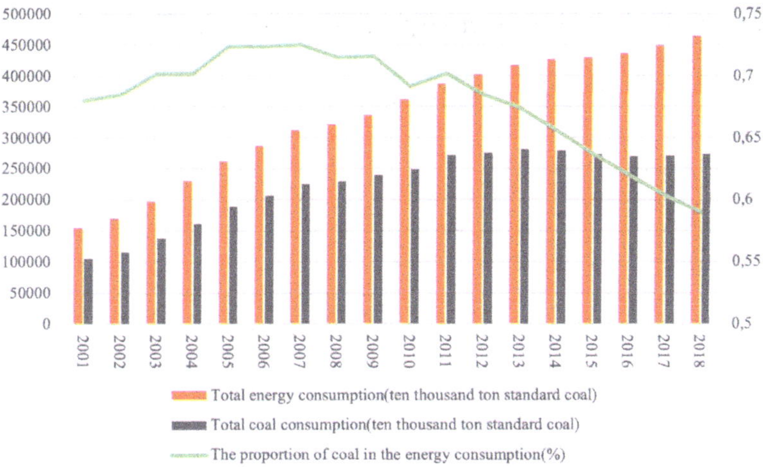

Figure 7. Total energy consumption and coal consumption of China
Data source: National Bureau of Statistics of China.

Traditionally, coal is used for urban heating in China, and the heating has caused a lot of coal consumption and carbon emissions especially in the cold north part of the country. In order to promote the clean use of fossil fuels, it is a good way to reduce the amount of coal consumption for household heating and to increase the proportion of electricity-producing coal. As the thermal power generation plants equipped with higher level of technologies and the modern equipment, they can be more efficient to make clean use of the coal and produce more coal-fired power to support the transformation project from "coal to electricity" for household heating. By 2018, China has completed the project for 2.74 million households, decreasing the end consumption of coal scattering around.

Another way to optimize the energy structure is to increase the supply of oil and gas to replace the higher-carbon coal consumption. The household heating project of transforming from "coal to natural gas" is a good example for the optimization. More than 2 million households have turned from "coal to natural gas" for heating by 2018 in China, decreasing the bulk coal consumption in order to have the emission reduction[24].

24. Ministry of Ecology and Environment of People's Republic of China.

Gradually, as reducing the dependence on fossil energy and increasing the utilization of non-fossil energy, the renewable energy and even some new clean energy are to consist of more in the energy supply system to achieve the coordinated and sustainable development of economy, environment, and resources. Fig. 8 shows the upward trend for the proportion of non-fossil energy sources in the primary energy consumption in China.

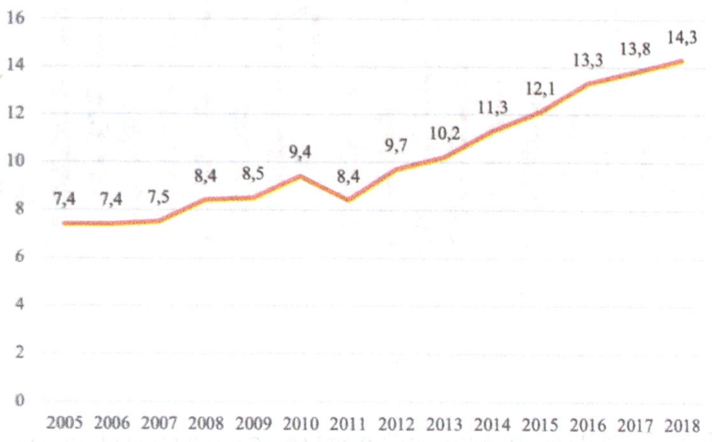

Figure 8. The percentages of non-fossil energy sources in the primary energy consumption in China
Data source: China Statistical Yearbook 2019

China is increasing the proportion of non-fossil energy in the total primary energy consumption to about 15% by 2020, and about 20% by 2030. As shown in Fig. 8, since 2005, the proportion of non-fossil energy consumption in China has basically maintained an upward trend with a slightly decline in 2011. Then it has been on a rapid upward trend since 2012 and reached 14.3% in 2018[25]. As China's total energy consumption in 2019 has grown at a low speed, the energy consumption and energy structure have continued to be cleaner and more efficient. Therefore, the target of 15% of non-fossil energy consumption in 2020 can be achieved apparently, which may contribute to the decrease of the carbon intensity in China.

1.3. Improvement of Energy Efficiency to Decrease Carbon Intensity

Since the promulgation of Energy Conservation Law of the People's Republic of China in 1998, the implementation of energy saving measures has

25. Data source: National Bureau of Statistics of China, retrieved from *http://www.stats.gov.cn/*

been guaranteed by the law. China has taken reducing energy intensity as a binding indicator and implemented strict annual assessment since 2006. Fig.9 shows that between 1998 and 2002, China's energy consumption intensity, defined as energy consumption per unit of GDP, falls by an average of 2.5%. From 2003 to 2004, while China's economy grows significantly, the intensity of energy consumption has increased. In this regard, the government quickly makes corresponding adjustments, and has issued and implemented a series of energy efficiency policies to save energy, reduce emissions, improve quality, and increase efficiency. Since 2005, China's energy intensity has continuously declined, with energy intensity falling by 39.8% from 1.08 tce/ten thousand CNY (2010 CNY) in 2005 to 0.65 tce/ten thousand CNY (2010 CNY) in 2017[26]. As the economy continues to grow steadily, China's total energy consumption has shown an overall growth trend over the last decade. However, due to a series of energy savings measures, China's energy intensity has declined, resulting in a slow-down growth rate of total energy consumption.

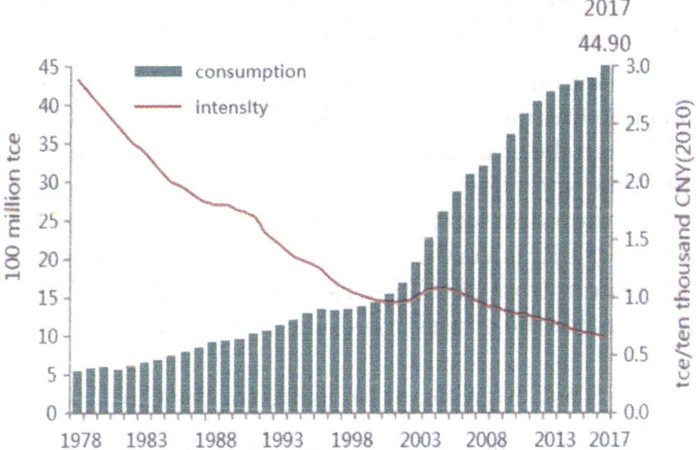

Figure 9. Energy Consumption and Intensity in China (1978-2017)
Data source: The Energy Efficiency Report of China 2018

In addition, since the implementation of the energy efficiency labeling system in 2005, the energy efficiency labeling system has covered 33 kinds of energy consumption products, involving more than 9000 enterprises and more than 900 testing institutions, and has achieved more than 441.9 billion-kilowatt hour energy-saving results. The system has effectively guaranteed

26. China Council for an Energy Efficient Economy, *Energy Efficiency China 2018*, retrieved from *http://www.cceee.org.cn/class/view?id=38*

the energy efficiency improvement of energy consumption products in China and promoted the development of national energy saving and emission reduction. It is estimated that by 2020, the implementation the system is to save 277.5 TWH of electric power, 129 million tons of standard coal and more than 110 million tons of carbon emissions[27].

As a successful case, the energy efficiency labeling system has enhanced the improvement of air conditioning energy efficiency level which further promotes the improvement of the energy efficiency standards in the air conditioning industry in China. The high-power with low energy efficiency air conditioning products are gradually eliminated from the market, and the upgraded high energy efficiency air conditioners prevail. Other industries producing energy consuming products follow the example to upgrade the energy efficiency of the products, and further promote the energy saving and emission reduction in China.

2. THE MEASURES ON CARBON REDUCTION FOR THE DECREASE OF CARBON INTENSITY IN CHINA

In addition to the energy saving activities, China also takes measures of emission reduction to achieve the decoupling of economic growth and carbon emissions, although the emission reduction measures are relatively lagging in the starting time and effects. In terms of reducing carbon emissions and achieving low-carbon development through emission reduction measures, EU's experience of ETS is very significant and China follows the example and draws the lessons from EU ETS so as to establish China's ETS with more effective measures for the emission reduction in China.

2.1. China's ETS as a Significant Measure for the Carbon Reduction

Emission trading scheme is regarded as an efficient market-based measure for emission reducing. EU ETS has implemented for more than fifteen years and has accumulated valuable experience in supervision and management for China. To follow the "cap and trade" mode of EU ETS, China learns to do and has the pilots for ETS. In October 2011, the National Development and Reform Commission of China has announced to have carbon emission trading pilots, approving 5 cities as Beijing, Shanghai, Tianjin, Chongqing, and Shenzhen, and 2 provinces as Hubei and Guangdong, to carry out carbon emission trading pilots which have been launched since 2013.

27. National Development and Reform Commission, *The 10th Anniversary Seminar of Energy Efficiency Labeling System*, retrieved from *https://www.ndrc.gov.cn/*

After more than four years of pilot operation, China's national ETS and the unified carbon trading market have been established. On December 19, 2017, with the approval of the State Council, the National Development and Reform Commission officially has issued China's national carbon emission trading market construction plan. The issuance of this document officially marks the start of China's carbon emission trading scheme. Although only one industry —the power generation industry— is included in at first, China's ETS, with the continuous development and improvement, would cover more energy intensive industries and other carbon intensive industries. China's carbon trading market is to be one of the most important carbon markets in the world.

China has carefully studied EU ETS offset mechanism, and China's pilots of ETS in the 5 cities+2 provinces have innovatively used the mechanism with creative ideas so that the industries which are not yet covered in China's pilot ETS are also motivated in activities of emission reduction. With the participation of more industries that are not even covered by the ETS, the carbon emission reduction in China is to be successfully implemented.

2.2. China's Pilot ETS Test Providing Successful Experience for the Implementation

China's pilot ETS in the 5 cities+2 provinces for emission trading before the establishment of a national emission trading market shows the practical and cautious ways of the Chinese government for policy making and implementation, since China is such a big country that any fault in the policy making, and implementation might cause serious results for a lot of people. Therefore, China always has pilots for some fresh and innovative ideas and policies in order to decrease the lost in case of failure and increase the possibilities for the success.

From June 2013 to June 2014, the 5cities+2 provinces pilot carbon emission trading markets have started one after another, and some of them, especially Hubei province have successively carried out the work. On December 22, 2016, Fujian Province voluntarily has launched the carbon emission trading market, becoming the eighth carbon emission trading pilot in China. Table 3 shows the rules of the 8 local carbon trading pilot markets. Some of the provisions of the pilots are similar, while others are quite different, because each of the pilot market is supervised in accordance with the local conditions by the local provincial government. The local autonomy for the pilot carbon markets provides the local authorities with the flexibilities to adopt the most effective modes for them, and with the motivation for the creativities in implementation. The enthusiasm of the local industries to participate in the carbon emission market is motivated and the different rules of the regional development lead to the different market performance.

Provinces and cities	Quota allocation mode	Quota allocation method	Carbon market coverage	Subject of carbon market
Shenzhen	Mixed mode: more than 90% of the quota be issued free of charge, and the quota from 2013 to 2015 be allocated in one time, considering the growth of the industry.	Based on the baseline method (the annual carbon emission quota of the enterprise is determined, based on its emission efficiency and its actual business volume), some industries adopt the competitive method to determine.	635 enterprises from 26 industries including power, gas, and water supply	Performing enterprises, institutional investors, and individual investment
Shanghai	Free distribution: 100% free, one-time allocation of 2013-2015 quota, with appropriate consideration of industry growth.	Baseline method and historical emission method (the carbon emission quota is determined, based on the historical emission level of the enterprise and the contribution of early emission reduction.)	197 enterprises from steel, petrochemical, chemical, metal, building materials, fiber industries, covering 57% of the city's emissions	Performing enterprises, institutional investors
Beijing	Mixed mode: more than 95% free allocation, distributed annually, based on the data of the previous year (without considering the increment).	Historical emission method	About 490 enterprises from power, heat, cement, petrochemical, and public construction industries covering half of the city's emissions	Performing enterprises, institutional investors
Guangdong	Hybrid mode: 97% of the free allocation for electric power enterprises in 2013 and 95% in 2014, distributed annually, considering the trend of economic and social development.	Historical emission method (based on the amount of emissions in 2010-2012), considering the characteristics of the industry.	239 enterprises from power, cement, steel, ceramics, metals, petrochemicals, plastics, and paper industries, accounting for 42% of the province's emissions	Performing enterprises, institutional investors

Provinces and cities	Quota allocation mode	Quota allocation method	Carbon market coverage	Subject of carbon market
Tianjin	Free distribution: 100% free allocation, annual quota for 2013-2015 are set at one time, which can be adjusted every year.	Historical emission method is adopted for stock and baseline is adopted for increment.	114 enterprises from steel, chemical, power, petrochemical, oil refining and other industries, accounting for 60% of the city's emissions	Performing enterprises, institutional investors, and individual investors
Hubei	Free distribution: 100% free allocation, no increment considered.	Stock: 80% of quota allocation is based on historical emission method, 20% is used for auction; increment: 15% quota reserved by the government	138 enterprises from iron and steel, chemical industry, cement, electric power and other industries, accounting for 35% of the total emissions of the province	Performing enterprises, institutional investors, and individual investors
Chongqing	Distribution free of charge: 100% free allocation, the upper limit for the total amount control of the annual quota is determined with an annual decrease of 4.13%, without considering the increment.	Historical emission method.	240 enterprises from cement, steel, electric power, and other industries, accounting for 30%–45% of total emissions	Performing enterprises
Fujian	Distribution free of charge: 100% free allocation.	Adopt the combination of baseline method and historical emission method.	Power, petrochemical, chemical, building materials, steel, nonferrous metals, paper, aviation, ceramics and other nine industries	Performing enterprises, institutional investors, and individual investors

Table 3. The rules of China's 8 local carbon emission trading pilot markets
Source from: Official websites of the development and reform commissions of the pilot provinces and cities.

Fig. 10 shows the volume and the turnover of the transactions per pilot in 2019. During this period, Hubei is the most successful pilot in China, with a carbon trading volume of 64.17 million tons and a turnover of 129.7142 million-yuan, which has accounted for more than 30% of the eight pilots in the country, ranking the first. Hubei has fully played a pilot role and provided the valuable experience for the building of the national carbon emission trading scheme. The second one is Guangdong with a turnover of 106.619 million yuan and the volume of 58.378 million tons[28].

In sum, the market performance of each pilot carbon market is quite different, which is related to the differences of the local energy consumption and carbon emissions, the economic development level, and the government supervision. The pilot projects of the local provinces and cities have made a very important contribution to the building of the national carbon emission market.

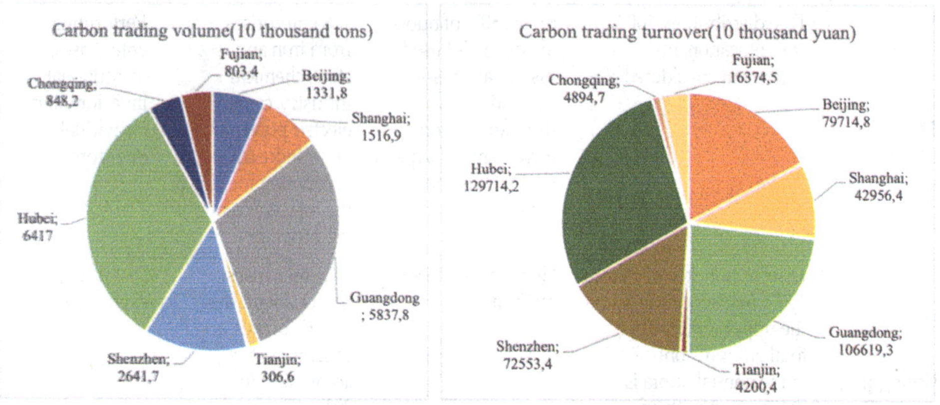

Figure 10. Trading volume and turnover of 8 carbon trading pilots in 2019
Data source: http://k.tanjiaoyi.com/

2.3. EU-China Cooperation in the Emission Reduction

EU ETS is the largest carbon emission trading scheme in the world, which makes a great contribution to the global carbon emission reduction by mandating carbon emissions for enterprises. EU ETS has implemented for three phrases. The first two phases adopt the decentralized governance model, while the third phrase adopts the centralized governance model. The Commission sets the overall quota and distribution rules, and member States are responsible for their implementation. The implementation of the market-based mechanism of ETS has achieved the purpose of EU's climate actions, while China is intended to adopt the market-based mechanism for the pilots. EU's approaches provide China with valuable experience in the implementation of ETS and China expects to cooperate with EU in the global governance of climate change.

28. Data source: *http://k.tanjiaoyi.com/*

In fact, China and EU have a long-standing cooperation on tackling the climate change. In 2005 the EU-China Partnership on Climate Change has provided a high-level political framework for cooperation and dialogue. In 2010, China and EU have issued a joint statement on climate change dialogue and cooperation. Recently, China and EU have issued a statement on climate change and clean energy, which has agreed to strengthen bilateral cooperation. China has learnt from the experience and lessons of EU ETS and EU also provides technical support for China in the design of the national ETS and the pilots of emission trading.

V. CONCLUSION

China's measures to achieve the decoupling between the economic growth and carbon emissions mainly replies on the decrease of energy consumption and increase of energy efficiency as a breakthrough for the carbon intensity reduction, while the emission reduction measures as the pilots of ETS have achieved successful experience, and the national ETS is on the way to be implemented in the country. As the decrease of carbon intensity is mainly due to the achievements of energy saving and emission reduction, China's measures on energy-activities as adjusting the industrial structure, optimizing the energy structure, and improving the energy efficiency are efficient and effective. The building of China's national carbon emission trading scheme, with EU's technical support in the design of the scheme and the projects of EU-China cooperation for carbon reduction, may have more contribution to the future decreasing of carbon intensity in China.

China has fulfilled the commitment made at the Copenhagen climate change conference to "reduce the emission intensity per unit of GDP by 40% to 45% by 2020" three years ahead of the schedule, with an average annual decrease of 4.9% for the carbon intensity[29]. Now China is striving to achieve the goals of the Paris Agreement for the Intended Nationally Determined Contributions (INDCs) as to reduce the carbon dioxide emission intensity per unit of GDP by 60%-65% compared with that in 2005, to increase the proportion of non-fossil energy in the total primary energy consumption to about 20%, and to peak the carbon dioxide emission around 2030 or before.

At present, China is improving the economic development and is turning from the quantity-focused growth of GDP to the quality-focused growth, and switching from the resource dependent development model, which is driven

29. The State Council Information Office, *SCIO briefing on China's Policies and Actions for Addressing Climate Change (2018)*, retrieved from *http://www.scio.gov.cn/*

by increasing the input of the factors, to the economic development driven by knowledge and innovation. According to what President XI says that the lucid waters and lush mountains are invaluable assets, China's economic development is to be greener, and the low-carbon economic development with more efficient measures on energy saving and carbon reduction is to decouple furtherly the economic growth and the carbon emissions in China.

The consumers´ Role: The Energy Industry Upside Down? The Growing Importance of Electricity Consumers

DAVID ROBINSON

PhD in Economics from University of Oxford. Senior Research Fellow at the Oxford Institute for Energy Studies

I. INTRODUCTION

This article analyses the growing potential for consumers to help lower the costs of the energy transition. On the one hand, through the penetration of intermittent renewables, the transition has created the need for decarbonised flexibility (of different durations) to balance the increasingly unpredictable supply of electricity. On the other hand, through electrification of energy markets, it has given electricity consumers the opportunity to be flexible, especially using electrified distributed energy resources (DER). The growing potential for demand-side flexibility (DSF) is also due to increasingly sophisticated digitalization and communications systems that enable the optimization of aggregated DER.

Although these trends have been apparent for many years and policies have been introduced to encourage consumer flexibility in some countries, the impact of these policies has been limited. However, the Russian invasion in Ukraine led to an energy crisis in Europe, with tight gas markets driving prices of gas and electricity to levels never experienced. This crisis reinforced the view that the energy transition is as much about energy security of supply and cost containment as it is about reducing greenhouse gas emissions. This has led to increased policy interest, notably in the European Union (EU) and the United Kingdom (UK) to reduce and ultimately replace (unabated) gas-fired generation[1] as a source of flexibility. One of the potential alternatives of

1. Unabated generation refers to gas-fired stations that do not install carbon capture and storage or other means of abating CO2 emissions.

decarbonised flexibility is DSF, either by individual consumers or through commercial aggregation and energy communities.

With the right policies, the demand-side of the power sector has the potential to reduce the costs of the energy transition. From a technological perspective, consumers and their representatives will increasingly be able to decide how much energy to consume, produce, store, share or trade, and how much to rely on the central electricity system. This has the potential to turn the energy industry upside down, with central planning having to adjust to the new resources available on the demand side.

The article is organized as follows. Section II summarises the evidence of growing penetration of intermittent renewables and of electrification, creating the need for decarbonized flexibility and the opportunity for consumers to provide it. Section III explores DSF in more detail, examining the system's demand for flexibility services, the potential sources and the economic viability of DSF, especially the role of aggregation in lowering costs. Sections II and III apply to all electricity systems, whatever their level of liberalization. Section IV explores the EU policies aimed at enabling DSF before and after the Russian invasion of Ukraine. Section V concludes.

II. THE ENERGY TRANSITION AND THE FLEXIBILITY IMPERATIVE

The energy transition requires deep penetration of decarbonized electricity in the form of intermittent wind and solar renewable power and the electrification of end markets that are currently supplied by fossil fuels, notably transport, heating and many industrial processes. This leads to a requirement for sources of decarbonized flexibility of different durations; some of which consumers can provide through the development of DER.

1. PENETRATION OF RENEWABLES AND ELECTRIFICATION

The IEA[2] expects the share of renewables (including hydro) in the global power generation mix to rise from 29% in 2022 to 35% in 2025. It projects renewables to be the dominant source of electricity well before 2050. For example, in its Net Zero Emissions by 2050 Scenario, the renewable share

2. International Energy Agency, "Electricity Market Report 2023" (2023), retrieved from *https://iea.blob.core.windows.net/assets/255e9cba-da84-4681-8c1f-458ca1a3d9ca/ElectricityMarketReport2023.pdf*

increases to more than 60% by 2030[3]. Renewables are growing everywhere. IRENA[4] reports that the share of renewable capacity (90% of which was wind and solar) in annual power capacity expansion in 2022 reached 83%, compared to 78% in 2021 and less than 60% in 2016.

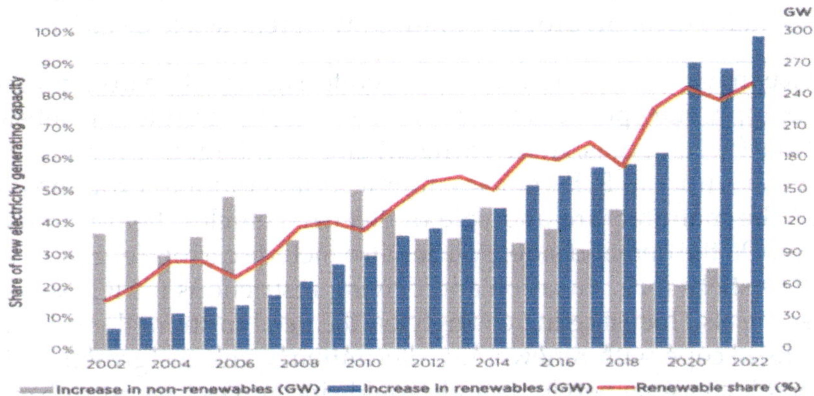

Figure 1: Renewable share of annual power capacity expansion
Source: International Renewable Energy Agency (IRENA), "Renewable capacity highlights" (2023)

In absolute terms, renewable generation capacity increased in 2022 by 295 GW. Of that, China accounted for 141 GW, well over half the total. Despite continued growth of coal-fired generation there, rapid growth of renewable energy is required for China to meet its carbon peaking and carbon neutrality targets. Over the longer term, one forecast projects wind and solar capacity of over 5,000 GW in China by 2050[5], compared to total global renewable capacity today of less than 3500 GW. Elsewhere in 2022, renewable capacity in Europe and North America expanded by 57.3 GW and 29.1 GW respectively, with rapid growth from a low base in developing and emerging economies.

Electrification is also accelerating rapidly, with electricity's share of global energy demand forecast to rise from about 20 % to between 40-70% by 2050.

---

3. International Energy Agency, "Renewable Electricity" (2022), retrieved from *https://www.iea.org/reports/renewable-electricity*
4. Source: International Renewable Energy Agency (IRENA), "Renewable capacity highlights" (2023), retrieved from *https://www.irena.org/Publications/2023/Mar/Renewable-capacity-statistics-2023*
5. Robinson, D. and Li, X., "How consumers can help to decarbonise the electricity system: The role of electricity demand-side flexibility (DSF) and policy implications for China", *Climate Strategies* (2021), retrieved from *https://climatestrategies.org/wp-content/uploads/2021/10/DSF-China-Policy-Brief-ENG_v2.pdf*

The IEA´s Net Zero Emissions Scenario has the share rising to 30% by 2030, a compound annual rate of around 3.5%, but it will have to grow even faster to meet the 2050 net zero target[6]. The Energy Transition Commission expects that the share of electricity in final energy demand could increase from 20% today to about 70% by 2050[7]. The share of electricity would be even higher if one includes green hydrogen produced with renewable electricity.

Polices have been introduced to accelerate electrification in end markets. On the supply side, polices include carrots (e. g., tax credits and subsidies) and sticks (e. g., quotas, more stringent emission targets, prohibitions on selling conventional ICE vehicles after a certain date) to promote a shift toward the manufacture and sale of electric vehicles, heat pumps and batteries. On the demand side, policies also include carrots (e. g., subsidies) as well as sticks (e. g., taxation and driving restrictions for ICE vehicles). Policies are also focusing increasingly on the need to strengthen electricity networks to cope with renewables intermittency and the growth of DER, develop EV charging networks and provide incentives to cope with energy shortages and excesses (when renewables exceed expected demand). As a result of electrification, the potential to provide DSF is growing through the use of DER.

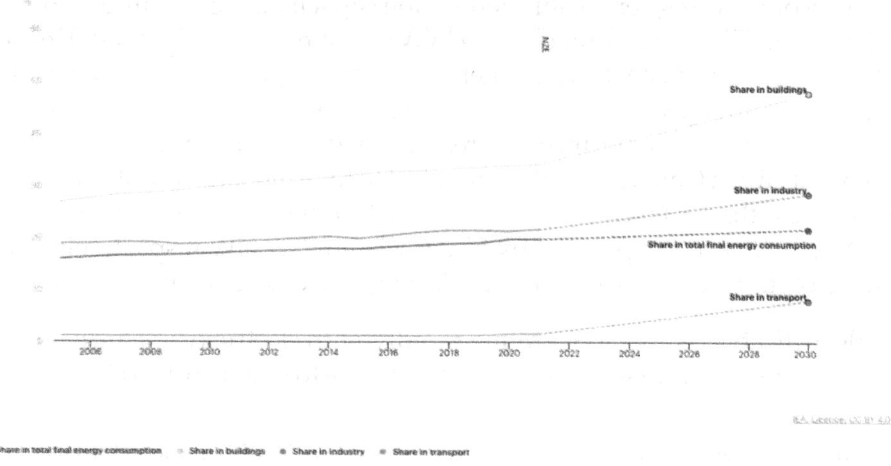

Figure 2: Share of electricity in total final energy consumption, 2005-2030
Source: International Energy Agency, "Electrification" *op. cit.*

6. International Energy Agency, "Electrification" (2022), retrieved from *https://www.iea.org/reports/electrification*
7. Energy Transitions Commission, "Electricity" (2021), retrieved from *https://www.energy-transitions.org/energy/electricity/#:~:text=Future%20energy%20systems%20will%20be,70%25%20by%20mid%2Dcentury*

2. THE FLEXIBILITY IMPERATIVE[8]

All electricity systems need flexibility to ensure that supply and demand are kept in balance. The IEA[9] defines power system flexibility as "the ability of a power system to reliably and cost-effectively manage the variability and uncertainty of demand and supply across all relevant timescales, from ensuring instantaneous stability of the power system to supporting long-term security of supply". Flexibility resources are available on the generation supply side, the demand side, and from the grid itself. Storage is a means of altering either the supply or the demand. Flexibility may be needed almost immediately or with a short delay and can be maintained for different periods of time, from minutes to months. It may be needed to resolve local congestion problems or system-wide imbalances.

Fossil and hydro generation are the overwhelming sources of flexibility. Electricity systems are typically referred to as "load following": generation capacity planning and operations assume that demand ("load") is inflexible and uncertain and that flexible generation is needed to adjust to changing demand. In some countries consumers have price incentives to reduce demand at times of system stress, but historically this flexibility was infrequently or never needed and often perceived as a hidden subsidy to large consumers.

New flexibility needs have emerged to cope with the uncertainty related to intermittency of renewable generation and increasing use of DER. A key reason to develop competitive sources of flexibility is the rising cost of balancing an electricity system with higher penetrations of intermittent renewables. Figure 2 shows that the average cost of balancing the UK power system as a share of the total cost of generation has been rising for a decade, in line with the increasing penetration of renewables. The increased costs were especially evident during the early Covid-19 period, reflecting an unexpected decrease in demand and wholesale prices, and a higher price for balancing services to manage excess renewable generation, for instance to stimulate demand and pay nuclear plant not to operate. This early Covid-19 experience may well be giving us a glimpse of the future, when renewables will make up a very large share of total generation and flexibility will be an important cost for the system[10].

8. Robinson, D. and Li, X., "How consumers can help [...]", *op. cit.*
9. International Energy Agency, "Status of Power System Transformation 2019: Power system flexibility" (2019), retrieved from *https://iea.blob.core.windows.net/assets/00dd2818-65f1-426c-8756-9cc0409d89a8/Status_of_Power_System_Transformation_2019.pdf*
10. Robinson, D. and Keay, M., "Glimpses of the future electricity system? Demand flexibility and a proposal for a special auction", *Oxford Institute for Energy Studies*

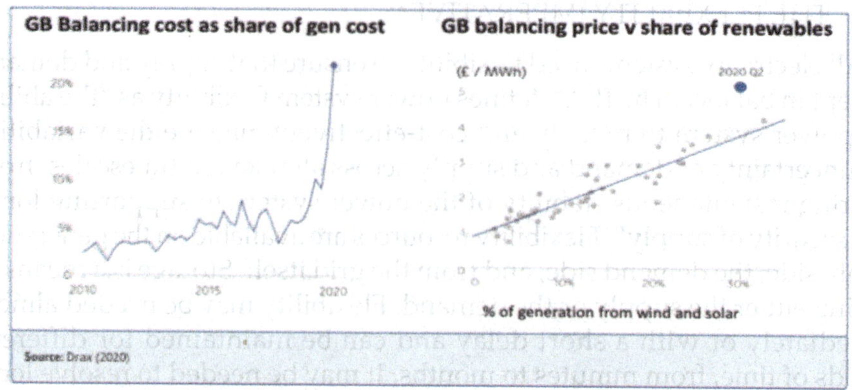

Figure 2: The Rising Cost of Balancing as Renewable Share Increases

Today, the logic of load-following systems is becoming less appropriate because generation is becoming less predictable with penetration of renewables. New sources of flexibility should be decarbonized and include storage, dispatchable generation, as well as network and demand management. The aim is to develop and use the flexible resources that minimize costs of system reliability and sustainability.

3. DISTRIBUTED ENERGY RESOURCES AND FLEXIBILITY

The penetration of intermittent renewables and electrification are the basis for the massive expansion of DER, including distributed generation (e. g., solar panels), fixed and mobile storage (e. g., EVs), electricity heating and cooling equipment (e. g., heat pumps), smart devices (e. g., thermostats) and demand management (e. g., shifting demand to periods when renewables are available). One flexible DER is renewable generation near the point of consumption. For instance, the IEA reports that 167 GW of distributed PV systems were installed globally between 2019 and 2021, with a combined peak output higher than the combined peak consumption of France and Britain[11].

Electrification increases power consumption and creates new power system opportunities, basically by enabling electrical equipment to vary net demand on the electricity system. DER includes digitalized electrical

(2020), retrieved from *https://www.oxfordenergy.org/wpcms/wp-content/uploads/2020/10/Glimpses-of-the-future-electricity-system.pdf*

11. International Energy Agency, "Unlocking the Potential of Distributed Energy Resources, Executive Summary" (2022), retrieved from *https://www.iea.org/reports/unlocking-the-potential-of-distributed-energy-resources/executive-summary*

devices, notably EV batteries and heat pumps, that can be managed directly by the consumer or remotely by third parties[12].

EV batteries are particularly important. In 2022 EV sales surpassed 10 million vehicles, accounting for 14% of all new cars sold in 2022, up from around 9% in 2021 and less than 5% in 2020[13]. The IEA´s Net Zero Emission by 2050 Scenario sees an electric car fleet of over 300 million in 2030, with EVs accounting for about 60% of new sales[14]. To provide an indication of the potential of battery flexibility, the battery capacity of EVs in China (which now accounts for half of global EVs) is expected to reach 5.7 TWh in 2030. This is equivalent to over one quarter of the average Chinese daily power consumption in 2020 (about 20.6 TWh)[15].

4. CENTRAL RESOURCES AND DISTRIBUTED RESOURCES

Electricity planning in most countries focuses on identifying the central system resources (mainly generation) that will minimize the cost of meeting uncertain and inflexible demand (i. e., load) with a security margin that corresponds to an acceptable probability of losing load (i. e., blackouts). These security margins are set by governments or their representatives and are typically subject to several distorting incentives that raise system costs. First, there is an incentive to build more capacity than needed to avoid the possibility of shortages. Second, because governments can pass the risks and costs to consumers, they have weak incentives to minimize costs and risks of mistakes. Third, governments and central planners do not have sufficient information about technology developments and about what mix of different technologies would be optimal. Fourth, governments tend to pick winners and their choices may be based on political criteria, such as favouring a local resource, rather than minimising cost. Fifth, at least in liberal democracies, governments change frequently and often change policies, leading to potentially very significant losses for investors; thereby raising the cost of capital. The result of these tendencies is to raise the overall cost of electricity, with many resources being underutilized[16].

---

12. Robinson, D. and Li, X., "How consumers can help [...]", *op. cit.*, p. 20.
13. International Energy Agency, "Global EV Outlook 2023: Executive summary" (2023), retrieved from *https://www.iea.org/reports/global-ev-outlook-2023/executive-summary*
14. International Energy Agency, "Electric Vehicles: Technology deep dive" (2022), retrieved from *https://www.iea.org/reports/electric-vehicles*
15. Robinson, D. and Li, X., "How consumers can help [...]", *op. cit.*, p. 20.
16. Keay, M. and Robinson, D., "The Limits of Auctions: reflections on the role of central purchaser auctions for long-term commitments in electricity systems", *Oxford Institute*

As the electricity system becomes more decentralised with growth of DER, the potential grows for alternatives to central system resources. This poses a major challenge, namely, to avoid central system plans to build resources that are not economically justified. When consumers can self-generate, store, manage demand and aggregate DER at costs that are lower than retail prices, they will try to rely less on the central system. Indeed, they will become competitors for the central system. Central planning methods need to adapt to reflect the increasing importance of DER and its implications.

III. THE NEW ROLE OF DSF AND CONSUMERS

This section introduces demand-side flexibility and examines the demand for flexibility services, the sources of flexibility and the economic logic of developing DSF.

1. DEMAND-SIDE FLEXIBILITY[17]

Demand-side flexibility (DSF) is the capacity of consumers or representatives on their behalf to change the consumer's net demand on the electricity system, in return for compensation or other benefits. DSF makes use of DER that respond to external information such as prices and the weather.

There are two types of DSF; implicit and explicit. "Implicit" DSF refers to consumer response to price signals, for instance with Time-ofUse (ToU) tariffs. ToU tariffs normally do not reflect real-time prices. The consumer has no obligation to respond to these price and this form of DSF is therefore not a firm commitment. However, these tariffs can provide useful signals[18].

"Explicit" DSF refers to consumers or representatives on their behalf selling flexibility into markets for energy, capacity, balancing and other services; as such it can be regarded as an explicit and firm commitment. Under explicit DSF, consumers or their representatives control the consumer's net demand on the system. Explicit DSF has previously applied only for large consumers. However, by providing lower costs and stronger incentives for large and small consumers to provide DSF, the explicit version is likely to become the main source of DSF in future.

---

for Energy Studies (2019).

17. Robinson, D. and Li, X., "How consumers can help [...]", *op. cit.* is a source for this section. This source also provides additional information on DSF policy and practice in the UK and offers background and policy suggestions for China.

18. An example of a successful ToU tariff is the UK Economy 7 tariff, which was originally introduced to give consumers a strong economic incentive to heat their electric water heaters at night.

2. DEMAND FOR DSF

Demand-side Flexibility was always considered "nice to have" as a way of reducing peak demand, thereby avoiding costs associated with investment in generation and networks. However, with the penetration of intermittent renewable generation and the withdrawal of fossil-fired generation, DSF will be essential. There will be increased need for DSF to increase and decrease total system demand at any time, as well as mange local imbalances. Furthermore, electrification of transport, buildings and industry will substantially increase electricity demand, adding to the complexity of managing the electric power system and the need for flexibility, especially on the distribution network.

The potential value for DSF depends in large part on the services it can provide and their economic value. This applies whether the system is liberalized or regulated. Every system will need to make investment and operational decisions based on competitive markets, regulation, or a mix of the two. One way to think of this, using the liberalized model as an example, is to identify the hypothetical revenue streams from a variety of markets. Cornwall Insight[19] prepared a graphic (Figure 3) of hypothetical revenue streams from the different UK markets in which DSF can potentially deliver value to customers and to the system: networks (investment and operations), the capacity market, the wholesale energy market, balancing markets and mechanisms and other ancillary services. This graphic is hypothetical. Actual revenue streams and avoided costs will depend on which markets are open to DSF, the size of the markets and the margins available in each.

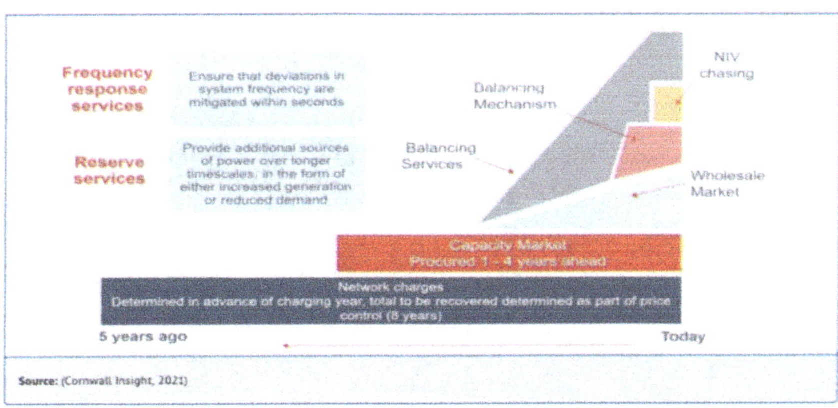

Figure 3: Overview of flexibility revenue streams in GB (revenue stacking)

19. Cornwall Insight, "Energy Spectrum: Capturing key developments across the GB energy sector" *Cornwall Insight*, n. 776.

It is important to recognize how DSF contributes to the security of energy supply and the limits of that contribution. First, by supporting integration of renewable energy (both distributed and in the central system), it reduces geopolitical risk associated with reliance on imported natural gas. Second, DSF allows for "islanding", that is DER operating on their own if the rest of the system is down, thereby reducing the cost of providing equivalent security through central system back-up. Third, DSF can provide the basis for starting up the rest of the system after a major system outage. Finally, by enabling consumers to benefit and participate, they give consumers a reason to support the energy transition.

DSF cannot provide all the flexibility services. DSF are particularly valuable for providing intra-day flexibility services (e. g., to manage the daily solar patterns), potentially longer. However, long-duration (i. e., seasonal) firm and flexible resources will very likely require large-scale storage or generation resources.

3. SUPPLY OF DSF[20]

The potential supply of DSF at a global level is substantial. In Table 4, IRENA categorises the sources by reference to the type of consumer (industrial, commercial, and residential), the specific technology sources and their maturity. All consumer categories can provide DSF and the sources differ for each category. This figure only includes DSF related to demand management and does not include distributed renewable generation or batteries, which are important sources of consumer flexibility.

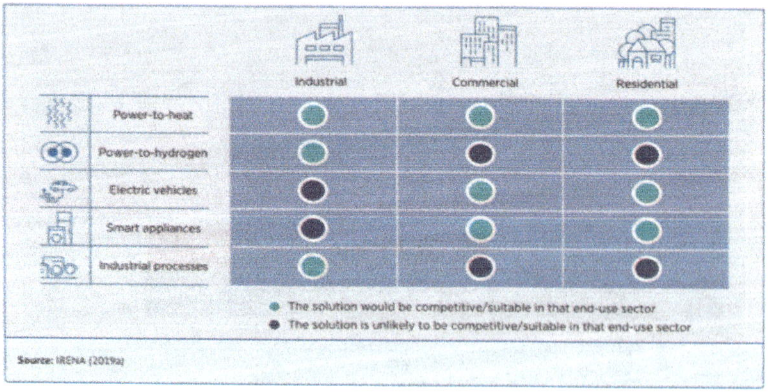

Figure 4: Sources of Flexible Demand
Source: International Renewable Energy Agency (IRENA), "Demand-side flexibility for power sector transformation" (2019).

20. Robinson, D. and Li, X., "How consumers can help [...]", *op. cit.*

To date, DSF has been provided by large industrial and commercial consumers willing and able to reduce their demand on a limited number of occasions, usually predictable. However, as explained above, the volume and range of required DSF have grown significantly. DSF is now technologically able to respond to shifting conditions in the energy market and on the networks and to do so very frequently. The challenge is to realize that potential; this depends on economic viability as well as policies to lower barriers. Below we examine the economic viability of explicit DSF.

4. ECONOMIC VIABILITY OF EXPLICIT DSF

The economic viability of explicit DSF depends on three main factors: the range of services provided, the economic value for each of those services, and the costs of providing the services. As illustrated above for the UK, DSF can now offer many services and the value of flexibility (for instance for balancing) is rising along with the penetration of renewables. But, are DSF competitive with alternative sources of decarbonised flexibility from existing or new resources?

The fact that electricity systems have often relied on explicit DSF from large consumers in emergencies suggests that the benefits of some sources of DSF outweigh the costs for the system and for the supplier of the DSF. However, for small consumers, the relatively limited involvement in providing explicit DSF, and even implicit DSF, suggests that the benefits were less than the costs, at least from the consumer perspective. This was largely due to poor regulatory incentive structures, the absence of smart meters to measure a consumer's contribution, and the low level of awareness and education on the consumer side. In short, the costs outweighed the benefits of DSF from the perspective of individual consumers[21].

However, there is now a concerted effort in many countries, notably in the EU and the UK, to reduce the costs of providing DSF and to provide a regulatory or market environment that encourages consumers to be more flexible. One possibility is to introduce dynamic tariffs to which consumers respond (implicit DSF). A second possibility is to encourage explicit DSF. For instance, distribution or transmission system operators may choose to buy demand response, as has been happening in the UK. Another possibility is to pool DSF from multiple consumers through energy communities or

21. Saviuc, I., Zabala López, C., Puskás-Tompos, A., Rollert, K. and Bertoldi, P., "Explicit Demand Response for small end-users and independent aggregators: Status, context, enablers and barriers", *JRC Science for Policy Report, European Commission* (2022).

aggregators that optimise the DSF and have the option to sell the aggregated energy and flexibility services into markets.

Aggregation may involve a single type of resource. For instance, aggregation of many EV batteries can provide demand flexibility by adjusting the timing of vehicle charging. Aggregators may now also use the battery to provide energy, capacity and services to meet their own commitments (if they are also retail companies) or to sell to the system.

However, the potential economic value of aggregation is much greater when many DERs are integrated into a Virtual Power Plant (VPP). A recent study by Brattle[22] compared the net cost of providing 400 MW of reliability from three resource types: a natural gas peaking plant, a transmission-connected utility-scale battery and a VPP composed of residential demand flexibility technologies. (See Figure 5.) The key findings include the following:

> "**Real reliability:** A VPP leveraging commercially-proven residential load flexibility technologies could perform as reliably as conventional resources
>
> **Cost savings:** The net cost to the utility of providing resource adequacy from a VPP is roughly 40-60% of the cost of the alternative options; 60 GW of VPP deployment could meet future US resource adequacy needs at $15-$35 billion less than the cost of the alternative options over the ensuing decade
>
> **Additional benefits:** 60 GW of VPP could provide over $20 billion in additional societal benefits — such as those related to emissions and resilience — over ten years".

The Brattle report reflects the potential for DSF to lower the costs of meeting the three objectives of the energy transition (security, sustainability, and efficiency). It strengthens the case for aggregation of residential DERs — which include technologies such as rooftop solar, smart thermostats, smart water heaters, EVs and distributed batteries. These DERs may be actively controlled by regulated monopolies or, in liberalised electricity systems, by supply companies (vertically integrated or independent), independent aggregators or by energy communities.

22. Hledik, R. and Peters, K., "Real Reliability: The Value of Virtual Power", *Brattle* (2023), retrieved from *https://www.brattle.com/wp-content/uploads/2023/04/Real-Reliability-The-Value-of-Virtual-Power_5.3.2023.pdf*

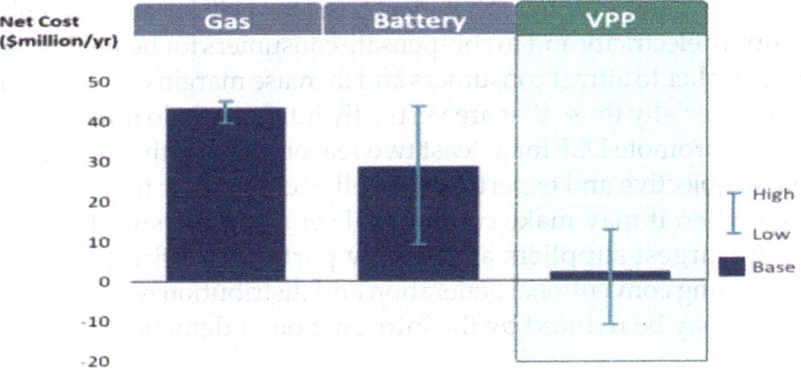

Figure 5: Net Cost of Providing 400 MW of Resource Adequacy

IV. EU DSF POLICY

This section summarises experience in the EU to encourage DSF before the Russian invasion of Ukraine began afterwards, with a focus mainly on the EU.

1. BEFORE THE RUSSIAN INVASION

The European Union formally recognised and regulated DSF (referred to as Demand Response in EU legislation) in the 2012 Energy Efficiency Directive. A 2016 report on the status of DR concluded that no Member State had completed the work of placing DR and supply-side resources on an equal footing, and that independent aggregation was only emerging in a limited number of countries.

In 2019, as part of the Clean Energy for all Europeans Package, the EU adopted Directive 944/2019 on common rules for the internal market for electricity[23]. A central feature of this legislation was the aim of enabling independent aggregators, defined as market participants engaged in aggregation who are not affiliated to the customer's supplier, especially when vertically integrated in networks and generation. In principle, aggregation by

23. Directive (EU) 2019/944 of the European Parliament and of the Council of 5 June 2019 on common rules for the internal market for electricity and amending Directive 2012/27/EU (recast), OJ L 158, 14.6.2019, pp. 125-199.

the customer's retail supplier is a logical basis for DSF because a combined offer to supply electricity and to compensate consumers for being flexible can assist the supplier to attract consumers and increase margins. However, most suppliers, especially those that are vertically integrated, do not have strong incentives to promote DSF for at least two reasons. One is that their primary commercial objective and expertise is to sell energy rather than to motivate DSF, even when it may make commercial sense for the supply business. Second, the largest suppliers are usually part of a vertically integrated group, including conventional generation and distribution networks, whose profitability may be reduced by the introduction of demand flexibility.

Article 17 includes the following measures, among others, to support DSF though independent aggregation. First, Member States shall allow and foster DSF through aggregation. Second, they shall allow final consumers, including those offering demand response through aggregation, to participate alongside producers in a non-discriminatory manner in all electricity markets. Third, they must also ensure that regulation contains the right for each market participant engaged in aggregation, including independent aggregators, to enter electricity markets without consent of other market participants.

The same article also introduces options with respect to paying financial compensation to other market participants or the participants´ balance party responsibility (BRP) when they are directly affected by demand response activation. This compensation provision is designed to relieve competitive supply companies of potential losses they would incur by committing in the day-ahead market to buy electricity for their consumers and then finding that their consumers bought less than anticipated. On the one hand, the legislation leaves it up to Member States to decide whether to introduce compensation; and in some cases, they do not require it, at least initially. Where it is introduced, the legislation states that financial compensation shall not create a barrier to market entry for market participants engaged in aggregation or a barrier to flexibility.

This legislation was therefore the starting point for a negotiation over whether affected suppliers should be compensated at all and, if so, who should pay that compensation, and what energy price should be used to determine it. The vertically integrated suppliers generally argue in favor of compensation and that independent aggregators should pay it, with the price being less important to the negotiation than who should pay. Independent aggregators do not oppose a compensation being paid to suppliers or their BRPs, but rather that the compensation is unnecessary and forbidden by the

Directive when an "uncorrected" model is used, i. e., in the current model where demand reduction creates positive imbalances for suppliers and where the TSO pays the supplier for the imbalances and then recovers the cost from all suppliers. However, the independent aggregators represented by DR4EU consider that a compensation may be paid to suppliers "where perimeter corrections are introduced", which means that the TSO is not paying a compensation for the imbalance. In that case, according to the independent aggregators, the compensation should be paid by all suppliers because they all benefit from reduced sourcing prices. They also argue that imposing compensation on aggregators will be a barrier to DSF and to market entry by independent aggregators. To support their position, they point to the US experience, where independent aggregation is permitted and no compensation needs be paid to suppliers, providing there is a net benefit for the system. The EU legislation supports that "net benefits" test: "...the aggregators or participating customers may be required to contribute to such compensation but only where and to the extent that the benefits to all suppliers, customers and their balance responsible parties do not exceed the direct costs incurred".

Since the EU legislation was passed, there has been limited progress with DSF, and almost none in many Member States. The legislation was supposed to be transposed by 31 December 2021. A report written for the European Commission[24] concluded that, first, the Directive was "ongoing" in most Member States, so was not completed. Second, on a more positive note, unlike in 2016, DR was now recognised and eligible to participate in at least one market. Third, the first possibility to engage in DR is made available through electricity suppliers. However, fourth, since suppliers are primarily focused on managing electricity, they are not always interested in exploiting the full potential of the available flexibility. The report argues:

> "Here is where the Independent Aggregator can improve the competition by offering an alternative to suppliers and retailers and thus realizing the potential of the flexibility resource. The possibility for the Independent Aggregators to effectively serve in this niche in the market requires a regulatory framework and a business case".

2. AFTER THE INVASION

Following the invasion and the very high and rising gas and electricity prices, the importance of DSF and storage became apparent, largely to reduce

24. Saviuc et al., "Explicit Demand Response for small end-users [...]", *op. cit.*

demand and prices for electricity generated by plants using natural gas at peak times. However, the subsequent war has acted as a stark reminder that the energy transition has to deliver both energy security and environmental sustainability at least cost. DSF would not only help to reduce demand when renewables were unavailable, but also to increase demand to avoid curtailment when renewable output was higher than predicted demand. For all these reasons, there was a need to replace gas-fired generation with decarbonized sources of flexibility, including DSF.

The new context has led to greater determination on behalf of the EU and the UK to deliver flexibility through sharper dynamic price signals to support implicit DSF and other measures to encourage explicit DSF, notably by independent aggregators, but also by supply companies and energy communities. There are three processes underway in the EU to deliver DSF. First, the European Commission (EC) is pressing Member States to transpose fully Article 17. Second, a Network Code drafted by ENTSO-e will soon be available to clarify the regulations for integrating DSF into the system. Third, the Commission has included several measures in their recent (March 14, 2023) Electricity Market Reform package, which is currently under discussion with Member States. The measures include: the requirement for Member States to carry out an assessment of flexibility needs; calling on TSOs and governments to develop programs to reduce demand at peaks; support for energy sharing among consumers and enabling system operators to take measures to encourage DSF, especially in short-term markets.

There is a long way to go before the potential for DSF will be fully realised. However, the combination of strong and growing political support to accelerate penetration of intermittent renewables and replace natural gas, along with the growing evidence that DSF and VPP can be economically viable, are good reasons to expect the demand-side of the energy sector to become increasingly important in the energy transition.

V. CONCLUSION

The energy transition is largely about the growing importance of electricity, which will in time account for at least half of energy demand. Today, the electricity system is based on the idea of "load following", where central system generation is planned and operated to meet uncertain and inflexible demand. Looking forward, penetration of intermittent renewables and electrification of end markets is making generation more uncertain and demand more flexible. With policies aimed at minimising the incremental costs of decarbonization and energy security, the future system should welcome the increasing potential of demand flexibility. It should enable consumers to express their preferences with respect to the extent of their reliance on the central electricity system, even if this means a reduced reliance on the central system resources. This will require a fundamental rethink about planning, operations, regulation and market design. It could well turn the traditional industry logic upside down.

The Consumers´ Role: A Legal Approach from The EU Clean Energy Package

JORGE GALÁN SOSA

PhD in Law from CEU San Pablo University. Partner at Villar y Asociados law firm

I. THE IRRUPTION OF THE CONSUMER´S POTENTIAL INTO THE EU LEGISLATION

The European Union law did not have binding provisions in the field of distributed generation prior to the *Clean energy package* (2018). The reason was simple; the third energy package (2009) was essentially intended to complete the promotion of competition between operators and the free choice of the supplier for energy consumers. This process of transition to competition began in 1996 with the aim of establishing an internal market in the electricity sector.

Under the third energy package, there were some isolated references to distributed generation in several legislative acts. For instance, the Directive 2009/28/EC on the promotion of the use of energy from renewable sources stated in its recital 6 that:

> "It is appropriate to support the demonstration and commercialisation phase of decentralised renewable energy technologies. The move towards decentralised energy production has many benefits, including the utilisation of local energy sources, increased local security of energy supply, shorter transport distances and reduced energy transmission losses. Such decentralisation also fosters community development and cohesion by providing income sources and creating jobs locally".

Likewise, article 13 of the same Directive contained a provision which compelled Member States to simplify the authorisation procedures for decentralised devices, like PV self-consumption.

Also, there was a specific allusion to self-generation in the Directive 2010/31/EC on the Energy Performance of Buildings. This reference consisted of obliging State Members to consider (before the construction of new buildings) decentralised energy supply systems, based on energy from renewable sources.

Apart from these isolated mentions, under the third energy package, there were no binding provisions for Member States referring to the deployment of decentralised activities.

Consequently, it is possible to state that this third regulatory package of the EU is inherent to the centralised energy system.

Under this system, the legal and administrative organization of the electricity sector is designed "top down", from production to supply. Moreover, a consumer is basically a passive agent, whose rights are essentially limited to the election of their supplier.

Nevertheless, since 2015, soft law instruments issued by the European Commission began to place consumers at the centre of the energy system as well as to highlight the importance of establishing a common legal framework for Distributed Energy Resources (henceforth referred to as DER).

A great example of the above is the Communication of the European Commission "*Delivering a new deal for energy consumers*"[1]. This Communication contained plenty of suggestions that would make possible the active participation of consumers in energy markets. For instance, this instrument states that "*consumers across the union should be free to choose their preferred form of active participation in energy markets*".

Also, the aforementioned Communication contained many allusions to self-consumption and distributed generation:

> "c) Reducing energy bills through self-generation and consumption
>
> The combination of decentralised generation and storage options with demand side flexibility can further enable consumers to become their own suppliers and managers for (a part of) their energy needs, becoming producers and consumers and reduce their energy bills.
>
> Decentralised renewable energy generation, whether used by consumers for their own use or supplied to the system, can usefully complement centralised generation sources. Where self-consumption exhibits a good match between

1. Communication from the Commission to the European Parliament, the Council, the European Economic and Social Committee and the Committee of the Regions *Delivering a New Deal for Energy Consumers*, COM/2015/339 final.

production and load, it can help reducing grid losses and congestion, saving network costs in the long-term that would otherwise have to be paid by consumers".

Even, as a part of this Communication, there was a specific paper called "*best practices on renewable self-consumption*"[2]. This working document contained several recommendations on the regulation of self-consumption for Member States and introduced the new concept of *prosumer* in the European framework.

In these Communications, the European Commission highlighted the need to incorporate in the European legal system the regulation of the new decentralised resources which, from the technological and economical perspective, were growing quickly.

Later, the *Clean energy for all Europeans* package of the European Commission included the reform of the renewable energy and electricity market Directives, among other legal instruments, with the intention of creating a European legal framework for the regulation of DER[3]. There was a need to provide a legal framework for the decentralisation process.

For this reason, both Directives incorporated new legal figures such as self-consumers of renewable energies, aggregators, energy communities (renewable and citizen) and active clients, with their corresponding rights and obligations. Moreover, the regulation of these new figures was accompanied by new legal provisions regarding the creation of new markets and services, such as flexibility services in distribution networks.

Overall, the purpose was to adapt the EU energy legal architecture to the new economic and technological realities.

At this point, several ideas related to the decentralisation of the energy system and its reflection on the EU energy law provisions should be stressed:

(i) The first one consists of the idea that, through new activities and figures, consumers can provide services to the system, for instance

2. Commission staff working document *Best practices on Renewable Energy Self-consumption* Accompanying the document Communication from the Commission to the European Parliament, the Council, the European Economic and Social Committee and the Committee of the Regions Delivering a New Deal for Energy Consumers, SWD/2015/141 final.
3. Communication from the Commission to the European Parliament, the Council, the European Economic and Social Committee and the Committee of the Regions and the European Investment Bank *Clean Energy For All Europeans*, COM/2016/0860 final.

through flexibility and the combination of self-generation and storage. Thus, in the new energy framework, the consumer is an active agent.

(ii) The second one focuses on the need to create new markets (e.g., local flexibility or capacity markets) to make possible the participation of consumers. Consequently, the decentralization of the electricity system implies major changes in market design.

(iii) Thirdly, in line with the previous point, there is a new meaning for the concept of liberalisation. Under the new energy framework, liberalisation is related to the new possibilities available for consumers to procure their energy supply and participate in the market either as individuals or through aggregation.

Once these initial considerations have been made, we will now move on to the regulatory changes in EU energy law, as well as to its subsequent transposition into Spanish legislation.

II. THE EU CLEAN ENERGY PACKAGE: THE LEGAL RECOGNITION OF *PROSUMERS*, ENERGY COMMUNITIES AND AGGREGATORS

In contrast to the third energy package, the *clean energy package* establishes a complete legal regime for the decentralization agents, making possible the participation of consumers in energy markets.

The incorporation of the new figure of active customers in the Directive (EU) 2019/944 represents, in my opinion, a turning point in the legal role of consumers. This is corroborated with the declaration of intent contained in the recital 27 of this Directive:

> "All consumers should be able to benefit from directly participating in the market, in particular by adjusting their consumption according to market signals and, in return, benefiting from lower electricity prices or other incentive payments. The benefits of such active participation are likely to increase over time, as the awareness of otherwise passive consumers is raised about their possibilities as active customers and as the information on the possibilities of active participation becomes more accessible and better known. Consumers should have the possibility of participating in all forms of demand response. They should therefore have the possibility of benefiting from the full deployment of smart metering systems and, where such deployment has been negatively assessed, of choosing to have a smart metering system and

a dynamic electricity price contract. This should allow them to adjust their consumption according to real-time price signals that reflect the value and cost of electricity or transportation in different time periods, while Member States should ensure the reasonable exposure of consumers to wholesale price risk. Consumers should be informed about benefits and potential price risks of dynamic electricity price contracts. Member States should also ensure that those consumers who choose not to actively engage in the market are not penalised. Instead, their ability to make informed decisions on the options available to them should be facilitated in the manner that is the most suited to domestic market conditions".

In this sense, it is important to highlight that the title of the chapter in which the regulation of this new agent is included is called *"consumer empowerment and protection"* (Chapter III), which constitutes a declaration of intent. Article 15.2 of the Directive (EU) 2019/944 contains a wide range of rights and obligations for active customers, from participating in energy markets directly or through aggregation to selling self-generated electricity:

"2. Member States shall ensure that active customers are:

(a) entitled to operate either directly or through aggregation;

(b) entitled to sell self-generated electricity, including through power purchase agreements;

(c) entitled to participate in flexibility schemes and energy efficiency schemes;

(d) entitled to delegate to a third party the management of the installations required for their activities, including installation, operation, data handling and maintenance, without that third party being considered to be an active customer;

(e) subject to cost-reflective, transparent and non-discriminatory network charges that account separately for the electricity fed into the grid and the electricity consumed from the grid, in accordance with Article 59(9) of this Directive and Article 18 of Regulation (EU) 2019/943, ensuring that they contribute in an adequate and balanced way to the overall cost sharing of the system;

(f) financially responsible for the imbalances they cause in the electricity system; to that extent they shall be balance responsible parties or shall delegate their balancing responsibility in accordance with Article 5 of Regulation (EU) 2019/943".

The only requirement for the active customers is that those activities do not constitute the agent's primary commercial or professional activity. This is a provision which is consequent with the nature of this figure because it is essential to distinguish active customers from electricity undertakings. An active customer can be a domestic consumer as well as a professional or a legal person (corporation) that develops a commercial or industrial activity. For that matter, it is increasingly frequent for companies that are engaged in other business segments / types of activities in which electricity represents a significant part of their costs to stand up for technologies that increase their energy efficiency, reduce their costs and ensure energy reliability.

Regarding self-consumption, the Directive (EU) 2018/2001 provides a complete legal regime for this activity and fills the previous legal gap existing on distributed energy resources.

The first thing to stress about the EU self-consumption regulation is that Directive (EU) 2018/2001 sets forth two legal definitions: renewables self-consumer and jointly acting renewables self-consumer. This distinction provides a clear regulatory framework from the perspective of the subjects (or agents).

According to these definitions, a renewable self-consumer is a final customer, either a legal or natural person, who has the right to generate renewable electricity, and to store or sell that electricity. These activities can be done individually or through aggregation (art. 2.14).

This right is recognised for non-household consumers, with the condition that those activities do not constitute their primary commercial or professional activity. Once again, this requirement is consistent with the objective to distinguish, in this case, between self-consumers and electricity undertakings.

The regulation of self-consumption in this Directive (EU) 2018/2001 lays the foundation to achieve a high penetration of this activity, establishing a complete regime of rights and obligations which grants legal security to consumers that decide to become self- consumers. In this respect, three points can be highlighted.

(i) In the first place, this regulation simplifies the requirements to become a self-consumer by obliging Member States to avoid disproportionate and discriminatory procedures. In this sense, excessive bureaucratic procedures constitute in many Member States (including Spain) one of the main regulatory barriers to this activity.

(ii) Secondly, this regulation allows consumers not only to obtain savings from their electricity consumption, but also from the sale of their electricity surpluses. In this way, the electricity consumer becomes a *prosumer*, because there is a clear distinction between saving energy or compensating energy surpluses and selling the surpluses to the market or to other agents.

(iii) Thirdly, this regulation incentivizes the participation of consumers in flexible mechanisms through aggregation, which demonstrates the connection between the new agents and new activities in the decentralised energy system.

In any case, two main aspects of the regulation on self-consumption in the Directive (EU) 2018/2001 should also be underlined.

The first one is the right to sell the excess production, which connects with the new concept of liberalisation mentioned above. Under this provision, not only the agents legally constituted as electricity undertakings (producers or suppliers) have the right to sell electricity; now consumers can sell their excess production, even to other consumers. This right recognised in the mentioned Directive is a radical change compared to the traditional configuration of the electric sector, under which consumers had to pay for receiving the provision of an electricity supply service.

The second one, on the downside, is the possibility to apply non-discriminatory and proportionate charges and fees to self-generated renewable electricity remaining within prosumers premises. Even though this option is limited to three specific cases, it does have echoes of the Spain's former "sun tax" (*impuesto al sol*) which had a detrimental impact on the activity[4].

This important question should be brake down into the following:

On the one hand, we must start from the premise that a higher level of penetration of self- consumption of electrical energy in the domestic, commercial and industrial sectors will imply a decrease in electrical energy demand and, consequently, lower returns for the current electrical system. For

4. This specific cases consists of the following: (a) when the self-generated renewable electricity is effectively supported via support schemes, only to the extent that the economic viability of the project and the incentive effect of such support are not undermined; (b) from 1 December 2026, when the overall share of self-consumption installations exceeds 8 % of the total installed electricity capacity of a Member State; or (c) when the self-generated renewable electricity is produced in installations with a total installed electrical capacity of more than 30 kW.

this reason, the establishment of this conditioned application of charges and fees makes sense in a scenario of massive penetration of distributed resources.

On the other hand, it should be highlighted that the application of charges and fees on self-consumed energy can have a discouraging effect on consumers, who may perceive it as a measure to restrict self-consumption. In addition, there are other more reasonable alternatives to the application of charges on the renewable energy generated on site, such as the application of a fix rate charge calculated according to the power of the installation.

In respect of energy communities, we must distinguish between the two types of communities that have been incorporated in the Directives of the clean energy package: renewable energy communities and citizen energy communities.

The common spirit of both figures is to represent an alternative to traditional energy operators and prioritize the economic and social interest of their activity. For that reason, these communities are open to the participation of final costumers.

Both communities allow their members to carry out a wide range of activities; to produce, consume, store and sell energy, including through power purchase agreements. However, there are also some clear differences between them, which entails that each one has its own legal regime. Renewable energy communities are regulated by the Directive (EU) 2018/2001 (art. 22) and citizen energy communities are regulated by the Directive (EU) 2019/944 (art. 16).

The main characteristic of renewable energy communities is the ownership of renewable energy projects (not only electricity projects). From the perspective of the subjects, renewable energy communities are legal entities formed and controlled by natural persons, small enterprises or local authorities, including municipalities. This makes a difference with the citizen energy communities.

Likewise, renewable energy communities are effectively controlled by members that are located in the proximity of renewable energy projects. This type of provision reinforces the local character of this entity which, at the same time, is connected to the income and employment creation objectives of local communities.

On the other hand, citizen energy communities can produce energy from non-renewable sources (this is one of the most important differences between both types of energy communities). Also, it is important to highlight that citizen communities can develop more activities than renewable communities. For instance, they are entitled to own, establish, purchase or lease distribution networks. This last provision is mostly important in the field of industrial areas to promote the use of power generation facilities at the local level and contribute to avoid grid saturation.

Furthermore, this kind of energy community can involve big energy companies provided they do not control the entity.

Finally, we must refer to aggregation, which is a key activity for the participation of consumers in energy markets. This activity, according to the definition of the Directive (EU) 2019/944, consists of combining *"multiple customer loads or generated electricity for sale, purchase or auction in any electricity market"* (art. 2.18). This basic definition is complemented with the definition of independent aggregator: *"a market participant engaged in aggregation who is not affiliated to the customer's supplier"* (art. 2.19).

The clean energy package contains dispersed but sufficient regulation on this market participant.

The Directive (EU) 2019/944 defines aggregation and independent aggregator, establishing the basic regulatory provisions for the development of the activity.

Among these provisions, we encounter the framework for aggregation contracts as well as several obligations for Member States to ensure the right of final costumers to participate, through aggregation, in all electricity markets.

With regard to aggregation contracting, Directive (EU) 2019/944 stipulates that *"member States shall ensure that all customers are free to purchase and sell electricity services, including aggregation, other than supply, independently from their electricity supply contract and from an electricity undertaking of their choice"* (art. 13.1). This provision broadens the scope of active customers' freedom to manage their energy resources and increases competition among different agents (e.g., suppliers and independent aggregators).

Likewise, the regulation of the aggregation in the abovementioned Directive (EU) 2018/2001 includes provisions intended to ensure that aggregators can participate in electricity markets.

Related to the latter, from the point of view of the agents, the independent aggregator must not be affiliated to the costumer´s supplier, as it is an autonomous agent.

Considering all the above, there is no doubt that the clean energy package of the European Union has created a legal architecture for a development of the final customer´s potential. This new legal framework has made possible a strong growth of some of the specific activities associated with the decentralization phenomena, particularly in the case of self-consumption of electric energy.

In this way, the clean energy package materializes the objective of the European Commission of placing consumers on the centre of the energy system.

On a critical note, we can say that some of the new legal agents originated in this energy package can lead to confusion in practice, so it is not easy to make a clear distinction in some cases. This is the case, for example, of two kinds of energy communities as well as the distinction between active costumers and self-consumers.

Also, it is important to emphasize that in the transposition rules applying to Member States, special attention should be given to the relations between traditional operators and new agents. As a matter of fact, one of the main aspects of Directive (EU) 2019/944 is that it focuses mainly on already consolidated operators and on not to set up unjustified restrictions with respect to new agents.

III. A BRIEF ANALYSIS OF THE SPANISH LEGISLATION

Spanish regulation of DER, particularly in the field of self-consumption, has moved from a very restrictive legislation to a more favourable regulatory environment.

Under the former regulation of this activity (2015), neither joint self-consumption nor the compensation of surpluses for small self-consumers (below 100 kilowatts) was allowed.

Furthermore, this regulation introduced the so-called *"sun tax"* (*"impuesto al sol"*). This was a charge applied over the self-consumed electricity with the aim of contributing to funding the backup role played by the electricity system. The philosophy behind this charge was clear; self-consumers that remained connected to the grid had to contribute economically to fund the support that they received from the electricity system when their renewable assets were not producing energy. In practise, this *"sun tax"* did not affect household self-consumers, because the installations below 10kW were exempted from paying this charge.

However, the *"sun tax"* had a deterrent effect on consumers, which explains the limited success of self-consumption during the four years that this regulation was in force.

The legal changes introduced in 2018 by royal decree-law and the subsequent regulation passed in 2019, have made possible a significant growth of the activity in Spain. Data on installed power for self-consumption reveals that during the 2018-2022 period, capacity has increased from 101 MW to 2.649 MW[5]. Therefore, there is no doubt that the regulation in force constitutes a successful development of this activity and that Spain has incorporated to its legal system the relevant provisions of European law.

Concretely, the provisions in force in Spain:

(i) Make possible the compensation of surpluses under a net-billing scheme for the installations under 100 kW.

(ii) Allow joint self-consumption.

(iii) Prohibit the application of charges and fees to self-generated electricity.

That said, there are immediate challenges for the regulation of Spanish self-consumption. Concretely, there are two main difficulties.

The first one is the need to recognise self-consumers who are not producers the right to sell their surpluses and not only the right to be compensated for them. In this sense, the rights established in the Directive (EU) 2018/2001 include the selling of surpluses, which is different from compensation. This regulatory change will enable self-consumers with smaller facilities not only to be compensated their surpluses by their retailer, but also to sell their surpluses to any other agent, for example, in markets through an aggregator.

The second one is the need to improve the regulation of joint self-consumption, which is subjected to several limitations, including the distance between the point of generation and consumption (which now is 2000 meters). These limitations are hampering the growth of this modality of self-consumption, especially in industrial complexes. Furthermore, companies with the aim of becoming self-consumers are reporting certain difficulties concerning distribution companies, from the point of view of access and connection to the electrical network, for the start-up of collective

5. See APPA Renovables, "2022 I Informe anual del autoconsumo fotovoltaico", APPA (2023).

self-consumption facilities. All in all, there is still considerable room for improvement as regards the installation and start-up of the facilities.

In contrast to self-consumption, the regulation of both types of energy communities and aggregation is pending in Spain; it requires a complete regulatory development. Despite both figures have been incorporated as legal agents in the Spanish electricity act, this recognition cannot have effects without its legislative and regulatory development.

In the case of energy communities, despite the absence of regulatory development, there is an important impetus from the energy policy field to promote the creation of these entities. According to this support, the implementation of energy communities has been incorporated with preferential character in some of the main energy policy instruments, such as the integrated national energy and climate plan or the "Plan + Seguridad Energética". In these types of instruments, the benefits that energy communities bring to the economy and employment at the local level, as well as the incentive they suppose for the participation of consumers in the creation of energy and energetic markets are presumably highlighted.

In addition, within the scope of competencies in the field of energy, some Autonomous Communities have passed acts that have tried to establish a legal framework for these entities, just like it happens in the Autonomous Community of Aragón[6].

In my opinion, this situation could create a problem of legal uncertainty, because many energy communities created under these regimes could incur in future legal incompatibility with the new national regulation. We must take into account that in April 2023, the Spanish government issued a regulation proposal to establish the legal framework of energy communities and to transpose the provisions regarding that matters of Directives (EU) 2019/944 and (EU) 2018/2001.

Moreover, it must also be remarked that, in the absence of a specific legal framework for the creation of energy communities, many of the projects that describe themselves as energy communities respond instead to a collective self-consumption system, giving rise to some confusion. Thus, it is necessary to precise that collective self-consumption is a very important tool for the implementation of energy communities. Nevertheless, energy communities are not limited to collective self-consumption and, as we have seen earlier, they can carry out a broader range of activities.

6. See Decreto-ley 1/2023, de 20 de marzo, del Gobierno de Aragón, de medidas urgentes para el impulso de la transición energética y el consumo de cercanía en Aragón.

Regarding aggregation, the recognition of the independent aggregator as one of the figures of the electricity sector in the Spanish law still does not have a proposal for regulatory development that allows the start of the activity of these agents. For this reason, its recent acknowledgement (2020) has no effect in practice. Considering the elapsed time since the approval of Directive (EU) 2019/944, it is important to pass the regulations that allow the activity of aggregators and independent aggregators without delay. Among other reasons, the reform of the internal market of the electricity in which the European Commission is currently working on, attributes a very important role to demand´s flexibility, to which aggregators activity is essential. Likewise, it is essential that the draft legislation related to storage and capacity takes into account the figure of aggregators.

IV. CONCLUSIONS

In view of the aforementioned, there is no doubt that EU energy law has been able to adapt relatively quickly to technological and economic changes which have given rise to a process of decentralization of the energy sector. Even more, since the approval of Directive (EU) 2018/2001, several new decentralized agents have been recognized, which at the same time it has been accompanied by the establishment of their legal regime, hence, making possible the success of activities such as self-consumption. Nevertheless, this new legal framework has been welcomed unevenly in Spain: very quickly in the case of self-consumption, but more slowly in the case of energy communities and aggregation.

Consequently, we can draw two main conclusions:

(i) On the one side, the European legal framework, after the changes introduced by the *clean energy package*, lays the foundation for a deep development of the decentralised figures and the empowerment of energy consumers. Concretely, the figures of self-consumption, energy communities and aggregators are key drivers for the transformation of energy markets.

(ii) On the other side, the Spanish legal framework should give priority to the full development of these new figures in order to drive the decentralisation process of the electricity system. More specifically, there is the need to regulate the details of these figures, not only their legal regimes, but also their relations with other subjects and with the system itself. In this sense, it is no use introducing new subjects in the legal system which are not properly developed.

Additionally, the development of these figures together with other activities and agents (such as storage or closed distribution networks) will lead to a strengthening of the distributed generation and to the participation of the demand in energy markets. In this way, the liberalisation of the energy sector is now related with the strengthening of consumers, instead of the *despublicatio* of the electricity system.

Greening the Transport Sector: Is the Recent Reform in Eu Law Heading Towards a Consistent Carbon Price?

DR. SÉBASTIEN E. WOLFF[1]
Post-Doctoral researcher at the Catholic University of Louvain (Belgium)

I. INTRODUCTION

Transport is an important part of everyone life. Commuting to work, catching the children at school, travelling to see family and friends are daily routines that have an important organisational impact. For most people, the main purpose is to minimise the time dedicated each day to transport. Its impact on the environment and the climate should however not be neglected.

Transport represents an increasing part of the human footprint on climate and on the environment. Travelling not only emits large quantities of CO_2 but also leads to increased artificialized surfaces for infrastructures. Today, in the European Union, transport represents an average of 25% of the total emissions of carbon dioxide. Interestingly, transport emissions increased slightly from 2011 to 2019, before decreasing in 2020 and 2021, noticeably because of the COVID-19 pandemic. However, emissions are expected to start increasing again in the coming years with economic activities resuming everywhere around the globe. According to an evaluation provided by the European Commission, transport is also responsible for two thirds of all NO_x emissions, and accounts for more than 10% for other pollutants[2].

1. Sébastien Wolff is a post-doctoral researcher at the Catholic University of Louvain (Belgium), lecturer at the University of Lorraine (France) and at the ICHEC Brussels Management School (Belgium). The opinions expressed in this contribution are his owns and do not necessarily represent the views of the institutions he is working with.
2. European Commission, *Proposal for a Regulation of the European Parliament and of the Council amending Regulation (EU) 2019/1242 as regards strengthening the CO2 emission performance standards for new heavy-duty vehicles and integrating reporting obligations, and repealing Regulation (EU) 2018/956*, COM (2023) 88 final, 2023, p. 2.

To fulfil its commitment to become the first carbon neutral economy, the European Commission has developed an ambitious plan to phase-out progressively all internal combustion engine means of transport using an internal combustion engine. The Fit-for-55 plan[3] is the execution plan of the Green Deal strategy[4] setting a milestone in 2030 with objective of a 55 % GHG emissions reduction and includes several legal initiatives in the field of transportation:

— As a first initiative to be analysed in this contribution, new regulations lay down stronger CO_2 requirements for new cars, vans[5] and trucks[6]. The objective is to reach a 90 % reduction of emissions coming from road transport in 2050 by setting decreasing targets to manufacturers for new cars and vans.

— A second initiative relates to the fuels used for air and waterborne navigation. In addition to the requirements laid down in the proposal for an Alternative Fuels Infrastructure Regulation[7] imposing Member States to offer aircrafts and vessels access to the clean electricity supply in all major ports and airports, the ReFuelEU Aviation Initiative[8] will oblige suppliers to offer on the market fuels with better sustainable

3. European Commission, *Communication from the Commission to the European Parliament, the Council, the European Economic and the Committee of the Regions "Fit for 55": delivering the EU's 2030 "Climate Target on the way to climate neutrality"*, COM (2021) 550 final, 2021.
4. European Commission, *Communication from the Commission to the European Parliament, the Council, the European Economic and the Committee of the Regions "European Green Deal"*, COM (2019)640 final, 2019.
5. Regulation (EU) 2023/851 of the European Parliament and of the Council of 19 April 2023 amending Regulation (EU) 2019/631 as regards strengthening the CO2 emission performance standards for new passenger cars and new light commercial vehicles in line with the Union's increased climate ambition, *OJ*, L 110 of 25 April 2023, pp. 5-20. The proposal was part of the Fit-for-55 package published in 2021: European Commission, *Proposal for a Regulation of the European Parliament and of the Council amending Regulation (EU) 2019/631 as regards strengthening the CO2 emission performance standards for new passenger cars and new light commercial vehicles in line with the Union's increased climate ambition*, COM (2021) 556 final, 2021.
6. European Commission, *Proposal for a Regulation of the European Parliament and of the Council amending Regulation (EU) 2019/1242 as regards strengthening the CO2 emission performance standards for new heavy-duty vehicles and integrating reporting obligations, and repealing Regulation (EU) 2018/956*, COM (2023) 88 final, 2023.
7. Regulation (EU) 2023/1804 of the European Parliament and of the Council of 13 September 2023 on the deployment of alternative fuels infrastructure, and repealing Directive 2014/94/EU, *OJ* L 234 of 22 September 2023, pp. 1-47.
8. European Commission, *Proposal for a Regulation of the European Parliament and of the Council on ensuring a level playing field for sustainable air transport*, COM (2021)561 final,

characteristics for aircrafts. A similar initiative is supported by the FuelEU Maritime Initiative[9] that will stimulate the uptake of sustainable fuels and zero emission technologies in this sector.

— A third initiative from the Commission intends to reform the EU Emissions Trading System (ETS)[10]. The newly adopted directives include many changes, from lowering the overall emission cap, to phase out the free emission allowances for aviation (by i.e., relying on the similar but not identical scheme "CORSIA" developed by the ICAO[11]). This fourth phase of the ETS aims also at addressing the lack of emissions reduction in road transport and building by the setting up of new schemes for fuel distribution for those activities. As it will be later discussed, "[T]hese measures are complemented by the revised Energy Taxation Directive, which will make cleaner fuels more attractive in all transport modes and close loopholes for polluting fuels" [12].

— An innovative European Carbon Border Adjustment Mechanism has been adopted recently by the European institutions[13]. The purpose

2021. The project ReFuelEU including both aviation and maritime sectors is a new initiative aiming at reducing the CO_2 emissions coming from these sectors.

9. European Commission, *Proposal for a Regulation of the European Parliament and of the Council on the use of renewable and low-carbon fuels in maritime transport and amending Directive 2009/16/EC*, COM (2021) 562 final, 2021.

10. Directive (EU) 2023/959 of the European Parliament and of the Council of 10 May 2023 amending Directive 2003/87/EC establishing a system for greenhouse gas emission allowance trading within the Union and Decision (EU) 2015/1814 concerning the establishment and operation of a market stability reserve for the Union greenhouse gas emission trading system, *OJ*, L 130 of 16 May 2023, pp. 134-202 ; Directive (EU) 2023/958 of the European Parliament and of the Council of 10 May 2023 amending Directive 2003/87/EC as regards aviation's contribution to the Union's economy-wide emission reduction target and the appropriate implementation of a global market-based measure, *OJ* L 130 of 16 May 2023, pp. 115-113.

11. CORSIA is the global Carbon Offsetting and Reduction Scheme for international Aviation from the International Civil Aviation Organisation (ICAO). The ICAO describes the CORSIA initiative as "a global market-based measure designed to offset international aviation CO_2 emissions in order to stabilize the levels of such emissions from 2020 onwards (CNG2020)." The offsetting of CO_2 emissions will be achieved through the acquisition and cancelation of emissions units from the global carbon market by aeroplane operators. (ICAO, *CORSIA implementation plan*, 2019, retrieved from *www.icao.int/environmental-protection/CORSIA/Documents/CORSIA%20Brochure/CorsiaBrochure_ENG-Mar2019_Web.pdf* on 9 June 2021).

12. "Fit for 55" communication, p. 9.

13. European Commission, *Proposal for a Regulation of the European Parliament and of the Council establishing a carbon border adjustment mechanism*, COM (2021) 564 final, 2021.

is to set a price on carbon emissions embedded in certain products. The mechanism aims at fostering emissions decline globally and to avoid "carbon leakage" in case of increase of carbon or energy taxes or fees within the European Union. However, it will be limited to a certain number of goods linked, where European manufacturing activities are already covered by the ETS.

— Finally, the European Commission ambitions to reform the Energy Taxation Directive[14]. The purpose of the initiative is to align the taxation of energy products with EU energy and climate policies but also to promote clean technologies — or rather clean sources of energy — and to repealed outdated exemptions and reduced rates that currently support the use of fossil energies[15].

In this chapter, we analyse the initiatives according to their policy nature: pure regulation, market-based instruments, and tax measures. Under the first category, new emissions standards for vehicles and mandatory delivering of electricity for crafts berthed in ports and aircrafts at airports will be further investigated; under market instruments, newly adopted amendments to the ETS legal framework will be analysed; the third category will cover specifically provisions relating to transport in the current drafting and expected upcoming modifications of the Energy Taxation Directive. The last section attempts to draw the impact of this bundle of measures on transport and to evaluate their ability to set a consistent price on carbon and related GHG emissions. For all subjects, a special attention is dedicated to the treatment of foreign entities operating on the Union territory and to global activities.

II. CHANGES IN PURE REGULATORY MEASURES TO ACCOMMODATE ENERGY TRANSITION

1. NEW EMISSIONS STANDARDS FOR CARS AND LIGHT- AND HEAVY-DUTY VEHICLES

Setting standards will have an impact on emissions that can be anticipated, since it will oblige manufacturers to comply with the new

14. European Commission, *Proposal for a Council Directive restructuring the Union framework for the taxation of energy products and electricity (recast)*, COM (2021) 563 final, 2021.
15. European Commission, *European Green Deal: Commission proposes transformation of EU economy and society to meet climate ambitions*, press release of 14 July 2021, retrieved from *ec.europa.eu/commission/presscorner/detail/en/IP_21_3541* on 10 June 2022.

maximum emissions requirements. The targets envisaged for cars and light commercial vehicles go a step further toward decarbonisation than just imposing new stringent thresholds for emissions by setting the obligation to have a reduction of the average emissions of 55 % by 2030 for new cars (under the previous regulation, the target was of 37,5% for the same date), and of 50 % for light commercial vehicles (previously 30%) based on an average of 95gCO_2/km and 147gCO_2/km respectively for cars and vans[16]. The absence of emissions at the tailpipe for non-commercial vehicles is foreseen for the 1st January 2035,[17] with the objective of a 100% reduction from the 2021 target endorsed in the Directive. In other words, starting from 2035 and under the condition that no amendment is later introduced to accommodate synthetic or biofuels, no more carbon dioxide emissions will come from new cars sold in the European Union. Based on this new standard, it will not be possible anymore for European and foreign manufacturers to commercialise cars equipped with an internal combustion engine, but only hydrogen or full electric cars. The double counting of cars emitting less than 50 gCO_2/km and the sampling of only 95% of the manufacturer production are now expired and will not be prolongated[18].

A similar proposal was recently published by the Commission for heavy-duty vehicles, setting the objectives of having a reduction up to 90 % from 2040 onwards. The regime seems however marginally suppler in the way average emissions are calculated, considering for instance that zero-emission vehicles include trucks emitting no more than 5gCO_2/t/km or 5gCO_2/km, which might let room to quite significant emissions considering that trucks have the ability to carry dozen tons of merchandises in average[19].

The use of standards is the most powerful tool for public authorities, allowing to reach net zero emissions from the use of cars and vans with an almost 100% certainty. Some derogative measures exist for small independent manufacturers (fewer than 10 000 passenger cars or fewer than 22 000 new light commercial vehicles) and for medium size manufacturers (between

16. Regulation 2019/631 of 17 April 2019 setting CO2 emission performance standards for new passenger cars and for new light commercial vehicles, *OJ* L 111 of 25 April 2019, p. 13, article 1. Regulation 2023/851 has introduced the new thresholds by amending the article 1.
17. *Ibid.*, reviewed Article 1(5a).
18. *Ibid.*, Article 4 and 5.
19. European Commission, *Proposal for a Regulation of the European Parliament and of the Council amending Regulation (EU) 2019/1242 as regards strengthening the CO_2 emission performance standards for new heavy-duty vehicles and integrating reporting obligations, and repealing Regulation (EU) 2018/956*, COM (2023) 88 final, 2023, p. 2, revised Article 3.

10 000 and 300 000 passenger cars), which benefit from adapted emissions reduction objectives or a tailor-made target taking into consideration their characteristics[20].

These new emissions requirements however are only for vehicles released on the European market[21]. Cars, vans, and trucks destined to be registered outside of the EU do not have to comply with this stricter decreasing carbon intensity obligation[22]. In other words, the application of these new European legislations does not preclude European manufacturers to produce internal combustion engine vehicles but only for export. From a climate perspective and setting aside the impact on economic activity and employment, it is regretful that the standard does not apply to all cars manufactured on the European ground, as it will serve the environmental objective by limiting the pollution coming from transportation of combustion-engine propelled vehicles globally and not only in the European Union. This regulation is also limited to direct emissions and do not take into consideration carbon dioxide release during the manufacturing process, neither of emissions during the recycling process — however, those processes will partially be subject to other policy tools, such as the EU ETS.

2. MINIMUM SUSTAINABLE FUEL TARGET FOR AIR TRANSPORT AND EMISSIONS REDUCTION REQUIREMENTS FOR SHIPS

A second important initiative from the Fit-for-55 package is the ReFuelEU program. This program aims at making air and waterborne navigation more sustainable and reducing their climate impact.

The proposal for ensuring a level playing field for sustainable air transport suggests imposing to fuel suppliers for air transportation to include in their products a certain proportion of sustainable aviation fuel[23]. The mandatory share of sustainable fuel remains modest until 2030, with only 2% of the volume to reach 70% in 2050, of which at least 50 % of

20. *Ibid.*, Article 10.
21. See European Commission, *Proposal for a Regulation of the European Parliament and of the Council amending Regulation (EU) 2019/1242 as regards strengthening the CO_2 emission performance standards for new heavy-duty vehicles and integrating reporting obligations, and repealing Regulation (EU) 2018/956*, COM (2023) 88 final, 2023, article 11(1).
22. Regulation 2023/851 for CO2 standards for cars and vans, article 13(3).
23. Regulation (EU) 2023/2405 of the European Parliament and of the Council of 18 October 2023 on ensuring a level playing field for sustainable air transport (ReFuelEU Aviation), *OJ* L 2023/2405 of 31 October 2023, article 4.

synthetic fuel[24]. The regulation has foreseen the potential refuelling by airlines in foreign countries and makes compulsory — we presume only for airlines based in the European Union — to refuel a minimum of 90% of the yearly aviation fuel required for a given aircraft under these conditions[25]. To ascertain the inclusion of sustainable aviation fuel, the future regulation will include several reporting obligations for airports and aviation fuel providers.

It is interesting to note that the manufacturing of aircrafts can be considered as a sustainable activity under the Taxonomy of environmentally sustainable activities. To be considered as sustainable, starting from 2028, the aircrafts must not emit any emissions at the tailpipe or being certified to operate on 100% blend of sustainable aviation fuels[26]. Two levels of ambition can then be observed: on the one hand, minimum requirements for the whole sector — under ReFuelEU initiative — and on the other, full sustainability with carbon sequestration or absence of carbon dioxide emissions for more advanced players in the energy transition.

Another proposal lays down similar requirements for waterborne transport, but by setting strict decrease requirements in carbon intensity, as for cars, vans, and trucks.

In this new regulation[27], a reduction is imposed by an incremental strengthening of the emission standard, reaching a 75% reduction in 2050. To take into consideration the size and the intrinsic characteristics of ships,

24. The definition of sustainable aviation fuel is provided with a reference to the Renewable Energy Directive (Directive (EU) 2018/2001 of 11 December 2018 on the promotion of the use of energy from renewable sources, *OJ* L 328 of 21 December 2018, pp. 82-209. Note that some amendments are planned in a short term within the Renewable Energy Directive in order to reassess the sustainability of the fuels considered as sustainable.
25. Regulation (EU) 2023/2405 of the European Parliament and of the Council of 18 October 2023 on ensuring a level playing field for sustainable air transport (ReFuelEU Aviation), *OJ* L 2023/2405 of 31 October 2023, article 5(1).
26. Commission Delegated Regulation (EU) 2021/2139 of 4 June 2021 supplementing Regulation (EU) 2020/852 of the European Parliament and of the Council by establishing the technical screening criteria for determining the conditions under which an economic activity qualifies as contributing substantially to climate change mitigation or climate change adaptation and for determining whether that economic activity causes no significant harm to any of the other environmental objectives, *OJ* L 442 of 9 December 2021, pp. 1-349, section 3.21.
27. Regulation (EU) 2023/1805 of the European Parliament and of the Council of 13 September 2023 on the use of renewable and low-carbon fuels in maritime transport, and amending Directive 2009/16/EC, *OJ* L 234 of 22 September 2023, pp. 48-100, article 4.

the calculation is based on yearly average greenhouse gas intensity by quantity of fuel consumed[28]. The regulation targets only ships with a gross tonnage above 5000t, because, according to the Commission, their emissions represent more than 90 % of the carbon dioxide released into the atmosphere from the maritime sector[29].

Another obligation will be for ships to connect to on-shore power supply and use it for all energy needs while at berth for at least two hours[30]. This requirement aim at tackling primarily the local air pollution (emissions of SO_4, NOx and fine particles) caused by the engines in operations when at berth, especially considering the ports are often located in large cities, but also at reducing GHG emissions and at promoting an increased reliance on renewable energies (and electricity made from them)[31]. In our opinion, a similar mandatory obligation should have been included for aircrafts and airport infrastructures, without further consideration to the fact that burning of aviation fuel in jet engines causes less air pollution.

III. MARKET INSTRUMENTS: REVISION OF THE EU ETS AND INTRODUCTION OF THE CBAM

1. REVISION OF THE EU ETS

1.1. General Context and Aim

The revised EU ETS is one of the cornerstones of the Green Deal and constitutes a major contributor to the Fit-for-55 plan for a 55% reduction of GHG emissions by 2030. The newly adopted amendments aim at filling the current loopholes of the system, mainly to end the free allocation of allowances and make auctioning the main method for market participants to acquire GHG emissions rights[32]. Furthermore, emissions coming from new sectors are now included within the EU ETS, namely carbon dioxide emissions from waterborne transport, building heating, commercial and small industrial activities, and transport.

28. *Ibid.*, art. 5.
29. *Ibid.*, article 2 and recital 11.
30. *Ibid.*, art. 6.
31. *Ibid.*, recital 35.
32. Directive (EU) 2023/959 of the European Parliament and of the Council of 10 May 2023 amending Directive 2003/87/EC establishing a system for greenhouse gas emission allowance trading within the Union and Decision (EU) 2015/1814 concerning the establishment and operation of a market stability reserve for the Union greenhouse gas emission trading system, *OJ*, L 130 of 16 May 2023. Hereafter: "2023 ETS Directive".

1.2. Waterborne Transport

The first important amendment to the current ETS legal framework consists in the inclusion of maritime transport within the its scope[33]. For waterborne transport, only intra-European journeys will have to be covered by allowances. In case the voyage departs from a port located into a Member State and arrives in another, the shipping company must report and hold permits for 50% in the departing country and for 50 % in the destination country[34]. The expected impact on GHG emissions remains limited, since the covered emissions are limited to carbon dioxide coming from intra-EU transport, representing only a few percent of the global traffic emissions. The increasing cost of shipping caused by the ETS might call for evasive transhipment activities at ports located near the border of the European Union, resulting not only in a diminution of the internalisation of the environmental cost of transport but also in a potential increase of the emissions from extra distance travelled to evade the application of the ETS and to transport the merchandises until their final EU destination[35]. Ultimately, as part of a global solution, the International Maritime Organisation could adopt its own market-based instrument, which will have to be coordinated with the new European system[36].

1.3. Air transport

Air transport has always been a more delicate affair, aircrafts being susceptible to flight across several (non-)EU national air spaces and international waters. In 2013, during the induction period of the third phase of the EU ETS, increased international political pressure leads the Commission to suspend the application of the EU ETS for extra-EEA flights[37]. Under the new provisions, flights not covered by the EU ETS — namely the flights arriving from or departing for a non-EEA Member States — will be subject to the Carbon Offset and Reduction Scheme for International Aviation (CORSIA) developed by the International Civil Aviation Organisation (ICAO). The adopted revision does not include any indication in the direction of including extra-European flights within the EU ETS. On the contrary, the

33. 2023 ETS Directive, articles 3a and 3h.
34. *Ibid.*, article 3ga.
35. *Ibid.*, article 3gg(3).
36. *Ibid.*, article 3gg(2).
37. Decision N.° 377/2013/EY of the European Parliament and of the Council of 24 April 2013derogating temporarily from Directive 2003/87/EC establishing a scheme for greenhouse gas emission allowance trading within the Community, *OJ* L 113 of 25 April 2013, p. 1.

revision of the Energy Taxation Directive potentially allows Member States to tax the fuel delivered to aircraft operating on international routes but without coordinating minimum mandatory levels of taxation with the target price for allowance on ETS markets[38].

1.4. New Activities: (Road) Transport and Building Heating

Covering road transport in emissions trading schemes has never been considered as an easy task, because of the difficulty to measure effectively and easily the quantities of emissions released within the atmosphere by millions of vehicles. A key element of an efficient policy applying to large population of end users is to set the permit surrendering obligation at a level of the distribution chain where economic operators are only few. Energy products used as propellant or for heating purpose are for some of identical chemical composition, whereas the differentiation is only for tax purpose. This fact has let the Commission to impose to distributors the obligation to hold allowances for all fuels released for consumption, independent of their final use (for heating or for propelling a vehicle). Distributors are not named *per se*, the text introducing a new concept of "regulated entity"[39], defined as any natural or legal person who is not the final user of the fuels and engages in one of the following activities:

- being an authorised warehouse keeper liable to pay excise duties (because the excise goods are departing from a duty suspension arrangement)[40]
- being another person liable to pay excise duties under the General Arrangement Directive or the Energy Taxation Directive[41]

38. See below for a more detailed discussion.
39. 2023 ETS Directive, article 1(3)(ae).
40. The 2023 ETS Directive makes a direct reference to the General Arrangement Directive of the excise duties legal framework (Directive 2020/262 of 19 December 2019 laying down the general arrangements for excise duty, *OJ* L 058 of 27 February 2020, p. 4). The reference is made to article 3 for the definition and article 7 for the conditions under which the warehouse keeper becomes liable to the payment of the duties.
41. A reference is made to the article 7 of the General Arrangement Directive for the persons who are not considered as warehouse keeper but are liable to pay excises but also, in the amended version, to the article 21(5) of the Energy Taxation Directive stating that electricity and natural gas are subject to taxation and become chargeable at the time of supply by the distributor or redistributor (Directive 2003/96/EC of 27 October 2003 restructuring the Community framework for the taxation of energy products and electricity, *OJ* L 283 of 31 October 2003, p. 51, art. 21(5)).

— any other person liable to pay excise duties under national provisions, including any person exempted under the article 21(5) of the Energy Taxation Directive

— in other cases, or if several persons are jointly and severally liable for payment of the same excise duty, any other person designated by a Member State.

The mandatory surrendering of emissions allowances for those activities follows then closely the liability to pay duties under the excise legal framework. Furthermore, the amendments relating to heating and road transport, constituting a new chapter IVa in the ETS Directive, include direct references to excise regulation for the definition of "fuels" and the concept of "release for consumption"[42]. This addition of road emission by the Fit-for-55 package leads to an increased interconnection within the legal framework, since the definition of fuels for the ETS is based on excise regulation, where the revised drafting of the Energy Taxation Directive aims at linking the definition of sustainable fuels and low-emissions fuels to the Renewable Energy Directive[43]. The fuels are then the ones currently subject to excise levies without any modification[44]. Small industrial or commercial facilities falling outside the ETS scope because of their size will in consequence have their emissions covered indirectly through their energy suppliers. On the contrary, certain fuels, mainly wood derivatives, are excluded because of the reference to the Energy Taxation Directive, despite having an impact on the environment[45].

However, not all activities carried on with the help of energy products falling within the scope of the Energy Taxation Directive are requiring the surrendering by the retailer of an allowance. Only the products released for consumption for buildings and road transport as defined in the 2006 IPCC Guidelines for National Greenhouse Gas Inventories are belonging to this new category of ETS activities[46]. Should then be covered by ETS allowances the emissions coming from:

42. 2023 ETS Directive, article 1(3)(c)(ag) and (ah).

43. Directive (EU) 2018/2001 of the European Parliament and of the Council of 11 December 2018 on the promotion of the use of energy from renewable sources (recast), *OJ* L 328 of 21 December 2018, pp. 82-209.

44. Council Directive 2003/96/EC of 27 October 2003 restructuring the Community framework for the taxation of energy products and electricity, *OJ* L 238 of 31 October 2003, pp. 51-70, article 2. See also: European Council, *Endorsed comprise text on files 2021/0211 and 2021/0202*, 2023, retrieved from *data.consilium.europa.eu/doc/document/ST-6210-2023-INIT/en/pdf*, revised article (2)(1)(x). See below for further detail on the Energy Taxation Directive.

45. *Ibid.*

46. 2023 ETS Directive, new Annex III.

— Road transport, which includes emissions from cars, light-duty trucks, heavy duty trucks and buses, motorcycles, evaporative emissions coming from vehicles, and urea-based catalysts, but without considering emissions from agricultural vehicles on paved roads.

— Energy consumption — for heating and other purposes — from commercial and institutional clients.

— Energy consumption — for heating and other purposes — from residential.

— Combined heat and power generation insofar as they produce heat for commercial and institutional sectors, either directly or through district heating network.

— Energy industries, which includes industries having as main activity electricity and heat production, petroleum refining, manufacture of solid fuels and all other energy industries.

— Manufacturing of iron and steel, non-ferrous metals, chemicals, pulp, paper and print, food processing, beverages and tobacco, non-metallic minerals, transport equipment, machinery, wood and wood products, textile, and leather; mining (with the exclusion of fuels) and quarrying and construction.

On the contrary, fuels used for combustion for transport and building heating should not be considered as falling within this activity when[47]:

— their emissions are already covered under another activity included in Annex I of the ETS directive (mainly industrial activities, aviation, and maritime transport), with the exception where fuels are used in activities of transport of greenhouse gases for geological storage or in installations emitting less than 2500 tons of CO2 equivalent annually, exempted from the ETS under national measures and authorisation;

— their emissions factor is equal to zero;

— their nature is of hazardous or municipal waste used as fuel.

The inclusion of transport in the EU ETS seems then to follow closely the design of excise duties, mainly due to the absence of connexion and

47. 2023 ETS Directive, new Annex III.

time correspondence between the holding of the allowance and the release of the emissions in the environment, as it is usually the case for other required holders. Regarding gases covered by allowances, only carbon dioxide emissions are included in the scheme for transport and heating[48]. The methodology for collecting revenues for new activities follows closely the one laid down in excise regimes.

The last-minute addition of these activities, including then energy industries, manufacturing, and construction, tends to support a potential future inclusion of other sectors within the ETS and subsequently the possibility to extend the Carbon Border Adjustment Mechanism[49] to all manufacturing processes. Since the CBAM is considered as an extraterritorial extension of the EU ETS, it is necessary that all activities included in the CBAM scope for foreign producers are subject to the EU ETS for European manufacturers to prevent the application of certain WTO mechanisms[50]. A simple inclusion within the system would not be sufficient to authorise the levy of an equivalent amount at the border, requiring a further extension of the auctioning for allowances to insure an unswerving price on primary and secondary markets.

Finally, it is worth noting that the social impact of including private and small businesses energy consumption within the ETS can be counterbalanced by a postponement until 2028 in case of high price for fossil energy products. It will be the case if the price on natural gas market is higher than in February or March 2022 or if the Brent price is twice the average of the five previous years[51].

48. 2023 ETS Directive, Annex III.
49. Regulation (EU) 2023/956 of the European Parliament and of the Council of 10 May 2023 establishing a carbon border adjustment mechanism, *OJ* L 130 of 16 May 2023, pp. 52-104.
50. On this topic, see English, J. and Falcao, T., *EU Carbon Border Adjustments for Imported Products and WTO Law*, 2021, retrieved from SSRN-id3863038.pdf on 4 June 2023; Venzke, I. and Vidigal G., "Are Trade Measures to Tackle the Climate Crisis the End of Differentiated Responsibilities? The Case of the EU Carbon Border Adjustment Mechanism (CBAM)" in *Amsterdam Law School Legal Studies Research Paper*, n. 2022-02, 2022; Espa, I., Francois, J., and van Asselt, H., "The EU Proposal for a Carbon Border Adjustment Mechanism (CBAM): An Analysis under WTO and Climate Change Law" in *WTI Working Paper Series*, n. 06/2022, 2022; Espa I., "Reconciling the climate/industrial interplay of CBAMs: what role for the WTO?" in *American Journal of International Law*, n. 116, 2022, pp. 208-212.
51. 2023 ETS Directive, article 30k.

2. THE CARBON BORDER ADJUSTMENT MECHANISM

The Carbon Border Adjustment Mechanism — or CBAM — is another key element of the Fit-for-55 package of the European Commission and has been published in its final version in the Official Journal on the 16 May 2023[52]. The CBAM was designed by the legislator with four objectives: firstly and mainly, to prevent the risk of carbon leakage — under the ETS more precisely —; secondly, addressing the climate impact of greenhouse gases embedded in goods manufactured outside of the EU; thirdly, to create incentives for the reduction of GHG emissions by operators in third countries; and finally, to reflect more accurately in the price of imports their carbon content[53]. As evoked in the previous section, the CBAM should be viewed as a complement to the EU ETS and aims at replacing carbon leakage prevention mechanisms included in previous ETS directives and in the Energy Taxation Directive. Going a step further, one could consider that the CBAM will serve as commercial protective mechanism for all energy-intense businesses, for both excise regimes and cap-and-trade mechanisms.

The CBAM applies to a limited number of goods during the first phase. They are designated by their numbering in the Combined Nomenclature — the taxonomy of goods used for custom duties[54]. They belong to six families of products: (1) cement, (2) electricity, (3) fertilisers, (4) iron and steel, (5) aluminium, (6) chemicals (but in reality, covering only hydrogen)[55]. The reasons for the inclusion of this sector lack of consistency, aluminium being included because manufacturers are highly exposed to carbon leakage, where hydrogen has been included due to the anticipated increased demand in the following years, notably as a consequence of the implementation of the Fit-for-55 package. For aluminium goods, the main exporting countries are Norway and Russia accounting for around 35 % of the EU imports, two countries located at the border of the EU[56].

One key element of the CBAM is that it includes both direct emissions — emissions of greenhouse gases caused by the production process and

52. Regulation (EU) 2023/956 of the European Parliament and of the Council of 10 May 2023 establishing a carbon border adjustment mechanism, *OJ* L 130 of 16 May 2023, pp. 52-104. Hereafter: "CBAM Regulation".

53. The term "carbon content" is used in the CBAM to include the direct and indirect GHG emissions embedded in imported products caused by their production process.

54. Council Regulation (EEC) No 2658/87 of 23 July 1987 on the tariff and statistical nomenclature and on the Common Customs Tariff, *OJ* L 256 of 7 September 1987, pp. 1-675.

55. CBAM Regulation, Annex I.

56. European Commission (2021), *CBAM impact assessment report*, Document SWD (2021) 643, p. 66.

during the time of production of goods until the import of those goods into the EU[57] — and indirect emissions — defined as "emissions arising from the generation of electricity used to produce goods[58]. However, not all imported goods must calculate their indirect embedded emissions, a distinction being made in the Annex II based on granular analysis of the combined nomenclature between different categories. In general, the more transformed the good is, the less it will be necessary to calculate the indirect emissions. Not all goods are treated equal when it comes to the GHG emissions expected to be covered with CBAM permits: aluminium products must also surrender allowances for perfluorocarbons, where the others must only cover the embedded emissions of carbon dioxide[59].

An important part of the regulation is dedicated to methodological instructions for emissions calculation[60]. To be certain that the methodology is correctly applied by the declarant, emissions reporting must be verified by an accredited verifier[61].

Another crucial point for a border adjustment mechanism in order to set a price on carbon efficiently and fairly consists in its ability to include in the calculation the price paid for carbon emissions under other systems[62]. There was a constant defiance during the discussion on the CBAM on the possibility offered to CBAM declarant to benefit from a reduction in the number of CBAM certificates to be surrendered in reason of the carbon price paid under another — non EU — system. The article 9 insists however on the requirements that the carbon price must have been effectively paid and that any rebate or other forms of compensation are disclosed[63]. For authorised declarants, a significant due diligence work will be required to collect evidence on all systems under which (parts of) the imported products have been subject to emissions pricing. The article 9 does not develop further the type of public measures whose must be considered as setting a price on carbon. Simple carbon taxes, as opposed to emissions trading system, also set a price on carbon, and can then justified to be accounted in the determination of the final price to be paid at the EU border.

57. CBAM Regulation, article 2.
58. CBAM Regulation, recital 19.
59. CBAM Regulation, Annex II.
60. CBAM Regulation, article 7.
61. CBAM Regulation, articles 8 and 18. The article 18 states that the accreditation of verifiers will be assessed by national authorisation body, based i. e., on the capacity of such person to apply the verification principles included in the CBAM regulation.
62. CBAM Regulation, article 9 and recital 46.
63. CBAM Regulation, article 9(2).

The CBAM certificates will be sold through national platforms, only to authorised CBAM declarants[64]. The system does not set a cap, meaning that there is not limitation in the quantity of certificates that a Member State is authorised to sell. The price will be aligned with the closing auction price for EU ETS allowances and will be adapted every week[65].

How transport will be affected by the CBAM? First, it should be noted that one of the aims behind the introduction of the mechanism is to incentivize manufacturers to locate their production near the consumption place. It could then result in a decrease demand for transport, affecting both shipping and road transport and the vehicles used to carry out these activities. At the same time, manufacturers of means of transport using products subject to the CBAM for their processes (aluminium, steel, iron) will see their price increased when produced outside of the European territory. A possible undesired effect of the CBAM introduction could be that non-European manufacturers will be tented to export to the European market finished products rather than raw or semi-finished goods, at least as long as the CBAM applies only to certain categories of — less-transformed — goods.

IV. THE ENERGY TAXATION DIRECTIVE REFORM TO PROMOTE GREENER TRANSPORTATION

1. CURRENT REGIME

Directive 2003/96 restructuring the Community framework for the taxation of energy products and electricity ("the Energy Taxation Directive")[66] has been the successor of the first directive from 1992 and sets a minimum level of taxation for all fuels used for transport, aviation fuel excepted[67]. The objective of the 2003 reform was to modernise the previous aging framework by including notably the electricity in the scope and by reviewing the ways EU Member States can differentiate taxation based on the intrinsic characteristics of each energy product.

Energy products used as propellant — which include gasoline, gasoil, LPG and natural gas — are subject to harmonised mandatory minimum

64. CBAM Regulation, article 20. A foreign manufacturer can be considered as an authorised declarant.
65. CBAM Regulation, article 20.
66. Directive 2003/96/EC of 27 October 2003 restructuring the Community framework for the taxation of energy products and electricity, *OJ* L 283 of 31 October 2003, p. 51. Hereafter: "Energy Taxation Directive".
67. Energy Taxation Directive, article 14.

levels of taxation for Member States[68]. The minima imposed by the Directive are based on the quantity — volume — of fuel, without any reference to a common denominator for all energy products[69]. Neither calorific value nor carbon content is utilised as a tax base measure, weakening the relevance of excise duties for tackling climate issues. Member States are however authorised to discriminate among energy products based on different criteria listed in article 5: quality, quantity consummed (but only for electricity and energy products used for heating purpose), specific uses (local public transportation, waste collection, armed forces and public administration, disabled people and ambulances) and business use[70]. Some Member States are using this faculty to support low-sulphur gas oil and gasoline[71] or to include in their calculation a "carbon" component, based on the carbon content of the fuel[72]. On the latter, it may be interesting to note that no country has a calculation based only on energy content or carbon content, since a share of the final rate is still based on the mass or volume of fuel.

The carriage of goods and persons by road with vehicles fuelled by gas oil may also benefit from a preferential regime in national laws, provided that the minimum level imposed by the Directive is observed[73]. "Commercial gas oil" may be subject to a lighter taxation when delivered to trucks (with a maximum permissible gross laden weight of not less than 7,5 tons) or for buses (as defined in the European homologation process[74]).

Air transport, in contrast, has always benefit from a preferential tax treatment at the European level. The reason for offering a more favourable tax regime to aircraft fuel is to be found in the Chicago Convention and in the development of bilateral tax treaties covering aviation activities. In the Chicago Convention, the article 24 has been interpreted as a prohibition of any tax on fuel, despite an equivocal drafting which could be interpreted that only fuel included in the tank shall be exempted but not quantities

68. Energy Taxation Directive, article 7. Annex 1 imposes a minimum of 421 EUR per 1000l for leaded petrol, 359 for unleaded petrol, 330 for Gas oil, 330 for kerosene, 125 EUR per 1000 kg for LPG and 2.6 EUR per megajoule.
69. Energy Taxation Directive, Annex I.
70. Energy Taxation Directive, article 5.
71. This the case in Germany, in Austria or in Belgium for instance.
72. See for instance the Irish and Swedish national laws.
73. Energy Taxation Directive, article 14(1)(b).
74. Directive 70/156/EEC of 6 February 1970 on the approximation of the laws of the Member States relating to the type-approval of motor vehicles and their trailers, *OJ* L 42 of 23 February 1970, p.1.

delivered to the aircraft on the territory[75]. Furthermore, the European Court of Justice seems to consider that the European Union is not bound by the Chicago Convention to a similar extent as its Member States[76]. Nevertheless, the article 14 of the Energy Taxation Directive exempts "energy products supplied for use as fuel for the purpose of air navigation other than for private pleasure-flying"[77]. Private pleasure-flying is defined as: "any craft used by its owner or the natural or legal person who enjoys its use either through hire or through any other means, for other than commercial purposes and in particular other than for the carriage of passengers or goods or for the supply of services for consideration or for the purposes of public authorities"[78]. This definition does not obviously include business activity, letting for instance fuel used by private jet services exempted[79]. Member States can limit the exemption to kerosene[80].

The article 14 provides an identical exemption of energy products supplied for waterborne navigation within the Community waters — including fishing —, other than private pleasure craft and electricity produced on board of a craft[81]. Under article 15, Member States are also authorised to

75. For an in-depth discussion on the international legal limitations applying to the aviation sector, see Havel, B.F. and Sanchez, G.S., *The Principles and Practice of International Aviation Law*, Cambridge: Cambridge University Press, 2004, p. 236: "Under the ICAO's reading, MBMs directed at offsetting emissions, such as cap-and-trade or eco-taxation, but which are unrelated to the provision of airport and air navigation services to international aviation, would constitute a charge "in respect solely of the right of transit over or entry into or exit" and would be impermissible under the Convention". See also ICAO Council, *ICAO's Policies on Charges for Airports and Air Navigation Services*, Doc 9082, 2012, para 3.
76. ECJ (2011), Case C-366/10 *Air Transport Association of America, American Airlines Inc., Continental Airlines Inc., United Airlines Inc. v. Secretary of State for Energy and Climate Change*, ECR [2011] I-13755, para 71, where the Court enounces that: "the powers previously exercised by the Member States in the field of application of the Chicago Convention have not to date been assumed in their entirety by the European Union."
77. Energy Taxation Directive, article 14(1)(b).
78. Energy Taxation Directive, article 14(1)(b).
79. Energy Taxation Directive, article 14(1)(b). private pleasure-flying is defined as "the use of an aircraft by its owner or the natural or legal person who enjoys its use either through hire or through any other means, for other than commercial purposes and in particular other than for the carriage of passengers or goods or for the supply of services for consideration or for the purposes of public authorities."
80. The code refers to Combined Nomenclature item 2710 19 21, jet fuel.
81. Energy Taxation Directive, article 14(1)(c). Again, the directive provides a definition of "private pleasure craft", meaning "Any craft used by its owner or the natural or legal person who enjoys its use either through hire or through any other means, for other than commercial purposes and in particular other than for the carriage of passengers

exempt energy products delivered for waterborne navigation within inlands water, as long as they are not used for private pleasure craft[82].

2. PROPOSED REFORM OF THE ENERGY TAXATION DIRECTIVE AND ITS IMPACT ON TRANSPORT

Transport has been at the core of the amendments proposed in 2021 by the Commission for excise taxation. A major point of the reform is the revision of the way fuels are treated, by asserting a clear reference to the Renewable Energy Directive for the definition of "renewable fuel from biological origin" and "low carbon fuels", both categories benefiting from a preferential treatment for transport in the Commission proposal[83].

The Commission proposal bases the new minimum levels of taxation on calorific value and environmental characteristics of the fuels and makes an important distinction between "classic fuels"[84], sustainable fuels and renewable fuels, reserving the most favourable tax treatment to renewable fuels and advanced sustainable biofuels and gases. As a general principle, "the ranking of energy products and electricity should be considered as a general principle equally applicable mutatis mutandis, whenever the Directive allows for differentiations"[85]. Moreover, the proposal supports electricity in an unconditional way, by stating in the explanatory memorandum that "electricity should always be among the least taxed energy sources in view of fostering its use, notably in the transport sector, and should be ranked together with other motor fuels and heating fuels"[86]. The minimum level of taxation for electricity is then aligned with renewable fuels, at 0,15 EUR per GJ[87]. Similar to the current regime, Member States will be authorised to offer reductions in the level of taxation for energy products and electricity used for the carriage of goods and passengers by rail, metro, tram and trolley

---

or goods or for the supply of services for consideration or for the purposes of public authorities."

82. Energy Taxation Directive, article 15(1)(f).
83. European Commission (2021), Proposal for a Council Directive restructuring the Union framework for the taxation of energy products and electricity, COM (2021) 563 final of 14 July 2021, revised article 2(4) and new Annexes. Hereafter: "2021 ETD proposal".
84. This category includes petrol, gasoil, kerosene, non-sustainable biofuels, LPG, natural gas, non-sustainable biogas, non-renewable fuels of non-biological origin, sustainable food, and feed crop biofuels.
85. 2021 ETD proposal, p. 14. The paragraph includes reference to articles 13 to 18 in their revised drafting.
86. 2021 ETD proposal, p. 14.
87. 2021 ETD proposal, redrafted Annexe I, Table A, B and C.

bus, and for local public passenger transport, waste collection, armed forces and public administration, disabled people and ambulances[88]. This time however, the minimum levels of taxation will have to be respected, the tax advantage being limited to a more favourable treatment compared to energy products for other activities in national law[89].

For air transport, the regime is entirely redrafted and is built on a more granular and nuanced analysis of civil aviation. To develop the new regime, commercial aviation is opposed to three other purposes:

a) "Business aviation", meaning the operation or use of aircraft by companies for the carriage of passengers or goods as an aid to the conduct of their business, flown for purposes generally considered not for public hire and piloted by individuals having, at the minimum, a valid commercial pilot license with an instrument rating.

b) "Pleasure flights" meaning, the use of an aircraft for personal or recreational purposes not associated with a business or professional use.

c) "Cargo-only flight" meaning a scheduled or non-scheduled air service performed by aircraft carrying revenue loads other than revenue passengers, excluding flights carrying one or more revenue passengers and flights listed in published timetables as open to passengers.

Those three definitions are the basis to differentiated tax regimes: energy products used to carry out business, commercial or pleasure flights are subjects to the standard minimum levels of taxation applicable to motor fuels and electricity[90]. Cargo-only flights benefit from an exemption, but Member States are authorised to apply a similar taxation as for commercial flights.

An important distinction is introduced between "intra-EU air navigation", defined as all flights between two airports located in the EU, including national domestic flights[91], and "extra-EU air navigation", which means a flight with an origin or a destination located outside of the EU. For extra-EU flights,

88. 2021 ETD proposal, revised article 17.
89. 2021 ETD proposal, revised article 17.
90. 2021 ETD proposal, p. 15.
91. 2021 ETD proposal, p. 40, new article 14(1).

Member States have the option to tax at the same level of taxation applied for intra-EU air navigation — and based on the distinction between business, pleasure, cargo, and commercial flights — or to exempt[92]. The advice from the European Parliament calls in contrast for a consistent application of the new minima for fuels, independent of the origin or destination of the flights[93].

The current exemption for waterborne navigation no longer exists in the proposed revised regime. A new article 15 will impose minimum levels of taxation for intra-EU waterborne navigation (Tables B of Annex I[94]), meaning that minimum levels for water navigation will be aligned with the ones for fuels used for business activities[95]. These new tax rates are identical to the minima for aquaculture works, reinforcing the coherence of the system. It concerns both energy products and electricity supplied to vessels — on board generated electricity is exempted[96]. The taxation is then not aligned with the one for air navigation or for other motorised transport, benefiting from a more favourable treatment, but must also respect the ranking of fuels of Table B in Annex I, based on environmental characteristics. The reason of the proposal to have lower minimum rates of taxation for waterborne navigation originates in the risk of ships retanking outside of the EU. For non-intra-EU waterborne navigation, Member States may exempt or apply the same levels of taxation as for intra-EU navigation. The distinction between inland and intra-EU navigation does not exist anymore in the revised regime.

V. COHERENCE OF THE REVISED SYSTEM WITH THE OBJECTIVE OF CARBON NEUTRALITY BY MID-CENTURY AND FOR SETTING A UNIFORM AND CONSISTENT PRICE ON CARBON

The European Commission is today bound by its objective of carbon-neutrality by the middle of the century and has pulled out all the stops to phase-out fossil fuels and related greenhouse gases emissions. Transport

92. 2021 ETD proposal, p. 40, new article 14(3).
93. Committee on Economic and Monetary Affairs, *Draft report on the proposal for a Council directive restructuring the Union framework for the taxation of energy products and electricity*, report 2021/0213, 2022, retrieved from *https://www.europarl.europa.eu/doceo/document/ECON-PR-719624_EN.pdf* on 5 April 2023, p. 39. The justification is the following: "The rapporteur is not in favour of discrimination according to the use of flights. This would hinder legal certainty, create loopholes, and hamper innovation and decarbonisation."
94. 2021 ETD proposal, p. 41, new article 15.
95. 2021 ETD proposal, p. 37, article 8(2) as redrafted.
96. 2021 ETD proposal, p. 41, new article 15.

is a victim of choice, representing roughly a quarter of all emissions for the European Union — but only 8% at the global level[97]. The tone is set for the manufacturing of new means of transports, with new stringent norms. Cars would become climate neutral in ten years, where trucks and vans will have to decrease sharply their emissions but benefit from an additional short amount of time for reaching climate neutrality. Materials used to build means of transports will be subject to carbon pricing under the EU ETS or the CBAM, depending on their production location. The taxation on fuels used to propel vehicles will be increased if the proposal reforming the Energy Taxation Directive is adopted by the European Council and the European Parliament. Under this new regime, all fuels used as propellant will be subject to taxation, including electricity, and ranked for fiscal purpose according to their environmental impact. Subsequently, the amount of carbon dioxide emitted by the fuel combustion in the engines will be covered by allowances due to the extension of the EU ETS to transport.

To summarise, road traveller and transporter will make a choice between having a vehicle with zero emissions and their fuel less taxed under the ETD — because it will be sustainable fuel, electricity or (carbon-neutral) hydrogen — or continuing to use a (older) vehicle with a more significant carbon impact, fuelled by an energy products subject to higher rate of indirect taxation and for which the distributor must purchase allowances under the ETS.

For aviation and waterborne navigation, the new requirements imposing the ability to plug crafts when berthed at port will improve the quality of European citizens living close to transport facilities. However, decarbonising a sector relying almost entirely on fossil fuels is an immense challenge and will require a large deployment of emerging technologies such as hydrogen aircrafts or electric vessels. For the moment, international non-EU transport remains untouched, with only CORSIA covering GHG emissions from international flights and the future possibility opened to Member States to tax fuels delivered to aircrafts and ships operating on global routes under the revised Energy Taxation Directive.

The right incentives exist under in this new framework to stimulate a large deployment of carbon neutral technologies. However, no consistent carbon price is set on energy products used for transport and the environmental impact of their consumption is not accurately reflected in prices, for different reasons.

97. Statistics from the International Energy Agency for 2021.

First, the EU ETS will set a cap on carbon dioxide emission but not a determined price or a prohibition of carbon products. The amount of tax paid by travellers will vary according to carbon market conditions and might not be a prefect reflexion of the progress achieved towards carbon neutrality.

Second, depending on the final usage of the fuel, the price for emitting a certain amount of greenhouse gas will be different. The Energy Taxation Directive provides a good example in this regard, by making a distinction for tax treatment between professional and non-professional use for a same energy product, with a different minimum level of taxation despite the energy product being identical or by grating a preferable treatment for other than climate reasons to certain fuels (GPL or electricity). For instance, a private car will pay more for using gas oil than a public bus or a tractor, and jet fuel for a long-distance flight departing from the EU is susceptible to be fully exempted under national law where the fuel consumed by a local private car to drive children to school must be imposed at the highest level.

Third, the CBAM is another complex example of how certain mechanisms have to cope with paradoxical reality: during the initial period, only certain goods entering the European Union market will have to buy permits covering the embodied emissions. Those activities are on the one hand the most carbon intensive ones and subject to the ETS in European law but on the other are also benefiting from derogatory regimes for energy intensive business under the ETS Directive and the Energy Taxation Directive.

Fourth, setting different dates to reach carbon neutrality for new vehicles depending on their size or use means stricter transition for some activities or people. Indeed, cars — and their private drivers — are the most pressed to switch to zero tailpipe emissions where aircrafts and ships are only requested to adopt their engines to more sustainable fuels and reduce — not annihilate — their climate impact in the short term.

Finally, because the European Green Deal includes both regulations and directives, measures are susceptible to vary broadly at the national level. Important differences in taxation rates are observed for excise duties currently, and the option let to Member States to tax the fuel delivered to aircrafts and ships operating on international roads could lead to the creation of transport hubs in non-taxing jurisdictions and the disconnection of certain areas of the European Union.

In the classical theory of environmental taxation, the rate of taxation must be proportional to the amount of pollution released into the environment and to the reparation of the damage caused by the pollutant behaviour[98]. This strict definition of what environmental taxes are calls for the setting of one price for all units of carbon dioxide released in the atmosphere, independent of its source. The future European regulatory framework fails to impose a unique and uniform price for carbon in the European Union, letting some transport activities unregulated and taxing more severely certain fuels and usages, without considering the real climate and environmental impact. The wind is turning however, with the recent broadening of the scope of the EU ETS and the adoption of a carbon border adjustment mechanism. Market and tax tools for reaching carbon neutrality by 2050 are sharpened and better coordinated. However, the ultimate change for transport is expected to come mainly from pure regulation: if vehicles released on the market are not anymore allowed to use fossils fuels as a powering mechanism, emissions from transport will plumet rapidly. Another question that remains unanswered until now is how or in which timeframe sustainable fuels for transport — including then hydrogen, electricity, and synthetic fuels — will be able to reach production on a large scale without relying on fossil technologies. A rapid deployment could be the crucial element of a successful and timely transition.

98. Pitrone, F., *Environmental Taxation: a Legal Perspective*, 2012, PhD Thesis, p. 91; Avi-Yonah, R. S., "The three goals of Taxation" in *Tax Law Review*, n. 60, 2017, p. 1; Avi-Yonah, R. S., "Taxation as Regulation: Carbon Tax, Health Care Tax, Bank Tax and Other Regulatory Taxes" in *Accounting, Economics, and Law*, vol. 1, n. 1, 2011; Yale, E., "Taxing Cap and Trade Environmental Regulation" in *Journal of Legal Studies*, n. 37, 2008, p. 535; Viessant, C., "La création d'une imposition environnementale : quel intérêt ?" in *Revue européenne et internationale de droit fiscal*, n. 4, 2015, p. 538. See also: Orsoni, G., "Quelle fiscalité de l'environnement ?" in *Innovations, créations et transformations en finances publiques*, Paris: LGDJ, 2006, p. 66 ; Lanneau R., "La fiscalité écologique : quelques éclairages sur l'écotaxe" in *Gestion & Finances Publiques*, n. 7/8, 2014, p. 126 ; Chiroleu-Assouline, M., "La fiscalité environnementale, instrument économique par excellence" in *RFFP*, n. 114, 2011, p. 25 ; Bachus, K., *The use of environmental taxation as a regulatory policy instrument*, 2017, retrieved from https://lirias.kuleuven.be/retrieve/483725 on 15 May 2023.

Rethinking and Greening Cities in Europe

ESTHER VALDÉS TEJERA
Professor and Director of the Urban Management Bachelor, Camilo José Cela University (Madrid, Spain)

I. CHALLENGES OF CITIES IN THE FACE OF CLIMATE CHANGE

In October 2019, during the C40 Global Summit of Mayors, António Guterres, the Secretary-General of the United Nations, stated that "Cities are where the climate battle will largely be won or lost" [1] and noted that Mayors were the first people to respond to the world's climate emergency. Although the phrase may seem somewhat exaggerated and typical of a speech prepared for the occasion, the reality is that it is very well-founded. The basis for these statements can be traced in numerous reports prepared by international organizations, top-level scientific articles, and professionals from different sectors that analyze the evolution of the environmental and social situation in the world, as well as their associated challenges and consequences. This section will review some of these reports to put Guterres' words in context.

1. A QUICK LOOK AT THE CLIMATE EMERGENCY AND ITS INTERRELATIONSHIPS

According to the Sixth Assessment Report (AR6) of the Intergovernmental Panel on Climate Change[2], greenhouse gas (GHG) emissions due to human

1. Guterres, A., *Secretary-General's remarks at C40 World Mayors Summit*, United Nations, Secretary General, 11 October 2019, retrieved from *www.un.org/sg/en/content/sg/statement/2019-10-11/secretary-generals-remarks-c40-world-mayors-summit*
2. Intergovernmental Panel on Climate Change (IPCC), "Summary for Policymakers" in Lee, H., and Romero, J. (eds.), *Climate Change 2023: Synthesis Report. Contribution of Working Groups I, II and III to the Sixth Assessment Report of the Intergovernmental Panel on Climate Change*, IPCC, Geneva, Switzerland, 2023, pp. 1-34, retrieved from *www.ipcc.ch/report/ar6/syr/downloads/report/IPCC_AR6_SYR_SPM.pdf*

activities have unequivocally caused global warming. The unsustainable use of energy and resources, the change in land use, production and consumption patterns, and lifestyles continue to cause an amount of GHG that carbon sinks cannot absorb and unequal development of regions, countries, and people. Earth's surface temperature is rising, causing extreme weather and climate events that harm the environment and people, and disproportionately affect those who have contributed the least to the climate crisis. The Report states that in urban areas, the impact of extreme phenomena affects human health and livelihoods, compromising the well-being of all. Critical infrastructure such as transportation, water, sanitation, and energy supply have been affected, causing economic losses. Once again, the most vulnerable and marginalized communities are the most affected. Adaptation and mitigation measures are being implemented in most countries and cities worldwide. However, its effectiveness is highly variable, and global financial funds are insufficient, especially in developing countries. During the 21st century, global warming is very likely to exceed 1.5.°C, and it will be difficult to limit it below 2.°C.

The good news from AR6 is that a rapid, deep, and sustained reduction in GHG emissions would stop global warming in about two decades, and actions taken now will last for thousands of years. Nevertheless, the window of opportunity to ensure a sustainable future is rapidly closing. Climate stabilization and social justice are critical objectives for resilient development. Political commitment and multi-level governance, laws, policies, and financial support are necessary for effective climate action. Efficient adaptation and mitigation policies will entail essential changes in lifestyle, such as a reduction in intensive consumption or the promotion of low-emission industries and activities. These actions, implemented mainly in developed countries, will benefit the well-being of all, especially developing countries, and will be the best way to achieve a just transition.

By 2030, six of the nine planetary boundaries have been surpassed[3]. Crossing these limits means irreversibly increasing environmental damage on a large scale, that will affect the people and ecosystems. Science has established the causes and consequences of the climate emergency and its relationship with the rest of the chained crises: the fossil fuel runout and the scarcity of raw materials, the decline or disappearance of biological diversity, the food insecurity, the crisis of migration, and the escalation of armed conflicts. The knowledge and awareness of governments and the

3. Richardson, K., Steffen, W., Lucht, W., *et al.*, "Earth beyond six of nine planetary boundaries" in *Science Advances*, vol. 9, n. 37, 2023, retrieved from *www.science.org/doi/10.1126/sciadv.adh2458*

civilian population are vital to overcoming a situation that puts the basic principles of life at risk. Just to mention a few aspects, the extinction of species is directly related to the proliferation of zoonoses and human health; the decrease in agricultural production that origins food insecurity, famine, and forced migration are related to the massive disappearance of pollinators, the depletion of soils due to intensive agriculture, or droughts and floods caused by global warming; heat waves, droughts and deforestation favor fires which increase CO2 emissions, feeding back the climate crisis; violence and wars have as a backdrop the lack of resources, decent housing, hunger, forced migrations and the inequalities above mentioned. Moreover, in a hyperconnected world, the historical relationships between the global North and South and its colonialist patterns are more visible than ever.

One fact that should be highlighted is the evolution of forced displacements worldwide. According to the Internal Displacement Monitoring Center[4], internal displacement[5] affected 71.1 million people at the end of 2022, representing an increase of 20% compared to the previous year. Of these, displacement due to natural disasters affected 8.7 million people in 88 countries and territories, with an increase of 45% by the end of 2022. For their part, 62.5 million are displaced by conflicts and violence, and this affects 65 countries and territories, an increase of 17% in the last year. Both kinds of displacements, due to natural disasters and caused by conflict and violence, affect developing and developed countries. Beyond political issues, there is a systemic problem related to the present and future scarcity of primary resources such as water, energy, or agricultural production, which affect the basic principles of people's well-being.

Against this background, the annual Report of the 2030 Agenda from 2022[6] indicates that the progress of the Sustainable Development Goals

4. Internal Displacements Monitoring Center (IDMC), *Global Report on Internal Displacement 2023. Internal Displacements and Food security*, Geneva, Norwegian Refugee Council, 2023, retrieved from *www.internal-displacement.org/global-report/grid2023/*
5. Internally displaced persons (IDPs) are "Persons or groups of persons who have been forced or obliged to flee or to leave their homes or places of habitual residence, in particular as a result of or in order to avoid the effects of armed conflict, situations of generalized violence, violations of human rights or natural or human-made disasters, and who have not crossed an internationally recognized State border". United Nations High Commissioner for Refugees (UNHCR), *Guiding Principles on Internal Displacement*, 22 July 1998, ADM 1.1,PRL 12.1, PR00/98/109, retrieved from *www.refworld.org/docid/3c3da07f7.html*
6. United Nations Department of Economic and Social Affairs (UNDESA), *The Sustainable Development Goals Report 2022*, New York, USA, 2022, retrieved from *unstats.un.org/sdgs/report/2022/*

has been compromised due to three factors: the effects of the COVID-19 pandemic, armed conflicts, and the climate emergency. As the Report highlights, these crises and their complex interrelationships seriously affect food security, health, education, the environment, and peace and security. The Report underlined the following data about the three factors.

According to the study, more than 15 million excess deaths can be associated with the pandemic, either directly or indirectly. Health systems were overwhelmed, leading to an uptick in other deadly diseases. Among the collateral effects of zoonosis, more than 93 million people were pushed into extreme poverty in 2020 returning to pre-pandemic levels of hunger. In addition, the decline in learning and education affected 147 million children, of whom 24 million at all educational levels were at risk of not returning to school or university. Women were significantly affected by job losses, unpaid work, and domestic violence. The unequal distribution of vaccines, supply chain challenges, and inflation and debt in developing countries exacerbated inequalities and social injustice.

Additionally, the world has experienced the most significant number of conflicts since the creation of the United Nations in 1946. Two billion people (a quarter of the world's population) live in countries in conflict. The war in Ukraine, among other wars, has raised the number of refugees to the highest in history, and the forcibly displaced in 2022 will be 100 million people (40% children). The rise in the price of food, fossil fuels, and fertilizers, as well as the breakdown of the supply chain, increased the problems and destabilized the financial markets.

For their part, greenhouse gas emissions continue to increase. If the agreements approved by the different countries are met, they will still grow by 14% until 2030. If the meetings fail, the consequences will be even worse. The effects of global warming and extreme weather events such as heat waves, droughts, and floods act as a multiplier effect for the above. It does not only affect the most vulnerable groups, but the damage to ecosystems is irreversible and impacts us all.

In light of these data, it is urgent to address the problem from a systemic point of view: multidimensional, multisectoral, multiscale, and planetary. The SDGs Report 2022 considers it urgent to promote commitment and coordinate action to overcome crises, rescue the SDGs, and create a green, inclusive, and fair global economy that works for everyone. Liu Zhenmin, United Nations Under-Secretary General for Economics and Social Affairs, highlights that "nothing short of a comprehensive transformation of the international financial and debt architecture will be required to achieve these goals and to avoid a two-track recovery, with developing countries left behind. The stakes could not be higher. If humanity is to survive, we must survive together, leaving no one behind"[7]. As will be seen later, the SDGs have been left behind in some aspects, and it is necessary to take the definitive step in economic matters to resolve the eco-social crisis.

2. THE CITY IN STATISTICS

According to the United Nations[8], 56% of the world's population (about 4.4 billion inhabitants) lives in cities nowadays. Forecasts indicate that the urban population will grow to 68% in 2050, meaning that almost seven out of ten people will live in cities.

As stated by the United Nations[9], the world's population could grow to around 8.5 billion in 2030 and between 8.9 and 12.4 billion in 2100. The reduction in mortality and life expectancy at birth causes the population to increase. However, it is expected that the development of the most disadvantaged regions and education will provoke a reduction in the number of births per woman from 2050 to stabilize population growth. If we look at the data according to the different areas of the earth, in 2022, the most populated regions were East and Southeast Asia and Central and South Asia. Nevertheless, the most significant population growth in the coming years will occur mainly in eight African and Asian countries[10]. For their part, highly urbanized areas and developed countries will experience a stabilization and even some decline in the urban population. Again, it will pose enormous challenges for everyone, especially developing countries.

Likewise, the World Bank[11] underlines that cities are the engine of economic growth and generate more than 80% of the world's gross domestic product.

---

7. *Ibid.*, p. 3.
8. United Nations Human Settlements Programme (UN-Habitat), *World Cities Report 2022: Envisaging the Future of Cities*, Nairobi, UN-Habitat, 2022, retrieved from *unhabitat.org/world-cities-report-2022-envisaging-the-future-of-cities*
9. United Nations Department of Economic and Social Affairs (UNDESA), Population Division, *World Population Prospects 2022: Summary of Results*, UN DESA/POP/2022/TR/NO. 3, 2022, retrieved from *www.un.org/development/desa/pd/content/World-Population-Prospects-2022*
10. The Democratic Republic of the Congo, Egypt, Ethiopia, India, Nigeria, Pakistan, the Philippines, and the United Republic of Tanzania. *Ibid*, p. 5.
11. Baeumler, A., D'Aoust, O., *et al.*, *Demographic Trends and Urbanization*. Washington, DC, World Bank, 2021, retrieved from *doi:10.1596/978-1-4648-1112-9*

However, they account for two-thirds of global energy consumption and emit over 70% of anthropogenic GHG. In the case of the European Union[12], more than two-thirds of the population lives in urban agglomerations, where 80% of energy is consumed and up to 85% of Europe's GDP is generated. Innovation, technology, and culture create employment opportunities and attract people, but they also generate slums, unemployment, segregation, and poverty. Cities and metropolitan regions have many pollution and environmental sustainability challenges. Concerning social sustainability and climate justice, the challenge is even more significant.

According to the World Bank[13], one in four urban inhabitants (1.81 billion people) lived in areas at high risk of flooding around cities, mainly in the river plains and urbanized coasts of developing countries. The increase in armed conflicts contributed to the urban pressure since 50% of forced displacements settled and sought new life opportunities in cities. However, the majority of displaced persons live in informal settlements. The number of urban poor now reaches 1 billion people. This uncontrolled and unplanned growth of cities means adding a built area of 1.2 million square meters by 2030, adding high pressure on land and natural resources that will be difficult to manage.

The COVID-19 pandemic made it clear that beyond competitiveness, cities must be designed to meet the needs of their inhabitants and allow a good life. More than 90% of confirmed COVID cases came from cities[14], which should push toward sustainable and resilient city models that enable them to navigate uncertainty. The data and projections of international organizations indicate that good urban planning and management focused on habitability, sustainability, equity, and resilience are crucial to confronting present and future crises.

Nevertheless, as pointed out, the challenges differ through regions and cities worldwide. The analysis of SDG 11, dedicated to Sustainable Cities and Communities[15], highlights the need to make cities and human settlements inclusive, safe, resilient, and sustainable. The Report defines five aspects that need to be focused on: informal settlements, air quality, public transportation, urban waste management, the risk of local climate

12. European Commission, *EU Regional and Urban Development*, available on *www.ec.europa.eu/regional_policy/policy/themes/urban-development_en*
13. The World Bank, *Urban Development overview*, 3 April 2023available on *www.worldbank.org/en/topic/urbandevelopment/overview#1*
14. UN-Habitat, *World Cities, op. cit.*, p. 245.
15. UNDESA, *SDGs Report, op. cit.*, p.18.

disasters, and the development of green spaces in cities[16]. It is worth it to see them in detail.

One of the objectives of SGD 11 is to reduce the proportion of the urban population living in slums. The SDGs Progress Chart 2022[17] indicates that the goal is a moderate distance from being met globally and experiencing deterioration. Developed countries made significant progress and achieved the goal. Most of Asia is far from reaching the target, and although considerable progress has been made, acceleration is needed. Latin America and the Caribbean, and the Pacific Island are also far from reaching the goal and have yet to progress. For their part, North Africa and Western Asia are also far from the target and have experienced deterioration during the last few years. The worst part of the results corresponds to sub-Saharan Africa, which is very far from the target and has experienced a significant deterioration. Of the 1 billion people living in slums and informal settlements, 85% are located in three regions: Central and Southern Asia (359 million people), East and Southeast Asia (306 million), and Sub-Saharan Africa (230 million), having the last one 50% of the population living in slums. If the population increase projections in these regions are met, the challenge will be enormous. Not only for these countries but also for the rest because of what it will mean in terms of migration.

Another significant challenge that threatens cities is air pollution. In 2019, poor urban air quality caused by traffic, industry, power generation, and household burning of waste and fuel caused more than 4.2 million premature deaths. Exposure to $PM_{2.5}$ polluting particles, among others, affects the health of citizens, increasing the risk of cardiovascular diseases, lung diseases, infections, or cancer 99% of cities exceed the guidelines the World Health Organization established in 2021 of 5 micrograms per cubic meter for $PM_{2.5}$. Once again, low and middle-income countries are the most affected by pollution. Thus, the three-year average between 2017 and 2019 in Central and Southern Asia was the highest (above 60 µg/m3), followed by Africa as a whole and East Asia (above 30 µg/m3), Latin America and the Caribbean were below 20µg/m3, Europe and North America somewhat above 10 µg/m3. Only Oceania fell below 8 µg/m3. The good news is that global $PM_{2.5}$ pollution has been reduced by 11% in the last decade, and more and more cities are monitoring air quality. It is a first step to take measures to reduce the cost of human lives and hospital expenses.

16. *Ibid.*, p.48-49.
17. United Nations, Department of Economic and Social Affairs (UNDESA), *The Sustainable Development Goals Progress Chart 2022*, New York, USA, 2022, p. 4, retrieved from *unstats.un.org/sdgs/report/2022/progress-chart/*

Related to the above are the transportation infrastructures of the cities. UN forecasts indicate that between 2015 and 2030, annual passenger traffic in cities will increase by 50%, and the number of cars is expected to increase in the same proportion. Thus, the existence of well-designed, low-emission, efficient, safe, and inclusive public transport is a crucial piece for the future of cities. The current situation indicates that developed countries in Europe, North America, and Oceania have public transport coverage in urban areas of more than 60%, allowing convenient access to public transport for more than 85% of the population. On the other end, Sub-Saharan Africa and Central and Southern Asia do not exceed 26% of public transport coverage in urban environments and cover less than 34% of the population. Investing in and developing a public transport network would reduce pollution, combat climate change, and allow access to jobs, educational centers, and health centers, reducing poverty and improving the living conditions of the most vulnerable.

Regarding the collection of urban solid waste, it is above 82% worldwide. However, its management in controlled facilities is at most 55%. Poor collection and management are related to the spread of infections, plastic pollution in rivers and seas, and the emission of GHG. The data by region are similar to the previous ones, which indicates that stricter environmental legislation and more significant investment and financing in developing countries are crucial. As for developed countries, it is necessary to improve waste management and work on developing the circular economy, reducing consumption, and eliminating planned obsolescence.

Between 2015 and 2021, the strategies and measures adopted to manage climate risks and natural disasters in cities have almost doubled. Local development plans are increasingly focused on taking adaptation measures to climate change. However, the risk in coastal cities and flood-prone areas is increasing. The rise in sea level and the increase in the frequency of extreme weather events strongly impact the most vulnerable regions. Although local measures are necessary, they must be accompanied by global measures to reduce GHG and the firm commitment of industrialized countries.

Finally, the SDGs Report 2022 highlights the importance of public space for the proper development of the social and economic life of the city. Parks and gardens, boulevards, and play areas allow people to interact, build support networks, and improve the quality of life. Data collected in 2020 in 962 cities worldwide indicated that less than 38% of urban neighborhoods have an open public space less than 400 meters away, which means that only

45.2% of the urban population has access to these spaces. Nevertheless, the benefits of green areas are social and economic and great allies in combating climate change.

A last important piece of information is the projection of the growth of cities in the coming years[18]. In 2020, there were 34 megacities with more than 10 million inhabitants, 51 metropolises[19] with a population of 5 to 10 million, 494 urban agglomerations with between 1 and 5 million, and 1,355 cities with 300,000 and 1 million people. According to future forecasts, there will be 48 megacities, 73 metropolises, 639 urban agglomerations, and 1,603 cities by 2035. The most significant growth in megacities and metropolises will occur in the Asia-Pacific region, followed by Africa. Eastern Europe will remain stable, and Latin America and the Caribbean, Western Europe, North America, and Oceania will grow very contained. This rapid growth in the size of cities poses enormous challenges in the construction of infrastructure, the provision of essential services, and the management of cities.

These data make it clear that cities can be both the source and the solution to current economic, environmental, and social challenges. Climate change is everyone's responsibility and affects everyone, although not in the same way or intensity. GHGs have been produced for decades, and fossil fuels allowed the development and well-being of the Global North's inhabitants. Meanwhile, their consequences affect the most vulnerable communities and developing countries in the Global South to a greater extent. It is time to face everyday challenges with equity through global governance and the cooperation of all countries and regions. A challenge in which the future of humanity is at

18. UN-Habitat, *Global State of Metropolis 2020. Population Data Booklet*, Nairobi, UN-Habitat, 2020, retrieved from *unhabitat.org/sites/default/files/2020/06/gsm-population-data-booklet2020.pdf*
19. In 2020, Un-Habitat agreed on a new definition for the metropolis based on the Degree of Urbanization, which combines population size and density, to facilitate international comparison. Three categories of human settlements were defined: cities, towns and semi-dense areas, and rural areas, thus allowing the rural-urban continuum to be captured. We use the terms metropolises, urban agglomerations, metropolitan areas, or metropolitan zones to include densely populated cities, not only urban but also peri-urban and nearby rural territories with economic and social interconnectedness. European Union, The Food and Agriculture Organization of the United Nations (FAO), the International Labour Office (ILO), the Organization for Economic Co-operation and Development (OECD), United Nations Human Settlements Programme (UN-Habitat) and the World Bank, *A recommendation on the method to delineate cities, urban and rural areas for international statistical comparisons*, Statistical Commission Background document, Fifty-first session, 3-6 March 2020, retrieved from *unstats.un.org/unsd/statcom/51st-session/documents/BG-Item3j-Recommendation-E.pdf*

stake can only be addressed through collaboration and a systemic vision. Understanding the earth as an interconnected system in which natural and anthropic dynamics are closely related is the basis for building tomorrow. Furthermore, each region and each city must seek solutions adapted to their circumstances. The experience and mistakes made by developed countries in the urbanization of cities during the 20th century should serve as an example to developing countries to avoid falling into the same mistakes. Well-planned urbanization and management have the potential to transform people's lives and make cities thrive, sustainable, inclusive, and resilient. The construction of affordable and decent neighborhoods and homes with a supply of water, energy, and sanitation, universal access to basic health care and education services, urban infrastructure such as public transport, open and safe green spaces, or clean air will ensure the level of well-being of all people. According to the United Nations[20] (UN-Habitat, 2022), a new social contract with minimum vital income and health and housing coverage is necessary. To "leave no one behind", all countries, especially developed ones, must do their part. Financial support and international aid to the most vulnerable countries and communities will be vital in achieving this goal.

II. POST-GROWTH AND URBAN CHALLENGES TO THE CLIMATE EMERGENCY

In this context, Antonio Guterres' statement about the importance of cities in overcoming the climate crisis is well understood. Furthermore, the search for new solutions based on global thinking must accompany local actions that improve well-being. A debate on the economic model will be seen in the first part of this section. In the second one, we will list the main issues that, according to us, should be considered to make cities levers of change for a sustainable future.

1. TOWARDS A CHANGE IN THE ECONOMIC MODEL

As the IPCC Report[21] highlighted, two primary objectives exist to address the climate emergency. One is stabilizing the climate, for which the drastic reduction of greenhouse gases is needed. The second objective must be towards social justice, where global governance is essential.

20. UN-Habitat, *World Cities op. cit.*, pp. 22-24.
21. IPCC, "Summary for […]", *op. cit*, 2023.

These two interrelated objectives can only be faced through a change in the economic paradigm, which debate on the need to overcome the idea of green growth has been opened recently. Most institutional approaches worldwide to confronting the climate crisis were based on a transition towards growth based on renewable energy. According to this assumption, new technologies would allow economic growth (measured by Gross Domestic Product) while protecting the Earth's dynamics that support life. Since the appearance of the notion of green growth at the Rio+20 Summit in 2012, this theory has been assumed in national and international policies, the 2030 Agenda, and the European fund from the Green New Deal. However, scientific research increasingly shows that it is impossible to decouple economic growth (even green growth) from the intensive use of natural resources and carbon emissions. Jason Hickel and Giorgos Kallis[22] review the most relevant literature on historical trends and prediction models to conclude the following:

> "(1) there is no empirical evidence that absolute decoupling from resource use can be achieved on a global scale against a background of continued economic growth, and (2) absolute decoupling from carbon emissions is highly unlikely to be achieved at a rate rapid enough to prevent global warming over 1.5.°C or 2.°C, even under optimistic policy conditions. We conclude that green growth is likely a misguided objective and that policymakers must look toward alternative strategies"[23].

Concerning green growth, Antonio Turiel[24] explains that renewable energies for electricity production and new technologies in development, like green hydrogen, will not be able to replace the workforce produced by fossil energies in the short and medium term. Every time, more scientists and researchers agree that infinite economic growth is incompatible with a planet of finite resources. They propose that the only way out of the climate crisis is to break the consumerist model and develop new economic and social models to overcome the systemic crisis[25]. It means changing growth

22. Hickel, J. and Kallis, G., "Is Green Growth Possible?" in *New Political Economy*, vol. 25, n. 4, pp. 469-486, 2020, retrieved from *www.tandfonline.com/doi/full/10.1080/14747731.2020.1812222*
23. *Ibid.* p. 1.
24. Turiel, A., *Petrocalipsis. Crisis energética global y cómo (no) la vamos a solucionar,* Madrid, Alfabeto, 2020.; Turiel, A., *Sin energía. Pequeña guía para el Gran Descenso,* Madrid, Alfabeto, 2022.
25. Valladares, F., *La Recivilización. Desafíos, zancadillas y motivaciones para arreglar el mundo,* Barcelona, Destino, 2023.; Reichmann, J., Simbioética, *Homo sapiens en el entramado de la vida (Elementos para una ética ecologista y animalista en el seno de una Nueva Cultura de*

based on GDP by other alternatives to reach well-being, and rethink people's relationship with others and the planet.

The alternative strategy that Hickel[26] proposes is based on post-growth or economic degrowth, which the author explains as a planned reduction in the performance of energy and resources, designed to return the economy to equilibrium with the living world to reduce inequalities and improve human well-being. If de-growth happened to be the solution, better to organize it. Planning is the keyword and what makes the big difference between degrowth and recession. Planned degrowth allows designing policies that reduce ecologically destructive and less socially necessary economic activities while investing in health, education, employment, transport, housing, and care sectors. For their part, recessions are not planned and usually have the opposite effect: massive unemployment, austerity in public services, loss of quality of life, increased inequalities, and discrimination, especially among women, migrants, and refugees. The recession caused by COVID-19 was an excellent example, and one of its consequences was the high increase in the gap between rich and poor. While large corporations saw their income vastly increase, millions were dragged into extreme poverty. According to the World Inequity Report[27], in 2022, the poorest half of the population owned 2% of the world's wealth, while the wealthiest 10% owned 76%. For this reason, Hickel[28] highlights that the decrease should not occur across the board. Most countries in the global South must increase their use of resources and energy to meet the needs of their inhabitants, while much of the global North must reduce them. The decolonization of the global South will impact the autonomous growth and development of southern economies. Furthermore, given that countries in the global North are responsible for most GHG, and those in the global South suffer the majority from its consequences, the time has come to balance the scales. A post-growth economy, Hickel concludes, will reduce economic elites› growth and capital accumulation and benefit developing countries› communities and ecology.

---

la Tierra gaiana), Madrid, Plaza y Valdés, 2022. González Reyes, L., and Almazán, A., *Decrecimiento: del qué al cómo. Propuestas para el estado español*, Madrid, Intervención cultural, 2023.

26. Hickel, J., "What does degrowth mean? A few points of clarification" in *Globalizations*, vol. 18, n. 7, pp. 1105-1111 pp., 2021, retrieved from www.tandfonline.com/doi/full/10.1080/14747731.2020.1812222

27. Chancel, L., Piketty, T., Saez, E., Zucman, G. *et al. World Inequality Report 2022*, World Inequality Lab, 2022, retrieved from *wir2022.wid.world*

28. Hickel, J., "What does degrowth mean? A few points of clarification", *op. cit.*

In May 2023, a conference entitled Beyond Growth[29] was held within the European Parliament. It was a multi-stakeholder initiative promoted by 20 European Members of Parliament from different parties, which included the participation of European and national public policy makers, academia, social partners, companies, and civil society organizations. The ultimate objective was to initiate the transition towards an economic, financial, social, and environmental model that is not based on GDP growth but on sustainable prosperity and well-being, which remains within planetary limits. Researchers, professors, and political advisors like Jason Hickel or Kate Raworth were developing new ideas and methodologies for the economic transition.

Fifty years have passed since the publication of the well-known report *The Limits to Growth*[30] of the Club of Rome, which warned about the severe consequences that the dominant model of production, distribution of goods, and environmental deterioration would have in the following hundred years. During the Beyond Growth Conference, the current co-president of the Club of Rome, Sandrine Dixson-Declève, underlined the interconnection between democracy and economic growth and the impossibility of having both simultaneously[31]. It is time, she said, to invest in social cohesion, where human well-being, economic security, and ecological resilience rest, and to build strong democracies capable of making historic decisions independent of corporate interests. She stated that a change in the economic paradigm and strong political leadership is necessary to achieve this.

In this same sense, the international Earth4all[32] initiative, which explores how to achieve the well-being of all people in this century while staying within planetary limits, proposed redefining the economic system and calling for action. The objective is to develop a well-being economy and place it at the center of public policy design, adopting new economic indicators and providing better results for people and the planet. Governments should

29. European Parliament, *Beyond Growth Conference 2023. Pathways towards Sustainable Prosperity in the EU*, 15-17 May 2023, retrieved from *www.beyond-growth-2023.eu/*

30. Meadows, D. H., Meadows, D. L., Randers, J., & Behrens III, W. W., *The limits to growth-club of Rome*, New York, Universe Book, 1972.

31. Dixson-Declève, S., "Opening plenary — Limits to Growth: where do we stand and where do we go from here?"; European Parliament, *Beyond Growth Conference 2023. Pathways towards Sustainable Prosperity in the EU*, 15-17 May 2023, video conference available on *www.beyond-growth-2023.eu/lecture/opening-plenary-limits-to-growth/*

32. Dixson-Declève, S.; Gaffney, O.; Ghosh, J.; Randers, J.; Rockström, J; Stoknes, P. E., *Earth4all: A Survival Guide For Humanity. Executive Summary*, Earth4all, September 2022, retrieved from *earth4all.life/publications/*

promote abandoning unsustainable consumption as a critical driver of GDP growth in high-income countries. Moreover, they should implement universal basic services and national universal basic dividends for a fair transformation, and promote sponsored citizen assemblies to debate what changes in economic systems people want to see. The initiative proposes measures that require extensive cooperation and extraordinary changes in the 2020-2030 decade. If achieved, stated Earth4all initiative, extraordinary results focused on five axes would be obtained. 1) achieve the end of poverty by 2060, favoring a GDP growth rate of at least 5% for low-income countries until GDP per person exceeds $15,000 annually; 2) reduce inequalities by increasing income and wealth taxes on the wealthiest 10% of society, until they own less than 40% of national income; 3) Empower women and other disadvantaged people in current systems to enjoy equal access to education, economic and social rights, power and assets by 2030. This will help stabilizing the world population to reach a maximum of 8.5 billion of people by 2040 and will unleash everyone's potential; 4) transform the food system towards regenerative and sustainable agriculture, providing healthy diets for people without destroying the planet, stopping the loss of biodiversity and protecting the global commons to ensure food for all; 5) transform the inefficient fossil energy system into a clean and optimized energy system to achieve a 50% reduction in GHG emissions by 2030, and net zero carbon emissions by 2050, while keeping temperature rise below 2.°C and guaranteeing sustainable energy for all[33].

These are some initiatives that scientists, organizations, and civil society are working on and that, through global governance, can be put into practice to overcome the systemic crisis. Science has been doing significant research and communication work for years. Collaboration between international organizations, administrations, companies, social agents, and civil society could give positive results in the short and medium term. In this process, cities are relevant actors.

2. RETHINKING THE CITY OF THE 21ST CENTURY

Let us now focus on the challenges cities face in different regions. According to the World Cities Report[34], the challenges of developed countries are managing cultural diversity, updating obsolete infrastructures, the demographic challenge in areas that are losing population, and the

33. *Ibid.*, pp. 13-29.
34. UN-Habitat, *World cities op cit.*, pp. 9-13.

aging of the population. According to this report, developing countries face increasing levels of poverty, a shortage of infrastructure and decent housing, high levels of youth unemployment, and the need to invest in secondary cities. In the worst scenario, the report highlights[35], extreme poverty will increase by 32%, economic uncertainty, environmental challenges, and war conflicts will have a high impact on cities, which will lead to the collapse of more vulnerable urban areas. Moving towards an optimistic scenario means favoring a collaboration, coordination, and multilateral intervention framework.

In this context, cities are an excellent opportunity to address some of these challenges in developing and developed countries. Learning from the mistakes made in the West to avoid making them in developing countries is a valuable lesson. Jan Gehl[36] explained that one of the significant errors of urban planning in the 20th century, derived from the Modern Movement, was the motorization of public space. The objective of promoting mobility by private vehicles in the city resulted in the design of cities out of human scale, which allocated more space to cars than to people and made social relations difficult. The urban planning model developed in the IV CIAM and included in the Athens Charter[37] defended the city's mechanization, functionality, order, and zoning. A model that celebrated the machine's use and promoted the motor industry and consumption in the West. With significant economic development and well-being advantages in some countries, it has proven to be a failed model in urban planning terms for different reasons. Designing the city for cars meant allocating much public space to private vehicles, reducing the space dedicated to pedestrians and the city's trees, and meeting and leisure spaces such as avenues, tree-lined squares, parks, gardens, or boulevards. The loss of places of coexistence and the omnipotent presence of vehicles on the streets had two main consequences. On the one hand, neighborhood community networks gradually reduce due to insecurity, the disappearance of children playing on the streets, the reduction of casual conversations between neighbors. On the other hand, the increase in the city's heat island and air pollution is due to the reduction of carbon sinks and the waterproofing of soils, among others. All of this led to the deterioration of the inhabitants' well-being and physical and mental health. It is essential to become aware of the causes and consequences of this failed model to

35. *Ibid.*, pp. 17.
36. Gehl, J., *Cities for people*, Washington D.C., Island press, 2013.
37. Congress Internationaux d'Architecture moderne (CIAM), *La Charte d'Athenes or The Athens Charter*, 1933. Trans J. Tyrwhitt. Paris, France: The Library of the Graduate School of Design, Harvard University, 1946.

improve developed countries' cities and avoid making the same mistakes in developing ones.

Many urban challenges and solutions can be implemented. UN-Habitat's New Urban Agenda[38] offered extensive practical urban planning and management guidance to accelerate the SDGs. Similarly, the Urban Agenda for the EU[39] aims to improve regulation in urban areas considering the significant differences between cities and regions and their challenges; advance financing programs by making them more accessible and favoring cohesion policies; build a base of knowledge, data, and good urban practices to ensure evidence-based policies and solutions adapted to different challenges. The priorities of the European Urban Agenda advance some of the challenges highlighted in the SDGs Report, such as air quality, circular economy, climate adaptation, energy transition, urban poverty, inclusion of migrants and refugees, and urban mobility. Likewise, they work on the challenges underlined for developed countries in the WCR, such as culture and cultural heritage, inclusion of migrants and refugees, digital transition, jobs and skills in the local economy, or sustainable use of land and nature-based solutions. The European Urban Agenda still has ample room for improvement in regulating and implementing post-growth measures. However, some cities are already developing new models that incorporate this vocation.

Before delving into the case studies, we want to make a compilation of ideas that should be the basis of the policies, planning, and management of future cities considering what has been explained so far. Given the challenges of climate change, there are many ways to adapt these principles in human settlements in developed and developing countries. Each city must find the solutions that best suit its circumstances.

a) Multi-scalar policies and actions: Given the population increase expected for the coming years, the development of national policies must contemplate multi-scalar actions, which provide solutions to territorial issues while working at a local scale. The planning of metropolises must go hand in hand with developing small cities, rural areas, and the rural-urban continuum. Excessive growth and the configuration of megacities are a challenge for managing and creating large pockets of poverty. Its growth will also relieve

38. UN-Habitat, *The New Urban Agenda: Habitat III. Conference on Housing and Sustainable Urban Development*, Quito, UN-Habitat, 2017, retrieved from *habitat3.org/the-new-urban-agenda/*

39. European Union, *Urban Agenda for de EU*, retrieved from *www.urbanagenda.urban-initiative.eu/urban-agenda-eu*

pressure on neighboring agricultural land, infrastructure, and services. The development of public policies to establish and attract the population in small cities and the rural world can avoid overcrowding and unsustainable expansion in large cities.

b) Multidimensional planning: The planning approach must be directed towards environmental, social, and economic resilience at the same time. The multisectoral approach and governance will be able to adopt measures that prevent new disruptors such as pandemics, extreme weather events, or the increase in pockets of poverty.

c) Governance: The collaboration of local governments, the third sector, and civil society must be permanent. Dialogue between international organizations, national and local governments, the private sector, and citizens must be prioritized. Only by listening to people and organizations and through multi-stakeholder understanding is it possible to develop full democracies, sustainable human environments, and peace.

d) New social contract: A new social contract with guaranteed income and basic services, decent health, and housing with water, sanitation, energy, or garbage collection must be a priority objective. As proposed by the new post-growth trends, the financing of local governments will grow by raising taxes on high incomes and companies. The prosperity of developing countries will require the forgiveness of external debt by developed countries.

e) Food security: The protection of communal lands, the creation of agricultural communities, the development of local and proximity agriculture and urban gardens, and the application of regenerative or ecological agriculture criteria not only promote food security, the protection of health and biodiversity, but it is a passport to peace.

f) Energy self-sufficiency: Promoting energy self-sufficiency in the territories so that they do not depend on others, developing renewable and low-polluting energy, and creating energy communities will allow for the reduction of greenhouse gas emissions and achieving net zero emissions in a short or medium time. A measure that a significant reduction in consumption in developed countries must accompany.

g) Local economy: Countries will promote policies to support businesses and strengthen the diversified local economy, avoiding relocating processes and favoring the reduction of supply chains. Greater independence from the outside world and jobs with decent and sufficient salaries allow for economic development capable of raising people's well-being, putting less pressure on the environment. The World Cities Report[40] is committed to stop the exclusion and harassment of informal workers, acknowledging and integrating them to build an inclusive urban future.

h) Green infrastructure and nature-based solutions: The city of the future must be environmentally sustainable and conceived from nature-based solutions. Redesigning cities and neighborhoods from the territory understood as an extensive green infrastructure offers the opportunity to connect cities horizontally and vertically. Measures such as promoting the development of urban forests, parks, and tree-lined squares, or using permeable pavements increase carbon sinks, regulate the temperature of cities, reduce the heat island, improve the composition of the soil, allow the recharge of aquifers and favor biodiversity. It will increase people's health and well-being, promoting compatibility between the earth's natural processes and human dynamics.

i) Social diversity and gender focus: City planning must think about the health and well-being of its inhabitants. They must be inclusive and integrate all population sectors, including older people, children, women, migrants, and other vulnerable groups. The gender approach is essential to break with old social structures and open the door to new forms of cooperation and care.

j) Mix of uses: Cities and neighborhoods must have a mix of uses and public services, such as residential, commercial, businesses and offices, health and educational centers, cultural and sports spaces, green spaces and leisure places, and public transportation. Furthermore, it is advisable to encourage the mixture of groups from different social classes, ethnicities, beliefs, and genders. Various uses and interculturality build more cohesive, equitable, safe neighborhoods and resilient communities.

k) Compact city and active mobility: The dense city model is more efficient in using resources and land. In developed countries, it is necessary to return the city to pedestrians, promote active mobility

40. UN-Habitat. *op cit*. p. 91.

(pedestrian and cyclist) and public transport, reduce car space by reintroducing nature, improve air quality, and promote social relations by designing inclusive and resilient public leisure spaces.

l) New technologies at the service of society: In a digitalized and hyperconnected world, technology offers the opportunity to serve the common good and improve people's lives. For this, developing effective regulation is essential to ensure the protection of citizens, truthful communication, and development in favor of equity, inclusion, and peace.

These are some ideas to change the concept of economic growth to prosperity in cities. Human settlements offer the opportunity to apply global solutions at a local level, fight climate change and social inequality, and build peace. As expressed, with a very high level of confidence, by the contribution of Working Group III of AR6, focused on Climate Change Mitigation:

"Urban areas can create opportunities to increase resource efficiency and significantly reduce GHG emissions through the systemic transition of infrastructure and urban form through low-emission development pathways towards net-zero emissions. Ambitious mitigation efforts for established, rapidly growing and emerging cities will encompass (i) reducing or changing energy and material consumption, (ii) electrification, and (iii) enhancing carbon uptake and storage in the urban environment. Cities can achieve net-zero emissions, but only if emissions are reduced within and outside of their administrative boundaries through supply chains, which will have beneficial cascading effects across other sectors"[41].

III. THRIVING EUROPEAN CITIES: THE CASE STUDIES OF AMSTERDAM AND PARIS

In the same vein as the Beyond Growth Congress, new economic and urban planning models are being developed and implemented in various cities. These case studies give us a glimpse of what future cities should be. At the same time, they confirm that there are better models to follow than those of the 20th century and, to a certain extent, they are closer to those

41. P. R. Shukla, J. Skea, A. Reisinger, R. Slade, *et al.* (eds.), IPCC, 2022, "Summary for Policymakers" in P. R. Shukla, J. Skea, R. Slade, A. Al Khourdajie, *et al.* (eds.), *Climate Change 2022: Mitigation of Climate Change. Contribution of Working Group III to the Sixth Assessment Report of the Intergovernmental Panel on Climate Change*, Cambridge University Press, Cambridge, UK and New York, NY, USA, p. 30, *doi: 10.1017/9781009157926.001*

existing in some developing regions. Thriving cities and regions do not require GDP growth, but rather the development and support of their own resources, local economies, and community networks.

1. THE ECONOMIC MODEL OF THE DOUGHNUT APPLIED TO THE CITY OF AMSTERDAM

British economist and Oxford lecturer, Kate Raworth, developed an alternative sustainable economic model that balances essential human needs with the planet's limits[42]. It is not founded on GDP growth but on prosperity and well-being. The model is represented as a doughnut and proposes the development of an economy whose principles try to solve the two significant challenges of today's society: social problems such as poverty, homelessness or loneliness, and environmental challenges derived from climate change. Raworth explains seven principles that should be followed to build tomorrow's economy and compares them with the current economic model. These principles are: change the goal, see the big picture, nurture human nature, get savvy with systems, design to distribute, create to regenerate, and be agnostic about growth. Raworth rethinks the economic model to build a new one that is environmental-friendly and guarantees minimum rights to everyone.

The doughnut model allows measuring and searching for strategies that meet two requirements. On the one hand and derived from the SDGs, there is a social floor that provides human well-being, in which all people should have their basic needs covered: water, food, health, education, income and work, justice and peace, political participation, social equity, gender equality, energy, housing, and networks and connectivity. On the other hand, based on scientific data, an environmental ceiling respects planetary boundaries and works for security and peace, reducing pressure on climate change, ocean acidification, chemical pollution, reduction of the ozone layer, the loss of biodiversity, and the extraction of freshwater among other dangers to the sustainability of the Earth. It is essential to understand that the health of all people, species, and ecosystems is interconnected and that the well-being of all and peace between nations depend on it. Only from the (scientific) understanding of this premise is it possible to work on the model. Suppose an organization that stays in the ring between the social floor and the environmental ceiling. In that case, it will be a safe and just space where

42. Kate Raworth, *Doughnut economics: seven ways to think like a 21st-century economist*, London, Penguin Random House UK, 2018.

everyone's needs will be covered and can thrive, and other species and the environment will be safe.

One of the advantages of this alternative model to economic growth is that it is easy to understand the repercussions of economic decisions on the well-being of people and the planet. Therefore, it could be possible to transform the economy and link it with social and environmental issues so that they are no longer considered externalities. Any organization (national or local governments, companies, or the domestic economy) could apply these standards to maintain their activity within the limits of the social floor and the environmental ceiling. Currently, 27 local governments and regions in the world, including Amsterdam, Brussels, Grenoble, Copenhagen, Barcelona, Glasgow or Bath and North East Somerset (in Europe), Toronto, Portland or Philadelphia (in North America), Mexico City, Santiago de Cali or Sao Paulo (in Latin America), Thimphu-Paro Region and Perak State (in Asia), and Wellington and Dunedin (in Oceania) are working on the implementation of the Doughnut Economy[43].

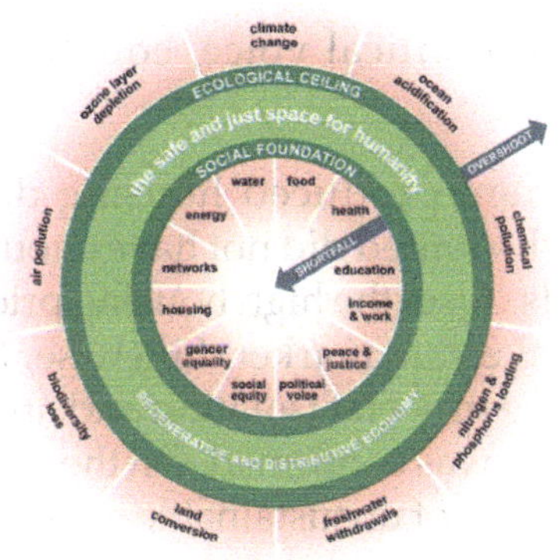

The Doughnut of social and planetary boundaries.
Source: Kate Raworth.

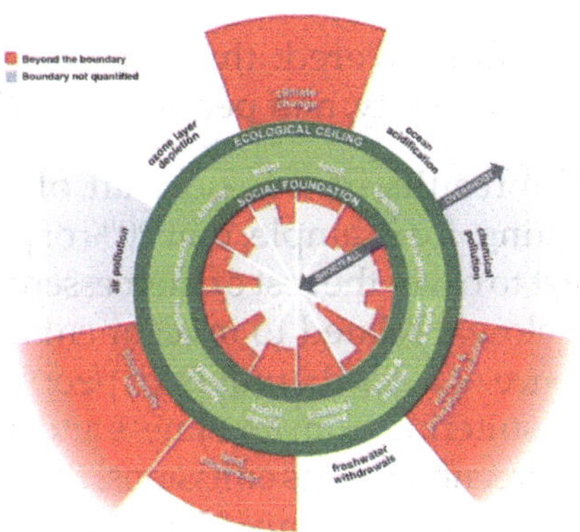

The state of humanity.
Source: Kate Raworth and Christian Guthier, 2017.

In 2020, Amsterdam (91,675 inhabitants)[44] envisioned becoming a prosperous, regenerative, and inclusive city for all citizens while respecting planetary boundaries.The city joined some initiatives, such as the circular

43. Doughnut Economics Action Lab (DEAL), retrieved from *www.doughnuteconomics.org/about-doughnut-economics*

44. Data as of January 1, 2023, Centraal Bureau voor de Statistiek, *Population Development*, retrieved from *opendata.cbs.nl/statline/#/CBS/en/*

economy, the Thriving Cities Initiative[45] of the C40 group of cities, and the Doughnut Economics Action Lab. The Thriving Cities Initiative was a crucial tool that offered a portrait of the city based on Doughnut's social and environmental limits, a starting point in which all social, ecological, local, and global indicators were evaluated. Numerous stakeholders from companies, organizations, and civil society were involved, resulting in the Amsterdam City Doughnut. Based on it, all stakeholders were invited to answer the question: "How can Amsterdam be a home to thriving people, in a thriving place, while respecting the well-being of all people and the health of the whole planet?"[46]

Four areas were analyzed with the following well-being indicators:

- Healthy: through food, water, health, housing
- Enabled: through education, energy, income, and employment
- Connected: through mobility, community, digital connectivity, and culture
- Empowered: through social equity, political voice, equality in diversity, and peace and justice

The results of this portrait of Amsterdam produced housing data indicating, for example, that 20% of people who rented did not have enough budget to cover the rest of their essential needs. Also, the high housing prices were closely related to investment in the real estate market. Likewise, the existence of a good number of people who live in social isolation and are at risk of suffering from loneliness and depression was confirmed. On the other hand, greenhouse gas emissions, the consumption of unsustainable materials in the city, and the impact of consumption patterns on people and nature in other countries were measured. Calculating the externalities of the city's economy in other places where the raw materials and products come from completed the picture of Amsterdam's social and environmental impact. It was found that 63% of Amsterdam's emissions were due to the import of materials, food, and consumer products that were produced abroad and that CO2 emissions had grown by 31% since 1990. The study provided other data, such as the port of Amsterdam being the largest importer of cocoa beans

45. C40 Cities, *Thiving Cities Initiative*, retrieved from *www.c40.org/what-we-do/raising-climate-ambition/inclusive-thriving-cities/thriving-cities/*

46. Doughnut Economics Action Lab (DEAL), Biomimicry 3.8, Circle Economy, and C40, *Amsterdam City Doughnut*, Amsterdam, March 2020, retrieved from *www.doughnuteconomics.org/amsterdam-portrait.pdf*

in the world, mainly from West Africa, where labor exploitation and child labor are joint. Once the reference data was known, specific measures began to be defined that would improve results and remain within the limits of the Doughnut. Amsterdam was the first city in the world to adopt the Doughnut Economy as a development strategy for the coming years.

One of the main objectives was to move towards the circular economy. The goal is to halve the use of new raw materials by 2030 and achieve a fully circular economy by 2050. One of the advantages of the circular economy is its potential for job creation. Fiscal measures to lower taxes on labor and increase taxes on raw materials would generate more employment and promote the circular economy.

Three areas that could significantly impact the city were chosen: construction, food, and consumer goods. Two hundred projects of very diverse types were known to be underway[47]. Some were focused on housing. The goal was to change the relationship between people's well-being and the city's economic performance. In traditional economics, rising housing prices cause local GDP to grow and are interpreted as a sign that the economy is doing well. However, in these circumstances, some people cannot cope with the price rise and are displaced out of the city. For this reason, the City Council is working to change this model and also co-finances some of the projects proposed by residents.

Among the measures taken is developing a support network with repair services, exchange platforms, second-hand stores, and online markets. Reducing the impact of construction has meant tightening sustainability regulations for buildings, encouraging the use of sustainable materials, such as wood, or introducing a materials passport that allows a record of the composition of buildings for future reuse.

New regulations and the involvement of the Netherlands and the European Union governments are needed to reduce waste. An environmental management pilot project has been launched, in which the city council is responsible for collecting and treating waste from a commercial area. The first result is a reduction in the number of garbage truck trips.

Another project aims to reduce the energy bill of people whose homes have poor insulation. This project provides thick curtains made by people

47. Marieke van Doorninck, M. and Schouten, S., "The Doughnut Model for a Fairer, Greener Amsterdam." *Green European Journal*, 15 October 2020, retrieved from *www.greeneuropeanjournal.eu/the-doughnut-model-for-a-fairer-greener-amsterdam/*

excluded from the labor market. The project combines the reduction of carbon emissions with the empowerment of vulnerable groups and the well-being of people while managing to strengthen community ties.

The city of Amsterdam developed the project during the worst moments of the pandemic when the relationship between people's health and the planet's health was evident. The model is being developed with the conviction that it will help create more jobs, improve people's well-being, strengthen community networks, and make the city and the planet more sustainable and resilient. More and more cities and regions are joining the initiative. However, for the model to be successful, it is necessary to promote it at the national and supranational level, as was done at the Beyond Growth Congress of the European Parliament. It will be necessary for more actors from other regions of the world to join.

2. THE 15-MINUTE CITY MODEL AND THE CASE OF PARIS

In 2016, Carlos Moreno, professor at the IAE Paris Sorbonne Business School and expert in urban planning, coined the term 15-minute city. The model tries to respond to challenges such as dependence on private vehicles, pollution, or social isolation. It is committed to bringing the basic needs of citizens (educational and health centers, shops, or green spaces) closer to a maximum distance walkable or cyclable, of 15 minutes from home. It is an approach based on promoting sustainability and people's well-being, trying to end the fragmented city, reducing the use of private vehicles, and rebuilding local communities. It is a familiar idea and retakes the traditional city concept. There are references in urban planning, such as Jane Jacobs[48], who defended mixed uses, public space, diversity, and citizen participation in New York in the 1960s; or Jan Gehl[49], who proposes transforming the city to return it to "the human scale". Placing people and their needs at the center of urban discourse means thinking about a compact, complex, and diverse city with mixed uses, soft mobility, and a commitment to the local. A well-designed and shared public space generates safety in the streets and develops bonds of coexistence.

The 15-minute city offers a vision of a polycentric and decentralized city where life can be done mainly in the neighborhoods. The new concept follows four major principles[50]:

48. Jacobs, J., *The Death and Life of Great American Cities*, Vintage Books, 1993.
49. Gehl, *op. cit.*
50. Moreno, C.; Allam, Z.; Chabaud, D.; Gall, C.; Pratlong, F., "Introducing the 15-Minute City: Sustainability, Resilience and Place Identity in Future Post-Pandemic Cities", *Smart Cities 2021*, n. 4, pp. 93-111, retrieved from *doi.org/10.3390/smartcities4010006*

- Proximity (temporal and spatial)
- Density (number of people and availability of amenities and services)
- Diversity (mixed-use neighborhoods and mixed culture and backgrounds)
- Ubiquity (digitalization)

Furthermore, each area within the city should be able to fulfill six social functions: living, working, commerce, caring, education, and entertainment. The model does not propose unique solutions because each neighborhood has its own identity. Identity is defined by its geography, the relationship with other places in the environment, the history and character of the place, and the people who live there. Working on the transformation of neighborhoods from their identity allows the space to be redesigned with people's needs in mind while, at the same time, educating and changing behaviors that are subject to improvement. The mix of uses and the diversity of inhabitants of different ages, origins, beliefs, genders, and conditions favor the configuration of more diverse, equitable, vibrant, and connected neighborhoods increasing levels of security.

Regarding sustainability, the proposal reduces GHGs by promoting active mobility and public transport, local production, the circular economy, and new business opportunities. Governance is also one of the primary keys since the projects are specific to each neighborhood and city. As a flexible model, it adapts to the conditions of each human settlement and can be applied to cities of different sizes, circumstances, and cultures. In this way, the quality of places is linked to the quality of the inhabitants' lives and manages to mobilize people and encourage them to work for the good of all.

City councils are usually the ones in charge of initiating the transformation. However, participatory processes carried out with organizations, companies, local groups, and citizens are the key to knowing the needs and proposals of all groups. Participation projects move forward with more support and confidence in the result. Prioritizing, supporting, and financing work in the most vulnerable or disadvantaged neighborhoods is the first step to moving together toward the set objectives.

The implementation of the 15-minute city began before 2020, but the problematic conditions of the COVID-19 pandemic gave it the definitive boost.

The initiative was adopted by the C40 Cities network, which, in collaboration with Arup, wrote a guide[51] that defines the path to achieving net zero emissions in cities. A neighborhood is defined as a place and a space people inhabit. On the one hand, it is necessary to consider infrastructure, buildings, public space, and green spaces and focus on reducing GHGs. On the other hand, residents, workers, visitors, and the needs of each group (of different ages, genders, races, and abilities or disabilities) should be considered to improve the quality of life of all people. The two pillars -reducing GHGs and improving people's quality of life — are complemented by ten interrelated approaches that respond to these pillars: complete neighborhoods, people-centered mobility, connected places, a place for everyone, clean construction, green buildings and energy, circular resources, green and nature-based solutions, sustainable lifestyle, and green economy. Using the neighborhood scale is a significant advantage because a neighborhood is large enough to favor efficiency and economies of scale and integrate different groups. It is also small enough to define limits and measurable objectives while encouraging stakeholder collaboration. Furthermore, the neighborhood scale is more straightforward for citizen participation and governance, the search and implementation of solutions, and financing. All of this allows the implementation of innovative policies with short-term results, which can then be scaled and applied at the city level.

Launching a 15-minute city project requires defining the participating actors, the association agreements, and the financing, always considering the context of the neighborhood and its surroundings, land uses, public space, transportation and connections, public services, and social and economic conditions. Measuring greenhouse gas emissions and quality of life indicators will provide knowledge to measure the future evolution of the process. Defining a vision for the neighborhood, the objectives and goals, as well as those responsible and a concrete action plan based on the ten approaches mentioned above, is the starting point.

In 2020, during Anne Hidalgo's electoral campaign for her re-election as mayor of Paris, she opted for the quarter-hour City project[52] launched by her advisor, Carlos Moreno. The center of Paris comprises 17 districts, delimited by a peripheral ring road, with a population of 2.1 million

51. C40 Cities and Arup, *Guidebook Green and thriving neighborhoods. A pathway to net zero, featuring the '15-minute city'*, 2021, retrieved from *www.arup.com/perspectives/publications/research/section/green-and-thriving-neighbourhoods*

52. Ville de Paris, *Paris ville du quart d'heure, ou le pari de la proximité*, 23 May 2022, retrieved from *www.paris.fr/dossiers/paris-ville-du-quart-d-heure-ou-le-pari-de-la-proximite-37*

inhabitants[53]. Furthermore, there are significant differences and inequalities between the north and south and between the east and west of the city, and each area has its characteristics and identity. The city of the quarter hour was proposed as a common base to transform the city to carry out various activities in the most zoned places.

The project began with participation processes in which the city council, the districts, and citizens identified, through an exhaustive analysis, the local, public, private, and associative facilities and services that exist and those that require rapid and efficient actions. The needs and ideas to improve the different neighborhoods were also defined. Changes in these spaces were proposed around three major themes: school, culture, and participatory democracy. Some examples implemented are using schools and universities on weekends to host cultural, sports, and leisure activities for neighborhood residents. "Artistic platforms" to carry out cultural activities outside the leading cultural institutions of Paris so that professionals and amateurs can share experiences and spaces. Likewise, "citizen kiosks" were created, spaces where people meet to ask for advice, with the support of the administration and other organizations. Sports clubs allow parents and children to do activities together or parents to play sports while their children are in a daycare center doing activities with other children. In some businesses, the "Make in Paris" brand promotes the network of local businesses and producers, craft stores, second-hand stores, and local logistics centers, among others. The needs for cleaning and security equipment are defined by the districts and the routes around school, commercial, or sports areas. Mobility is one of the main goals.

In the same way that in 2016, the old highways along the Seine were pedestrianized, now it is proposed to establish bike lanes, pedestrian areas, or ephemeral terraces. All these actions are making it possible to transform the city and make it more liveable, prosperous, and friendly while working for citizens' health and the planet's sustainability. A project that was launched during the time of COVID-19 has given excellent results since then. The model's flexibility has allowed its application in many places worldwide. It is the same idea with different names, such as Paris' 15-Minute City, Barcelona's Superblock, Portland's Complete Neighborhoods, Melbourne's 20 Minute Neighborhoods, Buenos Aires' Human-scale City, as well as Bogotá's Barrios Vitales.

53. 2.1 billion inhabitants in 2023, Statista, "Stimated population in Paris", retrieved from *www.statista.com/statistics/1046125/population-of-paris-france/*

IV. CONCLUSIONS

The forecasts of international organizations for the coming decades indicate that the future of humanity will be urban. The challenges cities face regarding demographics, poverty, health, and climate disasters are very different in the various regions, with those in the global South being the most affected. These challenges must be addressed through governance processes, providing global solutions that can be applied locally. Cities and regions offer the opportunity to adapt and implement each case's best projects and actions.

We are experiencing a systemic crisis with multiple derivatives (climate, geopolitical, social, energy, biodiversity crisis, among others) that can only be overcome through a change in growth and consumption models and public and financial policies that break with the economic model based on GDP growth. A new post-growth model focused on "the prosperity of regions and people" emerges as the best solution to ensure a socially, environmentally, and economically sustainable future. This model requires brave, broad-minded governments and bold, generous policies that resolve historical conflicts between countries and regions.

In recent years, new economic and urban planning models have been developed, such as the Doughnut Economy and the quarter-hour city, focused on rethinking the city locating people's and environmental prosperity at the center. Cities conceived from the territories in which they are inserted, through multidimensional and multisectoral planning, from governance to developing a new social contract, will be capable of working for healthy food and energy security, favoring local economies and new jobs. Promoting the compact city model, the mix of uses and services, and active mobility will favor social diversity and the gender approach that creates closer communities and makes cities safer and more vibrant. Developing a circular and collaborative economy that reuses, reduces solid waste, and recycles objects and materials will decrease GHGs. Expanding green infrastructure and nature-based solutions while lowering the space for private vehicles will raise carbon sinks and improve air quality, biodiversity, and health. Moreover, these models will provide time for people to share with loved ones, reduce loneliness, and improve mental health.

Implementing these models in cities of different sizes, like Amsterdam or Paris, offers a glimpse of a better future for everyone. They are flexible models that can be adapted to different contexts and human settlements anywhere in the world, both in developed and developing countries. It will be a considerable challenge, but a determined, committed, and multistakeholder performance can be the best option for many current challenges.

The Eu Climate Change Strategy: New Approaches in Taxation and Governance

MARTA VILLAR EZCURRA & MARINA BISOGNO[1]
San Pablo CEU University

I. INTRODUCTION

Europe faces strong urgent environmental and climate change challenges that pose risks to our health, to supply chains and production ability and, in turn, our well-being. As the secretary of the United Nations has stated, the era of global boiling has arrived[2]. Further to this, on-going megatrends (i. e. ageing population, changing migration patterns, increasing inequalities, global competition for resources, digitalisation and other technological changes) are influencing Europe's long-term environmental outlook[3].

The challenges of tackling climate change and energy transition are so great that they cannot be met without good governance. The foundations for transforming the economic model in this direction have been laid, both by the 2015 Paris Agreement and the development of its rules in Katowice, and by the 2030 Agenda for Sustainable Development. However, there is a consensus that the necessary changes can only be achieved through global and coordinated action. This requires a multilateral approach defined by common goals and creating space for new governance models that can involve different public administrations and civil society.

Globalisation has long been a catalyst for democratisation at the global level. However, in recent decades it has focused on promoting free trade flows

---

1. Marta Villar (vilezc@ceu.es) is full professor of financial and tax law and Marina Bisogno (marina.bisogno@ceu.es) is post-doctoral researcher in tax law Marie Curie fellow (her research project received funding from the European Union's Horizon 2020 research and innovation program under the Marie Skłodowska-Curie grant agreement No. 101024306), both at the Universidad San Pablo- CEU (CEU Universities) in Madrid (Spain).
2. See Antonio Guterres' speech to the United Nations on 27 July 2023.
3. European Commission, *Annual Report on Taxation 2023*, June 2023, p.101.

without paying sufficient attention to the need to protect essential public goods, such as those related to climate change, energy and environmental protection in the broad sense. As a result of this unequal globalisation, social and territorial inequalities have increased. At the same time, it has favoured the emergence of large global corporations that have been able to act in an oligopolistic manner.

In this complex context, the European Union (EU) has been pursuing an ambitious policy on climate action and has put in place an impressive regulatory framework to favour the achievement of its 2030 target for greenhouse gas emissions reduction. In particular, the reaction of the European Commission and the European Court of Justice (ECJ) to these developments seem to promote new approaches to governance in the European Union[4]. Tackling climate challenges and reaching the objectives of the Paris Agreement[5] are at the core of the so-called "European Green Deal" (EGD)[6]. The EGD relies on a new governance framework, multiple regulatory approaches ranging from soft law to hard law, and significant financial and fiscal commitments[7]. This is why environment and energy policy has recently moved from the periphery to the centre of EU policy, with the EGD and the REPowerEU[8] plan being the main drivers of its economic growth strategy.

4. Scott, J., Trubek, D., "Mind the gap: law and new approaches to governance in the European Union", *Eur. LJ.*, vol. 8, 2002, p.1.
5. At the 21st Conference of the Parties to the United Nations Framework Convention on Climate Change (UNFCCC), which took place in Paris from 30 November to 12 December 2015, the text of an agreement was adopted, concerning the strengthening of the global response to climate change. See Council Decision (EU) 2016/1841 of 5 October 2016 on the conclusion, on behalf of the EU, of the Agreement adopted under the United Nations Framework Convention on Climate Change.
6. The European Green Deal (EGD), presented in the Communication [COM (2019) 640] of 11 December 2019, sets out a detailed vision to make Europe the first climate-neutral continent by 2050, safeguarding biodiversity, establish a circular economy and eliminate pollution, while boosting the competitiveness of European industry and ensuring a just transition for the regions and workers affected.
7. See Jendrośka, J., Reese, M., Squintani, L., "Towards a new legal framework for sustainability under the European Green Deal", *The Opole Studies in Administration and Law*, vol. 19, n. 2, 2021, pp. 87-116, at 109.
8. The REPowerEU Plan aims to accelerate diversification and more renewable gases, frontloads energy savings and electrification with the potential to deliver as soon as possible the equivalent of the fossil fuels Europe currently imports from Russia every year. It does this with coordinated planning in the joint interest and with strong European solidarity. Particular short and medium-term measures are conceived, among other aims, to support investment and reform as well as to boost industrial decarbonization. See the Communication COM (2022) 230 final of 18 May 2022.

To implement the EGD by accelerating sustainable development goals in the EU, delivering greenhouse gas emissions reduction and meeting climate ambitions in line with the European Climate Law,[9] the European Commission has proposed a set of measures called the "Fit for 55" legislative package[10]. A broad revision of the relevant climate and energy legislation will be adopted in an integrated regulatory package covering, *inter alia*, energy taxation, renewables energies, energy efficiency, land use, CO2 emission performance standards for light-duty vehicles, effort sharing and the EU emission trading system (EU ETS). These initiatives are complemented by a huge financial package to accelerate the economic recovery in Europe.

This chapter considers some of the critical issues in the EU governance[11] related to climate change and taxation focusing on the role of legal principles (among others, the polluter pays principle — PPP), fundamentals and competences, and also on the legal trends in the field of taxation related to the climate change, environment and energy sector.

Accordingly, the chapter starts with an overview of the European legal framework for climate change, addressing the critical issues of EU environmental competence, key legal principles, public spending and State aid rules. The role of environmental taxation as an important tool for the achievement of the EU's ambitious decarbonisation goals is underlined by the identification of conceptual problems with regard to what is an "environmental tax' according to the criteria of the ECJ. Particular attention is also given to the core of the "Fit for 55' package and the EU plastic contribution as a new European own resource. Finally, it ends up with some conclusions.

---

9. Regulation (EU) 2021/1119 of the European Parliament and of the Council of 30 June 2021 establishing the framework for achieving climate neutrality and amending Regulations (EC) No 401/2009 and (EU) 2018/1999 ("European Climate Law").
10. European Commission, Communication: "Fit for 55": delivering the EU´s Climate target on the way to climate neutrality, Brussels, 14 of July 2021 [COM (2021) 550 final].
11. The expression "European governance" designates the body of rules, procedures and practices that relate to the way powers are exercised in the EU. The objective is to strengthen democracy at the EU level and to bring citizens closer to the EU institutions. Among others, it is based on the principles of respecting the principles of proportionality and subsidiarity, ensuring that each of the EU institutions and EU Member states explains and takes responsibility for what it does in the EU and that contributing to the global governance debate with a view to improving the operation of international institutions. *See* EUR-Lex Glossary of summaries.

II. THE EUROPEAN FRAMEWORK ON CLIMATE CHANGE

Originally the EU fundamental treaties did not mention the protection of the environment. Environmental concerns became part of the European policies in the Seventies with ancillary provisions linked to the common market. The European action and legislation in this sector have evolved significantly over time to the point that the protection of the environment and climate change concerns are now at the core of the EU political agenda.

1. THE ISSUE OF A GOOD GOVERNANCE: A REVIEW OF ENVIRONMENTAL AND ENERGY COMPETENCES

According to article 3 of the Treaty of the European Union (TEU), the Union is committed to a "high level of protection and improvement of the quality of the environment", which includes combating climate change. Other provisions of EU primary law develop this commitment. For example, environmental policy is based on articles 11 and 191-193 of the Treaty of the Functioning of the European Union (TFEU). Particular attention should be made of article 11 establishing that the protection of the environment must be integrated in the definition and implementation of other EU policies. This means that tax harmonization or State aid regulation should also contribute to raising the level of environmental protection. The greening of other related EU policies is also essential if effective progress is to be made.

The EU has progressively increased its relevant role (both intra-EU and extra-EU) in promote climate change and clean energy policies and is contributing in a very remarkable way to raising ambition in the objectives to be achieved, and laying the foundations for influential programs, financial plans, agendas and roadmaps. To this end, it has adopted European legislation and harmonised Member States' national rules in many areas, such as the strengthening of the role of environmental taxation and the use of tax incentives in support of environmental policy. It has also played a transcendental role, as a global leader, in climate summits. Overall, the EU is recognized as a committed leader, setting an example and seeking consensus to raise ambition in the protection of biodiversity, environment and the fight against climate change.

However, European regulatory action in the environmental field is still limited by a number of factors. Firstly, both environmental and energy policy fall within the area of shared competences[12]. Thus, the Union and

12. See Articles 11 and 191 to 192 of the TFEU. Article 192 (1) of the TFEU states that "The European Parliament and the Council, acting in accordance with the ordinary

the Member States may legislate and adopt legally binding acts in this area, covering among other fields, air and water pollution, waste management and climate change[13]. This means that EU legislative proposals on climate change have to pass the subsidiarity test with the result that sometimes there are conflicts among EU and Member States, who may have different priorities or rhythms. In addition, certain international challenges require global action and consensus, such as the important question of the design of the electricity market for the green energy target. The Union has the important task of participating in international negotiations and establishing commitments at bilateral, multilateral and global levels. All this demonstrates the need of a multi-level governance and the complexity of the issue[14]. Secondly, even if in the environmental and energy sector the ordinary legislative procedure is applied, for certain provisions primarily of a fiscal nature, the Council adopts unanimously after having heard the European Parliament. Reach consensus in the Council is not easy and many times the unanimity rule slowed down progress in environmental fiscal matters. Recently, emergency measures to mitigate the effects of high energy prices have been adopted by the Council on the basis of article 122 (1) TFEU. A "solidarity contribution" — exceptional and strictly temporary — is regulated at the EU level and should be applied by Member States for "Union companies and permanent establishment with activities in the crude petroleum, natural gas, coal and refinery sector in order to mitigate the direct economic effects of the soaring energy prices for public authorities budgets, final customers and companies across the Union"[15].

2. THE EU GREEN TRANSITION STRATEGY: FROM THEORY TO PRACTICE ON GREENING INVESTMENTS

Regarding green public spending, the EU has promoted important green investments through different programs and funds, such as the Environment and Climate Action (LIFE) program, as the EU's main financial instrument in environment for the period 2014-2020.

Moreover, the specific funds approved for fostering the economic recovery have considerably increased this spending for the next years as one third of

legislative procedure and after consulting the Economic and Social Committee and the Committee of the Regions, shall decide what action is to be taken by the Union in order to achieve the objectives referred to in Article 191".

13. Article 2 (2) of the TFEU.
14. See, among others, Scott, J., "The Multi-Level Governance of Climate Change", in Craig, P. and De Burca, G. (eds.), *The Evolution of EU Law*, OUP, 2012.
15. See Regulation (EU) 2022/1854 of 6 October 2022, recital 13 and articles 14 to 18.

it has to be devoted to the energy transition. It is an unprecedented exercise of solidarity that opens new expectations and benefits for the countries most damaged by the economic crisis. Precisely, REPowerEU is about rapidly reducing the EU dependence on Russian fossil fuels by fast forwarding the clean transition and joining forces to achieve a more resilient energy system and a true Energy Union. Besides, in consistency with other Union policies and contributing to the objectives of parts of the "Fit for 55" package that focus on the decarbonisation of EU industry, initiatives as the Net Zero Industry Act[16] and the Critical Raw Material Act[17] aim to implement the EGD.

However, despite the importance of these initiatives, there are still very important key issues to address to assure efficiency in its implementation. The financial support must be put into operation as soon as possible and to that aim all States must overcome bureaucracy deficiencies that continue to slow down EU countries compared to the more immediate reactions from other actors such as the US with the *Inflation Reduction Act*[18]; Besides, it is essential to ensure that the recovery funds are used effectively and considering opportunity costs. In the end, citizens will make judgements based on the results. Moreover, the public debt that is currently soaring, mainly in southern Europe, cannot be allowed to end up causing another

16. See the Proposal for a Regulation of the European Parliament and of the Council on establishing a framework of measures for strengthening Europe's net-zero technology products manufacturing ecosystem (Net Zero Industry Act, COM (2023) 161, SWD (2023) 68).
17. This initiative includes a Regulation and a Communication. The Regulation sets a regulatory framework to support the development of domestic capacities and strengthen sustainability and circularity of the critical raw material supply chains in the EU. The Communication proposes measures to support the diversification of supply chains through new internationally mutually supportive partnership. The focus is also maximizing the contribution of EU trade agreements, in full complementary with the Global Gateway strategy. See the Proposal for a regulation of the European Parliament and of the Council establishing a framework for ensuring a secure and sustainable supply chain of critical raw materials and amending Regulations (EU) 168/2013, (EU) 2018/858, 2018/1724 and (EU) 2019/102 of 16 March 2023 COM (2023) 160, SWD (2023) 160, SWD(2023) 161, SWD(2023) 162, SEC (2023) 360 and the Communication from the Commission, *A secure and sustainable supply of critical raw materials in support of the twin transition*, of 16 March 2023 COM(2023) 165 final.
18. The Inflation Reduction Act (IRA) signed by President Biden in August 2022 is one of the biggest investments in clean energy investment (USD 369 billion for clean energy and climate change mitigation initiatives). These provisions will likely make the United States one of the most competitive regions in the world. See Congressional Research Service, *Inflation Reduction Act of 2022 (IRA): Provisions Related to Climate Change* of 3 October 2022.

sovereign debt crisis in the eurozone. It is also important to ensure that the recovery funds are used to restructure weaknesses in all the European economies and that the financial instruments are conceived as being temporary measures that, can be extended beyond the current moment if successfully.

In addition to the above, the Union can also influence national public spending through its State aid control policy and contribute to promote green co-financing and investments by private actors.

In short, all these issues represent a complex task for the EU and for the new approaches needed to improve its governance. The approval of the European Climate Law was a crucial event to enhance a better framework because the objective of reaching climate neutrality in 2050 is now a binding EU legal target. Besides, this important Regulation establishes a European Scientific Advisory Board on Climate Change (article 3) which is embedded in the European Environment Agency. However, its effective implementation will depend very much on the way European institutions and Member States act consistently. In other words, only good strategies and the smartest combination of regulatory and economic instruments will assure the achievement of the ambitious long-term targets.

3. THE IMPORTANCE OF KEY LEGAL PRINCIPLES

The legal principles leading to better environmental governance in the EU have evolved throughout the amendment of the founding treaties. Nowadays, apart from the specific environmental policy principles[19] — precaution, prevention and rectifying pollution at source, and PPP — additional legal principles and values must be taken into consideration because other EU policies should also contribute to the environmental protection under the EGD.

For example, ensuring an effective EU internal market is at the heart of the EU process. It is reflected in many of the tax directives and therefore, the rationale behind each piece of legislation in the EU is not always aligned with the EGD. Precisely, to identify the mismatches is part of the EU agenda. In the energy sector, the sustainability principle is more important now than other principles — as reliable supply — in the new EU energy legislation packages. Another example could be the EU competition policy. There is a

19. For the global dimension see Eccleston, Ch. H. and Frederic March, F., *Global Environmental Policy*, Routedge, Taylor & Francis Group, 2011.

large room for greening it although it is controversial to what extent it should be done[20]. The reform of State aid control may be larger[21] because not only European funds, but also national funds will play a very important role. Many of these national funds will fall under the concept of "State aid" and be subject to the supervision of the European Commission.

Apart from the climate strategic actions to achieve decarbonization in the EU, one of the main building blocks of the EGD is the new circular economy action plan (CEAP)[22]. It targets how products are designed, promotes circular economy processes, encourages sustainable consumption, and aims to ensure that waste is prevented, and the resources used are kept in the EU economy for as long as possible. As a result, according to the subsidiarity principle, legislative and non-legislative measures have been implemented targeting areas where action at the EU level brings real added value. Although no international policy effort integrates circular-economy approaches, circularity principles would have an important role in helping organizations to hedge against volatility in the prices of commodities. This is why the European Commission is proposing that the product sustainability principles will guide broader policy and legislative developments in the future. The CEAP encourages the broader application of well-designed economic instruments, such as environmental taxation, including landfill and incineration taxes, and enable Member States to use value added tax (VAT) rates to promote circular economy activities that target final consumers, notably repair services.

Environmental taxation could be a suitable instrument and the right policy option to reduce plastic pollution in the current environmental emergency. It can also provide the right signal to citizens, producers and industry to change behaviours and contribute to meet the ambitious environmental targets. Taxes on single-use plastics for example (in the UK, Italy or Spain) have a vocation to be environmental but at the same time they can also pursue other goals, such as raising revenues for the economic recovery[23].

---

20. See Kingston, S., *Greening EU Competition Law and Policy*, CUP, 2011, and Holmes, S., D. Middelschulte, D. & Snoep M. (eds), *Competition Law, Climate Change & Environmental Sustainability*, Concurrences, 2021.
21. For a critical assessment before the reform, see Maillo, J., "Balancing Environmental Protection, Competitiveness and Competition: A Critical Assessment of the GBER and EEAG", *European State Aid Law Quaterly*, vol. 16, n. 1, 2017, pp. 4-10.
22. European Commission, Communication: *A new Circular Economy Action Plan. For a cleaner and more competitive Europe*, 11 March 2020, (COM) 98 final.
23. Villar Ezcurra, M. and Bisogno, M., "Are plastic taxes environmental or fiscal measures? A legal analysis of the Italian and Spanish cases under the circular economy strategy", in

The principle of national financing of environmental measures is included in the TFEU as an expression of solidarity within the EU. In this sense and without prejudice to the importance of certain measures adopted by the Union, Member States shall also finance and implement the environmental policy. This principle is accompanied by a rule that partially compensates the potential negative effects for national budgets: if a measure involves costs deemed disproportionate for the public authorities of a Member State, such measure shall lay down appropriate provisions in the form of temporary derogations, and/or financial support from the Cohesion Fund[24]. Particularly, the European funds for a just transition represent an important tool to condition access to the resources with the aim of reaching climate neutrality objectives. At least a minimum of 50% of co-national finance is required for the most advanced regions.

Currently, the EU financial support linked to Next Generation EU and the 2021-2027 EU budget are the basic lever for all the national ecological transition processes. The EU's 2021-2027 long-term budget, including the NextGenerationEU recovery instrument, amounts to €2.018 trillion in current prices. The package consists of the long-term budget, the 2021-2027 multiannual financial framework, which amounts to €1.211 trillion in current prices, combined with the temporary recovery instrument, NextGenerationEU, of €806.9 billion[25].

4. THE REINFORCEMENT OF EU STATE AID RULES ALIGNED WITH THE EGD

One important concern for good tax and climate change governance is the expansion of EU competition policy to tax issues and its effective contribution to the environmental objectives. The EU State aid rules are currently the major constraint on the tax sovereignty of national legislators[26] mainly because the expansion of the notion of "State aid" allows for a great intervention of the European Commission. If this is accepted, the question is whether the current approach to tax measures and their assessment in the environmental and climate areas are well balanced.

Weishaar S., Ashiabor H., Milne J., Andersen M. S. (eds.), *Green Deals in the Making, Critical Issues in Environmental Taxation*, vol. 24, Edward Elgar Publishing, 2022, pp.185-199.

24. See Article 192 paras. 4 and 5 of the TFEU.
25. See European Commission, *The EU's 2021-2027 long-term Budget and Next Generation EU. Facts and Figures*, April 2021.
26. See, among others, Schön, W., "Tax Legislation and the notion of fiscal aid: a review of 5 years of European Jurisprudence", in Richelle I. et al. (eds.), *State Aid Law and Business Taxation*, Springer, 2016, p. 3.

To answer this question, the two sides of tax incentives should be considered: on the one hand, any measure acting as an incentive is a useful tool to correct market failures, to support the national economy and to create new economic activities, and on the other hand, incentives can be a source of distortions of competition, significant costs to governments and opportunities for lobbying abuse. The assessment of a tax incentive for environmental purposes for example in an EU State aid context will depend on the balancing test applied between two different aims: (i) to protect market integration; or (ii) to ensure competition. This general statement is also valid in the fiscal field.

Any aid must be checked objectively against the notion of article 107 (1) TFEU under the well-known circumstances:[27] the existence of an undertaking, the imputability of the measure to the state, its financing through state resources, the granting of an advantage, the selectivity of the measure and its effect on competition and trade between Member States. With a view to contributing to an easier, more transparent and more consistent application of this notion across the European Union, the 2016 Commission Notice on the notion of State aid,[28] clarifies the different constitutive elements of the notion of State aid and reminds that "the notion of State aid is an objective and legal concept defined directly by the Treaty"[29].

The debate in the fiscal literature focuses around three overlapping concepts: the notion of "advantage", the notion of "selectivity" and the notion of "discrimination". While selectivity is clear when Member States adopt ad hoc positive measures benefiting one or more undertakings, the situation is usually less clear for fiscal aid. In such cases, a three-step analysis should normally be used to assess the "material selectivity" of the measures. The first step is to identify the system of reference[30]. Secondly, it should be determined whether the measure constitutes a derogation from that

27. Art. 107 (1) TFEU states: "Save as otherwise provided in the Treaties, any aid granted by a Member State or through State resources in any form whatsoever which distorts or threatens to distort competition by favouring certain undertakings or the production of certain goods shall, in so far as it affects trade between Member States, be incompatible with the internal market."

28. See European Commission, Notice on the notion of State aid as referred to in Article 107 (1) of the Treaty on the Functioning of the European Union, OJ C 262/1 (19 July 2016).

29. See *ibid.*, at para. 5.

30. The reference system constitutes the benchmark against which the selectivity of a measure is assessed. In the case of taxes, the reference system is based on elements such as the tax base, the taxable persons, the taxable event and the tax rates. For example, a reference system could be identified regarding the corporate income tax system. See 2016 Commission Notice, at para. 134.

system in so far as it discriminates between economic operators who are in a comparable factual and legal situation, having regard to the objectives inherent in the system.

Assessing whether a derogation exists is the key element of this part of the test and allows a conclusion to be drawn as to whether the measure is prima facie selective. If the measure under scrutiny does not constitute a derogation from the reference system, it is not selective. Otherwise, if this is the case, the third step of the test is to determine whether the derogation is justified by the nature or general scheme of the (reference) system. If a prima facie selective measure is justified by the nature or general scheme of the system, it will not be considered selective and will therefore fall outside the scope of article 107 (1) TFEU[31].

In general, aid must be notified by the Member State to the European Commission according to article 108 (3) TFEU. As the compatibility of aid for environmental protection is often directly evaluated under article 107 (3) the Commission guidelines are a source of great importance for legal certainty.

In this sense, the new guidelines on State aid for climate, environmental protection and energy[32] recognised that "competition policy, and State aid rules in particular, has an important role to play in enabling and supporting the Union in fulfilling its Green Deal policy objectives. The EGD Communication specifically states that the State aid rules will be revised to take into account those policy objectives, to support a cost-effective and just transition to climate neutrality, and to facilitate the phasing out of fossil fuels, while at the same time ensuring a level-playing field in the internal market"[33]. These new guidelines reflect that revision in section 4.7 dedicated to "aid in the form of reductions

31. See *ibid.*, at para. 128. See also NL: ECJ, 8 Sept. 2011, Case C-279/08 P *Commission v. Netherlands*, para. 62; AT: ECJ, 8 Nov. 2001, Case C-143/99, *Adria-Wien Pipeline GmbH und Wietersdorfer & Peggauer Zementwerke GmbH v. Finanzlandesdirektion für Kärnten*; IT: ECJ, 8 Sept. 2011, Joined Cases C-78/08 to C-80/08, *Amministrazione delle Finanze, Agenzia delle Entrate v. Paint Graphos Scarl; Adige Carni Scrl, in liquidation v. Ministero dell' Economia e delle Finanze, Agenzia delle Entrate; Ministero delle Finanze v. Michele Franchetto*, para. 49 et seq.; and UK: ECJ, 29 Apr. 2004, Case C-308/01, *Gil Insurance Ltd and Others v. Commissioners of Customs & Excise*.
32. The new guidelines, applicable as from January 2022, create a flexible, fit-for-purpose enabling framework to help Member States provide the necessary support to reach the Green Deal objectives in a targeted and cost-effective manner. European Commission, Annexes to the Communication to the Commission. Approval of the content of a draft for a Communication from the Commission on the Guidelines on State aid for climate, environmental protection and energy, 21 December 2021 (C(2021) 9817 final.
33. Para. 4 of the new guidelines, *supra n.* 26.

in environmental taxes and parafiscal levies". Still, as laid down in previous guidelines, when environmental taxes are harmonized, the Commission may apply a simplified approach to assess the necessity and proportionality of the aid. In the context of Directive 2003/96/EC (the so-called Energy Taxation Directive, ETD) the Commission may apply a simplified approach for tax reductions respecting the Union minimum tax level.

Finally, a brief reference to the flexibility of these measures should be noted. The outbreak of the COVID-19 virus has had a significant economic impact. The various containment measures adopted by Member States, such as travel restrictions, quarantines and closures, have hit the cultural, entertainment and tourism sectors particularly hard. The Temporary Framework was adopted on the basis of article 107 (3)(b) TFEU and complements other possibilities available to Member States, in particular the possibility under article 107 (2)(b) TFEU to compensate certain undertakings or sectors for the damage directly caused by exceptional occurrences such as the virus outbreak. Amendments were adopted on 3 April, 8 May, 29 June, 13 October 2020, 28 January 2021 and 18 November 2021, extending the scope of the Temporary Framework[34]. The Temporary Framework allows for a more simplified approach to the promotion of green investments with public financial support and has been translated into an increased use of the approved COVID-19 measures. Although the flexibility created by the temporary State aid regime and the decisive action of the European Central Bank have created room for national action to prevent the economy from collapsing and to protect businesses, jobs and livelihoods, the large differences in the amount of State aid granted by EU Member States have the potential to distort a level playing field within the European Union.

III. ENVIRONMENTAL TAXATION CONCERNS

In the EU, national governments are free to decide how to exploit their energy resources, what mix of energy sources they prefer to rely on (with the exception of renewable energy for which national targets are settled at the EU level) and how they tax or subsidize energy. Taxes being a central aspect of national sovereignty, most Member States have introduced taxes on energy products. However, different approaches to energy taxation may create

34. A consolidated version of the Temporary Framework as adopted on 19 March 2020 and its amendments is available at *https://ec.europa.eu/competition-policy/system/files/2021-11/TF_consolidated_version_amended_18_nov_2021_en_2.pdf* (accessed 29 December 2021). The authentic versions of the Temporary Framework are those published in the Official Journal of the European Union.

obstacles to trade and some national regulations may come into conflict with EU law. As the establishment of the internal market is very close to the core of national tax sovereignty, most of the energy taxes are harmonized at EU level.

There is general scepticism over whether important societal values — like to protect the environment — can be achieved through the tax system[35]. Nevertheless, the role of regulatory taxes have been reinforced in these years because environmental challenges and tax law are closely related topics. The crucial position of taxes in achieving net zero carbon emissions is widely recognised in the economic literature[36]. Particularly, the so-called "environmental taxes" seek to provide the right price signals to the market and to promote changes in the national tax systems. In this sense, the UN 2030 Sustainable Development Agenda clearly indicates that taxes can play a key role in the implementation of the seventeen regulatory goals — referred to as the "Sustainable Development Goals" (SDGs) — that it includes. These goals are broad and ambitious, going from ending poverty (SDG 1) to ensuring access to affordable and sustainable energy (SDG 7) and achieving gender equality (SDG 5). Aside from the EU and the OECD, it is striking to note that the United Nations also perceives tax measures "as regulatory and as coordination instruments to achieve its 2030 Agenda"[37].

Climate change is one of the most urgent challenges that the international community currently faces. Based on the calculations of the European Commission, the costs of air pollution, GHGs and water pollution alone amount to at least €750 billion per year across the EU[38]. A broad range of policy instruments can be used to curb carbon emissions. Economic instruments, in particular taxes and emissions trading, are vital tools for any comprehensive mitigation strategy to implement the PPP in an effective way.

However, as the European Court of Auditors has confirmed, many opportunities for a more rigorous application of the PPP in the EU have still been missed[39]. In comparison with other existing alternatives (e. g., EU ETS),

35. Barker, W. B., "The relevance of a concept of tax", in Peeters, B. (ed.) *The concept of tax*, EATLP-IBFD, 2005, p. 29.
36. The idea of a tax that corrects negative externalities caused by pollution dates back to the early 1900s to the figure of Pigou, A. C., *The Economics of Welfare*, Palgrave Macmillan London, 1920.
37. Dourado, A. P., Pirlot, A., "Taxes and Regulation", *Intertax*, Volume 48, Issue 4, pp. 356-359.
38. European Commission, *Green taxation and other economic instruments. Internalizing environmental costs to make the polluter pay*, September 2021, p. 80.
39. European Court of Auditors, *The Polluter Pays Principle: Inconsistent application across EU environmental policies and actions*, Special Report no. 12, 2021.

environmental taxes have additional advantages: (i) easier implementation; (ii) less bureaucracy; and (iii) the possibility of using tax revenue to protect public interests[40].

As we have remarked in other contributions, environmental and energy issues intersect in a particularly strong way in the policy area of climate change, given the need to reduce emissions from fossil fuels and shift to clean energy practices. Precisely, in this context, it is important to clarify the impact of tax benefits on the energy sector, its design and the constraints of the European and international laws to the tax authorities to promote environmental protection. However, it can be difficult to reconcile trade with clean energy objectives. Indeed, governmental policy instruments that promote clean practices can distort market competition at the international, national or sub-national level. For example, they may intervene in the market by providing subsidies or tax benefits to encourage renewable energy and energy conservation or to protect industries at risk during the transition to a greener economy. This is why the integration of EU State aid policy and tax policy is of great importance in the field of energy taxation. In addition, the Commission's review of State aid rules is a priority, with regard to actions taken to facilitate investments, in order to allow targeted interventions to promote energy and environmental investments, ensuring a level playing field and respecting the integrity of the single market[41].

1. THE CONCEPT OF ENVIRONMENTAL TAX

One of the problems for improving the EU legislation on energy taxation is that there is not a common understanding of what is an environmental tax.

Frequently, economists adopt a broad concept using the expression of "carbon taxes´ which refers to the idea of setting prices at the right level by considering environmental externalities. In contrast, a strict concept is included in regulations and also defined in several judgments at national or European level. At the beginning the term "environmental tax" included

40. See Bowen, A., "*Carbon pricing: How best to use the revenues? Grantham Research Institute on Climate Change and the Environment*", Policy Brief, LSE, November 2015. Steenkamp, L. A., "A classification framework for carbon tax revenue use", *Climate Policy*, vol. 21, n. 7, 2021, pp. 897-911; Bretschger, L., Smulders S., "Challenges for a sustainable resource use: Uncertainty, trade, and climate policies", *Journal of Environmental Economics and Management*, vol. 64, n. 3, 2012, pp. 279-287.

41. See Villar Ezcurra, M., "State Aids and Taxation in the Energy Sector: looking for a new approach", in Villar Ezcurra M. (ed.), *State aids, taxation and the energy sector*, Thomson Reuters Aranzadi, 2017, p. 38.

all levies which had an environmental protection purpose or whose resources were allocated to the environment. Then, for statistical reasons, the European Commission started considering environmental taxes as levies whose tax base is a physical quantity with a proven negative impact on the environment[42]. However, one common characteristic is that by taxing bad behaviour, environmental taxation acts as an incentive for more sustainable behaviour.

The ECJ has defined what an environmental tax is, for different purposes, on numerous occasions. In the recent judgment handed down on June 22, 2023, *Endesa and TEAC* (C-833/21), it is insisted on the relevance of its configuration discouraging the consumption of a product harmful to the environment, according to the *polluter pays principle*, although this principle is not explicitly mentioned. The judgment considers that while the predetermined allocation of the revenue of a tax to budgetary purposes may be a factor to be taken into account in order to establish the existence of a "specific purpose", such an allocation, which is merely a matter of the internal organisation of a Member State's budget, cannot in itself be a sufficient condition for classifying a tax as environmental, since each Member State may decide to earmark the proceeds of a tax for the financing of specific expenditure, irrespective of the purpose pursued (para. 40). Even if there is no mechanism for earmarking the revenue for environmental purposes, such a specific purpose may be presumed to exist if the tax is structurally designed, in particular in terms of its objective and the rate of taxation, to influence the behaviour of taxpayers in such a way as to facilitate the specific environmental objective to be achieved, i. e. better protection of the environment, for example by taxing the products concerned heavily in order to discourage their consumption or by encouraging the use of other products whose effects are in principle less harmful to the environment (paras. 46, 50, 57).

Furthermore, according to the ECJ, this measure can be considered as having a "double effect", both as a contribution to the budget and as an influence on behaviour. Such measures are likely to generate substantial budgetary revenues when they are introduced, which will be reduced in the long term, once they have achieved their environmental objective, as taxpayers adjust their behaviour (para. 51). Therefore, it is concluded that "if a tax discourages the consumption of a product harmful to the environment, it should be considered as contributing to the protection of the environment" (para. 55). The Court points out that the structure of the tax is indeed capable of encouraging the use of energy products which are less harmful

42. European Commission, *Statistics on Environmental taxes*, 28 July 1996, p. 3.

to the environment and that this design, in itself, attracts an impact on the environmental objective. In support of its argument and in order to clarify what constitutes a specific purpose, it relies on two precedents, *Statoil Fuel & Retail* (C-553/13) and *Vapo Atlantic* (C-460/21).

Although there are other relevant cases that were not cited in the judgment, this particular instance reinforces the importance of identifying what the key features of an environmental tax are. The criterion developed in *Transportes Jordi Besora* on the issue of the relevance of considering the entire tax structure and the need for maximum specification of the extrabudgetary purpose of the tax is not taken into account in this judgment, although the direct link between the use of the income and the purpose of the tax in question has been recalled (*Transportes Jordi Besora*, C-82/12 para. 30). The *British Aggregates* case *T-210/02 REBV)* is also noteworthy, in particular with regard to the assessment of the existence of asymmetric taxation and possible tax differentiation liable to undermine the environmental objective pursued by the national legislation; this judgment was considered to fall within the scope of State aid law *(British Aggregates* para. 88 et seq.) Finally, *Austria v Commission* (T-251/11) showed the importance of the categorization of energy taxes in terms of the relevance of the distinction between harmonised taxes, non-harmonised taxes and special-purpose tax systems (*Austria v Commission*, para. 169).

The ECJ has again ruled on the conditions that must be met for a national tax to be regarded as a tax introduced "for environmental policy reasons". In other words, it determines when the tax has the character of an "environmental tax".

It is stated in this judgment that there are two alternative criteria to consider: on the one hand, the direct link or specific allocation of the use of the revenue to the extrabudgetary purpose and, on the other hand, the design of the tax structure, including in particular the tax base or the tax rate, in the sense that it influences the behaviour of taxpayers in a way that makes it easier to ensure better protection of the environment.

Besides, in the environmental tax reform's theory (ETR) the so-called "Pigouvian taxes" are conceived as figures created with the aim to allow a transformation of national tax systems. In its original frame, the new resources are supposed to allow a reduction of the fiscal pressure on labour incomes. However, as experience shows, recent waves of ETRs around the world no longer aim at a "double dividend" (financial and environmental), but at introducing new legislative packages including financial measures to support vulnerable situations. Therefore, the possible distributional effects of environmental tax reforms and the role of taxation in mitigating climate change should be highlighted.

In the European Union, the emission trading system (ETS) and the energy taxation directive (ETD) are both economic instruments setting carbon pricing in a complementary way. A carbon pricing instruments can also be used to prevent carbon leakage and a loss of competitiveness for domestic enterprises, as in the case of the CBAM recently approved. The reforms of the EU's ETS and ETD and the introduction of the CBAM are central to achieve the EGD objectives.

2. THE ROLE OF THE POLLUTER PAYS PRINCIPLE

The PPP was firstly affirmed in a recommendation adopted by the OECD in 1972 and subsequently set out in article 16 of the 1992 Rio Declaration on Environment and Sustainable Development. As for European sources, in 1987 it was established in article 130R of the Treaty of Amsterdam, and today it is recognised in article 191 (2) TFEU.

The interpretation of this principle is controversial. It has been subject to many analyses, including fiscal ones. It has not been always understood in the same way in all the Member States' legal systems. The fiscal interpretation of this principle justifies the application of fiscal measures to polluter, who must bear the costs in proportion to the pollution he causes, according to a remedial and preventive logic. Although it is mentioned in many provisions of the EU directives and regulations, a recent analysis by the European Court of Auditors states that its application remains incomplete in environmental legislation[43]. This means that to reach so important climate change objectives it is crucial to remark the role of the polluter pays principle also in the taxation field. In the end, the need to review national and EU legislation and particularly the use or "bad use" of tax incentives is crucial. In particular, this is clear in the reform process of the ETD as well as in the implementation of environmental tax reforms in the EU countries.

3. THE WINDFALL PROFIT TAXES

In May 2021 the European Commission published its REPowerEU communication[44] which aims to safeguard and secure energy supplies. To

43. European Court of Auditors, *The Polluter Pays Principle: Inconsistent application across EU environmental policies and actions*, Special Report no. 12, 2021.
44. European Commission, Communication: *REPowerEU Plan*, 15 May 2022, COM (2022) 230 final.

raise funds for new renewable energy products and mitigate high energy prices on consumers, the Commission called on Member States to consider temporary tax measures on windfall profits.

The legal basis used by the Regulation (EU) is article 122 (1) TFEU, which allows the adoption of "measures appropriate to the economic situation, in particular if severe difficulties arise in the supply of certain products, notably in the area of energy". The temporary solidarity contribution has therefore not been adopted unanimously and legitimacy issues may arise, especially if levies or taxes established at national level change from temporary to permanent measures.

The rationale for the adoption of the measure is to provide a rapid and coordinated response at Union level, which allows, in a spirit of solidarity, to generate additional revenue for national authorities to provide financial assistance to households and businesses severely affected by the sharp rise in energy prices, while ensuring a level playing field across the Union. Two types of obligations are imposed on Member States. Firstly, the obligation to apply these measures to windfall profits, in accordance with the Regulation, on a temporary basis[45], unless they have enacted equivalent national measures and, secondly, the obligation to inform the European Commission of the measures adopted and the use of the public revenue generated by them[46].

The implementation of these kind of measure can jeopardize the internal market and in particular the electricity market. Indeed, the diversity of reactions at national level may lead to new legal problems with EU fundamental freedoms and principles since a solidarity contribution is still an economic burden — whether it is called a tax or not and whether it is a tax or not — which could have been resolved technically on the basis of tax directives or as a result of political coordination.

IV. THE CORE OF THE EGD: TOWARDS A FAIR AND GREEN TAX FRAMEWORK

A multidisciplinary and holistic approach is provided by the European Commission in the European Green Deal to develop an ambitious holistic strategy on climate change[47]. Its main objective is to transform the EU into

45. Article 18, Regulation (EU) 2022/1854.
46. Article 19, para. 4 Regulation (EU) 2022/1854.
47. European Commission, Communication: *The European Green Deal*, 11 December 2019, COM (2019) 640 final.

a modern, resource-efficient and competitive economy, ensuring zero net greenhouse gas emissions by 2050, decoupling economic growth from resource use and leaving no one behind.

1. THE "FIT FOR 55" LEGISLATIVE PACKAGE

In 2021 the European Commission presented the "Fit for 55" package in order to support its commitment to reduce net GGE by at least 55 per cent by 2030. The package represents a new policy action plan on how to reach Europe's climate targets, in line with its ambition to become the first climate-neutral continent by 2050. The package contains many legislative proposals to revise the European environmental legal framework. Some of the key measures to achieve the EU Green Deal's objectives are analysed in the in the following paragraphs: the extension of the ETS; the implementation of a *carbon border adjustment mechanism* (CBAM)[48]; the revision of the ETD.

Within the Council, the proposals are dealt with in four Council formations: Environment, Energy, Transport, and Economic and Financial Affairs. Most of the discussions in the Council have highlighted the strong linkages between the proposals. Some proposals have already been transposed into legislation (e. g. Regulation (EU) 2023/957, Directive (EU) 2023/959 and 2023/959 on ETS, Regulation (EU) 2023/956 on CBAM, Regulation (EU) 2023/955 on the Social Climate Fund, Regulation (EU) 2023/851 to strengthen standard emissions for cars) while others are still under negotiation.

1.1. The Revision of the Emission Trading System

Three proposals are dealt with under ETS reform[49]: a proposal to amend the ETS Directive, the Market Stability Reserve (MSR) Decision and the MRV

48. See Regulation (EU) 2023/956 of the European Parliament and of the Council of 10 May 2023 establishing a carbon border adjustment mechanism.

49. See all the Proposals and Regulations and Directives published on the Official journal of the EU L 130, Volume 66 of 16 May 2023. Regulation (EU) 2023/95 of 10 may 2023 establishing a Social Climate Fund and amending Regulation (EU) 2021/1060; Regulation (EU) 2023/956 of 10 may 2023, establishing a CBAM; Regulation (EU) 2023/957 of 10 may 2023 amending Regulation (EU) 2015/757 in order to provide for the inclusion of maritime transport activities in the EU ETS and for the monitoring reporting and verification of emissions of additional greenhouse gases and emissions from additional ship types; Directive (EU) 2023/958 of 10 may 2023 amending Directive 2003/87/EC as regards aviation´s contribution target and the appropriate implementation of a global market-based measure and Directive (EU) 2023/959 of 10 may 2023 amending Directive 2003/87/EC establishing a system for greenhouse gas

shipping Regulation ("general ETS"), a proposal to amend the ETS Directive as regards the aviation sector ("ETS aviation") and a separate proposal to amend the MSR Decision.

The ETS revision aims in particular to increase the ambitious reduction target for ETS sectors by 62% by 2030; to phase out free allocation in some sectors accompanied by the phase-in of the carbon border adjustment mechanism (CBAM); to gradually include maritime sector emissions into the EU ETS, with the obligation to surrender allowances rising from 40% of verified emissions in 2024 to 100% in 2026; to implement a new ETS 2 for buildings, road transport, and other fuel sectors, except agriculture and land-use, starting in 2027 or 2028 if energy prices are deemed exceptionally elevated; and to strengthen commitment to use ETS revenues to address distributional effects and stimulate innovation.

The ETS is at the heart of the EU climate policy. There seems to be a general consensus that the ETS will have to play its cost-effective part in meeting the EU's increased ambition. However, there are differing views on the proposed changes. In this context, there have been some calls to explore options to further increase the ambition of the ETS, but also concerns about the potential impact of certain parts of the proposals on both economic sectors and households, underlining the need to take into account different national situations.

Particular attention has been given to the proposed phase-out of free allocation in the ETS for sectors covered by the carbon border adjustment mechanism (CBAM).

1.2. The Adoption of the Carbon Border Adjustment Mechanism

Traditionally, CBAM are described as regulatory instruments that can be used to mitigate climate change, but also have a positive impact on trade, climate leadership and even public finance. The objective of the CBAM is to prevent that the emissions reduction efforts of the EU are offset by increasing emissions outside its borders through relocation of production to non-EU countries (where polices applied to fight climate change are less ambitious than those of the EU) or increased imports of carbon-intensive products. The EU CBAMs was adopted on 10 May 2023[50] and entered into

emission allowance trading within the Union and Decision (EU) 2015/1814 concerning the establishment and operation of a market stability reeve for the union greenhouse gas emission trading system.

50. Regulation (EU) 2023/956 of 10 May 2023 establishing a carbon border adjustment mechanism.

force in its transitional phase from the 1 October 2023, with the first reporting period for importers of certain energy-intensive products (cement, iron and steel, aluminium, fertilisers, hydrogen production and electricity) ending on 31 January 2024. The objective of this transition period is to serve as a pilot and learning period for all stakeholders (importers, producers and authorities) and to collect useful information on embedded emissions to refine the methodology for the definitive period. After the transitional period the mechanism would require importers to pay a carbon price equivalent to the price imposed in the EU. The price of the CBAM certificates will be calculated depending on the weekly average auction price of EU ETS allowances expressed in €/tonne of CO2 emitted. As Pirlot suggested CBAMs "can serve as straightforward multi-purpose instruments" and "the design of the EU CBAM is inconsistent with the Commission's main objectives of promoting fair competition and climate mitigation in line with the Paris Agreement" because the EU CBAM proposal is primarily an instrument of climate leadership[51]. The CBAM seeks to serve as an essential element of the Union's toolbox for meeting the objective of a climate neutrality by 2050 in line with the Paris Agreement by addressing the risk of carbon leakage that results from the Union's increased climate ambition. The CBAM is expected to also contribute to promoting decarbonisation in third countries[52].

1.3. The Important Role of the Energy Taxation Directive

The taxation of energy products and electricity plays an important role in the area of climate and energy policy. It can act as economic incentives driving a successful energy transition, driving low greenhouse gas investments and energy savings, while contributing to sustainable growth. However, the current legislation in force, Directive 2003/96/EC of 27 October 2003, introduced twenty years ago to ensure the proper functioning of the internal market is no longer aligned with current EU climate and energy objectives. In fact, it does not adequately promote greenhouse gas emissions reductions, energy efficiency and the take-up of electricity and alternative fuels (renewable hydrogen, synthetic fuels, advanced biofuels, etc.) and does not provide sufficient incentives for investments in clean technologies. Besides, the ETD *de facto* favours fossil fuel use. Highly divergent national rates are applied in combination with a wide range of tax exemptions and reductions which are not aligned with the objectives of the EGD. Finally,

51. See Pirlot, A., "Carbon Border Adjustment Measures: A straightforward multi-purpose Climate Change Instrument?", *Journal of Environmental Law*, Volume 34, Issue 1, March 2022, pp. 25-52.
52. See Recital 10 of the CBAM Regulation.

the ETD is no longer contributing to the proper functioning of the internal market as the minimum tax rates have lost their converging effect on national tax rates. Minimum rates are low as they have not been updated since 2003 although national rates are significantly above the ETD minima in most cases. In any case, the ETD minimum no longer prevents a "race to the bottom" nor do they constitute a floor for taxation. All this, joined to the existence of exemptions and reductions, increases the fragmentation of the internal market and distorts the level playing field between the different sectors of the economy that are involved. In addition, there are some aspects of the ETD that lack clarity, relevance and coherence, which creates legal uncertainty. These include, among others, the definition of taxable products and uses that are out of the scope of the Directive and the interpretation of the exemption related to motor fuels used in air and waterborne navigation.

The main changes included in the proposal[53] for a revised Directive addressed these problems with the following measures: (i) Fuels will start being taxed according to their energy content and environmental performance rather than their volume. This will better reflect the environmental impact of individual fuels, helping businesses and consumers to make cleaner, more climate-friendly choices; (ii) the way in which energy products are categorised for tax purposes will be simplified to ensure that the most polluting fuels are subject to the highest levels of taxation; (iii) exemptions for certain products and home heating will be phased out, so that fossil fuels can no longer be taxed below minimum rates and (iv) fossil fuels used as fuel for intra-EU air transport, maritime transport and fishing should no longer be fully exempt from energy taxation in the EU — a crucial measure given the role of these sectors in energy consumption and pollution.

2. GREENING THE EUROPEAN BUDGETS

To better support the objectives of Union policies and to reduce Member States' contributions based on gross national income to the Union's annual budget, the European Council held in July 2020 concluded that the Union will work in the coming years to reform the own resources system and introduce new own resources.

As a first step, a new category of own resources based on national contributions calculated on the basis of non-recycled plastic packaging waste was introduced in December 2020 in order to ensure the financing of the

53. Proposal for a Council Directive restructuring the Union framework for the taxation of energy products and electricity (recast), 14 July 2021, COM(2021) 563 final.

European Union's annual budget[54]. At the same time, Member States are free to take the most suitable measures to achieve goals related to the reduction of plastic packaging waste, in line with the principle of subsidiarity. This new resource to finance the EU budget is in force since January 2021. It is a national contribution based on the amount of non-recycled plastic packaging waste. Member States apply a uniform rate of euro €0.80/tonne on the amount of plastic resulting from the difference between what was produced and what was recycled. This contribution is accompanied by a mechanism to prevent excessive contributions from less wealthy Member States. The principal aims of this plastic measure are to encourage Member States to reduce the consumption of single-use plastic products, promote recycling and boost the circular economy. It is important to stress that the EU levy is not a tax and the European regulations neither recommend nor require Member States to introduce a tax.

Some critical issues concerning the introduction of this measure can be stressed. It complies with the EU environmental policy objectives and principles (particularly with the PPP, in fact the amount of the contribution increases as the amount of non-recycled plastic packaging waste increases) but as expressed by the European Court of Auditors it could lead to a decrease in revenues in the long run, if ecologically effective[55].

The European Commission proposed as a second step an amendment of the Own Resources Decision to introduce three new categories of own resources based on: (i) the CBAM; (ii) the revised EU ETS and (iii) a share of the residual profits of the largest and most profitable multinational enterprises that are allocated to EU Member States following the agreement by OECD/G20 Inclusive Framework on Base Erosion and Profit Shifting to address the Tax Challenges Arising from the Digitalization of the Economy (*OECD/G20 Inclusive Framework Agreement*). These revenues will be used for both the repayment of *Next Generation EU* and the financing of the Social Climate Fund. This proposal is consistent with and complementary to the proposals included in the "Fit for 55" package. The Commission emended its 2021 proposal by publishing an adjusted package on 20 June 2023[56]. It proposed to introduce a new temporary own resource, a national contribution calculated

54. European Council, Decision 2020/2053 of 14 December 2020 on the system of own resources of the EU and repealing Decision 2014/335/EU.
55. European Court of Auditors opinion n. 5, 2018, par. 42. This concern had been raised by the European Court of Auditors with respect to the plastic contribution proposed in 2018 but is still valid with respect to the one that entered into force in 2021.
56. European, Commission, Communication: *An adjusted package for the next generation of own resources*, 20 June 2023, COM(2023) 330 final.

as 0.5% of the notional EU company profit base, an indicator calculated by Eurostat on the basis of the national account statistics. This measure would later be replaced by a possible contribution from BEFIT (Business in Europe: Framework for Income Taxation).

V. CONCLUSION

In the EU, the future challenges associated with the energy transition cannot be tackled without a good governance and without fiscal tools. It is urgent to review the regulatory framework and the ETD in particular because the PPP is not sufficiently reflected in practice in EU Law, as the European Court of Auditors, among others, has stated.

There is some reason to be optimistic because new approaches in governance issues are remarkable. The European Court of Justice is playing an important guiding role by emphasising the conceptual autonomy of EU law and the legal relevance of different categorisations of taxes (harmonised and non-harmonised taxes, direct or indirect taxes, etc.). In some recent cases, particular attention is applied to the qualification of a levy as an "environmental tax" and the need to consider the definition of what its "specific purpose" is, to resolve the conformity of national tax measures with the legal requirements contained in the tax harmonisation directives. Additionally, the significance of non-budgetary allocation criterion is minimized by stating that the direct use of resources for regulatory purposes is a factor to consider when we are in the presence of an environmental tax or, in the words of the Court of Justice of a tax introduced "for reasons of environmental policy". All in all, the traditional criterion of the incentive effect to define an "environmental tax" is reaffirmed by the ECJ case-law when it is insisted that a tax that discourages the consumption of a product harmful to the environment must be considered as contributing to the protection of the environment, decoupling the assessment of the incentive effect of the use of the tax revenue and the budgetary or extrabudgetary nature of the tax considered. These rulings take a further step in the predominance of the finalist interpretation over more formalist criteria, such as the budgetary application of tax revenues and can be consider a good way to reinforce the role of the PPP.

Stronger governance, particularly in the areas of climate change, energy and taxation, is needed to mobilise investment and plan infrastructure and interconnections if the ambitious strategy of the EGD is to be truly successful. Not forgetting that the intersection of tax and competition policy (especially, State aid law) can also play a key role in promoting the right green investments to address the transition, both by Member States and private actors.

The European strategy to combat climate change is an interesting case study. Indeed, it appears capable not only of producing effects on the national legal systems of the Member States (due to the primacy of EU law), but also of influencing the response of other non-European countries (e. g. the implementation of CBAM). For this reason, strengthening environmental governance and promoting the use of environmental tax instruments at the European level could be a key element in tackling the energy transition and the climate neutrality.

The Eu-China Trade Partnership from a European Tax Perspective

ELENA MASSEGLIA MISZCZYSZYN, MARIE LAMENSCH, EDOARDO TRAVERSA, MARTA VILLAR EZCURRA & FABRIZIO PASCUCCI

I. THE EVOLUTION OF EU-CHINA TRADE PARTNERSHIP AND TAX-RELATED ISSUES

ELENA MASSEGLIA MISZCZYSZYN[1]

1. INTRODUCTION

The People's Republic of China ("China") nowadays is a strategic partner of the European Union ("EU"), as well as a strategic rival, proposing alternative models of governance in certain fields and being a leading technological power.

The EU-China trade relationship started officially in 1975. Since then, the soaring globalised economy and the intensification of digitalization broadened the connections between the two parties, and so the interactions of the tax systems who lead to an increase of the risk of tax-related barriers and distortions on the one hand, and on the other hand the exploitation of mismatches between different tax regimes by businesses operating internationally. International trade and taxation are strictly related.

Even if sometimes it is alleged the lack of transparency and of level playing field on the Chinese side, it is undeniable that the EU and China are still open to cooperation and that the EU is showing its intention to found a balance in trade and tax matters, insisting on reciprocity, to minimize the mentioned risks.

---

1. PhD candidate at the Université Catholique de Louvain.

2. EVOLUTION OF RELATIONSHIPS FROM THE 1978 TRADE AGREEMENT TO THE CAI AND THE BEPS ACTION PLAN: BRIDGING THE LINKS

Ten years after the creation of the EU Customs Union, a first agreement marked the beginning of trade relationships between the EU and China, despite the different nature of the interests of the two contracting parties underlying the signature —primarily economic for the first and political for the second[2]. On 3rd April 1978, the official signing ceremony took place in Brussels — it was the first occasion on which the institutions of the European Economic Community ("EEC") received a member of the Chinese government[3]— and on 1st June 1978 the *Trade Agreement between the European Economic Community and the People's Republic of China* entered into force[4] ("1978 Trade Agreement").

As far as tariffs are concerned, the two parties agreed to apply the most-favoured-nation ("MFN") clause[5]. So, any favourable provisions as regards customs duties and any taxes and charges in connection with importation and exportation of goods and services under other treaties with other contracting parties shall be accorded in the exchanges between the nine EEC countries[6] and China — exception made for customs unions, free trade areas, advantages to neighbouring countries and obligations undertaken under international commodity agreements. One of the main clauses of the General Agreement on Tariffs and Trade ("GATT")[7] were therefore included in this first agreement, even if China was not yet a member of the GATT/ WTO (*see below*).

2. ECC was interested in signing a trade agreement with China for "economic gains", while the reasons encouraging China to these negotiations were mainly political, see Xiaotong, Z. "Linkage Power. How the EU and China managed their economic and trade relationship", in Teló, M., Chun, D. and Xiaotong, Z. (eds.), *Deepening the EU-China Partnership. Bridging Institutional and Ideational Differences in an Unstable World, Routledge*, Oxon and New York, 2018, p. 155-156.
3. See European Communities: The Council, *Signing of the trade agreement between the EEC and the People's Republic of China*. Speech by K. B. Andersen, President in Office of the Council, Minister for Foreign Affairs of the Kingdom of Denmark, Brussels, 3 April 1978.
4. Council Regulation (EEC) No 946/78 of 2 May 1978 concerning the conclusion of the Trade Agreement between the European Economic Community and the People's Republic of China.
5. Art. 2 of the 1978 Trade Agreement.
6. Belgium, Denmark, France, Germany, Ireland, Italy, Luxembourg, Netherlands and United Kingdom.
7. Art. 1 of the GATT.

Moreover, China undertook to consider Community imports in a favourable light and the ECC of nine, for its part, committed itself to endeavour to increasingly liberalize imports of Chinese origin, extending the list of liberalized products and augment the amounts of quotas[8]. To boost the cooperation, they also agreed to create a Joint Committee.

Considering the satisfactory application of the 1978 Trade Agreement[9], the EEC and China decided to enter into a new trade agreement —the *Agreement on Trade and Economic Cooperation between the European Economic Community and the People's Republic of China* ("1985 Trade Agreement")— which was signed on 21st May 1985 and entered into force on 1st October 1985. As regards tariffs, the terms of the 1985 Trade Agreement were the same as those of the 1978 Trade Agreement: the MFN was reiterated. As it is evoked by the official title, the novelty aspect with respect to the previous treaty relates to the new provisions about the *economic cooperation*, including the promotion of investments and the enhancement of a propitious framework for the latter[10]. In any case, the EEC Members States were still allowed to undertake bilateral activities and conclude agreements relating to economic cooperation[11].

The mentioned two agreements are a manifestation of the trend reversal of the Beijing glance towards the outside world, opening the doors to foreign investment[12].

This change is also perceived in the purely (international) fiscal sector. It is during the Eighties that the first double tax treaties, including those with some of the EEC countries[13], were negotiated and signed. Moreover, starting from the 1979, several acts concerning the taxation of foreign investments were enacted to attract the latter and expand economic cooperation: on 1 July 1979 the Act of the People's Republic of China on Joint Ventures Using Chinese and Foreign Investment, on 10 September 1980 the Income Tax Act of the People's Republic of China Concerning Joint Ventures with Chinese and Foreign Investment, on 13 December 1981 the Income Tax Act

8. Art. 4 of the 1978 Trade Agreement.
9. Preamble of the Agreement on Trade and Economic Cooperation between the European Economic Community and the People's Republic of China.
10. Art. 12 of the 1985 Trade Agreement.
11. Art. 14 of the 1985 Trade Agreement.
12. Auyeung, P. K., "Taxation Trends and Issues in the People's Republic of China: 1984 to 2006" in *Bulletin for International Taxation, IBFD*, 2008, p. 249
13. E. g. with France in 1984, Italy in 1986, Netherlands in 1987, United Kingdom in 1984. See *www.oecd.org*

of the People's Republic of China for Foreign Enterprises (the two latter then replaced in 1991 by the Income Tax Act of the People's Republic of China for Enterprises with Foreign Investment and Foreign Enterprises)[14].

In the period at hand, the financial flow was mainly unidirectional: from the EEC companies to China and it is also confirmed by article 13 of the 1985 Trade Agreement which drawn attention on the different levels of development of the two contracting parties[15]. However, this was about to change.

China was determined to pursue the path undertaken as increasingly market-driven economy and therefore to participate in the multilateral trading system. In 1986, China requested the resumption[16] of its status as a GATT contracting party. An early accession of China to the GATT was supported by the EEC with which Beijing carried out bilateral negotiations[17]; but due to historical, economic and political reasons it was delayed until 2001, when China acceded to the Marrakech Agreement Establishing the World Trade Organization ("WTO Agreement") and thereby became a member of the World Trade Organization ("WTO"). One of the interests of the EEC, then —since 1993— the European Community ("EC"), was to improve "the climate for European investment in China"[18] and so also to significantly whittle Chinese import tariffs on industrial and agricultural goods as well as to ameliorate the establishment and trade conditions in China for foreign companies[19]. This goal was attained quite

14. WTO, *Accession of the People's Republic of China: Decision of 10 November 2001*, WT/L/432, 23 November 2001, pp. 75-76, retrieved from *www.wto.org*; Auyeung, P. K., "Taxation Trends and Issues in the People's Republic of China: 1984 to 2006", *op. cit.*, pp. 249-251; Bao, L., "China's Tax Policy toward Enterprises with Foreign Investment: A Comprehensive Appraisal" in *Intertax*, vol. 31, n. 2, 2003, pp. 66 et seq.

15. "In view of the difference in the two Contracting Parties' levels of development, the European Economic Community is prepared, within the context of its development aid activities, within the means at its disposal, and in accordance with its rules, to continue its development activities in the People's Republic of China. / It confirms its willingness to examine the possibility of stepping up and diversifying these activities".

16. China was a signatory of the GATT in 1948, but —after the revolution in 1949— the Taiwan government announced the withdrawal from the GATT. The Beijing government never acknowledged the latter withdrawal; however, it notified the resume of the membership in 1986. See WTO Press Release, *WTO successfully concludes negotiations on China's entry*, Press/243, 17 September 2001, retrieved from *www.wto.org*.

17. Commission of the EC, *Communication from the Commission. Building a Comprehensive Partnership with China*, COM (1998)181, 1988, p. 12.

18. *Ibid.*

19. *Ibid., pp. 12-16.*

successfully. From a tax perspective, a series of important commitments were undertaken by China, *inter alia*[20]:

1. The foreign individuals and enterprises will be accorded treatment no less favourable than that accorded to those in China (even as regards border tax adjustments);
2. The elimination of subsidy programs falling within the scope of article 3 of the Agreement on Subsidies and Countervailing Measures ("SCM Agreement");
3. China will ensure the compliance of customs fees, internal taxes and charges with the GATT;
4. The elimination of all taxes and charges on exports, except for those specifically provided in the Protocol or applied in conformity with Article 6 of the GATT;
5. The notification of subsidies pursuant to Article 25 of the SCM Agreement;
6. China bound tariffs for imported goods, it committed to decrease the average bound tariff level for agricultural and industrial products and it will eliminate several tariffs and reduce others mostly by 2004 and in any case no later than 2010.

Simultaneously, in 1997 the EC Council authorised the EC Commission to negotiate a customs cooperation agreement on behalf of the EC and in 2004 it approved the *Agreement between the European Community and the Government of the People's Republic of China on cooperation and mutual administrative assistance in customs matters* ("CCMAA"). Taking also into account that "operations in breach of customs legislation including infringements of intellectual property rights are prejudicial to the economic, fiscal and commercial interests of both Contracting Parties"[21], China and the EC decided to enhance the cooperation between competent administrative authorities in ensuring the accurate assessment of customs duties and other taxes. Customs cooperation covers all matters relating to the application of customs legislation[22], including exchange of information and expertise on

20. WTO, *Accession of the People's Republic of China: Decision of 10 November 2001, op. cit.*; WTO Press Release, *WTO successfully concludes negotiations on China's entry, op. cit.*
21. Council Decision of 16 November 2004 on the conclusion of an Agreement between the European Community and the Government of the People's Republic of China on cooperation and mutual administrative assistance in customs matters, 2004/889/EC.
22. Art. 6 CCMAA.

customs techniques and procedures, exchange of personnel and training, seeking a coordinate position in the context of international organisations as well as the assistance in ensuring the proper application of customs duties (*i. e.* recovery of duties, taxes or fines, arrest or detention) and prevention and fight against fraud[23]. More recently, to reiterate and increase the effectiveness of the mutual cooperation and assistance in the field of customs, the European Commissioner for Economic and Financial Affairs and the Minister of Customs of China has signed a *Strategic Framework for Customs Cooperation for the years 2018-2020*, which *inter alia* extends the collaboration to the e-commerce sector and supports the review of the CCMAA[24]. Then, in 2021 negotiations on Strategic Framework for Customs Cooperation 2021-2024 has started[25]. Subsequently, in 2006, discussions about the update of the 1985 Trade Agreement started. Unfortunately, they have been stalled since 2011, but the negotiations evolved and lead to a China's proposal of a free trade agreement ("FTA") and later, in 2012[26], to the launch of talks about a EU-China Comprehensive Agreement on Investment ("CAI") on the basis of the EU's objective to replace all the bilateral investment treaties ("BITs") concluded by the EU Member States with China[27]. In 2016 the parties established a joint negotiating text and the negotiations rounds about the CAI were still and frequently on the Brussels and Beijing agenda in order to conclude the agreement by 2020[28]. From a EU point of view, a unitary and reassuring legal framework was needed: the comprehensive agreement that EU Commission Directorate- General for Trade and the European External Action Service ("EEAS") are bargaining is a good legal instrument. Indeed, in the late 2020, the CAI has been approved in principle.

23. Art. 6-10 CCMAA.
24. The mentioned Framework follows the *Strategic Framework for Cooperation* for the period 2010-2012 and that for the period 2014-2017. See the note to delegation of the Council of the European Union, *Enhancing EU-China Trade Security and Facilitation: Strategic Framework for Customs Cooperation 2018-2020 between the European Union and the Government of the People's Republic of China*, 22 May 2017, 9548/17.
25. Council of the European Union, *Enhancing EU-China Trade Security and Facilitation — Strategic Framework for Customs Cooperation 2021-2024 between the European Union and the Government of the People's Republic of China — Approval of entering into negotiation*, Decision to use the written procedure, 5 March 2021, 6633/2.
26. Council of the European Union, Joint Press Communiqué of the 14th EU-China Summit, 14 February 2012, 6474/12 PRESSE 50, §11, p. 2.
27. Since the entry into force of the 2009 Lisbon Treaty, the EU gained the exclusive competence for foreign direct investment. See Art. 207 TFUE.
28. The last round (the 23rd) of the negotiations for the CAI has been held in Beijing on 23-24 September 2019. See European Commission Directorate-General for Trade, *Note to the file_ Report of the 23rd round of negotiations for the EU-China Investment Agreement*, 25 September 2019, retrieved from *www.trade.ec.europa.eu*

The CAI scope goes beyond the usual dimension of investment protection and additionally cover market access that goes also through taxation. There is also a tax provision to be included in the CAI. The EU Commission Directorate-General for Taxation and Customs Union were not effectively involved at the beginning since direct taxation is part of the general exemptions — one of the last provisions of the agreement. During the 34th round, discussions broadened to taxation matters and horizontal exceptions[29], which led to the inclusion of the tax provision — Article 11 of Section VI — aimed at protecting the taxing powers of the parties. Nevertheless, there are tax-related aspects — even sensitive — that have been debated, but that are still controversial, such as the case of disinvestments and tax measures that may amount to expropriation of investors' assets (*see* para. 1.3)[30].

In the light of the above, we can affirm that the register and the matters mooted have evolved, inasmuch China is not the same developing country with which the EU signed the 1985 Trade Agreement.

Another evidence of this change is the Beijing active participation in the international forum to tackle the *BEPS* issues to protect its tax base. China is a *key partner* —not a member— of the Organisation for Economic Co-operation and Development ("OECD"), it is a member of the Global Forum on Transparency and Exchange of Information for Tax Purposes and it is committed to implement the G20/OECD Base Erosion and Profit Shifting ("BEPS") Action Plan released in 2015[31], working closely with the EU Commission which takes part in the work of the OECD, together with the majority of the EU Members States that are also OECD members[32]. This is one of the direction of changes driven by the Belt Road Initiative ("BRI") — weather at treaty level that at domestic level — , combined with

29. European Commission Directorate-General for Trade, *Note to the file. Report of the 34th round of negotiations on the EU-China Comprehensive Agreement on Investment*, 24 November 2020, TRADE. B3/7906099.

30. European Commission Directorate-General for Trade, *Note to the file: Report of the 18th round of negotiations for the EU-China Investment Agreement*, 18 July 2018; European Commission Directorate-General for Trade, *Note to the file: Report of the 19th round of negotiations for the EU-China Investment Agreement*, 13 November 2018; and European Commission Directorate-General for Trade, Note to the file: Report of the 20th round of negotiations for the EU-China Investment Agreement, 1 March 2019, retrieved from *www.trade.ec.europa.eu*.

31. China has also deposited its instrument of approval for the Multilateral Convention to Implement Tax Treaty Related Measures to Prevent BEPS in 2022; see *https://oe.cd/mli*. See also infra sections III and IV.

32. Twenty-two of the thirty eight OECD members are also EU Members States.

the progressive removal of tax barriers to facilitate Chinese outbound investments, including the strengthening of collaboration between the China State Administration of Taxation with the local officers of other countries.

3. DISTINCTIVE CHALLENGES

The (trade) relationship between Europe and China is long-established and nowadays it is acknowledged the important role of China in international tax law making. Connections rises, they are increasingly closer, and we observe a growing need to address global challenges by global solutions.

Nevertheless, several issues — due to different approaches — come to light and it seems necessary to untangle them in order to proceed on the taken route.

At the EU level, transparency is increasingly becoming one of the operative words in the tax law sector (and even beyond) under the overarching concept of good tax governance[33], in order to tackle tax fraud, evasion and avoidance, protect the integrity of tax systems and foster fair taxation[34]. To this aim, the EU encourages positive changes through cooperation and this is always on the negotiations agenda between the EU and China, ranging from the general market model and the legal system to the economic and monetary policies as well as the food safety regime or the energy sector[35].

On the same wave, to ensure good economic relations between the EU and China, the state aid policies and the regulation of the Chinese state-

33. As regards good tax governance, see Hji Panayi, C., "The Europeanization of Good Tax Governance" in *Yearbook of European Law*, vol. 36, 2017, pp. 442-495; Mosquera Valderrama, I. J., "The EU Standard of Good Governance in Tax Matters for Third (Non-EU) Countries" in *Intertax*, n. 5, 2019, pp. 454-467.
34. Reference is made in particular to the Code of Conduct for Business Taxation (Resolution of the Council and the Representatives of the Governments of the Member States, meeting within the Council of 1 December 1997 on a code of conduct for business taxation) as well as the strengthening of the administrative cooperation in the field of direct taxation and in the VAT sector (Council Directive (EU) 2011/16/EU on administrative cooperation in the field of direct taxation —also known as "DAC"— as lastly amended in 2018; Council Regulation (EU) No 904/2010 of 7 October 2010 on administrative cooperation and combating fraud in the field of value added tax, lastly amended in 2018).
35. European Commission — High Representative of the Union for Foreign Affairs and Security Policy, *Joint Communication to the European Parliament and the Council. Elements for a new EU strategy on China*, JOIN (2016) 30 final, 2016, retrieved from *www.eeas.europa.eu*; European Commission Directorate-General for Trade, *Note to the file: Report of the 16th round of negotiations for the EU-China Investment Agreement*, 12-15 December 2017, retrieved from *www.trade.ec.europa.eu*.

owned companies are constantly under the spotlight — even tax measures can constitute state aid. Since 2001[36], the EU-China dialogue on competition policy has been intensified and, in 2019, a new *Memorandum of Understanding on a dialogue in the area of the State Aid Control and the Fair Competition Review* has been signed to enhance the exchange of good practices and an "effective, transparent and non-discriminatory state aid control and fair competition review"[37].

It happens that sometimes legal concepts are differently understood in distinct legal system. An example concerns taxation, disinvestment and the notion of expropriation. Investment implies the possibility of disinvestment and the latter could be usually subject to economic consequences, even tax levy. Nevertheless, if the taxation approximately amounts to the whole disinvestment it could be perceived as more than a levy and, rather, a disincentive to investment. In that case the tax measure imposed may consist in an expropriation and therefore not being compliant with the national treatment principle. In the context of the CAI, the EU and China have different positions as regards this aspect — and in particular, the identification of an expropriation as a result of a tax measures and the tax dispute exclusion clause in the CAI[38].

Lastly, the attention should be drawn on a slippery area that is mainly internal to the EU but that has an impact on the relationship with third countries: the EU competence as regards (international) taxation[39]. On the one hand, difference is made between direct and indirect taxation. With respect to direct taxation — taxes on natural persons and companies income —, it is still a competence of the Member States ("MS"), even if the principle of the primacy of the EU law over the MS domestic law applies[40] and the EU gave

36. See "Declaration on the start of a dialogue on competition by the EU and China" retrieved from *www.ec.europa.eu.*

37. Memorandum of Understanding on a dialogue in the area of the State Aid Control and the Fair Competition Review between the State Administration for Market Regulation of the People's Republic of China and the Directorate-General for Competition of the European Commission, 9 April 2019, retrieved from *www.ec.europa.eu.*

38. European Commission Directorate-General for Trade, *Note to the file: Report of the 16th round of negotiations for the EU-China Investment Agreement, op. cit.*; European Commission Directorate-General for Trade, *Note to the file: Report of the 19th round of negotiations for the EU-China Investment Agreement, op. cit.*; European Commission Directorate-General for Trade, *Note to the file: Report of the 20th round of negotiations for the EU-China Investment Agreement, op. cit.*

39. See, for example, the Reservations for existing measures applicable in the European Union in Annex I to the CAI.

40. *Inter alia* CJCE, 13 December 1967, C- 17/67, *Neumann/Hauptzollamt Hof/Saale*; CJCE, 13 December 2005, C-446/03, *Marks & Spencer*.

and is giving a framework to the national regulations[41] under article 115 of the Treaty on the Functioning of the European Union ("TFEU") which sets forth the approximation of MS legislations affecting the internal market. Concerning indirect taxation, we should distinguish between customs duties — which fall within the EU exclusive competence[42] — and the excise duties and the value added tax ("VAT"), which, instead, are "only" harmonised[43] under article 113 TFUE There is no homogeneity in the decision-making processes followed for the different taxation policies. Moreover, except for customs law, both in direct and indirect taxation, it is the Council who, upon the EU Commission proposal, adopts — acting unanimously — provisions for the approximation or harmonisation — the EU Parliament having a consultative role only. Also due to the unanimity clause, the EU has still limited powers in foreign tax policies, but if it is willing to strengthen the competitiveness of its tax system and to adapt quickly to changing economic realities, it should call for a more united voice. That is also the idea of the EU Commission, which is supporting the replacement of the unanimity principle with a qualified majority voting since "EU tax policy must be able to react and adapt quickly" and "a coordinated EU action in taxation is essential to protect Member States' revenues and ensure a fair tax environment for all"[44].

41. See, for example, Council Directive 2003/49/EC of 3 June 2003 on a common system of taxation applicable to interest and royalty payments made between associated companies of different Member States; Council Directive 2009/133/EC of 19 October 2009 on the common system of taxation applicable to mergers, divisions, partial divisions, transfers of assets and exchanges of shares concerning companies of different Member States and to the transfer of the registered office of an SE or SCE between Member States; Council Directive 2011/16/EU of 15 February 2011 on administrative cooperation in the field of taxation; Council Directive 2011/96/EU of 30 November 2011 on the common system of taxation applicable in the case of parent companies and subsidiaries of different Member States; Council Directive (EU) 2016/1164 of 12 July 2016 laying down rules against tax avoidance practices that directly affect the functioning of the internal market; Proposal for a Council Directive on a Common Consolidated Corporate Tax Base (CCCTB), COM (2016) 683 final, 2016; Proposal for a Council Directive on a Common Corporate Tax Base, COM (2016) 685 final, 2016.

42. The EU is a Customs Union which is governed by the Union Customs Code (Regulation (EU) No 952/2013 of the European Parliament and of the Council of 9 October 2013 laying down the Union Customs Code).

43. The directives allow a relatively little leeway in their transposition (albeit significant, as regards VAT, in terms of rates and exemptions). See Council Directive 2006/112/EC of 28 November 2006 on the common system of value added tax; Council Directive 2008/118/EC of 16 December 2008 concerning the general arrangements for excise duty; Council Regulation (EU) No 904/2010 of 7 October 2010 on administrative cooperation and combating fraud in the field of value added tax.

44. Communication from the Commission to the European Parliament, the European Council and the Council — Towards a more efficient and democratic decision making in EU tax policy, COM (2019) 8 final, 2019, p. 1.

4. CONCLUSIONS

Global challenges require international cooperation, and the tax sector is also concerned. The partnership between the EU and China has become progressively closer in a wider range of fields. The EU has always supported a greater integration in multilateral initiatives of global interest and both parties still promote a coordinated approach even towards exchanges of experiences to deal with tax matters this changing world is experiencing, for the benefit of all. The importance of cooperation in tax matters has been emphasised from both parties and a bilateral regulation between the EU and China could be an effective solution. The dialogue is consolidated, frequent and based on trust and respect, even if on some thorny topics the positions differ and they are the discourse priorities. Nevertheless, the main challenge for the EU is still internal: the actualisation of the internal market should not be the sole concern when it exercises its fiscal power. A broader outlook is needed and the EU should call for full unity among the Members States in cooperating with China to reach its full potential.

II. RETAIL DIGITAL PLATFORMS IN EU-CHINA TRADE

MARIE LAMENSCH, ELENA MASSEGLIA AND EDOARDO TRAVERSA[45]

Platforms have now become key players in the e-commerce sector. They also acted as catalyst in the development of the sharing economy sector. This central positioning raises new challenges as regards the taxes traditionally levied on companies (income tax and VAT).

1. INTRODUCTION

According to UNCTAD, global e commerce sales generated $25.3 trillion in 2015. An amount of $22,400 billion as business-to-business ("B2B") sales and an amount of $2,900 billion as business-to-consumer ("B2C") sales[46]. In 2021, they amounted to approximately $5.2 trillion. Nevertheless, the online retail sector has not yet reached its saturation point: it is estimated that by 2026, the amounts generated in this sector could reach $8,100 trillion[47].

45. Marie Lamensch is Professor of Taxation at the Université Catholique de Louvain. She is a member of the European Commission's "VAT Expert Group" and the OECD's "Technical Advisory Group on consumption taxes" and the Technical Editor of the International VAT Monitor (IBFD). Edoardo Traversa is Professor of Tax Law at the Université Catholique de Louvain and a lawyer at the Brussels Bar. Elena Masseglia Miszczyszyn is PhD candidate at the Université Catholique de Louvain.

46. UNCTAD, *Information Economy Report 2017: Digitization, Trade and Development*, United Nations publication, n. E. 17. II. D. 8.

47. Statista, *Retail e-commerce sales worldwide from 2014 to 2026*, 2022.

The development of online retail is strongly linked to the emergence of platforms, these new types of online intermediaries, which are now essential on the Internet. If initially, Internet was supposed to prompt a disintermediation process of the e-commerce — allowing direct access to a global base of potential customers — the reality showed a different trend: a strong reintermediation process. Moreover, in recent years, a limited number of "mega-platforms" (including Amazon and Alibaba) has indeed captured a significant portion of the overall B2C market. In addition to reintermediation, we are therefore also witnessing a process of concentration[48].

The emergence of platforms entailed new challenges in several legal areas and the tax law sector is not an exception.

2. INCOME TAXATION: OUTDATED RULES AND SLOW DEVELOPMENTS

The emergence of platforms raises several questions about the adequacy of current corporate income tax rules, in particular in an international context.

Indeed, the international rules currently in force concerning the allocation of territorial jurisdiction between countries limit the possibilities for the State where the economic activity is carried out to apply its tax rules in the absence of a Permanent Establishment ("PE").

Traditionally, the notion of PE refers to two different circumstances. On the one hand, the OECD Model Convention[49] defines the PE as "a fixed place of business through which the business of an enterprise is wholly or partly carried on"[50], definition which implies a certain level of physical

48. UNCTAD Secretariat, *Fostering development gains from e-commerce and digital platforms*, note for the meeting of the Intergovernmental Group of Experts on E-commerce and the Digital Economy held in Geneva on 18-20 April 2018, p. 7.

49. Treaties for the avoidance of double taxation signed by the Organisation for Economic Co-operation and Development ("OCDE") members —among which there are 21 EU countries— are largely inspired by the OECD's Model Tax Convention on Income and on Capital ("OECD Model"). The People's Republic of China is a "key partner" of the OECD and has entered into double taxation prevention treaties with EU member states in accordance with the OECD Model.

50. On the notion of permanent establishment, see in particular OECD, *Model Tax Convention on Income and on Capital 2017 (Full Version)*, OECD Publishing, 2019, Article 5 (including changes related to the BEPS process); OECD, 2018 and the reports to the 2009 Congress of the International Fiscal Association (Sujet A: "Is there a permanent establishment?" in *Cahiers de droit fiscal international*, vol. 94a, general report by Sasseville, J. and Skaar, A., and 40 national reports, including the Belgian report by Cauwenbergh and Claes).

infrastructure, such as offices or a factory. The OECD model excludes activities having a preparatory or auxiliary character, such as storage, exhibition, information collection, etc[51].

On the other hand, the concept of permanent establishments also refers to the presence of a person acting "on behalf of an enterprise and has, and habitually exercises, in a Contracting State, an authority to conclude contracts in the name of the enterprise" (OECD Model, Article 5.5, old version). This provision excludes the independent agent or broker acting as an intermediary without having the power to bind the company. Apart from the possible hypothesis of general or specific anti-abuse rules[52], or the prohibition of State aid under European law[53], which presupposes the fulfilment of conditions which are not always obvious to establish, it is therefore possible for a platform to play on the notion of permanent establishments to legally avoid the payment of income tax in the State of sale[54].

The reaction of public authorities to this phenomenon of non-taxation of platform revenues has been threefold: (a) a series of actions have been launched by the OECD on the basis of its BEPS plan[55]; (b) the European Commission has submitted several proposals to harmonise the taxation concerning the digital economy; and (c) measures unilaterally adopted by

51. Article 5, par. 4, OECD Model.
52. On tax abuse and avoidance in the European Union, see in particular Dourado, A. P. (ed.), *Tax Avoidance Revisited in the EU BEPS Context*, IBFD, 2017 (and the national reports included therein).
53. In Europe, countries such as Ireland, the Netherlands and Luxembourg have found themselves in the spotlight not only in the media but also in the courts, particularly with regard to the compatibility of certain tax arrangements concluded with multinational companies in the digital sector with the European state aid regime. See in particular Traversa, E. and Sabbadini, P., "Rulings et aides d'État fiscales: un état des lieux" in *J. D. E.* 2017/4, n. 238, pp. 138-141.
54. Companies operating in the e-commerce or digital economy sectors could (and still in many cases) relatively easily avoid to fall within one of the two mentioned hypotheses, being therefore able to sell goods and services in a territory without being taxed on the income generated by this activity. They usually concentrate the revenues in a company located in a State chosen on the basis of the leniency of the tax systems. Sometimes, incomes are even immediately deducted as costs (interest, royalties, remuneration for technical services, etc.) to a group entity located in a jurisdiction with even more favourable taxation (tax heaven).
55. For a description of the genesis and content of the BEPS action plan, see in particular the OECD website (*www.oecd.org*) and Traversa, E. and Possoz, M., "L'action de l'OCDE en matière de lute contre l'évasion fiscal internationale et d'échange de renseignements: développements récents" in *Revue Générale du Contentieux fiscal (R. G. C. F.)*, 2015, n. 1, pp. 5-24.

EU Member States targeting multinational companies operating through platforms on their territory (in particular as regards indirect taxation).

The OECD has published a series of reports under the project named "Base Erosion and Profit Shifting" (BEPS) covering 15 actions to be taken to tackle tax avoidance[56] and to adapt the international and national framework for the taxation of digital business income. These actions include in particular Action 1 "Addressing the Tax Challenges of the Digital Economy" and Action 7 "Preventing the Artificial Avoidance of Permanent Establishment Status".

The first report concerning the Action 1 describes the challenges which the tax systems are facing as a result of the emergence of new business models of the digital economy and highlights how they may exacerbate the BEPS risk[57].

The report on Action 7 of the BEPS plan[58] relates to the amendments to the notion of permanent establishment in the OECD Model, as well as in existing and future double taxation conventions, in order to address arrangements used to avoid falling within the scope of the permanent establishment notion, and thus avoid having a taxable presence in a jurisdiction under tax treaties. The goal is to strengthen the taxing power of the State where platforms carry out their activities.

Over 135 countries and jurisdictions are working together within OECD/ G20 Inclusive Framework on BEPS to implement the mentioned 15 actions.

At the EU level, the European Commission — working closely with the OECD — adopted two proposals in March 2018 aimed to adapt the corporate tax rules to the characteristics of digital businesses. The first — conceived as a temporary measure — sets out the common system of a tax on income

56. See OECD/G20 Base Erosion and Profit Shifting Project Final Reports 2015, OECD, 2015 (retrieved from *www.oecd.org*).

57. OECD, *Addressing the Fiscal Challenges of the Digital Economy, Action 1 — Final Report 2015*, OECD, 2015, *www.oecd.org*. This first report has been followed by an interim report, OECD, *Brief on the tax challenges arising from digitalisation: Interim report 2018, 2018, www.oecd.org*. A final report on the digital economy is expected by the end of 2019 taking into account the inputs raised on the occasion of the public consultation on the tax challenges of digitalization that took place at the beginning of 2019, concerning inter alia the identification of a taxable presence of a non-resident digitalised business. See OECD, "Addressing the tax challenges of digitalization of the economy", Public Consultation Document, 13 February-6 March 2019, *www.oecd.org*.

58. OECD, *Preventing the Artificial Avoidance of Permanent Establishment Status, Action 7 — 2015 Final Report*, 2015, *www.oecd.org*.

from the supply of certain digital services[59] ("Digital Services Tax" or "DST") as digital advertising interface, multi- sided digital interface which allows users to find and interact with other users, the transmission of data collected about users on digital interfaces[60].

This 3% tax on income generated by these activities only applies to certain companies with total revenues exceeding 750 million and 50 million in the EU. The second proposal[61] entails more fundamental changes as the objective is to establish a taxable nexus of a digital business in a jurisdiction by introducing the notion of "significant digital presence" — as a complement of the concept of permanent establishment — based on the revenues from digital services supply, the number of users of digital services or the number of contracts for a digital service. As regards the mentioned indicators, the proposals sets forth different thresholds: there is a significant digital presence in a Member State if one or more of the following criteria are met if (i) the revenues from providing digital services to users in a jurisdiction exceed 7 million in a tax period, (ii) the number of users of a digital service in a Member State exceeds 100 000 in a tax period, or (iii) the number of business contracts for digital services exceeds 3 000. This proposal is supplemented by a Recommendation addressed to the Member States for including provisions on a significant digital presence and in their double taxation treaties with third countries[62].

These two proposals, which are subject to the requirement of the unanimous approval by the EU Council, could not reach a sufficient consensus before the end of the 2014-2019 legislature.

Lacking the European compromise, some Member States have decided to take a step forward unilaterally by adopting different types of measures, still

59. Proposal for a Council directive on the common system of a digital services tax on revenues resulting from the provision of certain digital services of 21 March 2018, COM (2018) 148.

60. The following activities are thus excluded: retail activities (e-commerce); streaming services (digital interface consisting of the provision of digital content such as video, audio or text, either owned by this entity or that this entity has acquired distribution rights); game interfaces; crowdfunding; interfaces where user participation is not central to value creation (e. g., ensuring a secure environment, e. g. financing); provision of taxable services between entities in a consolidated group for financial accounting purposes.

61. Proposal for a Council directive laying down rules relating to the corporate taxation of a significant digital presence of 21 March 2018, COM (2018) 147.

62. Commission Recommendation of 21 March 2018 relating to the corporate taxation of a significant digital presence, C (2018) 1650.

within the existing framework of the international agreements they concluded (*e. g.* the double taxation conventions) and mostly following the European Commission proposal. These provisions aim to increase the platforms' taxable presence in the jurisdiction where they are carrying out their business. For example, in the United Kingdom the Diverted Profits Tax applies since 2015[63], the French Republic has approved the act concerning the so-called "taxe GAFA" on digital services in July 2019[64], in Italy, the "Web tax" has been approved in 2018 and implemented in 2021[65] and in Spain a law proposal related to a tax on digital services has been enacted in January 2019[66].

Nevertheless, a key element of the OECD/G20 Inclusive Framework's negotiations was to stop the proliferation of digital tax services (as those listed above) by replacing them with a consensus-based reallocation of taxing rights among the Inclusive Framework members, a measure going under the name of "Pillar 1", out of the two-pillar solution addressing tax challenges arising from the digitalization of the economy[67]. Considering the willing of the named countries to support the two-pillar solution, France, Italy, Spain and the United Kingdom, together with Austria, have agreed that as part of Pillar 1, they will withdraw all unilateral measures on all companies, including the digital tax services, and refrain from imposing new unilateral measures, upon the implementation of Pillar 1[68].

63. For a description see HMRC, *Diverted Profits Tax — Guidance*, December 2018, retrieved from *https://assets.publishing.service.gov.uk/government/uploads/system/uploads/attachment_data/file/768204/Diverted_Profits_Tax_-_Guidance December_2018_.pdf*

64. It is a 3% tax on the turnover realised in France applying to businesses with income deriving from the provision of digital services exceeding 750 million worldwide and 25 million in France, see *Loi n. 2019-759 du 24 juillet 2019 portant création d'une taxe sur les services numériques et modification de la trajectoire de baisse de l'impôt sur les sociétés*, retrieved from *https://www.legifrance.gouv.fr*

65. Art. 1, paras. 35-49, of Budget Act 2019 (*Legge n. 145/2018* as subsequently amended) sets forth the levy of a 3% tax on income of businesses supplying digital services (as advertising on digital interfaces, provision of a multilateral digital interfaces allowing connections between users, transmission of data collected and generated by the use of a digital interface) with a worldwide income higher than 750 million of which at least 5.5 million from digital services provided in the Italian territory. See also *Decreto-Legge n. 3/2021 Misure urgenti in materia di accertamento, riscossione, nonché adempimenti e versamenti tributari.*

66. The proposal regulates a 3% tax applying to businesses supplying digital services with worldwide income higher than 750 million and 3 million in Spain, see *Proyecto de Ley del Impuesto sobre Determinados Servicios Digitales* of 25 January 2019, retrieved from *http://www. congreso.es/public_oficiales/L12/CONG/BOCG/A/BOCG-12-A-40-1.PDF*

67. See OECD, *Statement on a Two-Pillar Solution to Address the Tax Challenges Arising from the Digitalization of the Economy*, 2021. For details on Pillar 2, see *infra* section 4.

68. For the moment of the withdrawal, *see* the Joint Statement from the United States, Austria, France, Italy, Spain, and the United Kingdom, Regarding a Compromise on

3. E-COMMERCE, PLATFORMS AND COLLECTION OF VAT

Countries are facing difficulties in collecting VAT due on sales via the platforms. Therefore, different solutions have been recently adopted at the EU level as well as at the national level — specifically in the United Kingdom and in Germany — aimed at involving the platforms in the collection procedures. Platforms are identified as allies by governments to protect their VAT revenues. To be noted that in contrast with the situation in the field of corporate income tax, there is no doubt that the transactions carried out by platforms are taxable in the State where the economic activity takes place and not in the State where the platforms are residing (irrespective of the existence of a permanent establishment in the market jurisdiction). Nevertheless, it might be difficult to enforce the collection of VAT when the platforms are non-resident.

Ensuring the correct collection of VAT on online sales has become a major challenge for governments around the world. Platforms facilitate cross-border trade and we observe a significant share of imported goods from Asia to the EU.

From a VAT perspective, as regards the supplies made through a platform, the taxable person is the underlying vendor, not the platform. One of the main difficulties is that for a State it is hard or even impossible (both legally and practically) to force companies established abroad to collect VAT on their behalf and to supervise them. The level of VAT compliance on cross-border transactions therefore largely depends largely on the "goodwill" of foreign companies. This lack of control over foreign companies has an impact on the income collected, but also on domestic companies, which are subject to real controls and face unfair competition from foreign companies that do not properly charge VAT on their sales.

At the OECD level[69], many countries are discussing about the best way to follow and the recently emerged trend is the identification of the platforms are as key actors in the collection process of VAT on the online purchases that

a Transitional Approach to Existing Unilateral Measures During the Interim Period Before Pillar 1 is in Effect, of 21 October 2021.

69. OECD, *International VAT/GST Guidelines*, retrieved from *https://www.oecd.org/ctp/international-vat-gst-guidelines- 9789264271401-en.htm* The World Customs Organization has also set up a working group on electronic commerce to map out possible policies that could be proposed. In June 2018, it published a "Framework of Standards on cross-border e-commerce" that addresses, *inter alia*, the collection of VAT/GST and customs duties on imports.

they facilitate when the vendors are non-established businesses, to increase the level of compliance.

From 1 January 2015 already in the European Union[70], platforms through which electronically supplied services[71] are provided to consumers established or usually residing in one of the Member States must be responsible for collecting and remitting the VAT due on their services[72]. A One Stop Shop ("OSS") system is available for the periodic payment of VAT in a single Member State (of their choice). In case the platform is not registered with the OSS, the registration in each Member State where the VAT is due is required.

Concerning the goods — for which the application of VAT rules is more complex as the location of the goods at the time of sale will be decisive for the characterization of the sale, an element over which platforms often do not have control — two approaches currently coexist in the EU.

3.1. The "First Line Enforcers" Approach

A first approach is to require platforms to ensure the payment of the VAT, without collecting the VAT directly, but imposing on them due diligence obligations. They have to check several information about the sellers they host (in particular, the validity of their VAT number; they must also collect information on sales made) and to block these sellers, either in case of doubt as to the validity of their registration with the tax administration or at the request of the latter. If they fail to comply with these due diligence obligations, the platforms are jointly and severally liable for the payment of unpaid VAT to the Treasury.

This approach has been followed by the United Kingdom since 2016 for non-established sellers[73] and since 2018 for all B2C suppliers passing through a platform[74], and by Germany (where all sellers supplying goods to German customers via platforms must obtain a VAT certificate) since January 2019[75].

70. See art. 5 of Council Directive 2008/8/EC of 12 February 2008 amending Directive 2006/112/EC as regards the place of supply of services.
71. For example, the supply of software, music or films for downloading and other applications that are supplied in a fully automated manner.
72. In order to simplify the collection, a one-stop shop system has been set up. Platforms register in a single Member State and remit the VAT due on services provided to all Member States.
73. Finance Act 2016 (UK), s. 124 introducing subsections 73B, 73C, and 73D into the VAT Act 1994.
74. Finance Act 2018 (UK), s. 38 amending s. 73B of the VAT Act 1994.
75. New Sections 22f and 25e of the German VAT Act.

3.2. The "Primary Liability" Approach

In December 2017, the Member States adopted the "VAT e-commerce package"[76]. The approach chosen, entered into force in 2021 (the German had therefore be rescinded to comply with it), consists, on the one hand, in requiring platforms to collect and keep (for 10 years!) details of transactions concluded via their interface and, on the other hand, in treating platforms as "deemed to have received and supplied those goods" themselves[77], and therefore as fully taxable person liable to collect and remit VAT on a periodic basis, when they *facilitate*:

- A domestic or intra-EU sale of goods by a taxable person not established within the European Un- ion to a non-taxable person ("distance selling")[78];
- An import of goods ("distance selling from a third country or territory") in consignments of an intrinsic value not exceeding EUR 150.

The VAT Implementing Regulation[79] defines the term 'facilitates' very broadly. According to Article 5b of the VAT Implementing Regulation, it covers the cases where an electronic interface allows a customer and a supplier, selling goods through the electronic interface, to enter into contact, resulting in a supply of goods through that electronic interface to that customer[80]. Only platforms that do not perform any of the following tasks will be excluded from this "primary liability" system[81]:

---

76. The package consisted of a Directive (Council Directive (EU) 2017/2455 of 5 December 2017 amending Directive 2006/112/EC and Directive 2009/132/EC as regards certain value added tax obligations for supplies of services and distance sales of goods) and two Regulations (Council Regulation (EU) 2017/2454 of 5 December 2017 amending Regulation (EU) No 904/2010 on administrative cooperation and combating fraud in the field of value added tax and Council Implementing Regulation (EU) 2017/2459 of 5 December 2017 amending Implementing Regulation (EU) No 282/2011 laying down implementing measures for Directive 2006/112/EC on the common system of value added tax).
77. Art. 14a Council Directive 2006/112/EC of 28 November 2006 on the common system of value added tax (hereinafter, "VAT Directive" and Art. 2, para. 2, Council Directive (EU) 2017/2455 of 5 December 2017.
78. As indicated above, the qualification of "domestic" or "intra-EU" will depend not on the location of the seller but on where the goods are. A seller established in China can therefore carry out a "domestic sale" of goods in Germany if the goods and the customer are located in Germany at the time of the sale. So, if the goods are located in Belgium and they are sold in France, but the company is based in China, the sale will be considered as an "intra-EU" supply.
79. Council Implementing Regulation (EU) No 282/2011 of 15 March 2011 laying down implementing measures for Directive 2006/112/EC on the common system of value added tax (hereinafter the "VAT Implementing Regulation") as amended.
80. Article 5b of the VAT Implementing Regulation.
81. *Ibid.*

1. Determine, either directly or indirectly, the general terms under which the supply of goods is carried out;
2. Participate, either directly or indirectly, in charging the customer in respect of the payment made;
3. Participate, directly or indirectly, in the ordering or delivery of the goods.

A platform will also be outside the scope of the mentioned "primary liability" regime if it only deals with one of the following activities[82]:

1. The processing of payments in relation with the supply of goods;
2. The listing or advertising of goods;
3. The redirecting or transferring of customers to other electronic interfaces where goods are offered for sale, without further intervention in the supply.

In the case of imports ("distance sales from a third country or territory") of consignments of an intrinsic value not exceeding EUR 150[83], unlike in the electronic services sector (*see above*), platforms falling within the scope of said provision are not required to register via the IOSS[84] (or to register in each Member State) and then remit VAT on a periodical basis. Indeed, they may opt to not register and, in that event, the postal operator will have to collect the VAT from the customer. However, they are required to provide the exact information enabling the carrier to fulfil its task.

The objective of this "primary liability" approach for platforms is to ensure a higher degree of compliance. Platforms are more likely to comply with VAT legislation than the thousands of vendors they host. However, several (non) legal issues arise in relation to that regime.

It should be borne in mind that the problem of undervaluing/ underreporting remains unresolved as such (whereas it is estimated that

82. *Ibid.*

83. This threshold follows the threshold of the customs duty exemption for consignments of negligible value under the Council Regulation (EC) No 1186/2009 of 16 November 2009 setting up a Community system of reliefs from customs duty. For the definition of "intrinsic value" see Article 1, point (48), of the Commission Delegated Regulation (EU) 2015/2446 of 28 July 2015 supplementing Regulation (EU) No 952/2013 of the European Parliament and of the Council as regards detailed rules concerning certain provisions of the Union Customs Code.

84. Import One Stop Shop.

more than 60% of imports are subject to underreporting)[85]. Member States can only hope that platforms remit the correct amounts of VAT or that they declare correct amounts to carriers without actually having the possibility to control them.

With respect to imported goods, it is also important to highlight the risk that platforms face when they register with the IOSS. In practice, in the event of registration to the IOSS, VAT must be invoiced to the customer when he buys (the chargeable event is the sale finalization[86] and the VAT has to be remitted via the IOSS on a monthly basis) and the physical entry of the goods into the EU (the importation) must then be exempt,[87] otherwise the supply is taxed twice. Conversely, if the platform is not registered, it will not charge VAT at the time of sale but the VAT will be due on the import. It is therefore necessary for the customs authorities to distinguish between imports that should be exempt (because VAT was invoiced at the time of sale and it will be remitted via the OSS at the end of the tax period) and those that should not be exempt. This distinction should be made on the basis of the submission (or not) of a valid IOSS registration number in the import declaration. In other words, a valid registration number will entitle you to an exemption. It is clear that there is a significant risk that foreign companies may use the number of one of the major platforms to obtain an import exemption (which is not confidential since it must be communicated to sellers active on these platforms so that they can obtain the import exemption when they organise the shipment of goods) even though the sale was not made by the platform and VAT was not charged at the time of sale[88]. The VAT Implementing Regulation sets forth that the platform are only liable for the declared and paid VAT on these supplies but they need to prove that it did not and could not reasonably know that the information provided by the supplier was incorrect. At this stage, for the Treasury no protection mechanism against this type of fraud seems to be put in place.

In any case, this legislative change at the EU level will have a significant impact on platforms, both in terms of internal procedures and cost terms.

85. Copenhagen Economics, *E-commerce imports into Europe: VAT and customs treatment*, 2016, retrieved from *https://www. copenhageneconomics.com/dyn/resources/Publication/publicationPDF/8/348/1462798608/e-commerce-imports-into- europe_vat-and-customs-treatment.pdf.*

86. Arts. 41a and 61b VAT Implementing Regulation.

87. Art. 369n(2)(4) VAT Directive.

88. For a detailed analysis of the flaws in the e-commerce package, see Lamensch, M., "Adoption of the e-commerce VAT package: the road ahead is still a rocky one" in *EC Tax Review*, vol. 27, n. 4, pp. 186-195.

In the long term, it could even favour the major platforms, which will be the only ones able to meet the new compliance obligations, discouraging the small platforms — and therefore the phenomenon of concentration mentioned in the introduction will be reinforced[89].

4. CONCLUSIONS

The platforms have fostered the spectacular growth of the e-commerce sector. They have also led States to rethink their strategies for protecting their incomes.

In the area of income taxation, the emergence of digital companies is forcing governments, the EU, and international organisations such as the OECD to thoroughly review the key concepts of international taxation used in bilateral double taxation treaties, in order to give to the source country (where the company actually operates) a broader taxing power and counteract avoidance strategies. This process has been launched, but is still evolving too slowly and it is too early at this time to know the exact contours of the notion of digital permanent establishment.

In the field of VAT, the future will tell us whether the cumbersome nature of the obligations recently imposed on platforms will have an impact on their diversity in the e-commerce sector or whether these obligations will reinforce the phenomenon of concentration that we are already observing nowadays.

III. INTERNATIONAL TAXATION BETWEEN BEPS AND THE BELT AND ROAD INITIATIVE. IMPLEMENTING BEPS IN THE EU

MARTA VILLAR EZCURRA[90]

1. INTRODUCTION

The People's Republic of China (hereinafter, the PRC) is the EU's second largest trading partner and the EU is the PRC's largest trading partner.

As OECD Secretary-General Angel Gurria has stated in 2015 "base erosion and profit shifting affects all countries, not only economically, but also as a matter of trust. BEPS is depriving countries of precious resources to

89. See Lamensch, M. and Millar, R., "The Role of Marketplaces in Taxing B2C Supplies" in Lang, M. et al. (eds.), *CJEU — Recent Developments in Value Added Tax 2018*, Linde Verlag, 2019, pp. 51-78.

90. Full Professor of Financial and Tax Law at the Universidad CEU San Pablo.

jump-start growth, tackle the effects of the global economic crisis and create more and better opportunities for all. However, beyond this, BEPS has been also eroding the trust of citizens in the fairness of tax systems worldwide. The measures we are presenting today represent the most fundamental changes to international tax rules in almost a century: They will put an end to double non-taxation, facilitate a better alignment of taxation with economic activity and value creation, and when fully implemented, these measures will render BEPS-inspired tax planning structures ineffective"[91].

"Base erosion and profit shifting" refers to "tax avoidance strategies that exploit gaps and mismatches in tax rules to artificially shift profits to low or no-tax locations"[92]. As called for in the OECD report on BEPS, *Addressing Base Erosion and Profit Shifting* (OECD, 2013)[93] the BEPS Plan (i) identifies actions needed to address BEPS, (ii) sets deadlines to implement these actions and (iii) identifies the resources needed and the methodology to implement BEPS Plan.

The 15 Actions have been identified as such: Action 1 "address the tax challenges of the digital economy"; Action 2 "neutralise the effects of hybrid mismatches agreements"; Action 3 "strengthen CFC rules"; Action 4 "limit base erosion via interest deductions and other financial payments"; Action 5 "counter harmful tax practices more effectively, taking into account transparency and substance"; Action 6 "prevent treaty abuse"; Action 7 "prevent the artificial avoidance of PE status"; Action 8 to 10 "assure that transfer pricing outcomes are in line with value creation"; Action 11 "establish methodologies to collect and analyse data on BEPS and the actions to address it"; Action 12 "require taxpayers to disclose their aggressive tax planning arrangements"; Action 13 "re-examine transfer pricing documentation"; Action 14 "make dispute resolution mechanisms more effective" and Action 15 "develop a multilateral instrument".

As M. Teresa Soler have pointed out "the main challenge is coordination and in this respect multilateralism and the work under Action 15, especially dealing with treaty issues is a key element on the process, although its final outcomes remain to be seen"[94].

91. OECD, Centre for Tax Policy and Administration, OECD presents outputs of OECD. Paper presented at G20 BEPS Project for discussion at G20 Finance Ministers Meeting, Lima, Peru, 5 October 2015.
92. See OECD website at *http://www.oecd.org/tax/beps.*
93. OECD, Action Plan on Base Erosion and Profit Shifting, OECD Publishing, 2013, retrieved from *http://dx.doi.org/10.1787/9789264202719-en*
94. See Soler Roch, M. T., "Consistency and Hierarchy among the BEPS Actions" in Dourado, A. P. (ed.), "Tax Avoidance revisited in the EU BEPS context", EATLP Annual

The BEPS project is still a work in progress and will continue to be so in the coming years. The EU has driving the implementation of BEPS forward in many respects. Some key-BEPS measures have been translated into binding EU law so they are implemented across the EU Member States.

Of the 15 BEPS Actions, the EU has already taken an active role in respect to 10 of them. For example, regarding Action 1, the European Commission issued two proposals for new Directives on digital economy and the Anti-Tax Avoidance Directive (ATAD) addresses the recommendations contained in BEPS Actions 2, 3, 4 and 6. In the context of Action 5, the EU has adopted the Directive on exchange of information of tax rulings; a Commission recommendation on the implementation of measures against tax treaty abuse that was adopted in 2016 urges Member States to implement general avoidance rules and to amend the PE definition in their treaties in line with BEPS Actions 6 and 7. The Directive on new mandatory transparency rules for intermediaries and taxpayers broadly reflects the objectives of Action 12 of the OECD BEPS Project; with the CbC Directive 2016/881, the EU introduced into legislation BEPS Action 13; and lastly, in line with the recommendations set out under Action 14, the EU has adopted the Tax Dispute Resolution Directive setting forth the rules for a mechanism to resolve disputes between Member States. Apart from the proposals on digital taxation, which are still awaiting adoption by the Council, and the Commission recommendation related to Actions 6 and 7 that has no binding effect, all the other EU measures have already been adopted and constitute part of the EU legislation[95].

Based on this premise, we would like to highlight two issues. On the one hand, that China has actively participated in both developing and implementing the BEPS project[96]. On the other hand, that the Belt and Road Initiative (BRI) will give rise to an unprecedented hybrid model of investment governance significantly shaped by transnational policy networks[97].

Congress Munich, 2-4 June 2016, EATLP International Tax Series, vol. 15, *IBFD*, 2017, p. 138.

95. This summary is based on the EY report, *The latest on BEPS — 2018 mid-year review A review of OECD and country actions in mid-year 2018*, retrieved from *https://www.ey.com/Publication/vwLUAssets/ey-the-latest-on-beps-2018-mid-year-review-now- available/$FILE/ey-the-latest-on-beps-2018-mid-year-review-now-available.pdf*.

96. China has been an active participant in the OECD-G2 project initially as a member of the CFA Bureau Plus in the first phase, and now in the Steering Group of the Inclusive Framework on BEPS. For further information about this topic see *https://data. oecd.org/china-people-s-republic-of.htm* and Avi-Yonah, R. and Xu, H., *China and BEPS*, Laws 2018, 7, 4; *doi:10.3390/ laws7010004*.

97. See Feldman, M., "China´s Belt and Road investment governance: building a hybrid model" in *Columbia Center on Sustainable Investment*, Columbia FDI Perspectives n. 244,

As China´s key trading partner, the EU is interested in coordinating a strategy to open up the doors to China´s investment. In this regard, the 19th EU-China Summit in 2017 advanced a bilateral strategic partnership, which has a global impact, and highlighted joint commitments to addressing global challenges and the promotion of multilateralism. This is why the European Parliament remarked the EU emphasis on a multilateral governance structure and on non-discriminatory implementation of the BRI[98]. Nevertheless, unilateral measures are taking place in some States[99].

Implementing BEPS in the EU raises a variety of interesting topics at the intersection between BEPS and the BRI, but there are probably two areas to highlight from the perspective of promoting foreign Chinese direct investment in the EU reducing the legal risks for companies: (i) the regulation of taxation and investment; (ii) and the need to strength cooperation in tax matters to assure and effective and efficient dispute resolving mechanism[100].

2. THE REGULATION OF TAXATION AND INVESTMENT

Mark Feldman remarks that "striking an appropriate balance between the ambition of a state-driven model and the inclusiveness of a transnational policy network model will be of central importance for BRI investment governance", as well as the significant roles played in rulemaking[101].

In the Forth Regional Meeting of the Inclusive Framework on BEPS for Eastern Europe and Central Asia (7-9 November 2018) the need to promote and to clarify the new rules to taxpayers and the main stakeholders was stressed (*e. g.* through Advance Pricing Arrangements (APA), Mutual Agreement Procedures (MAP) and exchange of information). Participants discussed there the role of tax consultants in ensuring consistent implementation and stressed the importance of consultation processes. Moreover, it was highlighted the need to enhance legislative organisational and human resource capabilities as well as cross- country co-operation.

2019, retrieved from *http://ccsi.columbia.edu/files/2018/10/No-244- Feldman-FINAL.pdf.*

98. See the European Parliament Report on the state of EU-China relations (2017/2275(INI). Committee on Foreign Affairs" (A8- 0252/2018), 10 July 2018.

99. See section 2.2., p. 13.

100. See Mejía-Lemos, D., *The Belt and Road Initiative (BRI) and International Tax Law: A Winter Note on Law-making and Dispute Resolution Issues Raised by the BRI*, retrieved from *https://globtaxgov.weblog.leidenuniv.nl/2019/01/23/belt-and-road-initiative-bri-and-international-tax-law-a-winter-note-on-law-making-and-dispute-resolution-issues-raised-by-the-bri.*

101. Feldman, M., "China´s Belt and Road investment governance: building a hybrid model", *op. cit.*

According to official data, since 2008, China has acquired assets in Europe worth USD 318 billion and since 2016, the PRC has become a net investor in the EU. Likewise, "the EU outward foreign direct investment (FDI) in the PRC has steadily decreased since 2012, particularly in the traditional manufacturing sector, with a parallel increase in investment in high-tech services, utilities, and agricultural and construction services, while the PRC's investment in the EU has grown exponentially over the past few years. Since 2016, the PRC has become a net investor in the EU. In 2017, 68 % of Chinese investments into Europe came from state-owned enterprises"[102].

To assure public resources in the jurisdiction where the value is created, transparency and legal certainty are, among others, key issues for investors and tax administrations.

3. FAIR TAXATION OF THE DIGITAL ECONOMY

The PE concept and the problem of the nexus are among the most important challenges regards in the way of finding a long-term solution to tax to the digital economy.

Under the OECD/G20 scope, from 2010 to 2018 different proposals have been held for the establishment of a fair taxation of the digital economy. The OECD recognised that "it would be difficult, if not impossible, to 'ring-fence' the digital economy from the rest of the economy for tax purposes because of the increasingly pervasive nature of digitalisation [...]. Beyond BEPS, digitalisation raised a series of broader direct tax challenges, which it identified as data, nexus and characterisation"[103].

On 21 March 2018, the European Commission issued two proposals for new Directives: as an interim solution, the one referred to as the Digital Services Tax (the DST)[104] and a longer-term Council Directive laying down rules relating to the corporate taxation of a significant digital presence (SDP or the Significant Digital Presence proposal)[105]. The DST proposal, which

102. See 2018 European Parliament report on the state of EU-China relations, 10 July 2018 — (2017/2274) (INI), par. 21. Retrieved from *https://www.europarl.europa.eu/doceo/document/A-8-2018-0252_EN.pdf*.

103. See OECD/G20, *Addressing the Tax Challenges of the Digitalisation of the Economy. Public Consultation Document*, 13 February-6 March 2019, p. 5.

104. Proposal for a Council Directive on the common system of a digital services tax on revenues resulting from the provision of certain digital services, Brussels, COM (2018) 148 final 2018/0073 (CNS), 2018.

105. Proposal for a Council Directive laying down rules relating to the corporate taxation of a significant digital presence, Brussels, COM (2018) 147 final 2018/0072(CNS), 2018. See *above* para. 2.2.

will apply only until the SDP solution has been implemented, is for gross revenues (i. e., turnover) tax, set at a uniform rate of 3% across all EU Member States. Consensus among EU Member States has not been reached on timing, but the DST proposal sets out proposed adoption of the Directive by 31 December 2019. The SDP proposal focuses on a new concept of digital PE, along with revised profit attribution rules.

According to the proposed Directive, Member States shall adopt and publish, by 31 December 2019 at the latest, the laws, regulations and administrative provisions necessary to comply with this Directive, and they shall apply those provisions from 1 January 2020 with respect to tax periods beginning on or after that date. In April 2018, the finance and economic affairs Ministers of the EU Member States discussed the above proposals at their informal Economic and Financial Affairs Council (ECOFIN) meeting in Sofia, Bulgaria. The Bulgarian Presidency of the Council of the EU scheduled a number of technical working meetings, starting on 2 May 2018, to discuss the proposals ahead of the next European Council meeting that took place in June.

4. THE ANTI-TAX-AVOIDANCE DIRECTIVE IMPLEMENTATION

Tax avoidance is a legal concept that emanates from the interpretation of either statutory general anti- avoidance rules (GAARs), sometimes also from targeted and specific anti-avoidance rules, from the judicial creation of GAARs or a principle of abuse, or from the reconciliatory interpretation of all the mentioned sources[106].

According to the EU Anti-Avoidance Directive (2016/1164) adopted on 12 July 2016 (ATAD), Member States must apply the anti-tax avoidance measures from 1 January 2019 by enacting new measures or amending existing ones. This Directive includes the implementation of the BEPS project in the EU and puts forward additional rules that establish a comprehensive framework against tax-avoidance.

According to its preamble, the ATAD should provide for a common framework in order to prevent a fragmentation of the market. The objective is to ensure a uniform implementation of the BEPS-package within the EU. However, Article 3 stipulates that the ATD provides for a *"de minimis"*

106. See Dourado, A. P., "Tax Avoidance revised in the EU BEPS Context", p. 3, in Dourado, A. P. (ed.), "Tax Avoidance revisited in the EU BEPS context", EATLP Annual Congress Munich, 2-4- June 2016, EATLP International Tax Series, vol. 15, *IBFD*, 2017, p. 138.

standard. This means that if the ATAD sets minimum standards, Member States can impose more restrictive ones and go beyond that standard[107].

5. THE EXCHANGE OF INFORMATION

The Directive on exchange of information of tax rulings (Directive 2015/2376, 8 December)[108] is a key legal issue for the BEPS actions implementations. The amendment of the Directive on administrative cooperation covers tax rulings going back five years from the date of implementation (that is, back to 1 January 2012) for cross-border, still valid, tax rulings, and three years (back to 1 January 2014) for those no longer valid.

The directive entered into force on 18 December 2015. Member States were due to adopt and publish by 31 December 2016 the laws, regulations and administrative provisions necessary to comply with the directive. The measures are being applied from 1 January 2017.

The Commission will receive a limited set of information for monitoring and assessing the proper application of the exchange of information, but this cannot be used for any other purpose. The exchange will be run over a six-month period.

6. THE NEED TO STRENGTH COOPERATION IN TAX MATTERS TO ASSURE AND EFFECTIVE AND EFFICIENT DISPUTE RESOLVING MECHANISM

For law making, it must be noted that, as of 2016, the PRC had concluded 54 double taxation avoidance agreements with BRI participating states. As Mejía-Lemos pointed out, "as for dispute resolution, it is anticipated that, like any major set of infrastructure projects, many disputes are likely to arise out of BRI projects and to be submitted to international arbitration. Expecting an increased demand for dispute resolution services, various arbitral institutions have updated, or are in the process of updating, their arbitration rules, and adopted specific guidelines (e. g. the various initiatives of the China International Economic and Trade Arbitration Commission (CIETAC),

107. See Popa, O. "An Overview of ATAD Implementation in EU Member States" in *European Taxation*, vol. 59, n 2/3, 2019.

108. The directive entered into force on 18 December 2015. Member States were due to adopt and publish by 31 December 2016 the laws, regulations and administrative provisions necessary to comply with the directive. The measures are being applied from 1 January 2017.

the Singapore International Arbitration Centre (SIAC) and the Hong Kong International Arbitration Centre (HKIAC)". The PRC government has also sought to address that demand, by establishing a Chinese domestic forum for the settlement of BRI disputes, in the form of international commercial courts, two of which were inaugurated in June 2018 by PRC's Supreme People's Court, the apex of the PRC state judicial branch (as reported in Xinhua news and discussed in other international legal media outlets). With particular reference to tax disputes, international arbitration may prove useful, in order to address some of the limitations of existing tax dispute resolution mechanisms, such as negotiation between tax authorities [also known as the "mutual agreement procedure" (MAP)][109].

Regarding tax disputes resolution, it should be noted that on 10 October 2017, the EU adopted the Tax Dispute Resolution Directive 2017/1852, setting forth the rules for a mechanism to resolve disputes between Member States when those disputes arise from the interpretation and application of agreements that provide for the elimination of double taxation. The Directive constitutes part of the EU's ongoing fight against aggressive tax planning and its efforts to resolve double taxation issues for businesses, and it is in line with recommendations set out under Action 14 on Making Dispute Resolution Mechanisms More Effective. Member States will have until 30 June 2019 to transpose the Directive into national laws and regulations. It will apply to complaints submitted after that date on questions relating to a tax year starting on or after 1 January 2018.

7. CONCLUSIONS

Further progress is needed to modernise and to stabilise the international tax framework[110].

109. See Mejía-Lemos, D., *The Belt and Road Initiative (BRI) and International Tax Law: A winter Note on Lawm-making and Dispute Resolution Issues Raised by the BRI*, 2019, retrieved from *https://globtaxgov.weblog.leidenuniv.nl/2019/01/23/belt-and-road- initiative-bri-and-international-tax-law-a-winter-note-on-law-making-and-dispute-resolution-issues-raised-by-the-bri/* For a discussion of the benefits (vel non) of international arbitration over the MAP in the context of PRC-ASEAN tax disputes, see Reuven Avi-Yonah and Haiyan Xu, "China and BEPS", *op. cit.*, p. 4 *et seq.*

110. OCDE, *OCDE Secretary-General Tax Report to G20 Finance Ministers and Central Bank Governors*, París, 2019, retrieved from *http://oecd.org./tax/oecd-secretary-general-tax-report-g20-finance-ministers-october-2019.pdf*. Implementing BEPS in the EU can help to stop unilateral tax measures and legal uncertainties for investments in the BRI scenario.

IV. INTERNATIONAL TAXATION IN THE POST-BEPS SCENARIO: A SIMPLIFIED INTRODUCTION TO THE OECD PILLAR TWO

FABRIZIO PASCUCCI[111]

1. INTRODUCTION

Taxation of cross-border business income follows a set of criteria resulting from a process of convergence between states which ignited over a century ago[112]. This process of convergence has increasingly led to the diffusion among countries of an articulated system of tax rules which reflect an essential idea: cross-border business income shall be taxed where income-producing activities might be located. This approach substantially results in that the (priority) taxing rights shall be allotted to source states, notably through the concept of a permanent establishment (PE)[113].

However, the international tax regime (usually referred to as this system of cross-border tax rules stemming from such convergence) is on the brink of an unparalleled reform, as the long-lasting paradigm seems to be profoundly altered. By reason of the evolution of multinational enterprises' (MNEs) business models, as well as the surge in international tax avoidance witnessed in the last decades, more than 130 countries agreed in 2021 to rethink the rules governing cross-border taxation on business income and adopted the so-called OECD Pillar Two[114], which essentially introduces the chance for (residence) states to exercise their taxing powers on foreign business income under the relatively simplistic assumption that such income has not been adequately taxed where it has been produced.

---

111. PhD candidate at the Université Catholique de Louvain and qualified tax lawyer.
112. The international tax regime may be regarded as the set of principles and rules embodied in the tax treaty network and in countries' domestic tax systems. According to some authors, such as Avi-Yonah, the international tax regime has been developed from the 1920s, when the League of Nations first introduced a set of comprehensive principles to avoid international double taxation. *See*, Avi-Yonah, R., *International Tax as International Law: An analysis of the International Tax Regime*, Cambridge University Press, 2007.
113. *See*, for example, Picciotto, S., *International Business Taxation: A Study in the Internationalization of Business Regulation*, Quorum Books, 1992, p. 24; and J. Kokott, "The "Genuine Link" Requirement for Source Taxation, in Public International Law" in W. Haslehner et al. (eds.), *Tax and the Digital Economy: Challenges and Proposals for Reform*, Kluwer Law International, 2019.
114. *See* OECD/G20, *Statement on a Two-Pillar Solution to Address the Tax Challenges Arising from the Digitalisation of the Economy*, 2021, retrieved from *https://www.oecd.org/tax/beps/beps-actions/action1/*

This short contribution proposes some theoretical observations to better understand the innovative approach that is going to be adopted in the post-BEPS tax scenario, as well as a (simplified) analysis of the process of determining and collecting the global minimum tax according to Pillar Two rules.

2. WHAT'S PILLAR TWO?

The OECD Pillar Two (or GloBE[115]) is essentially a minimum tax on MNE groups. This implies that regardless of *how much* income a multinational company has earned in a given fiscal year, and regardless of *where* such income has been produced, the effective tax burden (or Effective Tax Rate (ETR), according to the OECD terminology) must be not less than 15%.

The GloBE ETR is nothing more than the ratio between the taxes paid (numerator) and the income earned (denominator) in the concerned jurisdiction for a given fiscal year. Notably, the ETR shall be measured on a jurisdictional basis (i. e. by aggregating all the results of the entities in that jurisdiction) and according to *ad hoc* rules envisaged under Pillar Two[116]. Whenever the ETR so computed is below the 15% threshold, the gap shall be caught up and brought into charge by another jurisdiction (according to specific "charging mechanisms"[117].

Put differently, the OECD Pillar Two introduces a supranational tax regime that in some way overlaps internal tax rules (and tax treaties), entailing that — regardless of the corporate taxes paid in the jurisdiction where the activities are located (say, at source) — an additional amount (a "top-up tax", in the jargon) may be eventually paid in another country that proves to have a sufficient connection with the income (say, at residence)[118].

115. Which stands for "Global Anti-Base Erosion Rule".

116. Which do not necessarily reflect the internal tax rules of the concerned jurisdictions.

117. Thus, the underlying principle of Pillar Two is that — regardless of the reasons that led to such "inadequate" ETR (e. g. whether tax incentives have been awarded) — if the company has not been taxed in one country, then another country may "interfere" to make up the difference.

118. This passage accentuates one of the most critical aspects of Pillar Two, as this regime seems to go beyond the concept of territoriality (at least as traditionally intended). Indeed, in the pre-GloBE scenario, in order for a State to be able to exercise its taxing powers, a certain degree of connection between income and the territory was required. In other words, the additional taxing powers (i. e., the integration of taxation up to the threshold) are attributed to the different countries in which the multinational group operates regardless of the classic connecting criteria of residence and source, given that the subject who has produced the income (the investee company) is not resident in the State which exercises the additional levy (i. e. the State in which the participating

3. WHY PILLAR TWO?

As regards the purpose of Pillar Two and its role in the international tax landscape, it cannot be said that Pillar Two is a measure to tackle international tax avoidance *sic et simpliciter*. Indeed, Pillar Two seems to be lacking that element which mostly characterizes anti-abuse measures: the verification of the economic/commercial reasons underlying the transactions carried out by the taxpayer and the circumstances in which the allegedly abusive situation occurred. In the event that such economic/commercial reasons are adequately proven, the situation/transaction is to be regarded as non-abusive from a tax perspective.

Instead, Pillar Two rules do not require such an assessment and additional taxation is triggered upon the "mere" verification of elements which are based exclusively on numerical aspects. It could be thus said that the anti-abuse function of Pillar Two seems to be secondary when compared to the other objective of Pillar Two. Namely, to put a curb on tax competition[119]. Indeed, following the implementation of Pillar Two rules, business decisions concerning the location of investments should become less sensitive to the tax variable, as the benefits stemming from tax incentives offered by countries to attract foreign capital may be eventually captured according to Pillar Two rules by other countries[120].

For this reason, therefore, it could be argued that Pillar Two addresses two (interrelated) needs; i. e. to tackle harmful tax competition between states (as the main objective) and, through this, international tax avoidance (as a "collateral" objective).

4. HOW DOES IT WORK? A SIMPLIFIED APPROACH TO THE FUNCTIONING OF THE OECD PILLAR TWO[121]

The functioning of Pillar Two rules may be described by discussing three fundamental passages: the individuation of in-scope groups and entities; the determination of the GloBE ETR; and, finally, the collection of top-up taxes.

---

company is located), nor does the income produced by this entity have its source in the latter State.

119. See Mason, R., "The Transformation of International Tax" in *American Journal of International Law*, vol. 114, n. 3, 2020, pp. 353-402.

120. As explained, whatever the reason leading to an ETR below threshold, a top-up tax would be due and collected by some other countries, thereby sterilizing the incentive itself.

121. OECD/G20, *Tax Challenges Arising from the Digitalisation of the Economy — Global Anti-Base Erosion Model Rules (Pillar Two): Inclusive Framework on BEPS*, OECD Publishing,

4.1. Individuation of In-Scope Groups and Entities

The new rules only apply to multinational groups (i. e. MNEs), intended for Pillar Two purposes as those groups of companies that operate in at least two different jurisdictions. However, not all MNEs are subject to Pillar Two, provided that quantitative thresholds (set at EUR 750 million of global revenues) are envisaged to avert the application of these rules to "smaller" corporate taxpayers.

The computation of this quantitative threshold, as well as the determination of the MNE group's perimeter, are based on accounting data (namely, on consolidated financial statements) and, in principle, all those entities which are included in consolidated accounts[122] are subject to the Pillar Two rules. Nevertheless, the rules provide an array of exclusions (mostly due to policy concerns) and it is thus possible that certain entities (albeit included in consolidated financial statements), may be subsequently excluded from the application of the GloBE rules[123-124].

Once the in-scope entities have been identified, they shall be "located", as Pillar Two includes certain rules concerning the location of legal entities (and PEs) which are autonomous both from the domestic tax rules on tax residence and those included in the tax treaties that the concerned countries may have entered. It may be noted, though, that Pillar Two rules are not really dissimilar from the internal (and tax treaty) rules in terms of definitions and functioning, and quite often rely on the latter[125].

As mentioned, the location of entities is crucial for Pillar Two purposes, as the calculation of the GloBE ETR shall be generally performed on a

---

2021, retrieved from *https://www.oecd.org/tax/beps/tax-challenges-arising-from-the-digitalisation-of-theeconomy-global-anti-base-erosion-model-rules-pillar-two.htm*

122. As determined in accordance with the accounting principles used by the consolidating company.
123. Because, for example, it was considered that there are no avoidance risks associated with certain entities.
124. The effect of this exclusion is not only to relieve these entities from calculating the ETR (which may be quite burdensome at times), but also to deactivate any possible obligations that could arise as a result of Pillar Two rules, both in terms of reporting obligations and collection of taxes.
125. By means of a mere example, and without entering into details, the fundamental rule for legal entities is that they shall be located in those jurisdictions where they are regarded as tax resident according to the domestic tax rules. In the case of PEs, the criteria are based on the presence of a tax treaty between the jurisdiction of the head office (residence state) and the one in which the PE is recognized (source state); i. e. if a tax treaty is enacted Pillar Two relies on treaty rules, otherwise internal rules of the country where a PE is deemed to exist are to be followed.

jurisdictional basis by aggregating the income and taxes of those legal entities (and PEs) which may be located in a given territory.

4.1. Determination of the ETR

When the scope of application has been defined, it is necessary to proceed with the calculation of the GloBE ETR. The ETR is substantially the ratio between i) taxes on business income (or taxes which are regarded for Pillar Two purposes as "qualified" taxes[126]); and ii) corporate income earned in a certain jurisdiction as measured according to the GloBE rules. As mentioned, aggregated income taxes form the numerator and aggregated (net) income from the denominator of the (jurisdictional) GloBE ETR.

The income of the legal entities and PEs belonging to the MNE group shall be calculated according to the GloBE rules, i. e. irrespective of the applicable domestic (and tax treaty) rules.

The starting point in calculating the GloBE income is the (net) financial result for a given fiscal year as reflected in the accounts of the entity. That is, the set of financial data of the entity which are used in the preparation of consolidated accounts in accordance with the accounting standards used by the ultimate parent company of the MNE group[127].

Once the financial accounting net income or loss (FANIL, in the jargon) has been determined, the accounting figures shall be "rectified" to reflect those adjustments required under Pillar Two, which have been envisaged by the OECD to better align the computation of the GloBE income with the domestic tax rules of the states participating in the OECD Inclusive Framework.

As for the (income) taxes to be included in the numerator of the GloBE ETR, the starting point is yet again the accounting figures as adjusted according to Pillar Two rules (as an example, to prevent overstatements of the ETR, income taxes included in the financial statements of an entity shall be carefully analysed to exclude those amounts that may refer to e. g. taxes paid on income which is domestically taxable but excluded from the GloBE computations)[128].

126. Such as taxes on retained earnings or withholding taxes.

127. Before any consolidation adjustments (e. g., those adjustments which are performed to eliminate certain intra-group transactions).

128. The numerator also considers deferred taxation, to prevent purely temporal differences from giving rise to additional taxation. Like the GloBE income calculation, the tax calculation procedure also provides for specific allocation rules that must be taken into account in the case of particular situations.

Once GloBE income and taxes have been calculated, these figures must be aggregated to include all the results of the in-scope entities which are located in a given jurisdiction, provided that the calculation of ETR is ordinarily done on a jurisdictional basis[129]. This essentially means that all the results and taxes of entities of any legal form or PEs which are located in a certain jurisdiction for Pillar Two purposes flow, respectively, into the denominator and the numerator of the ETR for that jurisdiction.

Whenever the ratio (expressed as a percentage) is less than 15%, the difference (the so-called "top-up tax percentage") shall be applied to the (net) GloBE income in that jurisdiction and supplemented. More precisely, the top-up tax percentage multiplied by the net income produced in the jurisdiction represents the jurisdictional top-up tax for that country[130].

4.2. Collection of Top-Up Taxes

At this stage the jurisdictional top-up tax has been computed and allocated to each of the entities belonging to the MNE group in the jurisdiction. *Ergo*, it shall be now defined which jurisdictions will eventually benefit from it (i. e. which countries will be entitled to the additional levy).

To this end, there are three mechanisms for collecting the minimum global tax. Namely, the Income Inclusion Rule (IIR), the Under-Taxed Profits Rule (UTPR) and the Qualified Domestic Minimum Top-Up Tax (QDMTT). The application of these mechanisms takes place in a coordinated manner, in the sense that the application of the IIR takes place in priority with respect to the UTPR, and that the potential application of a QDMTT in a jurisdiction entails a reduction of the top-up taxes that can be collected through the IIR (and consequently through the UTPR) in other jurisdictions.

The IIR is to be regarded as the "primary rule" for collecting top-up taxes and essentially provides that if a controlled entity (i. e., an entity in which another entity of the MNE group has an investment) is considered as a low-taxed entity in the jurisdiction where located since the ETR in that jurisdiction is below the 15% threshold, then the controlling entity will be called upon under the IIR to supplement the difference (in the jurisdiction where such parent entity is located).

---

129. Exceptions are envisaged with respect e. g., to "investment entities", or minority-owned entities.

130. For the sake of completeness, once the whole amount of top-up taxes for a given country has been identified it shall be then allocated to each entity located in that country in proportion to the GloBE income share allocable to such entities and collected in another jurisdiction in accordance with the "collection mechanisms" (*see next section*).

More precisely, the application of the IIR follows a top-down approach, implying that the country in which the ultimate parent entity (UPE) is located is awarded additional taxing rights on the (low-taxed) income produced in the jurisdiction of its subsidiaries. Whenever this is not possible (because e. g., the UPE's jurisdiction has not implemented Pillar Two, or the UPE is an excluded entity), the IIR shall be applied by the "next" entity down the chain (i. e., the lower-tier parent company, defined as Intermediate Parent Entity under the terminology of Pillar Two)[131-132].

Whenever there is residual top-up tax to be allocated[133], the UTPR may be activated. In essence, the secondary mechanism provides that the taxing powers on the residual top-up taxes shall be attributed to those jurisdictions according to a formula which privileges countries with employees and tangible assets[134]. The concrete implementation and application methods for collecting top-up taxes under the UTPR are left to the jurisdictions, meaning that Pillar Two rules foresee those countries may choose whether to deny the deduction of expenses/items to the extent that the top-up tax due is integrated, or apply a corresponding taxation (e. g. in the form of withholding taxes).

This considered, it could be argued that the IIR and UTPR imply a re-allocation of taxing powers from those countries which have a "traditional" connection with the income (because e. g. the activities of the subsidiary are located therein) to those countries which exhibit some sort of an implicit *nexus* with the income (because e. g. the parent entity is located therein). This approach seems to rely on the assumption that if the income has not been sufficiently taxed where the company is located (say, at source), then another country may collect the "missing part" (say, at residence). This other country seems to be legitimized either because there is a parent company (in application of the IIR), or because there are indicators (i. e., physical assets or employees) which suggest that in some way the income have been surreptitiously diverted towards low-tax jurisdictions (in application of the UTPR).

131. The top-down approach provides for certain exceptions whenever in the chain there is an entity which owned by minority shareholders (not included in the scope of consolidation) in an amount of at least 20% (so-called Partially-Owned Parent Entity).
132. The objective of this top-down approach may be seen in allocating additional tax revenues to those jurisdictions in which the headquarters of the MNE group are located on the underlying assumption that the (low-taxed) income somewhat originated therein.
133. Top-up taxes which have not been allocated pursuant the IIR, or if it was not possible to apply the IIR in any jurisdiction.
134. The objective of the UTPR is to allocate additional taxes to those jurisdictions that have substantive activities located therein (i. e. because tangible assets and/or employees may be located in such jurisdictions).

For this reason, it has been decided at the level of the OECD to recognize the possibility for countries to implement a third mechanism which grant "low-tax" jurisdictions to preserve their taxing powers on that income that has been taxed at a rate below 15%. That is, a qualified domestic minimum top-up tax (QDMTT) which permits the ETR differential to be bridged at the domestic level (i. e. the top-up taxes due in a given jurisdiction may be collected domestically through the implementation of a QDMTT which follows the same set of Pillar Two rules). Whenever a QDMTT is applied, the amount of top-up taxes due in other jurisdictions shall be reduced correspondingly (i. e. to the extent that the gap has been filled up domestically as a result of this regime the IIR and UTPR shall credit the QDMTT).

5. PRELIMINARY CONCLUSIONS

It cannot be easily denied that the introduction of Pillar Two into the international tax landscape represents a game-changer, as this new set of rules not only involves the acceptance of a new approach when it comes to taxing cross-border business income, but extends to a supranational definition of income (and, hence, taxes on income), as well as to a new notion of international tax avoidance. Nevertheless, it is fairly impossible to express a holistic judgment on the effectiveness and, especially, on the soundness of this new "global regime", as this very much depends on the ability of countries to coordinate.

However (and regardless of the ability of Pillar Two to effectively put a limit on harmful tax competition and international tax avoidance), the attempt to harmonize tax rules must be welcomed, as this represents the first step towards the creation of a coordinated corporate tax system.

Regarding the EU-China relationships, the Pillar Two rules are to be implemented in the EU (as from 2024), whereas China has not set yet any definitive plans. Hence, it seems nearly impossible at this stage to foretell the potential impacts of Pillar Two on Chinese and EU MNEs, as these impacts will largely depend on the implementation phase.

Nevertheless, it shall be considered that tax incentives and exemptions (in their various forms) are a critical feature of China's corporate tax system and may be captured by Pillar Two, as the rules make no distinctions. Furthermore, it must be considered that Hong Kong (which might be regarded as a steppingstone for inbound and outbound investments involving China) could be targeted by the rules, provided that — albeit its nominal corporate tax rate is slightly above 15% — it adopts a territorial regime which could bring the GloBE ETR below threshold in different cases.

What is certain is that Chines tax policymakers will take into account all these factors in order not to demean the attractiveness for potential EU investors.

From Source-oriented to residence-oriented — China's International Tax Regime Reshaped by BRI?

JIE WANG
PhD candidate at Erasmus University Rotterdam

I. INTRODUCTION

The Belt and Road Initiative (BRI)[1] is a regional and transnational cooperative economic framework launched by China, which aims to revive its ancient economic ties with Eurasian countries[2] Announced by President Xi Jinping only in 2013, the geographic coverage and economic data that BRI has achieved are eye-catching. Up to July 2023, China has signed BRI "Cooperation Agreements" with 152 jurisdictions[3], which has shown the acceding parties' political commitment to further cooperating under the initiative. In the first 5 years (2013-2018) of BRI, the flow of foreign direct investment (FDI) from China to BRI countries had surpassed USD 90 billion, and the newly signed engineering project contracts valued more than USD 600 billion, with an annual increase rate of 11.9%[4].

1. The "Belt" is for "Silk Road Economic Belt", and "Road" is for "21st-Century Maritime Silk Road". In 2015, several ministries of China published the official English translation for BRI. Before that, the "Belt and Road" was also mostly known as "OBOR" for "One Belt and One Road" or "One Belt, One Road". See, for example, Yawen, Z., "The Establishment of a Multilateral Investment Treaty for the 'One Belt, One Road' Initiative", in *Special Issue Cambridge Law Review*, 2018.
2. However, as shown in Chart 5, BRI reaches out further than Eurasia, which has embraced Africa, Oceania, North and South America into its scope.
3. See Belt and Road Portal, *List of Countries that Have Signed "Belt and Road" Cooperation Document with China*, retrieved from *https://www.yidaiyilu.gov.cn/p/77298.html*, accessed 29 July 2023.
4. See Ministry of Commerce of China, *The Regular Press Conference of the Ministry of Commerce (MOFCOM)*, 18 April 2019, retrieved from *http://www.mofcom.gov.cn/xwfbh/20190418.shtml*, accessed 29 July 2023.

For China, BRI has been the strategic focus of the government since its launch. The Party and the central government ministries have been enacting guiding documents frequently to reform and regulate, and ultimately to facilitate the construction of BRI. Their efforts have covered multiple fields, including but not limited to infrastructure, technology, energy, environment, economy and so forth. Among those areas of rules, taxation has also been a key in advancing BRI.

The purpose of this article is to explore the implications of BRI for the development of China's international tax regime in general. It presupposes that there exists a mode of transformation that could be used to capture the evolution of an international tax regime. According to that, this article proposes that under the influences of BRI, there is a trend that the international tax regime of China ("ITRC"), is transforming from source-oriented to residence-oriented.

To start the verification process of the proposition, Part II lays down the background information about BRI and the ITRC. Part III elucidates the research proposition and the verifying approach. Part IV then turns to explore the top design of BRI with a special reference to tax policies. Part V and Part VI identify and analyze the BRI-driven changes of the two components of the international tax regime, respectively the domestic tax laws and the double tax agreements. For domestic part, the discussions cover the foreign tax credit system and the controlled foreign corporation (CFC) regime. For tax treaty part, this article inspects the changes in terms of breadth and depth. For breadth, the analysis looks into the general picture of China's bilateral tax treaty network, while the depth part discusses the content changes of sparing credit, the withholding tax liability, and the most-favored-nation clause. Based on all these discussions, this article is concluded by Part VII revisiting the proposition and presenting the result of the verification.

II. THE INTERNATIONAL TAX REGIME OF CHINA

1. BRI AND INTERNATIONAL TAXATION

Being a transnational framework, the key starting point of BRI is to connect the markets of China and its partners in the BRI. Yet comparing the level of development of China and most of BRI countries, the outbound investment from China outweighs China's inbound investment from BRI countries. As a result, such "inter-connection" implicitly advocates more for the removal of barriers to the Chinese outbound investment from both the China side and BRI countries. The other way round, facilitating the inbound investment into China, however, only gains normative weight in the framework of BRI.

Based on the above, inspecting how China adjusts itself to the demand and reality of BRI may provide valuable insights to understanding China's strategy and foreseeing its future actions as well. This article limits that inspection to the area of taxation, and more specifically, to the international aspects of business taxation.

2. CHINA'S INTERNATIONAL TAX REGIME

The international tax regime of China, or technically, China's foreign-related tax law has two components[5], the domestic tax law and the double tax agreements (DTA) signed with other tax jurisdictions. The composition generally reflects the basic norm of international taxation. The following only lays down some background information for the purpose of later and deeper discussions.

The current international tax model has been commonly accredited to the contributions made in the 1920s by the League of Nations[6]. To this day, if we compare the international tax law of China to the common international tax model, the former is still an "infant" to the latter, which is going to celebrate its 100th anniversary. The ITRC was created in the 1980s, for the facts that either its first DTA was signed in 1983[7], or that the first foreign-related enterprise income tax law was enacted in 1980 as well[8]. However, in modern times, China's international tax regime is closer to maturity, after going through its "adolescent" restlessness. That maturity can be partly explained by the so-called "latecomer advantage", in that Chinese international tax regime grows out of the modern international tax institutions[9].

For one thing, the ITRC is consistent with the *residence-source* model of international tax model. China taxes the worldwide income of residents while providing foreign tax credit to eliminate double taxation. For non-residents,

5. This relates to the nature of international tax law, see for example, Arnold, B. J., "Canada's International tax regime: Historical Review, Problems and Outlook for the Future" in *Canada in International Law at 150 and Beyond Paper*, at note 8, pp. 1-2.
6. De Wilde, M. F., "'Sharing the Pie'; Taxing Multinationals in a Global Market", 2015, retrieved from: *https://ssrn.com/abstract=2564181*, p. 12.
7. STA, *List of Double Taxation Agreements Signed by China*, retrieved from *http://www.chinatax.gov.cn/n810341/n810770/index.html*, accessed 29 July 2023.
8. Income Tax Law of China Concerning Chinese-Foreign Equity Joint Ventures.
9. Jinyan Li, *International Taxation in China: A Contextualized Analysis* (IBFD Publications 2016), para. 1.3.2.2.

the Chinese tax liability is limited to the income derived within China. As a result, to be well-functioning, the residence-source international tax model is in turn dependent on the delineation of residence and source concepts. For the concept of residence, China uses the test of place of incorporation and place of effective management[10], which is further supplemented by provisions of its DTAs (usually Article 4). The identification of source is generally aligned with the categorization of incomes, of which the foundational division is between positive (business) incomes and passive (investment) incomes.

For another, China now has one of the largest tax treaty networks in the world. By the end of April 2019, China has concluded DTAs with 107 jurisdictions[11], even though the network has been "weaved" only from 1983. The technical design of its DTAs draws on either the UN model or OECD model so that all these tax treaties are basically the same in structure, and the divergence of content is limited. It is expected that China's bilateral tax treaty network will further expand.

III. RESEARCH PROPOSITION AND VERIFYING APPROACH

This article, with a focus on the implications of BRI for the international tax law of China, proposes that under the influences of BRI, there is an emerging trend that the ITRC is shifting from *source-oriented* to *residence-oriented*. This pair of terms, the source-oriented tax (SOT) system and residence-oriented tax (ROT) system, will be refined in the following.

To validate the proposition, a comprehensive approach to inspecting and evaluating the implications of BRI for China's international tax regime must be designed. For that purpose, this article uses a two-fold approach, which consists of a conceptual approach as core to identifying an international tax regime as SOT or ROT, and a factual approach to systematically unfolding the concrete rule changes brought by BRI. The two sub-approaches work together to test the proposition.

1. CONCEPTUAL APPROACH — CATCHING THE TREND

The division of SOT and ROT is the conceptualization of and in line with a country's relative stance on the so-called "inbound" taxation and "outbound" taxation.

10. Enterprise Income Tax Law of China, Article 2.
11. STA, *List of Double Taxation Agreements Signed by China*, retrieved from *http://www.chinatax.gov.cn/n810341/n810770/index.html*, accessed 29 July 2023.

In the case of China, the inbound taxation is the taxation of non-residents, on their incomes sourced from China, manifested as *outflow* of taxable income from China; while the outbound taxation is the taxation of Chinese residents, on their worldwide especially foreign-source incomes, manifested as *inflow* of taxable income to China. As inbound taxation arises from the country being the source of taxable income outflow, it can be entitled "source-based" taxation (SBT). In the same vein, the outbound taxation can be named as "residence-based" taxation (RBT). In this article, SBT and RBT refer to the two integral modules of the international tax regime of a country.

SBT and RBT are inherently not overlapping or conflicting, for they are targeting different groups of taxpayers and incomes. They do embody and reflect distinctive policy objectives and value orientations. The design of SBT rules aims to effectively tax the income of non-residents on one hand, on the other, they can play the role of attracting foreign investment. These two dimensions either echo the benefit principle that justifies the territorial taxation, or relate to the capital import neutrality (CIN) or the legal principle of non-discrimination. Correspondingly, besides effectively taxing the foreign income, the residence-based tax rules can be designed to facilitating outbound investment, by removing tax barriers or lowering tax burdens. Not free from controversies, the RBT is constructed upon ability-to-pay and capital export neutrality (CEN).

	SBT	RBT
Policy objectives	Effective taxation on non-resident	Effective taxation on resident's foreign income
	Attracting foreign investments	Facilitating outbound investment
Foundations	Benefit principle	Ability-to-pay
	CIN	CEN

Table 1

Even as said that SBT and RBT are equally being key to the integrality of an international tax regime, different countries or a country in different stages may waver between the two. In other words, the relative weight of SBT and RBT is discrepant. For example, a developing economy that has barely any outbound investment is conceivable to have less sophisticated outbound or RBT rules, compared to that of a developed economy that relies much on foreign market and overseas investment. Or reversely, a traditional capital exporting country is expected to have less sophisticated inbound or SBT rules.

For the purpose of ongoing discussions, and based on the above comparison of SBT and RBT, this article further categorizes two modules of taxation, in delineation of a country's general orientation towards international taxation. That is what has been mentioned in the beginning, the *SOT* or *ROT*, which is determined by a country's inclination to or particular emphasis on SBT or RBT.

Being equally important in the purported proposition, another focus falls on the "trend". That firstly means that the purported proposition is not final or once for all, but is of the attribute of time, which is to catch the tendency of development within a certain period of time. In this article, it is for the period of BRI's construction. In other words, the proposition and its validation are not to grab the "destination", but the "scenery" during the journey. The efforts throughout this article does not touch upon the model of ITRC *before* the BRI, or to demonstrate that the ITRC has *already* finished its transformation.

To catch the trend of SOT or ROT, the key challenge then is to measure the weight of SBT or RBT of an international tax regime. It is unimaginable to accurately calculate their respective weight, either absolute or relative at an exact point of time. However, grasping the trend only entails inspecting the changes that are happening, and then distribute the changes to the weight of SBT or RBT to grasp the tendency.

In determining the trend of ITRC as source-oriented or residence-oriented, the *key* step is *"classification"*, meaning that the process of grouping a certain tax rule into either SBT or RBT. For that purpose, the policy objectives pursued by a relevant set of tax rules are accessible indicators for its classification. In cases where the rule is already in place, the focus is then to delineate the changes of the rule. As a result, it is introduced the *"maturtiy"* as an index factor of the "weight" of SBT or RBT. The maturity is in turn signified and materialized by the density or maturity of the rules in each camp, so factors like number, existence, robustness, or enforcement of rules are to be considered.

For illustration, it is supposed that a country introduces the CFC regime, being an anti-avoidance rule, of which the tenet is to safeguard the home taxing right on resident multinationals. The step classification groups the CFC regime into RBT, and it adds force to ROT. In comparison, if the country enhances the CFC regime to be more sophisticated, the classification step is supplemented by the consideration of the maturity of RBT. The CFC regime will be inspected in terms of its competency, practical implementation or other elements. All these improved elements increase the weight of RBT. If within a certain period of time, many other reforms of similar kind are adopted, a trend towards ROT can be established.

2. FACTUAL APPROACH

The factual approach is a method to firstly identify the changes of tax rules, and then organize the changes in a systematic way. The factual approach provides the "raw material" for the functioning of the conceptual approach. However, the application of the conceptual approach is not as visible as the factual approach, for normally the former is imbedded into the later.

The factual approach explores the rule changes effected by or in service of BRI from three aspects. The first aspect is the top-level system design, which is not strictly the law. However, in the context of law-making in China, usually it is the programmatic plan to guiding the future development of rules. The second aspect is the first element of a country's international tax regime, the domestic tax laws of China. The third aspect is the second element of a country's international tax regime, the bilateral DTAs of China. This aspect will research both the general picture of China's international tax treaty network, but also the material content of DTAs.

Beyond these three aspects, there are still two "controllers" underlying the factual approach, one external controller and one internal controller of inspecting the above three objects. The external controller is the time range. That is to say that only the new moves since the launch of BRI in 2013 can be taken into account. Normally, this is not a long time for exciting things to happen in taxation. However, the demonstration below will break the stereotype. The internal controller is the link at the surface or underlying between BRI and the rule changes, and it plays a fundamental rule in making the general analysis defensible. If a rule change has no link with BRI, it does then make no sense to count it in the follow-up analysis. It is not necessary to enumerate here all the forms of that link. Instead, the link will be explained when inspecting the rule changes.

IV. TOP-LEVEL POLICY DESIGN OF BRI

1. PHASE I: VISION AND ACTIONS

The so-called "top-level" refers to the policy documents issued by the Party or central government, in contrast to those by the provincial governments. During the period 2013-2015, the major policy reference to BRI is the milestone document ("Decision")[12] by the Party who led the government at all levels. The *Decision* is the programmatic plan for China's reform in the next 5-10 years. It positions BRI as one of the plans for the objective of constructing a new *open economy* system[13].

Before the State Council authorized NDRC[14], MOF[15], and MOFCOM to issue the first top-level BRI action plan[16] ("Vision and Actions") in 2015, there are no global guiding principles of BRI. Therefore, the *Vision and Actions* is the critical file to comprehending the guiding lights for the construction of BRI, in particular of taxation.

In the Vision and Actions, taxation is seen as one of the aspects regarding smooth trade and investment facilitation, among the priorities of cooperation. Specifically, in terms of taxation, the document calls on the parties to push forward the negotiation of DTAs. In this regard, the international tax treaty is saluted for its functions of eliminating investment barriers as well as protecting the interests of investors. Going further, considering China's advantageous positions to most of other BRI parties, either barrier elimination or investor protection gains more realistic significance for Chinese outbound investments and investors than their counterparties.

2. PHASE II: COMPREHENSIVE POLICYMAKING

After the guiding light shed by the Vision and Actions, there has been a clear boost of BRI policymaking. At the central government level, such policymaking has been comprehensively contributed by both the State Council and almost all the ministries. The below Chart 1 shows the policy fields covered, and Chart 2 shows the monthly issued quantity of BRI policies[17]. As shown in Chart 1, tax policy is obviously not among

12. Communist Party of China, *Decision of the Central Committee of the Communist Party of China on Several Major Issues Concerning Comprehensively Deepening Reform*, 12 November 2013, retrieved from *http://www.gov.cn/jrzg/2013-11/15/content_2528179.htm*, accessed 29 July 2023.
13. *Ibid*, chapter 7, point 26.
14. National Development and Reform Commission.
15. Ministry of Finance of People's Republic of China.
16. Ministry of Foreign Affairs, and Ministry of Commerce of the People's Republic of China, Vision and Actions on Jointly Building Silk Road Economic Belt and 21st-Century Maritime Silk Road, retrieved from *https://www.fmprc.gov.cn/eng/topics_665678/2015zt/xjpcxbayzlt2015nnh/201503/t20150328_705553.html*, accessed 29 July 2023.
17. The Chart is processed from the data in the research "黄凯丽, 赵频, 一带一路倡议的政策文本量化研究——基于政策工具视角, 情报杂志" 37.1, 2018, pp. 53-58. The authors collected the policy documents with the theme of BRI from the end of 2013 to May 2017.

the champions of fields issuing new BRI policies. However, that does not undermine the primacy of taxation in constructing BRI, as already evidenced by the Vision and Actions. The following focuses on the stance of State Taxation Administration (STA) in the BRI.

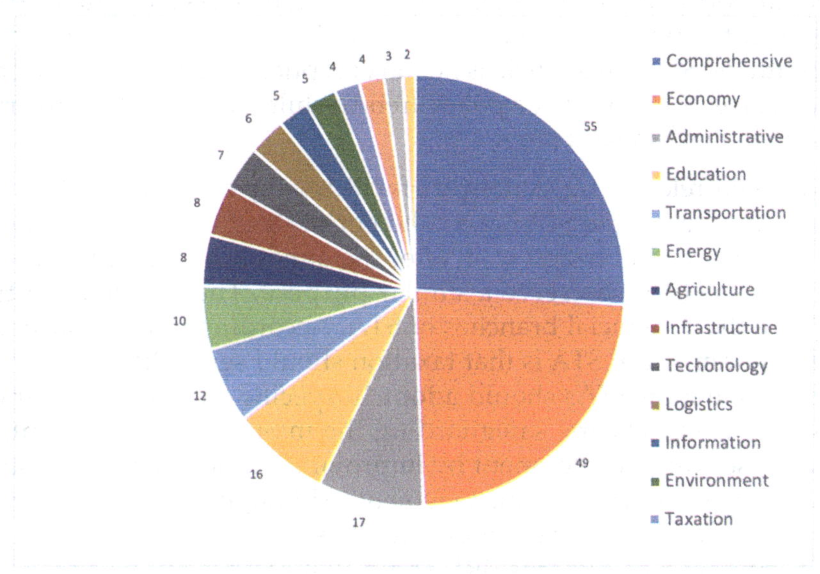

Chart 1

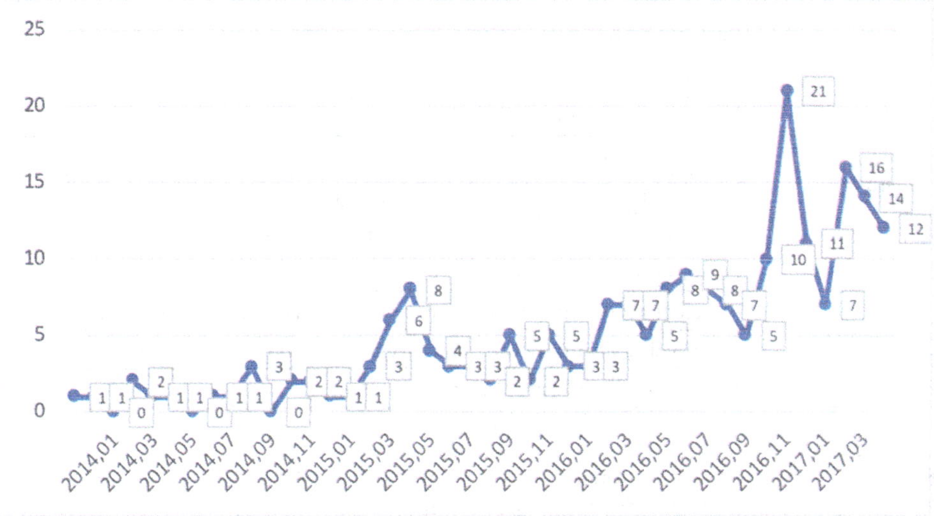

Chart 2

3. STA: TWO DIRECTIONS OF EFFORTS

The STA is the quasi-legislative as well as the administrative organ of taxation in China[18]. Its legislative power is broad, especially for the implementation matters of taxation "laws", of which the legislation is the reserved authority of the National People's Congress. As a result, for both the top-level tax policy orientation and the detailed tax rules, one must consult with the STA. This article is not an exception, it extracts its "macro" role as a source of knowing the policy trend, while leaves the "micro" role for further analysis in later parts.

STA does not release a legislation plan for BRI, so there is no straightforward way to know whether the STA has a coherent strategy for the rule changes. However, a Notice published soon after the announcement of the Vision and Actions in 2015 may serve a similar purpose. The recipients of this Notice[19] are the provincial branches of STA. According to the Notice, the general requirement of STA is that taxation should serve BRI proactively. In concrete, the local STAs should adopt 10 specific measures from three aspects. These aspects are, safeguarding the interests by implementing tax treaties, seeking development by improving services, and promoting compliance by standardizing management. Although these are mostly in the level of tax administration, they equally show at the macro level the work priorities of STA towards BRI. These 10 measures can be aligned by two directions of STA's efforts with regards to BRI, which are shown below.

Directions	Measures
Facilitating Outbound Investment	Establishing a country-by-country tax information center
	Creating BRI tax service website
	Tax training for outbound investors
	Setting up a "going out" seat on 12366 Hotline
	Encouraging intermediary agencies going out
	Enhancing the implementation of tax treaties
	Strengthening tax-related disputes resolution by bilateral negotiation
Managing the Risks	Perfecting the management of overseas tax Information declaration
	Reporting annually the tax analysis of outbound investors
	Establishing risk pre-warning mechanism

Table 2

18. Li, J., "International Taxation in China: A Contextualized Analysis", *op. cit.*, para. 2.5.1.
19. STA, *Notice of the State Administration of Taxation on Implementing the Action Plan on the Belt and Road Initiative and Effectively Conducting the Taxation Service and Administration*, April 2015.

Through these two directions of efforts in terms of BRI, it is known that STA intends to, on one hand, smooth the tax experiences for Chinese companies to investing overseas, on the other, to control the tax risks brought by the outbound investment. Even though for the latter point, the form and substance of the tax "risks" are not specified.

V. BRI-DRIVEN REFORMS OF DOMESTIC TAX LAW

Compared to the investigation of China's DTAs that often requires to see things behind the articles, the adjustments of Chinese domestic tax laws are more transparent. Even though there are many more changes in law enforcement, however, the following only focuses on the rule-based reforms. To testify the proposition, one of the characteristics of ROT is that a state is taking tax actions encouraging its residents to invest overseas. On the mirror side, the growing outbound investment may also challenge the effectiveness of the home country's RBT. The countering tax measures, therefore, constitute another thread demonstrating the proposition. Accordingly, two aspects of rule changes will be introduced and discussed. The first is the perfected and activated controlled foreign company (CFC) regime, the second is the improved foreign tax credit system.

1. IMPROVED FOREIGN TAX CREDIT SYSTEM

China's foreign tax credit (FTC) system has undergone substantial reform against the background of BRI. The tenet of the reform is to facilitate the going out of Chinese companies by providing more thorough credit of foreign tax. The original FTC system was effectively built up in 2009[20], which had imposed considerable restrictions on the sufficiency of tax credit. In 2017, STA reshaped the FTC system so as to adapt to the new situation brought about by BRI,[21] and that has released the restrictions tit for tat. Here the restrictions and the countering reforms are grouped as horizontal and vertical.

The horizontal feature of the old system marking those restrictions is the per-country credit mechanism. Under this mechanism, resident company deriving incomes from more than one countries is not allowed to combine and reuse the credit balance across countries. As a result, taxpayers' credit

---

20. MOF, STA, *Notice on Issues Concerning the Foreign Income Tax Credit of Enterprises*, n.125, 2009.
21. MOF, STA, *Notice on Issues concerning Improving the Tax Credit Policy for Overseas Income of Enterprises*, n. 84, 2017.

balances in low tax countries cannot be reused for the credit of high tax countries. On the other hand, foreign tax paid to high tax countries that exceed the credit limit as calculated by the Chinese tax rate cannot be credited currently. Therefore, insufficient credit exists under the per-country credit mechanism, which will adversely affect the cash flow of the taxpayer. The situation will be worse if one of the foreign branches has suffered losses, for under the mechanism such losses cannot be manipulated into calculating the taxable income in China or third countries.

The vertical restriction in the old FTC system is the three-layer credit mechanism, regarding the indirect credit for tax paid by the multi-layered foreign subsidiaries. Ideally, a perfect FTC system should provide unlimited credit to the end of the holding chain. Whereas apparently, this cannot be the case in reality. In China's old FTC system, the taxpayer can file credit for foreign tax at most until the third layer subsidiary. There are detailed standards to identify the qualified layer and subsidiary[22]. With the popularity of outbound investment, the business model that extends further than three-layer holding becomes common as well[23]. Restricting the credit chain to three layers makes the FTC halfway to its purpose, for double taxation is only partially exempt.

The new system aiming at facilitating outbound investment has targeted loosening both the horizontal and vertical restrictions. First of all, the per-country credit is supplemented by a global credit mechanism, which provides combined FTC regardless of the countries of source. In this case, the FTC obtained by the taxpayer will be more sufficient. The same spirit is found in the reform of the five-layer credit. It literally means that resident company can credit the foreign tax it has indirectly born all the way to the fifth-layer subsidiary. Although it raises higher standards of tax administration and compliance, the elimination of double taxation will be achieved to a greater extent.

The two measures, in horizontal and vertical aspects, have the direct effect of easing the tax burden of outbound Chinese investors. Besides these, there are also peripheral actions serving the same purpose. For instance, STA abolished the ex-ante approval procedure for FTC in 2015[24], now taxpayer

22. *Ibid*, articles 5 and 6.
23. See official reading of the new FTC policy: MOF, STA, *Senior Officials of STA and MOF Answering Questions on Improving the Tax Credit Policy for Enterprises' Overseas Income*, retrieved from *http://m.mof.gov.cn/czxw/201712/t20171229_2790745.htm*, accessed 29 July 2023.
24. STA, *Announcement on Issues concerning the Follow-up Administration after the Cancellation of the Approval Item of Confirmation of the Application of Simple Collection and Tax Sparing*

only needs to file for record of FTC. Another example is a BRI-tailored policy relevant to FTC. In general or sub-contracting or consortium engineering project, the entity that actually earns the foreign income is not who actually pays the foreign tax. The first entity then may not be eligible for Chinese FTC. STA issued a circular in 2017 to solve this inconsistency problem by adopting the principle of "substance over form"[25]. These actions taken together have formed robust policy support for improving the FTC system, to the direction of facilitating the outbound investment of resident companies.

According to the conceptual approach and the table 1, the foreign tax credit system should firstly be classified into the group of RBT rules. For that the FTC is a basic method to eliminate double taxation, which is the key consideration for cross-border factor movement. Secondly, in the level of maturity, the above reform of China's FTC system has made it more competent to achieve its normative goal. The reform can also pass the test of factual approach as well. Because STA had expressly alleged that the reform is to serve the "the need for new developments"[26]. Therefore, the improvement of FTC system has added weight to the RBT. Taken individually, it conforms to the trend in the research proposition regarding the ITRC's transformation to ROT.

2. ACTIVATED AND PATCHED CFC REGIME

CFC regime is designed to combat the artificial tax avoidance of resident companies by using foreign controlled entities, especially in low tax jurisdictions. CFC denies the potential tax deferral or avoidance by taxing currently the resident's proportionate income share in its controlled foreign subsidiaries. CFC regime is not sensitive to the worldwide or territorial tax system, in that in either system resident companies have the incentive to abuse the tax laws. On the other hand, the CFC regime is rooted in the rightfulness of residence taxing right, and the unreasonable tax deferral or tax avoidance by using CFC challenge such rightfulness. In this sense, the CFC regime maintains the RBT, and the development of it may manifest the changing weight of RBT.

The evolvement of China's CFC regime in recent years corresponds to the trend of strengthening RBT. The regime was introduced by China's

Credit to the Overseas Income of Enterprises, n. 70, 2015.

25. STA, *Announcement on Issues concerning the Tax Credit Vouchers for Overseas Contracted Engineering Projects of Enterprises*, n. 41, 2017.

26. MOF, STA, *Senior Officials of STA and MOF Answering Questions on Improving the Tax Credit Policy for Enterprises' Overseas Income*, *op. cit.*

first Enterprise Income Tax Law (EITL) in 2008[27], and materialized by STA subsequently in 2009[28]. However, it was still far from perfection, for it lacks operational guidelines on various elements. For instance, there are no comprehensive standards of "control"[29] in identifying controlled foreign entities. The same situation is there for "reasonable business operation". In addition, although the EITL refers to the individual holding CFC, STA cannot deal with the individual tax avoidance on behalf of Individual Income Tax Law (IITL). The IITL then did not intend to cooperate with EITL on this point. Furthermore, at the practical level, STA lacked the experiences of tackling the tax avoidance of residents using overseas resources.

Due to the lack of maturity of legislation and also the lack of realistic urgency, China's CFC regime had been frozen for a significant period of time. STA had never administered a CFC case, until 2014 and 2015 when STA improved the tax information collection of residents investing overseas[30]. The reform was enacted expressly to serve the construction of BRI, signaling that the increasing outbound investment is the factual impetus. Later on, in 2018, the new IITL also filled up the hole in CFC regime with respect to individual controlling cases[31]. While more patches can be put on the regime, the existing one can already basically function. It is found then a boost of CFC cases filed by STA since 2014[32], and by now STA has managed to administer CFC regime on a regular basis.

The above reforms around the CFC regime, either STA's legislative and administrative measures that have activated CFC or the patch made by IITL, have increased the effectiveness and competency of the regime. Being the rule of RBT in itself, the CFC regime, through the improvements, has contributed to the weighted RBT. As for the considerations of the factual approach, the link with BRI and the timing requirement are convincing as well. In

27. See article 45.
28. STA, *Notice on Issuing the Measures for the Implementation of Special Tax Adjustments (for Trial Implementation)*, n. 2, 2009.
29. In the above regulation, it is provided only the case of control by shareholding.
30. STA, *Announcement on Issues concerning Resident Enterprises' Reporting of Information Relating to Overseas Investment and Income*, n. 38, 2014; STA, *Notice on Effectively Conducting the Work of Resident Enterprises' Reporting of Information about Overseas Investment and Income*, n. 327, 2015.
31. Article 8 of Individual Income Tax Law (2018).
32. The first CFC case appeared in 2014, handled by Shandong Local Tax Bureau. There is an "outburst" of CFC cases ever since investigated by STA branches of, for example, Hai Nan and Xin Jiang (2015), Su Zhou (2016), Beijing and JinZhou (2017), Kun Shan and Qingdao (2018).

conclusion, the reforms of the CFC regime have added the persuasiveness of the research proposition, affirming again the ITRC's transformation to ROT.

VI. CHANGES IN BILATERAL TAX AGREEMENTS

The bilateral tax treaty is entered traditionally for the purpose of eliminating double taxation and tax evasion. However, that purpose has extended to objectives like developing economic relationship and improving cooperation on tax matters[33]. The proactive intent of the contracting parties whatsoever must be triggered by the realistic economic intercourse of the two countries. This is the fundamental reason for their delegates to sit down and argue. The same applies to BRI, which aims to (re)build the economic ties along the Belt and Road. Consequently, with the revival of the Belt and Road, there must come the need to establish the "tax ties" as well.

When questioning the implications of BRI for the general ITRC, and for now in terms of tax treaties, both the breadth and depth of China's DTAs should be considered. In this article, the inspection of breadth, which refers to the extensiveness of China's tax treaty network, intends to explore the expansion of the treaty network. "While for depth, the specific changes of treaties" articles are viewed as substantial evidence to knowing the tendency of ITRC under the influences of BRI. Only through the combination of both the breadth and depth aspects can we master the global transformation of China's stance on international taxation from the treaty perspective. However, what needs to be explained is that the breadth part and depth part are not always and do not need to be aligned by the same tax treaties. In other words, the treaties that signify the specific tendency of expansion do not necessarily show the noticeable content changes, which may lie elsewhere. This article views the two aspects as on equal foot and organically connected.

1. THE BREADTH OF CHINA'S TAX TREATY NETWORK

This section is unfolded by three charts, which are in turn processed with the data regarding China's DTAs and the development of BRI[34].

33. See Article 6 of "Multilateral Convention to Implement Tax Treaty Related Measures to Prevent BEPS", retrieved from *https://www.oecd.org/tax/treaties/multilateral-convention-to-implement-tax-treaty-related-measures-to-prevent-beps.htm*
34. See Belt and Road Portal, *List of Countries that Have Signed "Belt and Road" Cooperation Document with China, op. cit.*; STA, *List of Double Taxation Agreements Signed by China, op. cit.*

Chart 3 shows (in green area) the countries signing tax treaties with China. As can be seen, China's tax treaty network is already very comprehensive so far. With a few still not into force, China has signed bilateral tax agreements with 107 countries in the world, which makes China's tax treaty network one of the largest in the world. From the map in Chart 3, there are only two noteworthy grey areas, meaning that those are countries without tax agreements with China. One is in Africa, and another is in South America.

Chart 4 shows the number of tax treaties that China signed or updated with other countries each year from 1983 to 2019. This Chart supplements Chart 1 in that it introduces the time dimension into the analysis of China's DTA network evolution.

Combining the Chart 3 and Chart 4, the first thing to note is that over 30 years and of such extensive coverage, China's international tax treaty network is still growing, through either extending to new jurisdictions or refreshing the old treaties. Narrowing the lens down to only the period since the launch of BRI, it is found that even within only 6 years, BRI has clear influences on the expansion of China's treaty network. Since 2015, China's treaty network extends to eight new countries, who are at the same time the new members of BRI as well[35]. Even in the first five months of 2019, the tax treaties with New Zealand and Italy, being the new BRI countries respectively in 2017 and 2019, were totally renegotiated both in 2019.

Then, on the historical dimension, there are three more points of time shown in Chart 4 that are worth considering. The first is 2001, when China joined the WTO, marking its integration into the world and its twenty-year rapid growth of the economy. The new century is literally the new age of the economic China. The second point of time is that after 7 years of attracting foreign capital, China's dual corporate income tax system ended in 2008[36]. The third one is 2016, two years after the announcement of BRI, China has transformed from a capital importing country to net capital exporting country. As can be seen in Chart 4, nearly 70 out of 107 tax treaties were signed before 2001, when China has fewer capital outputs. The little triangle symbolizing the launch of BRI rests after the first two blue dash lines and ahead of the third one.

This has two aspects of instructions. For one thing, the status quo of China's tax treaties falls behind the fast-changing reality, both economic and

35. They are Chile, Zimbabwe, Cambodia, Kenya, Gabon, The Republic of Congo, Angola and Argentina. Argentina does not officially sign the BRI cooperation documents with China, yet it already has substantial projects going on in the name of constructing BRI.
36. See the evolution of China's enterprise income tax law at para. 2.2.1 of Li, J., *International Taxation in China: A Contextualized Analysis*, *op. cit.*

legal, in that the basis of those treaties have shifted dramatically. The second instruction relates to how should we view BRI's role in China's evolving tax treaties. When evaluating the implications of BRI for both the scope and content of China's tax treaty network, the efforts of isolating BRI from its general economic and legal background are futile. The changes brought by BRI must be seen in conjunction with the background it grows in. Therefore, it can be said that BRI has been accelerating the change of reality along the existed route, and in turn making the tax rule changes faster and more observable.

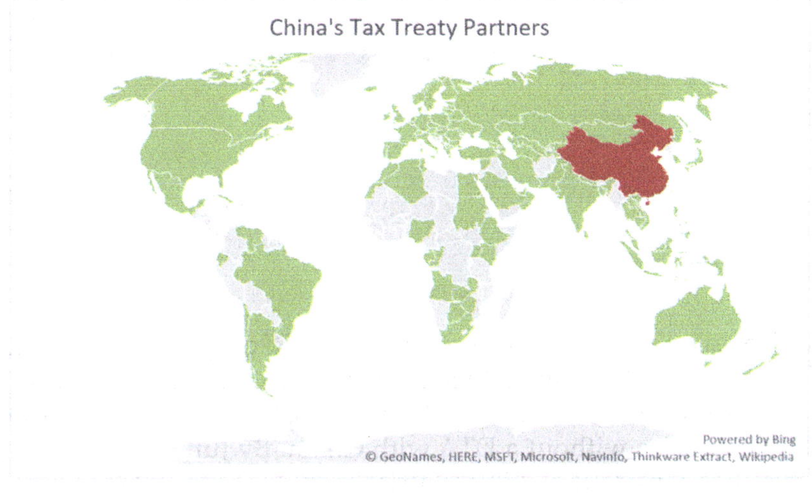

Chart 3

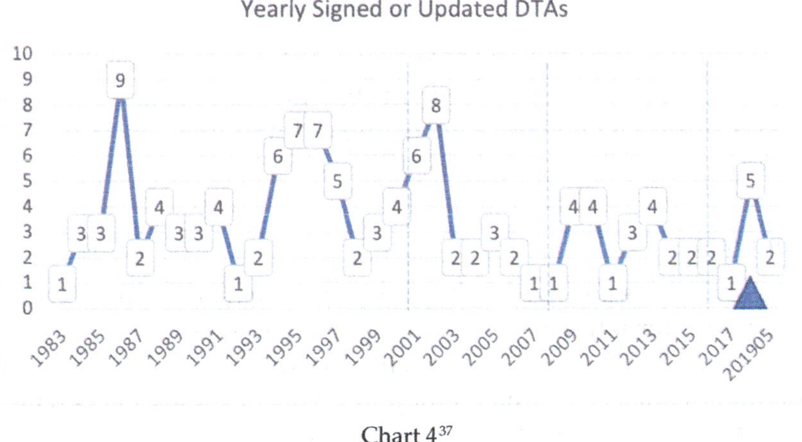

Chart 4[37]

37. The "updated" includes the re-negotiated ones.

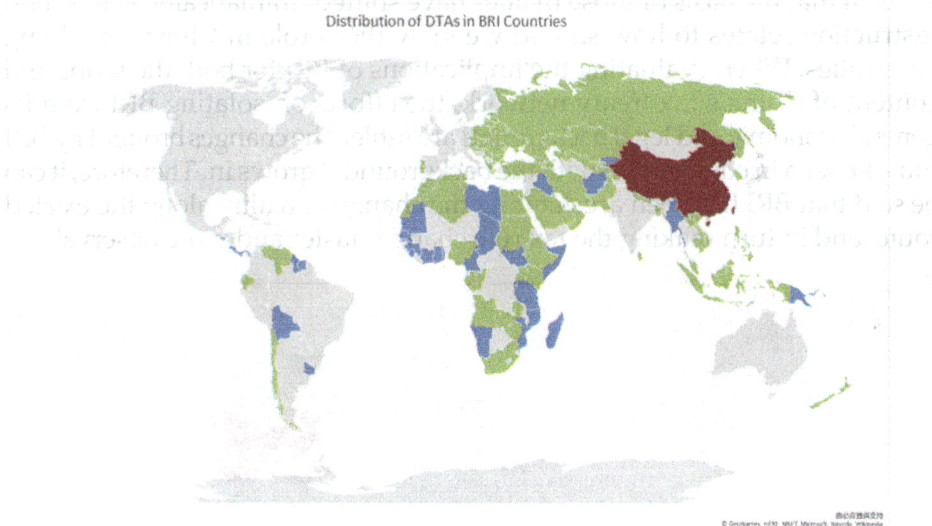

Chart 5

Chart 5 painted all the countries signing the BRI cooperation documents ("BRI Countries") with China either blue or green. The green areas in the map are the BRI countries with which China has a DTA, while the blue areas are the BRI countries without a DTA with China. By July 2023, the pained areas altogether consisted of 152 countries, which covered the majority of Africa and Euro-Asia continent. The BRI countries are mostly developing countries, for the noteworthy grey areas are all rich North America, Australia, and West and North Europe[38].

In terms of the distribution of DTAs in the BRI countries, it can be found that the majority of BRI countries, both in absolute number and geographic coverage, has already had bilateral tax treaties with China. That is attributed to the work done by STA largely before BRI.

1.1. Summary

The above analysis around the three diagrams has shown the network of China's current international tax treaties, and the evident role of BRI in its expanding scope. The analysis also touches upon why a transition of ITRC in terms of tax treaties is destined to happen. This part only deals with the breadth of the ITRC, and the next session turns to focus on the depth, the

38. See Chart 6 for detailed information about the distribution of BRI countries across the continents.

content of tax treaties so as to reveal the material changes. However, it does not mean the scope change of DTAs is of trivial significance. The key lies in that firstly, the bilateral tax treaty is critical to distributing income between countries by allocating taxing rights; secondly, bilateral tax treaty is itself an instrument to removing barriers to cross-border investment, which has been pointed out in the top design of BRI; thirdly, BRI has made a difference in the expanding tax treaty network, for the increased treaty partners may be attracted in by BRI.

The first decade in the chronicle of China's international treaties witnessed the agreements with most of OECD countries[39]. Through the latter two decades and under the influences of BRI, the network has included more capital-poor countries than capital-rich countries, with China as a benchmark. Even though sometimes the tax treaties are called "international", it is in fact only "bilateral". Yet China's international tax treaties seen as a whole, the general position of China in the DTAs must have been different from it ever was.

2. THE DEPTH OF CHINA'S TAX TREATIES

As said, the depth part deals with the content changes of China's DTAs, under the implications of BRI, with an aim to shed some light on the research proposition of this article. This part is not going to do a blanket search of all the article changes of DTAs, but only to identify the key articles that are relevant to the proposition. The direct objective of a bilateral tax treaty, as usually stated in its preamble, is to eliminate double-taxation and combat tax avoidance. To those ends, tax treaty determines the two contracting parties as either source or residence, and then divides the taxing rights between them. The identification of ITRC as SOT or ROT, while manifested in tax treaty, is firstly dependent upon China's position as source or residence, and further on the interests vested in the source or residence by the treaty. In general, the taxing right of the source is prioritized, and the residence state has the residual right to tax. According to this judgment, this article does find proof of the ITRC's move from SOT to ROT.

2.1. The Flexible Sparing Credit

Normally, in the double tax agreement, article 23 specifies the methods adopted by the two contracting states for eliminating double taxation. In

39. Li, J., *International Taxation in China: A Contextualized Analysis, op. cit.*, para. 4.2.2.

cases where they choose credit method, there are options for the residence state to decide whether to view the *de facto* unpaid tax as the payable tax in the other state, for the purpose of calculating foreign tax credit. The unpaid tax is the tax that would have been paid but otherwise is spared (exempted or reduced) as tax incentives to attract foreign investment.

Neither OECD or UN Model Tax Conventions provide sparing credit in its articles as an option for double-tax elimination. However, sparing credit has been common for the DTAs between developed and developing countries. However, being counterproductive for the popular propositions of neutrality and equity, sparing credit has lost its appeal for developed countries[40]. However, sparing credit may still attract those countries, mainly in that it increases the competitiveness of their outbound investors.

For developing countries, however, the inclusion of sparing credit in its DTAs prevents the other contracting state from nullifying their tax incentives under the top-up effect of credit method. The incentive benefits then will be accrued to investors, rather than the treasury of their home states[41]. The sparing credit method has been embraced as a tool for attracting and competing for capital from developed countries.

The sparing credit thus implicitly links SOT and ROT, for that different countries or a country in different phases may adopt sparing credit from different starting points. When a country adopts sparing credit in its DTAs, it is not difficult to identify its purpose as attracting foreign investment or facilitating outbound investment. Based on that, sparing credit adds weight to either SOT or ROT, and is able to show dynamically the transformation process between SOT and ROT.

2.2. The Redirected Role of Sparing Credit

The historical trajectory of sparing credit in tax treaties echoes the evolution of China's DTAs and is in concert with the tendency of ITRC from SOT to ROT.

Sparing credit was introduced by China as early as in its first DTA in 1983, which was with Japan. Since then, sparing credit has sprung up in its tax

40. Yan, X., "Thinking Over Questions Relevant to Sparing Credit" in *International Taxation*, vol. 12, 2016, p. 36 (熊艳. (2016). 对饶让抵免有关问题的思考. *国际税收*, (12), p. 36.).
41. Haugland Nilsen, K. R., *The Concept of Tax Sparing: A General Analysis, and an Analysis and Assessment of the Various Features of Tax Sparing Provisions*, Law School of the University of Oslo, p. 9, retrieved from *https://www.jus.uio.no/ior/english/research/projects/global-tax-tranparency/publications/the-concept-of-tax-sparing.pdf*

treaty network. Put that against the system background, China has operated a dual tax system which gives institutional incentives to foreign investors until 2008. Consequently, by the end of 2007, forty-nine in all ninety-two China's DTAs contain the sparing credit provisions, and most of them are treaties with developed countries.

In 2008, the first *Enterprise Income Tax Law* canceled the systematic preferential treatment of foreign investors, and only sectorial and regional incentives exist thereafter. The institutional basis thus falls away. After 2008, only 2 among the 33 newly signed or updated tax treaties contain the sparing credit provisions. The first one with Ethiopia included a restricted sparing credit, which was claimed to be a reluctant compromise made by China in 2009[42]. The second one, however, came late on 2016 with Cambodia, which used a standard clause of sparing credit.

This article holds that the tax treaty with Cambodia manifests a shifted role of sparing credit, and to a certain extent, it marks a new stance of China's tax treaty negotiation, in contrast to that a decade ago.

Although rather unlikely the treaty would specify its link to BRI in its text, that link, however, is genuine. The bilateral tax treaty and BRI cooperation agreement between China and Cambodia were negotiated along the same track and were signed simultaneously on 13th October 2016. The process is the reflection of the tenet of the *Vision and Actions* that China's tax treaty should be in proactive service of BRI. As a result, it can be said that the consideration of sparing credit can pass the test of the factual approach.

Needless to say, the mutual sparing credit, gains more attractiveness for Cambodia as an investment destination among other Southeast Asian countries. For China, the taxable income that would have accrued to the Chinese treasury, due to the credit mechanism, turns to be the income of the Chinese investors in Cambodia. What makes this even more meaningful for those investors is that China has operated a per-country credit mechanism until 2017. The credit balance for a specific country cannot be reused for another country's tax credit. Sparing credit thus reduces the "waste" of credit balance, and in a certain way alleviates the double taxation caused by the inadequate foreign tax credit. Therefore, the sparing credit included in the Cambodia-China DTA plays a redirected role from its predecessors that started from China being the location of investment, rather than an exporter of capital.

42. Yan, X., "Thinking Over Questions Relevant to Sparing Credit", *op. cit.*, p. 35.

Following the conceptual approach, the classification of sparing credit is flexible. The way to classify is not to look at the content of provisions, but to look through the motives of adopting it. As analyzed above, the redirected role of sparing credit renders itself into the category of RBT from the former SBT, which echoes China's shifted motives to facilitating outbound investment from attracting foreign investment. Compared to the arguments in Part V that prove more the destination of the trend, the analysis here has shown where the transformation comes from and where it leads to.

3. LOWERED WITHHOLDING TAX

In international taxation, the way to tax income of foreign investors is generally aligned with the categorization of incomes as active income or passive income[43]. The country of source can tax the active or business income on a net basis with a normal corporate tax rate, while passive incomes are taxed at a reduced rate on a gross basis. More particularly, the source tax on passive incomes is paid by the payer rather than the recipient. The scope and the special way of taxing the international passive incomes result in a unique category within the corporate income tax, that is, the withholding tax.

3.1. Withholding Tax and RBT/SBT

Withholding tax is a key design for international income sharing. For business income derived by the permanent establishment, the source country has abundant resources to tax such income. In contrast, the earner of passive incomes does not need to have a significant presence in the source country. Letting the payers pay the source tax out of the dividend, interest, or royalties to be received by foreign earner seems to be the best option. Withholding tax is thus key to realizing source taxing rights, leaving the residence country to tax the residual incomes. Withholding tax, together with other tax allocation regimes, affect the balance of income sharing between source and residence. The heavier liability of withholding tax results in the larger share in the source, and less income will accrue to the residence. Being a gross-based mechanism, withholding tax is more succinct than typical corporate income tax. Among others, the decisive factors of withholding tax liability are the scope and the tax rate, which is also simpler than the case of net-basis income tax.

On the other side of the mirror, the income sharing of residence and source concerns directly the interests of taxpayers. In the case where the

43. Avi-Yonah, R. S., *International Tax as International Law: An Analysis of The International Tax Regime*, Cambridge: Cambridge University Press, 2007, p. 1.

residence state adopts the credit method, the withholding tax affects the cash flow of the taxpayer. Or when the residence state uses exemption method to eliminate double taxation, the withholding tax will directly affect the overall tax burden. In either case, withholding taxation influences the interest of cross-border taxpayer.

Based on the above, it is reasonable to gauge the changing position of a country by looking into the trend of withholding tax in its tax treaties. The trend can be a rising, declining or stable withholding taxation. If over a certain period of time, a tax treaty has provided lower withholding tax liability in the source state, then that means the residence state has been sharing larger pie of the cross-border income. The residence country has gained stronger position than the source state in the game of international tax sharing. Translate that to contact the conceptual approach, the residence country that achieved lower withholding tax liability in a DTA obtains greater benefits for its residents. Consequently, residence country has the motive to reduce the withholding tax liability for both the treasury and to facilitate overseas investment. In short, lower withholding tax liability adds weight to RBT.

For the theme of this article, a preliminary conclusion can be drawn that the residence country may be transforming to ROT, if multiple such treaties can be found. Because any tax liability in a DTA is bilateral, the changing position as reflected by inspecting withholding tax should be considered with the underlying fact — the general stance of the contracting parties as exercising more source or residence taxing rights. For the tax treaties between China and BRI countries, as analyzed above, China plays more as the residence states. Consequently, the trend of lower or higher withholding tax liability prescribed by the treaty means the larger or smaller income pie share of China, which in turn renders China closer to ROT or SOT.

3.2. Cases of Lowered Withholding Tax

Through inspecting some of the recent DTAs of China, a clear trend of lower withholding tax liability can be found, and that will further back the proposition that the ITRC is heading towards ROT. Such a trend also has an indelible connection with the construction of BRI. The following introduces the details.

Non-exhaustively, this article has found some recent tax treaties that exhibit dynamically or statically the decreasing withholding tax liability. For the dynamical demonstration, the DTAs with Russia and Romania are good examples. China's first tax treaty with Russia was signed in 1994, in which the rates set for the passive incomes dividend, interest and royalties were all 10%. In 2014, the DTA with Russia was renegotiated, and the same rates were reduced. For dividend, a 5% rate applies with a modest threshold, otherwise, the rate is 10%. For interest and royalties, the rates were also reduced to 5% and 6%. This is not the end. In 2015, when China and Russia signed the BRI cooperation document[44], the delegates of the two sides also signed a tax protocol amending the new DTA. According to the protocol, the withholding taxing right on interest payment was exclusively conferred upon the residence state, while the source state gives up its taxing right. All in all, from 1994 to 2015, China has gained more and more residence taxing rights relative to the source taxing rights of Russia. The same conclusion can be drawn based on the observation of the DTA with Romania, which has reduced the withholding rate to around 3%. For static demonstration, the first DTAs with BRI countries Gabon, Argentina, and the Republic of Congo all set the withholding tax rate to a relatively low level.

Besides the above, there are proofs demonstrating that the aforesaid trend is real and that such trend is affected by BRI to a large extent. The proofs are the provisions in a number of DTAS exempting or lowering the withholding tax liability of the Silk Road Fund of China (SRF). Established in 2014, SRF is a state-owned fund with a focus on financing BRI projects. In DTAs with BRI countries Italy (2019)[45], Argentina (2018), Kongo (2018), Spain (2018), and Malaysia (2016), the withholding tax liabilities of SRF in those countries are set low or lowered, wholly or partially exempt. Although the preferential treatment can be attributed to sovereign immunity, that does not hinder it adding strength to the trend and reflecting the straightforward role of BRI in ITRC.

4. MOST-FAVORED-NATION CLAUSE

This part aims to link the changing position of the most-favored-nation (MFN) clause in China's tax treaties over the years with the research proposition. The analysis in the following is expected to contribute to the proposition that China is indeed gaining more dominance in negotiating tax treaties, and the ITRC is in turn heading towards ROT.

44. "Joint statement between the People's Republic of China and the Russian Federation on the construction of Silk Road Economic Belt and the construction of Eurasian Economic Union, retrieved from *https://www.yidaiyilu.gov.cn/zchj/sbwj/2427.htm*, accessed 29 July 2023".

45. The renegotiated DTA with Italy was also signed simultaneously with the BRI document.

In plain words, MFN clause is to ensure in a bilateral agreement between A and B that party A will not be subjected to a less favorable treatment than what B accords to C in their agreement of the same kind. In international trade or investment law, MFN is a "standard" clause[46], for that the major multilateral trade agreements including GATT, GATS, TRIPS, and NAFTA all contain it, and so do most of bilateral investment treaties[47]. However, it is well known that these agreements virtually do not touch upon tax especially direct tax issues.

Narrowing down the lens to tax treaties, the MFN clause has independent significance than that in international trade or investment law. For one thing, in international taxation, it is less possible for MFN to be a rule of customary international law. Unlike the popularity among international trade or investment agreements, MFN only exhibits limited existence in the global tax treaty network. Countries do not feel obliged to provide MFN treatment to its counterparty when negotiating bilateral tax agreement. As a matter of fact, either in academia or practice, the stances on MFN are far from united[48]. For another, taxation has direct and immediate impact on national welfare, which explains partly why tax issues are usually reserved in trade or investment agreements, and why a multilateral tax agreement is still staggering on its way. Therefore, it should be understood that the MFN clause enjoys different status and serves different purposes in a tax treaty than those in a trade or investment agreement.

4.1. MFN and Non-discrimination: Deviated but Connected

As reported by the International Law Commission, MFN clause does not stem from a country's general right to non-discrimination[49]. The OECD

46. OECD, *Most-Favored-Nation-Treatment in International Investment Law*, OECD working paper on international investment, n. 2004/2, September 2004, p. 16.
47. See Art. I of GATT, Art. II of GATS, Art. 4 of TRIPS, and the Art. 1103 (investment), Art.1203 (services) and Art. 1403 (financial services) of the North American Free Trade Agreement (NAFTA).
48. See generally the discussions in Dürrschmidt, D., "Tax Treaties and Most-Favoured-Nation Treatment, particularly within the European Union" in *Schriftenreihe Steuerinstitut Nürnberg*, n. 2, 2006, p. 202; Cordewener, A. and Reimer, E., "The Future of Most-Favoured-Nation Treatment in EC Tax Law — Did The ECJ Pull the Emergency Brake without Real Need? — Part I" in *European Taxation*, vol. 46, n. 6. 2006, pp. 239-249, and Weber, D., "Most-Favoured-Nation Treatment under Tax Treaties Rejected in the European Community: Background and Analysis of the D Case" in *Intertax*, vol. 33, n. 10, 2005, pp. 429-444.
49. ILC, *Report of the ILC on the work of its thirtieth session*, A/33/10, 1978, Chapter II, paras. 47 to 50.

Model Tax Convention (MTC) has never accepted MFN clause in its articles, while only considered it in the commentary for a while and later on removed it without substitution[50]. The OECD in Article 24 has provided four forms of non-discrimination in five paragraphs[51]. They are the non-discrimination of nationality, permanent establishment, payment and capital. Being separate aspects, the four lack an overarching rationale behind them[52]. The prevalence of non-discrimination clauses in tax treaties has contributed little to the status of MFN clause in tax treaties, simply because a third state cannot require the most-favored-nation treatment on account of the non-discrimination provisions. The status quo is that, among the MFN clauses that are included in the worldwide tax treaties, almost none of them are aligned with the non-discrimination article. Under most circumstances, instead of being applied overarchingly, MFN treatments are provided only to particular aspects of international taxation, like for the transportation income or permanent establishment[53]. Resting uncomfortably among the general non-discrimination provisions, the current status of MFN clause is closer to being an exception to them. For example, the tax treaty between country A and B contains the standard non-discrimination article, which enumerates several situations where both parties shall not discriminate the residents of each other. A's tax treaty with country C also has similar non-discrimination arrangement. Now B has negotiated a more favorable condition in its treaty with A, the question arises that whether C is reasonable to claim for its residents the same treatment that B's residents are newly having in A. The answer, under the existing development of treaty law, is obviously negative[54].

50. Art. 24 OECD Commentary 1977, n. 55, 2nd sentence, and it was deleted in the 1992 commentary. Hofbauer, Ines. Hofbauer, I., "Most-Favoured-Nation Clauses in Double Taxation Conventions-A Worldwide Overview" in *Intertax*, vol. 33, n. 10, 2005, p. 445.

51. OECD MTC 2018, retrieved from *https://www.oecd.org/tax/treaties/model-tax-convention-on-income-and-on-capital-condensed-version-20745419.htm*

52. Maisto, G. *et al.*, *Non-Discrimination in Tax Treaties: Selected Issues from a Global Perspective*, IBFD, 2016, p. 4.

53. For illustration, see the distribution of MFN clauses through the treaty articles at Hofbauer, I., "Most-Favoured-Nation Clauses in Double Taxation Conventions-A Worldwide Overview", *op. cit.*, pp. 449-453.

54. "As tax conventions are based on the principle of reciprocity, a tax treatment that is granted by one Contracting State under a bilateral agreement to a resident or national of another Contracting State party to that agreement by reason of the specific economic relationship between those Contracting States may not be extended to a resident or national of a third State under the non-discrimination provision of the tax convention between the first State and the third State", OECD, *Commentary on Article 24 Concerning Non-discrimination*, OECD, 2007.

Consequently, the *opinio juris* of countries to include MFN clause in their tax treaties barely exist. The autonomous revision of treaty conditions that may be triggered by MFN treatment with a third state poses risks to the reciprocal basis of tax treaty, unless the MFN clause is expressly provided in the treaty. In the above example, the claim of C will be justifiable if the A-C tax treaty has the MFN provisions written regarding its claim. Otherwise, the MFN treatment inappropriately deducted from non-discrimination will blur the border of the "two-sidedness" or "privity" of tax treaty.

While the realities of the non-discrimination article and MFN clause deviate, their underlying connections are touchable. First of all, the loosely aligned provisions of non-discrimination in the MTC are targeting the same negative consequences with that the general DTA aims to counter. Economic distortions can be caused by both double taxation and discriminatory taxation[55]. The equal tax treatment of nationals and non-nationals advocated by non-discrimination reflects part of the capital import neutrality (CIN)[56]. Discriminatory tax treatment in the source state hinders the free movement of capital and investment, and so do the double taxation of residence and source states.

Secondly, both non-discrimination in the MTC and MFN clause lead to equal treatment, while only the former is for resident and non-resident, and the latter is for non-residents. In the same vein with the first point above, what is justifying MFN is that discriminatory treatment among non-residents of different nationalities also creates distortions and reduces efficiency. Through the application of MFN clause, the differential tax treatment in a certain aspect will be eliminated, and that aspect will not be a factor for foreign investors in their business decisions. As a result, the efficiency will be safeguarded for both the investor and source state. In this regard, the MFN clause and non-discrimination article are connected by their common rationale and objective.

4.2. Driving Forces Behind MFN

Questioning why a country is driven to adopt MFN clauses in their tax treaties leads us to the purposes of those countries doing so. More importantly, the inquiry of the driving forces of MFN clause will also provide fulcrums

55. Richman, P., *Taxation of Foreign Investment Income, an Economic Analysis. Baltimore*, MD: Johns Hopkins Press, 1963.
56. CIN aims to lay down a level playing field for residents and non-residents, in the sense of the general international tax regime, which is wider than equal treatment in the source. Non-discrimination in the source states is necessary but not sufficient.

to think out the proposition of this article. Since the relative scarcity of MFN clauses in the global tax treaty network, MFN is not a reliable instrument to achieving international tax harmonization, as what MFN can effectively do in international trade and investment system. The deviated nature of MFN and non-discrimination also decides their different "destiny" in practice. As discussed above, MFN shares the value of non-discrimination, which means that even though MFN gains far less application, the situation does not prevent MFN from radiating its appeal to a single state. It is held that the MFN clause especially the unilateral type is relied upon by a state as a tool to attracting foreign investment.

To illustrate this point, the base case will be concretized by adding more details and another version. First of all, suppose that in the base case 1, A, B and C are all having tax treaties among each other, and all those treaties include MFN clause regarding the withholding tax rate on interest. The original rates in the three treaties are identically 10%. Now C has negotiated such rate as lowered to 5% with A in their DTA, which means A will impose a preferable rate on investors of C. The MFN clause between A and B will then be triggered, the same rate will apply to B's investors in A. If these MFN clauses in this triangle scenario all provide the two-way treatment, the same change will happen to B and C as the source states. The cross-border investments from and to either A, B and C will face only a 5% withholding tax on interest, the overall tax burden on investment within the group of ABC will be decreased. The consideration of taxation will be less weighted in capital movement.

However, a more realistic version of the base case is that the "conduction chain" of MFN clauses is often broken. When the mutual or group MFN treatment is not available, the unilateral MFN clause in a state's tax treaty with another country will especially attract investment from that country, for its the preferable treatment will be maintained in the state. For example, in the base case 2, A provides unilateral MFN treatment to B in their DTA, while C has MFN arrangements with neither A nor B. In this new situation, if A provides lower rate from 10% to 5% to C, A will also accord such rate to B. In contrast, if the rate for B further drops to 3%, C is not entitled to such favorable treatment. The base case 2 has identified that in the real world where bilateral or multilateral MFN is rare[57], a unilateral MFN can guarantee the target country is treated no worse than any other countries in the source

57. For the comprehensive collection of the existing MFN clauses in the global bilateral tax treaty network, see IBFD-Tax Research Platform-Treaties-MFN.

state. The source country can thus gain an advantage over its competitors attracting the target country's investment.

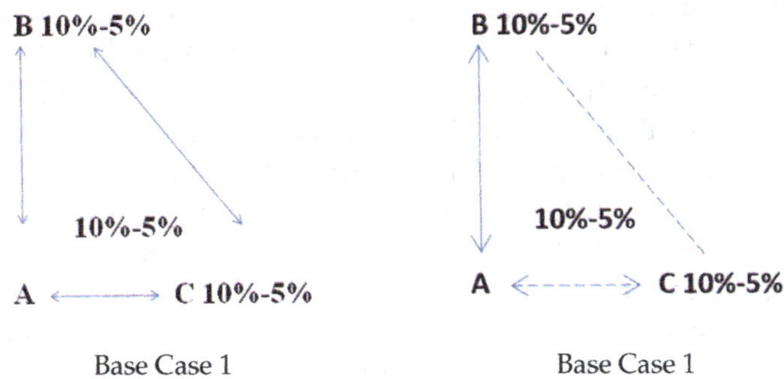

Base Case 1 Base Case 1

4.3. New Developments of MFN in China

In general, China has few MFN clauses in its extensive tax treaty network, consistent with the overall situation in the world. The recent move in the DTA with Chile, however, provides us with a new window to think through the implications of MFN. China and Chile signed their first tax treaty in 2015, and Chile officially endorsed BRI in 2018. The China-Chile tax treaty is annexed to a protocol, of which the article 10 has prescribed an MFN clause regarding the withholding rate on interest[58]. The MFN treatment is provided unilaterally by Chile to China, saying that in the case that Chile applies lower rate in the treaty with a third country for interest payment from Chile, the same low rate will then be provided to China as well. In 2018, two years after the China-Chile DTA took effect, the MFN clause was triggered since Chile had negotiated lower rate with Japan and Italy[59]. As a

58. "In the event that pursuant to an Agreement concluded with a country after the date of signature of this Agreement, Chile agrees to a lower rate of tax in paragraph 2 of Article 11, such new rate shall automatically apply under the same conditions as established in that other Agreement, for the purposes of this Agreement when the provision of the first-mentioned Agreement becomes applicable, in particular with reference to financial institutions wholly owned by the government. In such case, the competent authorities shall by mutual agreement settle the mode of application of this paragraph", retrieved from *http://www.chinatax.gov.cn/n810341/n810770/c1644352/part/1659942.pdf*

59. "I hereby inform you that the condition for this (MFN) clause to apply has been fulfilled, since Chile concluded after the date of signature of the Convention with China, a convention with Japan and another with Italy that contemplates lower source tax rates for interests than those contained in the Convention between Chile and China", Exchange of Notes of China and Chile tax authorities in 2018, retrieved from *http://www.chinatax.gov.cn/n810341/n810770/c1644352/part/3562025.pdf*

result, the two countries through the exchange of notes modified the original interest article in 2018.

The implications of this new development should be considered from both signatory parties. On one hand, it should be noted that before the treaty with China, Chile has already been veteran in adopting MFN clause in its DTAs. By now, there are 22 DATs that contain the MFN clause,[60] and the majority of them are with OECD countries. Combining with the earlier analysis, the intention of Chile embracing the MFN is clear, especially considering that most of OECD countries use the exemption method to eliminate double taxation. Chile aims to level the playing field at least in terms of certain tax aspects for those capital-exporting countries, the economic efficiency will be enhanced probably at the cost of reciprocity. The MFN clauses will increase the horizontal attractiveness over its fellow South American countries as well.

On the other hand, at the side of China, because the successful application of MFN clause with Chile, its competitive advantage of tax policy is sealed. The treaty with Chile is not the first that contains an MFN clause, even though the total number is indeed tiny. What makes the MFN clause with Chile of significance is not about the content, but the first of such being effectively activated and unilaterally given to China, which also denotes the willingness of China to innovate in DTA design[61]. The earlier MFN clauses are either bilateral like with Philippine[62], or unilaterally given to other countries like the Netherlands[63]. In any event, the MFN clauses remain on the paper. The activated MFN clause further adds forces to the position of China as both the largest trade partner of and exporter to Chile, among other capital exporters including Japan and Italy. It particularly relates to BRI which is expected to deepen the economic relationship of the two countries.

---

60. The data is extracted from IBFD Tax Research Platform, at https://research.ibfd.org.
61. Turley, C., *Coming of age — China's leveraging of BEPS*, International Tax Review, 2018, retrieved from *https://www.internationaltaxreview.com/Article/3848525/Coming-of-ageChinas-leveraging-of-BEPS.html?ArticleId=3848525*
62. Art. 2 of the Protocol to the Agreement Between the Government of The People's Republic of China and the Government of the Republic of the Philippines for the Avoidance of Double Taxation and the Prevention of Fiscal Evasion with Respect to Taxes on Income, retrieved from *http://www.chinatax.gov.cn/n810341/n810770/c1153616/part/1153618.pdf*
63. Article IX of Protocol to the Agreement between the Government of the People's Republic of China and the Kingdom of the Netherlands for the Avoidance of Double Taxation and the Prevention of Fiscal Evasion with Respect to Taxes on Income, retrieved from *http://www.chinatax.gov.cn/n810341/n810770/c1153196/part/1153200.pdf*

4.4. The Shifted Position of China

MFN clause has a special status in the general institutions of international tax law. Under the current circumstances that a multilateral or regional tax treaty is not around the corner, the reciprocity and privity of DTA are material obstacles to the acceptance of MFN clause. The adoption and practice of MFN clause in the global tax treaty network are thus not common. In contrast, the non-discrimination article, which shares the equal treatment principle with MFN, is routine in DTAs. The deviated reality of non-discrimination and MFN, however, does not cut the link that they both target the negative economic effect of unequal treatment. Based on that, countries should have been obsessed with MFN clause. Due to the restrictions though, countries may retreat to providing unilateral MFN treatment utilizing MFN clause as an instrument to attracting investment. On the mirror side, there may also be countries that demand the MFN treatment proactively in that it maintains their relative competitiveness.

The above case roughly echoes the track of MFN clause in China, which sheds some lights on the task of this article, for that the shifted position of China corresponds to the transition of ITRC from SOT to ROT. Before the China-Chile treaty, though remaining deactivated and with exceptions[64], the MFN clauses of China are introduced for the sake of its value of attracting capital. For example, China provides MFN treatment unilaterally to the Netherlands in 1987. The case of the United States is not that straightforward, but according to "substance over form", the MFN clause with the United States that specifies the sparing credit in their 1984 Exchange of Notes serves the same purpose for China[65]. In this phase, MFN is one of the characteristics that contribute to the so-called SOT system, when the focus of STA was to attract foreign capital or safeguarding its source taxing rights. In the more recent times, China either withdrawn the unilateral MFN treatment to other countries, for example, the unilateral MFN treatment to the Netherlands

64. For example, the exception is that with Vietnam, in which the MFN treatment is given unilaterally to China by Vietnam (see Exchange of Notes, retrieved from *http://www.chinatax.gov.cn/n810341/n810770/c1153436/part/1153443.pdf*)

65. As analyzed earlier regarding the function of sparing credit, here the MFN clause is a tool for China to attract investment from the United States. "Both sides agree that a tax sparing credit shall not be provided in Article 22 of this Agreement at this time. However, the Agreement shall be promptly amended to incorporate a tax sparing credit provision if the United States hereafter amends its laws concerning the provision of tax sparing credits, or the United States reaches agreement on the provisions of a tax sparing credit with any other country", Exchange of Notes of DTA between China and the United States, retrieved from *http://www.chinatax.gov.cn/n810341/n810770/c1153055/part/1153063.pdf*

was canceled in their renegotiated treaty in 2014, or as discussed, China was taking MFN treatment from Chile. Especially for the latter, STA opened a new door out of the sights of OECD or UN MTC serving the redirected goals of ITRC towards ROT against the background of BRI.

VII. CONCLUSION

The changes surveyed and analyzed in accordance with the approach illuminated earlier have verified the proposition made in Part II of this article. The international tax regime of China, propelled by the forces of BRI, has a clear trend of transforming from source-oriented to residence-oriented tax system. The STA, either in formulating domestic tax policies or negotiating double tax agreements, bears more and more residence than source thinking.

As explained in Part III, China has formed at the top level the systematic design for developing BRI, in which STA was assigned for advancing BRI in both facilitating outbound investment and managing the risks therein. This two-direction guideline can also basically cover the rule-based efforts made in domestic and DTA aspects. From domestic rule-making perspective, the improved tax credit system and CFC regime respectively ease the burden and defend against base erosion. More domestic measures that are not rule-based as seen in table 2 are skipped by this article, which operate along this same two-lane route as well. From the perspective of bilateral tax treaty, the expanding breadth of China's tax treaty network, among other dimensions, are paving the way for Chinese companies going global. In terms of depth, the changes of sparing credit, withholding tax liability and the MFN clause are both signaling the transformation of China's position in tax treaties.

The trend is real, and this article further holds that such transformation to residence-oriented taxation is an ongoing process. It does not mean China is loosening its taxing rights as the state of source. Actions have also been taken to attract foreign investment or combat source base erosion, but mostly they stay at the level of rule-administration rather than rule-making[66]. In contrast, it has been revealed from top to the bottom the rule-based changes that lead to residence-oriented taxation, and the construction of BRI has accelerated the transformation and made it more observable.

66. An exception is the STA, *Announcement on Issues Concerning Expanding the Applicable Scope of the Policy of Temporary Exemption of Withholding Tax on the Direct Investment Made by Overseas Investors with Distributed Profits*, n. 53, 2018.

Guía de uso

¡ENHORABUENA!

ACABAS DE ADQUIRIR UNA OBRA QUE **INCLUYE LA VERSIÓN ELECTRÓNICA.**
APROVÉCHATE DE TODAS LAS FUNCIONALIDADES.

ACCESO INTERACTIVO A LOS MEJORES LIBROS JURÍDICOS

FUNCIONALIDADES

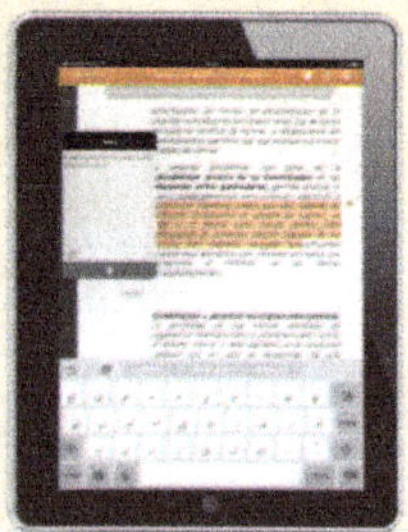

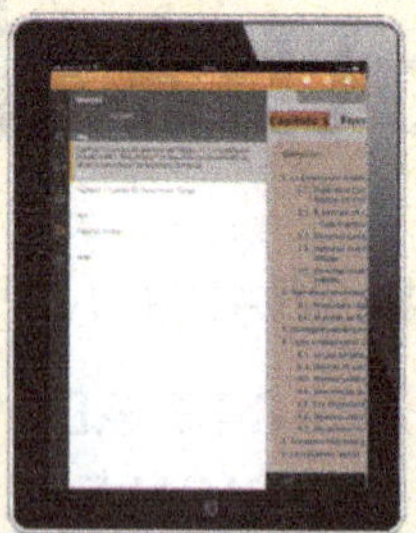

SELECCIONA Y DESTACA TEXTOS

Crea anotaciones y escoge los colores para organizar tus notas y subrayados.

USA EL TESAURO PARA ENCONTRAR INFORMACIÓN

Al comenzar a escribir un término, aparecerán las distintas coincidencias del índice del Tesauro relacionadas con el término buscado.

HISTÓRICO DE NAVEGACIÓN

Vuelve a las páginas por las que ya has navegado.

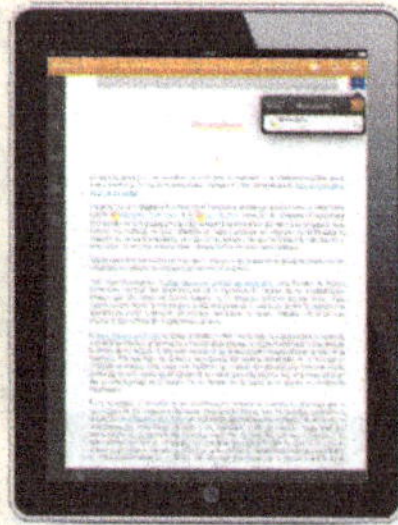

ORDENAR

Ordena tu biblioteca por: Título (orden alfabético), tipo (libros y revistas), editorial, jurisdicción o área del Derecho.

CONFIGURACIÓN Y PREFERENCIAS

Escoge la apariencia de tus libros y revistas cambiando la fuente del texto, el tamaño de los caracteres, el espaciado entre líneas o la relación de colores.

MARCADORES DE PÁGINA

Crea un marcador de página en el libro tocando en el icono de Marcador de página situado en el extremo superior derecho de la página.

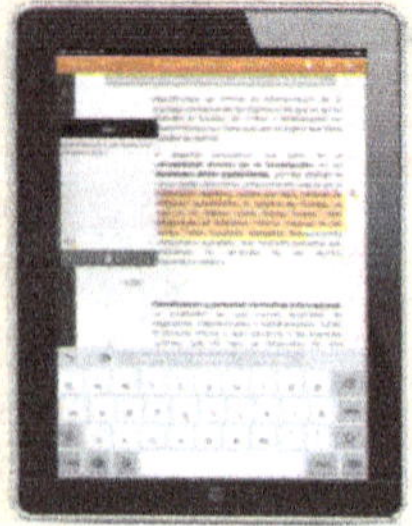

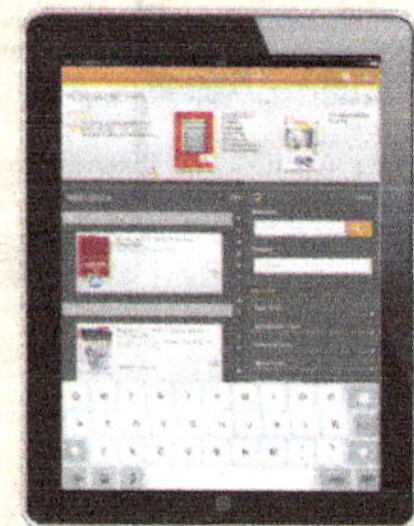

BÚSQUEDA EN LA BIBLIOTECA

Busca en todos tus libros y obtén resultados con los libros y revistas donde los términos fueron encontrados y las veces que aparecen en cada obra.

IMPORTACIÓN DE ANOTACIONES A UNA NUEVA EDICIÓN

Transfiere todas sus anotaciones y marcadores de manera automática a través de esta funcionalidad.

SUMARIO NAVEGABLE

Sumario con accesos directos al contenido.

INFORMACIÓN IMPORTANTE: Si has recibido previamente un correo electrónico deberás seguir los pasos que en él se detallan.

Estimado/a cliente/a,

Para acceder a la versión electrónica de este libro, por favor, accede a **http://onepass.aranzadi.es** Tras acceder a la página citada, introduce tu dirección de correo electrónico (*) y el código que encontrarás en el interior de la cubierta del libro.

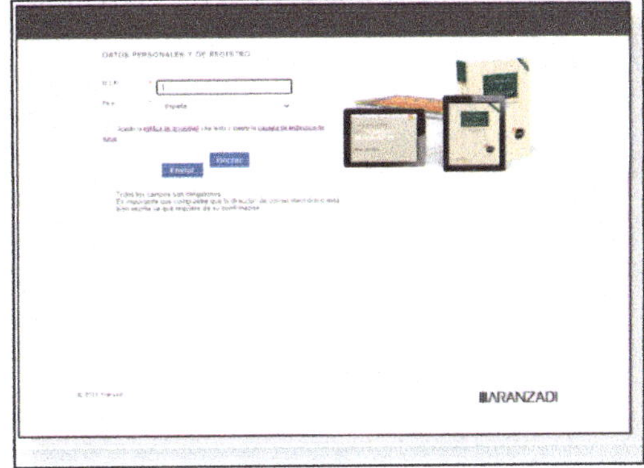

A continuación pulsa enviar.

Si te has registrado anteriormente en OnePass, en la siguiente pantalla se te pedirá que introduzcas el NIF asociado al correo electrónico.

Finalmente, te aparecerá un mensaje de confirmación y recibirás un correo electrónico confirmando la disponibilidad de la obra en tu biblioteca.

Si es la primera vez que te registras en **OnePass,** deberás cumplimentar los datos para crear tu cuenta y poder acceder a tu libro electrónico.

- Los campos **"Nombre de usuario"** y **"Contraseña"** son los datos que utilizarás para acceder a las obras que tienes disponibles a través del navegador en la ruta www.proview.thomsonreuters.com

Servicio de Atención al Cliente

Ante cualquier incidencia en el proceso de registro de la obra no dudes en ponerte en contacto con nuestro Servicio de Atención al Cliente. Para ello accede a nuestro Portal Corporativo y una vez allí en el apartado del Centro de Atención al Cliente selecciona la opción de Acceso a Soporte para no Suscriptores (compra de Publicaciones).